SOCIOLOGY
Contours of Society

Robert H. Lauer
Jeanette C. Lauer
U.S. International University

Roxbury Publishing Company
Los Angeles, California

Library of Congress Cataloging-in-Publication Data

Sociology: contours of society/Robert H. Lauer and Jeanette C. Lauer.
  p. cm.
  Includes bibliographical references and index.
  ISBN 1-891487-01-9
  1. Sociology. I. Lauer, Jeanette C. II. Title.
HM51.L34286 1998 97-13296
301—dc21   CIP

Sociology: Contours of Society

Publisher and Editor: Claude Teweles
Assistant Editors: Dawn VanDercreek and Renée Burkhammer
Copy Editor: Michelle Mimlitsch
Production Assistants: Kate Shaffar and Erin Record
Typography: Synergistic Data Systems
Cover Design: Marnie Deacon Kenney

Printed on acid-free paper in the United States of America. This paper meets the standards for recycling of the Environmental Protection Agency.

ISBN: 1-891487-01-9

ROXBURY PUBLISHING COMPANY
P.O. Box 491044
Los Angeles, California 90049-9044
Tel: (213) 653-1068 • Fax: (213) 653-4140
Email: roxbury@crl.com

CONTENTS

PREFACE

Why study sociology? A graduate student once told us she had decided to pursue sociology because when she took the introductory course "a whole new world opened for me." She said that she gained a fresh understanding of what was happening in her world and saw many things in a new light. "I was one of those who thought that all poor people had to do was to go to work and they would no longer be poor," she admitted. "I learned that poverty, like nearly everything else, has no simple solutions. Life is complex."

Her last phrase, "life is complex," is a telling one. It underscores the need for many different tools of understanding. Sociology is one of those tools. Using sociology to gain a new understanding of yourself and your world is the basic theme of this book. Our emphasis is on sociology as a unique tool of understanding. We view sociology not as an esoteric analysis of topics with little bearing on life, but as a pathway to a more realistic and comprehensive understanding. In other words, our purpose is to show you how to use what has been called the "sociological imagination" to understand yourself and your world and, by that, enrich your life.

Features

In Chapter One we discuss how this understanding is crucial to personal well-being and to intellectual growth. We have incorporated several features in this book that encourage a deeper understanding of social life.

First, we believe that jargon and stilted language are barriers to understanding. We have tried, therefore, to be conversational without using language that is patronizing or simplistic. We use the same language that we would use if we were discussing these topics with students in a classroom or in an informal setting.

Second, gaining a deeper understanding requires knowledge of, and use of, critical thinking. We devote Chapter Two to this important topic, showing you with numerous examples how to evaluate both popular and professional information sources. In the following chapters, we offer additional assistance in critical thinking. Early in each chapter, we furnish a specific example of critical thinking and, at the end of the chapter, provide a critical thinking exercise for you to complete. We recommend that, whenever possible, you collaborate with other students in completing these exercises.

Third, studies show that student involvement in the learning process greatly increases understanding. Like many educators today, we value collaborative learning involving groups of students working together. The *Explorations* boxes in each chapter are designed to encourage collaborative learning. Because collaboration is not always possible, we also suggest ways that you can complete these exercises on your own. In either case, the exercises will help you get involved in the learning process.

Fourth, learning to understand social life is easier when it is personalized. It is one thing to study about an issue like racial discrimination in the abstract; but it is another thing to read about a real person's description of suffering from racial discrimination. In each chapter, we offer an *Experiences* box that personalizes an important topic in the chapter. Although we relate personal experiences throughout the chapters, the *Experiences* boxes offer a more extensive account. These are actual experiences, and the individuals who shared them with us are real people. We have changed their names and background information to assure their anonymity.

Fifth, we stress the importance of maintaining a global perspective when examining social life. As we demonstrate in the text, no society is self-sufficient, each is influenced by other societies. In each chapter, we relate the topics to various nations. In addition, we focus on a particular nation or a group of nations in the *Extensions* boxes, usually making a comparison with the United States.

Sixth, we emphasize the importance of learning about diversity within nations. In every chapter, you will find materials comparing males with females. You will also find materials on people from differing racial/ethnic backgrounds and from various social strata. The point is, the nature of people's lives and the kind of experiences they have vary by whether they are male or female, by their racial/ethnic group, and by their socioeconomic level. Diversity doesn't mean that individuals in one group are completely different from those in another group. Yet the differences are substantial enough that you miss something very important if you don't recognize them.

Seventh, we maintain that a knowledge of theory and methods is necessary for sociological understanding. We try to make you comfortable with, and knowledgeable about, theory and methods. We offer an overview of theory and methods in the first chapter and highlight their use in subsequent chapters. In other words, we show how theoretical premises and concepts help explain research results and point out the method used to conduct the research. We do not, like many texts, segregate theories in a separate section in each chapter. Rather, we integrate theories and methods into the discussion so that you can see how they are used in sociological research.

Eighth, we utilize a variety of resources to enhance understanding. Although we want you to acquire the sociological imagination, we also draw upon the work of psychologists, anthropologists, political scientists, economists, and historians. Sociology is not meant to isolate you from other disciplines nor ignore the important work they are doing. Rather, it offers you a perspective and a set of tools for making good use of the work of these disciplines.

Finally, we believe that the most recent research and data are necessary for understanding. Accordingly, you will find data from the latest available government statistics and the most recent research. If you read something with a reference that is ten or more years old, you might ask (and we hope you will) whether there isn't later research on the matter. Our answer is: not that we know of at the time this book went into production. If you find more recent research, we would appreciate hearing from you. We sincerely mean this, for our hope is that this book will become what we have tried to make it—an ongoing discussion and learning process with you the student.

Organization

Certain topics are traditionally covered in introductory sociology courses and are included in this text. However, we also incorporate some topics that are not typically included. We begin with a discussion of sociology as understanding—how it can help you make sense out of social life. The chapter provides a discussion of the theories and methods used by those who exercise the sociological imagination in their research and analyses.

Chapter Two moves to the important topic of critical thinking. As you seek to understand, you will find yourself bombarded by information that often is inconsistent. How do you evaluate this information? We show you how to appraise both professional and popular sources.

In the next four chapters, we look at some fundamental concepts: culture (Chapter Three), socialization (Chapter Four), social interaction (Chapter Five), and social structure (Chapter Six).Understanding culture not only helps you to understand human behavior but also to recognize the diverse ways in which people solve their everyday problems of living.

Socialization deals with how you become the kind of person you are. It raises the issue of whether who you are is primarily the result of nature or of nurture. Socialization is a lifelong process. You will find yourself socializing, and being socialized, in every group in which you participate.

Social interaction explores the ways in which you relate to and influence others. We note certain recurring patterns of interaction and discuss the ways in which people manage interaction in order to present themselves in particular ways.

Social structure shows how human life is patterned. There are various levels of social structure, from small groups to nations. Chapter Six also discusses the topic of formal organizations and the misunderstood notion of bureaucracy.

The remaining chapters deal with substantive topics. We look at deviance in Chapter Seven. "Deviance" is not a negative term to sociologists. Deviance is behavior that violates social norms. To illustrate the meaning of deviance, we examine crime, drugs, and mental illness in some detail.

Chapter Eight discusses social stratification—how inequality shapes human life. We examine the meaning of stratification and types of stratification systems. Every society has some kind of system of stratification. Your position in the stratification system makes an enormous difference in your life style and in the quality of your life.

In Chapter Nine we look at racial and ethnic groups. You may be surprised when you read how scientists regard race. But you should not be surprised by reactions to race and ethnicity or to the differences race and ethnicity make in people's lives. Prejudice and discrimination, and patterns of race/ethnic relations are addressed in this chapter.

Chapter Ten deals with gender and gender roles. What are the differences between males and females? Are those differences rooted in biology or socialization? Is gender inequality inevitable? These and other important issues are discussed in this chapter.

In Chapter Eleven we examine the family. Many people believe that the family is the foundation of a strong society and a primary source of intimate relationships. We agree. But what is happening to the family? Is its existence being threatened by divorce? We respond to these questions as we look at various issues in the areas of family, marriage, and sex.

Chapter Twelve covers two institutions: religion and education. Historically religious organizations have been a primary source of education. And both religion and education involve the search for meaning and knowledge. We discuss such topics as the functions of religion and education in American life, the ways in which social stratification intersects with religion and education, and problems facing religion and education today.

Chapter Thirteen also explores two topics: government and the economy. These two topics are tied together because each affects the other in crucial ways. We consider such things as the functions and forms of government, power, types of economic systems and their development, and the changing nature of work.

The topics of science, technology, and health are discussed in Chapter Fourteen. Science is seldom highlighted in introductory texts. This seems an unfortunate omission to us. In this chapter, we discuss the nature of science and show how science is a social process. We explore the ways in which technology affects society and social factors bear upon technological development. And we examine an important outcome of scientific and technological endeavors—health and health care. You may be surprised by the extent to which your health reflects social factors.

Chapter Fifteen focuses on population, urbanization, and the environment. You will see how these three dimensions of social life are crucially linked. Population deals with more than sheer numbers and is a problem in the United States as well as other nations. Population growth is accompanied by urbanization. Urbanism, or the way of life in cities, can be conceptualized in various ways. Environmental issues pose vexing problems that are intensified by population growth and urbanization. Steps taken to resolve one difficulty always seem to generate new environmental problems.

Finally, Chapter Sixteen deals with social change and social movements; that is, how people and societies are transformed. We discuss why people resist change (no, it isn't human nature). We investigate the various factors that cause change. We look at important patterns of change, including modernization. And we consider the ways in which social movements inhibit or promote change and why people participate in social movements.

Thus, we cover the waterfront of topics that deal with social life. As you read the various chapters, we hope that you learn about yourself as well as your world and that your journey into the sociological imagination is as exciting as it is informative.

Acknowledgments

We are grateful to the following reviewers whose careful criticisms and numerous insights were invaluable in the final product:

Deborah A. Abowitz (Bucknell University)
Janet Bogdan (LeMoyne College)
Roy Childs (University of the Pacific)
Rachel Einwohner (University of Washington)
James A. Glynn (Bakersfield College)
John Heeren (California State University, San Bernardino)
Jeremy Hein (University of Wisconsin, Eau Claire)

Thomas M. Kando (California State University, Sacramento)
Peter Kivisto (Augustana College)
Michael Lovaglia (University of Iowa)
Suzanne B. Maurer (Syracuse University)
Brenda Phillips (Texas Women's University)
Scott Sernau (Indiana University at South Bend)
Peter J. Stein (William Paterson College)
Kathleen Tiemann (University of North Dakota)
Mark A. Winton (University of Central Florida)

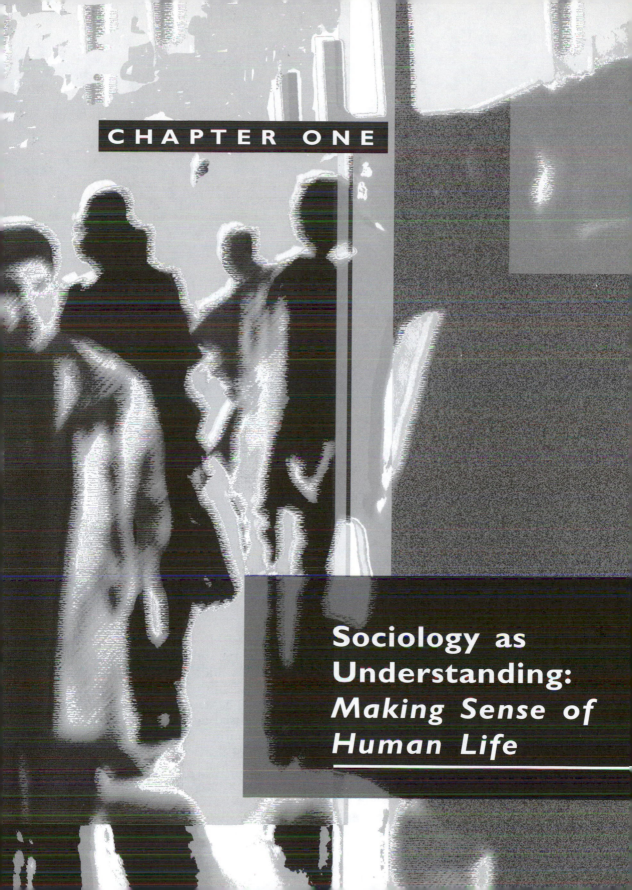

CHAPTER ONE

Sociology as Understanding: *Making Sense of Human Life*

On March 22, 1997, thirty-nine Americans committed suicide in their luxury home at Rancho Santa Fe, California. They were members of the Heaven's Gate cult. Led by a man known as "Do," they convinced themselves that a spaceship would pick them up and take them to a better life. A man and woman, calling themselves "Bo" and "Peep" and claiming to be from outer space, started the cult in the 1970s. They lectured in rented halls and sought followers to join them as part of their crew for a spaceship that would carry them all to a higher plane of life.

Bo and Peep persuaded a number of people to abandon their families, change their names, and take a vow of celibacy in preparation for a higher plane of life, a plane above that now known to humans. Part of the appeal of the group was the leaders' conviction that the earth's people were self-destructing. Only those who joined the cult would be saved.

The cult's fortunes rose and fell over the years. Some members abandoned the group when nothing seemed to be happening to fulfill their predictions. Peep died in 1985. But Bo continued the work, eventually renamed himself "Do," and taught his followers that the appearance of the Hale-Bopp comet was the sign for which they had been waiting. On their web site early in 1997, the group wrote: "Our 22 years of classroom here on planet Earth is finally coming to conclusion—'graduation' from the Human Evolutionary Level." They were "happily prepared" to leave this world and enter the spaceship.

It was not the first time that news of a mass suicide had stunned Americans. An even more dramatic incident occurred nearly twenty years earlier in a cult group led by Jim Jones. Jones started a church in Indianapolis. Its ministry, which focused on the poor and needy, included a soup kitchen, clothing distribution, job placement for ex-addicts and felons, and efforts to desegregate public facilities.

Over the years, Jones became increasingly concerned about the threat of nuclear war. In 1965, he and a hundred of his followers moved to a town in California that was considered one of the safer places to be in the event of attack. By 1971, Jones' church had about

2,000 members. For reasons known only to himself, Jones decided to move again and purchased property in Los Angeles, San Francisco, and Guyana (South America). The San Francisco church, his primary headquarters, offered a free clinic and dining hall, a legal aid office, and a drug rehabilitation program.

Jones began to preach more and more about the evils of racism, fascism, and what he believed to be the coming nuclear holocaust. He also began talking about a way to escape those evils through mass suicide. In 1977, Jones learned that an expose about his church was to be published by reporters from *The New West* magazine and the *San Francisco Chronicle*. A number of defectors claimed that church members had been beaten as a form of discipline and that funds were being misused. Jones and 800 of his followers promptly departed for their jungle retreat in Guyana.

The next year, some of Jones' followers ambushed and killed Congressman Jim Ryan and most of those who had come with him to Jonestown to investigate the group. When Jones heard of the killings, he directed his followers to line up and drink from a tub of strawberry-flavored liquid laced with tranquilizers and cyanide. Armed guards forced those who were reluctant. In the chaos that followed, an unknown assailant murdered Jim Jones. It was November 1978; 912 people—men, women, and children—lay dead in the jungles of Guyana.

The Need to Understand

Incidents like those of Jonestown and Heaven's Gate raise many questions. Why do people join an organization where one person holds such absolute power? How can people remain in a group where cruel and bizarre behavior occurs on a regular basis? How can so many people willingly go to their deaths and even poison their children? How can a man like Jones, supposedly committed to social justice and actively involved in projects to help people, end up being so murderous and destructive?

That such questions are raised reflects a basic fact: people strive to make sense out of the world in which they live. They want, indeed they need, to understand why things happen and why people behave as they do. In addition, individuals need to understand themselves: What kind of person am I? Why do I think as I do? How do I make sense out of my emotional experiences? Why do I have aspirations or values or attitudes that are different from those of my parents or siblings? And so on.

We do not use the term "need to understand" lightly. The drive to understand has five important functions or purposes. It helps satisfy human curiosity, and it provides a basis for emotional security, interpersonal relationships, organizational behavior, and policy decisions.

We will examine each of these functions and show how **sociology**, the scientific study of social life, is important to each of them.

A Means of Satisfying Curiosity

One important function of understanding is simply to satisfy curiosity. For instance, are you curious about Heaven's Gate and Jonestown? Do you wonder how such things can happen? A member who defected from Jones's congregation before the move to Guyana told why she would have willingly taken poison. It would have been an "easy way out," she said, because everyone was exhausted. Group meetings lasted until three or four in the morning and featured not only Jim Jones's sermons but also films of concentration camps and torture. She explained, "We were so tired, we were so weary, we weren't thinking" (Mills 1982, p. 169). At Heaven's Gate, "Do" thoroughly indoctrinated members with the belief that they could achieve a higher level of life if they followed his guidance. Both groups were relatively isolated from contact with outsiders.

Physical exhaustion, isolation from outside influences, and indoctrination are well-known techniques for brainwashing. If you understand the power of these techniques to manipulate thought and behavior, you can understand why people, who are otherwise quite rational, can accept the bizarre directives of a cult leader.

A Basis for Emotional Security

Another important function of understanding is to provide a basis for emotional security. Such security doesn't depend on any particular kind of understanding, just one that makes sense to you. Thus, members of the Jonestown and Heaven's Gate cults found emotional security in the understanding of life provided by their leaders.

We can illustrate the importance of understanding by considering an extreme: a world in which no understanding is possible. In other words, a world that is senseless. Try to imagine what it would be like to live in such a world. Nothing would be predictable. All events, all relationships, all experiences would be, from your point of view, completely random.

For example, in this kind of world, you would never know what to expect from your professors. A professor might lecture, or sit and stare silently, or hurl rotten tomatoes at you. And when you received a grade (if you received one), you would not know how to interpret it. Perhaps your grade would reflect the professor's feelings toward you, or the quality of your work, or the professor's mood when assigning the grades.

This illustration is absurd, to be sure. Yet it illustrates the point that a senseless world is a highly stressful and anxiety-provoking world.

Here's a more realistic illustration. A manager was stressed by his work, quit his job, and went back to college to get another degree. One of the classes he took was Sociology of Organizations. He told the professor:

> This class makes me realize that I was stressed in my job because I was so naively idealistic. Now I understand the things that went on in that firm. I still don't agree with many of the firm's policies, but I think I could handle the situation now.

Understanding does not guarantee good mental health, but it is a necessary basis for it.

A Guide for Interpersonal Relationships

Another function of understanding is to guide interpersonal relationships. In part, this understanding involves knowledge of **norms** (the shared expectations for behavior). In both Jonestown and Heaven's Gate, the norms prescribed minimal contact with outsiders and unquestioning respect for the leaders.

Norms cover a wide range of behavior. For example, what is the proper way to greet someone when you first meet? You would probably offer to shake hands. In some societies, the proper greeting is very different. It might be the joining of hands and separating them with a pull so as to make a noise; or stroking your face with the hands of the other person; or licking your hands, drawing them over your face and then over that of the other person; or smelling each other's cheeks. So, it's important to know the norms of a society in order to relate in an acceptable way.

But understanding also involves knowledge of cause-and-effect relations: "If I do this, I can expect these consequences . . ." And "These kind of people are likely to behave in this fashion. . . ." For example, most parents try to motivate their children to achieve. What is the best way to do this? A common way is to point out where a child is falling short. A father looked over his daughter's report card, which contained four A's and one B. His only comment was: "What happened in the class where you got the B?" He intended for his comment to encourage her to get all A's the next semester. But his plan backfired because he misunderstood the cause-and-effect relations in this situation. His comment only discouraged his daughter and left her feeling unappreciated. "I can never do enough to please him," was her reaction.

The father was well-intentioned. Yet good intentions cannot override the damage that results from a lack of understanding. An understanding of human behavior is essential for healthy and rewarding interpersonal relationships.

A Guide for Organizational Behavior

A substantial part of your life involves dealing with or functioning in organizations. Birth, education, marriage, shopping, health care, and work are all likely to take place in organizations. As the stressed-out manager noted, your understanding—or lack thereof—of organizational processes can make a crucial difference in the quality of your life.

Recall that this manager left his job in frustration to pursue a university degree. He told his professor that he had repeatedly been disappointed in his attempts to advance in his former position. He had believed that if he did his job well, his superiors would take note and promote him. He had not understood the political nature of his organization. As one researcher has noted, in some organizations the rules include such things as telling your boss what he or she wants to hear even when the boss claims to want your honest opinions (Jackall 1988, p. 109).The manager had frequently broken this rule and others. Consequently, he was consistently passed over for promotion in spite of his excellent performance record.

Similarly, those who could not follow the rules in Jonestown and Heaven's Gate either left the groups or were ejected. Every group takes its own rules seriously, however nonsensical those rules appear to outsiders.

A Basis for Policy Decisions

Why are some Americans poor? The answer a person gives to this question will make a difference in the kinds of governmental policies that he or she is willing to initiate or support. For instance, a great many Americans believe that people are poor because they are lazy or unwilling to work (Lauer 1997). If you believe this, you are unlikely to support governmental programs aimed at helping the poor.

Researchers find, however, that the willingness to work has very little to do with poverty. There are complex causes to poverty, as we shall discuss in Chapter Eight. Here, we want to point out that the most impoverished group in the nation is single mothers and their children. And millions of Americans who live in poverty are aged, disabled, or working full-time at low-paying jobs (Lauer 1997).

In other words, to deal realistically and effectively with various problems and issues facing the nation, you must have an understanding of the factors at work in creating and maintaining society's ills. So far, the suicides at Jonestown and Heaven's Gate have not led to policy decisions, but some relatives of those who took their lives believe that government action is needed to curtail the power of these groups.

Thinking Sociologically

Given the need to understand, and given the fact that a sociological perspective is an important part of that understanding, what exactly does it mean to think sociologically?

You Are a Social Creature

To acquire a sociological perspective, we begin with the affirmation that humans are social creatures. Or, to put it another way, we begin by denying what we call the *myth of the autonomous individual*. The myth is reflected in the statement "I am the captain of my fate"—a statement widely accepted by Americans. It is reflected in the notion that any child (or any boy, as they used to say) can grow up to be president of the United States. It is reflected in the notion that you can become whatever you want if you are only willing to work hard. It is epitomized in the notion of the successful, "self-made" individual.

But how autonomous are you? To what extent are you a self-governing, independent person? In denying the myth, we are not denying the fact that you exercise some control over your life. We are underscoring the fact that numerous social factors influence who you are and what you do. In order to understand why you think as you do, why you act as you do, and even why you experience emotions as you do, you must not only look at the kind of person you are but also at the many influences in your life.

Those influences include the people with whom you interact, the particular context in which the interaction occurs, and the sociocultural system in which you participate. For example, assume that someone insults you. How will you respond? Your response will depend upon, among other things, the amount and kind of interaction you have had with that person in the past. You may react differently to a long-time friend than to a stranger. Your reaction also depends upon the context in which the insult occurs. You might react differently if the two of you are alone than if other people are around. You may react differently if you are in your friend's home rather than on an athletic field or at church. Your reaction will also depend on the sociocultural system of which you are a part. The norms of some groups would require you to exact revenge, while those of other groups would lead you to ignore an insult or withdraw (Frijda and Mesquita 1994).

It is important to keep in mind that the social factors that influence people are not necessarily consistent. You may, for example, encounter norms among your friends that differ from those of your parents. Or they may have expectations in particular situations that contradict your own inclinations. A classic **experiment** by Richard LaPiere (1934) illustrates this. He went with Chinese friends to a number of West coast hotels and restaurants where prejudice against Asians was high. In most cases, they were not refused service. Yet several months later, LaPiere sent a questionnaire to the establishments and over 90 percent indicated that they would not serve Chinese people! Clearly, the behavior of these establishments contradicted their attitudes toward the Chinese. Many of them went against their own preferences in serving the Chinese (perhaps only because LaPiere was also there). Like the restaurant owners, you are a social creature. What you do is not just a reflection of the kind of person you are but also of the social context in which you function.

Social Factors Affect All That You Think, Feel, and Do

Because you are a social creature, social factors affect every aspect of your life, including your thinking, your emotions, and your behavior. Thus, sociologists who study attitudes and values about premarital sex want to know not merely the proportion of people who oppose or accept it, but the way in which those attitudes and values are shaped by social factors.

The point is, a particular stand on premarital sex is more than just a reflection of an individual's moral standards. A Gallup survey reported that the proportion of people agreeing that premarital sex is *not* wrong was higher for males than for females, the young than the old, college graduates than those with less education, nonwhites than whites, and Catholics than Protestants (Hugick and Leonard 1991). Your attitudes and values tend to be consistent with the social groups to which you belong.

The social groups that influence you are many and diverse. Included are both small groups like family, friends, school and religious organizations and larger groups like the nation. Also people are influenced simultaneously by many different group memberships. A study of attitudes and values about family relationships among some American, Chinese, and Mexican students illustrates national and gender-based differences (Chia et al. 1994). The researchers found that Americans gave less importance to the family and believed more in sexual equality and independence than did students in the other two nations. But within the national groups Chinese women were more traditional than Chinese men, American women believed in equality between the sexes more than did the American men, and Mexican men valued independence more than did Mexican women.

Clearly, the various groups to which you belong strongly influence your attitudes and values. Social factors also affect emotional experiences (Kitayama and Markus 1994). They help determine the kind and the intensity of emotions, as well as the extent to which people suppress or feel free to express emotions. Your own experience probably confirms this. Think of the difference in the emotions most people experience when watching a televised sporting event alone versus watching that same event in the packed stadium where it is being played. The mere presence of other people tends to intensify emotional experiences. And the presence of other people freely expressing intense emotions helps release any inhibitions you might have about doing the same.

Group memberships also are important in emotional life. Your gender, your family, your friends, your country, and even the region of the country in which you live can make a difference in your emotional experiences. A study of one hundred Italians, half of whom were from northern and half from southern Italy, reported some interesting differences (Galati and Sciaky 1995). Southern Italians worried more than did northern Italians about the negative behavior of others. Northern Italians were more worried about their own achievement. And the northerners feared personal harm more than loneliness, while the southerners were more fearful of not having good relationships.

Finally, social factors influence your behavior. Take dating, for instance. Dating is an important way for you to learn how to relate intimately to others and thus helps prepare you for sexual relationships. Logically, you might expect young people to start dating as a result of sexual maturation—reaching the age of puberty. Because puberty does not occur at the same chronological age for every young person, you might also expect the starting age for dating to vary. But these expectations were refuted by Sanford Dornbusch (1982) and his associates. Using national data, they found that chronological age explained onset of dating far more than sexual maturation (as measured by physicians' ratings of such things as pubic hair development).In other words, those teenagers whose biological development is slower or faster than their peers still are likely to start dating at the same age as their peers. Social pressures exert more influence than do biological ones.

Stanley Milgram's (1974) classic experiment provides a more dramatic example. Before we describe the experiment, answer the following questions. Would you be willing to deliver a severe and dangerous electrical shock (450 volts) to someone? Would you be willing to do this if you were part of a scientific experiment that was based on the premise that punishment can help people learn?

Milgram recruited volunteers for an experiment on human learning. Imagine that you were one of the volunteers, and you were chosen—by drawing lots—to be a teacher in the experiment. Here is what would have happened. A middle-aged man, another volunteer, is your pupil. He is strapped into a chair. Paste and electrodes are applied to his arms. You hear the experimenter say that the paste will avoid burns and blisters. You also hear the experimenter assure your pupil that, while the shocks might be painful, they will cause no permanent tissue damage.

The experimenter then takes you into an adjoining area and shows you the machine you will use to deliver the punishing shocks to your pupil. You have thirty switches that give shocks, ranging from 15 to 450 volts. The experimenter gives you a word test to administer to your pupil. Your pupil has buttons to push to indicate his answer. If he gets an answer wrong, you are to deliver the first electric shock—the 15 volt shock. Each time your pupil gives a wrong answer, you increase the voltage.

Your pupil begins to make mistakes, so you start administering the shocks. When you reach the 75-volt level, you hear a grunt of pain from your student. When you press the button for 120 volts, your pupil shouts at you about the painfulness of the shocks. At 150 volts, your pupil screams at you and says he doesn't want to participate any more. At 300 volts, your pupil cries out that he will no longer respond to you at all. The experimenter, who has been standing by you throughout, tells you to treat no response as a mistake and continue pushing buttons, increasing the voltage each time.

Let's return to our original question. Would you continue until you had administered the 450 volt shock? Incidentally, your machine has labels below the buttons, ranging from "slight shock" beneath the 15 volt button to "danger: severe shock" beneath the 375 volt button to "x x x" beneath the 450 volt button.

Of the forty males and forty females who first participated in the experiment, twenty-six, or 65 percent, of each gender continued until they had pushed the 450 volt button. The experimenters were astonished. Psychiatrists, social scientists, and graduate students had all predicted, prior to the experiment, that no more than 2 or 3 percent would continue to the end, and that they themselves would *not* continue to the end.

Had you been a participant, you would have been debriefed. Only then would you have learned that no shocks were actually given and that your "pupil" was actually a confederate of the experimenter. He only pretended to be in pain, and he deliberately made mistakes in order to see how far you would go.

When we've asked students whether they would be willing to administer a 450 volt shock as part of a research experiment, most say that they would never do it. But two-thirds of Milgram's subjects did. Had they been asked prior to the experiment, most of them probably would also have said that they would not administer such a severe shock to someone. How, then, can their behavior be explained? Personality factors did not account for it. Rather, Milgram explained it as "obedience to authority." Many of the "teachers" did not want to continue when they heard cries of pain from their pupils. However, the experimenter stood beside them and quietly but firmly directed, even insisted, that they continue. It was the authority of the scientist that led them to do something they did not want to do.

Consider the question again. Would you do the same? It is difficult to know in advance what a person will or will not do when confronted with the demands of a legitimate authority. "Legitimate" here means that you accept the authority as valid and as rightfully having some power over you. If you regard a scientist as an authoritative figure, you may obey him or her even when commanded to do something that goes against your conscience or better judgment. This may be why some Germans were willing to tolerate or even engage in, the murder of millions of Jews during World War II. To them, the authority of their government was legitimate and if the government said these actions were necessary, they were willing to carry out its orders (Fischer 1995).

In sum, it was not an individual factor—personality or personal standards—that best explained the behavior of the subjects in Milgram's study. Rather, it was a social factor—the tendency people have to obey a legitimate authority even when that authority commands something that is against their inclinations, their desires, or even their consciences. Please note our use of "tendency." Remember that a third of the subjects in the initial experiment did *not* continue, even though they were given the opportunity to do so. For them, the influence of other social factors—for example, parental training or religious beliefs—was stronger than the influence of scientific authority.

The Sociological Imagination

As you think about human behavior in terms of the social factors that help shape it, you are exercising the **sociolgical imagination**. C. Wright Mills (1959) coined the term "sociological imagination" to stress the point that people not only need information; they also need a way of thinking about and analyzing this information in order to gain understanding. In particular, he pointed out, people need to understand the effects of culture, the society, and group memberships on their behavior.

The validity of Mills's argument is underscored by our earlier examples of how thinking, feeling, and behavior are influenced by social factors. We'll reinforce it further by raising the kind of question that researchers ask: Why is the unemployment rate consistently higher among African Americans than among whites? The information provided in the question is correct: nationally, the unemployment rate of African Americans has remained at about double that of whites since 1948. The question is, how do you make sense of this information? Those who believe that every individual is responsible for his or her own destiny might argue that African Americans simply don't want to work. Others might attribute the difference to prejudice, and no doubt some prejudice is involved.

But what are the larger social factors at work? Two researchers who investigated the matter began with an interesting observation: the difference between the black and white rates varies by region (Cohn and Fossett 1995).They found greater inequality in employment in the Northeast and Midwest than in the South and West. Looking into the matter further, they discovered that African Americans fare better in areas with strong economies (so that whites and African Americans are not competing for scarce jobs), smaller average firm size, and lower levels of unionization (unions have frequently impeded the efforts of African Americans to break into some specialized areas of work).

In other words, you must go beyond simple explanations such as prejudice if you want to understand something like unequal access to jobs. The sociological imagination considers the social, cultural, and organizational factors that are at work. We want to make three additional points about the sociological imagination.

The Sociological Imagination Does Not Negate the Individual

When first exposed to the great variety of social influences upon their lives, some students wonder if sociologists claim that the individual is nothing more than the sum of these influences. The answer is no. Sociologists are aware of biological factors in human behavior (Udry 1995).They know that individual needs and drives, such as the sex drive, vary because of genetic makeup. They are aware that some aspects of personality, such as whether you are an introvert or an extrovert, seem to be present from birth and, therefore, have a genetic basis. However, the study of the genetic component of behavior and the impact of personality on behavior is the province of other scientists.

The individual, then, is not merely the sum of multiple social factors that impinge upon his or her life. Individuals both affect and are affected by social factors (we shall explore this point more fully in Chapter Four).

At the same time, sociologists agree with other behavioral scientists that individuals are not aware of all the factors that come to bear upon their behavior. For example, people at a football game or a political rally probably do not acknowledge to themselves, in the excitement of the moment, that their emotions are more intense because others are present. Similarly, individuals who regard themselves as highly ambitious are more likely to define themselves virtuous than as exemplars of a success-worshipping society. Those who affirm that abortion is wrong probably think of themselves as moral advocates rather than as the products of family and religious ideologies and it is unlikely that most people whose parents divorced before they reached the age of twenty-one regard that divorce as a factor in how long they will live. Yet a long-term study of giftedchildrenfoundadifferenceoffouryearsin the life span between those whose parents divorced and those whose parents remained married (Friedman et al. 1995). And this was true for both men and women.

In other words, while not denying the importance of genetic makeup, personality, and individual choices, sociologists stress the importance of studying the social factors that are essential for understanding human life and human behavior. The sociological imagination does not provide complete understanding, but it does furnish a necessary component of that understanding.

The Sociological Imagination Discovers Probabilities

All of the sciences that study human behavior discover probabilistic rather than deterministic relationships. That is, you never can predict exactly how an individual will act, or what will happen in a group, or in what way a nation will change. Rather, you can talk about the probabilities of certain outcomes.

Thus, Milgram's experiment can increase your understanding about a number of things. For example, it shows that if you get others to accept you as a legitimate authority, you will have considerable power over them. Followers regarded both Jim Jones and "Do" as their religious authorities, and this helps explain why the two leaders had so much control.

You can also learn from Milgram's experiment that, when directed by a legitimate authority, people will do things even they themselves think they would not do. Before they were members, it is probable that few of the Jonestown and Heaven's Gate members thought themselves capable of committing suicide. Remember that people who were told of Milgram's experiment typically believed that they themselves would not continue pushing buttons to the end.

It is clear, then, that legitimate authorities have enormous power over people's lives. Still, some members escaped from Jonestown and Heaven's Gate before the mass suicide. And a third of Milgram's subjects refused to continue the experiment. So social scientists can say that the majority of people will comply with an authority, but also know that a certain number will not. Thus, relationships are probabilistic, not deterministic.

The Sociological Imagination May Be Exercised at Various Levels

Sociologists are interested in all levels of human life—from the individual to the global levels. Table 1.1 shows various levels and some of the kinds of things that sociologists study.

In subsequent chapters, we will discuss phenomena at all of these levels. The point here is that whatever the level—from the individual to the global—sociologists look for the social factors that enable them to exercise the sociological imagination to enhance their understanding.

Table 1.1	Examples of Sociological Studies at Various Levels	
	Level	**Some Representative Studies**
	Individual	Attitudes about premarital sex. How people are taught to manage their emotions.
	Interaction	How people define an intimate relationship as fair. Controlling the impressions they make on others.
	Organizations	The impact of private schools on public schools. How the size of the company affects job rewards.
	Institutions	Factors affecting family breakup. How education affects income.
	Community	Community characteristics that bear upon crime rates. Exercising power in a community.
	Society	Population shifts. Patterns of drug use. patterns of modernization.
	Global	Inequality among nations. Comparative

How the Sociological Imagination Developed

Throughout human history there have been thinkers who displayed the sociological imagination. However, the development of sociology as a discipline did not occur until the nineteenth century—a century of turbulent change. The first sociologists wanted both to understand their changing world and also to alleviate the social ills they saw all around them. In other words, sociology developed as an effort to understand and control social processes so that the quality of life would be enhanced.

Auguste Comte (1798-1857) is known as the father of sociology. He named the discipline and argued that it should become a science of human behavior. The name, sociology, is taken from the Latin word *socius* (which means associate or companion) and the Greek word *logos* (which means word, and is the suffix for a number of sciences). Thus, sociology literally means the science of human association.

Indeed, Comte said that sociology was not only a science, but the latest and greatest of the sciences. He helped to make it a science by insisting that sociological findings be based on observations and that those observations be systematized. This was an enormous advance over past thinkers, who relied more upon reason (which means what was reasonable to them) than upon data.

The early sociologists included both men and women of various nationalities. Comte was French. An English woman, Harriet Martineau, translated Comte's works into English and wrote the first social science methods book. An English man, Herbert Spencer, popularized sociology in the English-speaking world. Another Frenchman, Emile Durkheim, was the first to study social phenomena using rigorous scientific methods (including statistical analysis). And a German, Max Weber, insisted that, if they are to understand social life, researchers must know how people think and feel about things, as well as how they behave.

In the United States, Lester Ward, William Graham Sumner, Jane Addams, and Ida Wells-Barnett made important contributions to the new science. Ward argued that all science must benefit humankind in some way. Addams and Wells-Barnett demonstrated how to better the lives of people. Addams founded Hull House, which was designed to help integrate immigrants into American life. She won the Nobel Peace Prize in 1931. Wells-Barnett, an African American, initiated a one-woman anti-lynching crusade in 1892 (Berkin and Norton 1979). She used facts and figures, rather than speculation or opinion, to counter the rationalizations people gave for mob violence.

Sumner's most important contribution to sociology was his classic work, *Folkways*. The book is a study of patterns of behavior in preindustrial societies. He argued that as people found ways to meet their needs, these ways—**folkways,** he called them—became the established ways of behaving. They were also the patterns of behavior that served people's interests.

As folkways pass on to succeeding generations, however, a subtle change occurs. People become convinced that they are not merely ways that work, but ways that are essential to the welfare of society. That is, the folkways are viewed as the only acceptable form of behavior. Then, they become the **mores**, and those who violate them are viewed as a threat to the group and face punishment.

Both folkways and mores are types of norms. And they illustrate the fact that not all norms are equally important. For example, if you don't comb your hair you are breaking a folkway. No one will arrest or assault you, though some people may keep their distance or stare at you. On the other hand, if you view your mission in life as combing everyone else's hair, you will probably be arrested at some point. For you have now broken the mores, which set limits to what you can do to other people (even if the act is relatively harmless).

Whether particular behaviors are folkways or mores can change over time. They can also vary from one group to another within the society. For instance, a professional man who wore a beard was pressured to shave it off when he was a student at a small, religious college during the 1960s. The college administration viewed the beard as a symbol of rebellion and, therefore, a threat to the community. None of those who felt threatened by the beard appeared to notice the irony that a portrait of the college's founder, sporting a full beard, occupied a prominent place in the administration building!

In sum, the pioneers set the tone for the discipline of sociology. They established it as a science—one that would be used for the betterment of humankind. Let's turn to the question, then, of what it means to say that sociology is a science. Clearly, it is not a science like chemistry or biology, but it does share certain characteristics with those sciences. In particular, sociology employs both theories and specific methods in its quest for understanding.

Sociological Theories

"Even the word **theory** makes me yawn," a student told us. We pointed out that everyone uses theories. For in simplest terms, a theory is simply a reasonable explanation about something. More formally, a theory is a set of logically related propositions that explain relationships of social phenomena to each other.

Why Is Theory Important?

Protestants are more likely to commit suicide than are Catholics. How would you explain this fact? An associate explained it to us by noting that for Catholics, suicide is a mortal sin: "If you commit suicide, you spend eternity in hell. So no matter how rotten their lives are, Catholics are not about to commit suicide."

This explanation sounds reasonable until you realize that Catholic rates were lower even during the nineteenth century when Protestants also considered suicide sinful and evidence that a person was probably not a Christian (Durkheim 1951; orig. 1897). Durkheim provided a more sophisticated explanation in his classic investigation of suicide. He looked at suicide rates among various groups and tried to make sense of the variations. He came up with a number of different types of suicide, one of which he called "egoistic suicide."

The following set of logically related propositions summarizes the notion of egoistic suicide:

1. Humans are social creatures.

2. As social creatures, humans have a basic need to have relationships with other humans—to be integrated into some group or groups.

3. When basic needs are not met, negative consequences follow.

4. Therefore, humans who perceive a deficit of meaningful relationships in their lives (that is, a lack of integration into groups) will suffer some kind of negative consequence, ranging from illness to self-destructive behavior.

5. The more a group's structure and processes facilitate a perceived deficit (or, the lower the integration of a group), the higher the rate of suicide among members of that group.

Durkheim pointed out that Protestantism is a highly individualistic (less integrated) religion, while Catholicism places greater emphasis on the group than the individual. Protestantism, therefore, is more likely to create the relational deficit in members' lives that increases the chances of suicide. Thus, it is not a particular belief that makes the difference in the rates, but the social order that the religion creates.

The theory suggests that differing suicide rates exist among other groups. In particular, the greater the group's integration, the lower the suicide rate. Accordingly, Durkheim found that the suicide rates were lower among families with children (domestic integration increases with children in the home) and during times of national crisis (an external threat makes a society more integrated).

In sum, theory is important both because it enables us to make sense out of data and events and because it stimulates us to do additional research. Durkheim's work has stimulated a great deal of research. For example, if suicide is related to relational deficits, you would expect higher rates among single than among married people. Three researchers who tested this notion among white males found that divorced or separated men and those who live alone have significantly higher rates of suicide (Kposowa, Breault, and Singh 1995).The rates were not higher, however, for never-married or widowed men, suggesting that such men have other kinds of social ties which provide them with a sense of being integrated into groups.

Major Theories of Sociology

What, then, are some major theories of sociology? We should note, first, that sociologists employ many different theories, including "middle-range" theories which apply to a specific area. Durkheim's theory of suicide is a middle-range theory. There are also broader theories that provide a perspective, a way of looking at, and understanding, all kinds of phenomena. Four such broad theories are: **structural-functionalism**, **conflict theory**, **symbolic interactionism**, and **feminist theory**.

Structural-Functionalism

According to structural-functionalism (often simply called functionalism), you must learn to look at phenomena as systems. Systems have many parts, and each of these parts contributes to the functioning of the system as a whole. Moreover, the system tends to be stable, held together by shared values and adjusting to outside forces with minimal internal change.

For example, if you want to examine an entire society, then the parts of that system would include such things as the government, the economy, the law, and the family. If you want to examine a family, the parts are the various members—mother, father, son, daughter. In either case, each part contributes something important to the functioning of the system, and the system tends to remain stable over time. At the family level, therapists see an interesting phenomenon in this stability—the tendency of a troubled family to remain troubled even when the apparent problem seems to be resolved. An adolescent female whose father was away from home for long periods of time due to his work had ongoing problems at school—both behavioral and academic. Therapy revealed that the girl was using these problems to gain her father's attention. On occasion he would return home ahead of schedule to deal with her problems. The father rearranged his work life so that he would be at home more, but the family remained troubled. The parents' quarreling increased, and the daughter became the family mediator. It seems that this family found its cohesion in problem solving; if one problem was solved another took its place so that the family system remained stable.

Comte, Spencer, and Durkheim all contributed to structural-functionist ideas. Comte insisted that you need to understand social order before you can understand social change and advocated the use of sociology to bring about a stable social system. Spencer viewed society as an organism, a system of interdependent parts that must function together to maintain the system. Durkheim (1933; orig. 1893) raised the question of what holds a society together. He answered the question by positing two kinds of social solidarity—mechanical and organic.

Mechanical solidarity involves shared ideas and tendencies, the dominance of the group over the individual, and strong sanctions against anyone who deviates from group norms. Mechanical solidarity is found in primitive societies in which people do the same basic kinds of work and share the same world view.

Organic solidarity arises as a society develops and the division of labor becomes more complex. The people are held together by their interdependence, not through shared ideas and sentiments. In organic solidarity, individual rights are strong and individual uniqueness is recognized. However, people also recognize their need for each other. Organic solidarity is found in developed, modern societies.

Structural-functionalism became the dominant theoretical perspective in the United States after World War II. One of the more influential modern advocates of structural-functionalism is Robert Merton (1957).

Merton fine-tuned the notion of functions by pointing out that both latent and **manifest functions** are found in social systems. A manifest function is the intended and recognized consequence of social action. People generally can identify manifest functions. Why do you vote? To help shape the kind of government you have. Why do you go to school? To get the education necessary for a desirable job. Why do you work? To get money to fulfill your needs. Why do you buy a stereo system? To get the relaxation and enjoyment of listening to music.

These are not the only manifest functions of the behaviors, of course. Each of the behaviors also has latent functions—the unintended and unrecognized consequences of social action. Thus, your stereo system may also function to give you a certain amount of prestige (if your system is top-of-the-line); enhance your social life (you can have friends over to listen or to talk about systems or the best CDs); and strengthen your identity as a member of a particular generation (in contrast to your parents, a stereo system is considered essential among your peers).

Conflict Theory

In contrast to structural-functionalism, which stresses stability based on shared values, **conflict theory** emphasizes the diverse and contradictory interests of individuals and groups. It also highlights the inequalities which typically exist because of the scarcity of things that people desire, the resulting conflict as individuals and groups struggle in behalf of their own interests, and the ongoing change that results from that conflict.

In sociology, conflict theory has been heavily influenced by the **dialectical materialism** of Karl Marx (1818-1883) and Frederick Engels (1820-1895). According to dialectical materialism, history is a process driven by material forces (rather than ideas) that exist together but that are in contradiction with each other. If there is progress, then, it is not because leaders are motivated by noble ideas such as democracy and justice, but because there are contradictions in the society that drive the change. For instance, the ownership of the bulk of resources by a small proportion of the population drives the majority into increasing poverty. A contradiction exists between the effort to accumulate wealth and the inability of the masses to support continuing economic development. Ultimately, the impoverished masses rebel against the privileged few and establish a new social order.

Marx and Engels, like the pioneer sociologists, wanted to know how society changes in order to enable the masses of people to seize control of the historical process and gain their freedom. As Marx put it, the point of philosophy is not merely to understand history but to change it by ridding the world of the savage inequalities that exist in societies.

Although structural-functionalism was dominant after World War II, conflict theory became increasingly prominent in the 1960s, advanced by the work of Ralf Dahrendorf. The essence of Dahrendorf's (1959, p. 162) ideas are found in four propositions:

1. Every society is at every point subject to change.

2. Every society is at every point characterized by dissent and conflict.

3. Every element in a society contributes to that society's disintegration and change.

4. Every society involves the coercion of some of its members by other members.

In the four propositions you have the elements of conflict theory: inequality (coercion), contrary interests (dissent), conflict, and continual change. An apt example of the utility of conflict theory is the struggle of women for equal rights. In the United States, women continue to battle such things as career discrimination, income discrimination (men tend to have higher average incomes in every occupational category), and barriers to full political participation (Lauer 1997). However, 1992 was labeled the "year of the woman" by some political observers because of the "many" women elected to national office. Nevertheless, by 1995 women—who are 51.2 percent of the population—comprised only 8 percent of the U.S. Senate, 11 percent of the House of Representatives, 21 percent of state legislators, and 20 percent of elected officials in local governments (U.S. Bureau of the Census 1996d, pp. 279-83).

How can you explain the inequality between men and women? Conflict theorists have a ready answer: the interests of men and women diverge, because they are competing for the same scarce resources—power, wealth, and prestige. Indeed, after World War II, the competition was openly acknowledged as many women were urged or even required to leave their wartime jobs so that returning soldiers would have work.

Symbolic Interactionism

Structural-functionalists and conflict theorists approach the quest for understanding from the top down—i.e., from the larger social and cultural factors that operate in human life (called the macro level). Symbolic interactionism, in contrast, is a quest for understanding that begins at the level of the individual and of interaction between individuals (called the micro level).

Symbolic interactionists view humans as cognitive creatures who are influenced and shaped by their interaction experiences (Lauer and Handel 1983). Humans act on the basis of meaning, and the meaning of any situation depends in part upon the nature of the interaction itself. In other words, what happens in interaction is not merely the result of the kind of people who come to the interaction, but of the interaction itself. Thus, a typically nonaggressive individual might become aggressive in a particular situation because of the nature of the interaction. Or a man who determined to give himself wholly to a career might change his mind as a result of interacting with a particular woman.

At the core of symbolic interactionism is the proposition that behavior must be understood from the point of view of the actors. The meaning of a situation depends, as noted above, on the nature of the interaction itself, but more particularly upon the way in which the actors interpret and understand the nature of the interaction. This notion is captured in the important concept of **definition of the situation** (Thomas 1937)—a concept which asserts that when you define a situation as real, it is real in its consequences. For example, a man may define himself as ill even though physicians can find nothing physically wrong with him. He will continue to feel ill, and that "illness" will affect the way he functions and the way he interacts with other people.

Symbolic interactionists, then, underscore the importance of the actors' points of view. For example, you might expect that women working in an organization and getting less pay than men in similar positions would be outraged and would protest the inequality. But when one of our graduate students, as part of his master's thesis, surveyed women faculty members at a small college where females received less pay than their male colleagues, he found that most of the women felt neither deprived nor angry at the college administration. The student had defined the female professors as victims of discrimination, but they did not define themselves this way and did not react as victims. Rather, most of them considered themselves well off compared to women who did not have such prestigious careers.

Similarly, two researchers who studied a **sample** of African Americans could not explain marital quality on the basis of objective measures such as income, education, or occupation (Clark-Nicolas and Gray-Little 1991). Rather, the subjects rated their marital quality by subjective factors such as their perceptions of the adequacy of their incomes to meet their needs. In essence, actors' perceptions of a situation may differ from those of an observer, and it is the actors' perceptions rather than the observer's assessment that are important for understanding the actors' behavior.

Symbolic interactionism is sometimes called social constructionism, because "reality" is viewed as a social construction and not merely something out there waiting to be perceived. You will see examples of this in subsequent chapters. Here, we will give one simple illustration. Are you afraid to walk alone on city streets at night? Many people are. And many are who, objectively, would be at almost no risk because they walk in neighborhoods that are virtually free of crime. But if you are afraid, you have created a reality—the streets are unsafe at night. Objective data that show you are wrong will not change that reality.

Feminist Theory

As Chafetz (1988) has pointed out, there is no single feminist theory. Some feminist theorists use ideas found in conflict theory, while others use ideas from symbolic interactionism, from Freud, or from other perspectives. But all feminist theories contain four elements.

The first, the "acid test," is that the theory is useful for challenging, refuting, or changing "a status quo that disadvantages or devalues women" (Chafetz 1988, p. 5). Theory, as noted earlier, is meant to facilitate understanding. From a feminist point of view, theory must enable you to understand and counter the disadvantaged position of women. If a theory can be used to support the status quo, it is not feminist. (In Chapter Ten, we will show how structural-functionalism can be used to support the status quo.)

Second, the theory focuses on gender. A prime argument of feminists is that all of social life is gendered, in the sense that men and women are treated differently. Gender, therefore, is at the center of analysis. Third, the theory views gender relations as problematic. They are problematic because of inequalities and struggles between men and women. Fourth, the theory asserts that these problematic gender relations are neither inevitable (the result of nature) nor unchangeable. Social systems can change so that men and women are equal.

We can illustrate feminist theory by looking at how it explains gender inequality. That is, why is it that women are, and always have been, disadvantaged with respect to men? Feminist theorists look at the matter in different ways, but most point to the role of women in bearing and rearing children. In the earliest human societies, an efficient division of labor was for men to provide the food while women bore and cared for the children. This made women more dependent on men than men were dependent on women. Men controlled the means of survival, and they used this control to dominate women.

But why does inequality persist into later societies? The theorists typically point to economic power as the continuing basis for male dominance. The modern homemaker is not as dependent upon her husband as was the primitive woman, but many divorcees can testify to the fact that a woman pays a heavy financial price for the breakup of her marriage (see Chapter Ten). In addition, the theorists assert, because men have always had control of the economic sphere, they will act in ways to insure their continued dominance (such as restricting women's opportunities or supporting the idea that a woman's place is in the home).

A Summary and Critique

Each of the theories makes important points. Structural-functionalism sensitizes you to the need for seeing the whole picture (the system), for understanding the way in which the various parts of the system function together, and for identifying those things that integrate the system into a unified, stable whole. Conflict theory teaches you to look for the inequalities, the diverse interests, and the factors that bring about change. Symbolic interactionism reminds you to take the individual actors into account, understand their viewpoint, and remember that individuals are always more than the sum of social forces that impinge upon them. And feminism sensitizes you to the pervasiveness of male-female inequities and the role of social factors in creating and perpetuating those inequities.

Each theory also has shortcomings. Structural-functionalism doesn't explain conflict or change well. Many sociologists have criticized it as being too conservative, for it states that all the parts serve a useful function in the system and that the system resists change. How then are people to respond to a system that does not serve them well? The point is, a particular system—like a slave society—may be working quite well, in the sense that all parts function appropriately to maintain the whole. Yet the slaves are more concerned with knowing how to change that system than with marveling at how well it works.

Conflict theory, in contrast, doesn't explain social integration well. If every society is characterized by diverse interests and by conflict, what holds it all together? Can't you say anything positive about a society in spite of the inequalities that exist? And how do you account for the fact that some people, who clearly come out on the short end of the good things that a society has to offer, vigorously defend it?

Symbolic interactionism, in overcoming the shortcomings of the other two at the micro level, has difficulty bringing in the important macro level factors. It may be true that the way individuals define a situation is crucial to understanding their behavior in that situation. But how do such things as family, the media, the economy, and religion affect the way individuals define situations? And what of those factors that clearly influence individuals but of which they are unaware?

Finally, in the course of focusing attention on gender, feminist theorists may overlook the similarities between men and women as well as the relative importance of the various factors that bear on human behavior. How do you explain men who are feminists? How do you explain women who oppose feminist objectives? How do you account for the fact that white women, on the average, earn more than Hispanic men?

Clearly, none of the theories alone is adequate to answer all questions. Just as clearly, each of the theories directs attention to important aspects of social phenomena and, thus, provides guidelines that are important to your understanding. Each theory, in other words, provides a way of understanding the data of social life. To help you grasp the significance of the theories, we will highlight places in subsequent chapters where a theory is used to enhance understanding.

Social Research

Now let's turn to another important question: How do you get the data of social life that you can use to understand yourself and your world? We noted that Comte and other pioneers wanted to make sociology a science. Science is one way to address a perennial human concern—how to gain knowledge and solve human problems. Some people have responded to that concern by appealing to a supernatural authority, such as astrology. Some have looked to human authority. Thus, the Western world was dominated for many years by the philosophy of Aristotle, and even scientists were expected to agree with some of Aristotle's erroneous statements.

Other people have claimed that you only need to exercise common sense. As one student put it: "It seems to me that sociology is just using some big words to describe what we all know through common sense." But what is common sense? Frequently, it means the exercise of reason which has been informed by information that is common but came from research. In any case, common sense can be wrong. In subsequent chapters, we will see a number of examples of commonly believed things that are wrong. Meanwhile, consider this: What are the chances that two people in your class were born on the same day of the same month? What does your common sense lead you to say? Undoubtedly it would not lead you to conclude what can be proved from probability theory, that the chances of two people being born on the same day of the same month (such as June 23) are about equal if there are 27 people in the group, about 7 out of 10 if there are 30 people, and about 97 out of 100 if there are 50 people.

Again, what does your common sense tell you to expect about the suicide rates of whites and African Americans? Do more African Americans commit suicide because they experience more deprivation? Common sense might lead you to think so. But actually the suicide rates are higher among whites than among African Americans. In fact, the white suicide rate is twelve times higher than the black rate (U.S. Bureau of the Census 1996, p. 95)!

Science, then, is a way of acquiring knowledge that does not depend upon such things as speculation or common sense. Science must be both theoretical and empirical. You have already seen some of the theoretical approaches of sociology. What does it mean to be empirical? Empirical means that science is based on observation or experience and gathers data. There are four major ways that sociologists and other social scientists gather data: **survey research**, **participant observation**, experiments, and official records and other existing data.

Survey Research

In survey research, interviews and/or questionnaires are used to gather data. The researcher typically gathers the data from a sample, a relatively small number of people selected from some larger population. We will discuss samples further in the next chapter. Surveys provide information about two aspects of the social world. First, they can tell how people are distributed along some question or issue. For example, you could survey people to find out how many favor, are neutral about, or oppose abortion, premarital sex, incumbent politicians, or gun control.

Second, surveys furnish information on the relationships among **variables**. A variable is any trait or characteristic or social factor that has multiple values to which numbers can be assigned. For example, sex is a variable, for one can be either male or female, and the numbers 1 and 2 could be assigned to the two. "Male" or "female" alone is not a variable, however, because one is not more or less male or female. Attitude toward abortion is also a variable, because a person's attitude can vary from strongly approve to strongly disapprove.

Now if you measure attitudes toward abortion, and also get such data about the respondents as sex, age, race, and so on, you can find the relationship between the variables. That is, you can tell whether women are more supportive of abortion than are men (they are), whether the young are more supportive than the old (they are), and whether there are any racial differences (African Americans are somewhat more supportive than are whites).

We'll illustrate the utility of survey research by looking at attitudes about the homeless. In the 1990s, the problems of the homeless concerned many Americans. Who do you think would be more sympathetic to the plight of the homeless—the highly educated or those with less education? And who would be more supportive of economic aid for the homeless? Some students to whom we posed the questions said that those with less education would be more sympathetic and more supportive of aid because they probably earned less and would understand the struggles of the deprived better. Other students thought that those with more education would be more sympathetic and more supportive because they would have more understanding.

Four researchers used survey research to address these questions (Phelan, Link, Stueve, and Moore 1995). They found that the more educated respondents were more sympathetic toward the homeless, but less supportive of aid to the homeless! That sounded like a contradiction to most of the students with whom we talked (this underscores again the dangers of relying on "common sense"). However, the researchers pointed out that in their sympathy for the homeless the respondents reflected the American value of equal opportunity and equal respect, while in their resistance to economic aid they reflected the American conviction that no society will have equal outcomes for all its citizens. Such research, incidentally, is useful to policy makers who want to address the problem of homelessness and who need to know what their constituencies think about the issue.

Participant Observation

Participant observation has been used extensively by symbolic interactionists and involves observation of the social situation in which the researcher is also participating. In other words, the researcher is not a detached onlooker and gatherer of information, but one who gathers data on variables by being an involved observer. For example, suppose you wanted to find out the extent to which people involved in a social movement, such as the pro-life movement, differed in their perspectives from the general population. You could use survey research, and distribute questionnaires to a sample of the general population as well as a sample of people who belong to organizations in the movement. Then you could compare the results.

Or you could join a pro-life organization, talk to members, make notes of things they say and activities they support, and use the data to draw conclusions about the perspectives of pro-lifers. Incidentally, ethical and legal questions arise over whether researchers should identify themselves when joining the organization. Some social scientists believe that researchers should always let their identity and purpose be known, while others argue that much research can be done only if the researcher's identity and purpose are unknown to other members of the group.

An example of knowledge gained by participant observation is the work of Ruth Horowitz (1982) on Hispanic gangs. Gangs are usually thought of as an adolescent phenomenon. However, Horowitz found that some inner-city Hispanics maintained their gang affiliations after they were adults, married, and even parents. Horowitz made her identity known and participated for two years in the gang when the members were all adolescents. She attended meetings and engaged in various activities with them. Four years later, she renewed her contact, again participating in various activities.

As adults, the gang members still approved of certain kinds of illegal activity, mainly drug dealing. They also approved of the use of violence when they felt it was necessary to defend their honor. One factor that helps explain the group, Horowitz found, was the limited financial success of the men. They had jobs, but were not doing well financially. As a result, they sought "their sense of who they are largely in the world of the excitement of the streets" (Horowitz 1982, p. 10).

Another factor that helps explain the group is the Hispanic culture's emphasis on honor. A man may lose honor by being unable to pay for his family's needs or by being treated with disrespect. The willingness to use violence and to engage in some illegal activities reflects the need to maintain honor. Through participant observation, then, Horowitz explained the unusual case of a gang that persisted into the adulthood of its members.

Experiments

Although they use other methods more often, sociologists do appreciate and use the results of experiments. Experimental research is complex, but in essence, the experiment is a method of manipulating some variables, while controlling others, in order to measure the outcome on still other variables.

The variables that are manipulated are called the **independent variables**, while those that are measured are the **dependent variables** (because changes in it depend on the independent variable). There may be a **control group** in the experiment which is not subjected to the independent variable. Only the dependent variable is measured. The control group increases the chances that the effects observed in the experimental groups are indeed due to the independent variable because, hopefully, no such effects occur in the control group.

To understand these concepts, consider the classic experiment by social psychologists Bandura, Ross, and Ross (1963), which addressed the question of whether children become more aggressive as a result of watching violence in the mass media. The researchers divided 48 boys and 48 girls in a nursery school into four groups. One group watched an adult punch and kick a five-foot inflated Bobo doll. A second group watched a film of the adult punching and kicking the doll. The third group watched a cartoon in which a model dressed like a cat engaged in the same aggressive behavior as the adult. The fourth group was not exposed to any aggressive behavior. This last group was the control group.

Because frustrating situations tend to make people more aggressive, the children in each group were then put into a mildly frustrating situation—a room with appealing toys that they were not to touch. Shortly afterward, the children were brought into a room with other toys, some of which could be used for aggressive behavior and others of which could not. The three groups of children exposed to aggression had nearly double the rate of aggressive behavior with the toys as did the fourth group.

In the experiment, the dependent variable was the children's aggressive behavior. The independent variable was the observed aggressive behavior. In addition, the use of the control group increased the researchers' confidence that the rate of aggressive behavior in the children was higher than normal and a result of watching the aggression.

Official Records and Other Existing Data

There are a number of available data banks. The United States government is a dependable source. The various agencies of the government regularly publish a monumental amount of information. For example, suppose you are interested in how much progress minorities have made in income since the civil rights movement began in the 1950s. You could go to the *Statistical Abstract of the United States* and find that information. You would discover that in 1955 the median income of minority families was 55.1 percent that of white families. By 1994, the figures were 60.4 percent for African American families and 59.5 percent for Hispanic families (U.S. Bureau of the Census 1996d, p. 466).In terms of income, African Americans and Hispanics were only slightly better off relative to whites in 1993 than they were in 1955, a fact which is contrary to the perception of many white Americans. It is true that some African Americans have made great progress, but many others have fallen farther behind, so that the median income remains low.

The Bureau of the Census, Department of Health and Human Services, and Department of Justice publish an abundance of data that are useful to your understanding. A number of private organizations, such as the National Opinion Research Center and the Gallup, Harris, and Roper polling organizations, also provide various kinds of useful data. In addition, the World Bank has data available for countries throughout the world.

Finally, sociologists make use of existing data in the communication and printed media. Frequently, such data are analyzed by **content analysis**, which is the determination of the relative frequency of particular ideas, words, or kinds of behavior in the materials. For instance, you could watch children's television shows, and count the number of violent incidents per hour. Or you could read various newspapers to see how they handle a controversial subject and, therefore, how they attempt to shape public opinion.

Another example of content analysis is the study of children's picture books. These books have an impact on children's ideas of what it means to be male or female. What, then, do children learn from such books? Lenore Weitzman and her associates (1972) examined award winning books in the early 1970s and found that females tended to be "invisible," because most of the books were about boys or men or male animals. When females were shown, they were often insignificant or inconspicuous and were generally passive in contrast to the active males.

In the late 1980s, a group of researchers updated the Weitzman study and reported some changes (Williams et al. 1987). Females were then as likely as males to appear in the books. However, their roles were still unattractive or even offensive. Finally, a 1994 study found that the books still tend to portray girls and boys in traditional roles, with girls more likely than boys to use household items and boys more likely than girls to use nondomestic items (Crabb and Bielawski 1994).

Through content analysis, therefore, you can see some progress in the way children's picture books portray females as equal to males. Even in the 1990s, however, the books still teach children that females are more domestic than are males.

Summary

You need to make sense out of the world in which you live. You need to understand both yourself and your world. Understanding has five important functions for you. It helps satisfy your curiosity about yourself and your world. It is a basis for your emotional security. It guides you in interpersonal relationships. It guides organizational behavior. And it is a basis for policy decisions.

Sociology is an important tool in gaining understanding. You learn to think sociologically by understanding humans as social creatures. Social factors affect the totality of your life—all that you think, feel, and do. When you think this way, you have developed the sociological imagination. The sociological imagination does not negate the individual. Rather, it trains you to look for the social factors that affect behavior, and to discover probabilistic relationships at various levels of human life.

The sociological imagination is evident among some ancient thinkers. But sociology as a discipline took shape in the nineteenth century. Auguste Comte is called the father of sociology. Herbert Spencer, Harriet Martineau, Emile Durkheim, Max Weber, Lester Ward, Jane Addams, Ida Wells-Barnett, and William Graham Sumner were among others who made important contributions. These pioneers set the tone for the discipline—that it would be a science of human behavior and that it would enhance human well-being.

Science is both theoretical and empirical. Theory is an important component to our understanding. Structural-functionalism focuses attention on stable systems and their interrelated parts which are held together by shared values. Conflict theory focuses attention on contrary interests and inequality in society, and on the resulting conflict and change. Symbolic interactionism focuses attention on the micro aspects of social life, including the point of view of the actors. And feminism focuses attention on gender as a central factor in social life.

The empirical part of sociology includes four major research methods. Survey research involves the use of interviews and/or questionnaires to gather data. Participant observation is the method of participating in, as well as observing, what is being studied. Experiments employ the manipulation of some variables to see their effects on others. Finally, researchers may use official records and other existing data.

Glossary

conflict theory a sociological theory that focuses on contradictory interests, inequalities, and the resulting conflict and change

content analysis the determination of the relative frequency of particular ideas or words in the content of communication or printed materials

control group an experimental group in which there is no manipulation of the independent variable and only the dependent variable is measured

definition of the situation when you define a situation as real it is real in its consequences

dependent variable the variable in an experiment that is affected in some way by the independent variable

dialectical materialism the theory that history is a process driven by material forces (rather than ideas) that exist together but that are in contradiction with each other

experiment a test designed to verify or disprove a theory by means of the manipulation of some variables, while controlling others, in order to measure the outcome on still other variables

feminist theory a sociological theory that focuses on explaining women's disadvantaged position in society

folkways norms that are defined as not essential to social well-being, thereby incurring only mild sanctions when broken

independent variable the variable in an experiment that is manipulated in order to see how it affects the dependent variable

latent functions unintended and unrecognized consequences of social action

manifest functions intended and recognized consequences of social action

mechanical solidarity a type of social solidarity in which there are shared ideas and tendencies, the dominance of the group over the individual, and strong sanctions against anyone who deviates from group norms

mores norms considered essential to the well-being of the group, thereby incurring severe sanctions when broken

norm a shared expectation for behavior

organic solidarity a type of social solidarity based on people's need of each other in a society with a complex division of labor

participant observation the study of the social situation in which the researcher is also involved

sample a small number of people selected by various methods from a larger population

sociological imagination a way of thinking that enables people to understand the impact of culture, society, and group memberships on their behavior

sociology the scientific study of social life

structural-functionalism a sociological theory that focuses on social systems and how their interdependent parts maintain order

survey research the use of interviews and/or questionnaires to gather data

symbolic interactionism a sociological theory that focuses on the interaction between individuals and the resulting construction of social life

theory a set of logically related propositions that explain relationships of social phenomena to each other

variable any trait, characteristic, or social factor that has multiple values to which numbers can be assigned

CHAPTER TWO

Critical Thinking:
How to Evaluate
Information

How would you answer this question: What are the major problems facing public schools today? A survey of schools in the 1940s found that the main problems were: 1. talking; 2. chewing gum; 3. making noise; 4. running in the halls; 5. getting out of turn in line; 6. wearing improper clothing; 7. not putting paper in wastebaskets. In contrast, a survey in the 1980s reported that the major problems were: 1. drug abuse; 2. alcohol abuse; 3. pregnancy; 4. suicide; 5. rape; 6. robbery; 7. assault.

These two surveys were cited by, among others, a former U.S. Secretary of Education, a Harvard University president, a former chancellor of the New York City public schools, and a number of newspaper columnists. The surveys were used as evidence of a decline in American morality and of an increase in problem behavior in the public schools. Was the evidence provided by these two surveys sufficient to reach these conclusions?

A Yale business professor, Barry O'Neill (1994), was intrigued by the results of these surveys and investigated the matter further. He looked for corroborating evidence as well as for the source of the surveys. He found some contradictory information in a 1984 Gallup poll in which teachers said the two biggest school problems were parent apathy and lack of financial support. The teachers put drugs near the bottom of the list of problems. Moreover, O'Neill couldn't find any polls of teachers that supported the accuracy of these two surveys.

Eventually, O'Neill located the man who had created the surveys. He was a Texas businessman who was concerned about the quality of education in public schools. It turns out that he had not actually conducted surveys. Indeed, the lists of public school problems produced by his surveys were a product of his personal opinions. He explained that he had been in school in the 1940s so he knew what the problems were then. And he knew what the problems were in the 1980s because he "read the newspapers."

The businessman shared the results of his "surveys" widely as he tried to generate concern about the schools. He succeeded in gaining national attention. Some of those who publicized his findings added their own modifications. For example, a former Secretary of Education claimed that they were part of an "ongoing" survey that had asked teachers the same set of questions over the years. A conservative radio talk-show host added a few offenses to the 1980s list. In addition, the Wall Street Journal reprinted the results from another source, which listed the date of the second survey as 1990, thus making it seem more current.

Interestingly, until O'Neill pursued the topic, no one seemed to question the source. Who had conducted the surveys in the first place? No one questioned the sample. How many teachers in what parts of the country were asked to identify the problems? And no one questioned the validity of the conclusion that the surveys revealed moral and academic decline. Even if the teachers' perceptions of school problems had changed so dramatically, was this evidence of a moral decline in American society or of academic deterioration in American public schools?

Such questions illustrate the process of critical thinking. Critical thinking is a crucial component of understanding because it is the way you evaluate the mass of information you face every day. Of course, few people have the time or inclination to pursue the validity of information the way Barry O'Neill did. But that's not necessary. Simply raising the question of who did the research and finding no answer should be enough to make you challenge the results.

At the outset, we'd like to make an important point. Critical thinking is not meant to turn you into a cynic; rather, its purpose is to develop scientific skepticism. The difference is enormous. The cynic sees the negative in everything and believes nothing. Scientific skepticism, in contrast, is part of the scientific frame of mind. It involves a willingness to consider new evidence or evidence that is contrary to what you already believe, and to evaluate carefully all evidence before accepting it as valid.

The Process of Critical Thinking

You have probably heard the phrase, "The facts speak for themselves." If this were true, there would be no need for critical thinking. You would only have to get the facts. In actuality, however, the facts rarely, if ever, "speak for themselves" in the sense that their meaning is clear and that their meaning is the same for everyone.

Facts Must Be Interpreted

Consider, for example, these facts. Kitty Genovese, a 28-year-old woman was stabbed to death in New York City. Her assailant attacked her, left for a short time, then returned and killed her. The attack lasted about half an hour. At least 38 people heard or saw the incident, but no one tried to intervene and no one called for help. These are the facts.

The question is, why didn't anyone try to help Kitty Genovese? The incident took place in 1964 and spawned a good deal of research as social scientists tried to answer this question.

At the time, many people thought they knew how to interpret the facts. The most common interpretations included: people are apathetic and just don't care; or, people are afraid to get involved. Perhaps some of those 38 people were apathetic or afraid. However, a number of social scientists were not satisfied with these "common sense" interpretations and, in response, set up experiments to address the issue of why people don't help in an emergency. For instance, in one experiment, college students were put in a one-person cubicle, provided with a microphone and headphones, and asked to talk about college life with another student, who was in a similar setup nearby (Darley and Latané 1968).

Imagine yourself as one of the volunteers in the experiment. The other person begins the conversation and tells you he is an epileptic—a condition which has caused him problems because seizures can occur when he is stressed by his studies. He stops and you talk a bit. Then it is his turn again, and he returns to the topic of his seizures. As he talks, it is clear that he is beginning to have a seizure, and he soon asks for help.

Would you leave your cubicle and try to help or at least find help? If you did, you would find that you had been talking to a taped voice; there was no young man in the cubicle. The point was to see how you would respond to the emergency. The experimenters made an interesting discovery—over 80 percent of the students tried to help. But when they set up the experiment differently and led the students to believe that either they were one of a group of three or one of a group of five talking together, the likelihood of trying to help decreased significantly. Only 62 percent of those who thought a third person was listening, and only 31 percent of those who thought four other people were part of the discussion, tried to help.

In other words, this experiment showed that the more people there are around, the less likely is any one individual to help. Why? In part, a diffusion of responsibility occurs in a group setting. With many people around, few if any are likely to feel "this is my responsibility." Furthermore, many situations are ambiguous. This one was not, but what if you saw a man and woman struggling together on the street? Is it an attack? Or a domestic dispute? If you intervene in the former, you might be a hero. But most people would hesitate to intervene in the latter.

So why didn't anyone help Kitty Genovese? The facts are plain: at least 38 people saw or heard the attack, and no one helped. The interpretation of the facts is more problematic. Perhaps some of the people were apathetic. Perhaps some were afraid. Perhaps some thought that others who were around, rather than they themselves, would do something. And perhaps some of them weren't sure if the situation really was an emergency that required intervention.

We could make similar points about any set of facts. They don't speak for themselves. They must be interpreted. And critical thinking is an important tool for interpretation.

A Model of Critical Thinking

Shepelak, Curry-Jackson, and Moore (1992) have developed a four-stage process of critical thinking that is useful for sociologists. The first stage, "understanding," involves a careful reading of, or listening to, someone's work. The point is to understand exactly what the author or speaker is saying.

The second stage is "evaluation." In this stage, you make a judgment about whether you accept the work. Do you believe that what was presented was valid and true?

The third stage is "reason for the evaluation." Here you identify the bases for your acceptance or rejection of the work. There are both "low-level" and "high-level" bases. The low-level bases include such things as: the work agrees with what you already believe; you found the information amusing or interesting; you accept the authority of the person or persons responsible for the work; and you didn't detect any problems or errors. The high-level bases include such things as: the work was presented in a logical way; the conclusions were supported by empirical work; and the work followed good scientific procedure.

The final step is "creative resolution." If you accept the work, what additional ideas or further action would you suggest? If you reject the work, what do you propose as an alternative?

In this chapter, we will focus on stages one through three. In particular, we will concentrate on matters you should consider and questions you should ask in evaluating what you read and hear in both the popular media and the professional literature.

Understanding the Information

As Shepelak, Curry-Jackson, and Moore (1992) suggest, the first stage of critical thinking—understanding—requires careful effort. We suggest two steps that can help you gain understanding: reading or listening carefully and then reconstructing what you have read or heard for someone else.

Read or Listen Carefully to the Information Source

As university professors, we both have had the experience of hearing a student comment on a position that he or she believes that we have taken in an earlier lecture. And more than once, the reply has been: "No, you misunderstood. That's not my position. I was just presenting a position taken by another scholar."

The point is, you must carefully attend to any source of information. You cannot listen half-heartedly or read without concentrating if you want to understand the information. As you read or listen, identify the main points being made. Note any causal connections being suggested. At the end of listening or reading, summarize the main message or argument in one or two sentences.

You cannot do the above if you listen to, or read, only part of the information. For instance, a good deal of information is available in newspapers. Take care that you don't simply read a headline and assume you know what the article says. The local paper once ran a story with the headline that a survey ranked our city "number 10 in high car costs." When we read the entire article, we discovered that the "survey" only included twenty cities. In other words, our city ranked in the middle of those surveyed. But the headline had led us to believe that we lived in one of the most expensive cities in the nation for operating an automobile!

Here is another example of how headlines can mislead. In 1996, newspapers around the nation reported the discovery by an astronomer at the University of Pittsburgh of a solar system that is 8.2 light years from Earth. Headlines varied, but four of them were as follows:

"Astronomer may have found star with planets right in the neighborhood" *The Chicago Tribune*.

"Solar system hints at other life forms" *USA Today*.

"Data suggest planetary system around nearby star" *The New York Times*.

"Scientists find planet system like our own" *The Orlando Sentinel*.

If you had read only the headlines, what would you have concluded? Certainly, the second headline raises the possibility of life on other planets in our solar system. The fourth might also lead you to speculate about the possibility of life elsewhere in the universe. Note also that the first and third headlines are more tentative about the discovery than the other two.

In reading the articles, however, we found that most pointed out that the astronomer noted that the star was too faint to create enough heat to support life. At the most, his discovery means that there may be other planetary systems like ours in the universe. Even if they are similar, they will not necessarily contain life. Those who believe that there are other life forms in the universe will not be able to use this discovery to buttress their argument.

Reconstruct the Information

Once you have carefully listened to, or read information, reconstruct it for someone else. If you have listened to someone and have the opportunity, review what was said with the speaker. He or she can then tell you whether you have gotten the message accurately. If you do not have such an opportunity, share what you have learned with someone else.

When you reconstruct something that you have read or heard, you will become aware of whether the information is clear to you. A man lecturing at a public seminar confessed to us that he was in the midst of teaching a complex idea when he realized that the idea wasn't completely clear in his own mind. He said: "Thank heavens no one raised a question." He didn't realize that his own understanding was deficient until he tried to teach it.

We have often urged students, only half jokingly, to share what they learn in class with a date, with family members, or with friends. Such sharing is not to impress others, but to clarify the material in your own mind. At any rate, the first essential step in critical thinking is to make sure you understand. Once you do, you are ready for evaluation.

Evaluating Information in the Professional and Popular Media

One of the traps people easily fall into is the unquestioning acceptance of authority. Just as Milgram's subjects acquiesced to the authority of the scientist, you may find yourself unthinkingly accepting the authority of not only the scientist but also the physician, the plumber, and the auto mechanic. Indeed, because no one is an expert in all things, it is necessary to depend upon others' knowledge. Still, no expert, nor even any group of experts, is infallible.

Furthermore, even if you read a study in a professional journal and judge it solid in terms of theory, methods, and conclusions, keep in mind that there are generally a number of possible interpretations of the data. For example, South and Lloyd (1995) found that a substantial proportion of men and women who divorce are romantically involved with someone other than their spouses prior to the divorce. That's the fact, but what does it mean? Are they romantically involved because they are unhappy in their marriages? Or are they unhappy in their marriages because they have become romantically involved—intentionally or not—with someone else? Was the romantic involvement a factor in the divorce, or would they have divorced in any case?

In other words, you need to evaluate information in the professional as well the popular media. We will offer some guidelines for your evaluation. First, however, we want to underscore one of the reasons for evaluating: the fact that neither the science of human behavior nor the social scientist is infallible.

Social Science: Fallible People Using More-or-Less Precise Methods

Again, this discussion is designed to make you a critical thinker, not a cynic. We just don't want you to unthinkingly accept any information simply because it comes from a recognized authority.

Scientists Are Human

To say that scientists are human is simply to recognize that, like everyone else, scientists can be wrong, can make mistakes, and can have their thinking distorted by biases. Consider, for example, the findings of two psychologists who examined all articles published in four journals in their field over a one-year span (Hernandez and White 1989). They checked 1,278 quotations against the original sources. They could not find 89 of the quotations in the cited original source. And they found errors in 519 other quotes that ranged from the trivial (punctuation differences) to the significant (the meaning was changed by alteration from the original).

An illustration from sociology is the widely quoted and influential conclusion of Weitzman (1985) regarding the financial impact of divorce on women. Within a year after a divorce is finalized, Weitzman (1985, p. 339) claimed, "men experience a 42 percent improvement in their . . . standard of living, while women experience a 73 percent decline." Weitzman's work was cited in hundreds of professional and popular sources as well as in a number of court cases and was a major factor in the passage of new legislation in California.

Other research had found that men, on the average, experience an improvement and women, on the average, experience a decline in standard of living after divorce. However, Weitzman's figures were far more dramatic. In fact, they were so dramatic that Richard Peterson (1996) did a reanalysis of the data. While he did not have the exact same data that Weitzman used, and the situation is more involved than we will discuss here, the bottom line is that he found a 10 percent increase for men and a 27 percent decline for women—figures more in line with the work of other researchers and far below Weitzman's earlier calculations. In response, Weitzman (1996), while cautioning not to overlook the rest of her work or the fact that a significant disparity exists, acknowledged that her figures were inaccurate.

So, scientists do make mistakes. There have been a few reported cases of fraud (in both biomedical and social scientific research), in which scientists faked data or engaged in other unethical or illegal behavior (Froelich and Moe 1985; Boffey 1987), but most of the cases are simply human error. Scientists, like other people, are not invulnerable to mistakes.

Social Scientific Methods Are More or Less Precise

If you think that true science gives only precise and unambiguous results, consider the following, which is only one of many illustrations that could be given. Two biomedical studies published in the October 24, 1985 issue of the *New England Journal of Medicine* came to opposite conclusions (Winkler 1985).One of the studies followed 1,234 post-menopausal women over the age of 50 for eight years. The 24 percent of the women who were using estrogen, the researchers concluded, had a 50 percent *greater risk* of cardiovascular disease than women who did not use the hormone. The second study surveyed 121,964 female nurses aged 30 to 55 over a four-year period. Among the 32,317 women in the sample who were postmenopausal, those who had used estrogen had a lower risk of cardiovascular disease than those who did not use the hormone!

As with the other sciences, social scientific conclusions must always be viewed as tentative because the methods are more or less precise. Each of the methods we discussed in the last chapter has its strengths and its weaknesses. For example, survey research can yield quite different results depending on the way the questions are worded. Two public opinion surveys on affirmative action came to quite different conclusions (Langer 1989).One survey asked people: "All in all, do you favor or oppose affirmative action programs in employment for blacks, provided there are no rigid quotas?" Nearly three-fourths of the respondents favored such programs. The other survey asked: "Because of past discrimination, should qualified blacks receive preference over equally qualified whites in such matters as getting into college or getting jobs, or not?"Nearly eight of ten of the respondents opposed such affirmative action.

Sometimes the differences in wording may sound very trivial. A case well-known to social scientists is the 1940 survey in which one sample was asked, "Do you think the U.S. should forbid public speeches against democracy?" while another sample was asked, "Do you think the U.S. should allow public speeches against democracy?" In the first sample, 54 percent agreed that the U.S. should forbid such speeches; in the second sample, 75 percent said that the nation should not allow such speeches. The majority was against the speeches in both samples, but the proportion against was strikingly different.

Each of the other methods also has shortcomings. Participant observation clearly depends upon the ability and perspective of the researcher and is based on the debatable assumption that the researcher's presence does not alter what happens in the group. Experiments put people into artificial situations, making the debatable assumption that they will behave in real situations as they do in the experimental one. And the use of official records makes the debatable assumption that those who gathered the data were accurate and unbiased and that the data are trustworthy.

What such shortcomings mean is not that you can learn nothing by using the methods, but that you must not regard any conclusions as the unassailable truth. When a number of different researchers, using various methods, come to the same essential conclusion, confidence in that conclusion is greatly strengthened. Social science, like all science, is a cooperative effort in which researchers build upon and depend upon each other's work as they strive for greater understanding.

Questions to Ask When Evaluating Professional Sources

Critical thinking requires, among other things, that you know what questions to raise. If the information comes from a professional source, the following questions are pertinent:

What Was the Sample?

In order to determine the **generalizability** of a study, you must have information about the sample. Generalizability refers to the extent to which the results of the study apply to other subjects, groups, or conditions. For example, suppose you survey a **representative sample** of students in a particular college or university. A representative sample is one that typifies the population from which it is drawn. In other words, your sample would have the same proportion of males and females, of racial and ethnic groups, of age range as the entire school. There are ways to obtain such samples, but the important point here is to be aware of whether the sample is representative, and, if so, of what population (an organization or group of organizations, a city, the nation, etc.).

Let's suppose that, in your survey, you discover that the males in the sample are twice as likely to use illegal drugs as are the females. To whom can you generalize the results? Can you say that males generally are twice as likely as females to use the drugs? Or can you generalize to those in your city, or those in the same age group, or to all college and university students? Actually, you can only generalize to the school itself. If the sample was representative, you can say that males in your college or university are twice as likely as females to use illegal drugs.

Of course, you would like to generalize as widely as possible. You would like to make statements about all males and females, not just those in one college or university. Yet you can only do this if the sample is representative of the entire population to which you want to generalize.

As you read the professional literature, you will find that samples range from the nationally representative to samples of convenience (the students in one or more of the researcher's classes). Because representative samples require considerably more resources (time, money, organizational help) than other kinds—resources which are not available to all researchers—you will find a great many nonrepresentative samples. Research based on such samples is still useful, but you must take care about generalizing from it. At most, you can say that the findings may apply to larger populations, but additional research is required.

To illustrate, consider the question of dating violence: how much violent or abusive behavior (ranging from mild acts such as shoving to severe violence such as beating or rape) occurs in dating situations? No national study has been done, so we must rely on those taken in various local areas. And the results vary considerably. In a sample of 644 high school students, 12 percent said they had been involved in abusive behavior on a date (Henton et al. 1983). Incidentally, the use of "abusive behavior" rather than "violence" creates another possible reason for variation: if you don't ask exactly the same question, you won't get totally comparable results. In another sample, of 256 high school students, 35.5 percent said they had experienced some kind of violence on a date (O'Keefe, Brockopp, and Chew 1986). Among college-age and older, from two-thirds to three-fourths report abuse in a dating situation (Laner and Thompson 1982; Marshall and Rose 1990).

What can you conclude? The proportion of Americans who experience violent or abusive behavior on a date isn't known, but the chances of being a victim depend on where you are and your age. Even in the best of situations, the probability may be higher than most people imagine.

Are the Conclusions Reasonable?

We do not mean "reasonable" in terms of your own experience or expectations. Research sometimes uncovers information that is contrary to your—and even the researcher's own—experience and expectations. Rather, conclusions are to be evaluated as reasonable in two ways. First, are they reasonable in terms of other research and existing knowledge? If a piece of research is contrary to all past research, you must be very tentative about your acceptance of it.

For example, we noted earlier that many researchers had found an increase in men's and a decrease in women's standard of living following divorce, but no one had come up with figures as dramatic as Weitzman's. Peterson raised the appropriate question of whether Weitzman's findings were reasonable and doubted that they were. Weitzman's sample was of California women, so it could be possible that those women suffered far more of a loss than, say, women on the East Coast. However, Peterson discovered that California women suffer a standard-of-living loss comparable to women in other states where research has been conducted.

The other sense in which it is appropriate to ask about whether the conclusions are reasonable is: Do they logically follow from the results of the research? Generally, they will. But you may find that the researchers state the conclusions in a way that is not warranted by the methods they used.

For instance, how much does the extent to which you believe your father takes an interest in your activities affect your self-esteem? One study of this issue found, among other things, that adolescents in two-parent families who perceived their fathers as more interested in their siblings than in them had lower self-esteem than those who perceived their fathers to be as interested in them as their siblings. Note the "perceived" interest. The researchers did not ask the fathers about their interest in their children. Some or even most of the adolescents could be wrong in their perceptions. Yet recall that symbolic interactionist theory points out the need to understand the actor's point of view. If an adolescent, for whatever reason, defines the father as having less interest in him or her than in a sibling, that adolescent's self-esteem is likely to suffer even if he or she is wrong about the father.

For the most part, the authors of the study are careful to indicate that the interest is perceived. However, in their closing discussion, the authors state that "the results of the present study support the idea that adolescents whose fathers' interest in them is low may have a more difficult time preserving self-esteem" and "paternal favoritism toward a sibling may be disadvantageous to self-esteem" (Clark and Barber 1994, p. 613). These statements are inaccurate and misleading because you don't know how much interest the fathers actually displayed, only the subjects' perceptions of interest. Yet one can imagine someone reading the article and reporting in a popular source that some adolescents suffer from low self-esteem because their fathers are not interested in them.

Does Statistical Significance Mean Substantive Significance?

This is a difficult but important question. In much of the professional literature, you will find various kinds of statistical analyses. Many of these analyses involve some kind of **test of significance**, which is simply a technical way of determining the probability that the findings occurred by chance.

Thus, in the study cited above about adolescents' self-esteem and their perceptions of their fathers' interest, the researchers found the relationship to be statistically significant. This means that there is a high probability that the relationship between self-esteem and perceived paternal interest is a real one rather than one which could have occurred by chance. Further, because it is statistically significant, you could expect to draw other samples and find the same relationship (rather than finding that perceived father's interest makes no difference in self-esteem).

However, statistical significance only means that the relationship was probably not a chance finding that is unlikely to be repeated. It does not tell how important the relationship is, or whether there are real-life consequences of the relationship. In the Clarks' and Barbers' study of adolescents, the researchers reported an average self-esteem score of 5.05 for those perceiving high paternal interest, and 4.53 for those perceiving low paternal interest. The question is, does an average 0.52 difference in self-esteem scores make any difference in adolescents' lives? Does it affect school performance, or interpersonal relationships, or life satisfaction? We don't know.

Let's explore the matter a little further by looking at the way self-esteem was measured. We don't have full information, but the researchers tell us that they had the subjects respond to three questions, such as "How often do you feel good about yourself?" on a scale of one (never) to seven (daily).The report doesn't state whether they assigned names to the other numbers (such as two equals rarely, three equals seldom, etc.). While an adolescent who scores four on such a scale is significantly lower in self-esteem statistically than one who scores five, how much difference will that make in their lives? Again, we don't know. It could make a good deal of difference. Or it could make no difference. The point is, statistical significance does not necessarily translate into important substantive differences.

How Could the Emphasis Given to Conclusions Be Changed?

Researchers typically work on the basis of one or more hypotheses, which are tentative statements about the relationships between phenomena. Hypotheses can be constructed on the basis of theory, other known research, or both. An example of a **hypothesis** is: The higher an adolescent perceives paternal interest to be, the higher the adolescent's self-esteem. In the research we have been discussing, the hypothesis was supported. What should be emphasized in the conclusions? You could simply emphasize the importance of perceptions of paternal interest for adolescent self-esteem, and this is what the researchers tried to do. Or, in light of the discussion above, you could also emphasize the fact that it isn't known if the self-esteem differences found here have any important impact on adolescents' lives.

Or you could emphasize something else. The researchers reported a total of 446 subjects in the high interest, high self-esteem category, and 255 subjects in the low interest, low self-esteem category. So you could emphasize the fact that in this sample of Michigan students nearly two-thirds reported high paternal interest. Or you could believe that all fathers should show such interest and stress the fact that fully a third of the students perceived low paternal interest.

The point is, there are various ways to emphasize the results of any research. In the Milgram research discussed in the last chapter, the emphasis is typically given to the fact that two-thirds of the subjects were willing to administer 450 volts to another person. What about the fact that a third of the subjects, even in the face of pressures from a scientist, refused to continue the experiment? Thus, there are various ways to state conclusions, and it can be both interesting and useful to emphasize the findings in different ways.

Questions to Ask When Evaluating Popular Sources

It's important to give careful attention to the evaluation of popular sources for several reasons. First, popular sources are the basis for much of what is called the "conventional wisdom"—the things that "everyone" knows to be true but which may be only partially true or untrue altogether. Many people, for example, "know" that people are apathetic. They "prove" their position by noting public response in the Kitty Genovese murder or the proportion of registered voters who vote in local elections. Thus, the facts have been interpreted. The interpretation seems to provide a reasonable explanation. And enough people accept the interpretation so that it becomes a part of the conventional wisdom.

Second, popular sources contain useful information which may be derived, in part, from professional sources. Yet whatever the source, the information must be carefully evaluated before being accepted.

Third, popular sources regularly report, and frequently distort, the results of social scientific research. A social scientist may draw a tentative conclusion from a piece of research only to find the popular media reporting it as a proven fact. Or the popular media may simplify the results of a complex piece of research to such an extent that a full understanding is impossible.

An example of distortion and possible misunderstanding is a newspaper article entitled, "Violence is darker side of self-esteem" (Torassa 1996).The article began with an assertion made by a psychology professor: The effort to enhance self-esteem "as an antidote to violent behavior is not only fruitless, it may even lead to aggression."A check of the article shows this statement to be misleading. The primary conclusion of the authors was that people who engage in violent behavior do not suffer from low self-esteem, that low self-esteem does not lead to violence, and that "certain forms of high self-esteem seem to increase one's proneness to violence" (Baumeister, Smart, and Boden 1996, p. 26). The forms that might increase proneness to violence are those found in such people as "arrogant narcissists and conceited, egotistical bullies," the individual whose "self-appraisal is unrealistically positive" and who has an "exaggerated impression of being superior" (Baumeister, Smart, and Boden 1996, pp. 27-28).

In sum, the newspaper article could leave you with the impression that only harm can come from continuing efforts to raise people's self-esteem. The professional article, on the other hand, cautioned against regarding high self-esteem as a cure-all for violent behavior and noted that the excessive, unrealistic self-esteem of the egocentric individual is associated with the proneness to violence.

In evaluating popular sources, then, we suggest that you carefully read or listen. Then ask a number of questions.

If an Author's Name Is Given . . .

What else do you know about the author? Is the author an authority on the topic? Does the author have an axe to grind? The author of the "surveys" of high school problems that we discussed at the beginning of this chapter is clearly not an authority and just as clearly had an agenda of his own.

An important point to keep in mind here is that no one is an authority on everything. Sometimes people who are noted experts in one field speak out on a topic unrelated to their field, and their statements gain a certain credibility because of their credentials. In the 1960s and 1970s, a Nobel Prize winning physicist, William Shockley, engaged in a personal crusade to convince the world that African Americans are, intellectually, genetically inferior to whites. At the time of his crusade, he was a professor of engineering science at Stanford.

No doubt because Shockley was highly respected as a physicist, some people felt that Shockley must be correct. Yet why would Shockley be more believable than anyone else who made the same claim? And why would he be more credible than all the social scientists who disputed his claims? The point is not that you should dismiss the views of anyone who is not an authority in a particular field. The point is that you should exercise caution and not accept someone's opinion simply because the person has significant achievements in an unrelated field.

If a Claim Is Made or a Conclusion Is Drawn . . .

Half of all marriages end in divorce. Correct? Actually, the idea that half of all marriages end in divorce has become a part of the conventional wisdom of America. We published an article in a popular magazine in 1985 on the results of our research on the factors that result in marriage being both lasting and satisfying. Without our knowledge or permission, the editor added a sentence at the beginning of the article—probably as a hook for readers—about the "fact" that half of all marriages fail.

How did the myth arise? It might have been a misinterpretation of the data (Lauer and Lauer 1997). In 1981, there were 2.4 million marriages and 1.2 million divorces in the nation—one divorce for every two marriages. But one divorce and two marriages involves three couples, only one of which was divorced. In that year, in addition, there were 54 million couples who had married prior to 1981 and whose marriages remained intact. Some of them would eventually divorce, of course, but the point is that computing the number of marriages that will eventually end in divorce is a very complex process.

Actually, divorce rates vary a good deal by generation. Among some age groups, half or more of the marriages will probably fail. But the divorce rate would have to continue at its 1981 rate well into the twenty-first century before it would be true to say that half of all marriages end in divorce. Moreover, divorce rates have declined somewhat since 1982. Overall, only about a fourth of adults who have ever been married have also been divorced.

Whenever you see a claim, therefore, it is always appropriate to raise these questions: upon what is this claim based and can the information be checked? Sometimes the information may be difficult to verify, such as the proportion of marriages that end in divorce. And sometimes it is impossible to verify. We once heard a man claim on a radio program that newspapers had reported the facts until after World War II when they were taken over by the "liberal establishment." It is hard to either accept or dispute such statements because they are so subjective and cannot be validated.

If "facts" are presented and a conclusion drawn, ask whether the data support the conclusion. Be alert for a **non sequitur**, a conclusion that does not logically flow from a premise or from data which presumably support the conclusion.

For example, advertisements for a widely used mouthwash touted the product's ability to kill millions of germs and thereby help prevent colds. Even if the mouthwash killed the germs, however, does it follow that it would also help prevent colds? The federal government didn't think so, and forced the manufacturer to change the advertisements.

If a Causal Connection Is Made . . .

We are usually interested in cause-and-effect relationships. What caused the Second World War? Why do working women have better health than those who do not work? Why are millions of Americans unemployed? What has caused the so-called mainline Protestant denominations in America to decline in members? And so on.

The newspaper article referred to above, regarding self-esteem and violent behavior, suggested that building people's self-esteem could actually increase their propensity for violence. This causal conclusion, as we noted, is misleading. Another way results can be distorted is to confuse statistical **correlation** with causation. Even professionals sometimes make this error, so you need to understand the meaning of correlation.

Professional papers frequently report a statistically significant correlation between two or more variables. Correlation is a statistical procedure that refers to the extent to which two phenomena vary the same way, from 0 to 100 percent. Thus, if you look at income level in communities and crime rates, a high correlation would mean that the higher the income, the higher the crime rate. A high inverse correlation would mean the higher the income, the lower the crime rate. The higher the correlation, the more the income levels and crime rates follow the pattern. A zero correlation means that there is no relationship at all between income level and crime rates.

Yet correlation does not mean causation. In other words, without additional information, you cannot say that income level causes crime rates (such as lower-income people commit more crimes) or that crime rates cause lower income level (such as well-to-do people move out of high-crime areas). Both claims may be true. Or they may be false. But you cannot make either claim on the basis of a correlation.

Take for example the research into perceived fathers' interest and self-esteem. The researchers actually used a different statistical procedure than correlational analysis. However, a correlation undoubtedly exists between the two scores, and this means that those with higher perceived fathers' interest also tend to have higher self-esteem. But the correlation itself would not say that the relationship is a causal one. It is possible that high perceived fathers' interest does lead to higher self-esteem. The opposite causal connection is also possible—that high self-esteem in an adolescent causes him or her to perceive higher father interest. It is also possible that some other factor, not considered in the research, causes the level of both perceived father interest and self-esteem.

A humorous example of another factor is the story of the man who drank vodka and water on Monday, gin and water on Tuesday, whiskey and water on Wednesday, and tequila and water on Thursday. He got drunk each day, and concluded that water—the common element—was the cause.

If the popular source indicates a causal connection, you may need to check out the source to see whether the researcher indicated only a correlation or actually did the kind of analysis that would support a causal conclusion.

If a Poll Is Reported . . .

As with the professional literature, you should always question the sample. The poll might consist of people who listen to, and responded to, a particular radio program. Or people who took the time to call in their responses to a question on a 900 number. Or people who took the time to fill out and mail in a magazine's questionnaire. Such polls are not useless, but they must be used with great caution.

Consider the question of how many Americans get involved in extramarital affairs. A *Cosmopolitan* magazine poll some years ago reported that 54 percent had affairs, while a *Ladies' Home Journal* poll put the figure at 21 percent. What can you determine from such figures? The magazines' figures are based on readers who responded to their polls, and it isn't known if those who responded were representative of all readers. So you can only say that 54 percent of those who responded to the *Cosmopolitan* poll and 21 percent of those who responded to the *Ladies' Home Journal* poll had affairs. You can't even be sure if those numbers apply to all readers of the magazines, much less to the American public.

A more scientific and recent piece of research, based on a national survey of 3,432 American men and women between the ages of 18 and 59, found that about a fourth of married men and 15 percent of married women acknowledged that they had an affair (Laumann et al. 1994). Clearly, the *Cosmopolitan* poll was misleading in terms of being generalizable to the American population. Still, the poll was not useless. You can at least say that the kind of people who read *Cosmopolitan* (and the magazine can give you a profile of its readership) and who take time to respond to its poll have a higher rate of infidelity than the American population generally.

If Quotes Are Given . . .

All people have "red flags," words or phrases that are likely to elicit an emotional response from them. It is important to know what kinds of things are red flags for you, so that your critical thinking processes are not turned off by an emotional response.

Many politicians seem to use red-flag words and phrases as they run for election or re-election or as they press their agendas. Moreover, they have been doing this from the earliest days of the nation. "Presidential politics have been rude, nasty and highly personal since George Washington's election" (Tackett 1996). Critics accused Thomas Jefferson of taking one of his slaves as a mistress and of planning to outlaw Christianity. Lincoln was said to have an illegitimate daughter. Critics called Samuel Tilden, the 1876 Democratic candidate, a "drunken, syphilitic swindler."

Similarly, politicians may use emotionally charged words as they press for or resist a piece of legislation. Many social welfare programs have been labeled "creeping socialism." For some people, the word "socialism" causes an immediate and strong negative reaction. Rational discussion is likely to stop if they accept the idea that a program or proposed program is socialistic.

For the past several years, the question of women in military combat has been debated. In 1995, a U.S. congressman addressed the issue by arguing that women are not generally suited for combat: "If combat means living in a ditch, females have biological problems staying in a ditch for 30 days because they get infections" (Englemann 1995). Such a statement is more likely to generate arguments and charges of sexism than rational discussion.

The point is, a position is neither true nor false because the individual uses emotionally charged words or phrases. The question to raise is not whether the individual is racist, sexist, or chauvinist, but what the individual's position is and how can you rationally evaluate that position.

If Numbers Are Used . . .

Few things impress us more than numbers. "You can't argue with numbers" is a statement used to rebut opposing arguments. Yet numbers can be tricky. For example, considerable concern exists in the nation about the relative earnings of men and women. From 1985 to 1990, the median weekly earnings of male wage and salary earners increased by 19.5 percent, while those of females increased by 25.6 percent (U.S. Bureau of the Census 1995, p. 433).What would you conclude? Perhaps that women were making great gains in their struggle for equality in the workplace.

Now look at the figures differently. In 1985, the median weekly earnings of women were $129 less then men's, while in 1990 they were $137 less than men's. Now what would you conclude? Perhaps that women had lost ground over the five-year period. Finally, look at the figures in a third way. What are women's earnings as a percentage of men's? If there is perfect equality, they will be 100 percent—that is, equal. In 1985, women earned 68.2 percent as much as men, while in 1990 they earned 71.8 percent as much. Now what would you conclude?

Think about the ways you could use these numbers to support a particular position. You could use the percentage increase and argue that women have made considerable progress. You could use the female percentage of male earnings and argue that women have only made moderate progress. Or you could use the absolute difference between the two figures on earnings and say that women have lost ground.

Why do the differences compute differently than the percentages? The answer is in the base. Men's weekly earnings in 1985 were $406, while women's were $277. Because the figures for men derive from a larger base ($406), it is possible to have both a smaller percentage increase for men than for women and a larger absolute difference between the two groups.

Whenever percentages or differences are given, then, you need to ask about the base. What would you think if you read that the murder rate in your community had risen 100 percent since last year? Would you feel differently if the article pointed out that there were two murders this year compared to one last year versus 200 murders this year and

100 last year? Of course, the percentage increase is still the same in either case.

Or consider this 1996 newspaper headline: "Dramatic increase in cholera in U.S. spurs warning." Cholera is a disease of the small intestine that can cause death within hours. It is a significant health problem in parts of Asia and can lead to massive numbers of deaths. We read the article and calculated that the annual number of cholera cases in the United States from 1992 to 1994 was 960 percent higher than the annual average from 1961 to 1991! Clearly, the increase was "dramatic." Unless you looked at the actual numbers. From 1961 to 1991, there was an average of five cases of cholera per year in the United States. From 1992 to 1994 there was an average of 53 cases per year, nearly all of which were acquired from foreign travel.

Another question to raise about numbers is their substantive meaning. This is similar to the question we raised about the difference between statistical and substantive significance for professional articles. As an example, a cigarette ad from a popular magazine claims the lowest tar of all cigarettes. The advertised product has only three milligrams of tar, while other brands have anywhere from four to seven milligrams.

What does this mean? Are three milligrams safe? Or are they significantly safer than those with four or five milligrams? Should a three milligram cigarette be exempt from the Surgeon General's warning about the hazards of smoking? Or does it simply mean that it will take longer to die if you smoke cigarettes with three milligrams than those with four or more?

If a Mean or Median Is Given . . .

Two numbers are also frequently cited that merit additional attention—the mean and the median. The **mean** is simply the average, all of the scores divided by the number of cases. The **median** is the number below which are half of all the scores and above which are the other half. Note that we used the median figure in the illustration about men's and women's weekly earnings. The government typically uses median figures for income because means can be misleading when dealing with income. Think of it this way. Suppose you read that the mean income in a particular neighborhood is $180,000. Would your sense of that neighborhood change if you read, instead, that the median income is $50,000? Table 2.1 illustrates how this could happen. Note that there are three families above and three below the median. But the family with the $1 million income raises the mean considerably without affecting the median. If you only had the figure for the mean income, therefore, you might have a distorted notion of the financial state of the families in the neighborhood. Both the mean and the median provide important information, but it is important to understand the kind of information each gives.

Table 2.1	Income in a Hypothetical Neighborhood	
	Family	**Annual Income**
	1	$1,000,000
	2	60,000
	3	55,000
	4	50,000
	5	40,000
	6	30,000
	7	25,000
	Mean income:	$180,000
	Median income:	$50,000

If a Graph Is Shown . . .

Graphs are useful for assisting understanding. To see a line graph or bar graph may be more helpful than a paragraph of numbers and explanation. However, graphs can also mislead. Look at figures 2.1 and 2.2.

Each gives the same information, but not the same impression. If you did not look carefully at the numbers, you could assume a much greater decline in marriage rates from figure 2.2 than from figure 2.1.

Would the popular media mislead you by drawing a graph in a particular way? We would not say that the distortion was intended, but Orcutt and Turner (1993) have documented such a case. In early 1986, various news media took information from annual surveys of student

Figure 2.1   Marriage rates, per 1,000 population

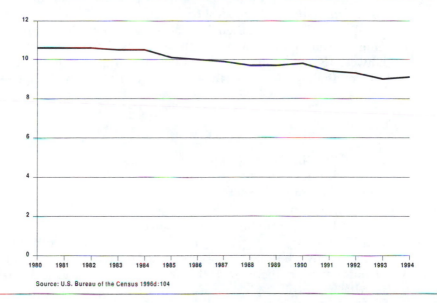

Source: U.S. Bureau of the Census 1996d:104

Figure 2.2   **Marriage rates, per 1,000 population**

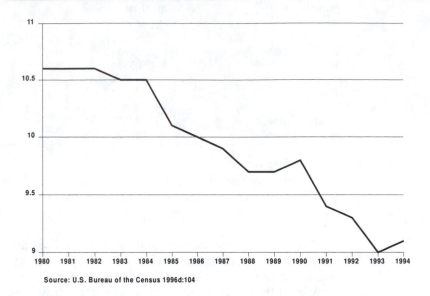

Source: U.S. Bureau of the Census 1996d:104

drug use, depicted it graphically, and declared that the nation had, as one source put it, a "coke plague." If you computed the numbers, you would find a 7.4 percent increase from 1984 to 1985. However, a national news magazine drew a graph that, visually, made the 1985 figure appear to be double that of 1984! The graph gave the impression that the nation was experiencing a dramatic rise in cocaine use when in fact the increase was a relatively modest one.

If a graph is given, then, look at the numbers. What are the beginning and end points of the graph? What is the percentage difference between the beginning and end points? The graph will give you the right information, but it may or may not give you the correct impression.

Summary

Critical thinking is a crucial part of your understanding. It is the process by which information is evaluated. Critical thinking means scientific skepticism, not cynicism.

Critical thinking is necessary because facts must be interpreted. One model of critical thinking for sociologists involves four stages. The first is understanding, or carefully reading or listening in order to understand exactly what the author or speaker is saying. The second stage is evaluation, a judgment of whether the information is valid and true. The third stage involves giving a reason for your evaluation, the bases for your acceptance or rejection. And the fourth stage is creative resolution, in which you advance in some way beyond the work you have evaluated.

Understanding requires you to read or listen carefully to the entire information source. Getting just part of the information can be misleading. To make sure you understand, try to reconstruct the information for someone else.

Professional sources need to be evaluated for a number of reasons. Social scientific methods are only more-or-less precise. Each of the methods has weaknesses as well as strengths. Social scientists are fallible. There have been a few cases of fraud, but most mistakes are human error. And data are generally subject to a number of different interpretations or emphases.

When evaluating professional sources, a number of questions should be raised. What was the sample? You need to know the kind of sample in order to know the extent to which the findings can be generalized. Are the conclusions reasonable in terms of other research and existing knowledge? Are the conclusions reasonable in the sense that they logically follow from the results of the research? Does statistical significance mean that the results have substantive significance? And how could the emphasis given to the conclusions be changed?

When evaluating popular sources, it may be useful to examine any professional source which is cited as a basis for information. If an author's name is given, ask about the author's qualifications. If a claim is made or a conclusion drawn, ask upon what basis the claim is made, whether the information can be checked out, or whether the data provided support the conclusion. If a causal connection is made, ask whether the research supports causation or only correlation.

If a poll is reported, ask about the sample. If quotes are given, watch for any emotionally charged words or phrases. If numbers are used, ask about the base for any percentages, see if you can manipulate the numbers in other ways, and raise the question of the substantive meaning of the numbers. If either a mean or median is given, keep in mind how the figure not given might differ from the one given. If a graph is shown, check the beginning and end numbers and compute the percentage change shown on the graph.

Glossary

correlation the extent to which two phenomena vary in the same way, from 0 to 100 percent

generalizability the extent to which the results of a study apply to other subjects, groups, or conditions

hypothesis a tentative statement about the relationship between phenomena

mean the average, or all of the scores divided by the number of cases

median the number below which are half of all the scores and above which are the other half

non sequitur a conclusion that does not follow logically from what precedes it

representative sample a sample that typifies the population from which it is drawn

test of significance a technical way of determining the probability that the findings occurred by chance

CHAPTER THREE

Culture: *How Social Life Varies*

In word association, someone gives you a word and you respond with any additional words that pop into your mind. For example, what do you think of when you hear the word "kissing?" You probably have a positive reaction, and you no doubt link kissing with romance. Yet kissing has many different meanings, and not all of them are positive. Depending on the social context, a kiss may be a sign of friendship, a sexual act, a show of respect, a form of ritual, a health-threatening act, or a disgusting act that merits condemnation.

In the United States, the kiss runs the gamut from the romantic to the religious—from the torrid embrace in movies to the "holy kiss" practiced by some fundamentalist Christians as a part of their worship. The kiss is also a common form of greeting among family and friends as well as a sign of respect—as when a Catholic priest kisses the ring of his bishop.

In other societies, the kiss may have a very different meaning. Among certain groups in Oceania, Africa, and South America, mouth-to-mouth kissing is considered as disgusting as you would find "sticking one's tongue into a lover's nose" (Tiefer, 1978, p. 30). The Thonga, an East African tribe, laughed when they first observed Europeans kissing: "Look at them—they eat each other's saliva and dirt" (Ford and Beach, 1951, p. 49).

The form of kissing also varies. Some South Sea Islanders kiss by sucking the lips and tongues of each other, and others kiss by touching lips and drawing in their breath. The Lapps kiss the mouth and nose simultaneously (Tiefer, 1978, p. 28).

How can you account for such variation? To understand the diverse forms and differing meanings of the act, you need to look at the concept of **culture**.

What Culture Is

In popular usage, culture means the "highbrow" elements of society. Popularly, a person might describe a "cultured" individual as one who drinks wine rather than beer, enjoys classical rather than country music, is a patron of the arts, and dresses in accord with the latest Paris fashions. In sociology and anthropology, however, culture has a very different meaning. In essence, culture refers to everything created by people, including their **technology**, their system of **knowledge** and **beliefs**, their art, their morals and **laws**, their customs, and all other products of human thought and action.

By asserting that culture is the creation of human thought and action, sociologists stress that social life is the result of human interaction and human decisions rather than instincts (most social scientists no longer accept the notion that humans are instinctive creatures). Humans act. They do not merely react, either to external or internal stimuli. The lower animals and insects build complex social orders on the basis of instinctive reactions to stimuli, but their range of creation is extremely narrow. Only humans are able to create various kinds of social orders, consciously modify their social order, and incorporate both the past and the future into their creative activities.

As a noted anthropologist Clyde Kluckhohn (1960, p. 21) put it, culture is the "design of living" of a people. It is a shared way of life that provides people with socially acceptable ways of thinking, feeling, and behaving. If, for example, you dress more formally than usual for religious services, feel pride when you see the American flag or your school's football team, eat cereal rather than rice for breakfast, shake hands rather than bow when you meet someone, watch television rather than share stories for recreation, accept the notion that a man should only have one wife at a time, and learn your job skills at school rather than from your parents, you are acting out the dictates of your own culture—the design of living created in the United States. In other cultures, these ways of thinking, feeling, and acting might be defined as abnormal or be nonexistent.

Material and Nonmaterial Culture

The basic components of culture include both material and nonmaterial phenomena. **Material culture** refers to those objects which are made and used by people. **Nonmaterial culture** refers to shared beliefs, attitudes, **values**, and norms.

Material Culture

Material culture includes such basics as fire, food, housing, and tools. Significant advances in material culture bring about significant changes in the character of a society.

Material culture includes technology. Indeed, the level of technological development is a common way to classify societies and to characterize social evolution over the course of human history (Lenski,

Lenski, and Nolan 1994). The earliest type is the **hunting and gathering** society, in which the people survive by hunting animals and gathering plants. Technology is very simple. In the more advanced hunting and gathering societies, people have spears, bows, and arrows, which greatly increase their ability to get food.

The **horticultural society** emerges as people develop the technology of growing plants in gardens—the hoe and the digging stick. Metal tools and weapons emerge in the advanced horticultural society. The addition of the animal-drawn plow for cultivation paves the way for the development of the **agrarian society**. Iron tools and weapons appear in the advanced agrarian societies. There are also fishing, herding, and maritime societies, which are roughly at the same levels of development as the horticultural and agrarian societies, but which have different technologies for securing food.

The **industrial society** develops when new sources of energy (coal, petroleum, natural gas, etc.) are available, and industry rather than agriculture is the primary source of wealth. The industrial society achieves new highs in the standard of living. Finally, the **post-industrial society** emerges when the majority of workers are neither in agricultural nor industrial jobs (see Chapter Thirteen).

Nonmaterial Culture

Although we discuss them separately, material and nonmaterial culture are intertwined. For instance, Americans have historically placed a high value on the acquisition of material possessions. This value is part of the nonmaterial culture of Americans. On the other hand, the relative lack of technological progress among some societies reflects a different kind of nonmaterial culture. Both China and Japan were confronted by a challenge from the West in the nineteenth century. Japan responded by embarking on a course that led to a modern nation within a generation. China, however, remained technologically backward for decades. Why did the two nations respond so differently? The question has no simple answer, but one reason is found in the nonmaterial culture of the Chinese.

The Chinese were strongly oriented to the past (Lauer 1981). Some Chinese leaders were visionaries and forward-looking. But for the most part, the Chinese venerated the ancients and traditional society. A potential change might be declared as wrong not because it failed to meet people's needs, but because it deviated from past truths. Attempts to adopt Western technology, therefore, were not very successful. They justified the few that were adopted by claiming that they came originally from China and were further developed in the West. Moreover, reformers had to justify any proposed changes by showing their consistency with Confucian thought. It's not surprising, then, that the nonmaterial culture of the Chinese constrained the development of their material culture.

Characteristics of Culture

Anthropologists and sociologists tend to agree on certain characteristics of culture. First, culture is created. It is the product of human behavior. It is a necessary product because culture is the foundation of human society. There can be no human society without tools, houses, beliefs, and values.

Both material and nonmaterial culture enable us to adapt to the environment. The role of material culture is obvious, but the importance of the nonmaterial culture may not be so readily apparent. Harris (1974, pp. 36–41) offers an interesting example of that importance, however, in his explanation of the Jewish prohibition on eating pork. Why, he asks, should God have condemned "a harmless and even laughable beast whose flesh is relished by the greater part of mankind?"

The various explanations offered in the past, such as the problem of getting trichinosis from eating undercooked pork, do not hold up under scrutiny. Rather, Harris argues, the prohibition on pork was a "sound ecological strategy." The pig is mainly a creature of the forests and shaded riverbanks and unsuited to the arid, hot land of Israel. Moreover, it thrives best on nuts, fruits, tubers, and grains, making it a com-

Thinking Critically

People tend to assume that the material culture enhances the quality of their lives. Occasionally, evidence suggests that certain aspects of that culture may also be harmful. Two researchers studied 699 drivers who had cellular telephones and who were involved in auto accidents (Redelmeier and Tibshirani 1997). Examining billing records, the researchers found that the risk of a collision when using the cellular was four times higher than when the phone was not in use. Do the results suggest that the use of cellulars while driving should be discouraged or even prohibited?

Perhaps. But we have two questions. First, what would the results be if the sample included all drivers? The researchers only studied those with cellulars who had accidents. We don't know from the research that you are far more likely to have an accident if you use a cellular while driving. We only know that those who had an accident were more likely than not to be using the cellular at the time. What if a sample of all drivers showed no difference in the accident rate between those with and those without cellulars?

The second question is, what is the actual risk of having an accident while using a cellular? Remember, the researchers only studied people who had accidents, not all those with cellular phones in their cars. So how many accidents do drivers with cellulars have? We don't know, but if the figure is something like, say, one per hundred thousand miles driven, then the risk is about four per hundred thousand miles driven while using a cellular phone. The point is, without knowing the actual risk, we can't really interpret the meaning of "four times higher." If your chances are four in a hundred thousand, the risk is minor. If your chances are four in ten, the risk is high. Without more information, we're not ready to agree to a ban on cellular phones in automobiles.

petitor with humans for the available food supply. Finally, the pig is not a source of milk and is extremely difficult to herd for long distances. Clearly, whatever the religious implications might be, the prohibition against eating pork was ecologically sound and facilitated the Jews' adaptation to their environment.

A second characteristic is that culture is learned. Indeed, because humans do not act on the basis of instincts, culture *must* be learned. The fact that culture is learned enormously increases the possibilities for diverse kinds of behavior. The lower animals engage in some very complex behavior, but they have little flexibility because they act on instinct rather than learning. For example, some wasps feed their young by paralyzing a cricket and placing it in the nest with the eggs. Before the female carries the cricket into the burrow that forms the nest, she leaves it on the threshold and inspects the nest. Once inspected, she drags in the cricket. When the eggs hatch, the young grubs feed on the cricket, which is still alive but unable to move.

The remarkable behavior of the wasp appears at first glance to be purposive, almost "human." But the wasp cannot vary from a fixed routine. If the cricket is moved a few inches while the female is inspecting the burrow, she will come out, drag the cricket back to the threshold, then re-enter the nest for another inspection before bringing in the cricket. No matter how many times the cricket is moved, she continues to engage in the same behavior. She cannot bring in the cricket unless it lies on the threshold just after she has inspected the interior. The wasp's behavior is qualitatively different from human behavior.

Cultural transmission is the process by which you learn your culture. Each generation must learn the culture from previous generations. What is given by the older generation is never exactly what they received; rather it is what they received plus changes that occurred along the way. And what is learned from them is never exactly what they pass on; rather people interpret their legacy through current experiences and understandings.

All societies have both formal and informal means of transmitting culture to the young. In American society, formal education plays a significant role in transmission. In other societies, direct teaching by parents and/or other adults or imitation of adults by children may be the major form of transmission.

Among preindustrial people, **rites of passage** ceremonies that mark the transition from adolescence to adulthood, are an important part of cultural transmission. For example, the Okiek, a tribal group in Kenya, initiate boys into adulthood between the ages of fourteen and sixteen (Delaney 1995). The ritual begins with a ceremonial circumcision. The boys then live in seclusion from adult females for one to six months. They paint their bodies white so they look like wild creatures. And men of the tribe pass on to them secret knowledge, including knowledge of a beast that will haunt them while they are in seclusion. They hear the beast's roar at night. What they actually hear is a sound the elders produce with an instrument. When each boy has discovered the source of the roar and successfully used the instrument to produce it themselves, the ceremony is complete. The boys are now full-fledged adult members of the tribe, and they possess a more complete understanding of tribal culture.

A third characteristic of culture is that it is shared. Culture is a collective rather than an individual enterprise. Individualistic habits or beliefs are not a part of culture, although they can become a part of culture if others adopt them. An American who believes that the sun revolves about the earth does not have a cultural belief but an idiosyncratic one. On the other hand, there are some beliefs and habits which are divergent from the mainstream but which are shared by others. Among the divergent patterns are those groups of Americans who believe the earth is flat, those who handle poisonous snakes as a part of their religious ritual, and those who refuse to use modern technology (including electricity and automobiles). Thus, "shared" does not mean uniform throughout a society. It simply means that your design for living is not a purely individualistic affair but part of a collective creation.

Fourth, culture is cumulative. In the ongoing quest for a more satisfying life, people continue to add to the culture. "More satisfying" here means anything that people define as adding to their comfort, well-being, enjoyment, wealth, or growth. For example, Americans in recent decades have become increasingly focused on personal growth. This interest has produced a wide range of new therapies and books that tell them how to maximize personal fulfillment and increase their well-being. Some of these therapies are basically nonmaterial, such as "primal scream" therapy. Others employ material elements such as electric vibrators which are used for massage therapy, crystals, herbs, mineral waters, and candles.

The new elements in a culture, however, do not necessarily bring about a more satisfying life. Sometimes, in fact, people are severely stressed by the change, particularly when it's imposed on them. In Brazil, for example, an epidemic of suicides began in the mid-1980s among the Guarani Indians (Ellison 1996). Suicides were rare until that time, but since then the suicide rate has been fifty times the rate for Brazil as a whole. And half of the suicides are children or adolescents.

The suicides are both a form of protest and a sign of despair. The Guarani Indians, who once freely roamed over thousands of square miles, have been pushed into small reservations which are too crowded for their cultural or even their physical survival. They do not have enough land for farming. Fathers are forced to leave home for months at a time to cut sugar cane, and they return home with very little money to show for their efforts (they must pay for their own food and lodging out of very meager wages).

Thus, the cumulative nature of culture does not mean that the people are generally enjoying a more satisfying way of life. Guarani culture has changed, but the changes have generated intense dissatisfaction and despair.

The Elements of Culture

Cultures, then, are systems used by people to adapt to their environment and fulfill their needs. Because people everywhere face some of the same problems and sense some of the same needs, it isn't surprising that all cultures share certain elements, including language, knowledge and beliefs, systems of **social control**, values, technology, and art and recreation.

Language

What makes you different from other animals? Many scholars would give language as the answer. All animals engage in some form of communication. Yet there is a qualitative difference between communication at the infrahuman and human levels. For only humans have language. In fact, human culture rests upon language. A language system is a set of **symbols** or arbitrary signs with shared meanings. Humans are symbolic creatures, in the sense that they respond to their environment by first interpreting it through language.

A wink, a crucifix, a cry, or a bed of flowers brings no automatic, invariable response. You first define the meaning of the wink, the crucifix, the cry, the flowers, then respond appropriately to that definition. In other words, you endow objects, people, and situations with meaning through your language. A crucifix may be simply an oddly shaped piece of metal to someone who has never been exposed to Catholicism. It may be a sacred object, meriting reverence, to the devout Catholic. To a fundamentalist Protestant, it may be a sacrilegious object that epitomizes the corruption of the faith. The meaning of the crucifix depends upon the way you interpret it. You do not, of course, consciously interpret each time you see a crucifix. Yet your response is still based upon an interpretation, the meaning that you give to the object.

The lower animals, by contrast, respond to signs rather than to symbols. You can train a dog not to run through your flowers. The flowers become a sign to the dog, a sign that warns it away. However, the dog can never exult in the beauty of flowers nor use them to express love or appreciation or sorrow.

What about the primates? Chimpanzees are now taught to communicate with people and can use a vocabulary of a few hundred words. The chimpanzees are taught their languages in a variety of ways—by using sign language, plastic pieces of differing shapes and colors, or cards with figures on them, and by punching keys tied into a computer. Yet this communication is still different from the human use of symbols because the range of meaning the chimps assign to words is quite limited.

This capacity for functioning in a symbolic environment makes humans unique. No other creature can create, manipulate, and use symbols to direct its own behavior and influence the behavior of others. As a symbolic creature, you can accumulate and store more information than any other creature. You learn more, adapt more easily and successfully, and incorporate a far greater temporal range (both the distant past and the distant future) into your behavior than any other creature. You can step "outside" of yourself and see yourself as others see you. You can, in short, create a culture, share it with others in a meaningful social order, and pass it on to succeeding generations. Only humans have such a capacity.

Some social scientists have carried the significance of language even farther. Proponents of **linguistic relativity**, or the Sapir-Whorf hypothesis, argue that language systems shape your experience of the world and direct your interpretations. Benjamin Whorf studied the language of the Hopi Indians and claimed that his studies showed that human thinking reflects the structure of the language:

> No individual is free to describe with absolute impartiality but is constrained to certain modes of interpretation . . . thus . . . all observers are not led by the same physical evidence to the same picture of the universe, unless their linguistic backgrounds are similar, or can in some way be calibrated. (Whorf, 1940, p. 214)

The Sapir-Whorf hypothesis overstates the impact of language on thought and experience. It is possible to conceive of things or ideas that go beyond the bounds of your language. For instance, philosophers often coin new words to express thoughts that cannot be captured in the existing language. Moreover, the grammar of a language is not as constraining as Whorf believed, for he asserted that the differences between Hopi and English grammar resulted in differing conceptions of time. Hopi language, he noted, is "timeless." The verb has no tense, no way of distinguishing between past, present, and future. Thus, the Hopi do not have a conception of linear, mathematical time.

However, the argument does not hold up when we look at other languages. For instance, the ancient Hebrew language did not have past, present, and future tenses in the verbs, while ancient Greek had a more complex tense structure than English has. The Greek tenses made finer distinctions, such as one tense that indicated action at punctuated intervals and another that suggested action that began at a certain point in the past and continued indefinitely into the future. Yet, the Jews had a real sense of both the past and the future (their hope in the coming Messiah) and a linear notion of time (ongoing progress). The Greeks, on the other hand, had a cyclical view of time, believing that the various states of the universe are regularly repeated rather than the idea that there is linear progress to existence. Although they produced some noted historians, the Greeks generally had little sense of history and little regard for the past.

At the same time, people with differing language systems—and there are about 6,000 languages in the world—do have diverse experiences of the world in which they live (Diamond 1991). Arabs who live around camels have thousands of different words related to the camel. They will look at the animal and see the same physical entity as an American. But the Arab's experience of the camel will differ from that of the American because of the Arab's symbol system. This is not to say that the American could not gain the same experience by an expansion of his or her own language.

An analogous situation is one in which an electronics expert and someone with no knowledge of electronic equipment look at the inside of a television set. They both see the same physical objects, but their experience of those objects is quite different. The expert can interpret the complexities of the set in a way that is unavailable to the untrained person.

Knowledge and Beliefs

All cultures have systems of knowledge and beliefs. Beliefs are propositions which are unverified or unverifiable. They are part of the so-called conventional wisdom of a people, the propositions which are generally accepted without question. For instance, many Americans accept the proposition that men are absent from work because of illness far less than women. This belief is unverified by them; in fact, if they tried to verify it they would discover that it is false. Some beliefs are unverifiable. Most Americans believe in God, but the existence of God is a matter of faith because neither God's existence nor God's nonexistence is verifiable by scientific method.

Knowledge refers to those propositions for which there is empirical evidence. People can know such things as the nature of the atmosphere, the cause of tuberculosis, the occupational structure of the nation, and the extent to which family size has changed over time. Beliefs may be discarded or they may become a part of knowledge as empirical evidence supporting them grows. Thus, when most people believed that the earth was the center of the universe, Copernicus believed that the earth actually revolved around the sun. His belief eventually became a part of human knowledge, while the unverified belief of his contemporaries passed into the realm of fallacy.

Of course, you do not necessarily make the distinction between beliefs and knowledge. Sometimes you might ignore empirical evidence for various reasons. You may ignore knowledge because it contradicts your ideology or threatens you in some way. For example, some Americans assert that those who are poor have only themselves to blame. In support of the assertion, they cite the "rags to riches" idea—the notion that anyone willing to acquire the necessary skills and work hard can be successful in this country. They continue to believe the idea either because this means they can become financially successful or because the story explains the financial success they have already achieved.

Similarly, the Bamileke of Cameroon believe that repeated sexual intercourse during pregnancy is important both for bearing a healthy child and for the child's bonding with the father (Feldman-Savelsberg 1996). Undoubtedly, many of them would not like to have those beliefs challenged by scientific knowledge because they enjoy the frequent sexual relations.

Another reason that you might not necessarily distinguish between beliefs and knowledge is that the evidence is ambiguous. The preindustrial man who calls on the witch doctor to heal his illness knows that the witch doctor can cure him. Before you label the man as naive, keep in mind that many of the witch doctor's patients do get well again, including some who suffer from emotional problems of various kinds. Also keep in mind that it was not until the first decades of this century that an American could go to a physician and have a better-than-even chance of benefiting from the visit, and that psychiatrists disagree considerably about both the diagnosis and treatment of many cases (Lauer 1997). Whether treatment is provided by a witch doctor or a physician or a psychiatrist, there is uncertainty in the healing process.

Values

Values are shared conceptions of what is desirable or undesirable, right or wrong. Values are a source of, and a justification for, norms and behavior. For example, because of the value on individualism, early childhood education in the United States stresses activities that develop individual initiative. In contrast, because of the value on the community, childhood education in Japan involves more large-group activities—such as singing together and putting on skits—that develop commitment to the group. People's behavior, in all cultures, tends to reflect their values. We will explore further the variations in values when we discuss

EXTENSIONS

The Koro Epidemics

As symbolic interactionist theory reminds us, when you define something as real, it has real consequences (Thomas 1937). Beliefs which are unrealistic from the viewpoint of an observer will still have real consequences for those who hold the beliefs. Koro, unknown to most Westerners, is a condition that illustrates the point. Cheng (1996) used existing data, including the results of some survey research, to investigate Koro, a condition in which the victim believes that his or her sex organs are shrinking and that the outcome is death unless the process of shrinking is stopped. Koro is found primarily in southern China and Southeast Asia. Generally, only a small number of cases are reported, but a few Koro epidemics have occurred, affecting hundreds of thousands of people. A 1984–85 epidemic lasted for a year and affected more than 3,000 people.

Koro begins when victims somehow get the impression that their sex organs are shrinking. Intense anxiety then grips the victim because of the fear of death. Victims may turn pale, shiver, hyperventilate, sweat, or faint. The victims, or those around, use various devices and methods to try to stop the shrinking. Bruises, bleeding, and infections frequently result from the effort.

A study of victims in one county found that 85 percent were male, 78 percent were unmarried, and most were relatively poor and uneducated. Perhaps Koro will no longer afflict people if their educational level rises. However, education does not always change beliefs. And as long as people believe in Koro, cases and even epidemics will continue to occur.

cultural diversity. Here, we will look at some of the major values of American culture.

American Values

Sociologist Robin Williams (1970), in a dated but still widely accepted study, has identified major values in American society. They include equality of opportunity, success, working hard, material comfort, efficiency, progress, science, freedom, conformity, democracy, and group superiority (e.g., whites are valued more than those of other races and males are valued more than females). Not all Americans today accept all of these values. Yet many are still widely held.

For example, consider the value placed on achievement and success. Americans strive to achieve in the workplace. They assume that they have "made it" if they hold a high-status job, which provides a high income and feelings of fulfillment and self-worth. Closely related to achievement and success is the value placed on activity and work. American society has typically been noted for its activity and "busyness." Children are taught early in life that "idle hands are the devil's workshop" and that they "work before play." For the most part, they learn these lessons well. Of course, activity and work are necessary for achievement and success, so these values complement each other.

American values do not all complement and support each other, however. Some are contradictory. For instance, Americans value humanitarianism—concern and helpfulness given to others, generally with "no strings attached." This value, however, may clash with the American value of individualism, which stresses the importance of each individual pursuing his or her own destiny and forging his or her own pattern of life.

Among the other values mentioned by Williams are efficiency and practicality (Americans like to do things that have some practical use and do them in a way that is cost effective in time and money); progress (Americans believe that they have control over their destiny and that can create a better society); material comfort (Americans believe that their desires should be realized and that they should find quick relief from any pain or problem); equality (Americans affirm equal opportunity; and even though it has often been denied to many citizens, the value itself has been the basis for legal action and change); freedom (Americans do not like to be coerced, dependent, or restricted); conformity (while this value clashes with those of individualism and freedom, Americans still expect external conformity; imagine the reaction to someone who refused to stand for the National Anthem); science and rationality (Americans believe that these are the foundation of their progress and so pursue and support them vigorously); nationalism-patriotism (Americans have historically viewed their nation as the hope of all humankind, a blessed society to be admired and emulated by all peoples); democracy (Americans believe that majority wishes should rule although minority rights must always be protected); and group superiority (Americans believe in the superiority of the American way over the ways of other nations).

Such values, as *structural-functionalists* point out, are what integrate American society. But as *conflict theorists* note, not every American holds to all of these values. This will be evident when we discuss subcultures and countercultures below.

Social Control

All cultures have systems of **social control**, mechanisms for regulating behavior in socially approved ways and, thereby, for maintaining cultural values. In other words, social control mechanisms tend to produce the kind of behavior that reflects the dominant values of the culture. Furthermore, individuals do not function well in a capricious environment. They need order, and that order is maintained through the system of social control.

Norms

Norms are one of the most important mechanisms of control. Norms let you know what society expects of you. As such, norms are generally consistent with the values from which they arise. For example, because Americans value education (which reflects the value placed on

Explorations

What Is Beauty?

Americans value beautiful bodies. They spend an enormous amount of time and money to make their bodies as attractive as possible. The same is true of well-to-do Asians (Gee 1996). As the director of Image Workshop in Hong Kong puts it: "No other credentials are as visible as your looks." Asians now spend billions of dollars on beauty products, treatments, and plastic surgery. In Tokyo, for example, someone worried about underarm odor can secure a gland treatment to get rid of the problem. Japanese brides can take advantage of a full-body whitening treatment that makes their skin look childlike for four days.

The question for you to explore is, what is beauty? Do all people have the same notion of a beautiful body or are there variations? Divide the class into groups, and let each member of your group interview six people. Assign each member to interview a different race, ethnic group, or nationality. Ask respondents to describe their ideal of a beautiful female body and a beautiful male body. Be sure to get shape, height, and coloring. Note respondents' sex, age, and race/ethnic/national group.

Are there differences in people's ideals? How do the respondents' ideals compare with your own? Are there differences between the ideals of males and females? Between people of differing ages or differing racial/ethnic/national groups?

If you do this as an individual project, select people from a racial, ethnic, or national group that is different from your own, and compare their ideals with yours.

rationality, science, and progress), teachers expect students to listen attentively, students expect teachers to be prepared, and administrators expect teachers to be competent and to maintain classroom order.

You learn and abide by norms according to the various groups of which you are a part. Thus, the norms you actually follow may or may not be shared by the majority of people in your society. Some individuals follow norms that are considered outrageous or even immoral by most others.

For example, you may belong to a group—a fraternity, sorority, church, or civic organization—that has some type of initiation ceremony. What would you think of a group whose initiation ceremony was a severe beating? "That's disgraceful and unacceptable!" you say. But this is precisely the way that some youth gangs initiate new members. Vigil (1996) described initiation into some Chicano gangs as a kind of "street baptism." New gang members are initiated around the age of twelve or thirteen. A number of existing gang members attack the initiate, who is expected to fight back and to show no fear or weakness. The beating may be more or less severe, depending upon the initiate's background (those with relatives in the gang are beaten less) and the state of the attackers (beatings are more severe when the attackers are intoxicated). While you may find the practice objectionable if not disgusting, keep in mind that the gang members are doing, in one sense at least, what we all do—abiding by their group's norms.

Norms vary in a number of ways. First, they vary in the extent to which they are generally accepted. Some are more universally accepted than others. For example, most people in American society expect mothers to be concerned about their children. The norm of motherly concern is widely accepted. On the other hand, while most Americans do not expect children to drink alcoholic beverages, some do give alcohol to their children either as a part of religious ritual or because they believe that it is a way to teach them to enjoy a drink in moderation.

Norms also vary in terms of their clarity. Some norms are very clear to members of the group while other norms may be somewhat ambiguous or may be in the process of development. Ambiguity is likely when a new organization is formed. It is also likely in intercultural contacts (see Experiences, this chapter).

Third, particular norms may change over time. Behavior that breaks a norm in one generation may become normative in another generation. For example, in 1830 a quiet, religious man by the name of Joseph Palmer moved into a town in Massachusetts. The man was greeted with suspicion and then anger. The citizens broke his windows. Women crossed the street rather than walk on the same side as him. Children threw rocks at him. The church refused him communion. One day four men assaulted him on the street, and when he resisted and defended himself with a knife, he was arrested and fined. He refused to pay the fine and was imprisoned for a year. The cause of his persecution? He wore a beard! In 1830, no one in the town wore beards, and no one was expected to wear one. In another generation, it would be the beardless man who would be out of step and the bearded man would be following the norms of the society. But in 1830, Joseph Palmer was defined as a threat to the welfare of his community because he broke a norm (Corson, 1965, p. 403).

Finally, norms vary in terms of their perceived importance to the welfare of society. As we saw in Chapter One, some norms are considered far more important than others, leading to the distinction we noted between folkways and mores. Here we will add a third distinction—the norm that is incorporated into law.

Laws, the third type of norm, are formalized norms that are enforced by the state because of their defined importance to social well-being. In many preindustrial societies, the mores are sufficient to enforce behavior. However, as societies become larger and more technologically complex, laws are needed along with the folkways and mores. Often laws simply reflect existing norms, such as those against arson, murder, or other felonies. Sometimes the laws are established to change existing norms, such as the planning and zoning laws that restrict what people can do with their property.

There is a popular notion that you can't legislate morality, that you can't make people behave morally by passing laws. People often argue against a law on the basis that it will not be effective if it contradicts the mores. In some cases, this is true. Prohibition was one of the more notable examples of the failure of law to alter norms (although it should be noted that drinking patterns did change, with many Americans refraining from alcohol during Prohibition). Yet often laws can change people's attitudes, their behavior, and, ultimately, even their morality.

The American Medical Association bitterly resisted the passage of Medicare in 1965, but within six months after the legislation took effect a dramatic shift occurred in the attitudes of physicians. Only 38 percent of a sample of physicians had approved of the main part of Medicare—hospitalization for the elderly—before the bill passed; six months after the bill was implemented, the proportion who approved had jumped to 81 percent (Colombotos, 1969). Similarly, civil rights legislation in the 1960s drastically changed voting behavior in the nation, and public opinion polls showed that the proportion of Americans who believed in

Experiences

Doing Business in Japan

Even cultures that are fairly similar have certain differences. For instance, people in southern European countries such as Italy and Greece touch each other while conversing more often than do people in northern European countries such as England, France, and the Netherlands (Remland, Jones, and Brinkman 1995). Thus, an Italian might perceive the Englishman he is talking to as cold and indifferent; while the Englishman might feel that the Italian is invading his personal space by frequently touching him.

It's not surprising, then, that when the cultures are quite different, intercultural interaction can be challenging. An American businesswoman whose firm does business in Japan tells of some difficult moments she had in her first encounters with Japanese businessmen:

Today, companies train their people who travel to other countries to conduct business. I had very little training before my first trip to Japan. And I had little knowledge of the Japanese other than what I had seen in movies.

My first mistake came when I tried to be friendly and invited the Japanese executive with whom I was working most closely to lunch. He accepted, but he seemed to stiffen. I later discovered that it embarrassed him to have a woman invite him out alone. Apparently, his colleagues really gave him a hard time about it.

I made another mistake when I accepted the invitation of the Japanese businessmen to go to a hostess bar after dinner. I knew better than to be involved in a one–on–one situation again, but I thought nothing about going with the group. I soon discovered that Japanese men make sexual advances toward the women who serve as hostesses. Worse, I realized that some of them—perhaps they had too much to drink—were treating me like I was one of the hostesses.

I've learned most of what a woman needs to do in order to survive doing business with Japanese men. But every so often I still find myself getting into an embarrassing or awkward situation. Because I tend to act as I would with Americans. And you can't do that when you're in Japan.

racial discrimination decreased dramatically from the 1940s to the 1990s.

Sanctions

Sanctions are rewards and punishments used to regulate behavior according to social norms. Sanctions may be formal and incorporated into law, such as the Congressional Medal of Honor or punishments for various crimes. Sanctions also may be informal, such as praise from your peers, the "cold shoulder" from your friends, or the rewards and punishments regularly meted out in a group to which you belong.

Informal sanctions can be as gratifying or as severe as the formal sanctions. For example, among the Old Order Amish, the most severe form of punishment is the Meidung or ban (Kephart, 1991). The Meidung is imposed only for the most serious infractions. Basically, the individual who is banned is treated as nonexistent. No one can even talk to the individual, including members of his or her own family. The Meidung exemplifies one of the harshest kinds of punishment a group can use.

Similar punishment is meted out in Bangladesh to unmarried women who get pregnant. The cultural ideal for women in Bangladesh is "to be virtuous, married, secluded, the mother of sons, and cherished by those sons in old age" (Wilson-Moore 1996, p. 173). Women get little in the way of information about sex but are expected to remain chaste. If an unmarried woman becomes pregnant, she not only dishonors herself but also her family. In the best of situations, the family may try to hide the pregnancy, secure an abortion, then arrange marriage between the woman and the man who impregnated her. If an abortion or marriage cannot be arranged, the family will disown the woman and send her away. Only a minority of such women keep their babies. They usually settle in an area where they can claim to be either widowed or deserted. If their true identity is discovered, they will be evicted from their home or even stoned to death in the street.

Obviously, sanctions can be of various types. Some are physically coercive, such as spanking or the threat of imprisonment. Some are psychosocial, such as praise or gossip or ridicule. Some are utilitarian, such as the giving or withholding of money or other material rewards. Frequently a combination of these types of sanctions may be used.

For most kinds of behavior, relatively mild sanctions are sufficient. For behavior considered extremely threatening, like the Amish man who violates community mores or the unmarried Bangladesh woman who gets pregnant, the sanctions are severe.

Groups and societies differ in the extent to which conformity is required and, hence, in the extent to which sanctions are used to ensure conformity. Some groups expect considerable or even total conformity.

In his utopian novel, *Erewhon*, Samuel Butler satirized the expectation of total conformity. The hero of the novel talks with a group of citizens of Erewhon, and expresses his belief that original thought should be encouraged. He quickly discovers that they are horrified by his belief. Rather, they insist, each person must think as the neighbors think, and heaven help a man who "thinks good what they count bad. And really it is hard to see how the Erewhonian theory differs from our own, for the word 'idiot' only means a person who forms his opinions for himself" (Butler 1968, pp. 243–44).

In some groups, by contrast, original thinking is encouraged and rewarded. Yet every group puts boundaries on nonconformity. It is just that some boundaries are far narrower than others.

Social Control and Self Control

Social control is more than external demand. People do not conform to norms simply because they receive rewards or punishments. In fact, the most effective form of control is **self control**, the internalization of norms that leads to self-regulation of behavior. Most Americans, for instance, do not subscribe to their form of government because they fear punishment or seek reward; they genuinely believe that it is the best form of government. Social control has become self control. Of course, people in many other nations feel the same way about their forms of government.

Self control means that rewards and punishments are self administered. You reward yourself by feeling good about certain kinds of behavior and punish yourself by feeling a sense of shame or guilt about other kinds of behavior. No individual, however, totally regulates his or her own behavior, no matter how much he or she has internalized the norms of the group. Every individual faces unexpected situations and unanticipated temptations when he or she is torn between a sense of duty and a desire to engage in disapproved behavior. You may exercise self control and conform to the normative order, but you are aided by the knowledge that sanctions await the outcome of your decision.

Technology

Technology is the organization of knowledge for practical purposes. Every society has technology, no matter how simple, because it enables people to survive, to adapt to their environment, and to improve their lifestyles. Technology is one of the most crucial elements of culture. Indeed, the nature of the society is intimately related to the level of technology.

There are common tasks performed by humans, that require some kind of technology. These include the gathering of food, cooking, the building of shelter, and making clothes. Technology can be relatively simple or complex for the same tasks. For example, an American farmer may use artificial fertilizer, tractors, and other expensive equipment to grow and harvest crops. But in other societies, farming is still done with a hand plow drawn by oxen and with animal manure as the only available fertilizer. Similarly, many Westerners prepare their frozen meals in a microwave oven, while many women in rural India use cow dung as fuel for the oven on which they cook the grain that they have cleaned and ground into flour themselves.

Technology may also be more or less efficient for the same tasks. People today have a variety of methods of birth control available to them. In ancient societies, there were also many kinds of contraceptives but these were developed and used without scientific knowledge about the process of conception. Nearly 2,000 years ago in Rome, for instance, Pliny suggested a number of possibilities:

> 'Mouse dung . . . applied in the form of a liniment' was one suggestion; another involved swallowing either snail excrement or pigeon droppings mixed with oil and wine; a third required the testicles and blood of a dunghill cock to be secreted under the bed. Further, he pointed out that if a woman's loins were 'rubbed with blood taken from the ticks on a wild black bull' she would be inspired 'with aversion to sexual intercourse'. (Tannahill, 1980:128)

You may think of technology in terms of such things as tools and equipment, but technology also includes nonmaterial techniques. In modern societies, for example, behavior modification is a nonmaterial technology. In behavior modification, an individual's behavior is changed by using rewards and sometimes punishment to eliminate undesired, and reinforce desired, behavior. Altering people's behavior by manipulating their environment is as much a form of technology as learning how to start a fire or make a plow.

Art and Recreation

Broadly speaking, art and recreation are found in all societies. They seem to reflect the universal human quest for creative expression and diversion. Art even includes the shaping and decorating of the body in order to enhance beauty. Virtually every part of the human body has been manipulated in some fashion in some culture somewhere (Rudofsky, 1971). The ancient Egyptians, the American Indians, and some rural French people practiced head elongation, by massaging or binding the head of the young infant. In some cultures, female obesity became a sign of affluence and beauty (because affluent women did little physical work, in contrast to poor women who worked hard and ate poorly).

Of course, art also includes sculpture, painting, pottery making, and weaving. These art forms appear to be universal. For example, the cave paintings created by the Cro-Magnons are of high quality even by modern critical standards. The paintings may not have been purely expressions of art, however, for they are typically located in deep, hard-to-find recesses of the caves. Quite likely, they were a form of magic. And because they were always of animals, they probably were intended as a type of hunting magic (Swartz and Jordan 1976, pp. 361–62). However, the cave paintings are art regardless of their purpose. They express the universal desire of humans to be creative in some way.

Art is also sometimes thought to be universal because its value and meaning transcend any nation or any group. From a *feminist* point of view, however, art is, and has been, male dominated (Pollock 1992). This domination may be seen in the portrayal of males and females in paintings, in the control of art institutions by men, and in the fact that for centuries female artists' work was identified as "women's art," a label that carried with it an inherent devaluation.

Recreation refers to the expenditure of time and energy in matters that are ends in themselves rather than the means to something else. As such, recreation is also found in all cultures. Recreation can be essentially nonviolent, such as dancing, or it may be fairly violent, such as American football.

Probably no one, however, can match the Yanomamo Indians of South America for violent recreation. The Yanomamo engage in chest-pounding and side-slapping duels (Harris 1974, pp. 92-3). The duels occur when two villages get together. A man from the host village will step into a clearing, spread his legs, put his hands behind his back, and thrust his chest out towards the guests. One of the male guests then comes out, adjusts the other's stance if he wishes, puts himself at arm's length, sets himself firmly, and hits the host with his fist as hard as he can on the upper chest. The host staggers and sways under the blow but remains silent. His fellow villagers urge him to take another blow. The guest will hit him a second time in the same place. And as the man sinks to the ground, the guest dances victoriously around him while the other guests cheer. The host may decide to take a number of additional blows. Eventually, with his chest swollen and red, he signals his opponent that he has had enough. He then may give the guest the same number of blows that he has received. In the side-slapping version, one man strikes the other with his open hand just below the ribs, typically causing the one struck to fall unconscious to the ground.

Cultural Diversity

As we have noted, there is considerable diversity among cultures. In a sense, cultures may be likened to people. People have the same basic features but there are considerable differences between individuals. Consequently, many of the things that Americans take for granted as "natural" in human interaction are learned patterns that vary between cultures.

There is also considerable diversity within any culture. We will illustrate both intercultural and intracultural diversity below by looking at variations in one particular element—values. Before we do this, however, consider the reasons for diversity.

How do you explain the diversity among and within cultures? First, diversity is inevitable because of the nature of human interaction. Individuals do not simply mirror their culture but act in ways that modify them to some extent. Billions of individuals interacting throughout the earth will inevitably create diversity. In addition, both intercultural and intracultural diversity are rooted in the reasons we gave above for why people create culture: adaptation to the environment and the quest for a more satisfying life. The harsh environment of the Arctic Eskimo requires different technology, clothing, and shelter than the environment of the Arizona farmer. Even the values and norms may reflect environmental adaptation, for some Eskimo groups leave their infirmed old people behind to die when they migrate to a new location, in order to assure survival of the group.

The quest for a more satisfying life also involves diverse habits. The Yanomamo do not have radios, magazines, or parks, but they seem to gain a measure of satisfaction (status and honor) from their chest-pounding duels.

Similarly, within the same society different groups will develop diverse ways as they adapt to their environment and seek a more satisfying life. Life in Minnesota imposes a different set of environmental constraints on people than does life in southern California or Florida. Urban and rural environments also impose different constraints. Moreover, as people seek satisfaction in life, they will create diverse patterns in accord with their circumstances. The well-to-do youth may expect to meet friends in Aspen for skiing. The ghetto youth may have learned to play the "Dozens," a one-up-manship verbal game in which each participant tries to outdo the other in insults. The normative behavior is very different, but the same quest for satisfaction underlies both kinds of behavior.

Intercultural Diversity

When you look at diversity of values (or any other cultural element) among cultures, you must first recognize that there are both similarities and differences. People everywhere, for instance, value health, friendship, and material well-being. But there are also considerable differences. The American value on individualism that leads you to admire the entrepreneur and the person who does it "my way," may or may not be valued in other cultures.

Using *participant observation*, including in-depth interviews with 49 men, Derne (1995) questioned how some Hindu men could act in an individualistic fashion in a society that values collective over individual decision-making. The men had chosen to select their own wives on the basis of love rather than have a wife chosen for them by their parents. Or they had opted to live only with their wives and children rather than with other family members as well.

Derne found that the men had learned to frame their decisions in a way that made them compatible with their societal values. For instance, a man who wanted to marry a woman he loved, rather than one his parents preferred, finally convinced his parents that his love marriage was not like the Western love matches they despised. He focused on the prospective bride's family, who was of the same caste as his parents, and assured his parents that his choice would not involve dishonor to the family.

Another American value, competition, is often viewed by Americans as the pathway to progress, achievement, and success. Many Americans even believe that competition is a part of human nature. Actually, you learn to be competitive (just as you learn to be cooperative). Other cultures may or may not value competition, and there may be more or less emphasis upon competition than there is in the United States. In Japan, for example, competition is intense during childhood, more intense than it is in the United States. Young children often take special courses or devote long periods of time to studying for the entrance exams as a way to get into the best schools and ultimately into the best jobs. Once employed, competition is channeled into vying with other companies. Within a company, however, the emphasis is on loyalty and conformity.

Intracultural Diversity

As conflict theory suggests, diverse and even contradictory values exist in any complex culture. Segments of the society will diverge from, as well as share to some extent, the dominant values. Such diversity can lead to conflict. For example, Samoans in Hawaii are at a disadvantage when facing possible eviction by a public housing board (Lempert and Monsma 1994). Their disadvantage stems from their values. For the most part, people in public housing who do not pay their rent plead factors beyond their control. They have been ill, unemployed, or have suffered theft. The housing board may extend the time allowed for such people to pay the rent. The board is less likely to extend the time to Samoans, whose excuses are not as acceptable.

The Samoan excuses stem from different kinds of demands on their money, demands that reflect their values. For one thing, because many Samoans are assisted in coming to the United States by their family, they are expected to send regular payments back to their families. Samoans also expect family members, including those living far away, to contribute money for such special events as funerals and weddings. And for most Samoans, support of the church is an obligation as well.

The net result of all this is that Samoans may not be able to pay their rent because of other obligations: "Central in Samoan life are the *aiga* (extended family), the *matai* (family chief), and, especially in the United States, the church" (Lampert and Monsma 1994, p. 902). The Samoans are penalized for living by values that most Americans admire.

In addition to diversity within a culture at a given time, there are changes (diversity) over time. For example, although success is one of the values identified earlier, it may be something less of a value than it was formerly. In a 1994 national poll that asked a representative sample of Americans to identify the "most important thing in life," over half named relationships with friends and family and 21 percent named religious faith or spirituality; only 5 percent identified career fulfillment and another 4 percent named monetary success (Figure 3.1).

Figure 3.1   **Most Important Thing in Life**

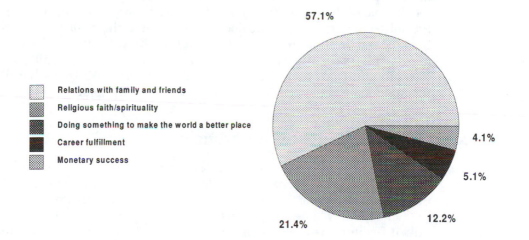

57.1%

- Relations with family and friends
- Religious faith/spirituality
- Doing something to make the world a better place
- Career fulfillment
- Monetary success

4.1%

5.1%

21.4%   12.2%

Source: Adapted from The American Enterprise, Nov/Dec., 1994, p. 98.

Subcultures

A subculture is a group within a society that shares much of the culture of the larger society while maintaining certain distinctive cultural patterns of its own. There are various kinds of subcultures; these include generational, racial and ethnic, regional, and religious groups. Generational subcultures involve people of a particular age group. Adolescents are a subculture because they have, to some extent, distinctive language patterns, clothing, recreation, values, and norms. Some of these distinctive ways—such as the hippie and punk styles—have caused horror, despair, disgust, and even outright hostility among adults.

Ethnic and racial subcultures exist to the extent that groups maintain unique cultural patterns. Ethnic groups, who live in the same area and continue to speak their native language and practice their native customs—such as the Samoans in Hawaii and Native Americans who have remained on reservations—are examples of ethnic/racial subcultures.

Regional subcultures exist in spite of the tendency toward a homogeneous society. There are regional variations in the United States in such things as language, values, and norms. A national survey reported in *The New York Times* on July 28, 1996, asked adults whether they would favor a law against interracial marriage. The proportion who said "yes" was 7 percent in the West, 17 percent in the Midwest, 26 percent in the South, and 12 percent in the Northeast.

Religious subcultures include the various sects and cults that have always existed in America. Male members of the Hare Krishna cult, for example, wear robes, beads, and shave their heads (Stoner and Parke 1977). Members refrain from eating meat. Celibacy is highly valued. Members who marry must refrain from sex except during the wife's fertile time of the month (because sex is only for procreation). Women are subservient to men; a wife does not even eat at the same table with her husband. In some instances, groups of Hare Krishnas have refused to obey local laws regarding property upkeep and noise control. Not all religious subcultures are as dramatically different as the Hare Krishnas, but all maintain some patterns that distinguish them from the larger society.

Ethnocentrism and Cultural Relativism

Cultural relativism is the proposition that each culture must be evaluated on its own terms rather than according to the standards of outsiders. The idea is that each aspect of culture, however immoral or inefficient it may appear to an outsider, should be evaluated in terms of how it fits into the overall culture. **Ethnocentrism** is the tendency to do the opposite—to consider your own culture as the right and the best way of life and to evaluate other cultures in terms of your own values and beliefs.

People everywhere tend to be ethnocentric, to judge the culture of others by how well it corresponds with their own. That is, people tend to think of their own ways as superior to those of others. The ancient Persians had a rule that a man who wanted to be a physician had to first practice on outsiders; if they lived, he could then practice on Persians. When the English first came to China, a land they considered primitive and barbaric, they found that the Chinese regarded *them* as barbarians and required the Englishmen to kowtow before the emperor like any other inferior group. Herman Melville captured the sense of American ethnocentrism in *Moby Dick* when he pointed out that the foreign-born comprised the crews of whale ships and the bulk of the construction crews in the nation, so that the American "liberally provides the brains, the rest of the world as generously supplying the muscles" (Melville 1966, p. 106).

Ethnocentrism has a number of consequences. It contributes to group solidarity by enhancing the value and appeal of the individual's own group. On the other hand, it can justify the exploitation of others (Europeans and Americans had few qualms about seizing "inferior" Africans and thrusting them into slavery) and can be used to legitimate destructive conflict (enemies are always castigated in time of war). Ethnocentrism can also blind people to the need for change in their society and to the valuable aspects of other cultures that they could profitably imitate. Finally, ethnocentrism inhibits knowledge and impedes the application of the sociological perspective in the quest for understanding. After all, an individual who already knows what is appropriate and best need not engage in social scientific analysis.

Instead of dismissing the practices of other people as irrational, immoral, or inefficient, then, you must see these in their own terms rather than in terms of the way you do things. A variety of practices can satisfy human needs. Practices that initially seem pointless or questionable to you may make sense when seen in the light of the whole (such as the Jewish prohibition on pork we discussed earlier).

Yet, we do not advocate cultural relativism in the sense that people must accept every practice everywhere as right or permissible. The fact that many peoples have felt it necessary to kill some of their infants in order for the group to survive does not mean that should you accept the practice as right. To condemn without understanding is a form of arrogant ignorance. But to understand is not necessarily to approve.

Cultural Change

The dynamic nature of social life means that culture is always changing. Two important mechanisms of cultural change are innovation and diffusion.

Innovation

An **innovation** is a discovery or invention that adds something new to a culture. A discovery is the perception or finding of something that already exists. Researchers discover new knowledge about the human body and human societies. People discover medicinal properties in herbs or plants. Astronomers discover new information about the nature of the universe. Invention, on the other hand, is the process of combining existing aspects of culture to form something that has not existed previously. The stirrup, the gasoline engine, the electric light, and the bicycle are inventions. Theories about the nature of humans, society, and the universe are inventions. Therapies for treating mental illness are inventions.

Innovation is a social process. Even if your innovation emerges out of hours of isolated study, you are the product of and function in an ongoing social structure and culture. Sir Isaac Newton is reputed to have said that he stood on the shoulders of giants. Indeed, any innovator stands on the shoulders of all those who have prepared the way in the continuing growth of culture.

Innovation can arise through conflict in a society. As various groups seek to improve the quality of their lives, they may bring about a variety of innovations. The gay bar, day-care facilities for the children of working mothers, Medicare, and Medicaid are social inventions that have emerged out of the struggles of the deprived to gain a more satisfying life.

In addition to the above, social scientists stress the social nature of innovation by noting the numerous cases of simultaneous and independent discoveries and inventions. Thus, both Scheele and Priestley discovered oxygen in 1774. Clausius and Rankine both proposed the kinetic theory of gases in 1850. And the telegraph was independently invented by Henry in 1831, and by Morse, Cooke-Wheatstone, and Steinheil in 1837. Innovation is a social process rather than the independent product of the few geniuses in a culture. If Jobs and Wozniak hadn't invented the Apple computer, someone else would have, for the culture itself had advanced to the point where such an invention was likely.

Diffusion

Diffusion is the spread of culture from one society to another or from one portion of a society to another. All cultures are a result of both indigenous activity and diffusion from other cultures. Some items have diffused throughout the world. Thus, two American tourists who planned to go across the Sahara desert in a jeep asked their guide where civilization ended. The guide asked what they meant by civilization. The

Americans replied, "When will we get to a place where they don't have Coca-Cola?" "Never," said the guide (Liedtke 1978, p. 38). Similarly, the Barbie doll, which appeared in the early 1960s, is now a worldwide phenomenon (Rand 1995). A Barbie is purchased somewhere in the world every two seconds.

Mass communications facilitate the diffusion of cola, Barbie, and other products. In earlier times, diffusion occurred largely because of traders and travellers. Kroeber (1948) gives the example of pipe smoking. Smoking originated in tropical America, where tobacco is an indigenous plant. Spanish explorers who came into contact with the Indians of tropical America picked up the habit and took it back to Spain. From there it diffused across Europe and Asia. Eventually, traders introduced it to the Eskimos, who did not smoke until recent centuries.

Diffusion is not a one-way process. When societies are in contact, there will generally be diffusion from each one to the other. For instance, few Americans are probably aware of the extent to which their culture has been influenced by Native Americans. As Beals (1967) pointed out, plants domesticated by Native Americans furnish nearly half the world's food supply. Those plants include the so-called "Irish" potato, corn, beans, squash, and sweet potatoes. A number of drugs used in modern pharmacology, including pain relievers (datura) and laxatives (cascara), were first used by Native Americans. Commercial cottons come mainly from a species cultivated by Native Americans. And Native American music has had an influence on a number of American composers such as Edward McDowell.

Change and Integration

Structural-functionalists emphasize **cultural integration**, which means that the various portions of the culture fit together into a more or less coherent whole. The point is that various parts of a culture tend to be mutually supportive and consistent with each other. However, cultural integration is much stronger in preindustrial than in modern societies. In modern societies, the integration occurs in the context of considerable diversity and conflict. Moreover, as conflict theorists point out, change tends to be more rapid and more pervasive in modern societies, increasing the tendency to create conflict and contradictions between the various elements of culture. Cultural change means that cultural integration is always a tenuous state. The extent of integration waxes and wanes with change.

Take, for example, the place of women in nineteenth century America. The prevailing belief in nineteenth century America was that a woman's place, if she could afford it, was in the home (Lauer and Lauer 1981). Various facets of the culture worked together to maintain that belief and to make many women domestic creatures. Americans generally believed that women were physically and intellectually inferior to men, incapable of functioning competently in men's tasks. Women's sphere of influence was within the home; this is where they could make their most effective contribution to society.

Even female dress conspired to keep women at home. Tight lacings, heavy petticoats, yards of material, and long skirts made a woman practically immobile. A complete outfit could weigh thirty pounds or more. Tightly corseted waists resulted in a literal rearrangement of the vital organs and prevented proper breathing. Tight garters prevented proper circulation in the legs. One nineteenth century reformer summed up the situation by pointing out that until women were allowed to have ankles there was no hope for their brains (Lauer and Lauer 1981, p. 124).

In sum, the various pieces of the culture fit together in a more or less coherent whole to reinforce the nineteenth century ideal of the American woman. But, as is clear from the case of the corset, cultural integration is not necessarily equivalent to individual well-being or to the well-being of particular groups within the culture.

Critical Thinking Exercise

An article in a popular news magazine reported a study of television news shows during a week in February (Whitman 1996). The study found a predominance of negative news stories. The article concluded that such shows may be causing Americans to view matters in a pessimistic way and may thereby contribute to the growing pessimism among Americans. Before accepting this conclusion as valid, what information would you want about such things as the sample, the methods, and the assumptions? Do you agree that pessimistic news stories can make people more pessimistic? Do you agree that Americans are growing more pessimistic? What kind of evidence do you need to answer these questions?

Summary

To explain the variations in human thinking, feeling, and behavior, you need to understand the concept of culture: everything created by people that becomes their design for living. Material culture refers to those objects made and used by people, while nonmaterial culture is comprised of the beliefs, attitudes, values, and norms shared by people.

Material culture includes technology, which is a crucial mechanism in the evolution of societies. Societies can be classified on the basis of change from simple to complex technology: hunting and gathering, horticultural, agrarian, and industrial societies.

Culture is created in the course of people adapting to their environment. The culture must be learned by each generation, a process known as cultural transmission. Culture is shared. That is, culture is what people have in common rather than the peculiar habits or beliefs of individuals. Culture is cumulative in the sense that it is continually changing as people search for a more satisfying life.

All cultures have a number of important elements. Language, in the opinion of some social scientists, is what distinguishes humans from the lower animals. Knowledge is propositions for which people have empirical evidence, while beliefs are propositions which are unverified or unverifiable. Values are shared conceptions of what is right and wrong. Social control involves mechanisms for regulating behavior in socially approved ways. Technology is organized knowledge used for practical purposes. Art and recreation reflect the universal desire to be creative and to have diversions.

Cultural diversity exists both among and within cultures. Such diversity is inevitable because of the nature of human interaction, and because of the ongoing needs to adapt to the environment and to find a more satisfying life. Intracultural diversity is illustrated by various subcultures.

Cultural relativism is the idea that individuals must evaluate culture on its own terms rather than by the standards of outsiders. Ethnocentrism is the universal tendency to judge other cultures by one's own, and to regard one's own as superior.

Cultures change continuously. Innovation and diffusion are two important mechanisms of that change. Cultural change makes integration of the culture problematic. Cultures are more or less integrated, depending upon the rate of change. In any case, integration is not necessarily equivalent to the well-being of individuals or of particular groups of individuals.

Glossary

agrarian society a society in which people survive by using animal-drawn plows for cultivating the land

beliefs propositions which are unverified or unverifiable

cultural integration the process whereby various elements of the culture fit together into a more or less coherent whole

cultural relativism the idea that each culture must be evaluated in its own terms rather than in terms of the standards of others

cultural transmission the process by which culture is learned by each succeeding generation

culture everything created by people, including their technology, knowledge and beliefs, art, morals, law, customs, and all other products of their thought and action

diffusion the spread of culture from one society to another or from one portion of a society to another

ethnocentrism the belief that one's own culture is the right and best way of life and the tendency to evaluate other cultures in terms of one's own cultural ways

horticultural society a society in which the people survive by growing plants in gardens

hunting and gathering society a society in which the people survive by hunting animals and gathering plants

industrial society a society with new sources of energy (coal, petroleum, natural gas, etc.) and industry rather than agriculture as its primary source of wealth

innovation a discovery or invention that adds something new to a culture

knowledge propositions for which there is empirical evidence

laws formalized norms enforced by the state

linguistic relativity the thesis that language systems shape people's experience of the world and direct their interpretations

material culture those objects and artifacts which are made and used by people

nonmaterial culture the beliefs, attitudes, values, and norms that are shared by people

post-industrial society a society in which agricultural and industrial jobs are a minority of all jobs

rites of passage ceremonies that mark the transition to a new status in a society

sanctions rewards and punishments used to regulate behavior according to social norms

self control the internalization of norms that results in self-regulation of behavior

social control a system of mechanisms for regulating behavior in socially approved ways

subculture a group within a society that shares much of the culture of the larger society while maintaining certain distinctive cultural patterns of its own

symbols arbitrary signs with shared meaning

technology the organization of knowledge for practical purposes

values shared conceptions of what is desirable or undesirable, right or wrong

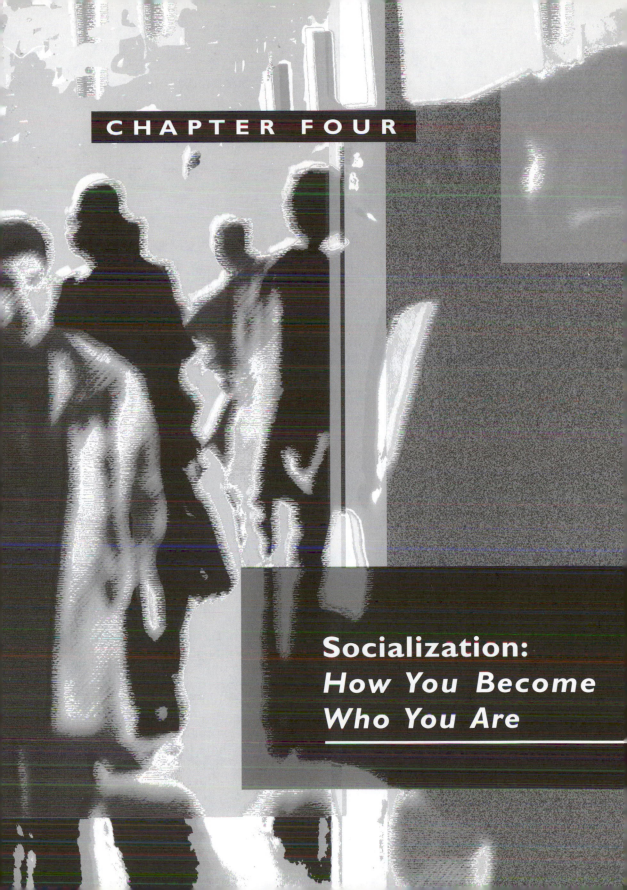

CHAPTER FOUR

Socialization:
How You Become Who You Are

What kind of person are you? For example, if you were asked to describe yourself in five or six words, what words would you choose? Would you include intelligent? logical? loyal? sensitive? attractive? ambitious? fun-loving? moral? strong? As you think about the words you chose, ask another question: Why are you this way? In other words, how do you explain the kind of person you are?

Now think about people who have hurt or angered you. What words would you use to describe them? How would you explain their character?

To what extent do you think that the traits you described in yourself and in this other person are due to heredity? To what extent did you think they are acquired? For instance, is intelligence something you inherit, or do you acquire it? Or is it a little of each? How about sensitivity? Are you born with it, or do you learn it? Or are both heredity and learning involved? These questions reflect a long-standing debate: can human behavior be best understood as the result of nature or of nurture?

Nature or Nurture?

David grew up with a mother and a stepfather. His stepfather was cruel and tyrannical; he severely abused David both physically and emotionally. In school, unfortunately, David encountered more abuse. It would be more accurate to say that he survived, rather than progressed through, school. When he graduated, he found only menial, low-paying work. Eventually, a great-aunt discovered David, learned of his difficult existence, and offered him help.

Based on your understanding of the effects of childhood experiences, what kind of outcome would you expect for David? It wouldn't surprise us if you, like most students we have had, predicted that he would have a difficult and troubled life in spite of his great-aunt's offer of help. However, he ultimately was both successful and happy.

You may have guessed, by this point, that David is David Copperfield, the creation of novelist Charles Dickens. And Dickens, like most nineteenth century English intellectuals, came down firmly on the side of nature in the nature/nurture debate. Thus, no matter how much David was abused, no matter how much he suffered, he came from "good stock" and ultimately his virtuous nature triumphed.

Early in the twentieth century, social scientists continued to think and argue about the nature/nurture issue in either-or terms. Some argued for nature—that it is your heredity that determines the kind of person you are. Others argued for nurture—that it is how you are reared that determines the kind of person you are. Today, however, social scientists are more likely to agree that both nature and nurture play a role (though there is not much agreement on precisely how and to what extent nature and nurture play their roles). The kind of person you are and the way you behave are the outcome of the interaction between your genetic makeup and your nurturing experiences.

Heredity: The Basic Materials

For many decades, heredity was virtually ignored by the social sciences; that is, those who argued for nurture won out over those who opted for nature. However, social scientists are once again looking at the role of heredity, or genetic makeup, in understanding human behavior. Studies of identical twins separated at birth provide evidence for a strong genetic component in such things as personality traits, likes and dislikes, and cognitive abilities (Pedersen, Plomin and McClearn 1994; Jang, Livesley and Vernon 1996). The field of sociobiology explores how biological factors interact with social factors to produce various kinds of behavior (Walsh and Gordon 1995).

A genetic basis, or a genetic component, has been claimed for many different kinds of behavior in recent decades, including homosexuality, the intelligence scores of African Americans, addictive behavior, and the math capabilities of women (Lauer 1997). Such claims generate considerable controversy. For, as *conflict theory* suggests, the claims not only involve contrary scientific positions but contrary group interests. For instance, if homosexuality is genetically based rather than a learned behavior or the preferred behavior of some individuals, how can people justify discriminatory laws and practices? In contrast, those who define homosexuality as a threat to social well-being prefer to see the behavior as a perverse choice that merits condemnation.

While controversy will no doubt continue, we believe that the best approach is to think of heredity as supplying the basic materials of life, with nurturing experiences giving specific shape to those materials. Put somewhat differently, your genetic makeup determines limits and your nurturing experiences determine where you will fall within those limits. For example, your life span has genetic limits.

Let's say that, genetically, you could live into your nineties. Barring such things as accidents, your lifestyle determines how many years within those limits you will actually live. Similarly, you have inherited a certain intellectual capacity. Whether you ever reach your full intellectual potential, however, depends upon your life experiences.

One question that must be raised about heredity, then, is what are the limits imposed by your genetic makeup? Another question is, to what extent are various traits and behaviors shaped by genetic makeup? For instance, some basic aspects of temperament, such as whether you are an extrovert or introvert, appear to be largely inherited (Kroeger and Thuesen 1988). Extroverts tend to talk a lot and find talking easier than listening. They are energized by interacting with other people. They feel comfortable meeting strangers and enjoy going to parties. Introverts, in contrast, tend to be quieter than extroverts and to find listening easier than talking. They need more private time than do extroverts because being with people drains them of energy. They prefer to be with just one other person, or a small group, rather than with a large group.

All of these characteristics seem to be present from an individual's earliest years. That is, people don't learn to be, or choose to be, extroverts or introverts. They simply are one or the other. But two additional points are important. First, the extent to which you are an extrovert or introvert can vary considerably; you could be extremely extroverted, extremely introverted, or somewhere in between. Second, temperament reflects a preference, not an unchangeable pattern. If necessary, introverts can learn to function like extroverts (some actors, actresses, and salespeople are introverts), and extroverts can moderate their behavior (a talkative extrovert can develop the skills of a good listener).

In sum, our position is that heredity provides the basic materials of your life. Heredity sets limits (though we have no way at present of determining what the limits are). Heredity is also more or less involved in your traits and your behavior. For example, genetically, you may have a predisposition to alcoholism, but your genes don't force you to become an alcoholic. Genetically, you may be an introvert, but that doesn't mean you can't enjoy parties or make public speeches. Your genetic makeup is important, but it alone can't explain who and what you are.

Socialization: Shaping the Materials

Instead of nurture, sociologists use the term **socialization**—the social process by which an individual develops and learns to function effectively in groups (Gecas 1981). Note the two emphases in socialization: the individual's own development as a unique creature and the individual's ability to be an acceptable member of various groups (e.g., the family, friendship circles, organizations). Both are part of a social process in which social influences shape the kind of person you are and also train you to function effectively in groups.

What If You Weren't Socialized?

If socialization is the shaping of your genetic materials, what would happen if you were not socialized; that is, if you experienced no social influences? In brief, without socialization you would not be fully human. Your very humanity depends upon your interaction with other people. This is not a new insight. As the American psychologist and philosopher William James (1950, pp. 193–94; orig. 1890) wrote, it would be a "fiendish punishment" for an individual to be treated as nonexistent by others:

> If no one turned round when we entered, answered when we spoke, or minded what we did, but if every person 'cut us dead,' and acted as if we were nonexisting things, a kind of rage and impotent despair would ere long well up in us, from which the cruellest bodily tortures would be a relief; for these would make us feel that, however bad might be our plight, we had not sunk to such a depth as to be unworthy of attention at all.

Actually, there is evidence of what does happen to an individual who lacks normal human interaction. There are more than fifty cases of children who were abandoned at or shortly after birth, presumably raised by some kind of animal, and later discovered by other humans. These "feral children," once found and brought into a human community, did not function as humans and generally died at an early age.

For example, the "wild boy of Aveyron" was found in the woods in France near the end of the eighteenth century (Lane 1976). He was about eleven years old, walked on all fours, and used no language. A physician began taking care of him, and the boy lived for another thirty years. Yet he never learned to speak nor to function like a normal human.

Some people believe that the feral children have all been severely retarded. Others argue that the children are normal but severely deprived. In any case, evidence about the effects of the loss of human contact—for example, prisoners kept in isolation—supports the same conclusion: you lose something of what it means to be human if you are cut off from other people.

Socialization and Culture

The way you are socialized reflects the culture. This is understandable because one of the major purposes of socialization is to enable individuals to function effectively in groups. The socialization process, therefore, will be more or less demanding, depending upon the extent to which group members expect conformity.

Thus, families are more or less flexible with children, depending upon the extent to which parents define obedience to their expectations as necessary and the larger community expects conformity. Socialization among the Hutterites of Canada in the early 1980s is an example of a rigid socialization process in which the goal was to make every child completely obedient to the church community (Huntington 1981). The Hutterites are a communal religious group who came to the United States from Europe and Russia in the last half of the nineteenth century. As pacifists, they were harassed and imprisoned when they refused to serve in the military during World War I. Most of them then moved to Canada.

Huntington found that, to insure conformity to their beliefs and strict code of behavior, the Hutterites raised their children in accord with a fixed pattern. For the first three years, children remained in their homes where they were taught to like people and to respond positively to everyone in the community. From ages three to six, they went to kindergarten where they learned "to obey, sing, sleep, memorize, and pray together" (Huntington 1981, p. 39). Children of that age were considered willful and useless, and a major purpose of kindergarten was to break their wills and teach them to be obedient. Among other things, kindergarten children were not allowed to be noisy around adults.

On their sixth birthdays, the children left kindergarten for German school. They remained in German school until the age of fifteen. During that time, they were under the care of their teachers, ate all meals with their peers, and did work for the community as assigned by the teachers. Finally, at fifteen the children were defined as adults. They moved from the children's dining room to the adult dining room, and from the children's group into the adult work force. As adults, they were given gifts of tools and clothes that they would use in their communal work.

Socialization: An Ongoing Process

Your development as a unique individual is a life-long task. Training to be an effective group member will occur at various points throughout your life. Socialization is an ongoing process.

Childhood Socialization

Some of the most important socialization occurs during your earliest years. Childhood socialization sets the direction of your life. A number of important and influential models of childhood socialization have been developed in an effort to understand the process. We will look briefly at three such models, proposed by Sigmund Freud, Jean Piaget, and George Herbert Mead.

Freud (1856–1939)

Freud (1961; orig. 1930) was an Austrian neurologist who believed that life and death instincts drive human life. Such things as destructive and aggressive behavior come from death instincts, while such things as love and sexual behavior come from life instincts. These instincts are part of the human biological makeup. Therefore, they drive all people.

Your instincts interact with the demands of society as you develop. Society, for example, requires you to keep your aggressive instincts in check and puts constraints on the way you express your sexual needs.

Freud posited that at birth, humans possess only one of three parts of human personality—the **id**. The id is the seat of the instincts, the source of all psychic energy. Initially, the id enables the infant to get gratification in the form of tension release through impulsive motions (such as waving hands or feet) and the formation of images (the memory of food).

These early forms of tension release do not suffice for very long, however. Cries or screams indicate that the formation of an image is no substitute for real food. Soon, therefore, the second part of the personality forms—the **ego**. The ego is a child's connection with the external world, the part of the personality that enables the individual to interact with the world in a realistic and effective way (eventually, crying and screaming will not achieve what the individual needs).

Finally, as a child learns what is and is not acceptable, the **superego** emerges—the conscience. Where the id prods the child to seek pleasure, and the ego prods the child to be realistic, the superego prods the child toward perfection (as perfection is defined by the child's social world). Perfection can be achieved both through striving for ideals and through feelings of guilt that lead to the abandonment of less-than-ideal ways.

Of course, in Freud's theory there is ongoing tension between the individual and the environment, between the id—which urges the individual to "do what comes naturally"—and the superego—which urges the individual to "do what is right." It is the task of the ego to manage this tension. A well-socialized child will develop an ego capable of the task and become a well-adjusted adult. The well-adjusted adult is one in whom the ego is "the executive of the personality, controlling and governing the id and the superego and maintaining commerce with the external world in the interest of the total personality and its far-flung needs" (Hall 1954, p. 28).

Freud asserted that there are significant sex differences in this development. Compared to men, he argued, women are more preoccupied with themselves, are more vain, have little sense of justice, and have less social interest. In sum, their superegos are less developed.

From a feminist perspective, this is nonsense and a good example of a theory that perpetuates the devaluation of women. Based on her interviews with women about their abortion decisions, Gilligan (1982) suggested that women have a more rather than a less developed super-ego. Gilligan concluded that women repeatedly think in terms of their responsibility to care about and care for others, while men tend to approach others with a philosophy of respecting rights and not interfering.

These are a few basic elements of a system that is far too complex to discuss thoroughly here. Some of Freud's ideas have been supported, and others have not, by research. For our purposes, his model underscores three important social aspects of human development. First, development is an ongoing process of interaction between a child's needs and social demands. Second, as a child develops, he or she internalizes many of those social demands (so that social control becomes self-control). And third, a key factor in development is identification, the process of becoming like other individuals with whom a child intimately interacts.

Thinking Critically

Freud and Freudian ideas have come under increasing criticism in recent decades. A severe criticism appeared in a respected British medical journal (Tallis 1996). The author argued that Freud based his theories on isolated examples and preconceived ideas of what his patients thought and felt. If the patient's understanding didn't fit his theories, Freud insisted that the patient was repressing memories. He kept using the same cases to support his arguments, giving the impression that he based his theories on numerous observations. And he made some disastrous mistakes, once treating a child for hysterical pain who eventually died of abdominal cancer.

Assuming that all of the above is true, would you dismiss Freud's ideas? Although feminists also criticize Freud, many of them use Freudian concepts and ideas to explain gender inequalities. In other words, they make a distinction between Freud's character and mistakes, on the one hand, and the scientific validity of his ideas on the other hand. Some of those ideas are not supported by subsequent research, but others are. Freud clearly made important contributions in spite of his various flaws.

Thinking critically, then, means to evaluate materials on their own merit. You may not like the kind of person Freud was. You may agree that some of his conclusions were based on his own biases. And you may be appalled at some of his mistakes. But such things do not of themselves invalidate either his entire theory or all of the conclusions he drew about human behavior.

Jean Piaget (1896-1980)

Jean Piaget, a highly regarded Swiss social scientist of this century, observed and experimented with children as he sought to understand their cognitive development. He concluded that experience and social interaction are crucial components of this development (Piaget and Inhelder 1969). He also identified four stages of development.

According to Piaget, in the first two years of life, a child is in the "sensorimotor stage." Lacking experience and language, the child understands the world through touching, sucking, tasting, listening, seeing, and hearing. At first, the child only understands what is immediately present; when mother leaves, she is, for the child, no longer real.

From ages two to seven, the child is in the "preoperational stage." The child is now learning to function in a symbolic world, using language to understand and interact with the world. But such complex forms of thinking as cause and effect are still beyond the child's capacity. Piaget found, for instance, that four-year-olds cannot grasp the relationship between peddling and making a bicycle move. Nor can they grasp abstract concepts. A child may understand that a particular object is appealing to look at but does not understand the abstract notion of beauty.

In the "concrete operational stage," lasting from ages seven to twelve, children learn to understand more complex cognitive processes. They understand cause and effect. They learn that multiple meanings can be attached to something (the dog is my friend as well as a watchdog for the house). Yet some cognitive tasks are still beyond their capacity.

Finally, at about the age of twelve, children enter the "formal operational stage" of Piaget's schema. They are now capable of abstract thought, able to reason about things they cannot see. Before this stage, a child would not know how to respond if you said, "If A is more than B, and B is more than C, is A more or less than C?" If the child saw five pennies, three pennies, and one penny, he or she would understand that the group of five is more than either of the other two. But putting it in terms of A, B, and C would make no sense.

In addition to showing the stages of development, Piaget contributed to an understanding of socialization by stressing the fact that the child is an active agent in the process, not simply a passive recipient. A child's development does not proceed automatically, but through social interaction. The outcome of the child's experiences is an individual capable of shaping, not merely responding to, the social world.

George Herbert Mead (1863–1931)

Mead, an American philosopher and social psychologist, is generally considered the father of *symbolic interactionism*. He raised the question of how you become a **self,** a creature capable of observing, responding to, and directing your own behavior. The newborn infant cannot distinguish itself from others. Only gradually children learn to see themselves as separate and unique individuals. Only gradually, as cognitive capacity and personality develop, does the child learn to observe, respond to, and direct his or her own behavior.

According to Mead (1934), the self is composed of the **"I"** and the **"me."** The "I" is the unpredictable, the novel, the impulsive part of the self. The "me" is the socialized part of the self. The "me" sets the socially acceptable limits within which the "I" can act.

In Mead's theory the self develops in three stages. In the first two years of life, a child imitates others. Seeing its mother purse her lips, for instance, the child will eventually try to do the same. In the play stage (at about three years of age), the child begins to function symbolically (use language). The child plays like various people he or she has encountered—mother, father, a relative, or a TV character.

For example, a girl might play at being her mother. She acts toward her doll the way her mother behaves toward her. She speaks to the doll, loves it, feeds it, and disciplines it. In doing so, she is doing two very important things. First, she is striving to understand her mother's perspective. Mead called this **role-taking**. Second, she is making herself into an object outside of herself; and this is a way to learn how to observe, respond to, and direct her own behavior.

The third stage of development of the self is the "organized game." It differs from the second stage in that the child must now take the roles of a number of other people simultaneously and understand how those roles relate to each other. In a ball game, for example, the child must understand both what each of the players expects of him or her as well as what each player will do. This understanding is the prerequisite for a child's internalizing the values and attitudes of his or her social world. He or she understands the differences between what one person might want and what people generally want and expect.

Mead, like Freud, made the point that socialization involves the gradual internalization of social standards by the child. Like Piaget, he focused on cognitive processes. All three portrayed socialization as something that transforms a newborn child into an individual capable of functioning in society. None of the three, however, was concerned with the continuing socialization of the adult—an important aspect of socialization.

Adult Socialization

Socialization does not end when you become twenty-one. Many adolescents mistakenly view adulthood as the time when they have worked through all their major crises and developmental challenges. However, socialization continues throughout your life.

In his pioneering effort to understand continuing development in adulthood, Erik Erikson (1963) viewed life as a progression through a series of stages. Each stage presents a critical issue or challenge that the individual must resolve.

Erikson identified three such stages for adults. In the first, early adulthood, the challenge is to form bonds of love and friendship. To fail the challenge is to sink into relative isolation and to fall short of healthy development. In middle adulthood, from the ages of forty to sixty, the issue is whether you will get involved in "generativity" (becoming a nurturer or mentor of the young) or will stagnate in an effort to maintain your youthful ambitions and activities. In late adulthood, the critical issue is whether you will achieve a sense of integrity (accept what you are and what you have achieved) or sink into despair (regret the course of your life and discount its meaning).

For Erikson, then, a healthy socialization requires the resolution of a succession of challenges. Other researchers have suggested a similar form of development—stages that demand the resolution of challenges (e.g., Gould [1972] and Levinson [1978]). The challenges they identify include formation of a stable marriage and family, finding a meaningful career, dealing with the mid-life crisis, and facing retirement, loss, and death.

These stages and their attendant challenges, we should note, may not apply to women and to other cultures. Although some of the researchers (Levinson 1978) claimed to have a model that was universally applicable, the research was done on middle-class, white, American men (recall the importance of knowing the sample). Yet models based on the study of men may not fully apply to women (Rosenfeld and Stark 1987).

Consider, for instance, Erikson's middle stage of generativity. At around the age of forty many women, whose children are now in school, are just beginning a career outside the home or accelerating an existing career. It is no longer a time for them to be involved in mentoring—which they may have been doing with their own children for years. It is a time for exploring their potential and expanding their experiences.

There are, however, a number of processes that do apply to all people in all places, including role change, anticipatory socialization, and resocialization. Each of these is a part of adult socialization.

Role Change

Popularly, **status** means prestige. In the social sciences, status refers to a social position that is evaluated. For instance, student, daughter, father, sales clerk, and professor are statuses and, in every society, some statuses are accorded more value than others. In the United States, the status of professor is evaluated higher than that of sales clerk (regardless of what you may think of any particular professor or sales clerk).

But what does a student or a daughter or a father do? What does it mean to occupy a particular status? The answer lies in role—the social expectations for behavior associated with a particular status. Your role as a student includes the kinds of things you do—study, attend classes, take tests, and so on. The point is, these are not things you have decided to do on your own; the behavior associated with being a student was already present when you became a student.

From time to time, you will engage in role change of some kind—losing roles and taking on new roles. When you graduate, you will no longer have the status of student nor engage in the behaviors associated with the role of student. And you will take on new roles when you do such things as marry, start a career, have children, or assume a new position at work.

Loss of roles can be painful and often requires a period of adjustment. For many students, graduation creates a sense of loss as well as of achievement. In addition, acquiring new roles can be difficult and may require a period of learning. For example, businesses frequently train new members for a year or more so that they can function effectively in the organization. And people who are about to marry or become parents may attend classes, workshops, or counseling sessions to prepare for these new roles. Socialization, then, is a part of all role change.

Anticipatory Socialization

In some cases, socialization for a new role begins even before the person assumes the role. **Anticipatory socialization** is the adoption of values, attitudes, and behaviors that an individual perceives to be associated with a role that he or she will, or would like to, assume. The graduate student who looks forward to an academic career and adopts the mannerisms or perspectives of a favorite professor is engaging in anticipatory socialization. The aspiring executive who reads biographies and autobiographies of successful business leaders and tries to imitate their behavior is engaging in anticipatory socialization.

Anticipatory socialization can help you function effectively in new roles. Yet its value will depend upon how accurately you understand those new roles. For example, a teenage girl shared this experience with us:

> Before I started dating, some of my more experienced friends gave me the impression that boys not only expected but wanted their dates to be sexually aggressive. So the first date I had with this really nice guy, I came on pretty strong. He didn't respond very much so nothing much happened. But he didn't ask me out again. I realized that I didn't understand what guys—especially the nice ones—wanted after all.

Resocialization

Some kinds of role change demand more drastic change than do others. **Resocialization** refers to socialization into a role that radically alters an individual's behavior. Resocialization is a time-consuming process because emotions as well as thought patterns must change if the new behavior is to become stable (Fein 1990).

Resocialization may occur in such contexts as prisons, mental hospitals, special education programs, the military, and cults. For example, people who entered the Jim Jones organization we discussed in Chapter One went through "almost total transformations of subjective social reality and personal identity" (Redlinger and Armour 1982, p. 88).

Five mechanisms were used to resocialize the members (Redlinger and Armour 1982). First, new members learned to interpret events in their own lives and in the world according to the ideology of the group. Second, new members developed close relationships within the group to replace those they had outside the group and regarded Jim Jones as a father figure. Third, older members became role models for new members. Fourth, membership involved a considerable degree of isolation from outside influences; most of the member's nonwork activities were with other members. And fifth, past events, including the member's previous life, were reinterpreted and seen as destructive. In fact, the only good thing about the member's past was that it prepared him or her for entry into the group.

Through these mechanisms members of the Jim Jones cult learned to despise their past and the world outside the cult. They learned that the only hope for a meaningful life lay within the bounds of the cult. Their behavior and thought patterns were radically changed. They eventually demonstrated the radical nature of this change by voluntarily killing themselves.

Resocialization, then, sometimes involves a socially desirable change—the transformation of a criminal offender into a responsible citizen. In other times it involves a socially undesirable change—the transformation of a responsible citizen into a member of a destructive group.

Agents of Socialization

We began this chapter by asking you to describe the kind of person you are, and we raised the question of why you are the way you described yourself. Here we examine six important social factors that will enable you to understand your own socialization (and that of others as well): family, peers, school, the mass media, social class, and experience.

Family

Socialization begins in the family at the moment of birth. The way parents hold their baby, look at it, talk to it, and respond to its needs tells the baby about the nature of its world—a world in which it can expect security and love or one in which it can expect only struggle and neglect.

As the child grows, different parenting styles can lead to quite different outcomes. Three researchers who studied 372 children in grades five, six, and eleven found that the children perceived four different parenting styles: authoritative (the parents put boundaries on acceptable behavior within a warm, accepting context); permissive (minimal parental control and parental approval of almost anything the child decides to do); and two types of incongruent parenting (mother and father have very different parenting styles, with either the mother or the father perceived as very controlling and/or rejecting)(Johnson, Shulman, and Collins 1991). Interestingly, those who perceived their parents as authoritative were likely to have higher self-esteem and higher academic achievement than those in the other parenting styles (Figure 4.1). Perceived permissive parenting was associated with the lowest academic achievement while the perceived incongruent styles were associated with the lowest self-esteem.

The authoritative style appears to be best for all races and all kinds of families. A study of about ten thousand high school students reported that those from homes with this parenting style tended to earn higher grades, be more self-reliant, report less anxiety and depression, and be less likely to engage in delinquent behavior (Steinberg et al. 1991). Similarly, a study of interaction patterns in nineteen Mexican families found that warm, supportive parenting tended to produce children who were supportive and able to express themselves well, while punitive and restrictive parenting tended to produce children who resisted others either passively or aggressively (Bronstein 1994).

The extent to which parents attempt to control their children and express affection for their children, then, are two very important aspects of socialization in a family. The structure and size of the family are also

Figure 4.1   Parenting Style, Self-Concept, and Academic Achievment

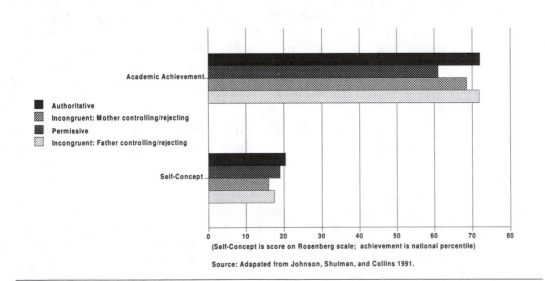

(Self-Concept is score on Rosenberg scale; achievement is national percentile)

Source: Adapated from Johnson, Shulman, and Collins 1991.

important. Children generally fare better in two-parent than single-parent families, particularly when the two parents are the child's natural parents. National data show that children who grow up with both biological parents are likely to receive more social, emotional, and material support than other children (Marks 1995). Children in stepfamilies have more behavior problems than those who live with both biological parents (Hetherington 1993). Children from divorced families also tend to be less sociable and less responsive at home, at school, and with their peers (Peretti and di Vitorrio 1993).

Finally, family socialization will vary from one culture to another. An investigation of child rearing practices in six different cultures—northern India, Okinawa, Mexico, Africa, the Philippines, and the northeastern United States—found differences in things such as the extent to which children are expected to be responsible for tasks, mothers feel and express positive emotions such as praise and warmth, and aggressive behavior toward peers and parents is tolerated (Lambert and Lambert 1973).

Experiences

'I Don't Have Any Common Sense'

Mark is a successful businessman. In spite of his achievements, he struggles with a problem that he has had since childhood—the nagging feeling that he lacks "common sense." He explains why he feels this way:

I don't have any common sense. At least, I really wonder if I do. When I was growing up, I heard my father say to me any number of times: "You don't have any common sense, Mark, or you wouldn't do such stupid things." Looking back on it, I realize that I did do some stupid things. But at least some of the time, I acted stupidly because my head was so messed up from my father telling me how inept I was.

One day before he left for work, my father told me to be sure and put out the bag in the garage for the trashmen to pick up. It was a large plastic bag, and I noticed it was filled with curios and pictures and things that I thought my parents would want to keep. But I remember thinking to myself that this time I was going to show my father that I could carry out his instructions. So I put the bag out.

Of course, it was the wrong bag. It was stuff my parents intended to keep. My mother had put another bag—the bag of junk—outside near the garage, but I didn't see it there. So I threw the wrong bag away. It was a stupid thing to do. But as I look back on it, I ask myself a question. Was my stupid behavior the *cause* of my father's comments or was it the *result* of his comments? I'm still not sure.

Mark raises an important question. Would a different parenting style have resulted in a different boy? Or was the conclusion of Mark's father correct? If parenting style is truly important, then we could say that Mark's father was a contributor to, and not merely an observer of, Mark's "lack of common sense."

Peers

Peers—those who are your equals in terms of such things as age and status—become increasingly important in your socialization after the first couple of years of life. Peers provide you with the first opportunity to associate with others as equals. Furthermore, while you cannot choose your family, you can to a large extent choose the peers who will be your friends.

Peers open up new possibilities that are not learned in the family. That is, if your family provided you with a number of options about what you can do and what you can become, your peers will add to those options. Peers, then, pave the way for you to become an independent and unique individual.

In fact, peer relationships can lead to family conflict when a child resists the parents' socialization (Stryker and Serpe 1982). Many parents of adolescents have found it difficult to enforce curfew rules when peers deride these rules as childish. By adolescence, peers are as important as family in influencing many kinds of behavior. Thus, whether a young person will engage in various kinds of delinquent behavior, including drug use, depends upon peer as well as family values and attitudes (Heimer and Matsueda 1994; Duncan et al. 1995).

School

Creating responsible citizens and facilitating the personal development of the young are among the explicit purposes of education (see Chapter Twelve). These purposes are achieved by socializing the young to accept and work within the context of cultural values. This socialization occurs through the use of various rewards and punishments such as grades and teacher approval or disapproval.

It is in school that you get a sense of how intelligent and competent you are. It is in school that you learn to value such things as democracy, achievement, self-discipline, and hard work. It is in school that you first learn how to function as a member of an organization. And it is in school that you learn how to obey authorities other than your parents. It is not merely the curriculum but the whole schooling experience that socializes you.

The atmosphere of fear in some schools is a grim reminder of the importance of the whole schooling experience. This fear is realistic. *Time Magazine* reported on January 25, 1993 that on any given day, at least 100,000 students have guns at school, 160,000 skip classes because they fear physical harm, 40 are hurt or killed by guns, and 260 are physically assaulted.

In this atmosphere, the schooling experience reinforces what many students have already discovered outside the classroom—life is violent and unpredictable. Moreover, the educational quality in these schools is questionable because research shows that "a safe, orderly environment" is necessary for academic success (National Center for Educational Statistics 1990, p. 58).

The Mass Media

Television, radio, movies, popular books and magazines, and newspapers all contribute to socialization. Debates have gone on for decades about whether the mass media make a positive or negative contribution to socialization. Do comic books produce violent behavior in children? Does rock music lead to self-destructive behavior? Does television turn children into electronic-age drones?

Actually, the media can have both positive and negative effects. For example, at least among younger viewers, watching television can enlarge vocabulary and expand knowledge of the world (Josephson 1987). A study of 59 children in the second through sixth grades reported that frequent television viewers were able to communicate emotions common on television (such as happiness and sadness) better than emotions that are uncommon (such as disgust and fear/surprise)(Coats 1995). Thus, television can make a positive contribution to both cognitive and emotional skills.

In addition, mass media campaigns against drugs have helped reduce the use of both legal and illegal drugs (Romer 1994). And television shows that have strong, altruistic messages (such as the value of helping others) have a positive impact on people's attitudes and behavior (Friedlander 1993).

On the other hand, there is an enormous amount of violence on television and evidence that those who watch it may either become more prone to violence or develop feelings of mistrust, vulnerability, and alienation (National Institute of Mental Health 1982). Three researchers set up an experiment in which they observed sixty-three four-year-old children at play (Singer, Singer, and Rapaczynski 1984). They counted the number of aggressive acts committed by the children. Over the next six years, they had the parents keep track of the number and kind of television programs the children watched, and the researchers measured the children's beliefs and behavior. The researchers concluded the more that children watched violent programs, the less they were able to behave with self-restraint, and the more likely they were to be aggressive, restless, and to believe that the world is a frightening place.

Social Class

We shall discuss **social class** in detail in Chapter Eight, but we need to include it here because of its importance in socialization. Social

classes are groups of people that are unequal with regard to things valued in a society, whose members share similar values and lifestyles.
Typically, we speak about upper, middle, working, and lower classes,
though finer distinctions are also made. In general, the higher your social class, the higher your income and education and the greater your
prestige.

The way that parents rear their children varies by social class. In
comparison to lower-class families, for example, middle-class families
tend to be more flexible about the roles of family members (Gecas 1981).
There is a lesser tendency to think of something as "man's work" or
"woman's work," and a greater tendency for any family member to be
expected to do every kind of task. Middle-class parents are also more
likely to stress the individuality and development of their children while
lower-class parents stress conformity (unquestioning obedience to parents and teachers). Middle-class parents also tend to be less narrow and
less punitive in matters of rules and discipline. Finally, the higher the
social class of the parents, the more likely their children are to be aware
of and to value cultural resources such as art, museums, concerts, and
libraries (Mohr and DiMaggio 1995).

To sum it up, depending on your social class background, you will
be more or less likely to value such things as openness, flexibility, self-
development, and the cultural resources of your community. This
doesn't mean you won't change. However, social class background gives
an initial direction to your life, and many people stay with that direction
throughout their lives.

Experiences

Of course, you have experiences in your family, school, and neighborhood. We include experiences as a separate category to emphasize
the fact that each individual has a unique set of experiences that go into
making that him or her a unique person. No two children, even in the
same family, have the same family experiences. (If you have siblings,
you can prove this to yourself by talking with them about their overall
impressions of your parents and how your parents related to each of
you.) No two children in the same class at school have precisely the same
experience in that classroom. (You can demonstrate this by talking with
fellow students in your class about such things as their impressions of
the teaching ability of the instructor and the value of the course content.)

Both positive and negative experiences enter into your socialization.
Williams (1993) illustrated the positive in his description of an African
American barbershop in New Orleans. Using *participant observation*,
Williams concluded that the barbershop was a place where black males
can go to learn how to become a black man, and black men can gather
to bond with each other. Through the tales told, the bonding occurs

among the men, and the children learn something of what their lives may be like.

Interestingly, eight years earlier Franklin (1985) had also studied an African American barbershop. He found some negative outcomes: interaction in the shop perpetuated stereotypes about men and women, fostered sexist attitudes, and justified inequality between the sexes.

Negative experiences can have both short-term and long-term effects. A rape victim might develop various physical and emotional symptoms and withdraw from people. She has learned that the world is a dangerous, unpredictable, and unjust place. Such consequences are typical in the short run, and they may persist for years or even a lifetime. Hopefully, "emotional relearning" will occur (Goleman 1995). Yet the victim may never be completely free from emotional twinges or periodic feelings of regret about the incident, even though she can successfully reorder her life.

Many people never fully recover from trauma such as rape, divorce, death of a loved one, or loss of work. Others, however, find ways not merely to cope but to use the trauma to develop into more competent and satisfied individuals (Lauer and Lauer 1988).

Becoming Who You Are

Many different social factors operate to help you become the person you are, but how exactly do they work? As noted earlier, George Herbert Mead stressed the importance of interaction. Let's look a little more closely at how interaction helps shape the way you think about yourself, your emotions, and your achievements.

How You Think About Yourself

According to symbolic interactionism, the way you think you appear to others is a crucial part of the process. Cooley (1902) called this the "looking-glass" self, and it involves both your thinking and your feelings. The way you think about yourself, and the kind of person you believe yourself to be, are the result of how you imagine that you appear to others, how you imagine others judge this appearance, "and some sort of self-feeling, such as pride or mortification" (Cooley 1902, p. 152).

For example, suppose you think that you are intelligent. You think of yourself in this way because important people—your parents, teachers, and friends—have indicated that they regard you as intelligent. They have admired this quality in you and thus have made you feel proud. Accordingly, you have incorporated "intelligence" into the list of qualities you believe you possess.

It is important to keep in mind that this process of "imagining" or perceiving how others regard you may or may not accurately reflect their opinion of you. You may believe that your friends all regard you as someone with immense sex appeal. Another person might interview your friends and find that they actually believe you have only average sex appeal. Nevertheless, you think of yourself as someone with extraordinary sex appeal. What matters for your behavior is your definition of the situation.

Your Emotions

Your genetic makeup inclines you to be more or less emotional. Some children smile and laugh a lot from their earliest days while others are more sober. Yet learning is also an important aspect of becoming an emotional creature. Both the kinds of emotions you experience and the way you express them are the result of your interaction experiences.

Oliver (1995) studied 186 undergraduates at a midwestern university and found that their perceptions of their family life helped explain some of their emotional experiences. In particular, those students who perceived a family in which there was a good deal of control but little affection were more likely to be depressed and less likely to feel good about themselves or about their ability to manage their lives well.

You also learn in your family about which emotions you are supposed to experience in various situations. You may learn to not laugh when someone is hurt, to cry when someone is dying, to feel happy when relatives visit, and so on. These are not mere reflections of common sense, and they are not true of all people. For instance, researchers found that Tahitian individuals whose spouses had died defined their subsequent feelings as an illness rather than as grief (Lauer and Handel 1983).

You learn not only *what* emotions you are supposed to experience but also *how* you are to express them from your family and the people with whom you interact. The Japanese, for example, learn to suppress their emotions in public. However, Ekman (1973) discovered that the Japanese exhibit the same expressions as Americans in private. He showed a group of students in Tokyo and another group in California a stressful film that caused feelings of disgust and anxiety. Unknown to the students, he videotaped their expressions while they watched the film. The expressions on the faces of the Japanese and American students were quite similar. But when the experimenter interviewed the students after the film, the Americans talked about the film with continued negative facial expressions while the Japanese talked about it with positive facial expressions. Their emotional experience was similar, but the public expression of the experience was quite different.

Your Achievements

When you achieve something, you like to think that the achievement is a reflection of your abilities. But it's more complicated than this, as illustrated by the terms "underachiever" and "overachiever." Why do some people with great ability achieve very little? Why do some people seem to achieve more than they should in terms of their abilities?

Interaction experiences enter into the extent to which you achieve. They especially affect your motivation to achieve. And those experiences may go back to your earliest years. David McClelland and his associates at Harvard have spent many years studying the motivation to achieve. In one research project, they interviewed a group of young adults whose mothers had been interviewed some twenty-five years earlier when their children were five-year-olds (McClelland and Pilon 1983). The young adults with the highest need for achievement were likely to have been reared by mothers who scheduled feedings and strict toilet training. In other words, the mothers of the high achievers were more demanding of their children (see Extensions, this chapter).

We noted earlier the impact that social class has on socialization. Among other things, those in the lower social classes are less likely to achieve highly in either school or work. What about those who do achieve in spite of their social class background? Luster and McAdoo (1996) addressed the question by using *existing data* that had been collected over a period of more than twenty years on a sample of African Americans from a low social-class background. The years of education that they had achieved by the time they were twenty-seven years old varied enormously, ranging from 6.5 years (less than an elementary school education) to eighteen years (a master's degree).

A number of factors explain the differences in educational achievement. Those with higher levels of achievement tended to have parents who valued education and who expected their children to attain a high degree of education. Their mothers were also more involved with their education from the time they started school. The students developed a high need for academic achievement, and that need, interestingly, was more closely related to achieving an eighth-grade education than was their IQ score. Clearly, interaction experiences are crucial to explaining achievement.

A Note on Human Freedom

Our discussion so far of how you become who you are may once again raise the issue of "nothing but." Are you "nothing but" the sum of the social factors that come to bear upon you? Are you determined by those factors? Does the notion of human freedom, the freedom to choose, have any meaning?

Yes, we believe in human freedom. No, we do not believe you are completely determined by social factors. Recall George Herbert Mead's description of the self as the "I" and the "me." The "I" is the unpredictable part of you. In a sense, Mead was affirming your freedom to act and to choose when he identified the "I" as one aspect of the self. The "me" may set limits, but it does not determine fully who you are and what you will do.

Similarly, Ralph Turner (1962) affirmed human freedom in his notion of **role-making**. Turner's point was that you not only take on roles, but you also act in ways that modify those roles. You may live out a role in a unique way. The judge who is known as the "hanging judge," the rich man who carries his lunch to work in a brown bag, and the women who first adopted the "braless" look are examples of individuals who modified roles. If enough people modify a role in a similar way, it may change over time so that the innovative elements become the norm. The dress of professors from the conservative fashion of the 1950s to the casual wear of the 1960s and the entry of women into previously all-male occupations are examples of role changes.

EXTENSIONS

Teaching Children to Be Successful In School

Asian Americans are noted for their academic success. In general, Asian Americans get higher SAT scores and higher grade point averages in both high school and college than individuals of other races of ethnicities. They also complete more years of school and receive higher scores on I.Q. tests. Even if you only compare individuals from the same social class, Asian Americans have higher grade point averages and more years of schooling than any other group (Chao 1996).

In an effort to explain the academic success of Asian Americans, Chao (1996) did *survey research* with a sample of forty-eight immigrant Chinese mothers and fifty white American mothers in the Los Angeles area. She interviewed each of the mothers about their parenting practices with regard to school achievement. The Chinese mothers differed from the white American mothers in a number of ways.

One of the most common things the Chinese mothers said was that they have high expectations for their children. They reinforce their high expectations with such things as assigning work to their children beyond that assigned by teachers and not allowing any play or television until homework is done. Some Chinese mothers even hire tutors and have their children participate in after-school study groups.

The white American mothers, in contrast, stressed social development. Some even said that too much stress on academic success is not good for children. They wanted learning to be fun for their children. And they sought to foster high self-esteem, which they believed to be the basis for success in life.

Thus, the two sets of mothers differed both in what they believed was most important and in the extent to which they directly participated in the education of their children. If you assume that all racial groups have equivalent proportions of intelligent individuals, the academic success of Asian Americans reflects their socialization experiences. Nurture, rather than nature, explains the success.

Barrie Thorne (1993) found examples of role-making in her observation of children at two elementary schools. As she watched the children at play, she realized that their behavior was not simply the outcome of adult socialization efforts. Rather, the children were, to some extent at least, creating their own notions about the meaning of male and female as they interacted with each other and created the rules of male-female relating.

Becoming Male and Female

We will discuss the issue of **gender** more fully in Chapter Ten. Here, we want to note that what it means to be male or female is also a result of socialization and not merely of your biological makeup. In fact, social scientists distinguish between sex, which is what you are biologically—male or female—and gender, which refers to males and females as social creatures. **Gender role** is the behavior associated with being either male or female.

Everyone agrees that there are differences between males and females. However, there is disagreement over the extent to which those differences reflect biological makeup or socialization. Even social scientists don't agree with each other. Sociobiologists, for example, stress the continuity of humans with other animals, pointing out that male-female differences reflect the evolutionary imperatives to survive and to perpetuate the species. Thus, sociobiologists argue that males are naturally polygamous and females are naturally monogamous. They maintain that the most effective way for males to perpetuate their own kind is to inseminate as many women as possible, while the most effective way for females is to get a male to protect them and help raise their children.

Some scientists who study the brain also affirm a biological basis for male-female differences. Indeed, there are neurological differences in male and female brains that could account for some differences in behavior (Kolata 1995). Yet many of the differences are small and even trivial (Hyde and Plant 1995). Moreover, as a biologist (Fausto-Sterling 1985, p. 77) noted, "extensive development of nervous connections occurs after birth, influenced profoundly by individual experience."

Furthermore, if male and female behavior is largely determined biologically, it is hard to explain some of the striking cultural variations. Margaret Mead studied three New Guinea tribes and concluded that most of the traits Americans think of as masculine or feminine are actually "as lightly linked to sex as are the clothing, the manners, and the form of headdress that a society at a given period assigns to either sex" (Mead 1969, p. 260). In one tribe she investigated, the behavior of males and females was very different from most Americans at the time of her study. The women ruled, took the initiative in things like mating, and dealt with such practical matters as fishing and trading. The men, on the other hand, spent a great deal of time attending to their personal appearance, their jewelry, and their efforts to get the attention of women.

Male and female behaviors, thus, reflect socialization. As *structural-functionalists* have pointed out, socialization aims at shaping males and females in a way that maintains the social order. Parsons (1955), one of the most influential of structural-functionalists, argued that girls are socialized to become ideal mothers and boys are socialized to become ideal fathers. They are socialized not merely to act accordingly—with men accepting the role of breadwinner and girls accepting the role of nurturer—but to think of their roles as *natural*. This socialization process, described by Parsons, accurately reflected and reinforced the social order of his time.

Of course, if you think of your gender role as determined by biology, you are likely to accept it unquestioningly. As Margaret Mead's and other studies show, however, the meaning of being male or female can vary considerably.

Explorations

Learning to Be Male or Female

Think about how your parents helped you to understand the meaning of being male or female. What kind of behavior did they model for you? What messages did you get from them about appropriate ways to think, to express emotions, to behave? What activities did they encourage for you? What aspirations did they have for your academic achievement and future occupation?

Divide the class into groups and discuss these questions. Then have each group member interview someone of the opposite sex. Do an in-depth interview, asking that person the above questions and any other questions you

may find helpful. Obtain as complete answers as possible. Summarize the findings of the group and have one member report them to the class. Discuss what kinds of similarities and differences you found in the ways that males and females are socialized.

If you do this assignment individually, interview a person of the opposite sex. Contrast and compare this person's experience to your own. To what extent were your experiences the same? To what extent were they different? What would you conclude about learning to be male and female?

Becoming a Moral Creature

"Everyone knows right from wrong," a student told us. "How do you know this?" we asked. "Because," the student replied, "everyone has a conscience." When we asked where one's conscience comes from, the student simply said: "You're born with it."

While it may be true that, apart from some mentally ill people, everyone "knows right from wrong," the problem is that one person's "right" is often another person's "wrong." Is it right or wrong to abandon your aged grandparent to die? Is it right or wrong to put your newborn daughter out to die? You might say that these actions are wrong, but societies who have practiced such behaviors would argue that they are not only right but also necessary for the survival of the group.

Right and wrong, in other words, are judgments that develop through socialization. You were not born a moral creature. You learn this, and the particular morality you learn reflects the culture of which you are a part.

Kohlberg (1969) developed an important model of different kinds of reasoning used to make moral decisions. His model has three levels of moral reasoning, each of which has two stages (Table 4.1). As shown in table 4.1, as an individual moves up the levels, he or she goes from what is essentially a premoral state to one where decisions are based on universal principles. In the premoral state, for example, a child may refrain from eating a forbidden between-meals snack not because the child agrees with the rule or even sees the point of it, but only to escape punishment (Stage 1); or the child may refrain not to avoid punishment but to obtain the approval of the parents (Stage 2). If a child reached Stage 6 of moral decision-making, he or she would refrain from eating the snack in order to maintain personal dignity as an individual who follows rules that enhance human well-being.

Table 4.1   **Kohlberg's Model of Moral Decision-Making**

Level 1 - Preconventional: Moral decisions based on the consequences of one's behavior for one's own benefit.
   Stage 1 - People act in order to avoid punishment.
   Stage 2 - People act in order to secure rewards.

Level 2 - Conventional: Moral decisions based on a desire to conform to expectations of others.
   Stage 3 - People act in order to please others.
   Stage 4 - People act in order to maintain social order and show respect for authorities.

Level 3 - Postconventional: Moral decisions based on principles that are universal rather than those of particular authorities.
   Stage 5 - People act in order to follow the will of the majority.
   Stage 6 - People act in order to be true to such universal principles as justice, equality, and human dignity.

While ideally an individual progresses from Stage 1 as a child to Stage 6 as an adult, the course of moral development is not automatic. Kohlberg found that most college students function between Stages 3 and 4. Some people never function at the higher stages. What then, facilitates moral development? Hart (1988) found that boys who identify with their parents are more likely than others to develop to higher stages. Of course, identification with one's parents only happens when parent-child relationships are warm and positive. In one *experiment*, parents of low-stage children were found to dominate parent-child discussions more than parents of higher-stage children (Walker 1991). In sum, when parents themselves function at higher stages, and when they use the warm, supportive parenting style we discussed earlier, their children are more likely to develop to the higher stages of moral reasoning.

There is a problem with all this, however. Kohlberg did his research on men and boys. Does the same scheme of development apply to females? Carol Gilligan (1982) found not. Based on her research, she argued that Kohlberg's model of a morality of justice applies to males, but that a model of caring is more appropriate for females. There is other evidence to support her claim (Ford and Lowery 1986; Wolfinger, Rabow, and Newcomb 1993). Female nurses, for instance, assert that a morality of caring better captures their experience than a morality of justice (Kuhse 1995).

It may be, however, that moral development is even more diverse, because cultural as well as gender differences are involved. Data collected from sixty Chinese students in Beijing, China, and sixty-one American students in Utah reported that the American women favored a caring orientation, while the Chinese women favored a justice orientation (Stander and Jensen 1993).

To sum up, becoming a moral creature is a process that requires many years. Through various kinds of interaction experiences, you can move from a premoral state to one of making moral decisions on higher principles. What principles are at the heart of the highest stage of moral development for you may depend on both your gender and your cultural background.

Becoming a Group Member

From the beginning of life, you learn how to be a member of groups. The first group you belong to is your family, and your parents spend a good deal of time training you for that membership. The next group you belong to might be a friendship group. What does it mean to be a friend? You learn this by interacting with others. Similarly, what does it mean to be a student or a member of a fraternity or sorority or an employee in a corporation or a member of a religious or political organization?

Most people experience some anxiety when they join a new group. The first day at a new school or the first day on the job may be filled with uncertainty and anxiety as well as anticipation—a reflection of the fact that socialization into a new group is taking place. Socialization into a new group involves a merging of the norms and goals of the individual and the group. The new member must learn the patterns of thought and behavior expected in the group, and the existing members must feel satisfied with the new member's degree of acceptance of those patterns.

The length of the socialization period can vary considerably. Fraternities and sororities use a pledge period to socialize new members. Corporations may take a year or more to socialize new employees, particularly those who are prospective managers or highly specialized technicians. In friendship groups, socialization may be a lengthy process as individuals learn what is acceptable and what is not with regard to such things as topics of conversation, teasing, and promptness.

In some groups, there is a two-stage socialization, with formal schooling in a particular field being the first stage and training in a particular organization comprising the second stage. And the way the new member performs may reflect the second stage more strongly than the first stage. Heck (1995) studied the performance of 148 new assistant principals in schools in a western state. He found that their schooling basically prepared them for the organizational socialization, and the latter significantly shaped their behavior as assistant principals.

In some cases, the socialization period is also a trial period—the group members are deciding whether they will accept the prospective new member. A study of law school interns in a prosecuting attorney's office found that those who were more completely socialized into the prosecutor role were regarded as "apprentice recruits," while those who were less well socialized were regarded as temporary help (Winfree, Kielich, and Clark 1984).

In sum, becoming a group member involves a process of socialization in which both the prospective new member and the existing members of the group determine whether the fit is acceptable. The prospective new member may drop out before being fully accepted, or the group may decide against full acceptance. If the prospective new member accepts the goals and norms of the group, full acceptance normally follows.

Critical Thinking Exercise

Traeen (1996) studied the socialization of Norwegian adolescents into sexual relations. The researcher had a sample of 920 young men and women. Of those who were sexually active, less than half were included in the analysis. He found that females were socialized to have sex for emotional reasons (e.g., love), while males were socialized to have sex for practical reasons (e.g., physical need). More males than females also reported having sex because the partner wanted it, from which the researcher concluded that males seldom use pressure if the females do not want sex. What kinds of questions would you raise about this research and the conclusion drawn? What additional information would you want? What other ways could you interpret the finding that more males than females reported having sex because the partner wanted it?

Summary

There is a long-standing debate about whether human behavior can be best understood as the result of nature or nurture. While some earlier social scientists insisted on one or the other, most now agree that behavior involves an interaction between genetic makeup and nurturing experiences, or socialization. Heredity provides the basic materials of life while socialization gives shape to them. Heredity sets limits and is more or less a factor in individual traits and behavior.

Socialization involves both the individual's personal development as a unique creature and the individual's capacity to function as an acceptable group member. Without socialization, individuals would not be fully human. The way they are socialized reflects their culture because they must learn to function in groups within the culture.

Socialization is a life-long process. Some of the most important socialization occurs in childhood, setting the directions for an individual's life. Freud, Piaget, and Mead all developed influential models of childhood socialization. All three portrayed socialization as a process that transforms the newborn child into a socially functioning individual.

Erik Erikson created a model of development that included both childhood and adult socialization. He viewed socialization as a process requiring the resolution of a succession of challenges. Adult socialization may vary by gender and by culture, but three processes that are universal are role change, anticipatory socialization, and resocialization. Role change includes both the loss and acquisition of roles. Anticipatory socialization occurs when an individual begins to act in accord with the perceived expectations of a particular role before actually assuming that role. Resocialization radically alters behavior.

Six important agents of socialization are family, peers, school, the mass media, social class, and experiences. In the family, differing parenting styles have quite different outcomes for children. Peers are influential because they provide individuals with their first opportunity to associate with others as equals. Schools socialize them to accept and work within the context of cultural values. The mass media can have both positive and negative effects on development. Social class impacts such things as values and parenting styles. And experiences contribute to the uniqueness of each individual.

Interaction experiences socialize you to become who you are. Such experiences help shape the way you think about yourself, your emotions, and your achievements. They also help you to understand what it means to be male or female, to become a moral creature, and to learn how to function as a group member.

Glossary

anticipatory socialization the adoption of values, attitudes, and behaviors that an individual perceives to be associated with a role that he or she will, or would like to, assume

ego the part of the personality that enables the individual to interact with the world in a realistic and effective way

gender social male or female, as distinguished from the biological male or female

gender role the behavior associated with being either male or female

"I" the unpredictable, the novel, the impulsive part of the self

id the seat of the instincts, the source of all psychic energy

"me" the socialized part of the self

resocialization socialization into a role that radically alters an individual's behavior

role the social expectations for behavior associated with a particular status

role-making acting in a way to modify a role

role-taking constructing the attitudes of another person in order to anticipate the behavior of that person

self the capacity to observe, respond to, and direct one's own behavior

sex biological male or female

social classes groups that are unequal with regard to things valued in a society, whose members share similar values and lifestyles

socialization the social process by which an individual develops and learns to function effectively in a group

status an evaluated social position

superego the part of the personality that distinguishes right from wrong and urges the individual to perfection

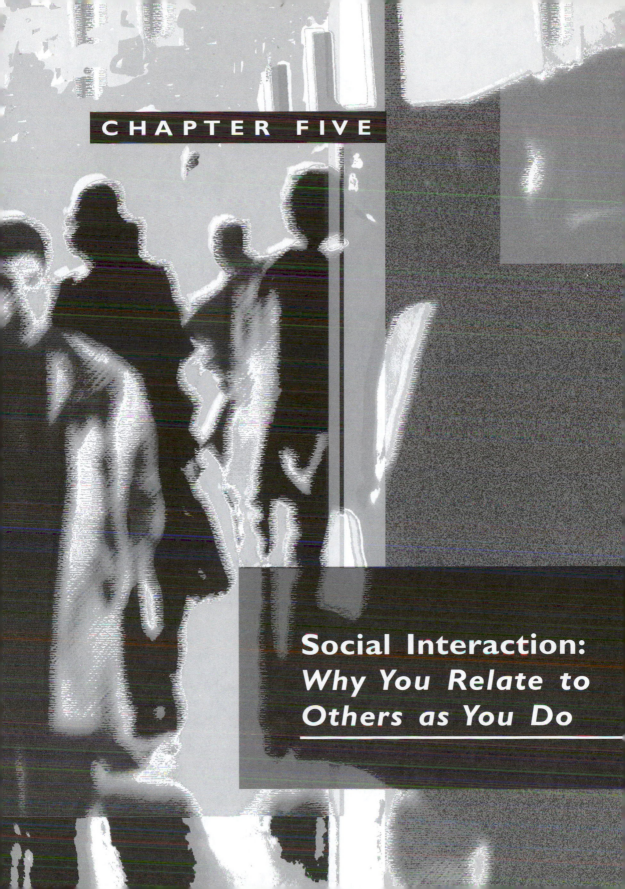

CHAPTER FIVE

Social Interaction: Why You Relate to Others as You Do

In her novel, *The Custom of the Country*, Edith Wharton describes the heroine's behavior as she sits talking with a group of new friends:

> . . . replying to their enquiries, and trying to think far enough ahead to guess what they would expect her to say, and what tone it would be well to take . . . it was instinctive with her to become, for the moment, the person she thought her interlocutors expected her to be." (Wharton 1989, p. 241; orig. 1913)

At times, at least, you behave in the way that Wharton's heroine typically behaved—you become the person you think those around you want you to be. For example, some female students have told us that they have on occasion acted less intelligent than they are in order not to threaten a male friend. And some male students have told us that they have on occasion acted braver and "cooler" than they felt in order to impress a female friend.

Think about your own interactions over the past few weeks. How many times did you behave in the way that you thought others expected rather than in the way you wanted to behave? How often did you try to become the person you thought others wanted you to be? In this chapter, we will examine why you relate to others as you do. To grasp this, you need to understand the functions, foundations, process, and patterns of interaction.

Functions of Interaction

Structural-functionalists argue that all social phenomena have particular functions or purposes. We agree that interaction has social functions. In particular, it has both a maintenance and a formative function. The maintenance function involves the affirmation and support by others of such things as your values and beliefs. It is important not only to have values and beliefs but also to know that there are others who share them.

In fact, this is how people manage to hold on to some unusual beliefs. For example, suppose that, in spite of evidence to the contrary, you believe that the earth is flat. Then you find out that there is an organization—The Flat Earth Society—that believes the same thing. Its existence encourages you and makes it much easier for you to persist in your belief.

Interaction, then, is crucial to the maintenance of values and beliefs. No person holds on indefinitely to a purely idiosyncratic value or belief unless he or she is mentally ill. You might stand against a strong majority, but only if you are sustained in your stand by others who agree with you.

Interaction also has a formative function. As discussed in the last chapter, interaction shapes the kind of person you are. We noted that if you perceive your parents to be authoritative but warm rather than permissive or coldly authoritarian, you are likely to have higher self-esteem. Moreover, the effect is likely to be lasting. A twenty-year follow-up study of youths in southern California found that those who reported warm ties to their parents continued to have higher self-esteem (Roberts and Bengtson 1996). In addition, using *survey data* from a national study, Elliott (1996) reported that marriage tends to improve self-esteem.

Your values and beliefs are also formed as well as maintained through interaction. Consider the belief that a person should willingly endure pain, if necessary, in pursuit of a particular activity. This is a belief shared by many athletes who risk ever more serious injuries as they continue to participate in a sport. In his case study of Sam, an amateur college wrestler, Curry (1993) showed how Sam learned through interaction with significant others to define pain and injury as an expected part of his career. As Sam reached higher levels of competition, he interacted with successful coaches and other wrestlers who had endured significant pain and injury. The result was that Sam learned not merely to accept but to value the increasingly serious injuries he sustained. They became his badge of honor; and Sam, in turn, became a role model for others who sought a similar career.

Interaction not only shapes the kind of person you are but also affects how you behave in a particular situation. The mere presence of others, even excluding any conversation with them, can affect how you behave. Thus, a series of experiments have shown that having an audience is likely to hinder your effort to learn a new task or skill, but once you have learned that task or skill an audience tends to facilitate your performance (Zajonc 1967).

The more intimate or personally important the person with whom you interact, the more the interaction tends to influence your behavior. Thus, a sales clerk who is cranky may not affect what you do or say as much as a friend or family member who is in a disagreeable mood. A negative comment by a stranger may not generate the same reaction as the same comment from your professor or employer.

Interaction, then, is not merely the arena where you act out your personality. It is also an important factor in maintaining and shaping who you are.

Foundations of Interaction

Think of yourself as about to interact with someone. What kinds of things affect what you will do? Three important factors—status, role, and self—are the foundation of all interaction.

Status

Recall that status refers to an evaluated social position. As a position, status may refer to any number of categories, such as occupation (mechanic, physician, teacher), kinship (mother, son, cousin), race (white, African American, Asian American), and gender (male, female). Implicitly or explicitly, people generally evaluate such positions as higher or lower in prestige, and this evaluation is an important part of the way they interact with each other. For instance, you would not interact exactly the same way with a grocery clerk, physician, best friend, and the president of the United States.

Both the kind and the amount of interaction you have with others depends on your statuses. *Survey research* on 2,077 workers in research and development teams in twenty-nine corporations found that the interaction experienced by an individual depended on that individual's education, gender, seniority, rank in the company, and leadership status (Cohen and Zhou 1991).

All people occupy a number of statuses simultaneously. You may, for instance, be a student, lover, friend, cousin, and part-time cashier. The positions are social because the place of each position in the overall structure is socially rather than individually determined. Thus, an individual might have an aptitude for mechanics and become an automobile mechanic. But he or she could not also opt to exert authority over the owner of the garage or command the high status of a physician in the community. The meaning of the status, "mechanic," cannot be manipulated according to the whims of the individual.

The social nature of statuses is also seen in the fact that statuses may have different evaluations in various societies and within the same society over time. The status of wife, for example, varies considerably from what it is in a South American Indian tribe, such as the Yanomamo, to what it is in the United States. Among the Yanomamo, wives are regularly beaten and are, in some cases, beaten to death (Chagnon 1992). Although wife beatings do occur in the United States, they are not considered the norm and, in fact, are illegal.

Or think about the way that the status of physicians in the United States has varied over time. In the early days of the nation, people viewed physicians with a combination of fear and contempt and preferred home remedies to those of the doctor. Today, the status of physician is one of the highest that an individual can achieve.

Thinking Critically

While a number of studies have shown that the ascribed characteristic of physical attractiveness is associated with other valued qualities, the studies always involve an evaluation of strangers. We can raise a number of questions about how to interpret the findings. Will attractiveness (or the lack of it) still affect your judgment after you get to know someone? Is this an ascribed status that quickly loses its impact, or does it continue to influence you? Does getting to know someone change your evaluation of their attractiveness? When you first see or meet someone, do you automatically assess their qualities by how attractive they are to you, or is that just something you would do when a researcher asks you to do it?

Such questions are not answered by the available research. But they are important questions to ask when deciding on what difference physical attractiveness actually makes in social life.

Ascribed Status

Ascribed status is a position that you have by virtue of the circumstances of your birth. Your gender and race are ascribed statuses. Your age group is an ascribed status—whether you are an adolescent or a senior citizen. And while modifications can be made by cosmetics and cosmetic surgery, physical appearance is also an ascribed status.

Clearly, people do not choose their ascribed statuses. Nevertheless, every society values some ascribed statuses more than others. In American society, for instance, people who are judged to be physically attractive are also perceived to have other valued qualities such as competence (Kalick 1988; Jackson, Hunter and Hodge 1995).

Achieved Status

Achieved status is a position you have as a result of your personal efforts. Your educational status, occupation, and marital status are examples of achieved statuses. In the area of occupation, the more you achieve, the more likely you are to attain the perquisites and rewards associated with such efforts. A study of the work situation of supervisors and non-supervisors in three government and three private organizations found that the supervisors had better office furnishings, more space, and greater ability to control access to themselves by others (Konar et al. 1982).

Most Americans like to think that ascribed status has little to do with achieved status in the United States—that any individual can achieve whatever he or she chooses. Yet achievement is always tempered by ascription. To be born black or female, for example, affects the course of an individual's achievement and may impede or limit that achievement. As *feminist theory* indicates (and as we shall show in detail in Chapter Ten), the only way you can completely explain such things as occupational and income differences between men and women is that the ascribed status of female is devalued in a male-dominated society.

Thus, the road to achievement is not the same for everyone. Ascribed statuses may make the road more or less difficult. In the United States the effects of ascribed status on achieved status may be seen in, among other things, the variations in income level by gender and racial/ethnic background (Table 5.1). Furthermore, even after you have achieved a particular status, you may find that your ascribed statuses continue to influence people's interaction with you. Although ascribed status and achieved status are often talked about as though they were two independent aspects of social life, in reality they are closely tied together.

Table 5.1	**Median Income of Full-Time Workers, 1995**	
	Male	**Female**
White, non-Hispanic	$35,605	$25,430
Black	24,798	20,801
Hispanic	20,553	19,843

Source: U.S. Bureau of the Census Website

EXTENSIONS

Ritualized Homosexuality and Manhood in Melanesia

We usually think that the status of an adult male is an ascribed status, involving nothing more than gender and age. But in some Melanesian societies, to be an adult male is both an ascribed and an achieved status. And the achievement part involves ritualized homosexuality (Elliston 1995). It is called "ritualized" because it is an integral part of a boy attaining manhood and is governed by rules.

The homosexual activity may last from ten to fifteen years, from the time of a male's first homosexual experience to the time of his marriage. A boy's first experience is to perform fellatio (oral stimulation of the male sex organ) on an older, unmarried male. The boy continues such experiences with various other unmarried males, and he both performs and, later, receives fellatio—sometimes on a daily basis.

The Melanesians explain the practice as necessary for boys to become men. Girls, they believe, become women naturally with the passage of time. Boys, on the other hand, do not become men naturally because being raised by women impedes their progress. The point of the ritualized homosexuality is to enable boys to become men by separating them from women and enabling them to take into themselves the strength of men by swallowing the semen of other males. The boys also learn to become men by being beaten by older boys. This, too, helps them to become strong, according to the group's beliefs.

The combination of physical violence and ritualized homosexuality is believed to make men out of the boys. They have become adult males not simply by being born male and aging, but by surviving the beatings and ingesting semen from other males. As adult males, they have a higher status than females; it is a status that is both ascribed and achieved.

Role

Roles—the social expectations for behavior attached to the individual who assumes particular statuses—always exist prior to the individual. That is, when you assume a particular role, you already have a set of behaviors that are expected of you. You do not determine the nature of the role according to your own whims. To accept a particular status means that you will fulfill the role expected of one who occupies that status.

Roles are important because the fulfillment of expectations helps maintain the social order, and this is important because humans do not thrive emotionally or mentally in disorder or uncertainty. In contrast, when expectations are fulfilled and the social order is maintained, you have some of the necessary conditions for interacting comfortably with others. If you go to a physician, for example, you have some sense of the kind of interaction that will and will not occur. You can be confident that the physician will not laugh at your illness, make sexual advances toward you, or advise you to see a faith healer. There is no need for you to set ground rules for interaction by informing the physician that your illness is real, that you are not interested in a sexual encounter, and that you prefer a doctor to a faith healer. The expectations associated with the physician's role allow you to take for granted that he or she will treat you with professional respect.

There are times, however, when expectations are violated. When this happens, the interaction can be very unsettling. It would be both disturbing and difficult to react appropriately if, for instance, your tennis coach suddenly decided to teach you chemistry or your physician began giving you tennis lessons. Roles facilitate social life and give us a sense of stability and security by providing us with a shared basis for interaction.

Role Variability

If pushed to the extreme, the fact that expectations for behavior are already present when you assume a role would result in a complete standardization of behavior. Thus, anyone who assumed a role would behave precisely the same as everyone else in the role. Behavior, however, is never totally prescribed. A person has some flexibility because social expectations are more like an outline than a detailed prescription. If a young man aspires to be the husband of a young woman, for example, you expect him to behave in a way that demonstrates his love. You don't expect him to bash her over the head with a club à la the comic strip version of the Neanderthals, or merely to assume that she knows of his love without being told. But he might demonstrate his love in a variety of ways, such as kissing her, telling her of his love, or giving her priority over other matters in his life. The role of husband-to-be carries the expectation of demonstrated love but does not give precise prescriptions as to how the love should be shown.

Individuals may take advantage of the flexibility available to them in roles to engage in what Goffman (1961) called **role distance**—the gap between social expectations and actual performance. A person engages in role distance to let others know that he or she is not to be defined totally in terms of the role itself. The individual says, in effect, "This is not the real me," or "This is not all there is of me." Thus, the major league baseball player who reads classical literature when he is traveling with the team is letting others in the room know that the totality of his being is not contained in the role of athlete. This role distancing serves the useful function for the individual of affirming a richer and more complex life than can be captured within the bounds of a single role.

Role distancing also provides people with a basis for justification if something goes wrong. For example, if a nurse is less than caring or sensitive to patients on a particular day, he or she may blame the demands of a spouse or difficulties with children for interfering with his or her patient responsibilities. The nurse is saying: "I am a spouse," or "I am a parent as well as a nurse. My whole life is not contained within the nurse's role. My mistakes today, therefore, do not reflect upon my nursing skills but rather arise out of the demands of other roles in which I am engaged." Of course, these justifications would not suffice if the nurse was never caring or always made mistakes in handing out medications. Yet minor flaws in performance can be dismissed on the basis of the individual's involvement in more roles than the one in question, an involvement which the individual has dramatized through role distance.

There is another reason why roles do not completely standardize behavior: interaction between individuals in various roles often results in modifications. Recall Ralph Turner's (1962) notion of "role-making." Role-making occurs because there is always some ambiguity about the expectations of a role. As you interact with others, you strive to make the expectations explicit and consensual. Thus, in acting out the role of friend, you may find that different individuals have somewhat different expectations of you as a friend. One friend may expect to share possessions (clothes, car, books), while another may regard that as an intrusion into privacy.

Over time, the expectations themselves change. Today, students who feel that an instructor is performing ineptly might complain to an administrator. Some instructors have been dismissed as a result of student complaints. A few generations ago, American students were wholly subservient to their instructors. In contrast, students in medieval Europe might hiss at or stone a professor who delivered what they considered an inept lecture. Roles, like social life generally, change over time.

Finally, roles vary from one cultural context to another. Even such fundamental roles as that of mother and father can vary, even between two groups that are culturally quite similar. For example, a study of a small number of Mexican and Mexican American mothers in the San Francisco area concluded that both groups of women viewed motherhood as their most important social role (Segura 1991). However, they differed on employment outside the home. The Mexican mothers saw employment as a way to improve the standard of living of their families and, thereby, to be better mothers. The Mexican-American mothers, in contrast, valued childrearing more than employment and tended to forego outside work or to take only part-time work in order to maximize the time they could spend with their children.

Role Set

The concept of role is even more complex than we have already indicated. In your status as a student, you relate to professors, to university officials and staff members, and to other students. Statuses always imply other statuses with which they are related. This means that roles always imply other roles. A "mother" makes no sense without a "son" or "daughter." A "teacher" makes no sense without a "student."

The expectations for a particular role vary somewhat depending upon other roles involved in the interaction. The role set is the "complement of role relationships which persons have by virtue of occupying a particular social status" (Merton, 1957, p. 369). Thus, the **role set** of a student is that cluster of behaviors expected of the student in his or her varied relationships with others—professors, university officials, and other students.

A particular role, such as student, is not a unitary phenomenon. Rather, when you assume the role of student you become embedded in a network of relationships. In each of the relationships you are a student, but somewhat different behavior is expected of you depending upon whether you interact with other students, a professor, or the registrar. These differing expectations are necessary, but they can sometimes result in role conflict, which we discuss below.

Some statuses involve a more extensive role set than do others because those statuses affect a larger number of your relationships. When you go into a store or sit in a classroom, for example, it probably doesn't matter that you are a son or daughter. Your gender status, on the other hand, is likely to affect the bulk of your relationships, including the way store clerks as well as professors relate to you.

Thus, in a *participant observation* study of the transition of a women's college into a co-ed institution, Canada and Pringle (1995) discovered very different patterns of professor-student interaction depending on the sex composition of the class and sex of the professor. When the classes were composed only of females, male and female professors initiated a similar amount of interaction with students in the classroom. When the professors taught in co-ed classes, the female professors initiated much more, and the male professors much less, interaction with the students. And the greater the number of males in a class, the less interaction initiated by students.

Throughout this book, we shall point out numerous other ways in which sex and gender influence the way you behave and the way others behave toward you. Again, the point is that some statuses involve a much more extensive role set than do others.

Role Conflict

When there are contrary expectations attached to the same role, or when the expectations of two or more roles are incompatible with each other, an individual experiences **role conflict**. An example of the first is Anna, a student whose long-time friend, Teri, began to abuse alcohol. In a short time, Teri's grades fell and she became increasingly despondent and withdrawn. She assured Anna that the problem was only temporary—the result of a troubled relationship with her boyfriend—and made Anna promise not to say anything to her family. One day, however, Teri's mother called and begged Anna to tell her what was happening to her daughter. It was her duty, the mother told Anna, to help her friend in this way.

In the role of friend, Anna faced contradictory expectations from Teri and her mother. "As my friend," Teri had told her, "I'm depending on you to not tell my parents about this. They wouldn't understand. It would only hurt them." "As Teri's friend," the mother had told her, "you must do something to help her. She is ruining her life, and I don't know why or what to do about it. You must tell me what's going on."

Examples of the other kind of role conflict—incompatible expectations between two or more roles—include the policeman who is called upon to arrest his brother for a crime and the female lawyer whose husband expects her to spend every evening with him while her firm expects her to spend a number of evenings at work.

Obviously, incompatible expectations do not indicate that the individual is insufficiently competent to handle all the demands. The incompatibilities, like the roles themselves, are social in nature. They grow out of interaction with particular others (the case of Anna), or they reflect the clashing demands of the diverse roles assumed by the individual (the policeman and lawyer).

Role conflict is not uncommon, and it is typically stressful. It's not surprising that people commonly employ a variety of means to reduce the stress. Both the conflict and the efforts to deal with the resulting stress are illustrated by Lloyd (1969) in his discussion of the African civil servant. Conflict arises because, in the context of a developing nation, the civil servant is expected by superiors in the government to be impartial in dealing with the citizenry, while relatives expect favors and even jobs. Lloyd noted four possible outcomes from the civil servant's efforts to cope with the conflict. First, the individual may be able, through negotiation, to redefine the nature of one of the roles (recall the notion of role-making). Second, the individual sometimes can compartmentalize the roles, keeping interaction with relatives isolated from interaction with superior bureaucrats and vice versa. Third, the individual may sever some relationships. Finally, when nothing else works, the individual may succumb to aberrant behavior such as aggression or fantasy.

Role Strain

The concepts of role set, role distance, and role conflict underscore the complexity, diversity, and incompatibilities that characterize social expectations and behavior. They also suggest that an individual may have difficulty in the course of meeting the demands of a role or a combination of roles. In such a case, the individual experiences **role strain**. In some cases, role strain may result from role conflict, though the two types of problems occur independently of each other. Role strain may also be rooted in the individual's dislike of a particular role, or lack of competency for the role, or in the fact that the role is not clearly defined. For instance, a man may experience role strain in his job as a salesman. He may dislike having continually to meet new people and the necessity of trying to gain rapport with them or convince them of the value of his product. Or he may lack the skills necessary to do a good job of selling. Or he may feel that his relationship with his manager and with other people in the firm is ambiguous so that he is never sure to whom he should report problems or ideas.

By definition, role strain is stressful. In his formulation of the concept, Goode (1960) suggested that people attempt to manage it through two techniques. One technique is the manipulation of roles and the other is bargaining over expectations. With respect to the first, a person might eliminate certain role relationships (as a student, you might give up a part-time job to concentrate on studying), delegate some obligations (as a woman, you might hire a housekeeper in order to pursue a career), or establish some barriers to role relationships (as an executive, you might have your secretary filter all calls and appointments). We will discuss the second technique below under "negotiation."

The Self

We include the self as one of the foundations of interaction because, as stressed in *symbolic interactionism*, you are never simply the sum of the social factors that impinge on you. You bring your own uniqueness and your impulses into all interaction. The way you act out your roles depends, in part, upon such things as your self concept and the way you define situations.

Your **self concept** is the set of beliefs and attitudes you have about yourself. People behave in ways to enhance or sustain their self concepts. Thus, if you think of yourself as a leader, you will tend to assume a leadership role in whatever situation you find yourself. If you think of yourself as someone with high sex appeal, you will assume that others find you attractive and you will act accordingly.

In fact, as an *experiment* involving 75 undergraduate students showed, people tend to seek out interaction with others that will support their self concept, even when some aspect of the self concept is negative (Robinson and Smith-Lovin 1992). The researchers had the students give a prepared speech and then listen to feedback on their social skills. All the students felt good when they were praised and bad when they were criticized. However, those with low self-esteem liked the negative critic better than did those with high self-esteem and actually preferred to interact with the negative critic rather than the one who had praised them! Viewing themselves as individuals with low competence, they were uncomfortable with someone who contradicted their self concept, even though that person was very positive about them.

Your behavior, then, reflects your self concept. It also reflects the way you define a situation. We discussed the concept of "definition of the situation" in Chapter One. In essence, the concept underscores the importance of knowing the actor's point of view in any situation.

For example, Chavez (1994) investigated the factors that would lead undocumented immigrants to stay in the United States. He found that, other things being equal, the one factor that made a difference was how they defined their status. Mexicans and Central Americans who defined themselves as part of a local community were four to five times more likely to stay here as those who didn't define themselves in this way.

Similarly, one of the factors in a stable and satisfying marriage is equity, or fairness, in the relationship. Yet how can equity be measured? One way is to measure the number of hours each spouse spends in doing household chores. This has been done; it turns out that, if there is an inequity in terms of time spent on chores, the spouses may or may not perceive the inequity. That is, many women who have outside employment and spend more time than their husbands in housework still regard their marriage as an equitable one. As long as the spouses perceive equity, they are satisfied with the marriage regardless of how much inequity a researcher might find.

Thus, as Greenstein (1996) points out, research on the division of labor in the home needs to focus on perceived rather than objective inequalities. He found that whether or not a woman perceived inequity in an inequitable situation depended on, among other things, how strongly she believed that marriage should be a 50-50 proposition.

In sum, when you interact with someone, you try to behave in a way that is consistent with your self concept and to direct the interaction in accordance with how you define the situation. You do not passively act out a predetermined role. Instead, you bring your uniqueness to the role and use this uniqueness to take advantage of the flexibility that every role offers.

The Process of Interaction: Your Life as Drama

There are many different ways to understand human behavior. An imaginative approach that emerged out of symbolic interactionism is called **dramaturgy**, a method of analysis that uses the imagery of the theater. A dramaturgical analysis uses terms like performance, setting, audience, roles, and so on. It emphasizes the way that individuals, like actors, attempt to manage the impressions they give of themselves to others.

Performances

In order to interact with someone, you need information about that person. You use this information to define the situation, to anticipate the behavior of the other, and to guide your own behavior.

Erving Goffman, who introduced the dramaturgical approach to sociological analysis, said that information is communicated through a performance. He defined this **performance** as "all the activity of a given participant on a given occasion which serves to influence in any way any of the other participants" (Goffman 1959, p. 15). A performance involves not only the behavior of the actor but the setting (including the physical environment) and the appearance and demeanor of the actor.

For example, you may wish to present yourself to an instructor as a highly intelligent person. You make an appointment to see the professor in his or her office. How do you communicate information that indicates your intelligence? You might rehearse what you are going to say, so that you speak with confidence. You attend to your clothes, so that you appear as a serious rather than a casual or fun-loving student. You carry a briefcase or a number of books so that you are seen as a person immersed in the written word.

The point of such a performance is not to deceive another person, although, as we shall note below, some performances have that aim. The point is, you want the professor to see you as you see yourself. You value intelligence, and it is important to you that other people recognize your intelligence. You, therefore, engage in the performance necessary—with others as well as the professor—to convey information about your intelligence.

At what age do you start engaging in conscious efforts to give a specific performance? Eighty-five children, aged six to ten, were asked to tell children at another school about themselves in three different ways (Aloise-Young 1993). First, they described themselves—the kind of people they believed themselves to be. Then, they tried to convince other children to pick them as partners in a game. Finally, they tried to convince other children who were highly motivated to win to choose them as partners in a game. The researcher noted the extent to which each child used self-promotion and ingratiation as a way to be chosen. Six-year-old children did not use specific tactics. But eight- and ten-year-old children did, and they used self-promotion more than ingratiation.

Performances begin at an early age, then. And as people mature, they tend to become increasingly adept at giving a performance.

Teams

Performances are not completely an individual matter. As in the theater, a number of people may be engaged in the performance. These people are part of the actor's team. A **team**, in Goffman's terms, is a group of people who work together to present a particular performance.

For instance, you might make an appointment with your professor to secure approval for a special project that you are planning with another student. This student goes with you to the meeting and comments about what a brilliant idea you came up with for the project. The student, thus, is functioning as a member of your team whose goals are to convince the professor of your intelligence as well as obtain approval for the project.

Performers on a team have a special relationship with each other. Team members are expected to be loyal and competent. Just as a play can be ruined by one actor who hasn't learned the lines or by a stage hand who misses cues, a performance can fail if a team member is disloyal or incompetent. The broker who continually gives poor advice can ruin the intended performance—an effective brokerage company. A nurse who sighs in dismay over a doctor's orders or who loses a patient's x-rays can ruin the intended performance—a hospital that gives expert medical care.

Again, the point is not to deceive people but rather to get people to define the situation in the same way as the team members do. The stock brokerage firm really thinks that it provides superior financial advice, and the hospital staff really believes that it provides expert medical care. Both groups would like others to see them in this way.

Frequently, however, a performance takes place in which the team attempts to get others to define a situation in a way that differs from the real position of the members. For example, we had a student who did a dramaturgical analysis of a beauty shop where she worked. Dramaturgy gave her a new perspective. In particular, the beauticians were all careful to give each customer the impression that she was a special person, so special that the beautician always remembered just what she wanted. In fact, a file was kept in a back room where the beautician could look up the customer's preferences. Moreover, in the back room the beauticians would speak in caustic and disparaging terms about a few of the customers they found to be difficult. They successfully gave a performance of caring about, and remembering the preferences of, each of the customers. In reality, they disliked a few of the customers and only remembered the preferences of a number of others by quickly looking in the files.

There is another possibility if you engage in a performance that does not fully reflect who you are: you might become more like the way you perform. A psychologist set up three experiments with over 200 of his students to see what, if any, were the effects of presenting themselves as sociable (Schlenker 1994). Some of the students were instructed to present themselves to an interviewer as very sociable, while others were instructed to not be sociable. Those who performed as sociable individuals later rated themselves more sociable than they did before the experiment and actually behaved more sociably in another situation.

The Audience

The nature of the performance you want to give depends, in part, upon the audience for whom you perform. You may be more concerned to present yourself as intelligent to your professor than to your friend or to a store clerk.

The way the audience can alter a performance is illustrated in studies of the difference between an audience of friends and an audience of strangers (Tice 1995). In essence, the studies show that people consistently strive to enhance themselves with strangers more than with friends. When they are with friends, they tend to be more modest about themselves.

Gender also affects performances. You may behave somewhat differently depending on whether the audience is mixed-sex, the same sex as you, or the opposite sex. Males tend to change their self-presentation when they are in the presence of females they consider attractive (Morier 1994). They present themselves as similar to the females in attitudes and beliefs.

Combining familiarity and gender, Leary et al. (1994) had volunteers keep a record for a week of every interaction that lasted ten minutes or more. The volunteers rated the extent to which they tried to make each of four impressions—that they were likeable, competent, ethical, and attractive. In general, the volunteers engaged in less effort to perform in particular ways with people of their own sex with whom they were familiar. They put more effort into their performances both with strangers and with people they knew who were of the opposite sex.

Explorations

Check Your Performances

As an extension of the Leary (1994) research discussed above, have each group member keep a record of interaction experiences for a week. For each interaction that lasts ten minutes or more, record the following information: the sex of the other person or persons; whether the other person or persons were strangers, acquaintances, or close friends; the particular impressions of yourself that you were trying to get across to your audience (make any additions necessary to the four impressions in the Leary research); the impressions you think the audience was trying to make on you (remember, from the point of view of your audience, *you* are the audience and they are the performers); and the extent to which any of the performances were part of a team effort (if so, what was the team and who were the other team members?).

In a group discussion, compare your results by discussing the following questions (if you do this as an individual project, write an analysis based on your answers to the questions). Did the performances vary according to the audiences' sex and degree of familiarity? If so, in what way? How many different kinds of performances did you engage in over the week? Were some of the impressions you were trying to convey (such as, e.g., that you are intelligent or attractive) more frequent than others? What kind of performances did you think others were putting on for you? How many of your performances were part of a team effort? What teams were involved? Finally, what conclusions would you draw about the usefulness of dramaturgical analysis for understanding human behavior?

Impression Management

A good deal of what you do in giving a performance is called **impression management**—the effort to manage the impressions that others gain of you so that they will define both you and the situation in the way you prefer (Goffman 1959). Symbolic interactionists and other social psychologists have used the concept "impression management" to analyze everything from male-female relationships to interaction in the business world.

We can illustrate the usefulness of the concept by reflecting on the purposes of fashionable clothes. Among other things, fashion is a tool of impression management for those who wish to enhance their status. Countless books and articles (including research articles in professional journals) have been written about the way that clothes are an integral part of how people convey information about themselves (Lauer and Lauer 1981). If you do not dress fashionably, many writers have insisted, the negative impressions given by your attire will negate any positive impressions you try to give through your words and behavior.

Because fashionable attire fosters good impressions, you can enhance your status by a careful selection of what you wear. Thus, the expensive-looking outfits you may sometimes see in impoverished neighborhoods are not evidence that the poor have more money than they claim. Rather, the clothing is an effort to gain some status by people who have little status generally.

A reporter who interviewed poor young men in a ghetto area of New York City wrote about the way they used expensive, fashionable clothing as a tool for enhancing their status (Lauer and Handel 1983, p. 137). One young man acknowledged that the outfit he was wearing cost him a week's income. And another summed up the value of his clothes: "They say to the world: 'I've got bread, man; so treat me with a little respect.' "

Lest you think that the young men are spending their money foolishly, keep in mind that they are only doing what all the rest of us do—maximizing their status in society. In fact, one of the ironies of impression management is that it can be literally hazardous to your health. Why else would people willingly risk skin cancer by sitting in the sun in order to get a tan? Leary (1993) found that those who seek a tan are motivated by self-presentational motives: they are highly concerned about their personal appearance and believe that a tan makes them more attractive. Leary (1994) also noted other kinds of health problems related to self-presentation and impression management, including HIV infection, eating disorders, and alcohol, tobacco, and other drug use.

Some Techniques of Impression Management

Many students find the notion of impression management distasteful. One reason for their distaste is that they think it is deceitful. However, impression management is not synonymous with deceit. Of course, deceitful people do use impression management, but so do the rest of us. Impression management is a technique for taking control of your life. Indeed, those who are more skilled in impression management also achieve more success and more of their goals (Gardner 1992). Here are several techniques of impression management.

Appearance, as we have shown above, is an important technique of impression management. For instance, think about the appearance of a mass murderer at the time he or she is apprehended and then when he or she goes on trial. Often the person looks disheveled when arrested. Yet you rarely, if ever, see a defendant in a criminal case looking unkempt in court. The defendant, or at least the defendant's lawyer, is concerned with presenting an upstanding individual who, at the very worst, got caught up in circumstances that would lead any normal person to behave in an unseemly manner.

There may be cultural differences in the extent to which people attend to their appearance. In a study of 74 African Americans, 93 whites, and 86 Asian Americans in both dating and nondating interaction with a member of the opposite sex, Aune (1994) measured the amount of time the subjects spent in managing their appearance—grooming their hair, straightening their clothes, and gazing at themselves in a mirror. Among the men, African Americans spent the most time, and among the women African Americans spent the least amount of time in appearance management. Asian Americans and whites spent similar amounts of time.

A second technique of impression management is speech pattern, including vocabulary, pace of talking, and nonverbal aspects like inflection and gestures. If you want to appear intelligent, for example, you should talk at a moderate speed and avoid punctuating what you say with such things as "uh." Faster talkers are not only regarded as more intelligent, but also are more persuasive and are rated more favorably by listeners (Maclachlan 1979). Perhaps the best way to grasp the impact of speech patterns is to think about qualities you admire, such as intelligence, attractiveness, sincerity, and caring. Then identify people who seem to possess those qualities and note carefully the way they speak.

Humor is a third technique of impression management. For one thing, humor enhances attractiveness. People in lasting and satisfying marriages say that the partner's humor was an important factor both in attracting them to the partner in the first place and in sustaining the vitality of their relationship (Lauer and Lauer 1986; Mackey and O'Brien 1995). To display a good sense of humor, then, is a way to tell others that you are attractive and would be a good partner in an intimate relationship. We should note that humor, like all other techniques of impression management, requires skill. Excessive humor (the person who jokes about everything) is a barrier to intimacy (Tannen 1990).

Humor can also be used to manage emotions in interactions (Francis 1994). In a situation of tension or conflict, humor can restore perspective and ease tension. We have seen couples in the midst of an increasingly tense argument change the course of their interaction when one of the partners made a humorous point that said to the other: "I'm not really a totally bad person; I just messed up this time." The humor put down the speaker, not the partner. The partner saw it as an apology and an offer of reconciliation. As a result, the tension lessened and the problem was resolved.

A final tactic of impression management that we will discuss is ingratiation—the use of deceit to enhance one's personal qualities in the eyes of another person. The deceit may be in what is said or in the nonverbal performance (such as a sincere look and voice that say "I really care about you" when the only motive is to manipulate the individual for personal advantage).

Ingratiation takes a number of forms (Jones 1964). One is enhancement of the other person or, to put it in everyday terms, flattery. If done well, flattery is extremely hard to recognize and to resist. The flatterer makes you feel good about yourself, and you therefore tend to like the flatterer and to believe what he or she says.

Opinion conformity is another form of ingratiation. People tend to like others more if they hold the same opinions. Think about your friends, for example. It is probable that you share a good many beliefs and values with them. Ingratiators, then, in an effort to raise their value in the eyes of others, will try to find as many areas of agreement as possible and will even invent some if necessary.

Doing favors is a third way people ingratiate themselves with others. The effectiveness of this technique is based on the norm of reciprocity, which Gouldner (1960) identified as a universal norm. The norm requires you to provide some kind of benefit to anyone from whom you receive benefits. You must, in other words, reciprocate when anyone does you a favor, such as bringing you a gift or complimenting you on something. And one way to reciprocate is to evaluate the one who rendered the favor more highly. Again, the ingratiator has achieved his or her purpose.

Finally, self-promotion can be used as an ingratiating technique. Those who skillfully present themselves as hard workers, devoted followers, or experts enhance their value. We say "skillfully," because the performance must come across as a statement of fact and not as bragging. For example, we knew a professor who presented himself as a hard worker and devoted teacher by saying such things as "while I was working on that report last night" and "the students did such a good job on their assignments that I was up until two a.m. grading them—I just lost track of time." In this case, however, the professor wasn't skilled enough. Eventually, other faculty members discovered that his words were far more impressive than his actual behavior.

Skilled ingratiators may use a combination of techniques, but the same ones are not always used equally by males and females. An investigation of 139 male and 92 female salespeople found that most used a number of techniques (Strutton 1995). Males and females used the enhancement of others and opinion conformity equally often. However, males were more likely than females to use self-promotion and the rendering of favors.

There are also cultural differences in ingratiation techniques. In India, for example, a number of additional techniques may be used in work situations (Pandey 1986; Shankar 1994). A worker may use self-degradation rather than self-promotion as a way of enhancing himself. A worker who degrades himself is, at the same time, highlighting the superiority of his boss and reducing his chances of being defined as a competitive threat to the boss' position. Another technique is asserting dependence on the boss in the hopes of gaining rewards. A final technique is name-dropping—emphasizing one's connections to important people and thus one's potential usefulness to the boss.

When the Performance Fails

We have stressed several times the importance of "skill" when using ingratiation and other techniques of impression management. The point is, a performance can fail when the actor is not sufficiently skillful. The professor who presented himself as a hard-working and devoted teacher ultimately failed because he was seen too often pursuing his own personal business and recreational interests. Students walked into his office and discovered him reading stock reports or real estate advertisements. Staff members reported seeing him at a local health club during his office hours.

Thus, a performance can fail because the actor's behavior and words are not consistent with each other. Or it can fail if the actor appears insincere or is unconvincing in the impressions he or she is trying to convey. Furthermore, it is true in real life just as it is in the theater that failed performances have painful consequences. We will look at one of the consequences that has been studied in detail by researchers: embarrassment.

Goffman (1967) pointed out that embarrassment arises out of social interaction in which something has happened that threatens or discredits the impressions that one or more of the participants is trying to convey. If you feel embarrassed, Goffman noted, it is not because you are maladjusted or lack social grace but because you are perceptive and have correctly appraised the situation.

Gross and Stone (1964) made an extensive study of embarrassment, gathering and analyzing approximately 1,000 cases. They argued that a successful performance—one that avoids embarrassment—has three requirements. Each actor must maintain an appropriate identity. Each actor must maintain poise. And the actors must sustain confidence in each other.

The failure to meet these conditions results in embarrassment. For instance, if you go into a store and bring an item to the checkout counter, you have established your identity as that of a paying customer. If you then discover that you left your wallet at home, you are likely to be embarrassed.

The failure to maintain poise was a major cause of embarrassment in Gross and Stone's research. They noted five ways in which a loss of poise can occur. First, an individual may violate the "space" of another person or persons. An example of this is when an individual breaks into the conversation of an animated group and realizes in the ensuing and awkward silence that he has violated their space. Second, an individual can lose control of one or more of the stationary elements in the setting—like the professor who turns around too quickly when lecturing and runs into the blackboard. Third, an individual can lose control of a movable part of the setting; for example, the adolescent who runs gracefully toward the bowling pins but drops the ball with a thud. Fourth, an individual can discover a flaw in his or her appearance, like the woman who notes a run in her stocking as she walks into a formal party. And fifth, an individual can lose control of his or her body; for instance, the nervous speaker we once saw who picked up a glass of water but whose hand shook so much that he was unable to drink from it.

The third requirement, maintaining confidence in each other, means that no person in the interaction can undermine the perform-ance of others. Failure here can occur if one person challenges the impressions being conveyed by another. A young woman, who enthu-siastically described a novel she was writing, was cut short and fell into an embarrassed silence when her male escort commented that she had actually done very little writing and probably would never finish the project.

Confidence can also be lost if one person acts in a way that is unexpected by other members of the team and, thus, disrupts the performance. A classic illustration of this is found in the old chil-dren's story of the emperor's new clothes. Recall that the gullible em-peror was deceived and went into public naked while thinking he was fully dressed in beautiful new clothes. He, of course, was engaged in a performance. But so were his subjects who pretended to admire the new clothes. It was only when a small boy cried out that the emperor had no clothes on that the performance failed. The boy acted in a way unexpected by other members of the team, and the performance came to an abrupt end in mass and massive embarrassment.

As the story illustrates, interaction is problematic once a perform-ance fails and one or more of the actors is embarrassed. The budding novelist noted above recovered after a short and embarrassed silence by retorting confidently: "That's true, but I've got the story in my head and I'm going to get it on paper. Then I'm going to write down your discouraging predictions on a piece of paper, make a sandwich out of it, and let you eat it." In other cases, however, the interaction may continue tensely or it may come to an end altogether.

Finally, cultural differences exist both in the extent to which em-barrassment is experienced and the manner of handling it. In a study involving embarrassing predicaments of 81 Japanese and 102 Ameri-can college students, researchers found a number of differences be-tween the two groups (Imahori and Cupach 1994). The Americans tended to identify embarrassing situations in terms of accidents that had happened, while the Japanese described them in terms of mis-takes they had made. The Americans were more likely than the Japa-nese to try to use humor to deal with the situation. And the Americans described their experience in terms of embarrassment and stupidity, while the Japanese were more likely to talk of a sense of shame.

Experiences

'The Memory Is Still a Horror to Me'

Some embarrassing experiences leave people a bit unsettled but are soon forgotten. Others may nettle people for years and affect their subsequent behavior. Joan, a department store buyer, recalls a childhood experience that was highly embarrassing to her and that has had a lasting impact on her behavior:

I was in first grade, and it was time for the annual school Halloween party. The teacher sent a note home that told our parents about the party and about the fact that we were to dress up in our Halloween costumes. My mother dressed me in an elaborate costume that she had made. I was a little angel, with a halo and a star-topped wand and a beautiful, flowing white dress. I remember feeling so proud as I walked to school. I could see some of our neighbors look at me and grin as I passed by. I knew they thought I was adorable.

The costume was so elaborate that I was a little late. I ran into my classroom with a big smile on my face. And I stopped short and looked in perplexity at the class. No one had a costume on! As it happened, my mother had dressed me up on the wrong day. I was the only kid in the class in costume. I was more than embarrassed. I was completely mortified. The memory still makes me shudder.

The teacher tried to console me, but I had to sit there all day in that costume. I could hear the other kids snickering about my bad timing. When I got home, I told my mother I was never going back to that school. Of course, I did. But not without a good deal of crying and protest. I wouldn't even look at the other kids for the next few days.

Even today, I am horrified by the thought of doing something embarrassing in a public situation. I won't go through a door until I'm certain it's the right one. My husband and I were invited to a party at a new friend's house, and I had him go to the door first to make sure we were at the right place. I guess the one good thing that came out of the experience was that I have always been careful to never embarrass my own children.

Patterns of Interaction

Patterns of interaction are additional considerations that are important in helping you to understand why you behave as you do. There are a number of patterns that are pervasive in human societies. We will examine four which we regard as fundamental: cooperation, exchange, negotiation, and conflict.

To illustrate the importance of the patterns, think about presenting yourself as an attractive and intelligent individual. You will do so differently in a cooperative situation than you would in a situation of negotiation. In a cooperative situation, for example, your aim may be to achieve greater intimacy with someone; thus, you will want to enhance your appeal for that person. In negotiation, you may aim more at gaining respect so that you and your position are taken seriously.

Cooperation

In cooperation, you work with others to achieve some goal and to share in the rewards. Cooperation is, by definition, an essential part of social life. Even in the simplest of societies, cooperation is necessary for survival. Among hunting and gathering groups, the meat of slain animals is usually shared among the members. They work together to hunt down their prey and then share in the rewards regardless of who actually killed the animals. From earliest times, humans found cooperation to be a vital element in their survival and development into more complex societies.

In a sense, an intimate relationship is a cooperative venture. Two people work together to create a closeness that will benefit each of them. Obviously, intimate relationships are also marked by conflict and the other patterns which we shall discuss. The point is, in any ongoing interaction, people are likely to experience all of the patterns although some may be more common than are others.

Cooperation is a learned form of behavior, and it is learned in a variety of contexts. In the family, you learn to cooperate with others in household chores and other shared activities. In school, you are taught to cooperate in classroom and playground projects. Religion also reinforces the value of cooperation in worship and social endeavors. And the mass media encourage people to cooperate, particularly in times of national crisis.

Clearly, people do not always cooperate with each other even when it is in their best interests to do so. An athlete may opt to be a star rather than a team player even though the latter would have a bigger payoff in the long run. A divorcing couple may choose to fight each other in court over the division of property even though both will wind up with much less than if they had cooperated. In experiments designed to sort out when people are more likely to cooperate, three researchers found that even cooperators were concerned with the rights and wrongs of a situation—they saw cooperation as right and competition as wrong in these particular circumstances (Beggan, Messick and Allison 1988). In other words, you are more likely to cooperate when you define cooperation as the morally correct thing to do in a given situation.

Cooperation occurs between groups and communities as well as between individuals. Diverse groups in the United States often cooperate on a particular political issue even though they may be at odds on most every other matter (leading to the aphorism that "politics makes strange bedfellows"). Communities cooperate in economic ventures or in the provision of services that will enhance the quality of life of their citizens. Cooperation is a pervasive process in the social structure because it is the means of achieving many desirable goals that cannot be achieved by individuals working alone.

Exchange

Exchange is a form of interaction in which people give and receive some kind of valued goods, services, or possessions. Again, this is learned behavior. In the family, you learn that obedience to family rules brings rewards of various kinds, including the parental approval which is so important to your emotional well-being. Religion teaches that spiritual rewards are contingent upon your beliefs and behavior. In the economy, you regularly use money (or credit) to purchase items that you desire. All of these are exchange relationships and, as the examples indicate, there are both economic and noneconomic kinds of exchange.

Social exchange theory (Homans 1961; Kelley and Thibaut 1978) asserts that people will only stay in a relationship if they receive as much as they give (the exchange, in other words, is an equitable one). This does not mean, however, that the situation is an ideal one. A woman, for example, might continue to work for an obnoxious boss because, on balance, the rewards of a high salary are greater than the price of her distaste.

Like cooperation, exchange is a pervasive social process, occurring between groups as well as between individuals. The Chamber of Commerce may support the local political administration in exchange for tax benefits to business. A small town may contract with its larger neighbor for fire protection, paying a specified sum in exchange for the service. Or a school in Vermont may exchange students with one in France on a short-term basis.

Exchange relationships are important because they involve the giving and receiving of things that are valued. People will strive, therefore, to maintain those relationships. Miller and Labovitz (1973) studied an organization of researchers fragmented by internal conflict. Some of the members eventually left to form a similar organization of their own. Each individual in the organization then had to decide whether to stay with the original group, join the splinter organization, or leave altogether. Miller and Labovitz examined the reasons for the members' decisions. Psychological influences such as job satisfaction and tension, relational factors such as social rewards and costs, and a number of factors external to the organization such as marital status and involvement in the community were considered. They found that the strongest factor in explaining individual decisions was the desire to preserve rewarding social exchanges with other members. In essence, the decisions were made more on the basis of friendship patterns, information contacts, and professional respect than other factors. The desire to preserve social rewards was the strongest factor in the decision-making process.

Negotiation

Negotiation is bargaining that leads to mutual agreement. Anselm Strauss (1978) has argued that negotiation is one of the ways that an individual or group can get things done. Alternative ways include coercion, education, persuasion, and an appeal to some authority. However, negotiation is typically used to gain a working consensus and so is present in every aspect of social life. When people interact, they rarely interact in a way that is maximally satisfying to them. That is, an individual comes into an interaction with certain goals or needs but rarely finds that they can be fully realized in the interaction. This is because others also have goals and needs. The group, whether it consists of two or twenty, must reach a working consensus that represents a viable compromise of the original goals and needs of the participants. This compromise is reached through negotiation. Lovers, husbands and wives, friends, employees, and politicians all negotiate in order to create a working consensus and get things done.

We indicated above that negotiation is one way to reduce role strain. People who experience role strain may negotiate with relevant others about expectations and obligations in order to reduce the role strain. A working wife may negotiate with her husband about the division of labor in the home to reduce her household obligations and the strain that they induce. A man who feels that a valued friend is making excessive demands on his time may negotiate with his friend over the amount of time they spend together.

Negotiation, in sum, is a method people use to reach an acceptable kind of relationship. Each party in the negotiation gains, and each party loses, some of what he or she wants.

Conflict

In Chapter One, we pointed out that *conflict theorists* assert that conflict is pervasive in social life. We agree, particularly when conflict includes: competition in which individuals or groups vie for scarce power, status, or resources; power struggles in which the aim is dominance or coercion; and violent struggles in which the objective is to harm or destroy another person or persons. Indeed, a survey of 319 high school sophomores and juniors found that they had an average of 7.74 conflicts on the day before the survey (Laursen 1995). The most common conflict was with mothers, followed by friends, romantic partners, siblings, fathers, and other adults and peers.

Conflict occurs at all levels of social life. A certain amount of conflict, like role conflict, is built into social life by the very nature of social arrangements. Racial conflict also reflects social arrangements. Racial minorities have historically been confined to the lower strata of society with fewer economic benefits, less power, less prestige, and less gratification than the white majority. Indeed, many sociologists have argued that racism is built into the policies and practices of organizations so that discrimination continues independently of the prejudice of those who lead those organizations. For example, a corporate manager may not be personally prejudiced and may even decry the discrimination that racial minorities have suffered. Yet if the firm has a "last hired first fired" policy, the manager may be required to lay off a disproportionate number of racial minorities during an economic recession in spite of the lack of personal prejudice.

There are various ways to handle interpersonal conflict. You can try to avoid facing up to it. You can give in to the other person or persons. You can compete, and aim at winning. You can compromise. These methods are not equally useful. For instance, in intimate relationships women may be more skilled than men in dealing with conflict (Metz, Rosser, and Strapko 1994; Minick and Gueldner 1995). Men are more likely than women to avoid dealing with conflict, a practice which is damaging to a relationship (Markman, Stanley, and Blumberg 1994).

It's important to point out that there is no *one* best way to deal with conflict in *every* situation. However, it is equally important to note that skill in handling conflict is crucial to the well-being of your relationships.

Critical Thinking Exercise

A newspaper article quoted a psychologist who said that ingratiation (in the form of "brown-nosing") can boost your career, but only if you also have the skills to do the job you were hired to do (Sammons 1997). On the basis of his review of seventy studies, the psychologist offered a number of tips on effective ingratiation: flatter the boss when you talk to other people and hope it gets back to her or to him; disagree sometimes so that you don't appear to be a "yes" person; and you can brown-nose a woman in front of other women, but brown-nosing a man in front of other men can backfire.

How would you evaluate such conclusions? What additional information would you want before accepting these conclusions? What questions would you ask about the research? What would you want to know about the seventy studies the psychologist used to draw his conclusions?

Summary

Social interaction has both a maintenance and a formative function. The maintenance function involves affirming and supporting values and beliefs. The formative function involves shaping people—their values, beliefs, and behavior.

Status, role, and the self are the foundation of all behavior. Status affects the kind and the amount of interaction people have. Ascribed status is the position a person has by virtue of the circumstances of birth. Achieved status is a position an individual has by virtue of his or her efforts. In reality, ascribed status affects the extent to which a person can achieve.

Roles provide people with a pre-existing set of expectations about how to behave. Roles help maintain social order. But individuals have some flexibility in how they will act out their roles. People take advantage of this flexibility to engage in role distance and role making. Over time, roles tend to change, and they also vary from one culture to another.

The role set is the group of role relationships an individual has as the result of occupying a particular status. Some statuses, such as gender, involve a more extensive role set than do others by affecting a larger number of relationships.

Role conflict occurs when there are contrary expectations attached to the same role or when the expectations of two or more roles are incompatible with each other. Role conflict is common and stressful. Role strain, difficulty in meeting the demands of a role or roles, may result from role conflict. Role strain also occurs when individuals dislike a role, lack competency for the role, or find that the role is not clearly defined.

The self is part of the foundation of interaction because people behave in ways which enhance or sustain their self concepts. They also behave according to the way they define situations.

Dramaturgy is a way of analyzing interaction by using the imagery of the theater. Interaction is viewed as a performance designed to influence the audience. Performances involve a setting as well as the actor's behavior, appearance, and demeanor. Some performances are efforts to deceive, but most are an effort to get others to define the situation as the actor would like and to see the actor as the kind of person he or she would like to be seen.

Performances may involve a team—the people who are important in presenting a particular performance. Performers on a team have a special relationship with each other and are expected to be loyal and competent. The audience affects the kind of performance given. The performance can vary depending on whether the audience is composed of friends or strangers, males or females or both.

Impression management is a major part of any performance. Some of the techniques of impression management are appearance, speech patterns, humor, and ingratiation. Ingratiation includes flattery, opinion conformity, rendering of favors, and self-promotion. In other cultures, self-degradation, asserting dependence on another, and name-dropping may also be used.

Embarrassment illustrates the problems that develop when a performance fails. Embarrassment occurs when something happens which threatens or discredits the impressions that one or more of the participants are trying to convey. Embarrassment can be avoided by maintaining an appropriate identity and poise and supporting the performance of others. Once a performance fails, and embarrassment occurs, subsequent interaction is problematic.

Some of the pervasive patterns of interaction among humans are cooperation, exchange, negotiation, and conflict. Cooperation includes intimate relationships and involves working with others to achieve some goal and share in the rewards. People are more likely to cooperate when they define it as the morally right thing to do. **Exchange** is the giving and receiving of something that is valued. People will only remain in relationships that they define as equitable in terms of the exchange.

Negotiation is bargaining that leads to mutual agreement. Negotiation is a way to establish an acceptable, rather than an ideal, relationship. Negotiation can be used to reduce role strain. Conflict is pervasive in social life and is built in to some situations. There are various ways to handle conflict, and skill at doing so is important to a person's well-being.

Glossary

achieved status a position an individual has by virtue of his or her efforts.

ascribed status a position a person has by virtue of the circumstances of his or her birth.

dramaturgy a method of analyzing human behavior that uses the imagery of the theater.

exchange a form of interaction in which people give and receive some kind of valued goods, services, or possessions.

impression management an individual's effort to manage the impressions others receive so as to control the way the others define the individual and the situation.

performance all the activity of an individual that influences others with whom the individual is interacting.

role conflict contrary expectations attached to the same role or incompatible expectations between two or more roles.

role distance the gap between social expectations and actual performance.

role set the set of role relationships involved in occupying a particular social status.

role strain difficulty in fulfilling role obligations.

self concept the set of beliefs and attitudes an individual holds toward him- or herself.

CHAPTER SIX

Social Structure:
How Human Life Is Patterned

Maria was fourteen years old when she walked up to a strange man and asked him if he would like to have sex with her. Maria did not find the man attractive. In fact, she found him somewhat repulsive. Moreover, she was not a prostitute and had no intention of asking him for money. Why did she offer him sex?

Carl was eighteen when he took a job at the checkout desk in the university library where he attended classes. One afternoon a distinguished looking man asked to have several books checked out. Although Carl recognized him as the dean who had spoken at orientation, he still insisted on seeing the man's I.D. card. After fumbling around in his pocket for a few moments, the Dean told Carl who he was and apologized for not having the proper identification. Carl insisted, however, that he couldn't let the Dean have the books, although he wanted to say: "I recognize you, Dean, so I'll go ahead and check you out." Yet he didn't. He refused to let the Dean have the books until a full-time staff member intervened and okayed the transaction. Why did Carl act as though he did not know the dean and refuse to check him out?

Kim was twenty-three, an introvert who loved to spend Sunday afternoons reading in her room. However, on a cold, November Sunday she went with an older woman to knock on doors in a strange neighborhood and hand out pamphlets to people she had never met. Kim was uncomfortable the entire time, more from having to meet a succession of strange people than from the cold. What motivated her to go against her natural inclinations and agree to the task?

In each case, these young people acted as they did because they belonged, or wanted to belong, to a particular **group**. Maria wanted to join a gang in her neighborhood. The gang's initiation ritual required her to walk up to the first male stranger she saw and offer to have sex with him. If he agreed, she had to submit to him. Carl was a new worker in the library, and his supervisor had told Carl in strong terms to allow no one—"and I mean *no one* including the President of the United States"—to check out books unless they had the proper identification card. As a new member of the library work force, Carl was afraid to break the rule even though he recognized the Dean. Kim was a relatively new member of Jehovah's Witnesses, and she was required to spend a certain number of hours going door to door to spread her faith.

Thus, in each case, you can understand the behavior when you recognize how it was shaped by the groups to which the individuals belonged or wanted to belong. All people belong to and are influenced by groups. A group is two or more interacting people who pursue some common goal or interest. In some cases, you choose to belong to a particular group. In other cases, you are part of a group because of the circumstances of your birth. Where you are in the **social structure**, then, reflects both the circumstances of your birth and choices you make.

The Structuring of Human Life: From Macro to Micro

What precisely is this structure into which you are born? What is this structure that encompasses your life and affects the way you think, feel, believe, and act? Social structure refers to regularities and patterns in social interaction. These regularities and patterns reflect the fact that people gather into societies. A **society** is comprised of those people who share a particular territory and culture. We discussed a number of different kinds of societies in Chapter Three (hunting and gathering, for example).

The regularities and patterns also reflect the way that societies are organized into groups and **institutions**. An institution is a collective solution to a problem of social life. All societies have institutions such as government, the economy, education, marriage and family, and religion. Each institution includes a variety of groups and organizations that address a problem of social life. For instance, one problem of social life is how to maintain law and order, and government is the institution that addresses this problem. This institution includes such groups as local, state, and federal governmental agencies, the police, and the courts. We discuss institutions in detail in later chapters. In this chapter, we will focus on the groups, including organizations, that comprise institutions.

Structure vs. Chaos

Patterns and regularities in social life mean that you live in an organized world. Organization is both necessary and nettlesome. It is nettlesome to the extent that the social structure imposes constraints and restrictions on your behavior. For example, many Americans distrust large organizations because these groups wield power over individual lives. A Gallup poll concerning opinions about the power held by various groups in American society found that, depending on the group named, from 12 to 63 percent of Americans believe the groups have too much power (Figure 6.1). In addition to the IRS and the entertainment industry (shown here), more than half of those polled believe that the advertising industry, the federal government, major corporations, and television news departments have too much power.

Perhaps you also have reservations about the power of these groups.

Figure 6.1   **Public Perceptions of Power**

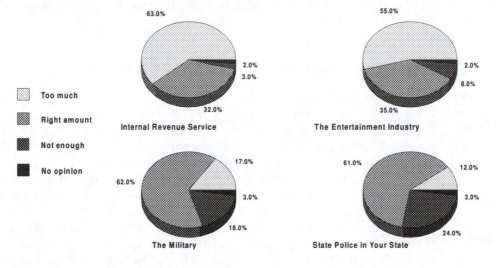

Source: Adapted from The Gallup Poll Monthly, October 1995, p. 11.

If you do, keep in mind that structure is important to your well-being, because the alternative is chaos—an intolerable state for humans. Imagine, for instance, a modern city in which there were no rules. Among other things, there would be no traffic lights or signs, no protection, and no set times for doing anything. Such a situation is inconceivable. You simply cannot function well in a situation devoid of rules. Rules may constrain behavior, but they also provide a context of order in which you can pursue your interests.

Under the illusion that "doing your own thing" is the ultimate in human freedom and happiness, some Americans have established small communities without any rules at all. These communities have either collapsed in a short time or have quickly shifted directions and developed some consensual rules about behavior. For example, a researcher found that the members of four modern communes were all ideologically opposed to having formal rules (Hawkins 1975). The resulting chaos led three of the groups to set up a certain number of rules, particularly regarding cooking, other kinds of work, and financial support of the group. The fourth group resisted the imposition of rules. However, the chaos and disillusionment intensified, and the group soon disbanded. Total freedom from external constraints may sound appealing, but it leads to social disintegration.

Structure and Process

Structure is the way things are organized and interrelated. Process is the way things change over time. All structures are in process. A building, for example, is a structure in which many materials are organized to form a place in which humans can function. But the building is also in the process of deterioration (or, at times, in a process of renovation).

In discussing the structure of social life, then, we are not talking about something that is unchanging. A totally static world would be as traumatic as a chaotic world. Fortunately, the world in which you live is neither chaotic nor unchanging.

For example, educational organizations are a part of the social structure. Yet the nature of education has changed over the course of American history. In colonial New England, the Puritans emphasized education because it empowered people to read the Bible. In the years following the Revolutionary War, the emphasis was on molding people into law-abiding citizens. Later, the Northwest Ordinance included a provision for the encouragement of education on the grounds that "religion, morality, and knowledge" are "necessary to good government and the happiness of mankind" (Parker 1975, p. 29). Still later, education focused on the training of people for the industrial economy. In more recent times, educators have emphasized development of each individual's full potential. Over the years, the purpose of American education has changed, the societal resources allocated to education have changed (illustrated by the enormous federal support for graduate education that began in the late 1950s), and the scope of education has grown to include females and racial minorities.

Thus, there are always rules and patterns, but these rules and patterns tend to be in flux. Some change rapidly and some change slowly, but social life is never a static affair.

Social Structure as Multilevel

Social structure includes both the **macro level** (large-scale social processes) and the **micro level** (small-scale social processes). The macro level refers to such things as societies, social institutions, patterns of inequality, and international relations. The micro level refers to such things as social interaction and behavior in small groups. Both levels affect you although you may or may not be aware of the effects.

For example, Millie is a branch librarian in a city system. On a particular day, she has little patience with a patron who is having a hard time finding what he wants. Millie's troubled interaction with the patron reflects the fact that, before coming to work, she and her husband had argued about their son's behavior. One of the groups to which she belongs—her family—is affecting the way she functions at work. Moreover, her impatience is intensified by some new library rules about record-keeping—rules that she regards as time-consuming and useless. Thus, another group to which she belongs—the library organization—is also affecting the way she behaves. Finally, her brusqueness is further aggravated by the news that the branch may be closed because of shortfalls in the city revenues. Thus, Millie's behavior is also affected by higher levels of the social structure—the city's economy and government. Millie may be unaware of the extent to which the national and international economies have also impacted her by depressing the local economy.

The point is, you are always being influenced by numerous social factors at various levels of social life. As structural functionalists point out, the various elements of the social structure are bound together in functional interdependence so that you are never influenced by only a single factor. Some of the elements of the social structure may be far removed from you or even unknown by you, but they still affect you.

The Micro Level: Social Groups

To how many groups do you belong? Before you begin reading this section about the various kinds of groups, write down the names of all groups to which you belong. When you come to the end of this section, review your list and think about whether you can make any additions or deletions.

Why Do People Join Groups?

What groups or organizations have you joined? Why do you think you joined them? How many of the following reasons apply to you?

One reason people join groups is to fulfill their need to relate to others. They need the intimacy they find in groups. Indeed, many people are lonely because of insufficient intimate relationships. Most people experience loneliness at some point in their lives, but chronic loneliness is detrimental to both physical and emotional well-being (Mahon, Yarcheski, and Yarcheski 1993). In a national survey of the problem of loneliness among Americans, Rubenstein and Shaver (1982) discovered nineteen problems associated with being lonely: feelings of worthlessness, a feeling that one just can't go on, constant worry and anxiety, irrational fears, trouble concentrating, feeling irritable and angry, guilt, crying spells, chronic tiredness, sleep problems, pains in the heart area, problems with breathing, poor appetite, headaches, digestive problems, loss of interest in sex, weight concerns, physical illness, and accident-proneness.

You are likely to join groups that help fulfill your need for intimacy. In fact, for some people intimacy needs are the only reason for joining, and the stated purpose of the group is almost irrelevant. We once knew a man who had been a member of numerous, incompatible movements throughout his life. At one time he was a member of the Socialist party. Later, he became a member of the John Birch society. He belonged to a series of other groups and movements that were either totally different from, or contrary to, each other. His behavior reflected his need for social interaction rather than a commitment to the cause represented by each of the groups.

There are, however, many people who join groups because they do believe in the cause. They illustrate another reason for joining groups: to accomplish something that an individual cannot accomplish alone. It is necessary for people to band together in order to create a business enterprise, get a law passed, challenge a governmental or corporate practice, battle against discrimination, and pursue certain interests such as playing ball and sky diving. It is hazardous at best, and foolish at worst, for an individual to pursue his or her interests by battling alone against a social order that is replete with large-scale organizations. Workers recognized this a long time ago and formed labor unions. Corporate leaders realized that they too could benefit by cooperating together; they formed the National Association of Manufacturers. The power of a group working together is illustrated by the National Rifle Association, which has managed to quell national legislation on gun control even though a majority of Americans favors some kind of control.

Some tasks can be accomplished alone but are still done in the context of groups. An individual, for example, can scuba dive, hang glide, play golf, or collect stamps alone. But people typically do such things with others or at least engage in some group interaction as a part of the activity. Participation in groups, then, usually involves more than a single motivation. People want to achieve something or accomplish some task, but they also want to interact with others. Furthermore, they want to share the achievement or accomplishment with others because this enhances its meaning and value.

Thus, you need groups in order to pursue your interests and maximize your well-being. At the same time, the groups in which you participate inevitably put constraints upon your behavior. Groups demand a certain amount of conformity in order to maintain their integrity and distinctive character as well as to demonstrate the commitment of members. The pressures to conformity are well illustrated by adolescent peer groups. Behavior—whether the adolescent smokes, wears certain clothes, uses particular words, or aspires to specific objectives—tends to reflect the friendship group and the school group. The adolescent will conform to the group's expectations in order to maintain his or her status in the group.

The same pressures to conform also occur in adult groups. The union can compel an individual to strike when he or she prefers to work. Getting married can alter a person's preferred pattern of recreation or daily schedule of activities. Joining a club can open up opportunities to pursue common interests but also can require an individual to engage in activities, or attend functions, such as membership drives or an annual dinner and dance, that he or she would prefer to avoid. People frequently do things and go places with friends that they themselves do not prefer; they compromise their preferences in order to maintain the friendship.

In sum, you necessarily pursue your own interests and needs in the context of various groups. This requires that you accept the constraints of those groups as well as the opportunities they provide.

Thinking Critically

Two researchers gave questionnaires to 41 female and 15 male freshmen to test the hypothesis that people with a propensity to join groups are psychologically healthier—a finding reported by other research (Wann and Hamlet 1996). They found that "high joiners" had significantly higher scores on scales measuring self-esteem and positive emotions and lower scores on a loneliness scale.

Do the results support the hypothesis? "High joiners" is a misleading term. The small sample of students indicated their *inclination* to join groups. We have no data on how many they actually joined. Moreover, the authors suggest that psychological health leads people to more readily join groups. But the relationship is correlational; if those who actually join more groups are healthier, it could be the joining and participation in the group that increases their psychological health rather than the health that leads them to join. Finally, the researchers found a mean self-esteem score of 5.97 for "high joiners" and 5.28 for "low joiners." The difference was statistically significant, but is it substantively significant? Without more information about the scale used, we are not convinced that it is.

Primary and Secondary Groups

It is important to distinguish between primary and secondary groups. **Primary groups** are those that involve face-to-face, personal, intimate interaction. **Secondary groups** are based on impersonal relationships and have a specific task. In other words, the groups represent two different types of relationships.

Primary relationships include those with families and close friends. These relationships are crucial to your sense of well-being and to your notion of who you are. Note that a primary relationship can both contribute to and detract from your well-being. An individual with an alcoholic father, for example, may have a long struggle in establishing satisfying intimate relationships. Yet even when a primary relationship is detrimental to well-being, it will require other primary relationships to rebuild that well-being. Wolin and Wolin (1993) studied resilient people—those who survive a troubled family and construct a meaningful life for themselves. The researchers point out that all of the survivors were able to find healthy intimate relationships to replace the troubled ones, and these healthy intimate relationships were a crucial part of their ability to overcome their troubled pasts.

Secondary relationships include such things as the interaction between a store clerk and a customer, an entertainer and an audience, and a teacher and students. These relationships are predominantly exchange relationships. They are based on specific tasks such as a purchase, recreation, or learning. Much interaction in modern society is secondary rather than primary. Indeed, it would not be possible to have a primary relationship with everyone because primary relationships, by definition, require a large investment of time and emotional energy.

Some secondary relationships, of course, evolve into primary ones. People who work together, for instance, can do things together socially and, as a result, become friends. Or a graduate student can eventually become a colleague and friend of his or her professor. The opposite can also occur. People who are friends may become estranged for some reason so that the primary relationship becomes a secondary one.

While primary relationships are most important in terms of their influence on people, secondary relationships can also have both short-

---

Explorations

The Most Influential Person in My Life

Let each member of your group write answers to the following four questions. Who is currently the most influential person in your life? What is your relationship to this person? Is this person a primary or secondary relationship? What is the reason for your selection of this person? Now answer the same four questions again, except change the most influential person to the one you would have chosen five years ago.

Discuss the answers along the following lines. Are the current relationships named mostly primary or mostly secondary? Are the most influential people of five years ago mostly primary or mostly secondary? How much, if any, change has occurred in the selections? Were there any common reasons given for the selections? Were the reasons given for current choices different from the reasons given for the choices of five years ago? What would you conclude about the relative importance of primary and secondary relationships if your data are true of the population as a whole? Are there any differences between the kinds of relationships chosen by males and females? To what extent do female respondents name females as most influential, and to what extent do males name males? What conclusions about gender differences would you draw from the results?

If you do this as an individual project, interview six other students. Ask them the same questions you have asked yourself and write down their answers. Analyze your results.

term and long-term influence. For example, an irritable and uncooperative clerk in a store can put you in such a bad mood that it has a short-term effect on your other relationships. Or you may strongly admire a professor who has a long-term effect on your beliefs and behavior. And the mass media have sufficient influence on people that one researcher has argued that they constitute a new kind of primary relationship, providing people with a time-efficient way to enjoy social interaction and substituting for other intimate contacts like family and friends (Cerulo 1992). We, however, prefer to think of the mass media as another example of a secondary group that has influence on people's lives.

Reference Groups

Recall that in dramaturgy, an offshoot of symbolic interactionism, there is always an audience for whom you are performing. A **reference group** is a special kind of audience, an audience that may or may not be present during a particular performance. A reference group is the audience that approves of the behavior. In other words, the reference group represents those people, real or imaginary, whom the actor believes will be pleased by the performance.

Thus, people wear certain kinds of clothes because they expect their reference group to approve and admire those clothes (Englis 1995). The reference group is not present when the clothes are purchased. In fact, the reference group may be, in part or whole, imaginary in the sense that the individual anticipates the admiration of others who see the clothes.

Another example of a reference group that is imaginary is the diarist who writes for "posterity." The diarist persists in writing even though no one alive reads the work. The diarist's reference group is not people who are alive but rather those yet to come who will appreciate the diary and the story it tells.

Of course, because reference groups are so important, many consist of people who are primary relationships. Parents, friends, lovers, spouses, children, and other relatives are among the important people who function as reference groups. The man who told us that he still acts in a way that he knows would have pleased his deceased father illustrates the power that primary relationships have as reference groups.

Reference groups are also an integral part of people's self concepts. A study of 370 male and female adolescents found that self-worth was related to perceptions of approval from peer reference groups (Robinson 1995). In fact, reference groups affect both positive and negative aspects of self concepts. For example, we have known individuals who struggled all of their lives with a sense of personal inadequacy because they could never measure up to their parents' expectations.

Ingroups and Outgroups

In Chapter Three, we discussed ethnocentrism. The term, coined by William Graham Sumner (1906), refers to a tendency for people to like their own groups and to dislike and/or distrust those in other **groups**. He named the former **ingroups** and the latter **outgroups**. An ingroup, then, is any group to which you belong and to which you are loyal; an outgroup is any group to which you do not belong and towards which you feel hostility, dislike, and/or competition.

The distinction between ingroups and outgroups is somewhat fluid. For instance, if you belong to a fraternity or sorority, you might regard other fraternities or sororities as outgroups. Yet if all the Greek societies come under attack by another student group, you are likely to band together and regard each other as threatened ingroups. Similarly, in World War II most Americans viewed the Soviets as part of the ingroup, the Allies, that waged war against the Nazi outgroup. However, when the war ended, the Soviet Union quickly became the outgroup and West Germany, a former enemy, became part of the ingroup.

The ingroup/outgroup distinction has both positive and negative social functions. Positively, it enables individuals to fulfill their need to belong and to have a sense of identity. Negatively, it adds to the amount of conflict in the world and can be used to justify the oppression and exploitation of people, as illustrated by the European conquest of the American Indians, the slave trade, and the Nazi effort to exterminate Jews.

Small Group Behavior

A **small group** is one in which face-to-face interaction is possible for all members. That is, each member can interact intimately with every other member. Friendship cliques, task groups in a work organization, seminar classes, and family gatherings are examples of small groups.

The Power of Small Groups

Small groups can exert a powerful influence on their members. For one thing, it is difficult for an individual to resist group norms. In a classic series of *experiments*, Solomon Asch (1958) set up small groups of male college students. The groups had the task of making visual judgments about the length of lines. The groups observed large cards on each of which they saw a standard line and, some distance to the right, three comparison lines. Their task was to identify which of the three comparison lines was the same length as the standard line. In every case, the correct answer was fairly obvious.

However, each group contained one volunteer who was unaware that other group members were Asch's confederates. During the experiment, the cards were shown, one at a time, to the whole group and each member identified aloud which of the lines was the matching one. Group members began by giving some correct answers, then offered a mix of correct and incorrect answers. The researchers arranged the seating so that the volunteer would answer last. What would the volunteer do if all the confederates agreed on a particular choice, but a choice that clearly violated the volunteer's own perception?

In one set of the experiments, the confederates gave wrong answers on twelve of eighteen cards. About a third of the volunteers' responses were in agreement with the incorrect responses of the confederates. The students openly agreed with judgments that contradicted their own observations!

Why did the volunteers do this? In follow-up interviews, Asch found that a few of the students actually came to believe that they saw the lines in the same way as the majority. Most of those who conformed said that they saw the correct answer but decided that the group must be right and, thus, their own observations must be wrong. And a few others admitted that they never believed the answers of the majority but didn't want to go against the majority opinion.

Keep in mind that the volunteers yielded to the group judgments although the members were strangers and even though the judgments contradicted something their eyes clearly saw. If the small group is composed of primary relationships or if the judgments are being made about something that is ambiguous, the pressure to conform is even greater.

Small Groups as Healing and Change Agents

In addition to exerting pressure to conform, small groups provide the context in which many people experience emotional healing and/or have their behavior changed. The power of small groups to achieve such results was recognized in the late 1940s when Kurt Lewin, a social psychologist, and his associates were training community leaders in conflict resolution and attitude change (Pizer and Travers 1975). When Lewin allowed some of the leaders to sit in on staff evaluation sessions, the social psychologists quickly discovered that this was a way for individuals to participate in small groups as well as learn about themselves and about human relationships.

Feedback and self-disclosure became a regular part of the sessions. In addition, sensitivity training, or the T-group, emerged as a small group process. In the T-group, individuals could talk freely about themselves and about others and, at the same time, get feedback from the group about what they were saying and feeling.

The T-group was designed to accomplish at least three things. First, members learned more about themselves and about social organization through participation in the group. Second, the members began to see themselves as others saw them. Third, members were able to consider various ways to change in a non-threatening setting.

A host of various kinds of small groups has grown out of the original T-group concept. Among the better known are the 12-step programs that are available for helping people deal with everything from alcoholism to neuroses to weight control. These programs have proliferated throughout the nation and have enabled many people to accomplish healing and change that they were unable to achieve on their own.

The Size of Small Groups

Although we define a group as two or more, we should note that the **dyad**, the group of two, is qualitatively different from all larger groups. Georg Simmel (Wolff 1950, pp. 125–42) discussed the qualitative differences by comparing the dyad with the triad—a group of three. The dyad is the locus of intimacy. Whatever the size and closeness of the groups to which you belong, intimacy ultimately occurs between two people, not between an individual and the group. Indeed, research has shown that people will disclose more intimate information and be more involved nonverbally as well as verbally in dyads (Solano and Dunnam 1985). The dyad also provides maximum scope for individuality. There is no majority to outvote the individual in a dyad, nor is the individual ever reduced to some average level.

The addition of one person dramatically alters the dyad. When this occurs, there is not only the direct relationship between the two members but also an indirect one based upon their common relationship with the third member. Moreover, no matter how close the members of a triad may be, there will always be some occasion when two of them regard the other as an intruder. It is also more difficult for three people to attain a common mood such as the desire to visit a museum or engage in some sport. Time constraints alone preclude this.

Gradually increasing the number of people in the group may not always make a difference. Asch found that the volunteers in his experiments were more likely to conform if they were in a group of four rather than a group of three. However, increasing the group beyond four did not further increase the conformity.

Nevertheless, increasing the size may affect the group members in various ways. Each new member adds heterogeneity. The more differences there are in the group the less likely it is that a majority will agree on all matters and thereby enforce conformity on the minority. Group size is also related to the productivity of a task group. Generally, increasing the size of the group increases the productivity. Yet on certain kinds of tasks—complex problem-solving tasks that require one member to discover a solution and then convince the other members of its utility—the group's performance will begin to decrease as group size grows (Littlepage 1991). At some point, the gain of additional brains is neutralized by problems of coordinating the group effort.

Social Networks

If you combine your participation in the groups and relationships discussed above with the organizations discussed in the remainder of this chapter, this constitutes your **social network**. In essence, a social network is the totality of your complex system of relationships and provides the vital resources available to you for achieving a meaningful life.

For example, as you seek solutions to a problem or help in advancing your career, you may find significant assistance from someone who went to the same school, came from the same town, or who knew someone in your family. Sharing these commonalities tends to make you part of an ingroup and gives the other person an extra incentive to help you. In reflecting upon our own careers, we recognize that many of the opportunities that have come our way—from university positions to writing opportunities—were the result of recommendations by friends and colleagues.

You may also receive assistance from people you have never met. A friend planned to travel to Italy. Instead of relying on a travel agent, she used an online computer service to contact people in Italy for their advice. She received an abundance of helpful suggestions that made her trip a memorable one. Being online is a method of enlarging your social network—a method that was unavailable to previous generations.

Sociological research is identifying numerous ways in which social networks influence behavior. For instance, those who join social movements may be motivated more by knowing someone involved than by belief in the cause itself (Tarrow 1997). People migrate to the United States to join the relatives who preceded them. And networks are the means through which individuals do everything from buying drugs to advancing their careers.

Formal Organizations

Human life is circumscribed by organizations. Consider the answers to the following questions. Where were you born? Where did you receive your primary school education? Where do you work? Where will you go if you are critically ill? Where will you be married? If you are like most people, every answer you gave referred to some type of organization. Organizations are pervasive components of human experiences.

Experiences

'Have We Forgotten About People?'

During his undergraduate years, Frank became enamored with history. He wasn't sure what he wanted to do with his life, however. So he joined the Peace Corps after graduation and served several years in Latin America before beginning graduate studies in Latin American history. When he completed his Ph.D., he eagerly sought an academic position. But his job search was not, as he tells it, a pleasant experience:

> By that time, I had a wife and two small children. I expected that with my life experience and a degree from a top university, I would have my choice of positions. Instead, I found very few openings. Unfortunately, those that existed either offered too little pay for me to support my family, or they were non-tenure-track positions that would force us to move every three to five years.
>
> But the worst part was the attitude of the people who interviewed me. I found no sympathy for my plight. Peo-

ple were willing to use me for the purposes of their organization, but no one was interested in helping me break into the discipline I loved. I finally gave up, found a job with a government agency, and am quite happy in what I now do.

Frank illustrates the way in which organizations circumscribe people's lives. One organization, a university, helped Frank develop his fascination with history. Another organization, the Peace Corps, gave him the opportunity to experience life in Latin America and to develop a consuming interest with that part of the world. A second university provided him with the Ph.D. credentials for a lifelong pursuit of his two major interests—history and Latin America. Other colleges and universities caused him to despair and impressed him with the way in which organizations can mute people's compassion. Finally, another organization gave him the opportunity to pursue a meaningful career.

The Nature of Formal Organizations

A **formal organization** is a secondary group that has been "deliberately structured for the purpose of attaining specific goals" (Etzioni 1961, p. 4). Schools have the specific goal of educating students. Factories have the specific goals of manufacturing products and selling those products at a profit. Hospitals have the specific goals of healing the sick and training physicians. As we shall discuss below, the goal orientation of organizations is not always as clear as these examples suggest. Nevertheless, organizations are established to pursue specific goals.

Clearly, your experience will vary depending on the type of organization as well as your role in it. Even in the same role—say, as a worker—you will have different experiences in a software-design firm than in a steel mill. Your experiences also will differ according to the way in which the organization is run. For instance, some organizations attempt to control workers through rewards while others use more coercive methods. Recognizing these differences, a number of researchers have attempted to classify all organizations into types (Hall 1982). Yet there is no consensus. We shall, therefore, examine a few of the important characteristics of formal organizations, then look at two types of organizations that are important and pervasive: the voluntary association and the **bureaucracy**.

Models of Work Organizations

You are likely to spend a good part of your life in some type of work organization. There are a number of models that attempt to capture the essence of work organizations. That is, the models attempt to explain basic patterns of behavior within the organizations.

Scientific Management

According to the scientific management model, workers are primarily motivated by the desire for money and managers by the desire for maximizing output. Frederick Taylor, the father of scientific management, believed that organizational efficiency could be maximized by "the segmentation of all tasks involved in production into a series of simple movements and operations" (Champion, 1975, p. 33). Each worker could be trained to perform certain relatively simple operations in the most efficient way and could be motivated to perform those operations through monetary rewards (including bonuses). As a result, output would be maximized. Because workers get what they want (money) and management gets what it wants (maximum output), everyone is satisfied.

Taylor initiated time and motion studies to determine the most efficient patterns for workers. Among his conclusions were: it is better for the two hands of the worker to begin and complete movements together; it is better to have a continuous, straight movement of the hands rather than jerking or zig-zag motions; and all tools and materials should be in a fixed place. Clearly, scientific management views the worker as a machine that can be manipulated for maximum output. It is manipulation because the real concern is output and not the workers' needs. The fact that workers want something more than money, and that scientific management falls far short of a true science of the workplace, was stressed by the human relations school (although some managers still try to fulfill their responsibilities in accord with the scientific management model).

The Human Relations Model

In the human relations model, workers are more than machines and more than economic creatures. This model views workers as social individuals who have a variety of needs and goals and who respond to work conditions as members of groups rather than as individuals.

The human relations model began with the work of Elton Mayo and his associates. They conducted the famous "Hawthorne Experiment" at the Western Electric Company's Hawthorne Works in Chicago (Roethlisberger and Dickson, 1939). They segregated one group of workers, who assembled telephone relays, in a separate room and observed their performance under various working conditions. The Taylorites had asserted, among other things, that proper illumination increases productivity. However, Mayo and his associates found that the productivity of the Hawthorne group continued to increase even when the illumination was decreased! The researchers then experimented with various patterns of work breaks, such as two five-minute breaks during the day versus one ten-minute and one fifteen-minute break. Yet productivity increased during the experiment independently of any changes made in the break pattern.

Eventually the researchers concluded that what had happened at Hawthorne showed the importance of the social nature of the worker. They believed that workers do not behave merely on the basis of their pay, but rather on the basis of their social relationships. The productivity of the Western Electric workers had risen because of their altered social situation—the special attention paid them by the researchers and their participation in decisions that affected their work. The result was a large increase in morale and higher productivity. Henceforth, the researchers pointed out, attention should be paid to social factors (including the needs of workers) in the workplace. In fact, the "Hawthorne effect" now refers to any instance of altered behavior resulting from the researcher's presence.

A more recent variation of the human relations school is Theory Z, described by William Ouchi (1981). Theory Z is modeled after the Japanese pattern of industrial relations. The "first lesson" in the Theory Z organization is mutual trust between management and workers. In addition, the Theory Z organization provides a more humane and secure situation for the worker. Workers have more job security (they are not laid off during times of economic setback). They engage in non-specialized career lines (they do not perform the same task for decades). They have a standard pattern of promotions, so competition between workers and "corporate games" are minimized. They participate with management in the decision-making process. And, finally, management has a "holistic" interest in workers. The employer is concerned about every aspect of an employee's existence—his or her family, health, personal well-being, and the overall quality of life—and not simply about the employee's work. Company efforts to find suitable wives for male employees and to establish meaningful recreation programs for employees illustrate this holistic concern.

One example provided by Ouchi will dramatize the difference between Theory Z and the typical American practices. In Japan during the early 1970s, the Mazda corporation had an enormous deficit. Management dealt with the deficit by cutting the pay of senior managers 20 percent, freezing the pay of middle-level managers, giving cost-of-living increases to lower-level workers, and keeping everyone employed. Some years later in the United States, Chrysler corporation faced its economic woes by laying off 28 percent of its blue-collar workers, firing 7 percent of its middle-level managers, and cutting white-collar salaries by about 5 percent. In other words, the Japanese strove to protect jobs of all personnel, even if the pay of some had to be cut and the corporation had to suffer losses. In the Chrysler situation, on the other hand, profits rather than jobs were protected.

The Negotiated Order Model

The negotiated order model emphasizes the dynamic nature of the organization. This does not mean that there is no stability or continuity. Rather, order is maintained in the face of continuing change through negotiations between members of the organization.

The negotiated order model was formulated by Anselm Strauss and his associates in their study of mental hospitals. They used *participant observation*, which included attending hospital meetings and following staff members around to observe their daily routines. The researchers discovered that "hardly anyone knows all the extant rules, much less exactly what situations they apply to, for whom, and with what sanctions" (Strauss et al. 1963, p. 374). In this kind of situation, continual negotiations were necessary. Professionals—psychiatrists, physicians, social workers, and nurses—negotiated with each other over procedures and even patient care. Strauss did not claim that all organizations are negotiated orders, only those in which there are ongoing change, uncertainty, ambiguity, ideological differences, inexperience of members in the organization, and problematic coordination. Thus, another study (Mellinger 1994) found that the work of nurses and paramedics in medical emergencies also involves a negotiated order.

In addition to health-care situations, the conditions of negotiated order have been found in special education programs (Hall and Hall 1982). As a relatively new area of education, special education involves professionals with diverse ideologies and knowledge who have to decide various matters in committees. They deal with students, for instance, on a case by case basis. Decisions about placement of students and development of the program are made through negotiations at committee meetings. Moreover, problems of space and adequate personnel require negotiations between the special education teachers, principals of schools, and district administrators.

The Conflict Model

The conflict model, as per *conflict theory*, assumes that the organization is composed of groups with diverse or contradictory interests. There is no single goal or set of goals that unites the members into a consensual group. Rather, the opposed interests of organizational members reflect their positions in the larger society (such as blue-collar workers versus management), or, as per *feminist theory*, their gender (women may face barriers to advancement as men seek to maintain their dominance in the organization), or the struggle for scarce resources (such as two different groups of professionals seeking to control an organization). The inevitable outcome is ongoing conflict, which, in turn, leads to changes in the organization.

The conflict model is illustrated by Jackall's (1988) study of corporate managers. The managers did not simply focus their thoughts on competing corporations but also had ongoing conflict with other segments of their own corporation. Thus, managers in production, marketing, sales, and finance all vied with each other to get their own ideas accepted and to maximize the productivity of their respective areas. In addition, line and staff managers fought over organizational resources and over the rules that applied to work. As a result, managers worked in a situation of relentless and painful anxiety.

The Search for New Models

The search for the best model of organizations continues. Some social scientists identify and use the concept of culture, which includes shared values and beliefs, as the "glue" that holds the organization together. The organization's culture fulfills a number of functions (Smircich 1983). It enables members to develop a sense of identity—a sense that they are an integral part of the organization. The culture also provides a basis upon which members can commit themselves to the organization. For example, some businesses foster the belief that their members are contributing to the well-being of the larger society. The culture facilitates stability through commitment of the members to a consensual ideology. Finally, the culture provides the guidelines for behavior in the organization.

Various other models continue to be offered. Senge (1990), for instance, argues for a learning model and identifies a number of "learning disabilities" that can cripple an organization's effectiveness. Yet no model so far can capture the essence of all organizations. The search for a model will surely continue, just as organizations will certainly continue as a powerful factor in people's lives.

Processes in Formal Organizations

Who's running things? How do you get something done? How do you find out what's really going on? People in organizations ask these questions all the time. Two factors—power and communication patterns—are vital in answering these questions.

Power and the Power Structure

Power is control over the behavior of others—with or without their consent—to attain specific goals. To get people to work harder or longer hours, to get people to grant one individual a greater share of rewards, or to get people to comply to a new program or policy that they do not prefer—these are examples of the exercise of power. The **power structure** is the way in which power is distributed among the various units and members of an organization. The power structure asserts who in the organization can exercise power.

As the concept of power structure suggests, status is one source of power. The various statuses in the organization are evaluated as more or less important to the achievement of goals and to the survival of the organization. Those in positions that are deemed most important have the greatest power. Thus, differential power is an integral part of the structure of an organization. In addition, however, power derives from the ability of individuals to fulfill their roles in the organization and to present themselves to other members as invaluable assets. Managers who are inept will have far less power than managers who are competent or able to convince others that they are competent.

Power is not something that is only exercised at the higher levels of an organization. In fact, it is important for all members to perceive themselves as having power. Those who feel powerless are likely to feel alienated and stressed and they may behave in ways detrimental to their own well-being or to the well-being of others. Kanter (1977) pointed out that such people in corporations get caught in a "downward spiral." Their efforts to cope with the lack of sufficient power are likely to be met with resistance and even further restrictions on their power. This can ultimately hurt their performance. For example, if they have supervisory responsibilities, they may render their subordinates ineffective. At the corporation she studied, Kanter noted one young trainee who was assigned to work under a low-power manager. The manager had become known as a chronic complainer, one who had problems in the organization and was not advancing in his career. The trainee had talent but needed guidance. Eventually, the negativism of the manager infected the trainee, who lost some of his motivation. The trainee became increasingly critical and decreasingly motivated to work. He expressed his hostility by letting his hair grow long, wearing shabby clothing, and showing disrespect toward people and things. Other people labeled the trainee a trouble-maker. Eventually, he resigned. No one in the corporation realized that the essence of the problem was the young man's interaction with the manager, who, in turn, was caught up in destructive behavior patterns that reflected his relative lack of power.

Communication Networks

All human enterprises involve communication. In organizations, there are both an official, or formal, and an unofficial, or informal, communication network. The formal network is simply the official organizational definition of who is supposed to say what to whom. In the formal network, information goes in various directions—downward from superiors to subordinates, upward from subordinates to superiors, or horizontally between peers.

Among the things that may be communicated downward are instructions about tasks, reasons for the tasks, information about policies and practices within the organization, and feedback about performance. Upward communication may involve such things as an individual's feelings about his or her performance and problems, problems of co-workers or fellow members, and thoughts about policies and practices in the organization. Horizontal communication is likely to involve not only organizational matters but also personal matters that give members support and fulfill emotional needs. Such information needs to be conveyed between various individuals and units, and the formal network both sanctions that flow of information and provides the mechanisms for it (such as memos, newsletters, and meetings).

The formal network is important in coordinating the work of the organization. Indeed, problems and frustrations can arise from inadequate communication, as the following remarks suggest: "No one told *me* that we have a policy about that"; "He always misinterprets what *I* tell him to do"; "How was *I* to know that the sales department was so touchy about that project?" and "Why didn't someone catch that mistake before it became so costly?" Unfortunately, communication problems can affect every kind of organization—from the student government to the local church to the international corporation.

The formal network does more than coordinate work. It also allows superiors to consolidate and maintain their power. To the extent that policies originate above and are communicated down to be followed without question, superiors continually underscore their positions of power. Moreover, there is power in the control of information. Those at the top, who know—or who convince others that they know—the kinds of things that are crucial to the organization's survival and success, can maintain their power by controlling the amount and kind of information they dispense to the rest of the organization.

The informal network is the flow of information that is outside the formal channels. The "grapevine" is one of the more prominent avenues of informal communication. Informal networks also include such things as casual conversations, friendships, rumors, and exchange relationships ("You owe me one, so tell me all you know about the boss's problem.").

The pervasiveness of the informal network is illustrated by a national survey of 30,000 employees (Graham 1984). When asked where they got most of their information about the company, 57 percent said it was through the grapevine. Organizational experts, therefore, advise managers to use the grapevine rather than suppress it. A manager, for example, can send messages that will alleviate anxieties even though the manager cannot formally make any announcement. The informal and formal networks are both indispensable to the functioning of the organization.

The informal communication network is one aspect of the **informal organization**, the unofficial, unplanned, but patterned relationships that develop in an organization. No organizational chart for the informal organization exists, but it is always present and always significant for the functioning of the organization. The informal organization develops out of socio-emotional needs (recall why people join groups), and the need of people to exercise some control over their existence. Individuals develop friendships and communication patterns that fulfill their needs for interaction, enhance their satisfaction, and provide them with the information channels and support to exercise some control over their work situation.

The informal organization can make an organization more effective as members establish meaningful relationships and work together in a pleasant atmosphere to achieve goals. The informal organization can also create various problems. For example, we once worked in a university where faculty members intensely disliked a particular administrator and cooperated with each other continually to subvert the administrator's programs.

Voluntary Associations

A *voluntary association* is an organization that people choose to join to pursue a particular interest or to support particular ideals. There is an enormous number of different kinds of voluntary associations, ranging from those that are basically sociable (such as the Elks and other fraternal groups) to those that focus on service (such as the Rotary Club) to those that are oriented to political action (such as pro-choice and pro-life groups in the abortion controversy). In terms of membership, religious groups are the largest type of voluntary association (see Extensions, this chapter).

Voluntary associations have important functions. For the individual, the association may provide a primary group and status in the community. For the larger society, voluntary associations provide a way of channeling conflict over social problems. People who feel strongly about an issue such as abortion, racial discrimination, or

EXTENSIONS

Voluntary Association Members in 15 Nations

Not all people participate equally in voluntary associations. Using *existing data* from the World Values Survey, three researchers compared voluntary association membership in fifteen countries (Curtis, Grabb, and Baer 1992). The countries consisted of the United States, Canada, Japan, Australia, and eleven European nations. The researchers found higher rates for joining voluntary associations among more educated individuals, older people, the employed, and, to some extent, males rather than females, and rural rather than city dwellers.

However, there were also differences between the nations. As Figure 6.2 illustrates, the percentage of people belonging to voluntary associations varies considerably from one nation to another. If church membership is included, Americans are more likely than people in other nations to join a voluntary association. When religious organizations are excluded, Australians, the Dutch, Norwegians, and Swedes all are more likely to be joiners.

It is difficult to explain the differences between joining rates in nations. Some observers have suggested that Protestantism might be one cause because of an emphasis on personal responsibility for helping others. This emphasis may have led to the formation of a larger number of associations. Yet, while many of the nations that have high rates of joining are Protestant nations, two of them—Canada and Belgium—do not have a large Protestant majority.

Another possible explanation is the degree to which a nation has a strong, centralized government. If the national government has a great deal of control, it could inhibit the growth of local associations. Indeed, three of the nations with relatively low levels of joining—Japan, France, and Spain—have such governmental structures. Yet it is difficult to measure and compare the strength of the central government, and the explanation does not work for all the nations in any case.

In sum, whether people join a voluntary association varies considerably from country to country, ranging from 72.7 percent of Americans to 25.9 percent of Italians. The United States, when compared to other nations and particularly when religious membership is included, is truly a nation of joiners.

Figure 6.2   Percentage of People in Voluntary Associations

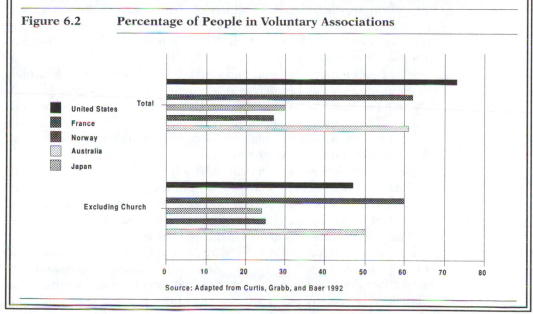

Source: Adapted from Curtis, Grabb, and Baer 1992

sexual inequality can express their feelings through an organization that supports their perspective. These organizations help prevent more serious forms of conflict such as mob violence. As long as people feel that they can accomplish their aims through an organization, they will probably not engage in the more violent forms of protest. And indeed, a number of voluntary associations have been effective in bringing about change: the NAACP (National Association for the Advancement of Colored People) has furthered civil rights for racial minorities, NOW (the National Organization of Women) has helped bring about new legislation that benefits women, and the AARP (American Association of Retired Persons) has been a powerful lobby in Congress on behalf of senior citizens.

Bureaucracy

Bureaucracy. The word itself makes most Americans grimace with disgust. Yet you will probably spend a significant part of your time in the bureaucratic organizations that are pervasive in modern society. They are pervasive because, contrary to the popular stereotype, they are the most efficient and effective form of administration.

What Is a Bureaucracy?

Max Weber identified the features of a **bureaucracy** (Gerth and Mills 1946, pp. 196–98). He pointed out six elements in the bureaucratic form of organization, each of which contributes to effectiveness and efficiency. Weber's description was an "ideal type" of bureaucracy. The six elements he identified are each found more or less in actual organizations.

The first element is "fixed and official jurisdictional areas" which are governed by regulations. That is, a bureaucracy has subgroups, each of which is a more or less permanent domain of authority and responsibility. The subgroups specialize in particular aspects of the overall work of the bureaucracy. This specialization should improve the performance in each area and, thereby, the overall achievement of goals.

Second, the subgroups are ordered in a hierarchy of authority. There is a clear and firm system of supervision of lower subgroups by higher ones. This gives management considerable power over workers, but it also means that managers can coordinate the various specialized areas.

The third element is the management of an organization on the basis of written documents, which are kept in their original form. The bureaucracy uses written evidence rather than verbal understandings. The written documents are a source of irritation to both members and clientele of bureaucracies (e.g., filling out everything in triplicate). But they are essential. A worker's "I was told that I could do it this way" is no substitute for "Here is the memo whose instructions I am following."

Fourth, the management of the bureaucracy requires thorough training. The division of labor along specialized lines implies expertise. People are hired on the basis of expertise or on the basis that they can be trained to become experts. Other matters, such as the fact that an individual is related to one of the managers, should not be considered.

Fifth, the officials of the bureaucracy must be full-time employees. Those who run the bureaucracy cannot hold their jobs part time or regard them as a secondary activity. This ensures that the officials will be committed to the organization and will devote full attention to its effective and efficient running.

Finally, the management of the bureaucracy is based upon general rules "which are more or less stable, more or less exhaustive, and which can be learned" (Gerth and Mills 1946, p. 198). In theory, there should be a rule to cover every contingency that arises in the organization so that the bureaucrat can deal with each situation by applying the pertinent rule. Bureaucrats are not supposed to "play it by ear" or make decisions based on extraneous factors (such as how much he or she likes the person or persons involved in the decision) or spend the time treating each decision as a unique case.

The above description makes the bureaucracy into a very rational type of organization. In fact, Weber defined the kind of authority exercised in a bureaucracy as *rational-legal authority*. Such authority is based on a belief in the legality of the rules and the right of those in authority under such rules to issue commands (Weber 1947). In contrast, *traditional authority* rests upon the belief in the sanctity of timeless traditions and the right of those in positions of authority under the traditional scheme to exercise that authority. And *charismatic authority* is rooted in the personality of the leader who elicits unquestioning devotion from the followers. The bureaucracy offers a superior form of organization for the achievement of goals because it follows a rational procedure rather than the whims of the leader or the unbending burden of traditions. As a rational organization, the bureaucracy treats everyone equally. It tolerates no favoritism based on blood relationships, friendship, or other nonrational factors. In theory, then, the bureaucracy should maximize effective and efficient achievement of goals.

Is Bureaucracy a Four-Letter Word?

For many people, bureaucracy connotes the worst aspects of organizational life. Both popular and professional observers have portrayed the evils of bureaucratic organization and either prophesied or yearned for its demise. Yet evidence suggests that this picture may be too drab.

Let's look first at the problems and then at some positive aspects of bureaucracies.

The Bureaucratic Personality

Some critics have argued that people who work in bureaucracies tend to develop a personality that is characterized by "trained incapacity." Trained incapacity means that an individual's training leads to incompetence because the individual is so concerned with following the rules that he or she becomes inflexible and even blind to the goals of the organization (Merton 1957). A bureaucracy, according to Merton, exerts pressure upon individuals to be "methodical, prudent, disciplined." Successful operation of the bureaucracy demands reliable behavior that conforms to established rules. This rigid adherence to rules leads clients of the bureaucracy to anger or exasperation. Moreover, the bureaucrat who is so ritualistic in his or her behavior may get involved in a displacement of goals; that is, the rules themselves rather than the situations the rules are designed to address become the end value. For instance, rules in nursing homes are necessary for efficiency and for proper care of patients. However, rules rigidly followed can interfere with staff members' ability to give warm, supportive care to patients (Foner 1995).

There is no doubt but that some bureaucrats do function in a rigid way. They stick to the rules with infuriating tenacity, even when the rules are not really applicable to a particular case. Carl, the young librarian we mentioned at the beginning of this chapter, furnishes a mild example of this. But do bureaucracies create such a personality? The findings of Kohn (1971) say no. It may be that the bureaucracy, by its very nature, does exert pressure on people to be inflexible in following the rules. Yet other factors—including educational level and organizational norms—may intervene to prevent widespread development of such rigidity.

The Peter Principle

According to the **Peter Principle**, employees in a bureaucracy tend to rise to their level of incompetence, so that every position in the organization tends to be occupied by someone unable to perform his or her responsibilities (Peter and Hull 1969). This happens because people who are competent at one level of the bureaucracy are often rewarded by being promoted to a higher level. At some point, unfortunately, they will be promoted to a level at which they cannot perform competently. For instance, a competent professor may become an incompetent department chair or an ineffectual dean. In fact, the very qualities that made the professor a good teacher—such as spending a lot of time with students and focusing on keeping up with a professional field rather than on reports and records—may result in incompetence at a higher level.

The Peter Principle asserts that the reality of bureaucracy (the presence of great numbers of incompetents) is the opposite of the ideal (the filling of every position with an expert). Again, there is no doubt but that some bureaucrats are incompetent. But does everyone who is promoted eventually reach a level of incompetence? Are all bureaucracies run by people who are incapable of fulfilling their duties? The Peter Principle was originally offered as a somewhat tongue-in-cheek commentary on the bureaucracy, but some people have accepted it literally. No doubt, some bureaucrats are incompetent, but this doesn't mean that all—or even most—are actually incapable of doing their jobs well.

Parkinson's Laws

C. Northcote Parkinson developed a number of "laws" about bureaucracies. Perhaps the best known asserts that "work expands to fill the amount of time available for its completion." Thus, given a certain task, an individual may complete it in one, two, or four hours, depending upon the amount of time allocated to its completion. Another of **Parkinson's laws**, which is less well-known, states that a bureaucracy will continue to expand independently of the amount of work to be done (Parkinson 1970). The organization, thus, will continue to get larger over time even though it has no additional tasks or even has fewer tasks. Parkinson illustrated his argument with figures from the British admiralty. In 1914, the British navy had 542 vessels, 125,000 officers and sailors, and 4,366 admiralty officials and their clerical staffs. By 1967 the number of vessels fell to 114, and the number of officers and men declined to 83,900. But the size of the admiralty officials and their staffs grew to 33,574! Thus, a 79 percent decline in vessels and a 38 percent decline in officers and sailors was accompanied by a 669 percent increase in the size of the bureaucracy.

Parkinson's Law of expansion is more likely to apply to governmental bureaucracies than to other kinds. In government, as Stevenson (1986, p. 307) put it, "managers respond to pressures for change by adding structures, regardless of increases in administrative cost and complexity, because bureaucratic structure is the legitimate, socially prescribed vehicle to accomplish bureaucratic goals." Most organizations could not afford such expansion. It is the nature of government rather than the nature of bureaucracy that accounts for the expansion.

Rationality and Goal Orientation

Some social scientists have questioned both rationality and goal orientation as fundamental characteristics of bureaucracies (Clark and McKibbin 1982; Perrow, 1982). It is not hard to understand why if you contrast what it means to be rational and goal-oriented with the behavior of people in organizations. One way a group could be rational and goal-oriented would be for the members to establish policies and practices that effectively and efficiently accomplish clearly-stated objectives. It is obvious to anyone who has functioned in an organization that such a rational, goal-oriented procedure is not always followed. Even when the procedure is consciously pursued, it may be deflected by accidents, unanticipated events, misunderstandings, and failures of various kinds.

Consider what goes on in some educational organizations. School administrators may prefer to think that they are engaging in a rational decision-making process. Yet the process they use actually falls short of the rational (in the sense of choosing the best means to reach specific goals). Instead, they use what has been called a "garbage-can" model. This model is a "collection of choices looking for problems, issues and feelings looking for decision situations in which they might be aired, solutions looking for issues to which they might be the answer, and decision makers looking for work" (Cohen, March, and Olsen 1972, p. 2). Rather than the selection of the means to reach goals, the garbage-can model involves the search for rationales to justify actions taken.

In other words, educators, like other people, frequently act first and then find reasons to justify their action. They also act from a variety of motives, many of which have little to do with formal organizational goals. They may, for example, act in order to consolidate their power, to protect their position, to improve their status, or to do a favor for a friend. There are numerous kinds of motivation that affect behavior and make the rational pursuit of organizational goals problematic.

Thus, things happen in organizations that seem to contradict both goals and rationality. This occurs because an organization is a collection of people with diverse interests and various motives and differing capabilities. There are formal organizational goals, but there are also individual goals (such as the goal of maintaining one's job or moving up in the organization) and goals of subgroups such as the board of trustees or the union. In addition, there are unanticipated events, chance occurrences, and individual failures. Consequently, organizational behavior may frequently appear to be, or actually be, irrational or contrary to formal goals.

In Behalf of Bureaucracy

Although the list of bureaucratic sins appears long, some researchers have challenged an overly negative portrait. Charles Perrow (1972) argued that the so-called sins of bureaucracies are either not sins at all or are the result of insufficient rather than excessive bureaucratization. For instance, what are the "sins" that people complain about in bureaucracies? Typically, they are such things as the lack of impartiality ("I didn't get promoted because I'm a woman rather than a man"), the lack of the exercise of authority ("who's in charge here? why can't someone make a decision about this?"), and the circumvention of authority ("that matter was *my* responsibility; you should have brought it to me rather than to Mr. X"). These complaints reflect inadequate rather than too much bureaucratization. In an ideal bureaucracy, the rules ensure that all people will be treated equally and impartially, and the hierarchy of authority provides clear guidelines for making decisions and assuming responsibility.

A friend of ours once worked as an electrical design draftsman in a large corporation. He was involved in designing new lighting for a building that was being remodeled. The blueprints lacked one necessary piece of information—the ceiling height in the remodeled areas. The supervisor did not know what the height would be but promised to find out. After a day or two, our friend reminded the supervisor that he still didn't have the necessary information. The supervisor acknowledged the problem and promised that he would get an answer as quickly as possible. For the next two weeks, our friend read books, worked puzzles, and chatted with co-workers while waiting for someone to decide on a ceiling height. The problem was insufficient bureaucratization. In a true bureaucracy, someone would have had the responsibility and authority to make the decision and would have provided the information quickly so that the work could proceed.

Thus, bureaucracy per se is not the demon it has become in the popular mind. Even if it is impossible to create an ideal bureaucracy in the real world, there are things to be said in its defense. In his study of working men, Kohn (1971) found no evidence for a bureaucratic personality. He interviewed 3,101 men to see how working in a bureaucracy affects people's values, social orientation, and intellectual functioning. He measured the extent of bureaucratization by the number of levels of authority in the organization. Kohn (1971, p. 472) reported that rather than having a stifling impact on personality, "bureaucratization is consistently, albeit not strongly, associated with greater intellectual flexibility, higher valuation of self-direction, greater openness to new experience, and more personally responsible moral standards." Kohn attributed this in part to the higher educational level of workers in bureaucracies. More importantly, he suggested, the working conditions of bureaucracies—such as greater job protection, higher income levels, and more complex work—tend to foster these characteristics in workers.

Critical Thinking Exercise

In his study of corporate managers, Jackall (1988) found that the managers believe in a number of "fundamental rules of bureaucratic life." The rules include: never go around your boss; always tell a boss what she or he wants to hear, even if the boss invites contrary views; and honor your boss's wishes to report or to cover up something, whatever your own views on the matter. The managers believe that it is necessary to follow these rules in order to survive in the corporate world.

If they follow these rules, how does their behavior differ from the actions of managers in an ideal bureaucracy? In what ways does such behavior cause an organization to deviate from an ideal bureaucracy? If a manager told you that the rules existed in her corporation, what kind of evidence would you want before accepting her observation as valid?

Jackall's data were gathered mainly from 143 in-depth interviews with managers in three different corporations. Would you accept his conclusions as valid for corporate life generally? Why or why not?

Summary

People always act in the context of a social structure—regularities and patterns in social interaction, including groups, organizations, and institutions. Social structure means an organized world—one which is necessary for people's well-being but also puts constraints on behavior. Social structure includes all levels from the macro to the micro and changes constantly.

The micro level consists of social groups. People join groups to fulfill their relational needs and to accomplish something that requires collective rather than individual effort. Primary and secondary groups are two different kinds of relationships. Primary relationships affect well-being and help form an individual's identity. Secondary relationships are mainly exchange relationships although they may evolve into primary relationships. Both primary and secondary relationships can have short-term and long-term influence on people's lives.

Reference groups are the audiences for whom people act and influence people's self concepts. Ingroups command people's loyalty and give them a sense of belonging. Outgroups are those toward which people feel competition, dislike, or hostility. The ingroup/outgroup distinction can lead to conflict and justify exploitation and oppression of those in outgroups.

Small groups with face-to-face interaction exert a powerful influence on people's behavior. It is difficult not to conform to the norms of such groups. Small groups also function as healing and change agents. The size of the group may or may not make a difference although there are significant differences between dyads and all larger groups. A social network is the totality of an individual's system of relationships. It is also a pool of resources for constructing a meaningful life.

Formal organizations—groups structured to achieve specific goals—are pervasive. A number of models of work organizations attempt to explain how those organizations influence members. Scientific management views workers as motivated by money and managers as motivated by the desire for maximum productivity. The human relations model views workers as having various needs and goals and as responding to work conditions as members of groups rather than as individuals. The negotiated order model views the organization as very fluid, and members as engaged in regular negotiations in order to fulfill their responsibilities. The conflict model views the organization as a number of groups with contrary interests, leading to ongoing conflict and change.

Important processes in formal organizations involve the power structure and communication patterns. All members have some power, although those in higher statuses have the most power. The formal communication network is useful for coordination and for the exercise of power by those in higher statuses. The informal network is part of the overall informal organization that arises out of people's social and emotional needs and the need to exercise some power.

People join voluntary associations to pursue particular interests or support particular ideals. Voluntary associations provide primary relationships and community status. They also channel conflict over social issues in constructive ways.

Bureaucracy is, in theory, the most efficient and effective method of administration, for it has specialization, a hierarchy of authority, written documents, expertise, full-time employees, and an extensive set of rules. Some criticisms of bureaucracies are that they develop bureaucratic personalities, follow the Peter Principle and Parkinson's Law, and violate the ideals of rationality and goal-orientation. Defenders of bureaucracy argue that all of the "sins" identified by critics are the result of an organization being insufficiently bureaucratic.

Glossary

bureaucracy   a form of organization characterized by specific domains of authority and responsibility, a hierarchy of authority, management based on written documents, expertise of officials and workers, management on the basis of rules, and full-time workers

dyad   a group of two people

formal organization   a secondary group set up to achieve specific goals

group   two or more interacting people who pursue some common goal or interest

informal organization   the unofficial, unplanned, but patterned relationships of an organization

ingroup   a group to which one feels one belongs and to which one is loyal

institution   a collective solution to a problem of social life

macro level   large-scale

micro level   small-scale

outgroup a group to which one feels one does not belong and toward which one feels some hostility, dislike, and/or competition

Parkinson's Law a bureaucracy will continue to expand independently of the amount of work to be done

Peter Principle individuals in an organization will be promoted to their level of incompetence

power control over the behavior of others—even if it is without their consent, against their will, or without their knowledge or understanding—in order to promote one's goals

power structure the way in which power is distributed among the various units and members of the organization

primary groups groups that involve face-to-face, personal, intimate interaction

reference group a real or imaginary group which is the audience that approves of an individual's behavior

secondary groups groups which are based on impersonal relationships and have a specific task

small group a group in which face-to-face interaction is possible for all members

social network the totality of an individual's complex system of relationships

social structure regularities and patterns in social interaction

society people who share a particular territory and culture

voluntary association an organization that people voluntarily join to pursue a particular interest or to support particular ideals

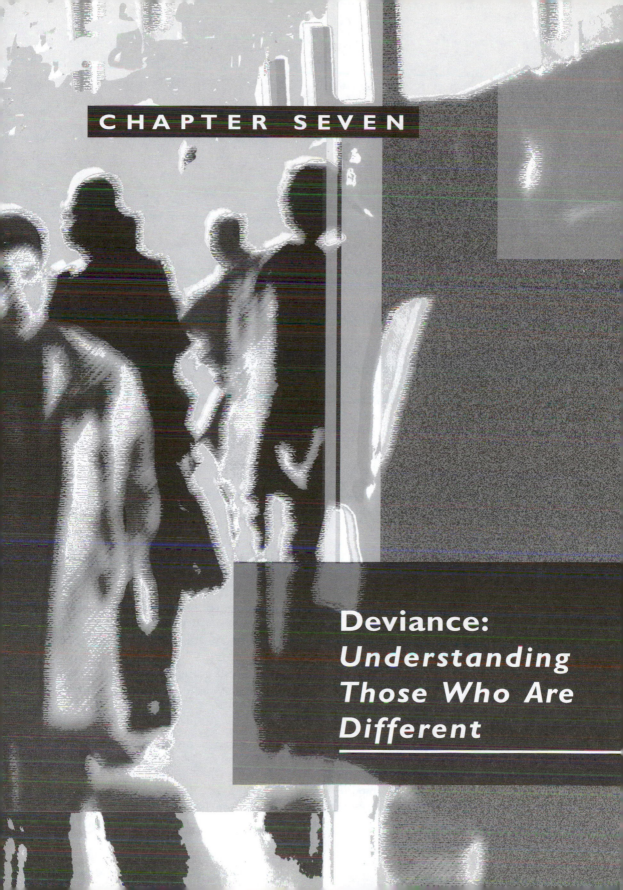

CHAPTER SEVEN

Deviance:
*Understanding
Those Who Are
Different*

What kinds of behavior do you think of when you hear the word "deviance"? Write down, or make a mental list of, at least five different behaviors you regard as deviant. How many of the five would you regard as immoral, illegal, harmful, or the result of a perverse choice by the individual engaged in the behavior?

Now consider the following incident. An adolescent stood before a judge in a midwestern juvenile court. The judge looked over the long list of offenses, including truancy, drug use, defacing walls with graffiti, and assault. He shook his head, and muttered: "I just don't understand why people do these things." The judge was perplexed, and so was the young man. He didn't understand the judge's comment because virtually everyone he knew did the things that baffled the judge. In the judge's circle of acquaintances, people regarded the offenses as behavior worthy of condemnation. In the young man's circle of friends, the offenses were both acceptable and expected behavior.

The incident illustrates an important point: what one person calls deviance, another person may define as normal. Think again about the five kinds of behavior you identified as deviant. Do you know of people who would defend any of these behaviors as acceptable and normal rather than as deviant? Why do you think people engage in such behaviors? We suspect that, by this time, you may be a bit perplexed. If so, that's good because too many people regard deviance as a straightforward topic that is easily explained. They are like the man who told us that everyone knows what is deviant because each person has a conscience and thus automatically understands what is right and wrong. Sociologists believe he was wrong. Understanding deviance is a complex matter. We'll begin by seeing what the term actually means.

What Is Deviance?

Sociologists use the term **deviance** in referring to behavior that violates social norms. It is important to keep in mind that the term does *not* indicate something that is evil or perverse or abnormal in a psychological sense. Some people define the behavior this way. And, of course, the behavior *may* be illegal or *may* be considered immoral by most people. However, to sociologists the term "deviance" is not used to make moral judgments about behavior but, rather, to indicate that the behavior violates one or more social norms.

A couple of additional points and some examples will clarify the matter. First, the norms that are violated may be those of a particular group rather than the society generally. Thus, an individual who breaks the norm could be considered a deviant by group members, but still be defined as a responsible person by the larger society.

For instance, how would you feel about being honored publicly as an outstanding student? If your grades merited it, you probably would be thrilled by the public honor and would act in accord with social norms by attending the ceremony. In some ghetto schools, however, students who pursue academic achievement and try to remain free of gangs, drugs, and violence may find themselves facing intense pressure from other students to replace educational goals with peer goals. Arti Shanker (1994) wrote of one school where the award ceremony for outstanding students was kept secret because those being honored might not show up out of fear for their safety. One recipient was called to the stage to receive a reward and did so amid the sneering cat-calls of other students. To most of us, the honorees were behaving responsibly in attaining academic excellence; to many of their peers, they were acting deviantly.

Second, the violated norms may be held generally in the society, but the norms are folkways rather than mores. The violator, then, may be regarded as eccentric rather than as immoral or perverse. For example, people are expected to wear clothing appropriate to their age, sex, and situation. We were at a party once where an eighty-year-old woman showed up wearing leotards and sporting a new blonde wig. She was not condemned as immoral but she did enhance her reputation as an eccentric.

Third, the violated norms may be held by people generally and be defined as mores. The violator is then likely to be regarded as immoral, criminal, perverse, or sick although there may still be some people who regard the behavior as appropriate. The friends of the young man standing before the juvenile judge in the incident described at the beginning of this chapter considered his behavior to be normal and admirable rather than criminal. In war time, the majority of Americans consider patriotism to be a moral or civic imperative. Yet protestors and conscientious objectors have opposed every U.S. war. The opponents have been condemned and called everything from communists to traitors, but their behavior has been applauded and called courageous by fellow protestors and opponents of the wars.

Finally, keep in mind that norm violations are deviant behavior whether or not the individual consciously and willfully chooses the behavior. To say that certain behavior is deviant, therefore, is not necessarily to say that the individual consciously decided to violate a norm. In some cases, of course, a choice has been made. These include, for example: people who protest a war when most others are being supportive, those who speed in the face of posted limits, and those who knowingly violate the law in order to get high on some kind of drug.

In other cases, however, people may either be unaware that they are engaging in deviance or they may be unwilling deviants. For instance, a man may have sexual intercourse with a willing, thirteen-year-old girl whom he thinks is eighteen. Even if she initiated the sex, however, he is guilty of statutory rape. Although unaware of it, he has committed a deviant act.

Another example of unwilling deviance is mental illness. You may not have thought of mental illness as deviance, but many kinds of mental illness involve behavior that violates social norms. The compulsive petty thief, the schizophrenic who cannot hold a job, and the paranoid who treats others as dangerous enemies are acting in ways considered threatening to the well-being of society. Yet no one sits down one day and decides to become compulsive, schizophrenic, or paranoid.

In sum, whether a particular behavior is defined as deviant depends upon who does the defining, and the deviant individual may or may not have chosen to violate the norms. Let's look more closely now at the kinds of deviance that are considered detrimental to the well-being of society.

Explorations

How Deviant Is Your Community?

How much, and what kind of, deviance is there in your community? While you can't answer these questions precisely, you can get some sense of the types of deviance that come to public attention. Divide the class into small groups and, for one week, have members read the local newspaper and write down every instance of deviance they find. If the resources are available, assign groups to different newspapers or other media sources. Record the kind of deviance, the sex, racial/ethnic background, and age (if given) of the deviant person or persons, and the general location (e.g., northwest part of the community) where the deviance occurred.

Have the groups tabulate and report on their findings. How many total acts of deviance and how many different kinds of deviance were found? Did someone or a few students report something as deviance that most did not? What were the most common kinds of deviance reported? What were the demographics—sex, age, and racial/ethnic background—of the deviant people? Is there a particular area of your community that seems to have higher rates of deviance? Do you have any explanation for your results?

If you do this as an individual project, use the same procedure and questions to explore deviance in your community.

How Much Deviance Is There? And Why Does It Matter?

Would you consider yourself a deviant? If you define deviance only in terms of the violation of norms considered essential to social well-being, would you say that you have ever engaged in a deviant act? One way to answer these questions is to ask whether you have ever done something that could be punished by law. Your answer is probably yes. Indeed, nearly all people violate some laws (Adler and Lambert 1993). Many things—e.g., littering, speeding, possessing small amounts of marijuana, and taking school or office supplies for personal use—could be punishable by fine or jail.

The answer to the question of how much deviance exists, therefore, is "an incredible amount." Yet not all of it is of equal concern to people. In a Gallup poll that asked Americans to rate nine issues from 0 (not serious) to 10 (extremely serious), 52 percent rated crime, 45 percent rated drug abuse, and 29 percent rated the health care system as extremely serious issues for the nation (Golay and Rollyson 1996). Among the nine issues, violent crime and drug abuse were most frequently named as extremely serious, followed by moral values, the federal deficit, the welfare system, the health care system, public education, the economy, and the job market.

Most people, then, would not think of the eighty-year-old woman who wore leotards and a blonde wig as troublesome, but they would regard criminals, drug addicts, and the mentally ill as disturbing elements of society. We will look at several types of deviance in American society and note briefly why they are considered troublesome.

Crime

While crime is technically any violation of the criminal law, there are a number of different types of crime, including some that may not be prosecuted under the criminal law (Lauer 1997). **Predatory crime** includes those acts that result in loss of property or some kind of physical harm. One of the more commonly used measures of crime rates—the F.B.I. Crime Index—includes eight predatory crimes: murder and non-negligent manslaughter, aggravated assault, forcible rape, robbery, burglary, larceny-theft, auto theft, and arson. Note that a distinction is made between robbery, burglary, and larceny-theft. Robbery involves the use of force or threat, burglary includes unlawful entry to commit a felony or theft, and larceny-theft refers to stealing where no force or threat is used.

A second type of crime is **illegal services**, the rendering of unlawful services such as drug dealing or prostitution to a customer. **Public disorder** crimes constitute a third type; they involve behavior such as disorderly conduct or public drunkenness that are offensive to an audience.

Fourth are **crimes of negligence**, in which there is an unintended victim or potential victim (reckless driving, e.g.). Fifth are **white-collar crimes**, those committed by respectable people in the course of their work (Sutherland and Cressey 1955). The businessman who keeps two sets of books in order to defraud the government of taxes, the executive who embezzles money, the judge who accepts a bribe in order to render a favorable decision, the physician who submits false Medicare claims, and the business that charges customers for services not rendered all exemplify white-collar crime.

Finally, we include juvenile delinquency as a type of crime. Much of the behavior that is officially defined as delinquency—including fighting, truancy from school, and running away from home—is quite different from what most people think of as crime. But delinquency also includes such crimes as drug use and sales, assault, and theft.

Considering all the various kinds of crime, how much crime is there? The question is not a simple one to answer because different methods of measuring crime exist. The F.B.I. index shows that every two seconds a predatory crime is committed in the United States, and a violent crime occurs every seventeen seconds (U.S. Federal Bureau of Investigation 1994). A rape occurs every five minutes and a murder every twenty-three minutes.

Apart from murder, however, the F.B.I. figures underestimate the amount of crime because they are based on crimes reported to the police and, for one reason or another, many crimes are never reported. A more accurate count of crime, then, comes from *survey research* that asks a representative sample of people whether they were a victim of a crime over the past year. When the victims were asked whether they reported the crime to the police, only a little over a third said that they had (Bastian 1995). Table 7.1 shows the victimization rates (per thousand persons aged twelve and over) for various kinds of crimes. Note that during the year a little over 5 percent of Americans were victims of a violent crime and nearly a third were victims of property crimes.

You might think that because only 5 percent of Americans are likely to be victims of a violent crime in a particular year, the concern about crime is out of proportion to the threat. Yet 5 percent in one year does not tell you how many are likely to be victimized over a lifetime. Actually, at the rates reported, nearly all Americans will be victims of some kind of crime, and more than eight out of ten will be victims of a violent crime during their lifetime (U.S. Department of Justice 1988).

Thus, the threat of being a victim of crime affects all of us. The threat can make walking down a dark street at night an uneasy experience. This threat is heightened by the growth of juvenile gangs in recent years. More than a thousand American cities now have a gang problem (Klein 1995). You have read, no doubt, more than one account of innocent bystanders being shot or murdered as a result of gang fighting.

Table 7.1	**Victimization Rates**	
	(Per 1,000 persons aged 12 and older)	
	Crimes of violence	51.5
	Rape	2.3
	Robbery	6.2
	Assault	43.0
	Property Crimes	322.4
	Household burglary	60.0
	Motor vehicle theft	13.0
	Theft	242.7

Source: Bastian 1995

The unsettling conclusion, then, is that you will face both the trauma of being a crime victim at some time in your life and the threat of being a victim. Victimization, or the potential for victimization, is an ever-present reality for Americans. Furthermore, the threat affects behavior. For instance, growing robbery rates were an important factor in the flight of whites from central cities (Liska and Bellair 1995).

Crime also adversely affects people economically. Estimates of losses due to white-collar crime alone range from $40 to $100 billion per year (Croft 1994). Victims of violent crimes lose additional billions each year because of things like property loss, medical expenses, and lost pay.

In the light of these facts, it is understandable that crime is a top concern of Americans. It's not pleasant to reflect upon the fact that anyone from your banker to a gang member whom you happen to meet by chance could make you a victim of crime.

EXTENSIONS

Victims of Sexual Assault in Australia

Crime exists in all nations, but not all nations have the same kind of crime problems. For one thing, crime rates vary. If you look at murder rates, for example, you find that the United States has one of the highest rates among industrial nations. When you look at other aspects of crime, you will find similarities as well as differences between nations.

Similarities are illustrated in a survey of Australian victims of sexual assault (Easteal 1994). The researcher put ads in newspapers, requesting victims to participate in the study. Two television programs, which dealt with the problem, also publicized the survey. As a result, 2,852 victims, 96.2 percent of them females, answered the questionnaire. ☞

☞ Results revealed that, as in the United States, the victim was more likely than not to know the perpetrator of sexual assault. For the Australians, only 20.8 percent of the perpetrators were strangers. One fourth were acquaintances, 8.2 percent were dates, 21.7 percent were husbands or estranged husbands, 13.5 percent were family members, and the rest were known in some other way to the victims. Also as in the United States, a substantial number of the victims (47 percent) sustained injuries as a result of the assault. Injuries were most likely when the attacker was a husband (66.5 percent) or a stranger (55.6 percent).

While nearly two-thirds of the victims told someone about the attack, only about a fifth informed the police. The most common reason for not informing the police was shame. As one victim of date rape explained: "I think I felt shame because apart from struggling, kicking and screaming there came a point where I realized the inevitability of the act and . . . let myself go limp" (Easteal 1994:338).

Telling someone about the assault did not always bring a sympathetic response. Victims who made contact with a rape crisis service found the most support, while those who informed the police found the least support. One woman, raped by her estranged husband, said the police told her it would be "devastating" for her to go to court and almost impossible to prove her case. The police were more helpful in those cases where the attacker was a stranger.

At one time, there was no such thing as wife rape in the United States. In 1977, however, Oregon eliminated the spouse-immunity clause from its rape statute, and a man was tried for wife rape the following year. Other states followed the example of Oregon and began to change their laws. In Australia, all of the states and territories recognized the crime of spousal rape in the 1980s and early 1990s. Even so, according to this survey, few cases of rape by spouses were reported or tried in court.

Drugs

Drugs rank a close second to crime in terms of what Americans define as serious national problems. What is the drug problem? That is, exactly what drugs come to your mind when you hear the phrase "drug problem"? Did you name alcohol and nicotine—the drugs which damage the health and lives of the greatest number of Americans?

Table 7.2 shows the proportion of people who are current users, at the time of the survey, of the more commonly used drugs. Note the strikingly higher proportions of those who use alcohol and cigarettes. Note also that more males than females are current users of these drugs. More whites than African Americans or Hispanics use alcohol and cigarettes, while more African Americans and Hispanics than whites use marijuana and cocaine.

Table 7.2	Proportion of People Who Are Current Users of Selected Drugs					
Drug	Total	Male	Female	White	Black	Hispanic
Alcohol	49.6	57.4	42.5	52.7	37.6	45.6
Cigarettes	24.2	26.2	22.3	24.7	23.4	21.2
Marijuana	4.3	6.0	2.8	4.2	5.6	4.7
Cocaine	0.6	0.9	0.4	0.5	1.3	1.1

Source: U.S. Bureau of the Census 1995, p. 143.

Drug use varies by age (U.S. Bureau of the Census 1995, p. 143). For example, current alcohol users vary from 18 percent of those 12 to 17 years old to 62.8 percent of those in the 26 to 34 age category. The highest proportion of cigarette and cocaine users falls in the 16 to 34 age group (30.1 percent), while marijuana and cocaine use is highest among those aged 18 to 25 years (11.1 and 1.5 percent, respectively).

Drug use also varies over time. In 1995, about 12.8 million Americans were current users of an illicit drug. This number was far below the peak year of 1979 when there were 25 million users (National Clearinghouse for Alcohol and Drug Information 1996a). In other words, the use of illicit drugs by the U.S. population, aged fifteen and above, dropped from over 14 percent in 1979 to a little over 6 percent in 1995. Incidentally, peak use of alcohol and tobacco also occurred in 1979.

The seemingly good news about declining rates of drug use must be balanced by the fact that drug use among teenagers rose each year in the early 1990s (National Clearinghouse for Alcohol and Drug Information 1996b). In its annual survey of drug use by junior and senior high school students, the National Parents' Resource Institute for Drug Education (PRIDE) found significant increases in the use of tobacco, marijuana, cocaine, and hallucinogens. By 1995, use of cigarettes was the highest ever recorded by PRIDE: 15.7 of junior high students and 31.3 percent of senior high students reported monthly use of cigarettes.

As in the case of crime, the consequences of drug use and abuse are both individual and social. People suffer both physical and psychological ill effects from drugs. For instance, alcohol abuse is involved in 40 to 50 percent of traffic deaths, in nearly two-thirds of fires and burns, and in about a fifth of suicides (National Institute on Alcohol Abuse and Alcoholism 1989). Alcoholics also may have difficulty with problem solving, abstract thinking, memory tasks, and physical coordination. In addition, almost a fourth of Americans say that alcohol has been a source of trouble in their family life (McAneny 1992).

Clearly, it is not only the addict or abuser who suffers, but acquaintances, friends, and family members as well. Strangers may also suffer when they become victims, such as the woman killed by a drunk driver or the man mugged and robbed by an addict who needed money to support his habit. Moreover, the economic consequences to the nation are considerable. Again, as with crime, there are the costs of policing, health care, rehabilitation, and lost productivity. These costs run into billions of dollars. It has been estimated that the costs of health problems from tobacco use alone are more than $50 billion each year (Cimons 1990).

The cover story in a popular magazine (*Nation's Business*, February 1997), focused on challenges faced by the United States. One section of the article dealt with crime and drugs as well as the challenge of reducing the "surging" use of drugs. It supported the urgency of the matter by pointing out that drug-related arrests had reached the new high of 1.14 million in 1995 and that drug use among 12- to 17-year-olds had doubled from 1991 to 1995. These same two "facts" were also emphasized during the 1996 presidential campaign.

As we noted earlier, drug use has risen in the 1990s. But we don't know whether the high number of arrests is due to increased usage or to better law enforcement. Moreover, alarmist articles always give us pause. We decided to check out "the facts." When we looked for evidence, we were puzzled by the claim of doubled use among adolescents. Government data, available from 1991 to 1994, show a substantial increase only in the proportion currently using marijuana (4.3 to 7.3 percent). And the 1994 figure of 7.3 percent was considerably below the 1979 figure of 16.7 percent. Moreover, there was actually a decline from 1991 to 1994 in rates for use of stimulants, alcohol, and cigarettes.

An annual study conducted by the University of Michigan Survey Research Center is another source of evidence. Rather than current use, the researchers ask about any use in the last twelve months and during the respondent's lifetime. They found that the proportion of eighth graders taking any illicit drug in the preceding twelve months *nearly* doubled from 1991 to 1995, and that rates also rose among tenth (20 to 33 percent) and twelfth graders (27 to 39 percent)(University of Michigan News and Information Services 1995). Marijuana use accounted for about half of all use in 1995. Again, we didn't find any evidence of a doubling—only a *near* doubling among eighth graders.

In sum, we believe there is cause for concern about adolescent drug usage. But exaggerating and misleading figures only produce skepticism about the need for concern.

Mental Illness

The term "mental illness" includes a broad range of problems from mental retardation to multiple personality disorder. As noted earlier, mental illness is deviant behavior because it involves people acting in ways that violate norms. An obsessive-compulsive man who brings his own cup to breakfast because he fears germs on the restaurant's cups is deviant. A schizophrenic woman who believes that she is immortal and walks fearlessly into heavy traffic is deviant. A paranoid man who is convinced that his co-workers are trying to have him fired and who believes he must take action against them to protect himself is deviant.

Clearly, some forms of mental illness are more threatening to social well-being than others. However, all are deviant because they involve a violation of norms. The difference between the mentally ill and other kinds of deviant behavior is that, as we noted earlier, people do not consciously or willingly decide to become mentally ill.

How many Americans struggle with this kind of deviance? The most comprehensive information comes from structured psychiatric interviews with a national probability sample of 8,098 Americans between the ages of fifteen and fifty-four (Kessler et al. 1994). Among the findings and conclusions of the research are:

- Nearly half of the respondents reported having at least one lifetime disorder and nearly 30 percent reported a disorder in the previous twelve months;

- At any given point in time, 3 to 5 percent of Americans are in serious need of psychiatric help;

- The most common disorders are severe depression, alcohol abuse, and phobias.

- Fourteen percent of the population accounted for more than half of all lifetime disorders (i.e., the people with three or more disorders in a lifetime).

Not everyone is equally likely to become mentally ill, however. The research found that women have more disorders involving anxiety and emotions (particularly depression), while men have more problems with substance abuse and the antisocial personality disorder (a disorder in which the individual seems to have no conscience and acts in ways designed only to please himself regardless of the cost to others). Twice as many women as men struggle with depression, with the highest rates found among African American women in the 35 to 44 age category (Blazer et al. 1994). Rates of disorders are also higher in younger age groups and in lower social class levels.

Overall, then, you stand a one in two chance of becoming mentally ill at some time in your life (but keep in mind that this includes all kinds of mental illness, not just the more severe forms). To put it another way, the chances that mental illness—whether your own or that of someone with whom you associate—will affect your life at some point are fairly high.

How does mental illness affect people? Those who are afflicted with it, of course, endure considerable stress and suffering. If you ever have the occasion to visit a locked psychiatric ward in a hospital, you will understand more clearly how much the patients suffer and how deprived they are of the essentials of a satisfying life.

As with criminals and drug abusers, the mentally ill bring trauma into the lives of others—family members and friends and co-workers. In addition, the economic costs run into the billions of dollars. Thus, the fact that an individual may be an unwilling victim of mental illness does not alter the detrimental effects of this kind of deviance to social well-being.

Becoming Deviant: Why?

You would probably answer the question of why someone becomes deviant very differently depending on whether you were addressing crime, drug abuse, or mental illness. It's not surprising, then, that considerably different explanations of deviance have been developed, each of which seems to apply more appropriately to some kinds of deviance than to others.

Before looking at the various explanations, we want to underscore the point that we regard none of them as exhaustive. That is, none of the explanations can explain all kinds of deviance and none can totally explain any single kind of deviance. Deviant behavior has multiple causes at various levels of the social structure (Lauer 1997).

For example, we shall look at labeling as an explanation of mental illness. A convincing case can be made for the usefulness of this approach. But such things as roles, family experiences, the economy, and social class are also causal factors in mental illness. The traditional role of women is a factor in proneness to depression. Childrens' mental health is closely related to the quality of their relationships with parents. A rise in unemployment is accompanied by an increase in rates of mental illness, including suicide. And deprivation in the lower classes is associated with higher rates of mental illness. Therefore, we present the following explanations as useful but not as exhaustive.

Deviance as Built In

In accord with the emphasis on the interrelatedness of all parts of a system, *structural functionalism* approaches deviance as that which is built into the system and necessary to, or at least inevitable in, the system. Durkheim's theory of crime and Merton's theory of deviance illustrate this approach to deviance.

Durkheim's Theory of Crime

Durkheim argued that deviance—in particular, crime—is both normal and necessary. It is normal because every known society has crime. In fact, "the fundamental conditions of social organization . . . logically imply it" (Durkheim 1951, p. 362). One of those "fundamental conditions" is the fact that, while crime offends community standards, the absence of crime would mean that every member of the society shared exactly the same standards. This is impossible. Consequently, crime is normal.

Crime not only exists in all societies, but also performs important social functions. Therefore, it is necessary as well as normal. Durkheim explained one function this way. If everyone in a society agreed on everything, there could be no progress. Crime offends people, but it also forces them to consider alternative social arrangements and prepares the way for changes (Durkheim 1938; orig. 1893). Thus, what is criminal in one generation may become the norm in a later generation. For example, the Greek philosopher, Socrates, was a criminal, but his criminality was actually the new morality and faith of the future—namely, the right of people to independent thought.

Durkheim did not argue that every crime, nor that every kind of crime, serves a useful purpose. Obviously, Socrates' insistence on independent thought is quite different from a serial killer's random murders. The point is not that every crime has a useful social purpose, but that crime as a type of human behavior has such a purpose.

Another function of crime is to clearly mark social values and put boundaries on acceptable behavior. The kind of boundary established defines the nature of crime. For example, in some societies the boundaries are religious, and crime takes the form of religious aberrations. The Amish, a Protestant sect, regard behavior such as driving an automobile or using electricity in the home as a violation of religious beliefs (Kephart 1991). They may punish violators by isolating them. The violations help sharpen the community values and set boundaries for behavior by defining what members can not do. In addition, the punishment reinforces those values and boundaries by showing that there is a price to be paid for deviant behavior.

Thus, crime helps a community or society to clarify its values. When the community or society responds to crime with sanctions, it is asserting its moral primacy over the individual and building solidarity among its members. Consequently, crime is useful.

Merton's Theory of Anomie

A variation of Durkheim's approach is the **anomie** theory of Robert Merton. Anomie is a condition in which norms are weak, inconsistent, or lacking. Durkheim introduced the term, and Merton applied it to the study of deviance. In an early formulation, Merton (1939) argued that rule breaking is normal for at least some segments of any society. All societies have cultural goals and a limited number of legitimate means for reaching those goals. This means that there are individuals or groups in these societies who are blocked from using the legitimate means for reaching the cultural goals. Merton called this situation "anomie," a contradiction between socially approved goals and the socially approved means available to some people to reach those goals.

For instance, financial success is a socially approved goal in the United States. Yet some Americans (such as many of those born in impoverished circumstances) are blocked from socially approved means (such as education and hard work) to reach this goal. Those who are blocked may opt for various alternatives.

Merton (1957) defined five different responses to the challenge of socially approved goals and means. Conformists are those who succeed by accepting as legitimate and desirable both the socially approved goals and the socially approved means for reaching the goals. Ritualists accept the means but do not strive to reach the goals for themselves; however, they may urge their children to achieve what they have failed to achieve. Retreatists reject both the goals and the means and may resort to deviant behavior such as alcoholism or mental illness.

Innovators accept the goals, but not the means. They may try to succeed through crime. The fifth type of response, rebellion, involves not merely a rejection of socially approved goals and means but the substitution of alternatives. The rebel becomes a political radical and presses for changes in what he or she defines as a destructive social system.

Merton did not argue that these five types of response explain all deviant behavior. In fact, he specifically denied that all crime is the result of an innovative response in which deviant means are used to pursue a socially approved goal. However, he insisted that a good deal of deviance can be understood in terms of people's responses to the challenge of using approved means to reach approved goals. This is an easier challenge for some segments of society than others and is impossible for at least a portion of the society.

Some students react negatively to the "impossible" in the last sentence. They accept the ideology that anyone in the United States can, by persevering effort, better his or her situation in life. Here are two examples that illustrate what we mean by impossible. The first is Evelyn, a young African American woman who grew up in an impoverished and unloving family. She dropped out of school in the eighth grade to search for work to help support herself and her parents. As a result of her hunger for the love she never received from her parents, Evelyn got pregnant by a man who then abandoned her. Now, at age twenty-three, she supports her child by working for minimum pay—less than the monthly welfare payments for which she is eligible. Unfortunately, this is the only kind of work she can find because of her limited education. What are her chances, by her own efforts and without outside help, of bettering her lot in life?

The second illustration is Sam, a forty-year-old white man who grew up in a middle-class family. He received an A.A. degree in a paralegal program from a local community college. He married and had three children. His wife, however, left the family to "find" herself, and her whereabouts are unknown. Both of Sam's parents are dead, and he has no siblings. A shortage of positions in law firms in his city has left Sam without work as a paralegal. He, like Evelyn, can only find work at minimum wage, and this doesn't begin to support his family at the level they once had. What are his chances, by his own efforts and without outside help, of bettering his lot in life?

In both cases, we would argue that the chances are close to nil. As we shall discuss further in the next chapter, millions of impoverished Americans are working hard. They are exerting great effort. But they remain in poverty. Millions more live at levels below what they consider to be a decent standard of living. These people face the challenge of goals and means that Merton identified. In a society that puts a high value on material success, at least some of them will resort to deviant behavior in an effort to cope with the challenge.

If Merton's analysis is correct, you would expect higher rates of deviance in the lower strata where deprivation is most severe and the chances of improving one's lot are least likely. Thus, it's not surprising that considerable research indicates higher deviance rates among the more impoverished segments of the population (Hagan and Peterson 1995).

For example, McNamara (1995) used *participant observation* to study young, male prostitutes in the Times Square area of New York City. After gaining the confidence of the young men, who were mostly teenagers, he was able to observe the way they solicited business. He also interviewed a number of them. Among other things, he found that the young men, most of whom identified themselves as heterosexual, plied their trade in order to survive. Without homes, families, or jobs, prostitution meant the difference between going hungry or eating and between doing nothing or seeing a movie. In Merton's terms, these young men were innovators; they had the same goals as other Americans but saw deviance as the only means available to them to reach those goals.

Deviance as Conformity

You may think of conformity in terms of behaving in a conventional, socially acceptable manner. However, recall the incident of the adolescent in juvenile court, discussed at the beginning of the chapter. From the perspective of the young man, his behavior was an attempt to conform to his group's norms. In other words, deviance may indicate a lack of conformity or it may represent conformity, depending upon the reference group involved.

Edwin Sutherland, who produced the notion of white-collar crime, also developed **differential association** theory to explain crime and delinquency. Sutherland (1939) defined differential association as exposure to more favorable than unfavorable definitions of illegal behavior. People learn to be criminals as they interact with primary relationships. Everyone is exposed to differing ideas of right and wrong behavior, and people accept that behavior which is most commonly defined as acceptable in their primary groups. The delinquent or criminal, like everyone else, is conforming to the norms of his or her reference group.

Again, considerable research supports the validity of this perspective. For example, a study of 2,213 males in 87 high schools concluded that interpersonal violence is more likely in those schools where a substantial minority of the students value such behavior (Felson et al. 1994). Another study looked at the drinking habits of 153 pregnant women (Testa 1995). Those who continued to drink heavily after learning they were pregnant did so because their peers approved of drinking during pregnancy and typically served alcohol at social gatherings. Finally, a national sample of youths reported that delinquency among both boys and girls involves the consideration of, and conformity to, the perspectives of significant others (Heimer 1996).

While much of the work on deviance as conformity has looked at the behavior of adolescents, you can also understand some adult deviance as conformity to group norms. The pregnant women noted above provide an example of adults yielding to peer pressure. Other examples are furnished by corporate executives who agree to fix prices at higher levels than competitive prices to maximize profits and drug-abusing workers who report that their families and friends are also abusers (Lehman et al. 1995).

Deviance as a Labeling Process

Labeling theory comes out of *symbolic interactionism*. According to labeling theory, people become deviant as they are defined and treated as deviants. To understand, therefore, why an individual becomes deviant you must see the process by which other people attach a deviant label to that individual, a process that includes the acceptance of the label by the individual.

The labeling process usually begins with the individual violating some norm. At this point, the individual is engaging in **primary deviance**—deviant behavior by someone who still defines himself or herself as conforming rather than deviant (Lemert 1951). Consider, for instance, the young male prostitutes whom we discussed above. We pointed out that the majority of them define themselves as heterosexual even though their services are homosexual. They accept the necessity of engaging in deviant acts in order to survive, but they do not define themselves as homosexuals.

Some of the young men, on the other hand, do define themselves as gay. Imagine them talking to one of the heterosexuals, telling him that he really is gay—just as they are—because otherwise he would not be offering his services to men. If he ultimately accepts their label, he will enter the stage of **secondary deviance** and define himself the way others have labeled him (Lemert 1951). In other words, he will think of himself as a homosexual rather than as a heterosexual who engages in homosexual acts in order to obtain needed money.

A crucial part of the process, then, is the reaction of significant others to the deviant acts. If they define the acts as aberrant behavior of a conforming individual, the behavior may not go beyond the stage of primary deviance. If they define the acts as the expected behavior of a deviant individual, the label may be incorporated into the individual's self-concept and the individual will enter the stage of secondary deviance.

Thomas Scheff (1966) used labeling theory to explain mental illness (though he cautioned that his analysis does not explain all mental illness and supplements rather than replaces psychiatric explanations). Scheff argued that people who are labeled as mentally ill are likely to have broken the norms that govern common decency and the view of reality that prevails in the group. For example, a person who regularly spits on the floor in restaurants is violating a norm of common decency, and a person who insists that he or she regularly talks with aliens is violating most people's view of reality. The violators could be defined as mentally ill.

Scheff acknowledged that there are different reasons why people break rules. However, their motivations are irrelevant in the labeling process. The only question is whether other people notice the rule-breaking and, if so, whether they decide that it is a sign of mental illness. People could conclude that the person who spits on restaurant floors is crude rather than mentally ill and that the person who regularly converses with aliens is simply harmlessly eccentric.

Whether or not a particular violation of the rules is defined as mental illness depends upon the image of mental illness the observers learned in childhood and still retain. That is, every individual has an idea of how both mentally ill people and normal people behave. When someone behaves in accord with your image of a mentally ill person or violates the rules you believe are followed by normal people, you may label that person as mentally ill.

Once someone is labeled as mentally ill, others relate to him or her accordingly. You may be more cautious, more guarded, more worried, or more nervous when you deal with someone you regard as mentally ill. Your response reinforces the label and can lead the individual more readily to accept the designation and thereby move into secondary deviance.

Labeling theory underscores the power of significant others to affect an individual's self-concept and behavior. The significant others apply the label in the first place. They then reinforce it by the way they relate to the labeled person. They can further strengthen the label and facilitate the individual's commitment to the deviant identity by sanctions (Ulmer 1994). For example, an ex-convict carries the label of "criminal." Ex-convicts face sanctions when employers refuse to give them legitimate employment and can be forced back into crime in order to survive. Or consider the case of a woman who is severely depressed, unable to function in her varied roles, and eventually hospitalized for treatment. After her release, her family is afraid to let her fully assume her former responsibilities. They reprimand her when she tries to do more than they feel she is capable of doing, thereby pushing her back into the role of a mentally ill person.

Experiences

'When She Told Me I was Crazy, I Believed Her'

You can not predict with certainty whether an individual who acts in a deviant way, is labeled, and enters into **secondary deviance** would have stopped short of the latter stage if the labeling had not taken place. But, as the experience of Vicki, a thirty-year-old bank clerk, illustrates, the labeling can facilitate the process. Vicki was nineteen when she was hospitalized with clinical depression. She recalls some incidents that led up to her entering the hospital as well as the nature of her struggle with the illness:

Do you know what it's like to be mentally ill? It is hell. Literally, it is hell on earth. As I look back on the days when I was at my worst, it was as though I'd take a step and find no ground beneath my feet. My words were like an uncontrolled mass of foreign objects coming out of my mouth. I was not living. I was groveling and crying, and searching for someone who would show me the most basic kind of caring.

I've always been prone to depression. Before this dreadful episode, I had always managed to survive and live in a reasonably normal way. But my mother and father had divorced some years earlier. I think that as my mother's frustration with her marriage intensified, she became increasingly unable to handle my bouts of depression. I guess I was just one more source of pain in her life.

One day when I was slumped in a chair and feeling as though something was sucking the life out me, she suddenly shouted at me. She screamed that I should get off my rear end and do something with my life and that she couldn't cope any longer with a mentally ill daughter. She practically screeched as she told me I was crazy and had to get help.

That was the first time that she had ever called me mentally ill or crazy. I hadn't really thought about my troubles in those terms. I knew that I got more depressed than other people, but I never thought about it as being crazy. At first, I shrugged it off as her problem rather than mine. But I remember vividly the day when she once again told me I was crazy, and I believed her. And that quickly led me into a tailspin and the worst depression I've ever had—before or since.

Eventually, a psychiatrist put me in the hospital—a true stretch in hell. Now I had hell within me and hell around me. I saw patients stripped naked by staff and strapped to their beds. I saw people defecate on the floor or in their clothes. I saw people violently attack others while hallucinating. I sometimes think that if the treatments hadn't made me better, the sheer terror of that place would have either forced me out of the depression or led me to kill myself.

I can still feel it in the pit of my stomach when I talk about the experience. I don't blame my mother. Maybe I would have been hospitalized eventually in any case. Still, I never thought of myself as mentally ill until she said I was. And the day I finally believed her was the day my plunge into depression got out of control.

In other words, whether the sanctions arise from fear, a desire to punish, or a desire to help, they can reinforce a deviant identity. Labeling cannot explain all deviant behavior, but it seems clear that labels are powerful social forces that can both lead to, and keep someone in, secondary deviance.

Deviance as a Power Struggle

From the perspective of *conflict theory*, deviance is another manifestation of the struggle between groups with contrary interests. The groups may be those represented by different races or sexes or social classes. In any case, the point is that those in the society with the most power are also those who define what is deviant and what is not. They are most likely, of course, to define the things they typically do as non-deviant and the things that those in other groups do, particularly those things they find threatening in some way, as deviant.

Those in the upper social classes clearly have more power than those in the lower classes. They hold positions of influence and authority in government and in the business world. They use their social clout to influence such things as the definition of crime. Thus, employee theft is treated as a crime but misleading advertising and exploitation of naive consumers are not. Ironically, Americans probably suffer greater losses to their health and their pocketbooks every year from the actions of corporations—everything from fraud to environmental pollution—than they do from street criminals (Lauer 1997).

What is the difference between a man who robs a bank of $10,000 and a corporation that robs people of millions of dollars by overcharging them for a product? The difference is that the bank robber can be prosecuted under the criminal law, charged as a felon, and sentenced to prison. The corporate executives, on the other hand, may only be reprimanded and/or fined by a federal agency and ordered to change their practices.

An interesting example of deviance as a power struggle is the legislation passed by Congress after concern developed over the use of crack cocaine, a crystallized form of powdered cocaine that appeared in the 1980s (Tonry 1995). Crack cocaine became the drug of choice for minorities because it was cheaper than powdered cocaine, which was preferred by white dealers and users.

Although many drug experts believe that the two forms of cocaine are equally potent, members of Congress were convinced that crack was worse than powder. They debated how much more serious the penalty should be for using crack than for using powdered cocaine. Concern intensified when a popular University of Maryland basketball star died of an overdose. Initially, reports said it was from crack. A year later, it turned out he had used the powder. At any rate, Congress passed legislation that mandated the same sentence for possession or sale of one ounce of crack as for 100 ounces of powdered cocaine. Whatever the intent of the legislation may have been, the result was a law that disproportionately punishes poor African Americans who use crack and made the penalties harsher for them than for the white suburbanites who use the powdered cocaine.

As a final example of crime as power struggle, *feminist theorists* point out that men have more power than women. Rape is primarily an act of violence, an expression of rage against women and, at the same time, a way of maintaining domination (Lauer 1997). Thus, although it was an act of deviance, before Emancipation it was not a crime to rape a black slave in this country. As noted earlier, there was no such offense as wife rape until 1977 when Oregon removed the spouse-immunity clause from its rape statute.

Deviance as Opportunity

In his later work, Sutherland noted that even if individuals are exposed mainly to definitions that favor illegal behavior, they may not become criminals unless they have the opportunities for criminal behavior. In essence, opportunity means that the potential offender is in the right place for a crime and unlikely to encounter law enforcement officials or others who could prevent the criminal activity.

A study of crime in Minneapolis illustrates the usefulness of this approach (Sherman, Gartin, and Buerger 1989). The researchers looked at crime patterns for a year and found a limited number of "hot spots"— areas in which a large proportion of the city's crimes occurred during the year. In all, nearly 324,000 calls came to the police from 110,000 locations. But 3 percent of the locations accounted for half of the calls! Looking at specific crimes, the researchers found that half of the robberies occurred at 2.2 percent, half of the rapes at 1.2 percent, and half of the thefts at 2.7 percent, of the locations. Obviously, some locations presented far greater opportunities for crime than others. These more active locations had a larger number of criminals living nearby and a greater number of potential targets (such as stores and banks).

Another study used a national sample of more than 1,700 youths age 18 to 26 to examine how the lack of authority figures can contribute to deviance (Osgood et al. 1996). The researchers found that the more the youths socialized with each other in unstructured activities that lacked authority figures—e.g., riding around in a car for fun, getting together with friends informally, and going to parties—the greater the amount of criminal behavior, heavy alcohol use, illicit drug use, and dangerous driving they engaged in. The point is, unstructured activities provided the youths with more opportunities for deviant behavior, and many of them made use of those opportunities.

The opportunity for deviance is affected by many factors, including government and business action, and technological advances. Periodically, local governments go on a crusade against prostitution and, for a time, reduce the prostitute's opportunities in a particular location. Anti-drug programs by governments and schools can make the purchase of illicit drugs more difficult. Petty deviance, such as employees stealing paper and pens from the workplace, can be minimized by accounting systems that keep records of all materials distributed.

Changing technology can both increase and decrease opportunities for deviance. Cameras in stores can reduce the amount of theft. Electronic marking of books cuts down on the number of volumes stolen from libraries and book stores. However, technology also opens up new opportunities. Computer technology, for example, offers new chances for pursuing sexual deviance (Durkin 1995). By using on-line bulletin boards that focus on particular kinds of sexual behavior, an individual can communicate with others around the world who share similar interests. Indeed, an individual who would hesitate to be seen going into a pornographic shop to purchase items may have no hesitation in going on-line to view and purchase those materials.

Evaluation

So which explanation is correct? We hear this question from students after we review the various explanations given above. The answer is: all are correct and all are incorrect. That is, each of them has something valid to say that can add to your understanding. Yet none of them explains all types of deviance, and none provides a completely sufficient explanation for any type of deviance. Let's start with the ways that each explanation fails to aid understanding.

First, consider the position of those who maintain that deviance is built into the system. The assertion that deviance is necessary because it serves useful social functions is of little comfort to victims and certainly doesn't apply to all types of deviance. It isn't necessary, for example, to have murders in a society in order to teach people the value of human life. Furthermore, in the case of Merton's theory even his explanation requires explanation. That is, among those who do not succeed in achieving approved goals by approved means, why do some people choose innovation while others opt for ritual, retreat, or rebellion?

Deviance as conformity also fails as a complete explanation. For one thing, it does not explain many types of deviance like mental illness or more individualistic forms like rape and the sale, or use, of child pornography. For another thing, it does not help us understand why some people conform and others do not even though they are subject to the same proportion of definitions that favor deviant behavior.

Deviance as labeling can help explain most kinds of deviance once the behavior begins. Yet it does not explain why the individual behaved in a deviant way in the first place. And certainly there are people who are labeled deviant because they have already become deviants; the label no doubt helps maintain the deviance, but it does not create it. And what of those people who resist the label? How can we explain, for instance, the child who is labeled as retarded, but who thwarts the process by becoming a high achiever?

If deviance is nothing more than a power struggle, we would have a hard time explaining laws that punish white-collar criminals. If the most powerful people in society are able to wholly define what is moral and immoral or legal and illegal, President Nixon and Vice-President Agnew would never have had to resign their offices. Moreover, deviance as a power struggle is not helpful in understanding something like mental illness.

Finally, deviance as an opportunity also fails to be useful in understanding such forms of deviance as mental illness. And it does not help us understand why some people make use of the opportunities while others do not.

Having laid bare their shortcomings, we want to reiterate the point that the explanations are useful. Each contributes to an understanding of particular kinds of deviance and, in some forms of deviance, they may all make a contribution. Consider a fictional young man who is a composite figure of criminals coming from a ghetto area. He was born into an impoverished family, joined a gang in early adolescence, and became wealthy by controlling drug sales in his neighborhood.

What do the various explanations have to offer in this case? First, the young man's deviant behavior was built into his social structure in that he accepted the American goal of financial success but was blocked from this goal by the circumstances of his birth. He chose to be an innovator, getting into drug sales in order to make the money he couldn't possibly earn in any legitimate job open to him.

However, he reached that point by first becoming a gang member and conforming to the behavior expected of all the members. In addition, early on he ran into trouble with the juvenile authorities and was labeled a delinquent. Local officials knew him by sight and viewed him with suspicion. He also accepted their label of him as a nonconformist. As far as he was concerned, the drug sales were no more contrary to public morals than were the bribes accepted by the policemen who patrolled the neighborhood. Besides, many of his sales were to successful white professionals, who made their purchases on their way from the office to their suburban homes.

He, of course, didn't use the term "power struggle" when he thought of the police or the white professionals. Yet he was aware of the fact that they made the rules and viewed him with contempt. He also could see little difference between what he did and what they did except that he was more likely to be punished by the law than they were.

Finally, he was able to maintain his business because he lived in an area that gave him the opportunities. He was around other young men who came from impoverished backgrounds and were eager to work with him. His base of operation was a neighborhood through which white customers traveled on their return home from the office. In addition, he was sufficiently knowledgeable about the activities and routines of police to avoid getting caught. As you can see, then, each of the explanations contributes to an understanding of the young man's criminal career.

Controlling Deviance

Because deviance is often defined as threatening to society, efforts will be made to control it. People's explanation of the deviance determines the method of control. For example, if you view alcoholism as a disease, you probably will recommend therapy. If you see it as a sin, you might urge repentance. If you view it as conformity to the alcoholic's group, you might try to change the pattern of association. If you see it as a result of labeling, you might apply new labels and change the way that people relate to the alcoholic. If you define it as a crime, you will support some form of punishment such as a fine or jail term.

In other words, the way people explain deviance is crucial in how they decide to control it. We will examine various ideas about how to exercise control, beginning with the idea that without adequate control nearly everyone would be deviant.

Control as a Social Bond

Merton's anomie theory is based on the assumption that people tend to be conformists, and only when conformity doesn't work for them will they use other means to achieve their goals. In contrast, Travis Hirschi (1969) began with the assumption that people tend to be nonconformists, and only when social controls are sufficiently strong will they conform. According to Hirschi, what needs to be explained is not why people are deviant but why they conform. They conform, he argued, when they are bonded to the society.

Social bonding depends on four things. One is commitment. If you are to be a part of the social bond, you must commit yourself to groups and activities that follow conventional ways. This commitment is based on a rational assessment of the costs and benefits of conforming or of deviating. The second is attachment—an emotional tie to conventional groups and activities. If commitment leads you to say, "It wouldn't pay to risk the deviant way," attachment leads you to say, "I couldn't do that to my parents." Commitment is your rational investment and attachment is your emotional investment in conformity. Because an intimate relationship involves both commitment and attachment, it is not surprising that an examination of the criminal pursuits of more than 600 serious male offenders found that the men were less likely to commit crimes when living with a wife (Horney, Osgood, and Marshall 1995).

A third factor in social bonding is involvement. The more time you spend interacting with conforming people the less likely you are to opt for deviance. The fourth factor is belief in the morality of conforming behavior. If you believe, for example, that laws against the use of marijuana are morally correct, you will most likely to obey them; but if you believe those laws are a violation of your right to engage in something that gives you pleasure, you may opt for deviance.

We don't agree that virtually everyone would engage in deviant behavior without adequate social controls. Yet Hirschi's idea of social bonding makes intuitive sense. Moreover, it has helped to explain the amount of certain kinds of crime and delinquency in society (Rosenbaum 1987; Sampson and Laub 1990). Those who engage in such activities as pimping, selling drugs, and stealing automobiles are likely to have weak social ties. The four elements of social bonding do not, however, appear to control such deviance as embezzlement or fraudulent advertising or other forms of white-collar crime (McCaghy and Capron 1994).

Control as Political

If the control of deviance requires social bonding, then families, religious groups, and schools have a heavy responsibility to help people develop the necessary beliefs, commitment, attachment, and involvement. In fact, we would argue that developing these inner qualities is the most effective method of control. In essence, it means that social control has become self control. The individual conforms not because of external threat but because of internal desire.

However, to the extent that families, religious groups, and schools fall short and to the extent that additional factors are involved in people becoming deviants, other institutions will have a part in social control. Because deviance is a violation of social order and the government is the institution for maintaining that order, the government plays a major role in deviance control. In particular, the criminal justice system—the criminal code, the police, the courts, and the jails and prisons—is set up to deal with deviant behavior.

The way the system actually deals with deviance is complex. In a typical situation, when a victim reports a crime to the police, the first step is to identify and apprehend the suspect. Once the police make an arrest, the prosecutor decides whether formal charges are to be made. If charged, the accused appears before a judge and is informed of the charges. The judge decides whether there is sufficient evidence to detain the accused. For minor offenses, the judge can render a decision at that point. For more serious offenses, the process continues.

The next step may be a preliminary hearing to determine whether there is probable cause to believe that the accused committed a crime that falls within the jurisdiction of the court. If the judge finds probable cause, the case can be turned over to the grand jury, which will hear evidence and decide whether a trial is justified. If so, the grand jury issues an indictment, and the accused is scheduled for arraignment where he or she will enter a plea to the charges.

At this point, the accused may decide to plead guilty in order to take advantage of plea bargaining. Plea bargaining allows way for the offender to get a lighter sentence without totally escaping penalty for the crime. The advantage of a plea bargain for society is that it saves the time and expense of a trial. If the accused pleads not guilty, however, the case will go to trial. It may be a trial by jury or one decided by a judge. If the trial results in a conviction, an appeal can be made to a higher court. If appeals are rejected, the accused must submit to the sentence imposed by the judge or jury.

Clearly, there are many points along the way where an accused can escape the process. One government study reported that, of 100 typical cases of arrests for felonies, twenty are rejected at the initial screening, and thirty more are dismissed by the prosecutor or court. Of the remainder, 45 enter guilty pleas and five go to trial; 49 of them are convicted of either a felony or misdemeanor, and 29 offenders go to jail or prison (U.S. Department of Justice 1983).

These facts lead many Americans to believe that the criminal justice system is too soft on criminals, but this view needs to be balanced by three considerations. First, the United States has a higher proportion of its population in jails and prisons than any other nation in the world. From 1970 to 1993, the American population increased 26 percent, but the prison population increased 3,633 percent (U.S. Bureau of the Census 1995)!

Second, getting "tough" on crime may bring about laws and practices that violate personal freedoms. Should the government wiretap all telephones in order to catch more criminals? Should freedom of speech be curtailed in order to ban the printing of materials that some people regard as offensive? Clearly, you are confronted with a dilemma. Perhaps nothing illustrates the dilemma better than abortion. If you favor a woman's right to decide whether or not to have an abortion, you must recognize that there are millions of Americans for whom "getting tough on crime" includes making abortion a criminal offense. If you are against abortion, you must recognize that there are millions of Americans for whom "getting tough on crime" includes making any efforts to obstruct abortions a criminal offense.

Finally, those who advocate a "get tough" policy need to recognize the extent to which crime is supported by respectable citizens. It is, for example, only in recent years that the customers as well as the prostitutes themselves have been subject to arrest. Prostitution is a crime, but it could hardly survive without the large numbers of respectable citizens who support it.

Similarly, a considerable number of the purchasers of illicit drugs are respectable citizens with good incomes. In fact, illicit drugs are big business worldwide, generating more revenue than the gross national products of three-fourths of the world's national economies (Stares 1996). The drug trade is one of the largest commercial activities in the world. Furthermore, there is little incentive for impoverished nations like Peru and Myanmar to stop growing coca leaf or opium poppies when doing so would only impoverish them further.

The point is, for some Americans getting tough on crime means getting tough on the supply side—cracking down on people like prostitutes and drug dealers. However, the supply side goes beyond the individual prostitute or drug dealer, and, in the case of drugs, becomes an international issue. And as long as substantial numbers of respectable citizens maintain a demand, the supply will never be fully stopped.

In sum, the political control of deviance is necessary but also poses some dilemmas and complex challenges. Durkheim and others were right when they asserted that there are no human societies without deviance. The most people can hope for from government, then, is to keep socially harmful deviance at a minimum.

Control as Medical

If a person is caught stealing in some Islamic nations today, the thief's hand can be cut off. The same practice occurred in England in the not-too-distant past. The practice may have kept theft rates down, but it never totally eliminated the deviant behavior. As noted in the last section, punishment by the authorities is limited in what it can accomplish.

Punishment, along with the social bonding generated by families, religious groups, and schools, has been the most common method of social control. In the twentieth century, however, a new approach developed: the medicalization of deviance. In the medical model, the deviant is no longer viewed as someone who is morally or legally guilty, but someone who is "sick."

The medical model leads to very different efforts to control deviance. Instead of putting drug addicts into jail, it prescribes sending them to a detoxification center and then to therapy. Instead of imposing capital punishment on a man who assassinates a political leader, it puts him into a hospital for the criminally insane. Instead of imprisoning a mother who abuses her child, it requires her to go to a psychiatrist.

The medical model implies that deviants are not fully responsible for their behavior. The deviants are incapable of controlling the behavior or unaware of what they are doing. Clearly, according to the model, it does no good to punish such a person.

The medical and criminal models clashed in the 1980s when John Hinckley attempted to assassinate President Reagan. Hinckley was found not guilty by reason of insanity. Shortly thereafter, a number of states passed legislation to allow an offender to be declared guilty but mentally ill. Those convicted under such a law are treated at a mental hospital but still face a prison term and/or fines when released.

As with the varied explanations of becoming deviant, we regard each of the diverse methods of control as valid. Deviance will be minimized to the extent that the social bond remains strong, the criminal justice system is thorough, and medical intervention helps some people alter their behavior.

Critical Thinking Exercise

A researcher studied 755 Canadian boys from low socioeconomic backgrounds over a seven-year period to see if "individual characteristics" or peer influences were linked to drug abuse (Dobkin 1995). She concluded that individual characteristics (fighting, hyperactivity, oppositional behavior) more than peer influence led to drug abuse before the age of fourteen. What questions does this brief description raise? What additional information do you need in order to evaluate the conclusion? What other factors might be at work that could explain both the individual characteristics and the drug abuse?

Summary

Deviance is behavior that violates social norms. The norms violated may be those of a particular group rather than the society generally. They may be folkways rather than mores. Or they may be mores which are held generally in the society. In the latter case, the violator is likely to be defined as immoral, criminal, perverse, or sick. Norm violations are deviant even if the individual breaks the norm unknowingly or unwillingly.

There is a great deal of deviance in any society, but some is considered more serious than others. Substantial numbers of American regard three kinds of deviance—crime, drug addiction, and mental illness—as troublesome in the society.

Many different types of crime exist, including predatory crime, illegal services, public disorder crimes, crimes of negligence, white-collar crimes, and juvenile delinquency. At current crime rates, virtually every

American will be a victim at some time during his or her lifetime, and eight of ten will be victims of a violent crime. The threat of being a victim generates fear in people, and this fear affects such behavior as where people are willing to go or to live. The economic costs of crime run into the billions of dollars.

The most commonly abused drugs in America are alcohol and tobacco, followed by marijuana and cocaine. Drug use varies by age and over time. The peak year for drug use in the United States was 1979, when a little over 14 percent of the population admitted to using an illicit drug. Physical, psychological, and interpersonal problems result from drug use and abuse. The economic costs reach billions of dollars per year.

Because it involves a violation of norms, mental illness is a form of deviance. About half of Americans have a mental disorder of some kind during their lifetimes. The kind of mental illness people are most likely to have varies by gender and race.

A number of explanations help us understand why people become deviant. Deviance can be viewed as built in; it is a form of behavior that actually has useful social functions such as clarifying social values. In Merton's approach, deviance is the outcome of people being blocked from using socially approved means to gain socially approved goals.

Looked at from the point of view of interaction patterns, deviance can be seen as conformity to group norms. Deviance can also be explained in terms of a labeling process. The label pushes the individual from primary into secondary deviance. Once there, the label is a powerful social force that tends to maintain the secondary deviance. Labeling theory can be used to explain mental illness.

Viewed as a power struggle, deviance is that behavior which is defined as abnormal or unacceptable by those with the most power. Finally, deviance as opportunity underscores the importance of a potential offender being in the right place at the right time.

All societies attempt to control deviance. Social control theory emphasizes the role of the social bond, a bond formed through commitment, attachment, involvement, and a belief in the morality of conformity. The government is an essential element of control, but can only minimize, not eliminate, deviance. And the medical model attempts control through psychotherapy that creates or restores the individual's awareness and capacity for control of deviant behavior.

Glossary

anomie a condition in which norms are weak, inconsistent, or lacking
crimes of negligence crimes in which there is an unintended victim or potential victim

deviance behavior that violates social norms

differential association the theory that illegal behavior results from exposure to more favorable than unfavorable definitions of that behavior

illegal services crime in which unlawful services such as drug dealing or prostitution are rendered to a customer

labeling theory the theory that people become deviant as they are defined and treated as deviants

predatory crime crime involving loss of property or some kind of physical harm

primary deviance deviant acts or behavior by an individual who still defines himself or herself as conforming rather than deviant

public disorder crimes crimes such as loud conduct and public drunkenness that are offensive to an audience

secondary deviance deviant acts or behavior by an individual who defines himself or herself as a deviant

white-collar crimes crimes committed by respectable people in the course of their work

CHAPTER EIGHT

Social Stratification: How Inequality Shapes Human Life

Susan is the president of her own job-training company. Few people who knew her when she was growing up would have expected her to reach this position. Susan was the youngest of six children. Shortly before she was born, her father was killed in an auto accident. As a result, Susan's mother was forced to move her children into a more affordable two-bedroom house in a poor neighborhood. Susan's mother worked long hours at low wages to support her family. They had no car. All of Susan's clothes came from a nearby thrift store. At times, the family was perilously close to having their electricity cut off because they had difficulty paying the bills.

None of Susan's brothers and sisters attended college, but Susan was determined to go herself. She not only went but continued until she had obtained a master's degree. After graduation, she worked for a company involved in employment training. Then she quit in order to start her own company. Her company now grosses over $1 million a year and has 24 employees.

How many of the following principles do you believe Susan's story supports?

- With perseverance and hard work, anyone in America can succeed.

- Although poverty exists in America, no one must remain poor because educational and occupational opportunities are available to all.

- It is not government programs, but initiative and determination that lead to success.

- America is still the land of opportunity, offering better chances to "move up" than any other nation.

Many Americans believe that all of these principles are valid. Yet Susan's story doesn't fully support any of them and even contradicts one of them. We'll explain why later.

Susan's story, however, does illustrate the reality of inequality. At one time, she was one of the underdogs. Today, she is one of the success stories. There are others with similar stories, but there are also stories of underdogs who never succeeded. And, of course, some successful people were never underdogs at all. How can you understand such inequalities?

Social Stratification: Everyone Lives in a System of Inequality

Social stratification is the division of a society into groups that are unequal with regard to things valued. In modern societies, "things valued" are property, income, power, prestige, and gratification of emotional and physical needs. In other words, your income, the amount of social power you can exercise, the prestige you possess, and your chances for a happy and healthy life all depend to some extent upon your position in the stratification system.

Of course, your position can change. That's because you are part of a class system (discussed below). Other societies have different systems of stratification. Let's begin by describing three major types of stratification systems and addressing the question of whether a society without inequality is possible.

Caste Systems

A **caste system** is a closed form of stratification based on ascription (Tumin 1985). "Closed" means that people don't have the opportunity to change their positions. People can't better their lot, no matter how hard they work. At least, they can't move up into a higher caste where they will receive more social prestige and greater opportunities for a higher standard of living. They remain at the level into which they were born.

Although caste systems have existed elsewhere, the system developed most completely in India as an outgrowth of Hinduism. Traditionally, there were five castes. The castes, from the highest to the lowest status, were: Brahmins (the priestly caste), Kshatriyas (the warrior caste), Vaishyas (traders), Shudras (servants and laborers), and the Untouchables. Only people in the first three castes were allowed to study the Hindu sacred Scriptures and perform certain religious rituals.

The five broad groupings were broken down into jati, thousands of small groups that engaged in a traditional occupation and had a certain amount of cultural, religious, and legal autonomy. As modern occupations developed in India, the upper castes found jobs in professional and managerial work, while the others settled for more menial types of labor.

The caste system is justified, in part, on the grounds that the circumstances of an individual's birth are no accident. Hinduism teaches reincarnation—that people continually die and are reborn as new individuals until they have lived so well that they are released from the ongoing cycle of birth, life, and death. An individual's status in the next life depends on his or her present life. Thus, someone born as an Untouchable has obviously lived badly in a previous life. By living well as an Untouchable that person can move to a higher level in the next life.

The caste system was never a part of the law of India. In fact, the 1950 constitution abolished the lowest caste, the Untouchables, and the law now prohibits discrimination on the basis of caste. Nevertheless, people continue to relate to each other on the basis of caste, and few people in India transcend the caste position into which they are born. The tenacity with which class distinctions are observed is illustrated by a 1978 Reuters News Service report of 78 deaths which occurred when a bus was caught in a flood. When the bus stalled in the rising waters, a shop owner waded out to it with a rope he had tied to a truck that was parked on high ground. He told the passengers to haul themselves to safety along the rope. But the higher-caste riders refused to share the same rope with the lower-caste riders. They stayed on the bus, were swept away, and died.

Estate Systems

Estate systems are also closed, but position is determined by law as well as by birth (Heller 1969). Estates occur in feudal societies. Each estate has clearly defined rights and duties. A typical breakdown of estates, from highest to lowest status, is: the royal family; landholding aristocrats and priests; merchants and craftsmen; free peasants and serfs.

In medieval Europe, peasants and serfs were typically not allowed to leave the place where they were born. The serfs literally belonged to the land and, thereby, to whomever owned the land. The peasants and serfs lived in villages of from 20 to 200 households (Blum, Cameron, and Barnes 1966). Each house was a crude, one-room structure with no windows. In winter, livestock usually shared the house with the family because there were no barns. The villages were located near the castles or manor houses where the feudal lord or his representative lived. The villagers were responsible for the entire care of the estate and were taxed for everything they had and did in order to support the lord and his family.

Class Systems

In contrast to the rigidity of the caste and estate systems, a **class system** of stratification is an open system that, theoretically, is based on achievement. Position in the class system is determined not by the circumstances of birth but by educational and occupational achievements.

The nature of a class system will become clearer when we discuss the American class system below. Here we want to point out that the divisions of the class system are arbitrary, the result of social scientific analysis. In the caste and estate systems, the groups were divided along clear social categories—priests, untouchables, royalty, landowners, and so forth. Class systems are divided into **social classes**, which are groups that are unequal with regard to things valued in the society and whose members share similar values and lifestyles. (Social classes are often called socioeconomic strata.) Yet both the number of classes and precisely how to distinguish these classes from each other are based on the decisions of social scientists rather than on recognizable social categories.

Thus, social scientists' divisions of social classes in the United States have ranged from three to eight. The most common breakdown, and the one we shall follow, has four: upper, middle, working, and lower classes.

Is Inequality Necessary?

When we ask students if they believe in perfect equality—that each person in a society should have the same wealth, for example, as everyone else—most agree that perfect equality is not their ideal. But when we discuss the extent of inequality in American society and ask if this is acceptable, most say their ideal would be for less inequality. Then comes the tough question: Because you accept the fact that there will always be some inequality, just how much is acceptable? Often the only thing students agree on in grappling with this question is that there should be equal opportunity. As long as there is equal opportunity, the amount of resulting inequality is not at issue.

In other words, our students reject the idea of perfect equality. They accept the inevitability of some inequality and affirm the ideal of equal opportunity. We will look briefly at each of these three ideas.

Equality and the Classless Society

Karl Marx's *conflict theory* is a model of social change that leads to a classless, or communist, society (Marx 1959, 1964). Even Marx did not advocate perfect equality, however. His dictum of "from each according to ability and to each according to need" suggests that some people shall require more and therefore receive more than will others.

Still, Marx's ideal of a classless society involves only minimal inequality. Marx believed society would only emerge, however, after a prolonged struggle between the social classes. Marx defined a social class as a group of people who perform the same function in the organization of production. Thus the two major classes in a capitalist society are the capitalists who own the means of production (such as factories, tools, and materials), and the laborers who do the work. The two classes have an inherent conflict of interest because the goal of the capitalists is to maximize their own profits, and this necessarily must be done at the expense of the workers.

Marx argued that the capitalists take advantage of their property and power to exploit the workers, who receive wages that are worth far less than the products of their labors. As the industrial society matures, the capitalists become increasingly wealthy and the laborers become increasingly impoverished. Ultimately, he theorized, the workers will rebel against the system and establish in its place a classless society.

In the classless society, each individual would give according to his or her ability and receive according to his or her need. Although this is a form of inequality, it is acceptable, according to Marx, because the society would be one of abundance. That is, all people in the classless society would have their needs fulfilled.

Contrary to Marx's prediction, the communist revolutions that occurred throughout the world did not take place in capitalist nations. Nor did the nations that became communist succeed in abolishing social classes or even in moving toward a classless society. Rather, the members of the communist parties became a new, privileged elite.

For example, a study of the life histories of a sample of residents in Beijing and Shanghai, China, from 1949 to 1993 found that the communist-controlled government determined the educational and work opportunities available to people (Zhou, Tuma, and Moen 1996). People's fortunes in life, therefore, could be drastically affected by changes in government policies. During the Cultural Revolution (1966–1979), the government restricted access to college education, and many people moved into low-status occupations and organizations. Yet in other years, the government encouraged education, and those who were members of the Communist party were more likely to have access to education and to the higher-status occupations.

Is Inequality Inevitable?

Looking at stratification from a *structural-functionalist* perspective, Kingsley Davis and Wilbert Moore (1945) asserted that inequality is necessary. They pointed out that all societies have positions that are more important than others to social well-being. These positions typically require more skill and training. If all positions were rewarded equally, there would be no motivation for an individual to engage in the rigorous training necessary for the more important positions. Why, for instance, would anyone expend the money, time, and energy necessary to become a physician if he or she could make as much money by working as a store clerk? Why would anyone make the personal and interpersonal sacrifices necessary to pursue a career in politics if the same prestige and income could be gained by working in a factory?

One reason inequality is necessary, then, is to get the most qualified people into the most important positions. Another reason is that rewards are necessary to motivate people to perform their work at the highest level possible. Lawyers make more money than carpenters because their work is more essential to social well-being (a point that would be argued by more than a few people). And the best lawyers make more money than mediocre lawyers because they perform in a superior fashion.

The Davis-Moore theory can be, and has been, attacked at every point. First, people enter particular occupations for more reasons than the material rewards involved. You might choose to be a carpenter rather than a lawyer because you love working with your hands. Or, even if the pay were the same, you might opt to become a physician rather than a clerk because you find medicine more challenging and more stimulating. Second, people perform well in their jobs for more reasons than the pay or prestige they receive. They may be motivated by a sense of integrity or personal pride in a "job well done."

Third, who is to say which occupations are more important to social well-being? Are the most highly paid occupations, by definition, the most important? In that case, rock musicians, professional athletes, and Hollywood stars must be some of the most important people to social well-being. Scientists like Arthur Fleming, who discovered penicillin and who worked for a modest salary all of his life, must be relatively unimportant. Finally, the Davis-Moore approach ignores such things as the pool of unused talent in any population, the effects of social class background on people's chances of getting the training needed for the more important positions, and the fact that inequality may be far more beneficial to the elite of any society than to the overall social well-being.

Whether inequality is inevitable and/or necessary, then, remains a matter of debate. Yet one fact is indisputable—inequality is universal in human societies.

Is Equal Opportunity the Answer?

We noted above that most of our students are willing to accept inequality as long as equal opportunities exist for all members of society. Equality of opportunity is the ideal for most Americans. Using *survey research* on a national sample, the National Opinion Research Center asked people whether they favored equal opportunity (everyone can compete for jobs and wealth on a fair and even basis) or equal outcomes (all Americans are guaranteed a decent standard of living, with only small differences in wealth between the top and bottom levels). Seventy-seven percent of African Americans and 89 percent of whites said they preferred equal opportunity (The Public Perspective 1996, p. 34). In a

Roper Center poll, 67 percent of African Americans and 77 percent of whites agreed that any American who works hard can get ahead (Roper Center 1996, p. 34). The majority of Americans, thus, both believe in equal opportunity and that it exists in this country.

In spite of such beliefs, as we will show in this and the following two chapters, the circumstances of your birth as well as your achievements are likely to affect your ultimate position in the class system. According to American ideals, everyone should be able, like Susan, to move upward by dint of hard work. In practice, the story is somewhat different.

The American Class System

If you were asked to what social class you belong, what would you say? If you were asked what difference your social class makes in your life, how would you respond? You may regard these questions as only of minor importance to you. We hope to convince you in this section that the matter of your social class position is crucial to the quality of your life.

How Social Class Is Measured

One way to measure social class is to ask people the same question we just asked you: to what class do you belong? Or you could ask people to place themselves in the upper, middle, working, or lower class. When people rank themselves in this way, it is called **subjective social class**.

You probably answered the questions the way most Americans do. Namely, you are likely to think of yourself as middle class or working class. Polls over a forty-year period show that the proportion of Americans who define themselves as lower class varies between 4 and 7 percent, while the proportion who define themselves as upper class varies between 2 and 6 percent (Ladd 1986). The rest—90 to 94 percent—classify themselves as either middle or working class.

Reference group theory helps explain why most people—in Europe as well as in the United States—place themselves in the middle of the stratification system (Kelley and Evans 1995). Most people decide their class location by comparing themselves with those around them—family, friends, coworkers. Because most people are similar in education and income to those around them, they see themselves as average. Moreover, even those in the higher levels recognize that there are others who are still higher, and those in the lower levels are aware of others still lower than they are. The upshot of all this is that most people define themselves as somewhere in the middle.

Subjective social class can be useful for some purposes. However, social scientists use **objective social class**, which is determined by some combination of income, education, and occupation, to measure class and its impact on the quality of people's lives. Subjective social class measures indicate that nine out of ten people are in the same class, which suggests little differences in the income, education, and occupational prestige of the vast majority. In point of fact, however, the differences are considerable.

We should note that some *feminist theorists* point out deficiencies in the way the concept of social class is used (Ferree and Hall 1996). For instance, you can't really understand how people end up in particular occupational categories without recognizing the way in which gender affects the selection. The same, of course, is true of race and ethnicity. As we shall see below, and in Chapters Nine and Ten, Americans are unequal with regard to income, education, and occupation, but the inequalities within each of the three also vary by gender and racial/ethnic background.

Income

Look at income first. Table 8.1 shows the proportion of families in various income categories in 1993, ranging from families that have less than $10,000 a year to those with more than $75,000 a year. This translates into considerable differences in standards of living.

Table 8.1

Income of Families: Percent Distribution

Income level	White	Black	Hispanic origin
Under $10,000	7.3	25.8	17.9
$10,000-14,999	6.6	11.4	12.5
$15,000-24,999	15.1	18.6	22.2
$25,000-34,999	15.1	13.7	16.6
$35,000-49,999	18.8	12.9	14.0
$50,000-74,999	20.6	10.9	11.4
$75,000 and over	16.6	6.9	5.5
Median income	$39,300	$21,542	$23,654

Source: U.S. Bureau of the Census 1996c, p. 468

Note that there is inequality both within and between the racial/ethnic groups, a topic we will discuss further in the next chapter. The proportion of African American families in the lowest income bracket is 3.5 times that of white families, and the proportion of Hispanic families is nearly 2.5 times that of white families. At the other end of the scale, the proportion of white families in the highest income bracket is 2.4 times that of African Americans and 3 times that of Hispanics.

Looking at all families, the top 5 percent receive about 20 percent of the income (U.S. Bureau of the Census 1996, p. 467). This means that the top 5 percent receive nearly four times what they would if all families had the same income. Another way to look at it is this: the lowest income of families in the top 5 percent in 1993 was $113,182, while the highest income of families in the bottom 20 percent was $16,952. Or still another way to look at income inequality is to take a pie and divide it among five people. The pie represents the total income in the nation, and each of the five people represent 20 percent of the population. If you divide the pie into five pieces, the richest person gets two and a third pieces, while the poorest person gets a quarter piece.

Is such income inequality important? You have probably heard the old saying that money can't buy happiness. There are, no doubt, some wealthy people who live in chronic gloom. However, poverty is even more ineffective than money in buying happiness. Surveys in 55 nations, including the United States, show that people's sense of well-being is positively correlated with income (Diener, Diener, and Diener 1995). Money can't buy happiness, but your chances of feeling good about yourself and your life are better to the extent that your income is high rather than low.

Education

Large differences also exist in educational attainment. In 1995, nearly 30.5 million American adults had not completed high school (U.S. Bureau of the Census 1996, p. 160). At the other end of the scale, nearly 13 million adults had an advanced degree. As with income, considerable differences existed between whites, African Americans, and Hispanics (Figure 8.1).

The fact that years of education correlate closely with income is one of the reasons that educational inequality is a vital concern. In 1993, for instance, the mean monthly income of those who had not graduated from

Figure 8.1   Years of School Completed

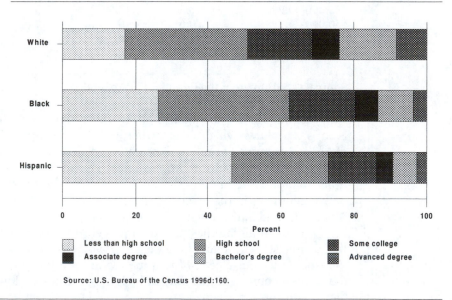

Source: U.S. Bureau of the Census 1996d:160.

high school was $906, compared to $1,380 for high school graduates, $2,625 for college graduates, $3,411 for those with master's degrees, and $4,328 for those with doctorates (U.S. Bureau of the Census 1996d, p. 160).

Educational inequality is also a vital concern because, to the extent that education achieves its purposes, it enriches people's lives. That is, one of the purposes of education is to free you from ignorance and facilitate your personal development. Education can help build your self-esteem and give you a greater sense of control over your life, both of which are positively correlated with happiness (Myers and Diener 1995).

Occupation

Recall that status refers to an evaluated position. People generally prefer a higher rather than a lower status because the higher status means greater honor or prestige. What kind of statuses bring the most prestige in American society? Social scientists answer the question in terms of occupations. For many decades, survey researchers have asked Americans to rank various occupations by prestige. In general, it found that people give high prestige to the kinds of occupations that yield high incomes (National Opinion Research Center 1993). For example, physicians, astronauts, and lawyers are among the occupations evaluated the highest, while shoe shiners, panhandlers, and janitors are among those evaluated the lowest.

Researchers have assigned prestige scores to each of the occupations. These scores can be used as a measure of social class because occupational prestige is correlated with income and education. However, a more common way to use occupational prestige as a measure of social class is the categorization developed by the Census Bureau, shown in table 8.2. The median weekly earnings are for full-time wage and salary workers in 1994. The table also shows the inequality in earnings between males and females, a point we shall pursue in Chapter Ten.

Note that the categories with larger incomes also tend to require the most education and are likely to yield the highest occupational prestige. You can get a better sense of this when you look at some of the specific occupations in each of the categories. The managerial and professional category includes business executives and managers, scientists, engineers, physicians, lawyers, writers, entertainers, teachers, and athletes. Technical, sales, and administrative support includes health and science technicians, sales representatives, computer operators, bookkeepers, and bank tellers. Precision production includes mechanics, electricians, and carpenters. Operators, fabricators, and laborers includes machine operators, production inspectors, truck drivers, and freight handlers. Service workers includes child care workers, cleaning people, fire fighters, police, dental assistants, hairdressers and barbers. And the farming, forestry, and fishing category includes all those who work in those three areas, including hunters and trappers.

Table 8.2   **Occupation and Median Weekly Earnings, by Sex**

Occupation	Males	Females
Managerial and professional	$829	$605
Technical, sales, and administrative support	556	383
Precision production	534	371
Operators, fabricators, laborers	413	297
Service workers	357	264
Farming, forestry, fishing	294	249

Source: U.S. Bureau of the Census 1996d, p. 426

While there are some exceptions, in general the higher the prestige of an occupation the more education is required and the higher the income level. For this reason, any of the three—income, education, or occupation—as well as a combination of them can be used as a measure of social class.

The Consequences of Social Class Position

Marx conceived of stratification as basically an economic phenomenon. Max Weber (Gerth and Mills 1946) modified Marx by adding two additional dimensions: power and prestige. Property, power, and prestige, according to Weber, are three distinct but linked dimensions of inequality. Property (income and wealth) differences are manifest in classes, power differences are reflected in political parties, and prestige differences are seen in status groupings.

Weber used these distinctions to make the point that property differences have significant consequences for life chances, and status differences have significant consequences for life styles. Life chances include such things as physical and mental health, longevity, and marital status. Life styles include such things as the type of home and neighborhood where an individual lives and leisure pursuits. Thus, both life chances and life styles deal with aspects of the quality of life and vary considerably for those in differing social classes.

Life Chances

A great number of studies have consistently shown that the higher the social class position, the lower the rates of illness and death (Fein 1995; Nickens 1995). This is true in countries around the world. Moreover, the advantages of the higher classes have increased over the past half century (Fein 1995). The health problems of those in the lower strata include higher rates of both chronic and acute diseases; more days of restricted activity because of illness; less use of health-care services; and a lower rate of such preventive health measures as vaccinations, proper diet, and not smoking (Ross and Wu 1995; National Center for Health Statistics 1995).

Mental as well as physical health is adversely affected by low social class position (Robins and Regier 1991). For children, living with various kinds of deprivation is associated with mental health problems (McLeod and Edwards 1995). For adults, both deprivation and the kinds of occupations held by those in the lower class are factors in depression (Link, Lennon and Dohrenwend 1993). It is, of course, understandable that people in low-paying, dead-end, routine kinds of work would find their situation depressing.

The chances of being a crime victim are also higher in the lower strata. The victimization rates (per 1,000 persons age twelve or older) for violent crimes in 1993 were 93.5 for those with less than $7,500 family income, 51.9 for those earning $25,000 to $34,999, and 40.9 for those with family income of $75,000 or more (Bastian 1995, p. 4).

Finally, marital status is included in life chances. A stable and satisfying marriage is associated with fewer health problems and longer life (Lauer and Lauer 1997). How does social class position affect the chances of people having such a marriage? Almost every time we raise this question, the majority of students respond that divorce rates are higher in the upper strata. Yet the opposite is true. The higher your class position, the less likely you are to divorce. It is probable that the financial pressures on those in the lower strata make their unions more precarious. Hernandez (1993) reported that couples with children who are below the poverty line are nearly twice as likely to divorce as those above the poverty line.

Thinking Critically

An aspect of mental health that is frequently related to social class is self-esteem. Those from the lower strata tend to have lower self-esteem than those from the upper strata. Two researchers illustrated good critical thinking processes by asking whether the way self-esteem is measured would make any difference in this relationship (Francis and Jones 1996). They gave three different measures of self-esteem to 711 subjects and used occupation as a measure of social class. They found a correlation between social class and self-esteem on all three measures, but one of the measures of self-esteem showed the relationship to be much stronger than did the others.

It is always good to ask how something was measured. If someone claims that self-esteem is related to social class, for instance, you should not be as comfortable with the result if the researcher measured self-esteem by a single question (such as, "on a scale of one to ten, how good do you feel about yourself?") than you would if a complex, validated scale were used. And you can be even more confident with the finding when three different measures yield the same result.

Life Styles

Unlike Weber, who linked life chances with property and life styles with status, sociologists now recognize that the diverse life styles that characterize various classes arise from such things as education, occupation and income as well as people's status groups (Tumin 1985). Clearly, the house and neighborhood in which a family lives reflect the income of that family.

Income affects consumption patterns generally—from the kind of watch you wear (a Timex or a Rolex) to the house you buy (the renovated urban house for under $100,000 or the $1 million suburban house). Of course, not everyone who can afford it will buy a Rolex watch or a million-dollar home. Values and tastes enter into consumption patterns.

Culture also affects consumption patterns. In his classic analysis of consumption patterns, Thorstein Veblen (1953; orig. 1899) coined the phrase "conspicuous consumption" to describe the purchase and display of goods in order to show off an individual's wealth. Wearing the most expensive clothes, living in the swankiest neighborhood, and taking costly trips are ways to indulge in conspicuous consumption.

A cultural historian has pointed out, however, that contemporary society calls for inconspicuous consumption (Hughes 1996). Hollywood stars are buying ranches in Montana or Wyoming or Idaho. Well-to-do people tend to focus not on the most expensive clothes but rather on who can look the most comfortable or the most casual. An important status symbol is having the best computer in your home. Of course, these status symbols are as costly as ever, but they may be a bit more subtle than the symbols of Veblen's day.

Life styles involve more than consumption patterns. Class differences exist in political behavior. For one thing, those in the higher strata are more likely to vote than those in the lower strata. Using education as a measure of social class, for example, in the 1994 elections 63.1 percent of those with four or more years of college, 40.5 percent of those with a high school education, and 23.2 percent of those with eight years or less of education, voted (U.S. Bureau of the Census 1996d, p. 286). Also a greater proportion of Democrats are in the working and lower classes, while a greater proportion of Republicans are in the middle and upper classes. Again using education as a measure of social class, in 1994 those with a grade school education reported the following party identification: 52 percent Democrat and 17 percent Republican. Among those with a high school education 37 percent reported being Democrats and 24 percent Republicans. And among those with a college education 30 percent reported being Democrats and 37 percent reported being Republicans (U.S. Bureau of the Census 1996d, p. 285).

Although the evidence is dated, sociologists tend to agree that parenting patterns also differ among the classes (Wright and Wright 1976; Kohn 1977). Lower-class parents pay less attention to their children than do middle-class parents and are more likely than middle-class parents to use physical punishment. Working-class parents stress conformity and neatness with their children while middle-class parents tend to emphasize initiative, creativity, and self-control.

Leisure activities in the area of sports furnish another example of life style differences (Eitzen and Sage 1993). Those in the higher strata tend to choose individual sports like tennis and golf; those in the lower strata are more inclined to engage in sports that emphasize physical strength or team play (such as weightlifting and softball). Which spectator sports are associated with the various social classes? Those in the upper strata are more likely to watch yacht races and polo. The middle class tends to enjoy watching tennis, skiing, and golf. And people in the lower strata are more likely to prefer bowling, boxing, professional wrestling, and the Roller Derby.

A Brief Portrait of American Classes

We have identified several factors that distinguish the classes and have shown some of the class differences in life chances and life styles. Now we will draw brief portraits of the upper, middle, working, and lower classes. Our portraits will be painted in broad strokes and will primarily be drawn from the work of Rossides (1990) and Gilbert and Kahl (1993).

The Upper Class

About 1 to 3 percent of Americans are identified as upper class (recall that class boundaries are based on researchers' judgments). The upper class controls a disproportionate amount of wealth and power. People in the upper class can afford luxuries: exclusive and custom-built homes, household help, high-priced cars, yachts, lavish parties, and costly vacations in exotic locations.

Those at the top of this class—the upper-uppers—tend to have "old" money, wealth that is inherited from past generations. They are listed in the *Social Register*, along with names like Rockefeller, Vanderbilt, and du Pont. They send their children to exclusive, expensive, private schools. Their social life is with their own kind, and marriage outside their social circle is rare.

Those in the bottom half of this class—the lower-uppers—are the "new" rich, people who have earned great sums of money through their own achievements rather than inheritance. Because new money is looked upon with more suspicion than old money (even though the old money may have been acquired initially through questionable activities), the lower-uppers may be barred from some of the exclusive activities of the upper-uppers.

The Middle Class

The middle class can also be subdivided into the upper-middle and lower-middle. The upper-middle class, from 10 to 15 percent of the population, consists of those who have been successful in the managerial and professional occupations: physicians, lawyers, engineers, business executives and managers, and college professors. The income of the upper-middle class is above average, with a median family income of perhaps $75,000 or more a year.

Those in the upper-middle class do not exercise as much power nor enjoy the lavish consumption patterns of those in the upper class. By world standards, however, upper-middle-class people are extremely wealthy. They can live in well-appointed homes, enjoy vacations abroad, and send their children to college. They can be influential in their communities, holding leadership positions in voluntary associations and government-related committees. They are likely to be career-oriented with both husband and wife pursuing careers. Their families tend to be democratic, with all members participating in household chores and family decision-making.

The lower-middle class, about 30 to 35 percent of the population, includes owners of small businesses, some lower-level professionals (teachers, police, and social workers), lower-level business managers, and higher-level clerical workers and sales people. The median income of lower-middle-class families is about half that of the upper middle class, and this lower income means that their standard of living is relatively modest compared to the upper-middle and upper classes. But relative to most of the rest of the world it is still very high.

Individuals in the lower-middle-class are less likely than those in the upper-middle class to participate in voluntary associations and to exercise influence in their communities. They are family oriented, and their families are democratic. They tend to focus on their children's well-being and strive to help their children move up in the class structure.

The Working Class

The working class, about a third of the population, is composed of those who work largely in the third, fourth, and fifth categories of Table 8.2—blue-collar and service workers. Some of those in the working class, particularly trade-union workers such as electricians and plumbers, may have higher incomes than those in the lower-middle class. For the most part, however, working-class people have less education and lower incomes than those in the middle class. They also have less job security and experience more layoffs than middle-class workers.

Because of the combination of lower incomes and lower job stability, many working-class people face an ongoing financial struggle. They are unlikely to have much, if anything, in the way of savings. They are unlikely to afford the vacations or the nice cars and homes that middle-class people enjoy. Their children may not go to college, either because they do not value a college education or because they cannot afford to go. Often the major goals of a working-class family are to avoid slipping into poverty and to maintain respectability.

The Lower Class

About 20 to 25 percent of the population fall into the lower class. Lower-class people work at menial jobs for minimal salary, or are frequently unemployed, or are unemployable (disabled, chronically ill, elderly). People in the lower class live from hand to mouth. They have run-down housing or are homeless. They are likely to wear clothes purchased from thrift shops. Their diets are inadequate. They experience more illness than those in other classes, but they are unlikely to have health insurance or to receive adequate health care. And their children suffer both physically and emotionally from living in a state of relentless deprivation (McLeod and Shanahan 1993).

In spite of their deprivation, not everyone in the lower class is officially poor according to government guidelines. But the 14 percent that are officially poor (U.S. Bureau of the Census 1996e) and the 6 to 11 percent that are just above the poverty level are sufficiently alike that we will look at them as a group in the next section.

Explorations

The Invisible Lower Class

As noted in the text, from 20 to 25 percent of Americans are in the lower class. That translates into more than 52 million people! Where are they? How many do you observe in any given week? How many Americans are aware of the fact that tens of millions of their fellow citizens engage in a daily struggle to survive a dismal existence?

Perhaps one of the reasons that the lower class is invisible to many Americans is that a prime source of information—television—has little to say about the matter. For one week, assign each group member to watch a particular hour or two of prime-time television. Include news programs in the assignment. For each person you see, including those in commercials, note your perception of that person's social class position. Keep a record of the data as follows:

First, record the number of people you see in each of the social classes. Second, use colored pencils to code the individuals by type of program. For example, you may want to use black for sitcoms, red for news programs, green for commercials, etc. Third, make notes about the lifestyles of people in the various classes.

At the end of the week, write up an analysis of the results. How visible or invisible are the various classes? Does this vary by type of program? In what ways were the portrayals of lifestyles consistent with or different from the information given in the text?

If you do this as an individual project, select a single channel and follow the above procedures.

Poverty in America: Is It Inevitable?

More than one student has told us that poverty can never be eliminated. If you substitute inequality for poverty, we would agree. Yet is poverty really inevitable? In this section, we'll discuss how many Americans are poor, who those Americans are, and some of the efforts that have been made to address the problem.

America's Poor

In 1994, the official poverty line was an annual income of $7,547 for an individual or $15,141 for a family of four (U.S. Bureau of the Census 1996c). This meant that 38.1 million Americans—14.5 percent of the population—were officially poor. In 1995, the numbers dropped to 13.8 percent of the population, or 36.4 million Americans (U.S. Bureau of the Census 1996e).

Who Are the Poor?

Have you heard the term "welfare deadbeat"? Consistent with the labeling theory of *symbolic interactionism*, this is one of the terms used to stigmatize the poor and to blame them for their plight. In this view, people are poor because they lack the effort or the morals necessary to get out of poverty (Wilson 1996). These labels are a way of saying to the poor, "You are responsible for your miserable situation." It's also a way of disavowing any social responsibility for the impoverished.

We don't doubt that there are some welfare deadbeats, people who prefer to be supported by the state rather than to support themselves. Yet when you look at the poor, you see a far different picture from a large group of deadbeats (U.S. Bureau of the Census 1995, 1996c, 1996e):

- The most impoverished group in the nation are single mothers; more than 35 percent of all single mothers live below the poverty line.

- A high proportion of children live in poverty—about 21 percent of all children under eighteen.

- About a third of African Americans and 30 percent of Hispanics live in poverty—nearly three times the proportion of impoverished whites.

- Poverty rates vary by state; Louisiana's rate is three times as high as that of Hawaii and twice that of Kansas.

- Of all adults (sixteen and over) living in poverty, over 40 percent work during the year, and about one out of ten work full-time and year-round.

If it surprises you that one out of ten of those living in poverty works full-time, keep in mind that these people work at menial jobs with low pay. If an adult with one dependent had a minimum-wage job ($5.15 an hour as of September 1997), he or she could not earn enough in a year to rise above the poverty line.

During the 1980s, attention focused on the homeless—a subgroup of those in poverty. Estimates of the number of homeless range between one-half to one million, a third of whom are families with children (Toth 1991). Most of the homeless are relatively young (under fifty), have no more than a high school education, and have high rates of mental illness and drug abuse (Lehman and Cordray 1993). Some of them work, but do not earn enough money to afford housing (Bohanon 1991).

One other factor to consider for those who view people in poverty as deadbeats is the small proportion who are impoverished for an extended period. A longitudinal study over a 19-year period found that only 1.1 percent of the households were poor throughout the period, but 38 percent were poor for at least one of the years (Devine and Wright 1993).

In other words, many people *are* able to escape poverty. But not without help. Recall the story of Susan at the beginning of the chapter. We said that her story does *not* support the ideas that anyone in America can, with initiative, perseverance and hard work, become a success and that these individual characteristics rather than government programs are what lead to success. What we did not tell you is that Susan's mother depended on government assistance to support her children for years after her husband's death. Without this aid, Susan would have been forced to leave school and get a job. Certainly, Susan does have initiative and does work hard, but without government assistance she might be working in a menial job today instead of running her own company.

The War on Poverty

The nation embarked on a "war on poverty" in the 1960s with high hopes that poverty could be completely or nearly eliminated. This didn't happen. Poverty rates did decline, but still about one out of every seven Americans lives in poverty.

The welfare system—a primary method for helping the poor—has been increasingly attacked as useless. Even supporters of welfare recognize flaws in the old system. For example, welfare discouraged people from working by reducing benefits as soon as a recipient started earning money; as a result, many discovered that they were no better off, or even worse off, by trying to work than by simply taking their welfare money. In addition, two out of three Americans believe that recipients of welfare are cheating the system (Golay and Rollyson 1996, p. 74). And people are frustrated by the fact that poverty rates remain high after decades of government programs to eliminate the problem.

The disillusionment with the welfare system led to new federal legislation in 1996 (Church 1996). The federal government no longer provides long-term help to the poor. States are given money to run their own programs. The states have discretion over how the money is used as long as no family receives welfare for more than five years. In addition, if the head of a family does not find work within two years, the family loses its benefits.

In essence, then, the approach now is that people must find work to support themselves. Welfare will provide only temporary support. It remains to be seen if this approach will be more effective, but a number of questions must be raised. Are there enough jobs available for every able-bodied person to work? What about the elderly, the disabled, the mentally ill? What about the people who are already working full-time and are still living in poverty? What about single mothers and children who are a large segment of those in poverty? Should these mothers be required to work and let someone else take care of their children? Can they find jobs that will pay enough both to lift them and pay for child care? Actually, the great majority of welfare mothers prefer to work (Edin 1995). Yet many of them have already found that they are no better off financially when they work (because of low wages), and no matter how hard they work their jobs never lead to better jobs.

The point is, any assault on poverty faces perplexing challenges. The most effective war on poverty has been waged in Scandinavian nations under social democracies. Americans are unlikely to support policies that include much higher rates of taxation in order to lift up lower-class income by redistribution of wealth. This demands, then, that the questions we raised above about the various groups who are poor must be addressed with some new and creative answers.

Experiences

'My Six Months in Hell'

Every year a few million Americans who were living above the poverty line fall below it. Janet's fall was both long and hard. She was divorced, childless, in her late 40s, earning good wages, and enjoying a comfortable lifestyle in Oregon. Then her father became too sick to take care of himself. As his only child, she quit her job and moved to his apartment in another state. After a few years, he died and her life came apart at the seams:

My father didn't have any life insurance. And I had used up all my savings while taking care of him. I was worn out physically and emotionally. And I was over fifty, which was over the hill as far as most employers were concerned. So I took the little money I had left and went back to Oregon. I stayed in a cheap motel but I couldn't find work. Finally, I realized that I would have to live in my car. I drove around to find a place where I would feel reasonably safe overnight and settled on a hotel parking lot. Ironically, I once had business lunches in the same hotel.

☞ A car is not a pleasant place to sleep. That first night I woke frequently and left before daybreak so that no one would see me there. It was the first night of my six months in hell. Six months living in a car. Being alone, being uncomfortable, being bored, being afraid, and sometimes being hungry. I never realized before how great it is just to have a toilet available when you need it. Or a bath tub. I would go to McDonald's early each morning and give myself a quick sponge bath in the restroom. I once shampooed my hair in the restroom of a public library.

During the day, I had plenty of time—agonizing time—to think about the way I had lived before. I got to a point where my evening meal was a can of tuna fish or a couple of pieces of fruit. I was rapidly getting to the point of total desperation. I had never really considered suicide before, but it no longer seemed so repugnant. In fact, it even seemed like a welcome relief from my misery.

During this time, Janet had continued to search for work. She finally found a clerical job. It took a couple of paychecks before she had enough money to rent an apartment, so she kept living in her car for two months after she started working. Janet now lives at a much lower standard than she did before her father's illness, but it's a much higher standard than during her brief stint in poverty. And she appreciates, as never before, how quickly poverty can grind the luster out of human existence.

Social Mobility: Moving Up or Down

What are your occupational and financial aspirations? Whatever they are, it is likely that they are at least as high, or higher, than those of your parents. Most Americans value upward **social mobility**, which is movement to a higher class standing. However, social mobility, movement within or between social classes, can be downward as well as upward. Thus, people can end up at a lower level than their parents enjoyed.

There is a distinction between **intergenerational mobility**—movement in class position from one generation to the next—and **intragenerational mobility**—movement in class position by an individual or group. If your parents owned their own small business and you become a corporate executive, you have experienced intergenerational mobility. If you begin your work career as a sales clerk and end up as a college professor, you have experienced intragenerational mobility. You could also have the experience of being downwardly mobile during your working life (e.g., see the case of Janet in Experiences, this chapter).

How Mobile Are Americans?

When people say that the United States is the "land of opportunity," they imply that the opportunities for social mobility are very high and are, in fact, higher than in any other nation. This is a nation in which people can literally go from rags to riches. To what extent is this true? The story of Susan, at the beginning of the chapter, certainly illustrates the possibility. However, her story does not prove the principle that

America is the land of opportunity. To do this, her experience would have to be replicated by a great many people. You need to look at the evidence of just how much mobility there is before making a judgment about whether or not America is the land of opportunity.

Because occupation is an integral part of your socioeconomic status, a common way of measuring mobility—particularly intergenerational mobility—is by occupational categories. A historian looked at various evidence from the nineteenth century and drew a number of conclusions (Weber 1975). First, many Americans worked hard without ever becoming mobile. Second, many others moved up, but only a small amount. Third, the likelihood of success depended on where an individual began. Sons of wealthy businessmen were much more likely to succeed than were the sons of laborers. Native whites were more likely to succeed than were immigrants, and immigrants were more likely to succeed than were African Americans or Mexican Americans. Finally, a very few individuals did go from rags to riches.

Weber's conclusions are consistent with various studies carried out since the 1960s that look at mobility in the twentieth century (Blau and Duncan 1967; Featherman and Hauser 1978; Gilbert and Kahl 1993). There is a good deal of mobility, but most of it is relatively modest. That is, people move up or down in small increments. There is more upward than downward mobility. Your chances of upward mobility are greater if you are male rather than female, and white rather than a member of a racial or ethnic minority. However, upward mobility diminished in the 1980s. In fact, each successive cohort of baby boomers (those born between 1946 and 1964) has faced an increasingly greater chance of being poor (Browne 1995).

In addition, your chances of upper mobility (or of remaining in a high position) are much better if you start out in the middle or upper strata. For example, among males in upper white-collar occupations (professionals, managers, officials, and nonretail sales workers), 60 percent had sons and 51 percent had daughters who entered upper white-collar jobs (Gilbert and Kahl 1993). Among males in lower manual occupations (service workers, laborers, and operatives), only 27 percent had sons and 24 percent had daughters who entered upper white-collar jobs. A study using existing data on the education, social backgrounds, and careers of 2,729 managers in 208 major corporations concluded that a degree from a prestigious school and an upper-class background both increased the likelihood of reaching the top ranks of corporate management (Useem and Karabel 1986).

What of the notion that the United States is the land of greatest opportunity? Actually, the relationships between class origin, education, and mobility are fairly similar among industrial nations (Ishida, Müller, and Ridge 1995). The chances of moving up a large distance into the elite may be somewhat higher in the United States (Wong 1990). Yet for the most part, all industrial nations offer roughly similar opportunities for social mobility.

What Accounts for Social Mobility?

What makes the difference in whether or not someone will be upwardly mobile? Many believe that such factors as initiative, determination, and hard work are the major ingredients in an individual's mobility pattern. These factors, however, did not prevent Janet (see Experiences, this chapter), and others like her, from being downwardly mobile. Nor do they guarantee that you will be upwardly mobile. Other than the fickle finger of fate (you win the lottery or discover oil in your backyard), there are five factors that help explain the social mobility in any society: structural causes, differing fertility rates, immigration, class interchange, and changes in occupational rankings.

Structural causes involve changes in technology and the economy (Hope 1982). These changes account for more mobility than individual effort because they result in more positions opening up in the higher strata. After all, if all the top positions are filled, it doesn't matter how talented or hard-working you are. Yet as the economy grows and technological developments open up new and highly-valued jobs, there are additional positions at the top to be filled.

The differing fertility rates within the various social classes also create the potential for mobility (Gilbert and Kahl 1993). In medieval Europe, the upper classes had more children than did the masses, creating a trend of more downward than upward mobility. In the United States today, the lower classes tend to have more children than the upper, creating the possibility for upward movement as the children of the elite are unable to fill all available positions.

Immigration can create some mobility because immigrants typically have a lower status than natives and are recruited for lower-status jobs. At the same time, immigrants represent an expanded market that may open up new jobs for natives.

Class interchange refers to the fact that some people will be downwardly mobile because they are either not capable or not willing to maintain the high positions their parents held. Their downward mobility opens up some positions for others to fill.

Finally, occasional changes in occupational rankings can lead to both upward and downward mobility. For instance, when computers first began to proliferate in the workplace, data processing appeared as a job with good status and good pay. Over time, both the prestige and the relative pay have declined. The chances of an entire occupation gaining or losing in social value is not great, but it does happen.

Even within the context of these five factors, however, an individual must still get the necessary education and engage in the necessary effort in order to be upwardly mobile. The point is, whether you are upwardly or downwardly mobile, or not mobile at all, depends upon a good deal more than your own efforts.

Global Stratification

Nations as well as individuals and families can be ranked in a stratification system. In fact, **world system theory** treats the entire world as one economic system with a division of labor along national lines (Wallerstein 1979). The varied economic tasks of the world are not distributed equally among the nations. Rather, there are certain "core nations" that, like the capitalists in Marx's theory, dominate and exploit the rest of the world. In the core nations (the United States, Japan, and the countries of Western Europe), free labor engages largely in skilled work. In peripheral nations (the poor nations in Asia, Africa, and Latin America), labor is coerced and unskilled. There are also a number of "semiperpheral" nations, such as Taiwan and South Korea, that have a mix of labor types and are better off economically than the peripheral nations. Differences between core nations and peripheral nations are similar to those between the upper and lower classes in the United States.

World system theorists argue that the gap between the rich and poor nations is growing. Why does the exploited bulk of the world's population tolerate such inequality? Wallerstein (1979) offers three reasons. First, the core states have superior military strength. Second, people accept the ideology that says that their well-being depends upon the continuation of the world economic system. Third, and most importantly, the three layers help the system to survive. The core nations do not face unified opposition from the rest of the world. Instead, the semiperpheral nations act as a buffer and maintain stability because they are both exploited and exploiters.

We will not go into the merits of world system theory, but undeniably large disparities do exist between nations. Table 8.3 shows some of the extremes that exist in gross national product per capita and life expectancy at birth. The figures are only a few of those that dramatize the fact that hundreds of millions of people on earth live in poverty and fail to get the proper diet for an active and healthy life (Lauer 1991). Even the numbers themselves cannot capture the extent of human misery involved. For instance, one of the differences that economic well-being makes is in the infant mortality rate—the number of deaths of children under one year of age per 1,000 live births. The rate in the United States is 6.7, compared to 55.3 for Brazil, 71.1 for India, 96.8 for Pakistan, and 149.7 for Afghanistan (U.S. Bureau of the Census 1996d, p. 831). In other words, the grief and disruption that attend the loss of an infant is seven times more likely in Brazil, nearly ten times more likely in India, more than twelve times as likely in Pakistan, and nineteen times more likely in Afghanistan than in the United States.

You could argue that, based upon such data, world inequalities are more severe than are those within the United States. Nearly 82 percent of the world's population is in Asia, Africa, and South America. If you view those continents as comprising most of the lower class, then eight out of ten Americans would have to be in the lower class if the United States stratification system mirrored that of the world.

Unfortunately, efforts to reduce world wide inequalities face some of the same dilemmas and challenges that exist within nations. For example, foreign investments and foreign aid appear to be a direct way to help a poorer nation. However, some evidence indicates that such investment and aid actually increase the inequality within countries and decrease the relative rate of economic growth in the long run (Bornschier, Chase-Dunn, and Rubinson 1978; Chan 1989). Yet this isn't always true. Taiwan and Kenya have both experienced high rates of economic growth while receiving considerable foreign aid and investment (Barrett and Whyte 1982; Bradshaw 1988).

Table 8.3	**Inequalities in the World System**
Gross National Product Per Capita:	
Japan	$34,630
United States	25,860
Germany	25,580
South Korea	8,220
Brazil	3,370
India	310
Nigeria	280
Mozambique	80
Life Expectancy at Birth:	
Japan	80
United States	76
Germany	76
South Korea	70
Brazil	66
India	59
Nigeria	56
Mozambique	46

Source: Population Reference Bureau 1996

In sum, reducing inequality in the world system is a perplexing challenge. Moreover, the pressure to do something about it is intensifying. Increasingly, the people of the world are not content with lives of silent desperation.

EXTENSIONS

Being Poor in Asia

When you think about poverty in the United States, you may have an image of shabbily-dressed people crowded into a ghetto apartment in a run-down area of a city. What kind of image does poverty in Asia generate in your mind? What is it like to be poor in a part of the world that is low in the international stratification system?

Look first at poverty in a prosperous area: Hong Kong (Gargan 1996). The gross national product per capita of Hong Kong places it among the wealthier areas of the world. Two of the ten richest men in the world live in Hong Kong. But about 10 percent of the population is poor. And the poorest live in cage homes—steel mesh boxes, stacked in twos and threes in old tenement houses—that barely hold a mattress and one person.

Ma Kwai-han typifies the cage dwellers. He came to Hong Kong in 1955 because there was no food in China. Now he sees little difference in his life in Hong Kong and what it would have been in China. He gets up at 4:15 A.M., rolls out of his cage, and washes in the tiny bathroom available to the twenty-five people who live in the cages stacked in the room. He walks to the restaurant where he works and earns about $273 a month. He pays $41 for his cage because he can't afford the cost of anything better.

Ma Kwai-han, like most of the poor in the United States, does have food and shelter of sorts. In India, one of the poorest nations of the world, poverty has a different face (Banerjee 1992). Millions of homeless beggars struggle every day to find food and shelter. A fifty-three-year-old Calcutta woman survives by picking up rotten vegetables and fish entrails in a market near a railway station, cooking them, and selling them to other homeless people. To buy such food, a beggar may have to pay everything he or she collected for the day.

The woman is one of a community of beggars and street urchins who exist from day to day in Calcutta by begging or stealing. Part of what they obtain must be paid to the railway police for the privilege of leaving them alone. Even so, the police may beat them and drive them off for the benefit of a visiting official. They always return, however, for the passengers who give them money and the rotting food cast away in the market are their only means of surviving for another day of a brutish existence.

Critical Thinking Exercise

In announcing the reshaping of California's welfare system, the governor said that he was finally ending a "system that for too long has unfairly trapped families in dependency and denied them the ability to . . . learn the self-esteem that comes only with self sufficiency" (Wilkie 1997). His belief about the effects of welfare are shared by many Americans. Using information in this chapter, what kind of response would you make to the governor's statement? What additional information would you need in order to assess the statement?

Summary

Social stratification is the division of any society into groups that are unequal with regard to things valued in that society. The things valued in modern societies are wealth, power, prestige, and emotional and physical gratification. Three major types of stratification systems are the caste, estate, and class system.

Caste systems are closed forms of stratification based on ascription. The Indian caste system grew out of Hinduism. It is justified on the basis that each individual is born into a position that he or she merits because of a past life. The caste system is not a part of the law but is a powerful influence.

Estate systems are also closed, but position is determined by both birth and law. Estates occur in feudal societies, and each position is governed by law. In medieval Europe, the peasants and serfs were not allowed to leave the place where they were born. Along with the villagers, they were responsible to maintain the lord's estate and life style.

Class systems are open and based on achievement. Social classes, or socioeconomic strata, are the arbitrarily-determined divisions in a class system. In the United States, four classes are typically identified: upper, middle, working, and lower.

Is stratification inevitable? Karl Marx theorized of conflict between classes that would ultimately lead to a classless society. However, communist nations that follow Marx have not moved toward a classless society.

Structural functionalists argue that inequality is necessary in order to fill the more important positions in society. Inequality exists in all societies, but this doesn't necessarily mean that it is necessary or inevitable. Americans are not opposed to inequality in outcomes as long as there is equality of opportunity.

Social class can be measured subjectively—by asking people to which class they belong, or objectively—by using some combination of income, education, and occupation. Subjectively, most people locate themselves in the middle of the system. Objectively, however, considerable differences exist in such things as income, education, and occupation.

The consequences of social class position can be summed up in terms of differences in life chances and life styles. The higher the class position, the lower the rates of death, illness, victimization, and divorce. The higher the class position, the richer the consumption pattern and the greater the participation in political life. Different parenting styles and leisure activities also exist in different social classes.

About 1 to 3 percent of Americans are in the upper class, which controls a disproportionate amount of wealth and power. The upper-middle class, 10 to 15 percent of the population, is career-oriented and affluent. The lower-middle class, 30 to 35 percent of the population, is family-oriented and lives modestly. The working class, about a third of the population, tends to face ongoing financial struggles; working-class people strive to maintain solvency and respectability. The lower class, 20 to 25 percent of the population, suffers various kinds of deprivation as they struggle to survive.

A substantial number of Americans live in poverty. Poverty rates are highest among single mothers and children. African Americans and Hispanics have higher rates than do whites. Many of the poor work, and some work full-time. There is considerable movement in and out of poverty. Government efforts to reduce poverty include the welfare system, which has now become largely a workfare system.

Social mobility is movement up or down in the stratification system. There is a good deal of mobility, but most of it is over a short distance. The chances of mobility are greater for whites and for males. The chances of reaching the top are greater for those who start near the top. Upward mobility opportunities have been diminishing and are generally no better in the United States than in other industrial nations. Mobility is possible because of structural causes, differing fertility rates, immigration, class interchange, and changes in occupational rankings.

The world may be viewed as a stratification system. World system theory treats the world as an economic system with a division of labor along national lines. The core nations dominate and exploit the others, leading to enormous disparities between nations of things valued. To reduce international inequality is a perplexing challenge because some programs that appear useful on the surface—such as investment and aid—may turn out to be counterproductive.

Glossary

caste system a closed form of stratification, based on ascription

class system an open form of stratification, based on achievement

estate system a closed form of stratification, based on law as well as birth

intergenerational mobility change in social class position from one generation to the next

intragenerational mobility movement in social class position of an individual or group

objective social class class position as measured by education, income, occupation, or some combination of the three

social classes groups that are unequal with regard to things valued in a society, whose members share similar values and lifestyles

social mobility movement of individuals and groups within or between social classes

social stratification the organization of any society into groups that are unequal with regard to things valued

subjective social class the ranking that people give to themselves in the class system

world system theory analysis of the world as an economic system with a division of labor along national lines

CHAPTER NINE

Racial and Ethnic Groups:
Understanding Differences

Early on a June morning in 1995, about 50 skinheads went on a rampage in a large city. They used iron rods and baseball bats to attack every black person they encountered. About a week later, two white youths were stabbed by a gang of young black men, apparently in retaliation against the violence of the skinheads. Additional attacks by whites against blacks and blacks against whites occurred over the next few days.

Government officials were appalled by the attacks which, they believed, violated a long tradition of racial tolerance. Indeed, racial tolerance seemed to be the norm in this city—Lisbon, Portugal. The Portuguese had assimilated Africans from former colonies into their society with relative ease. But in recent years, racist attitudes and behavior have surfaced.

It seems that no society is immune to the misunderstandings, tensions, and violence that occur between groups of people from diverse racial and ethnic backgrounds. How do you explain this kind of conflict? What can be done to minimize it? We begin by looking at the meaning of **race** and ethnicity.

Race and Ethnicity: Myth or Reality?

Is there such a thing as race? You may think that the answer is obvious. Yet, as we shall discuss below, the answer is not at all straightforward. Nevertheless, people are classified as belonging to a certain race or ethnic group. Even preschool children recognize differences of skin color or manner of speaking and may use the ingroup-outgroup distinction to berate or exclude those who are different (Van Ausdale and Feagin 1996). For race, children employ the same criterion used by most people—skin color. Is this a valid way of defining race?

Race

Although most people think of skin color when they talk about race, we shall define **race** as a group of people that have distinguishing biological characteristics that affect their interaction with other groups. Why not skin color alone? For one thing, skin color is only one of many biological characteristics that can be used. Why not select blood type? Or the ability to taste the chemical phenylthiocarbamide (many Europeans, Americans, American Indians, and Chinese are among those who can taste it)? Furthermore, how do you classify people whose parents had different skin colors? Could you distinguish between some Asians and whites if you only took skin color into account? How would you classify the golf professional, Tiger Woods, who some believe looks like an African American, but who is one-eighth black, one-quarter Thai, one-quarter Chinese, one-quarter white, and one-eighth American Indian?

The point is, any classification method is arbitrary. One system commonly used in the past identified six major "stocks"—Mongoloid, White, Negroid, Australoid, American Indian, and Polynesian (Coon, Garn, and Birdsell 1950). The researchers subdivided the six stocks into thirty races. They defined the six major stocks by biological characteristics, but geographical distribution and population size were also used. They deemed skin color an insufficient indicator of race.

More importantly, people who use skin color as a sign of the biological superiority of a particular group or groups fail to understand that the entire human race is one biological species—*Homo Sapiens*—and that skin color is a minor biological characteristic. Some scientists would like to do away with the concept of race altogether. Only about one half of physical anthropologists accept the notion of human biological races (Lieberman and Jackson 1995). And geneticists tend to view the term race, as most people use it, as virtually meaningless. Three geneticists who analyzed a half-century of research in population genetics concluded that the races are remarkably alike except for minor traits such as skin color and size (Cavalli-Sforza, Menozzi, and Piazza 1994). They pointed out that there is more variation within groups than among groups.

Race, then, is a minor biological, but a major social, phenomenon. This is why we include its effects on interaction in our definition. The fact that your skin is one color and that of another student in your class is a different color has nothing to do, per se, with your abilities or your potential as a human. It has a great deal to do, however, with your prospects in the United States and in other nations of the world.

Thinking Critically

Although a minor biological factor, race is very important socially. For instance, you need to be cautious in making comparisons between the races. As we shall point out below, some people of every race tend to be prejudiced against people of other races. Who is the most prejudiced? It is difficult to say. Researchers at the University of Michigan measured **prejudice** by the use of attitude scales. They found that African Americans are more likely than whites to use the extreme choices (such as "strongly agree" rather than merely "agree") re-

gardless of the question asked (Fischman 1984). The researchers have no explanation for this tendency. But if African Americans tend to respond to a prejudicial statement with "strongly agree" and whites tend to respond with "agree," African Americans will show up as more prejudiced than whites. In reality, there may be no difference in how prejudiced they are. Thus, you should be cautious when making racial comparisons about prejudice or other attitudes measured by agreement/disagreement statements.

Ethnic Groups

An **ethnic group** is composed of people with a shared cultural background that leads them to identify with each other. The concept of ethnicity is complex, however, because considerable diversity exists within ethnic groups. In the United States, for instance, Hispanics and Asian Americans are ethnic groups. Ethnic members may share such things as language, type of food eaten, and various cultural traditions. Yet Hispanics can be of any race, including whites, blacks, Indians, Asians, and some who are a racial mix. Moreover, Spaniards, Cubans, Mexicans and other Hispanics are not exactly alike in language, food, and traditions. Similarly, considerable differences exist between Japanese, Chinese, Vietnamese, and other Asians. Most census data, however, refer only to Hispanics or Asian Americans as a group. Wherever possible, we will note differences between subgroups.

Ethnic groups persist as long as people maintain their traditional cultural ways. In the past, groups of Germans, Swedes, Italians, and other Europeans came to this country and, for a time, maintained their native culture and language. Gradually, they, or their children, became Americanized and lost their ethnic identity.

Ethnic and racial identities overlap. An individual is not only Swedish but white, not only Nigerian but Negroid, not only Taiwanese but Mongoloid. For nonwhites, then, Americanization has a different meaning than it has for whites. If nonwhites lose their ethnic identity over the course of the generations, they do not lose their racial identity. They continue to be a minority regardless of the ethnicity they discard.

Minorities

A **minority**, for sociological purposes, is a disadvantaged racial or ethnic group. The disadvantages range from economic position to social acceptance. Thus, individuals in a minority may receive a lower income than that earned by nonminority individuals doing the same kind of work. Even if a minority individual has a high-income profession, such as a physician, he or she may not be as socially accepted.

Many of the foreign born in the United States are likely to be part of a minority group. In 1996, the Census Bureau reported nearly 25 million foreign-born people in the United States, a third of whom have already become naturalized citizens (U.S. Bureau of the Census 1996a). The largest numbers were Mexicans (6.7 million), Filipinos (1.2 million), and Chinese (801,000). Other nations represented by more than 500,000 were Cuba, India, Vietnam, El Salvador, Canada, Korea, Germany, the Dominican Republic, and Jamaica.

In addition to the foreign born, various racial and ethnic groups also constitute part of America's minorities. As Table 9.1 shows, these groups now comprise more than a fourth of the population, and the proportion is growing. In fact, most of the racial and ethnic groups are growing faster than are whites (Figure 9.1). From 1980 to 1996 the non Hispanic, white population declined from 79.9 to 73.2 percent of the total. Both immigration and higher birth rates account for the decreasing proportion of the population that is white and non Hispanic. By the middle of the twenty-first century, white, non Hispanic Americans will be less than half the population if the present trend continues.

Figure 9.1   **Average Annual Rates of Population Growth, by Race**

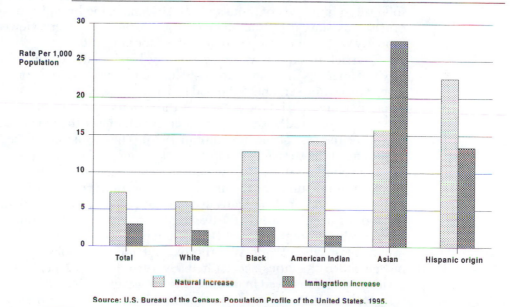

Source: U.S. Bureau of the Census. Population Profile of the United States. 1995.

Table 9.1	Racial Composition of the Population	
	Number (millions)	Percent
White, not Hispanic	194.3	73.2
Black, not Hispanic	32.0	12.1
Hispanic origin (any race)	28.0	10.6
Asian and Pacific Islander	9.1	3.4
American Indian, Eskimo, Aleut	2.0	0.7
Total	265.4	100.0
Total White, including Hispanic	219.8	82.8
Total Black, including Hispanic	33.7	12.7

Source: U.S. Bureau of the Census 1996f.

Racial and Ethnic Groups in the United States

You've seen the numbers. Now let's look at the people who fall into the various racial and ethnic groups. We begin with African Americans, the largest nonwhite group.

African Americans

There are more black people in the United States (33.7 million) than in most African nations. Only Nigeria, Ethiopia, and Zaire have larger black populations than the United States. Africans were first brought to colonial America in 1619. At that point they were probably considered indentured servants rather than slaves. But the economic value of slaves soon led to hundreds of thousands of Africans being brought to North America as slaves. By the eighteenth century, slaves were viewed as property with no civil or personal rights (Jordan 1970).

Even before slavery was a legal reality, blacks suffered discriminatory treatment in the courts. In 1640, for example, a Virginia court sentenced two white servants, who had run away, to serve their masters for an additional year and the colony for three years. But a black runaway servant was ordered to serve his master, or whomever the master designated, for the rest of his life (Jordan 1970). This decision marked the beginning of the transformation of blacks from persons into property.

The abolition of slavery by the Thirteenth Amendment to the Constitution, unfortunately, did not resolve the race problem. Until the 1940s, most African Americans lived in rural areas. Although many began moving to cities early in the twentieth century, this migration slowed considerably during the Great Depression because of the lack of jobs in urban areas. When World War II broke out and many jobs opened up, movement to the cities accelerated. By 1950, about 62 percent of all African Americans lived in urban areas. However, unlike other poor rural people who throughout the nation's history improved their lot by moving to the cities, African Americans continued to find most doors of opportunity closed to them. Indeed, they found that social mobility in a segregated society was virtually impossible.

The nature of black protest and the manner in which the race problem is defined have changed frequently since slavery ended (Meier, Rudwick, and Broderick 1971). Booker T. Washington, a prominent black educator of the late nineteenth century, urged social, economic, and moral development of African Americans. Washington believed that African Americans could make significant progress even though they lived in a segregated society. He failed to recognize the extent to which such things as sharecropping, corrupt relief agencies, and restricted opportunities would prevent African Americans from sharing in the nation's prosperity.

The National Association for the Advancement of Colored People (NAACP), founded in 1909, inaugurated an era of legal protest in contrast to the accommodation to **segregation** advocated by Booker T. Washington. However, when legal victories failed to achieve equality, direct nonviolent actions emerged, most notably under the leadership of Rev. Dr. Martin Luther King, Jr., a Baptist minister.

King's nonviolent protest movement developed out of the Montgomery Bus Boycott in the mid-1950s. On December 1, 1955, Rosa Parks, an African American, boarded a city bus in Montgomery Alabama and sat in the whites-only section. When she refused to move, she was arrested. King worked with groups like the local NAACP and the Women's Political Council (WPC). The WPC had tried to end **discrimination** on buses for a number of years prior to Parks' arrest (Garrow 1987). The leaders mobilized the black population to engage in vigorous protest, and the protest eventually went beyond segregated buses to segregation per se. King defined the problem as a moral one, urging that whites needed to be redeemed through the power of love and suffering.

Continuing white resistance to change, along with brutal treatment of nonviolent protesters, led to the black militancy of the 1960s. Militancy, however, gave way in the 1970s to renewed efforts to "work through the system." African Americans ran for political offices and emphasized the importance of political efforts in achieving equality and opportunity. Today, African Americans hold various ideas about the best way to redress the inequalities they continue to endure. Yet the majority believe that whites and blacks must work together and that, in spite of the obstacles African Americans face, the United States is still the best place to live (Roper Center 1996).

We noted examples of racial inequalities in the last chapter, including the far larger proportion of African Americans who live in poverty. Table 9.2 shows the amount of inequality in median household income in 1995. Note that table 9.2 is not inclusive because recent data are not available for all groups. For example, the latest data available on American Indians are for 1989, when family income was 63.2 percent that of whites and 27.2 percent lived in poverty (U.S. Bureau of the Census 1996d, p. 50). Note in Table 9.2 that the median income for African American households was 60.2 percent that of white households. How much progress does that represent? If you go back to 1970, some 15 years after the modern Civil Rights movement began, the median income for African American households was 60.9 percent! This represents an increase over the past but is less than that of 1978 when the this group's median income was at its highest point—64 percent. In other words, African American households, in comparison to whites, are at about the same level of income as they were in 1970, and lower than they were in 1978. Such figures are part of the answer to those who question why African Americans continue to protest about inequality.

Table 9.2	**Household Income, by Race and Ethnicity**		
		Median Income	**Percent of White Income**
	All households	$34,076	
	White, not Hispanic	37,178	
	African American	22,393	60.2
	Hispanic origin	22,860	61.5
	Asian American	40,614	109.2

Source: U.S. Bureau of the Census 1996a.

Some additional facts about the status of African Americans are (U.S. Bureau of the Census 1996b):

- In 1994, 55 percent of all African Americans lived in the South, 17 percent in the Northeast, 20 percent in the Midwest, and 8 percent in the West.

- Between 1987 and 1992, the number of African Americans owning businesses increased by 46 percent.

- The proportion of African American adults with a high school diploma increased from 51 percent in 1980 to 73 percent in 1994. In 1994, 12.9 percent of African American adults, compared to 23 percent of whites, had a bachelor's degree.

- In 1993, 54 percent of African American children under eighteen lived with their mothers only, compared to 16 percent of white children.

- In 1994, nearly twice the proportion of white males (27 percent) as African American males (15 percent) worked in managerial and professional jobs; for service jobs, the proportions were 20 percent for African Americans and 10 percent for whites.

The picture presented by these data shows both gains and losses for African Americans. But the gains are not as great as, and the losses are more severe than, those reported for whites. How can you account for such inequalities? The answers are found in the legacy of slavery, the experience of segregation, and the conditions of discrimination in which African Americans live. For instance, the high rate of children growing up in a mother-only household is a legacy of slavery which routinely broke up black families. As Ruggles (1994) has shown in his analysis of *existing data* on African Americans, black children have been two to three times more likely than white children to live without one or both parents since the end of slavery.

At any rate, the lack of educational and occupational attainment does not reflect a lack of motivation. Using *survey research* from a national study to examine differences in educational and occupational aspirations of high school sophomores, Solorzano (1991) found that African Americans have higher educational and occupational aspirations than Hispanics, who, in turn, have higher aspirations than whites. Clearly, something happens to thwart those aspirations.

Some scholars believe that social class rather than racial discrimination is the main problem facing African Americans today (Wilson 1987). They argue that black America has polarized into a growing middle class and an impoverished "underclass" that is largely trapped in urban **ghettos** (Landry 1988). No doubt, the lower-class blacks in urban ghettos face the typical dilemmas and obstacles of the lower class. In addition, as we shall document below, they may also face insurmountable hurdles of prejudice and discrimination.

Hispanic Americans

Hispanics include all those with Spanish as their native language or with a heritage of Spanish culture. Spanish explorers came to North America in the fifteenth century and established Spanish-speaking colonies, particularly in the southern part of the continent. The growth of the Hispanic population in the United States increased dramatically in the nineteenth century. First, as a result of the war with Mexico in 1848, vast areas of what is now the Southwest and West were added to the nation, and a considerable number of Mexicans suddenly became American citizens. Then, at the end of the Spanish-American War in 1898, the United States took control of several Spanish-controlled territories including Puerto Rico. As a result, many Puerto Ricans began to migrate to the mainland.

Mexicans, the largest group of Hispanic peoples in the United States, came in vast numbers after the 1910 revolution in Mexico (Baydo 1974). It was a bloody war in which more than 1 million Mexicans lost their lives and was followed by years of chaos and disorder. It's not surprising, then, that in the ten years following the revolution, more than a million Mexicans fled to the United States.

Another influx of Hispanics occurred after Cuba became a communist nation in 1959. Additional Hispanics have emigrated—for economic or political reasons—to the United States from the various nations of Central and South America. Thus, the term "Hispanic" includes a rather diverse group of people. Some Hispanics prefer a term that identifies their country of origin, such as "Mexican American." While all Hispanics share certain cultural characteristics, considerable differences also exist. You have seen, for example, that Hispanics have a lower median income and a higher rate of poverty than whites. Yet within the Hispanic community, economic well-being varies considerably, with Puerto Ricans by far the poorest. Unfortunately, much of the available information concerns the Hispanic population as a whole rather than as subgroups. Thus, we will treat them as a single group but will identify particular national backgrounds when information is available.

Hispanics currently constitute nearly 11 percent of the U.S. population and, except for Asians, have grown faster than any other group since 1980. High birth rates as well as immigration contribute to Hispanic growth (Garcia and Montgomery 1991). By 2020, if present trends continue, Hispanics will constitute the largest minority in the United States.

Because of larger family size, the Hispanic population is younger (median age about 26) than the total population (median age about 34) (U.S. Bureau of the Census 1996d, p. 23). Nearly a fourth of Hispanic families have a female head, compared to 14 percent of white families, 46 percent of black families, and 13 percent of Asian American families (U.S. Bureau of the Census 1996d, p. 62). Hispanics, however, are less likely than either whites or African Americans to be divorced.

Hispanics are only slightly better off economically than African Americans, with a slightly higher median income (Table 9.2) and a lower rate of poverty. They are better off than African Americans, but worse off than whites, in employment. Hispanic unemployment rates are generally one-and-a-half to two times that of whites and slightly lower than that of African Americans. The federal government has helped minorities as a source of employment. Nearly 17 percent of the more than 2 million civilian, non-postal employees of the federal executive branch are African Americans (U.S. Bureau of the Census 1996d, p. 346). However, Hispanics only have 5.7 percent of federal government jobs—less than their proportion of the population.

Although they have high educational aspirations, Hispanics have comparatively low educational attainment (U.S. Bureau of the Census 1996d, p. 159). In 1995, 53.4 percent of Hispanic adults completed high school (compared to 83 percent of whites and 73.8 percent of African Americans). And 9.3 percent earned a bachelor's degree or more (compared to 23.0 percent of whites and 13.2 percent of African Americans).

Hispanics, like African Americans, now look to judicial and political processes to help them make gains. By 1993, Hispanics held 5,170 elective offices in the nation (compared to 7,984 for African Americans). This number includes national, state, and local officials; therefore, Hispanics represent only a tiny fraction of all elected officials. At the local level, 1 percent of officials are Hispanics. Nevertheless, Hispanics are a political force with which to be reckoned. They live primarily in California, Texas, and New York—three states crucial to presidential elections. Political parties now actively court Hispanic support. Thus, the number of Hispanics in positions of political power is likely to increase.

Asian Americans

The Asian experience in the United States is a mixed one (Baydo 1974). The first Chinese to arrive in California after the 1848 discovery of gold at Sutter's Mill were merchants who came to set up businesses. They no doubt sent reports about the newly discovered gold back to China because 18,000 Chinese came to California in 1852. This was in marked contrast to the less than a thousand that had come in the years prior to 1850.

At first the Chinese were welcomed in the United States. However, as their numbers grew during the 1850s, particularly in mining areas, the Chinese were increasingly viewed as economic competitors. By the late 1850s, riots and violent attacks on Chinese were occurring in the mining areas. In the 1860s, thousands of Chinese found work constructing railroad lines. They worked hard for minimal wages but still failed to win respect from white Americans.

In fact, hostility—in the form of legal restrictions and violence—grew and culminated in 1882 when Chinese were forbidden to enter the country. Then, in the 1890s, Japanese immigrants began arriving in significant numbers. Most of the early arrivals were peasants who worked as laborers on farms or in factories. Later arrivals started successful businesses of various kinds, and their success again generated a hostile reaction. In the early 1900s, California newspapers warned of the "yellow peril" and called for exclusion of the Japanese. The most dramatic anti-Japanese action occurred during World War II when 112,000 West Coast Japanese (two-thirds of whom were American citizens) were forced into relocation camps.

In spite of the adverse experiences of the past, Asians continue to come to the United States in large numbers. A mass of refugees poured into the country from Vietnam following the end of the war in 1975. Between 1980 and the mid-1990s, Asians were the fastest growing group in the United States—largely because of immigration. More than 37 percent of all immigrants in the decade of the 1980s were Asian (Barringer 1992). Chinese, Filipinos, and Japanese are the most numerous of the Asians in the United States, constituting nearly 4 percent of the total population.

Although the Asian American community is not without complaints of mistreatment today, Asian Americans fare better than other racial and ethnic groups. Economically, as Table 9.2 shows, they even do better than white Americans, having the highest median income of any group. However, these figures should not obscure the differences within the Asian American community. Asian Americans tend to cluster in the higher and lower strata, with many doing quite well and many living in poverty. Dramatic differences exist between the wealthy Chinese Americans who live in suburban homes and those in the Chinatowns of New York, San Francisco, and Los Angeles (Takaki 1989). Differences also exist by nationality. Chinese and Japanese, for instance, tend to have higher incomes than Vietnamese. Moreover, the poverty rate among Asian Americans is slightly higher than that of white Americans. Still, as a group Asian Americans are doing well economically.

Asian Americans are also noted for educational achievements. A higher proportion of Asian Americans than white Americans completes high school (Bennett 1993). And 38.2 percent of Asian Americans complete four or more years of college, compared to 23 percent of whites, 13.2 percent of African Americans, and 9.3 percent of Hispanics (U.S. Bureau of the Census 1996d, p. 49, 159).

Their families' values account for the educational success of Asian American students (Chen and Stevenson 1995). Parents expect their children to be responsible, work hard, and do well. They do whatever is necessary to assure this outcome (including sometimes even giving children homework over and above what teachers assign).

Asian American families tend to be close-knit. They have lower rates of divorce and teenage pregnancy than any other group (Dunn 1994). As successive generations are born in the United States, however, the families tend to become more like other American families. For instance, Chinese American children resist parental control over matters, such as marriage, that involve their personal freedom and growth (Lin and Liu 1993).

If this sounds as though Asian Americans have virtually no problems, we will correct the impression when we discuss prejudice and discrimination. Here, we will note that there may be a price to pay for single-minded devotion to achievement. A comparison of 111 Asian American and 111 white college students found that the Asian Americans were more pessimistic, had more depressive and other psychological symptoms, and were more likely to cope with stress by avoidance and withdrawal (Chang 1996). Further, a study of ninth graders reported that the Asian Americans, compared to the white students, had less delinquent behavior and better academic records. However, they were also significantly more isolated, more depressed and anxious, and less likely to seek help for their problems (Lorenzo et al. 1995).

White Ethnics

White ethnics are the Europeans (other than the English and Scots) and their descendants who began to emigrate to the United States in large numbers around 1830. Germans and Irish were among the first of these large groups. The Germans, who tended to be fairly prosperous, quickly established themselves as farmers in the interior regions of the nation. But the Irish, who were poor and also Roman Catholic in a predominately Protestant nation, experienced prejudice and discrimination and were only slowly accepted into the larger society.

In the late nineteenth and early twentieth century a great wave of Eastern and Southern European immigrants entered the United States. These immigrants were predominately Roman Catholic or Jewish, didn't speak English, and were poor. They crowded together in ethnic ghettos in eastern cities. A ghetto is an urban area inhabited predominantly by one minority group. The size, high visibility, and cultural differences of the immigrants fostered an ethnocentric attitude in the nation. The newcomers were viewed as inferior and as a threat to the American way of life. As a result, stringent immigration restrictions were enacted in 1924.

European immigrants have tended to lose their ethnicity rather quickly and to disappear as an identifiable ethnic group. Indeed, the longer a family has been in the United States, the less likely it is for the present generation to speak the language of origin, to observe cultural traditions, and to live in ethnic enclaves. Of course, some white ethnics have tried to recapture their heritage and preserve their cultural roots (Schaefer 1993). Yet most think of themselves simply as Americans, even though they can list one or more European ancestries when asked.

The tendency to lose ethnicity is illustrated in Erdmans' (1995) study of Polish people in Chicago, where she found third-generation Polish Americans living among recent immigrants from Poland. Rather than feeling a sense of solidarity with each other, however, the two groups find themselves in conflict. One source of conflict is the recent immigrants' cultural orientation to Poland and the cultural orientation of the Polish Americans to the United States. The second source of conflict, as suggested by *conflict theory*, is the diverse needs and interests of the two groups. The immigrants have a need to learn the culture of their new country rather than remain embedded in the culture of Poland, while the Polish Americans have a need to maintain their attachment to American culture. When the immigrants act in accord with their traditional cultural ways, they generally receive neither sympathy nor understanding from Polish Americans.

Similarly, using *participant observation*, Stoller (1996) studied ethnic identity among second- and third-generation Finnish Americans. The Finnish Americans expressed pride in Finnish history and culture, but generally felt no attachment to issues which were of major concern to Finland. Rather, they engaged in selected and occasional ethnic activities, such as ethnic meals, an occasional Finnish phrase, and a Finnish twist to celebrating a holiday. Furthermore, involvement in Finnish culture was more pronounced among the older Finnish Americans. The younger were less likely than the older to be fluent in Finnish, to marry other Finns, to live in an ethnic neighborhood, and to be comfortable around fellow Finnish Americans.

White ethnics, in sum, have choices that those from other races do not have. They can maintain as much or as little of their ethnicity as they choose. The less they maintain, the more likely they are to be viewed as simply American, without any stigma of racial or ethnic difference attached to them.

Jewish Americans

You may think of Jews as a religious group, but they are also an ethnic group. Most Jews, but not all, practice the religion of Judaism. As a young Jewish woman told us, "I am a cultural Jew, but I am not a religious Jew." She identified with other Jewish people, but considered herself an agnostic.

There are nearly six million Jewish Americans, and nearly half of them live in the northeastern states (U.S. Bureau of the Census 1996d, p. 70). The first Jewish immigrants were 23 refugees from Brazil who came to New Amsterdam (New York) in 1654 (Reich 1994). The colonies discouraged Jewish immigrants by not allowing them to vote or hold political office. Yet they continued to come.

The number of Jewish immigrants was small until the last decades of the nineteenth century when large numbers came from various European nations where they faced persecution and death. For example, Jews in Russia were generally forbidden to own land or to live in cities (Conlin 1984). They faced arbitrary treatment by authorities and experienced harassment and death at the hands of authorities and citizens. Between 1881 and 1914, a third of the Jews in Russia left for other lands, most of them for the United States (Conlin 1984).

Anti-Semitism, prejudice against Jewish people, existed in the United States from the time of the first immigrants and intensified as the number of Jews increased. In the nineteenth century, some colleges and universities refused to admit Jews. As late as the middle of this century, some employers would not hire Jews, particularly for more prestigious jobs, and many exclusive social clubs refused to admit them. However, anti-Semitism may have reached its peak in the 1920s and 1930s when Jews were accused of being at the heart of a conspiracy to take control of the U.S. economy and government. Jewish Americans were openly treated with hostility and contempt by the Ku Klux Klan as well as by influential persons like Henry Ford (Marty 1984).

Since the 1930s, the Jewish American proportion of the population has been declining. The main issues for Jewish Americans are no longer anti-Semitism and economic survival, but the loss of identity as an ethnic group (Lipset and Raab 1995). Increasing numbers of Jewish Americans are neither affiliated with, nor concerned about, distinctive Jewish concerns and ethnic practices. In other words, they define themselves as Americans, rather than Jewish Americans.

Like Asian Americans, Jewish Americans have an impressive record of achieving high educational, occupational, and income levels (Lipset 1990; Chriswick 1993). More than half have college degrees, compared to 22.2 percent of the general population. A disproportionate number of Jewish Americans work in upper-level white-collar occupations. Although long excluded from top corporate positions, Jewish Americans have made significant contributions in science, education, and the arts.

The achievements of Jewish Americans result from many factors, including the high level of skills possessed by many immigrants. Social scientists also give credit to important elements in Jewish culture, such as the dietary and hygiene rules of the Jewish religion which enhanced their health, the strong sense of family, and the high value placed on education and learning.

American Indians

American Indians are numerically the smallest of the racial groups in the United States—2.3 million, or 0.9 percent of the population. This represents a considerable increase over the past few decades because the American Indian population tripled between 1960 and 1990. A substantial part of the increase ensued from people changing their official identities on the national census from non-Indian to Indian (Nagel 1995). In part, this switch resulted from political activism and the desire to reclaim cultural identity among the Indian population.

There are more than 550 Indian tribes and Alaskan native groups that speak more than 250 languages, and there are 278 Indian reservations under federal jurisdiction (Bureau of Indian Affairs 1992). From the time of initial contact, Europeans viewed the Indians as inferior. At best, they portrayed the Indians as "noble savages." At worst, they regarded them as "ruthless savages" who could be justifiably exterminated. For instance, a 1782 letter to a popular magazine advocated extermination, citing such things as Indian torture of prisoners and their general character:

> They have the shapes of men and may be of the human species, but certainly in their present state they approach nearer the character of Devils; take an Indian, is there any faith in him? Can you bind him by favors? Can you trust his word or confide in his promise? . . . The tortures which they exercise on the bodies of their prisoners, justify extermination. (Binder and Reimers 1988, pp. 19–20)

What to do with the "savages" has been an ongoing dilemma for the nation. The above writer was not alone in advocating extermination. As whites settled onto more and more of the land that once belonged to the Indians, violent conflict increased. Official policy became one of segregating Indians from the rest of the population. In the nineteenth century, this meant the forcible removal of many Indians from their traditional lands to reservations in the West.

Of course, the policy of "Indian removal" meant that existing treaties, which had given Indians certain lands east of the Mississippi "as long as the water runs and the grass grows," had to be broken (Conlin 1984, p. 241). Tragedy ensued as tribes rebelled and were defeated by military force. One of the more tragic incidents occurred among the Cherokees. The Cherokees were, by treaty, entitled to permanent residency on their established homelands and were even recognized as a semi-sovereign "nation" within the United States. Despite a Supreme Court ruling that said the state of Georgia had no authority over Cherokee territory, the Cherokees were forcibly removed from their lands in Georgia and other southeastern states. Their 1,200 mile forced march to Oklahoma was called the Trail of Tears, because thousands of Indians—a fourth of the Cherokee tribe—died from hunger, disease, and exposure.

Today, nearly half of American Indians live in the West and a third live in the South. They tend to have larger families than the general population, so that the median age (27 years) is lower than that of the total population (34 years). Slightly more than a fourth of American Indian families are headed by a female, and about two-thirds are headed by a married couple (U.S. Bureau of the Census 1996d, p. 50).

American Indians are the most deprived of the racial and ethnic groups. They have the highest unemployment rate of any group, averaging close to 45 percent for those on reservations (Cebula and Belton 1994). About two-thirds of adults are high school graduates (compared to 80.9 percent in the total population) and 9.4 percent have four or more years of college (compared to 22.2 percent in the total population). Median family income is only about 61 percent that of the national median, and the poverty rate is more than double that of the nation as a whole—nearly a third of all American Indians live in poverty (U.S. Bureau of the Census 1996d, p. 50).

As with others who are chronically deprived, American Indians experience high rates of crime, violence, and drug abuse. They also have the health problems associated with poverty and drug abuse (Kimball, Goldberg, and Oberle 1996). Life expectancy is only 42 years! Suicide rates are higher than in the general population. And infant mortality rates as much as three times the national average in some tribes (Kilborn 1992).

As with the other groups we have discussed, there are subgroup variations. In the case of American Indians, the subgroups are tribes. For example, the proportion of adults with high school degrees varies from 51.0 percent of the Navajo to 71.9 percent of the Iroquois (U.S. Bureau of the Census 1996d, p. 50). Poverty rates also vary—from one in five among the Iroquois to nearly half of the Navajo.

Explorations

Your New Friend

Reading about people in racial and ethnic groups different from your own is helpful in understanding group variations. But close contact with someone from a different group adds a new dimension to your understanding. Have each group member identify someone from a different racial or ethnic background in your school or neighborhood. If you do this as an individual project, follow the same guidelines:

Begin the acquaintance by telling the person that you are working on a school project and that you want to understand his or her racial or ethnic group better. Among the things you will want to explore are:

- How does the person's racial/ethnic identity affect the way that other people relate to him or her?

- How does the racial/ethnic identity affect the person's efforts to achieve his or her goals?

- How does his or her family traditions or practices differ from yours?

- What does the person think about race relations in America?

- In what ways does the person think that he or she is no different from other Americans?

Ask any other questions you need to obtain a full sense of what it is like to live in the United States as a member of that person's racial/ethnic group. Discuss your experiences in the group.

Prejudice and Discrimination: Racism in Action

Do you feel any hostility toward people who belong to racial or ethnic groups different from your own? Do you treat them any differently? Do you believe that they are generally inferior to members of your own group? The first question refers to **prejudice**, a negative attitude toward people in another racial/ethnic group that justifies discriminatory behavior. The second question refers to **discrimination**—arbitrary, unfavorable treatment of people in another racial/ethnic group. The third refers to **racism**, the belief that some racial groups are inherently inferior to others.

To what extent are prejudice, discrimination, and racism prevalent in the United States today? Your answer will vary depending on your own racial/ethnic background. In a national poll asking Americans how big a problem racism is, 68 percent of African Americans but only 38 percent of whites agreed that it is a big problem (Roper Center 1996).

As *feminist theorists* point out, your answer will also vary depending upon your gender. Thus, an African American woman experiences a double-edged prejudice, and it may be impossible to sort out whether the prejudice is rooted primarily in race or gender or in both. As a group of black feminists put it: "We also often find it difficult to separate race from class from sex oppression because in our lives they are most often experienced simultaneously" (Combahee River Collective 1992, p. 135). We'll examine gender in the next chapter; here we'll discuss what the research tells us about prejudice, discrimination, and racism.

Prejudice

A native-born white American, writing in 1838, recorded his reaction to a naturalization ceremony for new citizens (Binder and Reimers 1988, p. 240):

> It was enough to turn a man's stomach . . . to see the way they were naturalizing this morning at the *Hall*. Wretched, filthy, bestial-looking Italians and Irish . . . the very scum and dregs of human nature filled the . . . office so completely that I was almost afraid of being poisoned by going in.

Similar observations could be quoted about every racial/ethnic group in the nation. How widespread is such prejudice? Do only a few Americans hold such negative attitudes toward other racial/ethnic groups, or do many or all of us have some degree of prejudice? When we say "all," we mean literally all Americans. Sometimes prejudice is viewed as an attribute of whites toward other groups. Yet all groups exhibit some prejudice, and it may be true that few if any people are completely free of prejudice.

A national survey that asked people to identity typical attributes of others found that nearly a third of whites agreed that African Americans are more likely to be criminals, violent, dangerous, and lazy (Patterson and Kim 1991). On the other hand, 21 percent of Af-

ricanAmericanscharacterizedwhitesasgreedy,and14percentcharac-
terizedthemasdangerous.

Other researchers report similar findings. A comparison of African American and white students found that both groups had a typical ingroup bias toward the other (Wood and Allen 1996). An
examination of interview results on 153 police officers applying for
promotion reported that both white and African American interviewers gave higher ratings to members of their own race (Prewett-Liv-
ingston 1996).

Prejudice exists not only between whites and other groups, but
also among the various minorities. Some African Americans are
prejudiced toward Jews (Sigelman 1995). Moreover, African Americans, Hispanics, and Asian Americans are as prejudiced against each
other as they are against whites (Holmes 1994).

Prejudice is probably more widespread than the surveys indicate.
As Pettigrew (1994) has pointed out, prejudice against African Americans is more covert and subtle than it was at one time. It is no longer
socially acceptable to be openly prejudiced. You may even be among
the many people who do not want to be prejudiced. But give yourself
this simple test: honestly evaluate your emotional reaction when you
encounter strangers from various racial/ethnic groups. Do you feel
any twinge of anxiety or suspicion or hostility toward those who are
different from you? Do you have any sense of an ingroup/outgroup
distinction? These kinds of feelings are evidence of prejudice.

Prejudice also manifests itself in racist attitudes. Such attitudes
mean that people are treated as inferior even when they have demonstrated their competence. For instance, one of the complaints of
middle-class African Americans is that they encounter low expectations for their performance in business and the professions even
when their credentials and training indicate high competence (Cose
1993).

Prejudice, incidentally, is found everywhere. A study of people's
attitudes in twelve European nations found prejudice against immigrants and people of other races in all of them (Quillian 1995).
Furthermore, the prejudice was fueled by some of the same conditions as prejudice in the United States: the size of the immigrant
or racial groups and the perceived economic threat posed by the
groups.

Discrimination

Have you ever personally experienced discrimination? Has anyone
ever treated you badly or unjustly simply because of your racial/ethnic
background? How common do you think discrimination is in the United
States? In the world of work, a national poll reported that 13 percent of

Experiences

'Sometimes I Feel Like an Immigrant'

For most Americans, intergenerational mobility is a cherished ideal. But when that mobility occurs, it might not have quite the same luster for a minority family as it does for a family from the white majority. The Lopez family is black and Hispanic and lives in an affluent, mostly-white suburb. Carlos and Maria both came from working-class homes. He is a marketing executive and she is a public-relations officer. They have one child. Life is good. But not completely, as Carlos explained to us:

We moved into this neighborhood because we wanted our son to go to good schools. I think I know a good deal about our white neighbors, but they don't know much at all about us or the world we live in. What makes me angry sometimes is that I don't believe that they *want* to know us. Sometimes I feel like an immigrant, someone from a different world.

We live near a nice shopping center. Shortly after we moved here, Maria went to a department store to look for some jewelry. It was Saturday, so she wore blue jeans. She felt like she was being watched, and she was. A saleslady followed her around and watched her constantly, as if she might be trying to steal something. And we've both had this happen to us on other occasions. Just because we're black, people suspect us.

Or they don't think of us as professionals. One day I was cutting my front lawn, and a neighbor from down the street drove by and asked how much I would charge to do her lawn. Can you imagine that? Just because I'm black, she assumed that I was only working there instead of living there. She would never have just assumed that of a white man, no matter how dirty he was from working.

whites and 44 percent of African Americans believed they had personally been denied a job or a promotion because of their race (Roper Center 1996). The proportions of both races that actually suffered discrimination might be higher or lower than those figures. However, from a *symbolic interactionist* perspective, the important thing is the perception: more than one of every ten white workers and more than four of every ten African American workers believe they have been victimized and are therefore hurt, angry, and/or frustrated. These feelings fuel the ongoing tensions between the races.

Part of the evidence of ongoing discrimination in the nation is found in the income disparities shown in Table 9.2. Detailed analyses have shown that the disparities cannot be explained completely by educational differences or differences in occupational categories. When such factors are taken into account, African Americans and Hispanics still earn less than white non-Hispanics. In fact, the proportion of the earnings gap that *cannot* be explained by differences in qualifications (and is, therefore, a result of discrimination) has increased since the late 1970s (Cancio, Evans and Maume 1996). The increase in discrimination has coincided with the increased earnings gap between whites on the one hand, and African Americans and Hispanics on the other hand, over the same period of time.

Table 9.2 shows that Asian Americans earn more on the average than any other group. This does not necessarily mean that they face no discrimination (Zhou and Kamo 1994). Foreign-born Chinese do not earn as much as whites even when they have the same amount of education as whites. Furthermore, Chinese and Japanese born in the United States fall short of the earnings of their white counterparts in the state of California.

Discrimination is also evident in employment. Unemployment rates for African Americans have been roughly double those of whites since 1948 (Lauer 1997). This disadvantage is not unique to any particular area. African Americans in urban and rural areas and in different regions of the nation are similar in the disadvantage in employment they face (D'Amico and Maxwell 1995).

Once employed, minorities face discrimination in career advancement. African Americans may find themselves in a racially defined occupational line. Collins (1989) studied the careers of 76 black executives in white-owned corporations in Chicago. She found that they were most often in positions where they dealt primarily with black workers, mediated issues between white and black workers, or acted as public-relations persons with the black community.

Asian Americans, in spite of the income figures, see themselves as kept out of upper management positions. Indeed, a study of Asian Americans in engineering fields reported that they had achieved equality with their white counterparts in earnings but not in occupational advancement (Tang 1993). In particular, the Asian Americans were less likely than whites to advance to management positions.

Discrimination occurs in more than the work world, of course. We will give two additional examples that dramatize the pervasiveness of discrimination in American society. First, how would you feel about a hazardous waste site being constructed near your home? Or how do you feel about living in an area known for high levels of air pollution? One study found that minorities are much more likely to suffer exposure to waste sites, high levels of pollution, and other known hazards (Brown 1995). As a result, minorities are much more likely to suffer the adverse health consequences of exposure.

Second, how important is it to you that people treat you with respect? Have you had the experience of having someone view you as a possible criminal? Have you felt hostility from a store clerk or a waitress because you were of a different racial/ethnic background? In their interviews with 209 middle-class African Americans, Feagin and Sikes (1994) found countless illustrations of discriminatory treatment. Some of the respondents had been denied service or treated with hostility in hotels and restaurants. Others experienced various acts of rejection and humiliation: taxis that didn't stop, people who clearly showed their discomfort or distaste for them, and people who were obviously surprised that they were not menial workers.

Institutional Discrimination

Prejudice, by definition, justifies discrimination. Discrimination, in turn, tends to perpetuate prejudice. Indeed, one of the ways to reduce prejudice is to get people into close and sustained contact with each other as equals (Powers and Ellison 1995). As they do so, they discover their common humanity and can begin to relate to each other simply as people rather than as ingroup/outgroup members.

However, even if people have little or no prejudice, or even if they do not consciously act in accord with their prejudices, discriminatory behavior can still occur. **Institutional discrimination** is the maintenance of discriminatory behavior through the policies and practices of institutions. That is, whether or not people act out of prejudice, the operative policies and practices guarantee that minorities will suffer discriminatory treatment.

For example, many employers require new employees to have earned a bachelor's degree, a requirement that is even attached to jobs that have no direct connection between a degree and the skills needed for the work (Pincus 1994). Because most minorities are less likely than whites to have a college degree, this means that a greater proportion of them will automatically be ineligible for those jobs.

Another example is provided by comparing the wealth of whites and African Americans (Oliver and Shapiro 1995). Wealth is measured by total assets, and the wealth differences between the two races are even greater than the income differences. In fact, the median net wealth of black households is only about 10 percent that of white households—regardless of the socioeconomic level involved. Why, even among middle-class, college-educated African Americans, is there such a disparity?

Three factors seem to be involved. First, a greater proportion of whites either inherit money or borrow from their parents when they buy homes or start businesses. Second, because of the discriminatory policies of lending institutions, African Americans have, and always have had, more difficulty in securing home mortgages. This results in a greater proportion of African Americans living in rented accommodations. Thus, they don't get the tax breaks that facilitate the growth of wealth. Finally, when well-to-do African Americans in the past were able to purchase homes, they did so in all black neighborhoods. Those homes have not appreciated in value to the same extent that white homes have, resulting in less wealth to be inherited.

Like discrimination generally, institutional discrimination is pervasive. While examples can be found in all institutional areas, we shall give one more—in the area of higher education. We have pointed out that Hispanics lag behind many other groups in educational attainment. Colleges and universities have made efforts to recruit Hispanics and other minorities. However, in recent years a combination of rising admission standards and decreasing financial aid has hampered Hispanic enrollment (Halcon and Reyes 1991). The changes in standards and amounts of aid

EXTENSIONS

Our Tribal World

"We still live in a tribal world," a colleague of ours commented after reading about conflict in the former nation of Yugoslavia between Muslims, Serbs, and Croats. Putting diverse people into the same nation does not eradicate ancient animosities, particularly when the groups are largely segregated from each other. Even though they are of the same race, their differing ethnic backgrounds are the basis for prejudice, hostility, and violent conflict. Another bloody example involves the Hutu and Tutsi people of central Africa.

Most of the conflict between the Hutu and Tutsi has occurred in the neighboring nations of Rwanda and Burundi. Rwanda was the site of a particularly vicious massacre in 1994. Three ethnic groups inhabit Rwanda. The Hutu constitute about 90 percent, the Tutsi 9 percent, and the Twa 1 percent of the population of over eight million. The Twa are pygmies, and have played no part in the conflict. The fighting between the Hutu and Tutsi is long-standing and compounded by poverty, overcrowding (Rwanda is one of the most densely populated nations in Africa), environmental problems, and one of the highest rates of AIDS in the world.

The tribal rivalry is centuries old. The Tutsi came into the area from the north in the fifteenth century, conquered the Hutu, and became absolute rulers. They set up an estate system in which the Hutu were the serfs. The system lasted until the Belgians, who took over the area after World War I, forced the Tutsis to eliminate feudalism in 1958. The next year violence broke out between the tribes and the Tutsi king and some 200,000 of his tribe fled the nation.

Rwanda gained its independence in 1962. In 1963, some of the exiled Tutsi returned and attempted to regain control of the government. They failed, and the Hutu responded with a massacre of Tutsis. At the same time, Tutsis were killing thousands of Hutu in Burundi. Periodic outbreaks of violence continued until 1994, when both the Rwandan and Burundi presidents died in a suspicious plane crash. The Tutsis were suspected, and over the next few months a half-million Rwandans, mostly Tutsis and some moderate Hutus, were killed by the Hutu-dominated army. The Tutsis retaliated and killed thousands of Hutus. Virtually every family in the capital city of Kigali lost one or more members.

In 1996, it appeared that Burundi would follow suit as Hutu militants slaughtered Tutsis. The killing, as one observer put it, "left behind puddles of blood coagulated beneath simple beds, piles of charred children's bodies tossed into the corners of rooms and scores of hacked corpses lined up at the edge of the camp" (*Chicago Tribune*, October 21, 1996). The killings occurred in the aftermath of the massacre of thousands of Hutus by the Tutsi-dominated army of Burundi in the previous four months.

Because the aim of the conflict is extermination, women and children are killed indiscriminately along with men. In Rwanda, thousands of Tutsi women and girls watched their families being murdered and were then raped, tortured and kept as sex slaves by their captors.

As of this writing, the massacres and countermassacres continue to erupt. Estimates of the number of dead range up to a million or more. No one knows how many innocent people still face violent death simply because of their ethnicity.

Source: Varied editions of the *Chicago Tribune*, 1994-1996.

available were not intended to hurt minority enrollment, but this has been the result.

Affirmative Action: Solution or Problem?

What do you do when everyone agrees that minorities have suffered because of prejudice and discrimination? How do you rectify the situation? How do you establish justice? One answer has been affirmative-action programs, which require special consideration or special help to minorities with the goal of creating equal opportunity (such as scholarships designated for minorities and preference given to qualified minority applicants for jobs or promotions). Most white Americans believe that the programs have achieved their aim and are no longer needed (Golay and Rollyson 1996). Some have charged that the programs result in reverse discrimination, giving minorities an unfair advantage rather than an equal opportunity. Some minority members also agree that affirmative-action programs have served their purpose, arguing that it is insulting to believe that they need such programs rather than their own ability and effort to achieve success.

Unquestionably, affirmative-action programs have helped some members of minorities (although they have helped white women more than racial and ethnic minorities). Gandara (1995) studied fifty Hispanics who were born into poor families but obtained education at elite universities. All of their parents encouraged them to pursue their education, but many of the Hispanic students had difficulty getting into college-preparatory classes in high school. Because of their backgrounds, their teachers did not always regard them as college material. Yet they persevered, worked hard, and maintained high levels of aspiration. Many of them said they would not have continued their education if it had not been for the financial aid and special recruitment efforts arising out of affirmative-action programs.

Although there are some exceptions, minorities generally believe that affirmative-action programs are still needed. A national poll reported that 91 percent of African Americans believe that the nation needs to either maintain or increase affirmative-action programs (Golay and Rollyson 1996, p. 50). The future of these programs is in doubt, however, as a number of legislative and court actions now challenge them.

Forms of Interaction: Melting Pot or Salad Bowl or . . . ?

How have the diverse racial and ethnic groups related to each other in this country? Have prejudice and discrimination been the only experiences? Hasn't the United States truly been the land of opportunity for the various groups? In 1908, Israel Zangwill called America the "great Melting Pot," a fusing of various races and nationalities who work together to "build the Republic of Man and the Kingdom of God" (Conlin 1984, p. 484). Some sixty years later, the Rev. Jesse Jackson, a prominent African American leader, said America is more like vegetable soup than a melting pot: "There are separate pieces of corn, meat, and so on, each with its own identity" (Conlin 1984, p. 484). Others have used the analogy of a salad bowl to stress the fact that racial and ethnic identities remain distinct in the midst of the mixture of people who call themselves Americans.

The melting pot is an image in accord with structural functionism in which all the various parts of the system work together harmoniously for the good of the whole. Yet in fact unity is still elusive, as the vegetable soup and salad bowl images suggest. It is more realistic, we believe, to acknowledge that the relationships between the various racial and ethnic groups are as diverse as the groups themselves. Three primary kinds of intergroup relationships characterize the nation: conflict (including segregation), assimilation, and pluralism.

Conflict

From the perspective of conflict theory, racial/ethnic relations occur in the context of economic and power stratification (Feagin and Feagin 1994). Some theorists put it in terms of the white Anglo-Protestant settlers and their descendants exploiting people from other racial/ethnic groups by using them as cheap labor. The argument is that whites controlled the economy and used their power against the others—American Indians, Asians, Africans, and Hispanics—to maximize profits. The legacy is continuing stratification along racial/ethnic lines and continuing conflict among the groups as the dominants strive to maintain their position and those in the lower strata strive to move up.

Unquestionably, as we have already shown, a great deal of conflict has marked the experience of the various racial and ethnic groups. Even those who came as welcomed refugees—those whose interests the United States was officially seeking to protect—have encountered significant conflict. For example, the Indochinese refugees who came after the Vietnam war often found themselves in conflict with both the white majority and various other racial and ethnic groups as they tried to rebuild their lives in American cities (Hein 1995). Much of the conflict stemmed from perceived competition for jobs and from the perceived preferential treatment the government accorded the refugees as they sought housing and work.

One of the problems with the conflict approach, however, is that it doesn't take into account the fact that a great many whites—and not merely ethnic whites—have always been a part of the lower strata. It may be true that the racial and ethnic groups described above were exploited more than were Anglo-Saxon whites, but many of the latter are also exploited.

Nevertheless, it seems clear to us that any stratification system is inherently a system of conflict. By definition, only a limited number of people can get to the top. They will clearly do what they can to maintain their position, and those in the lower strata will do what they can do gain a bigger piece of the social and economic pie.

The point is, those at the top in the United States have been predominantly white. Other racial and ethnic groups have had to vie with the dominant Anglo whites as they strive to better their lot. The conflict has been cultural as well as economic. In any stratification system, those at the top tend to define what is best. Thus, the message from the top is: If you—the underdogs—want to get what we have, you must become more like us and do as we say.

For example, schools established for American Indians have typically geared the curriculum toward inculcating the dominant culture among the Indians. Students who resist, who want to maintain their traditional cultural ways, may do poorly at school and fail to make headway occupationally. In her study of Navajo youth, Dehyle (1995) found that the youth do better in school when their traditional culture is honored and maintained. They do poorly when they attend schools that ignore their culture and simply try to prepare them for lower-level jobs in the white person's world.

Segregation

One way for the elites of any society to maintain their power and position is to establish themselves as an ingroup that clearly possesses and controls those things valued in the society. The elites cannot intersperse themselves with the population generally; instead they must maintain their high-status identity and their solidarity. Thus, **segregation**, the physical and social separation of racial/ethnic groups from each other, has been a part of the experience of all the groups discussed earlier. In some cases, the segregation was voluntary and desired. Ethnic whites as well as Jews, for example, clustered in particular areas in order to give each other support as they established themselves in their new country.

Segregation, however, generally works to the disadvantage of minorities. Segregated housing is associated with segregated education (apart from busing children from one area to another) and segregated social life. This extensive separation means that people are unlikely to have the needed contact with each other to break down the prejudice, myths, suspicions, and hostilities that exist between the various groups (Powers and Ellison 1995).

How much segregation is there in the United States? A survey of Detroit residents shows that present interracial contact consists mainly of brief, superficial interaction rather than the sustained contact necessary for creating unity (Sigelman et al. 1996). Still, some progress has been made. In the 1950s, you could go into southern department stores and see signs at drinking fountains and rest rooms that read "colored only" or "white only." You could see signs at some exclusive clubs that openly stated that neither blacks nor Jews were allowed. The civil rights movement of the 1960s managed to eliminate such overt discrimination in public accommodations.

Segregated housing patterns have been more persistent. In recent years, however, some interesting patterns have occurred. African Americans are the most segregated, and this segregation is buttressed by racial prejudice (Bobo and Zubrinsky 1996). But, at least in metropolitan areas between 1980 and 1990, segregation of African Americans decreased somewhat while that of Asians and Hispanics tended to increase (Frey and Farley 1996). As long as such segregation exists, the nation can hardly be called either a melting pot or a salad bowl. It is more like an arena in which teams are struggling with each other to gain the prizes awaiting the victors.

The problem of segregation is not unique to the United States. For example, an analysis of existing data on American and Canadian cities found that segregation is not as severe in Canada as in the United States, but that black and Asian Canadians both are segregated to some extent from white Canadians (Fong 1996). Similarly, Brazilians are not as segregated as Americans, but residential segregation exists, and largely along the lines of skin color (Telles 1992).

Assimilation

The melting-pot image suggests a society in which newcomers are assimilated. **Assimilation** is a process in which a racial/ethnic group adopts the culture of the dominant group, thereby blending into the larger society and losing its distinctive identity. Certainly, many immigrants to the United States throughout the nation's history have been assimilated into the mainstream of American culture. In general, newcomers from Canada and Europe are assimilated more readily than those from Hispanic, Asian, or African nations (Saad 1995).

Assimilation, incidentally, is not a one direction process. Recall that cultures always influence each other. For example, American Indians and African Americans have influenced American culture through their art, literature, music and religion. To say that a racial/ethnic group is assimilated, therefore, is not to say that all of its distinctiveness is lost. The point is, that while the group has influenced the dominant culture, it has been shaped by that culture more than it has been the shaper.

Although few, if any, people view conflict as the desirable form of interracial contact, many do not accept assimilation as the ideal either. Why should racial/ethnic groups lose their distinctive identity? Isn't there some value in diversity?

Pluralism

In answer to the above questions, some people advocate **pluralism**, maintaining racial/ethnic identities along with equal rights and power. Some groups have maintained their identities. Chinatowns, little Tokyos, and various ethnic communities represent groups that have retained a distinct identity.

On the surface, pluralism might seem to be an ideal way to deal with racial/ethnic conflict. However, two problems arise. First, the maintenance of distinct identities means the potential exists for ingroup/outgroup distinctions to be made. Such distinctions easily slip into prejudice and discrimination. Second, while many people favor pluralism, assimilation is the choice of the majority. In a national poll, 27 percent of immigrants and 32 percent of natives favored the preservation of ethnic identities, while 59 percent of both groups favored assimilation (Saad 1995). And historically assimilation has meant conformity to the ways of the white majority.

In sum, opinions on the ideal pattern of interracial and interethnic relationships in the nation are as diverse as the groups themselves. In the foreseeable future, conflict, assimilation, and pluralism are likely to continue as patterns of interaction. Perhaps in the distant future some visionary will come up with a way to resolve the troubled relations among the United States', and the world's, varied racial and ethnic groups, and to achieve what appears to many to be an ideal situation—unity in the midst of diversity.

Critical Thinking Exercise

For some years, controversy has raged over the meaning of the gap between black and white I.Q. scores—the average of all blacks is about fifteen points lower than that of all whites. Some social scientists claim that at least a portion of the lower scores of African Americans is due to genetic factors (Herrnstein and Murray 1994; Rushton 1994). This would mean that African Americans are and will always be intellectually inferior to whites. Other social scientists dispute that interpretation (Goldberger and Manski 1995; Lauer 1997). Yet no one disputes the gap. Given that the gap exists, what explanations other than genetics could explain it? You may want to find out more about the meaning of I.Q. scores before you answer the question.

Summary

Scientifically, the concept of race has questionable meaning. Socially, it is very significant. Any classification method used is arbitrary. One of the more frequently used classifications identified six major "stocks"— Mongoloid, White, Negroid, Australoid, American Indian, and Polynesian.

Ethnic groups are people who share the same culture and identify with each other. People can lose their ethnic identity if they do not maintain their traditions. A minority is a disadvantaged racial or ethnic group. The various racial and ethnic groups in the United States are minorities. They now comprise a little over a fourth of the population.

African Americans are the largest of the nonwhite racial groups. Africans were brought to this country in 1619 as indentured servants and later as slaves. After slavery, their efforts to succeed in American society were marked by various strategies, including legal challenges to segregation, nonviolent protest, militancy, and cooperation. Some progress has occurred, but since the 1970s there has been little additional progress and even some losses. Compared to whites, African Americans are deprived in most of the things valued in the society.

Hispanic Americans, about 11 percent of the population, are also deprived in such things as education, job opportunities, income, and political participation. Asian Americans suffered some of the same prejudice and discriminatory treatment as other groups, but have the highest educational attainment and median income of any group, including whites.

White ethnics are the Europeans who emigrated to the United States after 1830. Many of their descendants today are blue-collar workers, and many have abandoned their ethnic identity. Jews came to the United States to escape persecution elsewhere. Anti-Semitism reached a high point in the 1920s and 1930s when Jews were accused of leading a conspiracy to take over the nation. Jewish Americans have high levels of achievements. Increasing numbers, however, are abandoning their ethnic identity.

American Indians, less than 1 percent of the population, are the most deprived of all the groups. They have higher rates of poverty, unemployment, drug abuse, and health problems than other groups. They have lower median incomes and lower levels of educational attainment.

Prejudice has been expressed by all groups against other groups. One manifestation of prejudice is the attribution of negative qualities to people in other groups. Another is racist attitudes. Prejudice is fueled in the United States and other countries by the perceived economic threat from minorities.

A substantial number of people believe that they have been discriminated against because of their race or ethnicity. And detailed analyses of income conclude that at least a part of the gap between the various groups can only be explained by discrimination. Other evidence of discrimination involves the probability of living near an environmental hazard and the likelihood of not being treated with respect.

Institutional discrimination means that some people will be short-changed even though no prejudice is involved. Many policies and practices of institutions guarantee such discrimination.

Affirmative-action programs were designed to rectify discriminatory treatment of minorities. To some extent, they have been successful. But they are under attack as no longer needed or as insulting to minorities.

The three major forms of intergroup interaction are conflict, assimilation, and pluralism. Conflict includes segregation as a way of maintaining the identity and power of the elite. Some groups have been largely assimilated, and some have tried to maintain a pluralistic society. However, the goal of unity in the midst of diversity is yet to be realized.

Glossary

anti-Semitism prejudice against Jewish people

assimilation a process in which a racial/ethnic group adopts the culture of the dominant group, thereby blending into the larger society and losing its distinctive identity

discrimination arbitrary, unfavorable treatment of the people in another racial/ethnic group

ethnic group people with a shared cultural background that leads them to identify with each other

ghetto an urban area inhabited predominantly by one minority group

institutional discrimination the maintenance of discriminatory behavior through the policies and practices of institutions

minority a disadvantaged racial or ethnic group

pluralism the maintenance of racial/ethnic identities along with equal rights and power

prejudice a negative attitude toward people in another racial/ethnic group that justifies discriminatory behavior

race a group of people with distinguishing biological characteristics that affect their interaction with other groups

racism the belief that some racial groups are inherently inferior to others

segregation the physical and social separation of racial/ethnic groups from each other

CHAPTER TEN

Gender and Gender Roles: *How Nature and Nurture Affect Identity*

When Machak turned six, she submitted to the ordeal that would make her an attractive Padaung woman—the placing of a ring around her neck (Mydans 1996). It is a tradition of the Padaung, who live in Myanmar (formerly Burma) and Thailand, to put rings around the necks of girls, increasing the number as the girls grow. The rings, by appearing to lengthen the neck, are regarded as a way to make a woman more beautiful. Actually, the rings do not lengthen the neck. Rather, their weight pushes down on the rib cage, causing the shoulders to slope dramatically. By adulthood, a woman's neck is no longer strong enough to support the head without the rings. If they are removed for any reason, the woman will require a neck brace and find it difficult to eat.

Machak's mother wound a coil of ten brass rings around her neck. They pushed against her chin and pressed on her chest, and she wept as she complained about their heaviness. Her mother, who wore a ten-pound coil of twenty-four rings around her own neck told her she would have to get used to it. For today, at least in Thailand, the "long-necked" women are a tourist attraction and the main source of revenue for the Padaung.

To outsiders, the women's appearance is somewhat bizarre. Yet the Padaung take pride in their rings. As one woman said: "It is most beautiful when the neck is really long. The longer it is, the more beautiful it is."

Perhaps you wonder how Padaung women could perpetuate a practice that involves such discomfort, not to mention a potential health hazard, in the name of beauty. In fact, however, the Padaung rings are no more uncomfortable or hazardous than many other women's fashions through the ages (Lauer and Lauer 1981). In the United States, women wore the corset for a hundred years because the hour-glass shape it produced was defined as beautiful. Yet corsets were clearly responsible for fainting spells, physical incapacity, health problems, and even deaths. Today, women opt for all kinds of cosmetic surgery, including silicone implants, in order to enhance their beauty.

Why are women willing to do such things? Are women that different from men? Do they have different needs and goals than do men? Are women and men, as the title of a popular book suggests, creatures from different planets? We will try to bring some clarity to these vexing and perplexing questions as we look at what it means to be female and male. We will see numerous factors at work in shaping males and females and their relationships. However, as feminist theorists point out, power differences pervade relations between the sexes. Throughout the world, and through time, men have had more power than women. Conformity to cultural standards of beauty in order to be attractive to the more powerful sex is only one of numerous illustrations of this power difference.

Sex, Gender, and Gender Roles

In Chapter Four, we defined sex, gender, and gender roles. We pointed out that the definition of what it means to be a female or a male is a social and not simply a biological matter. Here, we want to explore those ideas in further detail.

Sex and Gender

Your behavior is influenced by both biological and social factors. It is also influenced by your unique life experiences. What this means is that members of each sex are likely to share certain characteristics, but they do not all behave in the same way. Certainly, there are some ways in which females as a group differ from males as a group. Note that we say "as a group" because some individual females behave more like males as a group and some individual males behave more like females as a group.

The following are some of the differences researchers have found between males and females. The extent to which the differences are due to sex or gender or both may be debatable, but the differences do exist:

- Women live longer than men (79.0 and 72.3 years on the average, respectively) (U.S. Bureau of the Census 1996d, p. 88).

- Men tend to be more aggressive than women; they commit far more violent crimes, are far more likely to assault someone, and are consistently more aggressive than women even when they are not provoked (Kahn 1984).

- Women rate themselves higher on likability and morality than do men, while men rate themselves higher on giftedness and power than do women (Stake 1992).

- Women are more relationship-oriented than men; women value intimacy more and feel more responsible for the well-being of others than do men, while men value independence more than do women (Lang-Takac and Osterweil 1992; Beutel and Marini 1995).

- Women are more skilled than men in interpreting the nonverbal behavior of others (Kahn 1984).

- Women place less value than do men on materialism and competition, and more value than do men on finding purpose and meaning in life (Beutel and Marini 1995).

- Women suffer more distress (such as sadness, anxiety, anger, and physical symptoms) than do men, but men have higher rates of suicide, alcoholism, and drug abuse (Mirowsky and Ross 1995; Lauer 1997).

- Women and men have different conversational styles, with women striving for relational closeness and men striving to maintain or gain status (Tannen 1990).

- Women are better than men in grasping verbal meanings and in inductive reasoning skills, while men are better than women in spatial and number skills (Schaie 1994).

- Inequalities exist between men and women, with women coming out on the short end in such things as income, household work, and political participation (discussed below).

There are many other differences that we could list. There are also as many or more similarities. Furthermore, as noted earlier, the above differences do not apply to every individual. What they suggest, nevertheless, is that your life will probably be quite different depending on

Thinking Critically

Because of numerous differences between males and females, you always need to know the sex composition of the sample in order to interpret research results. For instance, a substantial amount of research, such as that on addictions, has been done using male subjects, but the results have been applied to both sexes (Brett, Graham, and Smythe 1995).

An interesting illustration of the importance of attending to sex differences is provided by research on the Pygmalion hypothesis, the notion that people tend to act as authoritative others expect them to act. The hypothesis has been confirmed in numerous studies, such as in classrooms where students tended to perform academically in accord with teachers' expectations. That is, students tend to do either inferior or superior work depending on a teacher's expectations about their ability. However, three researchers who conducted *experiments* with Israeli military trainees found that both men and women who were led by a man confirmed the hypothesis, but women led by a woman did not (Dvir, Eden, and Banjo 1995). Such results underscore the importance of always noting the sex of subjects in research, and of not assuming that what is true of one sex is true of the other.

whether you are male or female. Part of the reason for these differences are the social expectations about what it means to be male or female—the expectations that comprise gender roles.

Gender Roles

Gender roles are at the heart of the inequalities between men and women and of your own sense of what it means to be male or female. Think for a moment about the qualities that typically come to mind when you answer the question of what it means to be male or female. You may list many of the same qualities that occur to most Americans—that men are strong, independent, courageous, aggressive, and logical; women are gentle, dependent, nurturing, and emotional. These are called "gender-stereotyped" qualities.

These gender-stereotyped qualities exist in many societies, but they aren't universal. In nearly all societies, however, males are believed to possess more aggressive and dominant qualities than are females. For instance, adolescents in the Inuit (Eskimo) tribe living in Holman, Canada, identify females as sexy, shy, clean, quiet, friendly, and nice, and males as bullies, scary, aggressive, dirty, show-offs, and mean (Condon and Stern 1993).

The roles of men as breadwinners and women as homemakers fit well with the American gender-stereotyped qualities. These roles were the ideal for much of U.S. history. We call them the "traditional" gender roles. Yet even at the time when these roles were most highly idealized, a substantial number of women, particularly working-class and African American women, held other roles than that of homemaker.

In addition to the qualities of character, there are ideals about appearance for both women and men. Both men and women are expected to take care of themselves in ways that maintain the appropriate physical appearance. The ideal man is tall and muscular; the ideal woman is slender but shapely. Thus, men who think that they are too short may wear elevator shoes. Or if thinner or fatter than the ideal, they may try to shape up at a fitness center. However, women are under greater pressure than men to conform to the cultural ideal of beauty. As we have seen, during the nineteenth century women squeezed themselves into a corset to achieve a tiny waist, a requirement for the hourglass figure—the ideal of the day. Today, the ideal female is to be slender without being shapeless.

One way to achieve the requisite slender figure is by careful eating patterns. For some women, these patterns lead to eating disorders. **Anorexia nervosa**, self-starvation, and **bulimia**, repeated binge eating followed by "purging" through forced vomiting or laxatives, are disorders of those obsessed with being thin. Although only a small number of women go to such extremes, about two out of five adolescent girls are estimated to use less drastic bulimic behaviors or to follow an unhealthy diet (Graber et al. 1994). A researcher, who studied 400 students at Boston College after a rash of women with eating disorders appeared at the counseling center, concluded that the disorders reflected the "cult of thinness" (Hesse-Biber 1996). Many women sacrifice both their mental and physical health in an effort to achieve a culturally determined ideal of beauty.

Girdles also came back into fashion in the 1990s to assist women who hadn't achieved the ideal through dieting. Of course, the "girdle"—a garment rejected as a symbol of cultural bondage in the 1960s—has been resurrected with new labels. It's now a "body shaper." A shaper with a specific purpose is called a "Butt Booster," "Waist Cincher," or a "Tummy Terminator." One critic described these garments as "a compromise between not dieting and not accepting yourself" (Ager 1996).

Experiences

'I'm a Person Too!'

Many women have found the traditional female role constricting. They have opted for something other than, or in addition to, being a homemaker. And some have chosen a non-traditional direction after having lived for years in a traditional role. The transition is not without its struggles, as Wanda, a middle-aged wife and mother discovered. When the last of her four children started school, Wanda decided she wanted to complete her college education and become a teacher. Her problems began when she announced to her husband that she wanted to go back to school:

"What in the world do you want to do that for?" was his response. I told him I needed something more now that the kids were all in school and that I had always dreamed of being a teacher. I could tell he was puzzled and even a little angry at my proposal. He asked me all sorts of questions, like what would happen if one of the kids got sick, and how I could do both housework and homework, and what would happen if I finished and couldn't get a job.

Well, I started as a part-time student and loved it. I was thrilled with every class I took. When I tried to share some of my excitement with my husband, he just made caustic comments about 'egg-heads' and the difference between a class and the 'real world.' The two younger kids were fine with my new venture, but the two older ones felt that I wasn't giving them as much attention as in the past. And they weren't happy when I insisted that they take on some additional chores around the house.

I even got some negative reactions from friends. A lady at our church told me one day that she had seen my husband doing the grocery shopping and said how lucky I was to have such a 'patient husband.' Between people like that and my own family, I struggled alternately with anger, guilt, and depression. But one day when I was talking with my husband, something occurred to me. 'If *you* were the one going back to school,' I told him, 'no one would think a thing about it. They would call you ambitious. So why is it any different for me? I'm a person too!'

Fortunately, my husband is a loving and flexible person at heart. He finally came around. When he did, so did the kids. They're all supportive and proud of what I've accomplished. Today I'm delighted at being not only a wife and mother, but also a teacher.

Gender roles, then, are powerful influences on behavior. The Padaung women who wear their heavy, body-distorting rings are conforming to those roles, as are the American women who bear the discomfort of body shapers, opt for cosmetic surgery, or impair their health by an unwise diet.

How People Learn Gender Roles

Biological factors impose bounds and create predispositions. Thus, boys exhibit more aggressive behavior than do girls in all societies (Seifert, Hoffnung and Hoffnung 1997). Nevertheless, gender roles are largely learned. For example, while nurturance is a quality typically associated with women, evidence exists that small boys are no less nurturing than small girls. Until the age of four or five, boys and girls display an equal interest in babies and in their care (Melson and Fogel 1988). Boys exhibit some nurturing behavior after that, but eventually women become clearly more nurturing than men. What happens? It could be, of course, a gene that kicks in. But the study suggests that it is the result of differential socialization. Boys and girls both learn that it is the woman who is primarily responsible for the nurturing.

Before looking at how gender socialization occurs, we wish to make one additional point. We noted in Chapter Four that structural-functional theorists have argued that gender socialization maintains the social order. While we agree that people need to learn what it means to be men and women, there is no single type of gender role that is essential for social order. The society will not fall apart if people are not socialized in accord with the gender-stereotyped qualities noted earlier. However, some kind of socialization will take place. And it will take place in the family, through peers, at school, and from the media and religion. People learn about gender roles in multiple contexts, and what they learn tends to reflect and perpetuate the greater power of men.

Gender Socialization in the Family

Your first exposure to what it means to be a man or woman occurs in your family. One of the important ways you learn, of course, is by observing your father, mother, and other male and female relatives. If you never see your father express any emotion, you may believe that real men are rational creatures who seldom if ever display feelings. If you never see your mother try to repair anything, or take the car for an oil change, you may believe that real women are dependent creatures who require men in their lives.

It is not only through their behavior but also through the way they treat you that parents teach you about gender roles. Keep in mind the typical qualities mentioned earlier as you read the following. In the first two years of life, parents are likely to give their sons such things as sports equipment, tools, and various kinds of vehicles, while they are likely to give their daughters such things as dolls, child's furniture, and similar toys (Idle, Wood, and Desmarais 1993).

Researchers who have watched parents play with their preschool children report that parents are most likely to reward gender-stereotyped behavior (Seifert, Hoffnung, and Hoffnung 1997). They praise boys for playing with blocks rather than for playing with dolls and vice versa for girls. They encourage physical activity for boys more than they do for girls. As children reach school age, parents assign gender-stereotyped chores to them; girls are more likely to fold laundry and boys are more likely to take out the trash.

In general, parents reward children for following the gender-stereotyped qualities. They tend to reward their sons for being assertive, independent, active, and in control of their emotions; they tend to reward daughters for being dependent, more passive, and emotionally expressive (Fagot and Hagan 1991).

Parents even tend to talk differently with sons and daughters. An analysis of the transcripts of conversations between 17 white, middle-class parents and their children at 40 and 70 months of age showed that both mothers and fathers talked differently to daughters than to sons (Adams et al. 1995). They spoke more often about emotions, including a greater variety of emotions, with daughters than with sons. They mentioned negative emotions like sadness and dislike more often with daughters than with sons. As a result, by 70 months the girls were using a greater variety of emotion terms than were the boys. If such practices are generally true (the study involved a very small sample of white parents), it is little wonder that females are typically viewed as more emotional than males.

As children get older, parents continue to treat them differently depending on sex. They maintain higher educational aspirations for sons than for daughters (Adelman 1991). If a daughter wants to go into a traditionally male field like science, parents may not encourage her or provide her with the necessary resources (Hanson 1996). They tend to encourage their daughters to pursue careers in traditionally female fields like teaching.

Gender Socialization with Peers

The gender roles learned in the home are likely to be reinforced by peers. Play at an early age already shows an awareness of male-female differences. In preschool play, girls withdraw from a boy partner more often than from a girl partner, and boys obey a prohibition from other boys more often than they do from girls (Seifert, Hoffnung, and Hoffnung 1997). Both boys and girls respond more positively (in the sense of persisting in an activity) to compliments from same-sex than from opposite-sex playmates. In other words, preschool children already have a sense that they can, and should, respond differently to other children depending on their sex.

Peer pressures reach a high point in adolescence. A participant-observation study of conversations among middle school adolescents underscores the way in which peers reinforce stereotypical gender patterns (Eder, Evans, and Parker 1995). The researchers spent three years in a midwestern school, hanging out as friends with groups of seventh and eighth graders at lunchtime and listening to the patterns of their conversations.

The researchers found that adolescent conversations function, among other things, to maintain gender differences and to enable both males and females to gain status. Boys at the school gained status through their toughness, which they could show verbally by insults and humiliation. The boy who caused others to "lose their cool" achieved a superior status. The researchers pointed out that this verbal competition reflects a belief that boys are not responsible for the feelings of others; rather, each boy is responsible for his own feelings and is expected—if he wants high status—to control those feelings. Interestingly, boys who preferred not to participate in such activity were berated about their lack of masculinity by girls as well as other boys. Girls in the school gained status by physical appearance, a fact continually reinforced by gossip and insults from both boys and girls. For girls, who they were and what they did were secondary to how they looked.

We do not know how general these patterns are. But if adolescents generally behave as those at this midwestern school, men and women will continue to exhibit the typical gender-stereotyped qualities for years to come.

Gender Socialization at School

To some extent, schools have tried to counter gender-stereotyped tendencies. For instance, many high school subjects that were once considered either male (shop) or female (home economics) are now open to either sex. At one time, high school counselors discouraged girls from pursuing a college-preparation curriculum because they were expected to marry and have children after graduation. Colleges and universities have also reduced gender segregation in academic programs as well as gender inequality in sports.

Still, your educational experience is likely to vary in accord with your sex. Often the differences are subtle, such as the ways that teachers relate to boys and girls (Association of American Colleges 1982). Teachers tend to ask more difficult questions of boys and spend more time urging them to try again if they don't succeed. Teachers are also more likely to give boys instructions and to let them work on their own. On the other hand, they tend to lead girls step by step through a task. They may give girls direct answers to their questions and encourage boys to figure out the answers for themselves (Sadker and Sadker 1994). These practices teach children that boys are independent and capable and that girls are dependent and less capable.

Gender Socialization by the Media

Do you still have any picture books from your childhood? If so, study them closely and note how men and women are depicted. Picture books have changed over time. Before the 1980s they showed many more boys than girls, and the girls were typically passive while the boys were active. Since that time, girls are as likely as boys to appear in the books, but they are not portrayed as attractively as boys (Williams et al. 1987). The girls are "colorless" compared to the boys, with the boys still portrayed as independent and active and the girls as more dependent and passive.

Television is probably the most influential of all the mass media. What do you learn about gender roles from watching TV? Basically, television programs reinforce the gender-stereotyped qualities we have identified. The National Institute of Mental Health (1982) summed up the predominant ways in which males and females are characterized:

- When men and women interact, men are likely to be more dominant.

- Men are likely to appear as rational, ambitious, smart, competitive, powerful, stable, violent, or tolerant; women are more likely to appear as sensitive, romantic, attractive, happy, warm, sociable, peaceful, fair, submissive, or timid.

- Women are more likely than men to be shown involved in marriage and family life.

A study of 40 MTV videos reported that twice as many men as women appeared on the videos, and the men were typically aggressive and dominant while the women were more likely to be subservient and treated as sex objects (Sommers-Flanagan, Sommers-Flanagan, and Davis 1993). Because MTV is the fare of adolescent viewers, the gender roles it portrays are important. There is some indication that women are gaining more prominence on MTV, but until the mid 1990's little was shown that would change gender-stereotyped qualities. It appears that little is being shown on television to change gender-stereotyped qualities.

Gender Socialization in Religion

One way to assert dominance is to monopolize the most powerful and important roles. In most religious groups, these roles are held mainly or exclusively by men—priests, ministers, rabbis, bishops, imams (Muslim priests) and so on. This is not as true as it was in the past (Ostling 1992). In 1948, the African Methodist Episcopal Church became the first large Protestant denomination to approve the ordination of women, and other groups followed suit over the next decades. In 1980 the first female Methodist bishop and in 1992 the first female Lutheran bishop were appointed. However, men still hold positions of authority, and a number of groups continue to forbid the ordination of women.

Those religious groups that exclude women from positions of authority do so on theological grounds. Roman Catholics have argued that only men can be representatives of Jesus Christ at the altar because

---

Explorations

What I Learned About Gender Roles

How did you learn what it means to be a woman or a man? More specifically, what did you learn from your family, peers, school, religion, and the media? Have each group member write an account of his or her learning experiences, including both the things that were heard and the behavior observed, about gender roles. (If you do this as an individual project, follow the same instructions.)

For example, think about what you learned in your family. What did your parents say to you and your siblings that indicated how men and women should behave? Did you ever hear anything like "good little girls are always polite" or "little boys don't cry"? What did your parents' behavior teach you about what it means to be a man or woman?

Which of the five sources do you believe had the greatest influence on you? Why? In what ways do you differ in your own gender role from what you were taught or observed? Finally, what is your personal ideal for gender roles? What would have to happen in families, among peers, at school, in religion, and in the media for your ideal to be realized in coming generations?

Have one group member write a summary of the results and make a report to the class.

Jesus himself was a man (Ostling 1992). Southern Baptists, the largest Protestant denomination, refuse to ordain women on the grounds that all of the disciples of Jesus and all of the officials of the New Testament church were men. They point out that, in the New Testament, wives are told to be submissive to their husbands and to be silent in church. As a final example, the Koran, the sacred book of Islam, states that God has given men qualities that make them superior to women.

Clearly, devout believers in these faiths are likely to view gender roles differently from those in more moderate or liberal religious groups or those without religious beliefs. And because the authority of God is claimed as the basis for believing in the subordinate position of women, changes will be slow in coming.

Gender and Inequality

We once invited a member of an Eastern religious cult to speak to a social-problems class. The cult practiced what seemed clearly to be male dominance. For example, men and women ate separately, and the women served their husbands before eating their own meal in the kitchen. In the question-and-answer period following his talk, a female student raised the issue of sexual equality. "We believe in equality between the sexes," the man insisted. "People are equal when they each fulfill their God-given roles in life." In their group, it was men's God-given role to be served and women's God-given role to be the servers.

Our students were not satisfied. They insisted that what the cult practiced was not equality. Some of those same students believed that, in contrast to this cult, men and women are generally treated equally in American society. Others believed that they are not. The beliefs of the latter are supported by feminist theory which argues that inequality is pervasive. Before you decide one way or the other, consider the amount of gender inequality that exists.

Sexism: Illusion or Pervasive Obstacle?

Do you recall the story about the boy who cried "wolf" too often? He was responsible for protecting a flock of sheep and kept testing adults to see if they would come when he cried out that a wolf was attacking the flock. When the wolf did come, the skeptical adults decided he was simply crying out without reason once again and didn't respond.

Some Americans believe that the cry of **"sexism"** has been made too often. Sexism is prejudice or discrimination against an individual based on that person's sex. It is generally used, however, to refer to prejudice or discrimination against women. Do women face such prejudice and discrimination? Is it pervasive? Or is it merely an illusion perpetrated by feminists who detest men? As in the case of attitudes about racial and ethnic prejudice and discrimination, some Americans doubt that women suffer discrimination any longer. Furthermore, they define those who continue to press their demands or to talk about discrimination as troublemakers or radical feminists (Swim 1995).

We will look below at a number of areas of American life in which inequality exists between men and women. In each case, a portion of the inequality can be explained by nonsexist factors, but a part also is clearly due to prejudice and/or discrimination (recall from the last chapter that discrimination can occur even when people are not prejudiced). Here we will focus on a manifestation of sexism that many women experience—**sexual harassment**, unwanted sexual advances by someone in a position of superior power.

Both men and women experience sexual harassment, but women are far more likely than men to be victims. And the harassment occurs in all kinds of settings.

Consider a few of the results from various studies (Lauer 1997):

- 60 percent of women in 250 prestigious law firms say they have experienced sexual harassment at work.

- 79 percent of female auto workers report sexual harassment on the job.

- 11 percent of male faculty members surveyed in one study admitted that they had attempted to stroke, caress, or touch female students.

Perpetrators have been punished in a few noted cases. In the 1990s, Navy personnel were disciplined after widespread sexual harassment was uncovered, a United States Senator from Oregon resigned after a number of his female employees lodged complaints, and a number of clergymen lost their positions after evidence of sexual improprieties came to light.

These incidents underscore the way in which sexual harassment occurs between those of greater and those of lesser power. It is precisely the issue of power that makes women vulnerable. It is one thing to simply advise women to "just say no." It is another thing when you think about a patient whose therapist represents the power of healing, or the member of a congregation whose minister represents the power of salvation, or the student whose professor represents the power of knowledge (and perhaps the power to affect the student's future career).

Still, is sexual harassment a manifestation of sexism or is it simply, as one man put it, "stuff that has always gone on between men and women"? We view it as sexism because sexual harassment reflects a negative attitude about the nature of women, namely, that women are sex objects who do not need to be treated with the same dignity accorded to men.

Economic Quality

If there is economic equality in a society, then you could expect that people from various groups would have roughly equal work and income patterns. In comparing men and women, however, neither work nor income patterns are equal.

Inequality in Work Patterns

In the traditional gender role, women do not work outside the home. The increasing number of nontraditional women is reflected in the fact that the proportion of those who are married, living with husbands, and also working at a job or career outside the home increased from 23.8 percent in 1950 to 61.1 percent in 1995 (U.S. Bureau of the Census 1996d, p. 400). The largest increase occurred among women with children under six years of age.

Why are women going into the labor force in such large numbers? Basically, they go to work for many of the same reasons that men do. Often, the reason is economic necessity or, at least, the desire to maintain a certain standard of living. Thus, a family in which the wife and mother doesn't work might not go without food, but it might be forced to live in a less desirable area and enjoy fewer nice things.

Most married white and African American women who work indicate that they participate in the labor force for more reasons than economic necessity. Using data from a number of national surveys taken between 1973 and 1990, Herring and Wilson-Sadberry (1993) found that, over that period of time, both white and black women became increasingly like men in the reasons they gave for working outside the home. While some said it was economically necessary, more said it was out of preference. They find that work satisfies, in part, their need for personal development and fulfillment.

How do women fare in the job market? The unemployment rate is measured by the number of people actively looking for work but unable

---

Figure 10.1   Proportion of Women

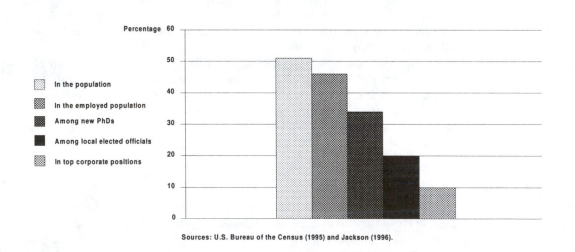

Sources: U.S. Bureau of the Census (1995) and Jackson (1996).

to secure it. Between World War II and 1990, the rates were nearly always higher for women than for men, but they have tended to be slightly higher for men than for women since 1990 (U.S. Bureau of the Census 1996d, p. 413). Since 1990, then, women have been slightly less likely than men to be unemployed.

Once in a job or career, the picture changes. If you are female, you are less likely than a male to be promoted and to achieve the higher positions in your field. Figure 10.1 shows that women, who comprise a little over 51 percent of the population and 46 percent of the employed population, hold only 10 percent of top corporate positions.

Recall that the highest occupational categories, in terms of prestige and income, fall into the managerial and professional category. Women hold 48.0 percent of these jobs (U.S. Bureau of the Census 1996d, p. 405). But the number is misleading. When broken down more finely, you can see that women hold a disproportionate number of the lower-level jobs (in terms of prestige and income) in the category. For example, women hold 84.1 percent of elementary teacher positions and 83.2 percent of librarian positions. They comprise only 8.4 percent of all engineers, 26.2 percent of all lawyers and judges, and 24.4 percent of all physicians.

An examination of specific occupational categories reveals that women tend to cluster at the lower levels (Lauer 1997). For example, while the overwhelming majority of elementary school teachers are women, a disproportionate number of men are principals of elementary schools. And while increasing numbers of women are entering medical schools, they may still be encouraged to pursue the traditionally "female" specialties such as pediatrics and psychiatry. Female surgeons are a rarity, and women are often actively discouraged from pursuing surgery as a specialty.

Women who go into careers or into organizations dominated by men often believe that they must prove their competence by doing the work even better than (not just as well as) a man (Williams 1995). By contrast, when men go into careers or into organizations dominated by women, their competence is more likely to be taken for granted.

We noted that there may be nondiscriminatory factors that account for a portion of the inequality. For example, although it is true that women comprise only 8.4 percent of engineers, this is a marked advance over twenty years ago when less than 1 percent of engineers were women. The figures may be low, in other words, because the inequality was even greater in the past than it is now.

The inequality may also reflect, in part, lingering gender-stereotyped behavior. The qualities of women that we listed earlier—gentle, dependent, nurturing, and emotional—are not the characteristics that corporations look for in their top executives. Yet whether women with the gender-stereotyped qualities do not go into business or replace those qualities if they do, there is no evidence that women are any less capable than men of being effective corporate executives. In fact, a study of 915 corporate workers conducted by the Foundation for Future Leadership reported that women do a better job than men in 28 out of 31 crucial management tasks, including problem-solving, planning, managing relationships, and leading (Zabarenko 1996). Women and men did equally well at delegating responsibility, and men did better than women in handling pressure and coping with their own frustration. The men also did better than women in an additional area: self-promotion. The women assumed that their performance would be recognized and rewarded without calling attention to it, while the men followed the old principle of "he that tooteth not his own horn, the same shall not be tooted."

Other possible nondiscriminatory factors in gender inequality are similarly either without foundation or they explain only a portion of the inequality. The contentions that women aren't seriously committed to work or career, or that women will quit as soon as they marry or begin a family, or that women take more time off from work for frivolous reasons have all been shown to be myths (Lauer 1997). The bottom line is, discrimination exists and it penalizes women as they strive to advance themselves in work or a career.

Inequality in work and career is not confined to the United States, of course. Women suffer similar kinds of discrimination worldwide, even in countries where equality is an official goal. Sweden, for example, has a standing policy promoting gender equality in work and, as in the United States, increasing numbers of married women have entered the labor force—a 300 percent increase from 1950 to 1975. Yet, analyzing a national sample of union members affiliated with the Swedish Confederation of Professional Associations, researchers found that almost 20 percent more men than women had supervisory positions and that professional women earned only 77 percent of what their male counterparts earned (Mueller, Kuruvilla, and Iverson 1994).

The researchers raised the question of whether some nondiscriminatory factors might be at work that would explain these findings. They looked at such things as whether the women had less experience, were disproportionately in professions where fewer positions of authority are available, or had family commitments that interfered with career advancement. Each of these factors accounted for a portion of the gender gap, but discrimination was the only explanation for about half of the gap.

Income Inequality

Most Americans would agree that your income should reflect such things as your expertise and job performance. However, few would argue that income should also reflect your gender. Yet it does. Table 10.1 shows the median income of men and women who work year round and full time. It shows that there are both racial/ethnic and gender inequalities and that the gender inequalities are greater. Note that the median income of white women is less than that of either white or black men, and the median incomes of black and Hispanic women is lower than that of men in any racial/ethnic group. Keep in mind that the figures are for individual income. If you look at figures for family or household income, those headed by women, compared to those headed by a married couple or a man, are even more disadvantaged.

Table 10.1	**Median Income of Year-Round Full-Time Workers**		
	Women	**Men**	**Women's as % of Men's**
White	$23,894	32,440	73.7
Black	20,628	24,405	84.5
Hispanic	18,418	20,525	89.7

Source: U.S. Bureau of the Census 1996d, p. 469

The median income of families with children and a female head is only 29.6 percent that of married-couple families with children (U.S. Bureau of the Census 1996d, p. 468)!

Again, there might be factors other than discrimination to account for the income inequality. Women might cluster in lower-paying jobs, or work fewer hours because of family commitments, or have less experience on the average than do men. Undoubtedly, the lower pay in female-dominated occupations (secretaries, librarians, etc.) is an important factor. Because many female-dominated occupations involve a nurturing type of work, it has been suggested that the lower pay they offer is itself a form of discrimination (England et al. 1994). Why should nurturing be worth less than producing or repairing?

The bottom line, however, is that when all the nondiscriminatory factors are taken into account, they still do not explain the income differences between men and women (Pfeffer and Ross 1990; Wellington 1994). Clearly, women suffer discrimination in the area of income.

As with career advancement, gender inequality in income is not confined to the United States and is found even in those nations with strong egalitarian ideologies and policies. The German Democratic Republic (East Germany) was a communist nation until 1990 when East and West Germany were reunified. Throughout its 40-year history, East German men and women were equal in terms of occupational qualifications and work experience (Sorensen and Trappe 1995). Nevertheless, women received less pay when they entered the labor force and continued to receive less than men throughout their work lives. The main reason for the disparity was the lower pay in job categories dominated by women, even though those categories required as much education and training as those dominated by men.

Gender Inequality in Education

Education is important to personal well-being. Among other things, career opportunities are dependent upon educational attainment. Surprisingly, it was not all that long ago in the United States that women were considered intellectually inferior to men and were not allowed to pursue a higher education. Today, educational opportunities at all levels are open to women. However, roadblocks still exist that prevent women from attaining equality in education.

Table 10.2	**Educational Attainment, by Race, Ethnicity, and Sex**	
	% Completed four years of high school or more	**% Completed four years of college or more**
White		
Male	83.0	27.2
Female	83.0	21.0
Black		
Male	73.4	13.6
Female	74.1	12.9
Asian		
Male	84.0	44.9
Female	77.2	35.4
Hispanic		
Male	52.9	10.1
Female	53.8	8.4

Source: U.S. Bureau of the Census 1996d, p. 159.

As Table 10.2 shows, while girls do about as well as boys in completing high school, men of every race are more likely than women to complete four years or more of college. Also while women receive more than half of all master's degrees, they received only 38.1 percent of all doctorates in 1993 (U.S. Bureau of the Census 1996d, p. 193).

Part of the reason for educational inequality may be the differing school experiences of boys and girls that we noted earlier—the fact that teachers tend to recognize boys and encourage their educational efforts more than they do those of girls. Combined with the probability of less support and encouragement from families, it is understandable that fewer women than men attain the highest levels of education.

The educational gender gap is even more severe in many other nations, particularly in the developing nations of Africa, the Middle East and South Asia (Hadden and London 1996). Women are less apt than men to attend school in these areas for a number of reasons. Typically, sons are responsible for supporting their aging parents, so educating sons is a form of social security. Moreover, the future job possibilities for daughters are more limited than they are for sons, and daughters contribute more to household tasks than do sons. Finally, when educated daughters marry they are likely (by cultural tradition) to join their husband's family. Thus, the husband's family, rather than the daughter's family, will be the main beneficiary of her education.

Unfortunately, in those nations where female education is minimal the society is missing out on enormous benefits. Using *existing data* from the United Nations, Hadden and London (1996) compared various nations of the world with differing educational practices. They found that people in nations with higher rates of female educational attainment have lower fertility rates, lower infant mortality rates, better health, and longer life expectancy. In addition, those nations also tend to have higher rates of economic growth. As a 1994 United Nations report summarized the matter: "In the long term, almost every other aspect of progress, from nutrition to family planning, from child health to women's rights, is profoundly affected by whether or not a nation educates its girls" (Hadden and London 1996, p. 31).

Political Inequality

Figure 10.1 shows that women represent only 20 percent of all local elected officials. The inequality increases at higher levels of office. In 1995, women comprised only 8 percent of the United States Senate and 11 percent of the House of Representatives (U.S. Bureau of the Census 1996d, p. 279). Clearly, women and men do not participate equally in the political process.

Is it important for women to hold political office? If you believe in equality, the answer is yes—for at least two reasons. First, the lack of women in political office reinforces the stereotype of male dominance. If most office holders are men, it is easy to slip into the assumption that political activity is the domain of men and that men rather than women are responsible for making the rules that govern the functioning of society.

The second reason involves the protection of women's rights. In the United States, women have historically occupied positions of legal subservience. Early in the nation's history, women didn't have the right to vote, and married women could not legally sign contracts, keep their own earnings, or retain title to inherited property. No doubt, women have made considerable progress over the years, but legal discrimination still exists. For example, some states still possess laws that give husbands certain rights over their wives' property or restrict a woman's right to sign contracts or engage in a business on her own.

In some cases, laws exist that were not designed to restrict or harm women but this is the effect they have. No-fault divorce laws have been passed to take some of the acrimony out of the process of dissolving a marriage. Yet their effect has been to impose serious financial hardship on women, particularly on women who have children. Typically, a man's standard of living following a divorce improves about 10 percent, while a woman's standard declines about 27 percent (Weitzman 1985; Arendell 1986). Many divorced women—whether white, African American, or Hispanic—find themselves living near, or in, poverty for the first time in their lives (Smock 1994). The problem exists because, under no-fault divorce laws, women receive less property and alimony than they did before the laws. Those who have been full-time homemakers and mothers are especially vulnerable to financial hardship under these conditions.

Finally, the protection of women's rights has required the passage of legislation forbidding discriminatory practices. For example, women have suffered discriminatory treatment in education and work but have been helped by affirmative-action programs that have rectified some past injustices. And laws against sexual harassment now can protect women who once had no legal recourse. As more women are elected to political office, they will increasingly have the power to protect women's rights through legislation.

Inequality in Household Tasks

As growing numbers of women enter the labor force, who is doing the work around the house? In the traditional household, it was the full-time homemaker who took care of most household chores. Who does them when the homemaker is employed outside the home? A number of national surveys indicate that a greater, but far from equal, sharing of those tasks occurs even when both husband and wife work full time outside the home (Goldscheider and Waite 1991).

Typically, wives who work outside the home spend twice as many hours as their husbands doing housework. Husbands are likely to do little housework unless both they and their wives believe in equality in gender and marital roles (Greenstein 1996). Even then, they are not likely to do equal amounts. Moreover, husbands and wives still tend to do gender-stereotyped tasks with the man taking care of household repairs and outdoor tasks and the woman attending to the cooking, dishwashing, housecleaning, laundry, and ironing (Blair and Lichter 1991). The net effect is that the woman comes home to what Hochschild (1989) calls a "second shift." In a year's time, an employed wife may work 700 or more additional hours than her employed husband because of her extra household tasks.

This is not a minor issue. Using a national sample, Suitor (1991) found that women's marital happiness is related more to satisfaction with the division of labor in the home than with such things as age, educational attainment, or the wife's employment status. Another national study reported that women are angry more frequently than men, in part the result of their greater child-care responsibilities (Ross and Van Willigen 1996). Fathers have assumed more child-care responsibilities in recent years but, as with most household tasks, the bulk of this care is still assumed by mothers.

Now let's combine a few of the inequalities we have discussed. Women are more likely than men to work for lower pay, to encounter obstacles in career advancement, and to assume the bulk of responsibility for household tasks. Two researchers studied these inequalities and their effect on women's sense of control over their lives (Ross and Mirowsky 1992). We'll discuss the results of their study below, but first we'll consider why a sense of control is important.

Think of it this way. The opposite of control is helplessness or powerlessness—feelings which are detrimental to your physical and mental health. Even animals deteriorate when they are powerless. In an *experiment* using rats, a researcher implanted cancerous cells in each of the animals (Seligman 1990). If a rat's immune system did not reject the resulting tumor, the rat would die. Then the rats were subjected to electric shocks. Some of them learned they could stop the shock by pressing a bar; others were unable to escape the shock—they were helpless. Within a month, the bodies of 70 percent of the former, but only 27 percent of the latter, rejected the tumor.

Similar results appear with humans. Researchers who studied a group of women whose Pap tests (the standard test for cervical cancer) showed "suspicious" cells, found that 11 of the 18 who felt hopeless in the face of stress, but only 7 of the 33 who felt some sense of control, developed cancer (Locke and Colligan 1986).

Ross and Mirowsky (1992) studied 809 Illinois adults, measuring sense of control by responses to statements such as "I am responsible for my own successes" and "I have little control over the bad things that happen to me." They asked how such things as work patterns and income and household tasks related to their subjects' sense of control. The researchers found that employed people generally express a greater sense of control over their lives than those who are unemployed. However, for married women the combination of low pay, jobs that afforded low autonomy, and high responsibility for household tasks negated the relationship between employment and sense of control. A sense of control is one of the benefits of employment, but it is less likely to be a benefit for married women because of the various inequalities in their lives.

Inequality in Personal Safety

One of the four cherished freedoms of Americans identified by President Franklin Roosevelt was freedom from fear. Men actually have more to fear in this area than women, because men are more likely to be the victims of violent crime. Men account for about 70 percent of murder victims and 60 percent of all victims of crimes of violence (U.S. Bureau of the Census 1996d).

Women, however, are more likely than men to be the victims of interpersonal violence. One form of violence is rape. The Justice Department estimates that about 500,000 women are raped each year (Futter 1995). Rape is one of the most traumatic experiences a woman can have. Rape victims may suffer both physical and emotional damage. Worse yet, the emotional damage can last for years and includes such things as nightmares, phobias, and sexual fears.

How many women are aware of being a potential rape victim? Or perhaps we should ask, how often or under what circumstances is a woman likely to be aware? A female student told us: "Every woman knows that she is a potential victim of a rapist." A survey of women

EXTENSIONS

Violence Against Women: A Global Problem

As with the other inequalities we have studied, violence against women is a problem throughout the world. In some societies, wives are routinely beaten by their husbands. In others, the abuse is not routine but there is no penalty imposed on the husband when it occurs. The following examples illustrate the pervasiveness of the problem:

- One out of every two women in Costa Rica will be victimized by violence at some point in their lives.

- In one year, 60 percent of those murdered in Papua New Guinea were women, and most were murdered by their spouses.

- About one of every four Canadian women will be victimized by violence during their lives, and for half of them the violence will occur before the age of seventeen.

- A survey of Sri Lankan female plantation workers found that three-fourths reported beatings by husbands or bosses.

- According to the Mexican Federation of Women Trade Unions, 95 percent of female workers are sexually harassed in the workplace.

- A fourth of all girls in Peru are sexually abused before they reach the age of sixteen.

- 95 percent of French victims of violence are women, and more than half of these are abused by their husbands.

In many nations, women are taking measures to help each other. In Tanzania, women have planned research projects and a National Day of Action with the goal of pressuring authorities to deal with the problem. Elsewhere women are organizing study groups, crisis centers, public forums, publications, and political action groups. These efforts, hopefully, will reduce the amount of violence women suffer; at the same time, they testify to the extent of the problem throughout the world.

reported that the major fears in their lives were rape, cancer, divorce, and losing a job (Gordon and Riger 1989).

A considerable amount of the violence in American society occurs in intimate relationships. In fact, over 13 percent of all violent victimizations take place between people who are intimates (friends or relations)(Zawitz 1994). And women experience ten times as many violent attacks by intimates as do men! For example, according to surveys taken in a number of states, 3.4 percent of new mothers have been physically abused by their husbands or boy friends in the 12 months before childbirth (Centers for Disease Control 1994).

The proliferation of shelters for battered women in recent years further dramatizes the problem. Unfortunately, some abused women either don't make their way to such shelters or can't find one to accommodate them. As a result, it is estimated that from a fourth to a half of homeless families are headed by a woman who ran away from a violent husband (Mason 1993).

Ending Gender Inequality: Fantasy or Possibility?

Can gender inequality be ended? On the one hand, gender inequality is not generally marked by the ingroup/outgroup animosity that tends to go along with racial and ethnic inequality. On the other hand, as with any kind of inequality, gender inequality benefits the dominant group, namely men. If women cluster in lower-prestige and lower-paying jobs, this leaves more of the higher-prestige and higher-paying jobs open to men. If women assume the bulk of household chores, this affords men more leisure hours. If women do not run for political office, this makes more positions available to men.

The point is, any privileged group is likely to defend its privileges. It is, therefore, unlikely that gender inequality will be reduced—much less ended—without struggle. And even if people want to end gender inequality, is it possible?

Is Gender Inequality Necessary?

Those who believe that gender inequality is rooted in biological differences insist that, no matter how much you value equality, gender inequality is an ineluctable fact of human life. Some base the argument on social as well as biological reasons. For example, *structural functionalism* views the relationships between the sexes as complementary and necessary to the harmony and effectiveness of society. That is, each sex has certain functions to perform, and the work of both sexes is necessary for social well-being. Moreover, the functions assumed by each sex are not assumable by the opposite sex. In hunting and gathering societies, for instance, men necessarily did the hunting because of their greater strength and because of the childbearing and child-care responsibilities of the women.

Even in modern societies, according to structural functionalists, the roles assumed by the sexes are not interchangeable (Parsons and Bales 1953). Mothers not only bear but also assume the primary nurturing responsibility for children. Mothers, thus, need expressive qualities like affection, caring, and sensitivity. Moreover, if women are caring for children and the home, men are necessarily in the workplace. There they need instrumental qualities like ambition, toughness, and rationality. Thus, women fulfill the expressive or relationship-focused roles and men fulfill the instrumental or achievement-focused roles in society. Structural functionalists argue that, while this arrangement gives the bulk of the power to men, male dominance is the inevitable outcome of the sexual division of labor and not some plot to deprive women of their rightful share of valued things. Consequently, gender inequality is not only inevitable but necessary.

According to *conflict theory*, however, gender inequality is neither necessary nor inevitable. Instead, it is the outcome of an ongoing struggle that arises out of differing and contrary interests and needs. The thesis is as follows. All societies have a sexual division of labor. Men and women have differing spheres of responsibility. Men's spheres have always been more powerful and prestigious than those of women. As Scanzoni (1972, p. 31) pointed out, "historically men saw to it that in their roles, both in and out of the home, they themselves possessed most of the rights and privileges."

In other words, most societies have been patriarchies. A **patriarchy** is a social system in which men dominate women. Sullerot (1974) pointed out four characteristics of patriarchy. First, a wife is primarily a "breeding machine" whose purpose is to perpetuate the male line of her husband and her group. Second, because the wife is primarily a breeding machine, she is largely confined to the home. Third, a woman is not allowed to own or dispose of property. Fourth, a woman has no role in civic affairs. Obviously, remnants of the patriarchal system remain. For example, while women in the United States are not excluded from civic affairs, the small proportion of elected offices they hold, along with the tendency for women to hold lower positions in government, are vestiges of a patriarchal society.

Male dominance and female subservience result in particular kinds of personalities and gender-appropriate behavior. People associate dominance with aggressiveness, rationality, and strength. They connect subservience with such qualities as passivity and mental and physical inferiority. Gender roles, in other words, are a direct outcome of the system of inequality. In turn, the roles tend to perpetuate the system. As long as men act dominant and women act subservient, the system will survive.

Both theoretical approaches have been criticized on a number of grounds. Many women's lives contradict the structural-functional assertion that the sexual division of labor leads naturally to female subservience and the exercise of expressive rather than instrumental qualities. As noted earlier, there is no inherent reason why women should be the primary nurturers in society because boys exhibit as much nurturing behavior as girls. Moreover, structural functionalism appears to justify and not merely explain gender inequality. Many critics have charged that the theory is inherently conservative, defending the status quo rather than providing directives for needed change.

Conflict theorists are criticized for overstating the amount of conflict between the sexes. Most women, like most men, are reasonably satisfied with their lives. Moreover, men are not uniformly the oppressors and women the victims. The Equal Rights Amendment to the Constitution that guaranteed men and women equal rights in all areas of social life was introduced into Congress repeatedly for half a century. It was finally passed in 1972 by a male-dominated Congress, but died in 1982 because not enough of the state legislatures ratified it. Interestingly, public opinion polls showed that a majority of Americans of both sexes favored the amendment. In fact, a 1980 Gallup poll reported that 61 percent of men and 54 percent of women favored the amendment. In sum, without minimizing the inequalities that exist and the seriousness of those inequalities, you must recognize that in everything from family life to political action there is a good deal of mutual respect and cooperation between men and women.

Some conflict theorists, particularly Marxists, argue that the end of gender as well as class inequality will only come with the establishment of communist societies. As the case of East Germany discussed earlier illustrates, however, communist governments have not eradicated gender or class inequality when they have come to power.

To return to the initial question, can gender inequality be ended? The answer depends on the kind of equality you want. Most Americans are not concerned about unequal outcomes as long as there is equal opportunity. Given equal opportunity, some women would opt to be full-time wives and mothers while others would opt for a career or employment outside the home. Women basically want the same thing that men want—to have options.

Attacking Gender Inequality

If you favor gender equality, you are a feminist. There are various kinds of feminists with diverse ideas about how to address the issue of inequality. We will look at the feminist approach to gender inequality, then examine a few programs and policies that support the feminist agenda.

The Feminist Approach

Feminism is the belief that all gender inequalities should be eliminated. There are, however, different kinds of feminists. For example, in the mid-nineteenth century, a number of American feminists called for full equality with men. Yet, a later group of feminists, the suffragists, focused on a single issue—gaining the right to vote for women. Today, some feminists—such as those represented by the National Organization for Women (NOW)—press for equality through legislation and reforms in the existing social structure. They believe that American society can become more egalitarian in the context of its capitalist economy and republican form of government.

Radical feminists, on the other hand, believe that nothing short of a revolution will bring about equality. They urge measures ranging from a Marxist-type revolution to the creation of a sisterhood of all women that will work together to achieve women's total control over their own destinies. Total control means such things as whether to be heterosexual or lesbian, whether or not to bear children, and whether—if a woman chooses motherhood—to care for her child full-time, work outside the home, or some blend of the two.

The feminist movement in the United States dates back to the 1840s (Flexner 1972). In the early nineteenth century, women were, from a legal point of view, not much better off than slaves. Those women who wanted to, or had to, find employment faced severe limitations. Even some of the jobs available to them, such as working in garment mills, offered debilitating working conditions and minimal pay.

In 1848, the first Woman's Rights Convention was held in Seneca Falls, New York. The convention adopted a "Declaration of Sentiments" that demanded women's rights as citizens (they could not vote at the time), new ways of thinking about gender, and new institutional practices. For the remainder of the nineteenth century, feminists engaged in various causes in addition to women's rights, such as temperance and child welfare. The suffragist movement gained momentum in the early years of the twentieth century, culminating in the Nineteenth Amendment to the Constitution in 1920.

For a variety of reasons, feminism waned after the passage of the Nineteenth Amendment and did not revive until the 1960s. Yet during these intervening years, the situation of women had been changing. For example, contraceptives had given women more control over their sexuality, and they were living longer. The net effect was that they had many potentially productive years after their last child started school. Not surprisingly, more women were working outside the home and many became involved in the social movements of the late 1950s and 1960s—particularly the civil rights movement.

In large measure, these changes spawned the modern-day feminist movement. NOW, a major force in this movement, held its first national conference in Washington in 1967. NOW's efforts were—and are—directed toward such concerns as inequality in income, sexual harassment, violence against women, child-care problems, the right of women to control their reproductive lives, and all forms of discrimination.

Reducing Gender Inequality

Many of the programs and policies advocated by NOW and other feminists would reduce gender inequality. For example, because they retain the bulk of child-care responsibilities, mothers—including single mothers—face more obstacles than do fathers when they try to work outside the home. Improved and expanded child-care centers and additional family leave laws (which provide time-off from work when a child is born or is seriously ill) would help equalize opportunities for women.

Women, like minorities, have been helped by affirmative action programs which are now under attack. As noted in the last chapter, many Americans believe that affirmative action is no longer needed. However, consider the amount of gender inequality in college sports. Affirmative action programs have helped reduce that inequality. But a survey of 23 Division I colleges found that women received less than one-fourth of the athletic scholarship money awarded even though women were a majority of the students in 16 of the schools (Blum 1994).

One final example of programs and policies that reduce inequality is **comparable worth**, the principle that equal pay should be given to work that is judged to be of comparable worth. Comparable worth arose as a way to deal with the fact that a disproportionate number of women are employed in such positions as clerical work and nursing. The jobs that are dominated by women also tend to pay less than those dominated by men. When jobs are of comparable worth, the argument runs, they should offer equal pay. Otherwise, gender inequality in income will not end in the foreseeable future.

The idea of comparable worth has been attacked vigorously. The critics ask: "Who is to judge whether two different jobs are comparable in worth?" Advocates reply with such questions as why should a woman who works as an administrative secretary be paid a fourth less than a man who is a grain inspector? Women employed by the city of Los Angeles raised a similar question—why should stenographers, who were mostly women, get $200 less a month than gardeners, who were mostly men? Not satisfied with the answer, they filed a complaint and won a 15 percent increase in pay. More than 20 states and a number of corporations have now adopted comparable worth plans.

Critical Thinking Exercise

According to a magazine article, a growing social problem in both the United States and Europe is the increasing number of uneducated and unemployed men (*The Economist*, February, 1997). The article supported the point by noting that: boys do worse than girls in school at every level except the university (and women are also closing the gap there); women dominate the jobs that are growing, while many men are trapped in jobs that are declining; women are entering traditionally male occupations, but men are not entering traditionally female occupations; and work and marriage are necessary for men to behave in socially responsible ways (such as obeying the law and caring for women and children).

How would you respond to the article? What questions would you ask? What information in this chapter bears upon the article's assertions? What additional information would you want in order to determine whether the assertions are valid?

Summary

Both your sex and your gender contribute to your behavior. Some of the typical differences between males and females are women's longer life span; men's greater aggression; women's higher self-ratings on likability and morality, and men's higher self-ratings on giftedness and power; women's higher value on relationships and men's higher value on independence; women's higher skill in interpreting nonverbal behavior; women's higher distress levels; diverse conversational styles; and numerous inequalities in things valued in the society.

Gender roles are at the heart of gender inequality. Gender-stereotyped qualities help perpetuate inequality. Gender roles include norms for appearance as well as qualities of character. Women are subject to more pressure than men to conform to cultural ideals of beauty.

Gender roles are learned in the family, at school, through peers, the media, and religion. Parents teach gender roles by their own behavior and the way they interact with their children. Peers tend to reinforce what is learned in the family. Schools have tried to minimize differential treatment of the sexes, but teachers still tend to give boys more attention and encouragement. Among the media, everything from children's picture books to television tends to support gender-stereotyped qualities and behavior. In many religions, women are either excluded from high positions of authority or hold only a small proportion of such positions.

Gender inequality is evident in sexism, prejudice or discrimination based on an individual's sex. A pervasive form of sexism is sexual harassment. Gender inequality in the economy is manifest in work patterns and income. Women tend to cluster in lower-level jobs and face more obstacles to advancement than do men. In income, there is more gender inequality than racial/ethnic inequality. A part of the inequality in work patterns and income can only be explained by discrimination.

Except for African Americans, there is gender inequality in educational attainment, and the inequality increases at higher levels of education. In the political sphere, women comprise only a small proportion of all elected officials. Getting more women into political office may be important for protecting women's rights.

Gender inequality also exists in household tasks. Even women with outside employment are likely to spend twice as much time as their husbands doing household chores. These women come home to a "second shift." This inequality in the home is detrimental to marital satisfaction and emotional well-being. The combination of household inequality with inequality in work and income reduces the benefits of outside work for women.

Another inequality is in personal safety. Women are more likely than men to be victims of interpersonal violence. Most of the violence occurs in intimate relationships.

Disagreement exists on whether gender inequality can be ended. Some argue on biological and social grounds that this inequality is inevitable and even necessary. Others argue that the inequality reflects contrary interests and needs and will only be ended through struggle. Feminism is the belief that all gender inequality should be eliminated. Different kinds of feminists have differing ideas on how to deal with gender inequality. Some feminists, represented by NOW, advocate reforms—some of which are already being implemented.

Glossary

anorexia nervosa an emotional disorder involving self-starvation

bulimia an emotional disorder involving repeated binge eating followed by "purging" through forced vomiting or laxatives

comparable worth the principle that equal pay should be given to work that is judged to be of comparable worth

feminism the belief that all gender inequalities should be eliminated

patriarchy a social system in which men dominate women

sexism prejudice or discrimination against someone based on that person's sex

sexual harassment unwanted sexual advances by someone in a position of superior power

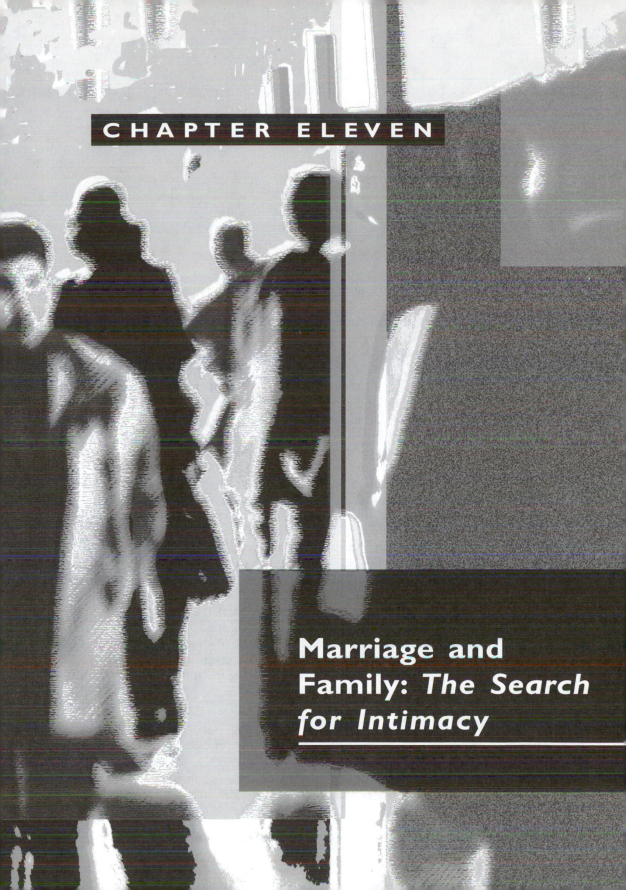

CHAPTER ELEVEN

Marriage and
Family: *The Search
for Intimacy*

When you think about your **family**, who comes to mind? Your parents and siblings? A stepparent and stepsiblings? A spouse? Bill and Nancy have a stable marriage and a strong commitment to each other. We were curious to learn about the families that they grew up in and were surprised by the complicated story they told us. Between them, as a result of multiple divorces by their mothers, they had nine different fathers! They were determined that their own children would not experience the pain that they had felt as they adjusted to a series of different fathers and stepfamilies. As a result, their commitment to each other and to their family is determined and unwavering.

For some people, then, "family" is a very complex affair. In response to our assignment to chart family relationships, a student brought an enormous poster to class. Her parents were divorced and both had remarried. Each of the new spouses had brought children to the marriage. Subsequently, the father's second marriage broke up. His second wife then married the oldest son of the man who had married his first wife. In other words, as the student explained, her stepmother had become her stepsister. Additional linkages also developed among the various children. Thus, the tangle of relationships was impossible to describe without the aid of the large poster.

While these two examples are not typical, they dramatize the fragile, complex, and volatile nature of family life today. Why is there so much family disruption? Why do people who have painful experiences in one marriage look for another mate and risk repeating the trauma? We will address these questions as we examine the institutions of marriage and the family.

What Is the Family?

Is a married couple with children a family? You would probably agree that it is. What about other arrangements? Is a married couple without children a family? Is a single parent and a child a family? Is a homosexual couple raising children a family? Certainly, there are some Americans who do not view the latter three as families. As one student put it, "That's not what I think of when I hear the word 'family'."

Defining the Family

Actually, we would include all four of the above as families. Some of the data we use in this chapter come from the United States Census Bureau, which defines a family as "a group of two or more persons related by birth, marriage, or adoption and residing together in a household" (U.S. Bureau of the Census 1996d, p. 6). By this definition, two or more siblings living together, a stepparent and stepchild, a married couple, and a lesbian who has adopted a child are all families.

Functions of the Family

Some form of the family is found in every human society. This suggests that the family has crucial functions for both individuals and society as a whole. Think about your own family experiences. What functions has your family served in your life? Do you think that another group could have served those functions as well? Do you think that anyone else would have been willing to do what your family has done for you?

Of course, the way you answer the questions will depend upon the kind of family life you have had. As we shall discuss later in this chapter, some families are very destructive. Others offer such loving closeness that people will die to protect them. As the anthropologist Ralph Linton (1949, p. 38) wrote, most family ties are so strong that if the human race ever self-destructs in a worldwide holocaust, "the last man will spend his last hours searching for his wife and child."

People in warm, supportive families know by experience the important functions of family life for them personally. But what about society? What important functions do families serve for society as a whole? The leading *structural-functionalist* theorist, Talcott Parsons (1967), wrote that all societies have a number of "functional imperatives" or challenges which must be met if the system is to survive. One of these imperatives is maintaining the values of the society and requires socialization of the young into those values. This task belongs to the family.

In addition to socialization, three other social functions of the family are: regulation of sexual relationships (in most societies, people are expected to confine sex to the spouse or spouses); reproduction (the family is the context for producing the next generation); and economic cooperation (the husband and wife work together to provide the necessary economic base for the survival of family members). However, socialization is the only function found in families in all human societies

(Reiss and Lee 1988). Exceptions can be found for the other three functions.

Some *feminist theorists* see a different function. The family (particularly the kind of family advocated by structural functionalists) reflects male interests and perpetuates male domination. At the center of a patriarchal society is "the individual family unit which originated with the idea of property and the desire to see one's property transmitted to one's biological descendants" (Rich 1992, p. 272).

We would add another function which we do not believe can be fully met apart from families: the fulfillment of intimacy needs. Recall that intimacy needs are fulfilled in primary groups, and for most people the family is the most important of all primary groups. "Blood is thicker than water" is a popular aphorism that reflects the special bonding that usually occurs in families. A family researcher (Blankenhorn 1990, p. xiii) has put it this way:

> The family is the basis for caring and nurturing relationships—the source, for most people, of life's greatest loves and most enduring commitments. In this regard, the family may be society's most important institution in determining the level of what might be called Gross National Happiness.

Actually, more than happiness is involved. Your physical and emotional well-being are dependent upon the fulfillment of your intimacy needs. *The Chicago Tribune* (March 31, 1991) reported a survey in which 1,505 psychologists were asked to identify the single greatest threat to mental health. The most frequent response was family breakup, followed by recession, unemployment, and drug abuse. In other words, when the family breaks up, a crucial foundation of emotional support breaks down.

The Changing American Family

If an American colonist had been asked, "what is a family?", he or she would probably have given a different answer than you would give. The reason for this is that family life varies not only among societies but within a particular society over time. We will first describe how American family life has changed over time and then look at some current trends.

Family Life over Time in the United States

Although men outnumbered women in colonial America, pressure was put on everyone to marry (Queen, Habenstein, and Quadagno 1985). A man might be single because no woman was available. If he stayed single when potential wives were available, however, he was viewed with contempt and, in several colonies, might even be punished. Sex was reserved for marriage. Premarital sex did occur, however, and frequently was punished if discovered.

A man was expected to be financially secure before marriage. Once secure, he had to get permission from the father of any woman he wanted to court. If she accepted his proposal, public notice of the proposed marriage was given. The marriage generally occurred in short order and was often followed quickly by children because little, if any, effective birth control was available. Families were large. With a combination of large families and shorter life expectancy, the median age of the population was quite low. In fact, as late as the 1800 census, the median age was only 16 (less than half the current figure of 34).

Colonial families were not always happy or healthy. Yet they were stable because divorce was stigmatized and difficult to obtain. The family was typically a self-contained economic unit, with all able members working together to produce most of those things necessary for their survival.

As the nation changed from an agrarian to an industrial society during the nineteenth century, family life also changed. And the change was substantial. As two historians put it, a grown man who was alive in both 1700 and 1800 would have found "little that was different in daily family life," but if that man were alive in both 1800 and 1900 he would have been "dumbfounded by family routines of 1900" (Scott and Wishy 1982, p. 174).

In particular, the nineteenth century family lost its function as a self-contained economic unit. Men, and sometimes women and children, went into the factories and mills in increasing numbers. Fewer families worked together as teams to produce what they needed. Instead, they increasingly worked as individuals outside the home and purchased goods and services.

Outside agencies—schools and governments—took over many of the functions that had been the responsibility of families. Providing a safe haven from an increasingly impersonal world and nurturing children became the primary functions of families. Americans "made a religion of domesticity, casting supernal light around mother, child, and home" (Scott and Wishy 1982, p. 178). Moreover, the traditional gender roles discussed in the last chapter became embedded in the nation's heart as cherished ideals.

In the twentieth century, life expectancy rose dramatically, the majority of people resided in cities, communication and travel expanded, and family disruption through divorce, desertion, and separation surged. Sexual "revolutions" occurred in the 1920s and 1960s; the rate of premarital sex rose dramatically. In recent decades, people questioned traditional gender roles, and many opted for alternatives of some kind. For the first time in American history, the traditional ideal of the **nuclear family** (a family of father, mother, and children) became a minority of all families in the nation (Figure 11.1).

Figure 11.1   Composition of American Households

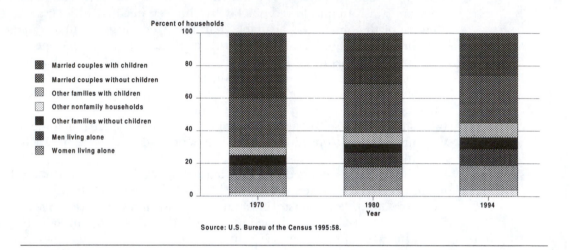

Source: U.S. Bureau of the Census 1995:58.

Recent Trends

During the last three decades the breakdown of traditional ideals has accelerated. In particular, fewer people are living out the ideals that sex should be confined to marriage, that all people should marry and have children, and that marriages should last until death. Consider the following trends:

- Among never-married women, 49.5 percent of those aged 15 through 19 and nearly two-thirds of those aged 15 through 44 have had sexual intercourse (Forrest and Singh 1990); among men aged 13 through 19, 79 percent—varying from 75.9 percent of whites to 80.5 percent of Hispanics to 95.8 percent of African Americans—have had sexual intercourse (Sonenstein, Pleck, and Ku 1991).

- Since 1970, the proportion of out-of-wedlock births has nearly tripled, involving more than three of every ten births (U.S. Bureau of the Census 1996d, p. 79).

- Since 1970, the never-married increased from 18.9 to 26.8 percent of adult men and 13.7 to 19.4 percent of adult women (U.S. Bureau of the Census 1996d, p. 54).

- Since 1970, the number of couples cohabiting has increased by 700 percent; more than 3.6 million couples are now cohabiting, including over 1.3 million who have children in the home (U.S. Bureau of the Census 1996d, p. 56).

- Since 1970, the birthrate per 1,000 women decreased from 87.9 to 67.6; it decreased for all races, so that the average size of families is smaller than it has ever been (U.S. Bureau of the Census 1996d, p. 77).

- Among married women, 63.5 percent of those with children under six years of age and a little over three-fourths of those with children between the ages of six and 17 are in the labor force (U.S. Bureau of the Census 1996d, p. 400).

- After 1965, the divorce rate rose dramatically, from 2.5 to 4.6 per 1,000 people; the 1994 rate was lower than the high rates of 1979 and 1981, but was still double the rates of the 1950s and 1960s (U.S. Bureau of the Census 1996d, p. 107).

These trends have occurred among all racial and ethnic groups although the numbers vary by groups. Table 11.1, for example, shows the proportion of those in various groups who were divorced in each of four years. The proportion of African Americans divorced is higher than the proportion of whites or Hispanics for all years, and a smaller proportion of Hispanics than either whites or African Americans is divorced.

Table 11.1   **Percent Divorced, by Race**

Year	White	Black	Hispanic
1970	3.1	4.4	3.9
1980	6.0	8.4	5.8
1990	8.1	10.6	7.0
1995	9.1	10.7	7.9

Source: U.S. Bureau of the Census 1996d, p. 54

What do these trends mean? Are they an indication that marriage and the family are doomed? To keep matters in perspective, the great majority of Americans still marry at some point in their lives. Only a minority of unmarried people are single by choice. Moreover, the preponderance of Americans say that a good marriage and family life is extremely important to them (Gallup and Newport 1991). Consequently, families are not disappearing, but they are becoming more diverse.

Thinking Critically

A popular magazine sponsored a survey of teenage girls about being unmarried and pregnant (Chassler 1997). Interviewers asked 720 girls what would prevent pregnancy among unwed teens. The overwhelming majority (96 to 97 percent) said that having parents they can talk to, having self-respect, being informed about sexual matters, and being aware of the responsibility of raising a child would all greatly reduce teenage pregnancies. A smaller majority mentioned several other factors such as not going out with older men.

The responses, according to the writer of the article, suggest a number of parental failings which contribute to the problem. They also identify concrete measures to address the problem. Or do they? Actually, only 6 percent of the respondents had been pregnant. Were the others speculating about what had worked in their lives, or what they think would be important generally? We don't know. Did the parents of those who got pregnant not talk openly with their children or try to build their children's self-respect? We don't know. Most important, were there differences between those who had been pregnant and those who had not in terms of their self-respect, sexual knowledge, and the extent to which they could talk to their parents? These were not measured.

We are not saying that the factors the girls mentioned are unimportant. Or even that they would not make a difference. But you should not readily accept speculations as solutions to a social problem. What is needed is research on those who have and those who have not been pregnant to see if there are differences on any of the factors mentioned in the survey.

Diversity in Family Life

Leo Tolstoy began his famed novel, *Anna Karenina*, with the observation that all happy families are alike and that all unhappy families differ from each other. Tolstoy was wrong. Both happy and unhappy families are diverse. Yet the obstacles or challenges to a happy family life can be greater among some kinds of families than others. What would you identify as obstacles or challenges to a happy family life in your own experience? As we discuss diversity in family life in the United States, think about how the families, and their obstacles and challenges, are similar to or different from, your own.

Single-Parent Families

"Why would anyone want to raise children on their own?" a harried mother asked us. Actually, few if any people prefer to be a single parent. Rather, single-parent families come about because of divorce, desertion, death, or because a person has a strong desire to have children and can't find an acceptable mate.

As Table 11.2 shows, single-parent families are a growing proportion of all families, a trend that holds for all races. Most single-parent families are headed by a mother, but fathers head 3 percent of white and 4 percent of African-American and Hispanic families.

Table 11.2   **Percent of Families With Children That Are Single-Parent**

Race	1970	1980	1990	1995
White	10	17	23	24
Black	36	52	61	67
Hispanic	NA	26	33	37

NA Not available

Source: U.S. Bureau of the Census 1996d, p. 65

This trend is not unique to the United States, incidentally. Single-parent families, and especially those headed by a mother, have increased in countries throughout the world, including Australia, England, Germany, Japan, Nicaragua, and Russia (Burns and Scott 1994). Furthermore, they are most likely to increase where the husband-wife roles are no longer complementary in the sense of a clearly defined sexual division of labor.

Single-parent families pose some special obstacles and challenges to both parent and child. First, think about the difficulty of being a single parent. Most couples who are parents will tell you about the stresses and time-consuming demands of raising children. All those stresses and demands fall on one person in the single-parent family. Thus, single parents are more likely than other parents to feel overwhelmed by the sheer number of responsibilities and tasks as well as by the emotional drain involved in parenting.

We don't want to paint a uniformly grim picture. We are not saying that all single parents are stressed or burnt out or standing at the edge of desperation. Nevertheless, single parents do face severe challenges, in part because of the greater likelihood of financial difficulties. As noted in Chapter Eight, female-headed families have the highest poverty rates of any group in the nation. And those single mothers who have never been married have far greater financial problems than those previously married (Thomson, Hanson, and McLanahan 1994).

Thus, it is not surprising that anxiety and depression are common among single mothers, or that single mothers as a group constitute one of the largest consumers of mental health services (Goldberg et al. 1992). In addition to the demands of parenting, single parents who were previously married may still be dealing with a sense of loss and/or betrayal. Thus, fathers who have the hardest time coping with being a single parent are those whose wives have deserted them (Greif 1985).

Children in single-parent families also face special obstacles and challenges. If a single-parent family results from divorce, the children may struggle with a sense of loss and/or betrayal. The rate of emotional and behavioral problems in children in single-parent families is more than twice that of children who live with both biological parents (Zill and Schoenborn 1990).

If the parent is working, the children may perceive less parental support and concern as well as less family cohesion than do those in two-parent families (Amato 1987). And, as survey research with 83 single parents found, if a single parent starts dating, the children may feel even more deprived of parental attention and may resent the people dated (Petronio and Endres 1985/1986). About two-thirds of the parents in the study believed that their dates had reservations about the children as well.

To balance these findings, most single parents find that the job becomes easier over time, and most believe that they possess one or more parenting strengths (Richards and Schmiege 1993). Moreover, while children in single-parent families perceive *less* cohesion than those in two-parent homes, they do not perceive a *lack* of cohesion. Finally, while the rates of emotional and behavioral problems are far higher than the rates in two-parent homes, the *majority* of children in single-parent families have adequate levels of physical and mental health.

In sum, single-parent families face certain unique obstacles and challenges to a happy family life, but many are able to cope with them. Generally, single parents enjoy being parents, feel competent as parents, and are satisfied with the experience of parenting (Mednick 1987).

Racial/Ethnic Families

Will your family experiences be different depending upon whether you are white, African American, Hispanic, Asian, or American Indian? Yes and no. American families, whatever their racial or ethnic background, are similar in many ways. Yet differences do exist.

African American Families

Among all racial/ethnic groups, African Americans have the lowest proportion of married-couple families—47 percent, compared 82 percent for whites, 81 percent for Asian Americans, and 68 percent for Hispanics (U.S. Bureau of the Census 1996d, p. 62). Black children are more likely than those of other racial/ethnic groups to grow up in single-parent families and to live with a mother who has never married.

The black family must be understood within the legacy of slavery, segregation, and discrimination that we discussed in Chapter Nine. Indeed, many of the obstacles and challenges they face are rooted not in race but rather in their disproportionate numbers in the lower social strata. If you are African American, you are more likely to grow up in a family that is impoverished. This means—for any race or ethnic group— higher rates of family disruption as well as physical and emotional problems. It also means less likelihood of financial support by one generation for another (Hogan, Eggebeen, and Clogg 1993).

In a study of Detroit families, Whyte (1990) found that African Americans were similar to whites in the division of power and labor in the home. Like whites, black women who worked outside the home often felt burdened by household tasks. In other ways, however, the African Americans differed from whites. For example, black women put more value on a high income, less value on sexual faithfulness, and reported less togetherness and lower marital satisfaction. Black families also have higher rates of violence than white families. In a national survey, black wives reported more than double the amount of severe violence from husbands as did white wives (Hamptom and Gelles 1994).

Again, however, you need to look at the other side of the ledger. In a sample of urban newlyweds, African Americans reported more disclosure, more positive sexual relationships, and less conflict than did whites (Oggins, Veroff, and Leber 1993). Whites also report a decline in marital satisfaction during the child-rearing years, but African Americans do not (Broman 1988). African Americans who are single parents also report more satisfaction with parenting and fewer problems with their children than white single parents (McKenry and Fine 1993). Finally, African Americans are less likely than whites to experience distress when their children leave home and the nest is "empty" (Borland 1982).

In sum, black families face a number of unique obstacles and challenges, most of which stem from their position in American society. Yet black families also display some unique strengths and have carved out happy family lives in spite of the obstacles and challenges.

Hispanic Families

Hispanic families are more likely than white, but less likely than black families, to be impoverished. Like African Americans, the major obstacles and challenges of the Hispanic family reflect their greater likelihood of being in the lower socioeconomic strata.

Hispanics have a lower proportion of married-couple families than whites but a higher proportion than African Americans. Hispanic men are more likely than white men, and Hispanic women are less likely than white women, to want to marry (South 1993). Once married, however, Hispanic women have more children than either whites or African Americans. They are also less likely to divorce than either whites or African Americans (Table 11.1).

Hispanics may have a somewhat different experience of marital satisfaction than do whites. In particular, a study of Mexican American families found that the women reported a successively lower marital satisfaction over time; among whites (and the Mexican American men), marital satisfaction tends to decline in the middle years of the marriage and then rise again (Markides and Hoppe 1985).

Martinez (1993) found that Mexican American mothers tend to use more punishment and more guilt in disciplining their children. The more frequent use of punishment probably reflects lower socioeconomic status, however, rather than ethnicity.

Finally, there is some evidence that Hispanics have closer bonds than do whites with a broad range of family relationships (del Castillo 1984). Uncles, aunts, cousins, and other relatives can be an important resource, offering financial and material help as well as emotional support.

Asian American and American Indian Families

Comparatively little research is available on Asian American and American Indian families, but as we showed in Chapter Nine they form a contrasting pair in terms of achievement and socioeconomic standing. Asian American families have the lowest divorce and teenage pregnancy rates of any racial group (Dunn 1994).

Major obstacles and challenges for Asian American families most often occur when a younger generation in the process of becoming Americanized clashes with the traditional ways of the older generation. Traditional Asian cultures consider the individual's needs to be subordinate to the group's needs and children to be subordinate to their parents. Women are expected to be obedient to men—to the father before marriage, to the husband after marriage, and to the eldest son if the husband dies. Thus, a study of Chinese immigrant families found that the children grew up accepting their responsibility to help and support their parents, but they resisted parental control in the areas of personal development and freedom (such as choosing their own marriage partner) (Lin and Liu 1993).

Poverty is the chief obstacle and challenge facing American Indian families. It's no wonder, then, that drug abuse, child abuse, and troubled family life are more common among American Indians than other groups. Nor is it surprising that American Indian adolescents have relatively high rates of depression and suicide attempts (Sack et al. 1994).

Tribal traditions affect American Indian family life in positive ways. Like Hispanics, American Indians tend to have larger extended families upon which they can depend for support. In fact, in most tribes parents are not expected to bear the sole responsibility for rearing children. In addition to parents, American Indian children may be loved and attended to by various other relatives living with or nearby the family (Bahr 1994).

Homosexual Families

How do you think a child is affected by being raised by homosexual parents? The evidence indicates that the sexual orientation of parents makes little or no difference—including no difference in the child's eventual sexual orientation. Contrary to what many people believe, homosexual parents are as able to raise normal, healthy children as heterosexuals (McCracken 1993; Tasker and Golombok 1995).

Although gay marriages are not legal in most places, a fourth to a third of homosexuals enter into informal marriages (Schulenburg 1985). These are generally committed, **monogamous** (married to one person at a time) relationships. In some cases, they involve children who were conceived in a previous heterosexual relationship.

Gay families face a number of unique obstacles and challenges (George and Behrendt 1987). One is the social stigma attached to being such a family. How do children explain the nature of their family to their friends? How is a gay couple received at a school's parents' night?

Homophobia, the irrational fear of homosexuals, is a second obstacle and challenge. Most homosexuals have grown up having contemptuous labels ("queer," "fag," etc.) applied to them. Homosexuals who are open about their sexual orientation may face hostility and threats (particularly since the onset of AIDS) and discrimination in the job and housing markets. Such things can affect the partners' sense of self-esteem or identity and can, in the process, adversely affect their relationship.

Traditional gender roles are also a source of problems for the gay family. If both partners have been socialized into those roles, they may encounter difficulty in their relationship. For instance, two males who are each relatively unemotional, competitive, and dominant—all aspects of the traditional male gender role—may have a difficult time establishing a loving, cooperative, supportive relationship.

In general, however, the same kinds of things create a satisfying relationship for both homosexuals and heterosexuals: commitment to the relationship, shared decision making, and emotional investment in each other (Kurdek and Schmitt 1986). Homosexuals, like heterosexuals, value an intimate relationship in which they can share feelings and activities, receive emotional support, and know someone cares deeply about them.

Single- and Dual-Earner Families

The traditional family, in which the husband is the sole breadwinner, now constitutes a minority of all families. In 1995, 61.1 percent of wives had jobs outside the home (U.S. Bureau of the Census 1996d, p. 400). As noted in the last chapter, even if they work full time outside the home, wives still tend to bear the major responsibility for household tasks. Thus, developing an equitable division of labor in the home is one of the major challenges for dual-earner families.

A second obstacle and challenge for dual-earner families is the stress that comes from conflicts between work demands and family responsibilities. More than a third of all couples report conflict of this sort (Lauer and Lauer 1997). The conflict is most severe when the partners are both engaged in careers (as opposed to simply having a job) and when there are children at home. A spouse who experiences the conflict is likely to be distressed, and this distress may lead to less marital warmth and supportiveness (Matthews, Conger, and Wickrama 1996).

Third, problems may arise if anyone in the family believes that the employment is harmful to the family. Surveys show that a majority of parents and 39 percent of children agree that preteen children suffer when both parents work outside the home (Roper and Keller 1988). Are these perceptions accurate? Actually, with the possible exception of mother-infant bonding, the research identifies no long-term problems as long as the children have close and warm supervision (Lauer and Lauer 1997).

Nevertheless, if family members perceive the work as troublesome, tensions and conflict can result. A study of eighth-grade students found more anger, stress, and family conflict among those who cared for themselves 11 hours or more a week because both parents worked (Dwyer 1990).

The obstacles and challenges are not insurmountable. On the contrary, comparisons of dual-earner and single-earner families find equal levels of marital satisfaction; the majority of dual-earner couples are able to deal satisfactorily with their obstacles and challenges (Smith 1985; Blair 1993). And in spite of the tendency for employed wives to do most of the household tasks, employed women report as much happiness as full-time homemakers, and women who are career-oriented are happier when they are able to combine a career with marriage and family (Benin and Nienstedt 1985; Pietromonaco, Manis, and Markus 1987).

Relational Choices

Until relatively recent times, if you chose not to be married, you might have been looked upon with suspicion. The common question was: what's wrong with someone who doesn't want to marry? If, on the other hand, you chose to live with someone without being married, you prob-

Explorations

A Different Kind of Family

How much do you know about families that are different from the one in which you were raised? Have each group member select one type of family discussed in this section that is different from his or her own—a single-parent family, a family from a different ethnic or racial group, a homosexual family, or a dual-earner family. Make an intensive study of this type of **family**.

Pursue the study in one of three ways (make certain each way is chosen by at least one group member):

1. Locate a real family. Interview the members in depth, exploring the topics covered in this and previous chapters. Include such items as gender roles, family rituals and traditions, division of labor in the home, how differences are handled, and relationships with other relatives. Compare your experiences with your findings. In what ways is your family similar to and different from the one you studied?

2. Research the kind of family chosen in the library. Be sure to check all sources— books, popular articles and professional articles. Cover the topics and make the analysis noted in 1) above.

3. Use an online service to get into an appropriate discussion group, find a member of a family of the kind you have selected, and follow the instructions in 1) above.

In a class discussion, compare the various types of families on each topic. Also compare the results obtained from the three ways of investigating the topic. If you do this as in individual project, select one of the three ways and write up your results.

---

ably would have been viewed as scandalous. The question asked was: how can people so blatantly flaunt morality?

Today, you may be free to choose between singlehood or **cohabitation** (living with someone in an intimate, sexual relationship without being married) or marriage. Of course, you may eventually make all three relational choices. You may choose to be single for a time, then cohabit and finally marry. Each of the choices, whether temporary or long-term, has different implications for your life.

Staying Single

As noted earlier, an increasing proportion of the adult population has never been married. In part, this is because people are getting married at a later age; some of those now classified as never married will eventually marry. Although the proportion who will never marry has increased, only a minority are single by choice. Apart from those who cannot find a suitable mate or whose life circumstances do not allow them to be married, why do some Americans choose the single life?

One reason for remaining single is career. People who are highly career-oriented may see marriage as an impediment. Most single women, for example, believe that staying single will help them advance in their careers (Rollins 1986). Indeed, women who remain single tend to attain more occupationally than those who marry.

Other reasons that singles most often cite for not marrying are personal freedom and the desire for personal growth (Simenauer and Carroll 1982; Greenglass 1985). Singles enjoy the freedom to go where they want and do what they please. They don't want a relationship that will inhibit the pursuit of personal interests.

What is the single life like? It may or may not mean living alone. Most singles prefer to live with someone—for financial reasons or intimacy needs or both. What about sex? Does the desire for freedom include the desire to have a greater range of sexual relations? The desire may be there, but sex experts point out that the best sex and the most frequent sex occurs in marriage. A national survey found that nearly 40 percent of married people, but only 25 percent of singles, report having sex twice a week (Laumann et al. 1994).

In addition to sex, singles are likely to be at a disadvantage compared to married people in a number of ways. Singles report more loneliness. Married people tend to be healthier and live longer than singles. Singles have more emotional problems, not only in the United States but in other nations as well (Mastekaasa 1994). And a greater proportion of married people than singles say they are "very happy" with their lives. For example, one survey reported that 39.4 percent of the married and 15.5 percent of those never married said they were "very happy" (Ward 1981).

In sum, singlehood, like any relational choice, has certain rewards and certain costs. Some singles find that the rewards are greater than the costs. Others find the opposite to be true.

Cohabitation

Why has the proportion of people who cohabit risen so much in recent decades? People cohabit for a variety of reasons (Lauer and Lauer 1997): to avoid being alone, to escape their parents' home, to fulfill sexual needs, to maintain an intimate relationship in which one of the partners is reluctant to marry, and to test the relationship's long-term potential in a type of trial marriage.

The most common reason we hear from students is the last one—cohabitation is a good way to test the waters, to get a sense of how well a marriage between the partners will work. Ironically, data from both the United States and Canada show that those who cohabit before marriage have a lower-quality marriage and a greater likelihood of divorce than those who do not cohabit (White 1989; DeMaris and Rao 1992; Stets 1993).

It isn't clear why cohabitation is not a good indicator of the quality of the marriage. But there are a number of interesting differences between cohabitors and married couples (Lauer and Lauer 1997). Compared to the married, cohabitors tend to: report more tension in the relationship; have less satisfying communication; report less happiness, more depression, and lower levels of commitment to the relationship; and have higher levels of violence.

These findings should be kept in perspective. For instance, to say that cohabitors have "less satisfying" communication is not to say that they are *dissatisfied* with their communication. It is simply to say that the experience is likely to be a more satisfying one in marriage than in cohabitation. If you choose to cohabit, it might be a very satisfying experience for you. However, your chances for a satisfying intimate relationship are higher in marriage than in cohabitation and higher in a marriage that has not been preceded by cohabiting than in one that has.

Marriage

Americans are delaying marriage. The median age at marriage is the highest it has been since records were kept—now 26.7 years for men and 24.5 years for women (Saluter 1996). Nevertheless, most people will eventually marry.

What are the qualities you desire in a life partner? A researcher conducted three *experiments* with college women in which he asked them to choose from among hypothetical partners with varying qualities (Cunningham 1996). When women chose between men with varying incomes and different levels of honesty and dominance, their top choice was a man with high income, honesty, and medium dominance. When women were asked to select a mate with one good trait and two bad ones, half opted for a man with good personality but low income and low physical attractiveness, while 29 percent chose high physical attractiveness combined with poor personality and low income. When asked to choose between a handsome cheater, an average-looking man who was loyal and helpful, a rich surgeon who had little time for his family, and a relatively low-income high school teacher who gave a lot of time to his family, 60 percent chose the high school teacher. The surgeon came in last. The experiments suggest that women value financial security, but not at the expense of other desired qualities.

In general, both men and women value such things as kindness, understanding, affection, and honesty in a life partner. Yet a gender difference also exists, and it exists in societies throughout the world: men tend to look for women who are younger and physically attractive, while women are more concerned with men who are likely to be good providers (Lauer and Lauer 1997).

As indicated earlier, marriage provides a number of benefits to people. Both men and women tend to benefit in terms of their physical and emotional well-being (Lillard and Waite 1995). For women, a secure financial status accounts for much of that well-being. For both men and women, the benefits of marriage tend to increase as the length of the union increases.

While both sexes benefit, men benefit more than women in terms of such things as mental health (Fowers 1991). Women generally have to make more adjustments than men—a situation which led Jessie Bernard (1972) to assert that every marriage is really two marriages—his and hers. In essence, his marriage yields more benefits and requires fewer adjustments than does hers. She is more likely to assume the major responsibility for household tasks and child care. She is more likely to drop out of the labor force and move to a new area to accommodate his career. And she may find that he is less attentive and less communicative than he was when he was courting her.

Thus, the experience of marriage varies by gender. It also varies by race and ethnicity. Two researchers who interviewed a sample of whites, African Americans, and Mexican Americans who had been married at least twenty years found a number of interesting differences (Mackey and O'Brien 1995):

- African American women had more ambivalence about the men they were to marry than did the other women.

- African Americans were more likely than whites or Mexican Americans to use mutual confrontation in dealing with conflict at the beginning of their marriages.

- Mexican Americans reported more mutuality in decision making than either whites or African Americans.

Thus, while there were more similarities than differences in the three groups, marriage is a somewhat different experience for people in various racial/ethnic groups.

Finally, the experience of marriage varies in terms of just how beneficial it is. The benefits range from virtually none for couples who have a highly conflicted relationship that ends in divorce, to short-term benefits for couples who have a satisfying marriage that deteriorates, to long-term benefits for couples who have a satisfying and stable marriage. What goes into the latter? In our study of long-term marriages, we found that husbands and wives agreed on the most important factors for a fulfilling relationship (Lauer and Lauer 1986). In essence, you are more likely to have a lasting and satisfying marriage if you both are committed to marriage and to a person you like, enjoy doing things with, and value as your best friend.

EXTENSIONS

Marriage Among the Siddis

Some form of marriage is found in all societies. But both the ideal and the practices vary among societies. The Siddis are a group of black Muslims who live on the western coast of India (Chakraborty 1994). They believe that marriage is essential; parents try to get their children to marry as early as is legally permissible—fifteen for girls and eighteen for boys.

Polygyny, a marriage involving one husband and two or more wives, is permitted in Muslim culture. Occasionally, a man will marry a second wife when the first is unable to bear children or when he falls in love with another woman. Most of the Siddis, however, are monogamous.

The Siddis also practice a custom that goes back to the time of the ancient Hebrews: if a husband dies, his widow may marry his younger brother. Among the Hebrews, the practice was mandatory if the widow had no sons. Among the Siddis, the practice is optional, depending upon the wishes of the two people. The Siddis also allow a widower to marry his deceased wife's younger sister if both agree to it.

Young people do not choose their marital partners, although their consent is taken into consideration before a match is finalized. Their parents make the choice, and usually a marriage proposal is initiated by a boy's father. Traditionally, the first choice for a marital partner is a cousin. If no such choice is available, a life partner is sought from within the village. Only as a last resort will a partner be sought outside the village.

Once a match is agreed upon, there is an engagement ceremony. The girl sits on a wooden stool while her fiance's sister puts a saree on her head and gives her a small sum of money and some silver ornaments. The girl's father is given a larger sum of money—the bride price. The girl's father provides lunch for any guests from the boy's side who come to visit during the engagement period. Usually, the engagement lasts only two or three months.

The marriage ceremony is a mixture of Hindu and Muslim rituals. Seven days before the wedding, specific relatives have specific responsibilities for the ceremony of "pithi." Among other things, the bride is smeared with a tumeric-based ointment, and a small hole—into which a copper coin, a betel nut and some rice are placed—is dug beside the door of the couple's future home. On the day before the wedding, the bride and groom are each given a purificatory bath, after which the groom rides around the village on a horse while his relatives accompany him and sing songs.

The wedding itself takes place in the evening. The most important part of the ceremony is when a flower veil is tied on the groom's forehead, the Muslim priest recites verses from the Koran, and the bride and groom are asked if they consent to the union. The marriage is then recorded in a notebook, the bride is given some utensils by her maternal uncle, and the couple go to their home. Three days later, some additional rituals occur, such as visiting and being blessed by elderly relatives.

Sex

What is the most intense form of intimacy you can experience? If you answered "sex," you have a lot of company. Yet sex can be alienating as well as bonding, a source of conflict as well as a source of gratification. For sex is not simply a physical act, it is also a social act.

Sex as Social

When we speak of sex as social, we mean that the experience of sex depends upon such things as gender roles and culture. For instance, men are more likely to be—and *expected* to be—the initiators of sexual activity. Men are more permissive than are women about casual sex, and tend to begin sexual relationships at a slightly earlier age (16 to 17) than women (17 to 18) (Seidman and Rieder 1994).

Culturally, enormous variations exist in sexual practices (Lauer and Lauer 1997). Frequency varies among South Pacific peoples from the Dani, who have sex so seldom that they barely maintain the population, to the young Mangaian males who have sex two or three times every night. Preferred positions for intercourse also vary. For example, among Trobriand Islanders, the preferred position is for the man to squat down and draw the woman toward him until her legs rest on his hips or elbows.

Finally, sex is social in the sense that norms about sex vary from one society to another and between groups within the same society. In American society, for example, most people regard sex as a pleasurable and desirable activity. But for a few very conservative religious groups, procreation is the main purpose of sex, and those who enjoy sex too much or want it too often may be defined as people without sufficient faith.

Premarital Sex

Traditionally, there has been a double standard in American society about premarital sex: It has been more acceptable and more expected for males than for females. To some extent, the double standard still exists. You can test this by asking yourself and some friends to evaluate a hypothetical male and a hypothetical female, each of whom is sexually promiscuous. The promiscuity may be condemned in both cases, but is the condemnation of the female greater than that of the male?

Apart from promiscuity, attitudes about premarital sex have changed considerably. Gallup polls show that the percentage of Americans who agree that premarital sex is "not wrong" rose from 21 percent in 1969 to 54 percent in 1991. As you might expect, the young are more likely than the old, and males are more likely than females, to approve of premarital sex.

Behavior has also changed. In the famous Kinsey studies of the 1940s, about a third of women experienced premarital sex. By the 1990s, about two-thirds of American women were having sexual intercourse before marriage. A number of social factors are related to the probability of having premarital sex. A study of Hispanic women found that those who are religiously active and from intact families are less likely than other American women to have premarital sex (Durant, Pendergast, and Seymore 1990). Rates of premarital sex are also higher among African Americans, among those with permissive parents, among those from broken homes, and among those whose siblings are sexually active (East, Felice, and Morgan 1993).

Marital Sex

Marital, as well as premarital, sex has changed in the United States. In the Kinsey studies, only a minority of married people engaged in oral sex, and most people used the "missionary" position (the man on top of the woman). By the 1970s, a majority of married people had some experience with oral sex, experimented with various positions, and engaged in more foreplay than did previous generations (Hunt 1974).

How important is a satisfying sex life to a satisfying marriage? In our study of long-term marriages, we found that both men and women rated sex as important but not as important as other things such as liking one's partner (Lauer and Lauer 1986). For some of the couples, sex was less frequent but more enjoyable over time. For others, both frequency and satisfaction remained stable over most of their years together. For a few spouses, there was a less-than-satisfactory sex life in the midst of a very satisfying marriage. As one wife explained, she had been previously married for a short time to a man with whom she had "great sex." But everything else about the marriage was miserable. Her present husband cannot engage in sex because of a physical disability, but they have a "great marriage."

A number of factors affect the frequency of marital sex. Sex tends to decrease in the child-rearing years. Poor health can diminish or even eliminate sex. A time- and energy-consuming career may depress the sex drive; as an ambitious, hard-driving husband told us, often he is "just too pooped to pop." In spite of such situations, however, marital sex is, as noted earlier, the best (most satisfying) and most frequent sex reported.

Contraception

Through most of human history, sexual relations generally resulted in pregnancy. Attempts to find an effective method of **contraception**, the use of devices or techniques to prevent fertilization, go back thousands of years when the ancient Egyptians used a mixture that contained crocodile dung. Many methods used in more modern times, such as the nineteenth century practice of a vaginal douche immediately after sex, have been as ineffective as the Egyptians'.

It was only after the work of Margaret Sanger in the 1920s and 1930s that contraceptives became generally available in the United States. Not all people use them, however. Probably few women want to get pregnant when they first become sexually active, but about a third use no contraceptive (Mosher and McNally 1991). Whites are slightly more likely than African Americans or Hispanics to use contraceptives.

Use of the condom has increased since the advent of concern about AIDS. However, the Pill is the most widely used method of birth control in the United States. Among married women, **sterilization**, a surgical procedure that prevents fertilization, is the most commonly used method. Forty-four percent of currently married women are surgically sterile (U.S. Bureau of the Census 1996d, p. 84).

Although most religious groups disapprove of premarital sex, and some disapprove of artificial contraceptives even for the married, the proportion of religious women who practice birth control is about the same as that of nonreligious women (Goldscheider and Mosher 1991). For reasons that are unknown, however, the preferred method differs, with sterilization being the most frequently used method for Protestants, the Pill for Catholics, and diaphragms for Jews.

There are various reasons why people do not use contraceptives. Among some unmarried, young women from poor or troubled families, the reason may be that they *want* to get pregnant (Musick 1993). These women often feel abandoned, unloved, and without purpose. They strive to fulfill their need for love and for doing something creative with their lives through sex and childbearing.

Abortion

Abortion, the expulsion of a fetus from the uterus, has generated a great deal of controversy. Abortion has long been used as a method of birth control. Until the Supreme Court's 1973 decision in the *Roe v. Wade* case, however, abortions were illegal in the United States. Roe v. Wade allowed women to have an abortion without resorting to a back-alley operation that threatened their health and even their life.

After 1973, the number of abortions rose dramatically but leveled off in the 1980s and 1990s. The latest Census Bureau data show a number of important facts about abortion (U.S. Bureau of the Census 1996d, p. 86). There are now more than 1.5 million abortions each year. For every ten pregnancies, between two and three are aborted. The abortion rate is lower among white women than women of other races. About a third of all abortions occur to women aged 20 to 24. And of those getting abortions, 83 percent are single and 17 percent are married.

A majority of Americans favor a woman's right to get an abortion. A minority claim that abortion should be illegal under any circumstances. Those who favor legalized abortion (the "pro-choice" camp) argue that women have a right to control their own fertility and to decide for themselves what is in their best interests. Those who oppose legalized abortion (the "pro-life" camp) argue that the unborn fetus is human and has rights, and that abortion is an act of murder. Despite efforts to reconcile the two positions, no end to the controversy is in sight.

Family Problems

Not everyone gains the beneficial effects of marriage and family. Some families nurture and enrich, but others are emotionally destructive to the members. Family life as a problem rather than a solution is suggested by *conflict theory*. We noted earlier that there is "his" marriage and "her" marriage in every union. The different marital experience of men and women reflect their diverse interests and needs. And, as noted in the last chapter, to the extent that women are subservient and accepting of lower benefits, men reap greater benefits.

Marxists carry the argument farther, arguing that women are not merely subservient but subjugated and miserable (Engels 1884). In a capitalist society, families are simply mechanisms for maintaining men's power and wealth and passing them on to their sons. As such, families help maintain inequalities between the social classes. Under communism, families will change along with other institutions and once again become the egalitarian groups they were in the pre-capitalist era of civilization.

Conflict theory correctly indicates that family life can be problematic, and not just for wives. Husbands and children can also be victims. Let us look at three kinds of family situations that pose a serious threat or challenge to people: violence in the family, divorce, and remarriage and the blended family.

Violence in the Family

Someone has said that, next to the military, the family is the most violent institution in American society. We include verbal as well as physical abuse in our definition of violence. Verbal abuse is emotionally destructive, while physical abuse is both physically and emotionally destructive. Taking both verbal and physical abuse into account, tens of millions of Americans experience violence in their homes every year. Murder is the extreme end of violence; 16 percent of all murder victims are killed by a family member (Dawson and Langan 1994).

We briefly discussed wife abuse in the last chapter. Husband abuse also occurs. In fact, a national survey found a slightly higher rate of husband than of wife abuse (Gelles and Straus 1988). However, the violence of wives against their husbands is often a matter of self-defense and is less likely to result in severe injury than is the violence of husbands against their wives. For women, domestic violence causes more injuries than automobile accidents, muggings, and rapes combined (Matlock, Slate, and Saarnio 1995).

Violence against children involves not only verbal and physical abuse but also neglect. Neglect can be both physically and emotionally destructive. Between one and three million children in the United States are known to be victims of such abuse each year (U.S. Bureau of the Census 1996d, pp. 217–18). Half of the victims are between the ages of two and nine, and 13.2 percent are infants a year old or younger. Girls are more likely than boys, and African Americans more likely than those of other races, to be victims.

Why is there so much violence in families? A number of social factors are involved. One is the norm that it is okay to hit someone who is misbehaving and does not respond to reason. Many Americans consider the physical punishment of children not merely acceptable but almost obligatory (Gelles and Straus 1988).

A second factor is the power structure of the family. Violence is less likely in egalitarian families than in those where one of the spouses is trying to be dominant (Coleman and Straus 1986). If all else fails, violence may be employed to gain and maintain the individual's power in the family.

A third factor involves the stratification system. A certain amount of abuse occurs in all the social strata, but both neglect and abuse appear to be more prevalent in the lower than in the middle or upper classes (Gelles and Straus 1988; Kruttschnitt, McLeod, and Dornfeld 1994). Incidentally, note carefully the words "more prevalent." Most lower-strata families are not violent, only a greater proportion of them than of those in the middle and upper strata.

Thus, the typical wife abuser is a young man with employment and financial problems who is dissatisfied with his life. The typical child abuser is also young and has serious financial problems and other stressors. In other words, the nature of life in the lower strata puts people under enormous stress and frustration that can erupt in violence against family members.

Divorce

The divorce rate reached a peak in the 1970s, declined through much of the 1980s, then leveled off. In 1994 there were 4.6 divorces per 1,000 population. This was lower than any time since the early 1970s, although it was still more than double the figure of 2.2 for 1960 (U.S. Bureau of the Census 1996d, p. 104).

Millions of Americans are affected by divorce every year, and most of the effects are negative. For spouses, a divorce typically involves a grieving process. Both physical and emotional problems are

Experiences

'My Beautiful Mother Abused Me'

Carolyn hadn't even meant to say it. She was in a marriage support group where members were discussing what they remembered most about their parents. And she just blurted out the words: "My beautiful mother abused me." Carolyn, an "I've-got-it-all-together" successful business woman, startled the group. She looked a bit sheepish, then explained her statement:

My mother really was beautiful. People said she looked like the movie star, Maureen O'Hara. She was red-headed, slender, very feminine. She was the stereotypical Southern lady. Always soft-spoken. Always polite. Always friendly.

I think everyone in our small Alabama town adored her. They certainly thought she was a perfect mother. That made it all the harder on me. People didn't see her other side, the side that made me wonder at times whether I even deserved to be alive.

She never abused me physically. But with her soft words she could cut my soul in half. I remember going with her to buy some shoes when I was ten. I was tall for my age. And my hands and feet were big—bigger than hers by that time. When we went into the store, she laughed—with that dainty laugh of a Southern lady—and told the clerk that he'd better bring the box because he probably didn't have shoes big enough to fit me.

Sometimes she shopped for clothes for me and brought them home. I can remember more than once when she would have me try on a new dress, then sigh and shake her head. I knew what she meant. In contrast to her, I was an ugly duckling. She always made me feel that way. We had a picture taken together when I was six. She looked at the proofs and sighed and said it was too bad I had smiled and showed my 'big ol' ugly teeth.'

It's a wonder I had any self-confidence at all. When I announced that I wanted to go to college, she stared at me, then frowned and said maybe it was a good thing because I would never be pretty. In her book, it was looks, not brains, that were a woman's most important asset.

Here I am in my mid-thirties, and whenever I go back home she still says things to put me down. And people in my home town still think I am so lucky to have such a wonderful, beautiful mother. So if you want to know what I remember most about my mother, that's it. And I don't suppose she'll ever be any different.

Carolyn has carved out a successful career and life for herself in spite of her mother's quiet verbal abuse. She is more fortunate than those who give up on themselves as a result of such abuse. And perhaps the best thing to come of her experience is that, if she has children, she is determined that they will know how talented and how appreciated they are.

common in the months following a divorce. Although most adults will experience a sense of normalcy within one to three years, a few divorced people experience anger, loneliness, and depression for ten years or more following a divorce (Wallerstein 1986).

The trauma and disruption of divorce is captured well in Arendell's (1995) study of 75 fathers who were divorced. Working within a *symbolic interactionist* framework, Arendell interviewed the men in depth, then constructed three types of divorced fathers: traditionalists, neotraditionalists, and innovators. Traditionalists defined themselves as masculine individuals and their ex-wives as their enemies. They had limited contact with their children. Basically, they perceived themselves as victims, and many talked either of further legal action or of physically assaulting their ex-wives.

The neotraditionalists also spoke about retaliation against their ex-wives. They discussed the difficulty of maintaining their masculine identity. They had more contact with their children than did the traditionalists, and defined their role in terms of being a masculine model for their children.

The innovators were more involved with their children and spoke more about parenting than did the other two types. They tried to cooperate with, rather than combat, their ex-wives. They, too, were angry with their ex-wives but tried to mute their anger for the sake of their children.

All three types of fathers illustrate the tension between strong animosity toward ex-wives and the desire to maintain meaningful contact with their children. Contact with children typically involves some degree of contact with the ex-wife. The divorced father, therefore, faces an even greater struggle than men without children who divorce.

Recall that divorced mothers also face greater struggles than divorced women without children, primarily because of financial problems. The financial disruption of divorce for women holds true for all racial/ethnic groups (Smock 1994).

Divorce is likely to be even harder on children than on spouses. There are both short-term and long-term consequences. In the short term, children, like adults, frequently experience a variety of emotional and physical problems. In the long run, the negative consequences of divorce for children—that is, consequences that last into adulthood—include:

- more health problems, depression, and divorce, and less educational attainment, income, and life satisfaction (Amato 1991; Kessler and Magee 1993);

- more negative attitudes about marriage (Gabardi and Rosen 1991);

- poorer relationships with parents (Cooney 1994); and

- greater difficulties in establishing and maintaining meaningful intimate relationships (Southworth and Schwarz 1987; Wallerstein and Blakeslee 1989).

An interesting gender difference exists in the way children react to parental divorce. Generally, girls adjust more easily than do boys to the divorce of parents (Hetherington 1993). Boys are particularly prone to depression and withdrawal and take a longer time than girls in adjusting to the divorce.

Given the emotional, physical, relational, and financial costs of divorce, why are the rates so high? The changed norms about divorce play an important role: both laws and attitudes have become far more accepting of divorce. The individual who wants out of a marriage is no longer likely to face severe legal or social barriers. In addition, researchers have identified a number of factors—not all of which can be easily explained—that are related to higher divorce rates (Lauer and Lauer 1997). In essence, the chances of divorce are higher:

- among those in the lower than in the upper socioeconomic strata;

- for whites who marry before, and African Americans and Hispanics who marry after, the age of 26;

- for African Americans than those in other racial or ethnic groups;

- among those who are not religious or nominally religious;

- when the couple has no children;

- among women who work outside the home;

- among women who are sexually active before marriage;

- for couples who have pervasive and intense conflict;

- for couples whose parents divorced.

Remarriage and the Blended Family

About 46 percent of all marriages in the United States are a remarriage for one or both partners (U.S. Bureau of the Census 1996d, p. 104). Many of these remarriages also include children from a previous marriage, forming a **blended family**. Among all children under 18, 14.6 percent of whites, 32.3 percent of African Americans, and 16.1 percent of Hispanics are living with a stepparent (U.S. Bureau of the Census 1995, p. 64).

Remarriages, particularly those involving a blended family, are more fragile than first marriages (White and Booth 1985). If one partner was single and the other remarried, the chances for divorce are about the same as for couples who are in a first marriage for both partners. But the chances increase 50 percent if both partners were previously married, and another 50 percent if one or both bring children into the remarriage.

Generally, the quality of a remarriage, in terms of such things as amount of interaction and level of happiness, is high (White and Booth 1985). However, the stepparent-stepchild relationship poses severe challenges and is the major cause of breakup in the blended family. For reasons unknown, stepmothers find it more difficult than do stepfathers to deal with stepchildren (MacDonald and DeMaris 1996). Blended families that include a stepmother are more likely than others to have serious conflict and poor adjustment (Ganong and Coleman 1994).

Once again, keep in mind that we are only dealing with greater or lesser likelihood. Most children in blended families are satisfied with their stepparents and have no more negative attitudes about themselves than do children in intact families (Ganong and Coleman 1993). The blended family is a greater challenge in terms of creating a meaningful and fulfilling family life, but it is a challenge that is often met successfully.

Critical Thinking Exercise

A newspaper article stated that the general consensus in the United States is that the breakdown of the family has resulted from "a debased popular culture, drugs, crime, and a debilitating welfare system" (Ventura 1995). The writer went on to say that because other nations without such serious problems are also experiencing family breakdown, the general consensus is wrong.

The writer gave no evidence to support his assertion about "the general consensus." Is there such a consensus? Is there a breakdown of the family? Is it happening in other nations? What kind of information do you need to answer the questions and evaluate the article?

Summary

A family is a group of two or more persons related by birth, marriage, or adoption and residing together in a household. Although families in modern societies have lost many functions, families are still the most important source for socialization and the fulfillment of intimacy needs.

Family life has changed over time in the United States. In colonial days, people were expected to marry, and families tended to be large and stable. In the nineteenth century, the family gradually lost its identity as a self-contained economic unit. An increasing number of functions came to rest in institutions and organizations outside the family.

In the twentieth century, life expectancy rose dramatically, the majority of people came to live in cities, communication and travel expanded, and family disruption surged. Sexual revolutions resulted in dramatic increases in premarital sex. The nuclear family became a minority of all families. Some recent trends include higher rates of premarital sex, out-of-wedlock births, never-married adults, cohabitation, childlessness, mothers who work outside the home, and divorce rates.

The number of single-parent families has grown for all racial and ethnic groups. Single parents face overwhelming responsibilities and demands. Single mothers have high rates of anxiety and depression. Children in single-parent families are more likely to have various physical and emotional problems and to perceive less parental support and concern.

White families are both similar to, and different from, those in other racial and ethnic groups. The black family, which is less likely than any other to be a two-parent family, must be understood in terms of the history of slavery, segregation, and discrimination. Poverty, not race, explains many of the troublesome aspects of black families. Black families exhibit some unique strengths in spite of severe obstacles.

Poverty is also a challenge for the Hispanic family. Hispanics are less likely to divorce and likely to have more children than white or black families. Hispanics are also more likely than whites to have a broader range of family relationships and to find financial and emotional support in those relationships.

Asian American and American Indian families form a dramatic contrast as they stand at opposite ends of achievement and socioeconomic status. Asian Americans have the lowest rates of divorce and teenage pregnancy of any racial group. Major challenges for Asian Americans occur from the strains that arise when one generation is traditional and a younger generation is becoming Americanized. Poverty presents the greatest challenge for American Indians. Tribal traditions have some positive effects on American Indian families.

In spite of the problems of social stigma, homophobia, and traditional gender roles, homosexual families are as healthy as heterosexual ones. Homosexuals gain satisfaction in the same ways as heterosexuals.

Single-earner families are in the minority. Dual-earner families face a number of challenges: how to establish an equitable division of labor in the home; dealing with the stress resulting from home-work conflicts; and dealing with the belief that it is harmful for both parents to work outside the home.

Singlehood is one of the relational choices available to people. Most are not single by choice but some opt for singlehood for reasons of career, personal growth, or freedom. Compared to the married, singles have more health problems and lower life satisfaction. Cohabitation is chosen by increasing numbers of people. When cohabitors marry, they tend to have lower-quality marriages than those who do not cohabit and are more likely to divorce than those who do not cohabit.

In general, both men and women value such things as kindness, understanding, affection, and honesty in a life partner, and both tend to benefit physically and emotionally from marriage. Men, however, benefit more than women.

Sex is social, in the sense that the experience varies by gender roles and culture. The rate of premarital sex has increased over time, and attitudes toward it have become more permissive. Sex is important, though not crucial, to marital satisfaction. Overall, married people report having the most satisfying sex lives. Contraceptives have been readily available only in recent decades. The Pill and sterilization are the most common methods of contraception. Between two and three of every ten pregnancies are aborted. The rate of abortion is lower among whites than other races, and lower among the married.

Family problems include violence, divorce, and life in a remarriage and/or blended family. Violence is more likely in the lower socioeconomic strata and among authoritarian families. Divorce has short-term and long-term negative consequences—including physical, emotional, and interpersonal problems—for both adults and children. Divorce rates are higher in the lower socioeconomic strata. Remarriages, particularly those involving blended families, have higher rates of breakup than first marriages. The stepparent-stepchild relationship is exceedingly challenging, though many people manage it successfully.

Glossary

abortion expulsion of a fetus from the uterus

blended family a remarriage in which one or both spouses bring in children from a previous marriage

cohabitation living with someone in an intimate, sexual relationship without being married

contraception the use of devices or techniques to prevent fertilization

family a group of two or more persons related by birth, marriage, or adoption and residing together in a household

homophobia the irrational fear of homosexuals

monogamous married to one person at a time

nuclear family a family composed of husband, wife, and children

polygyny marriage of one husband with two or more wives

sterilization a surgical procedure that prevents fertilization

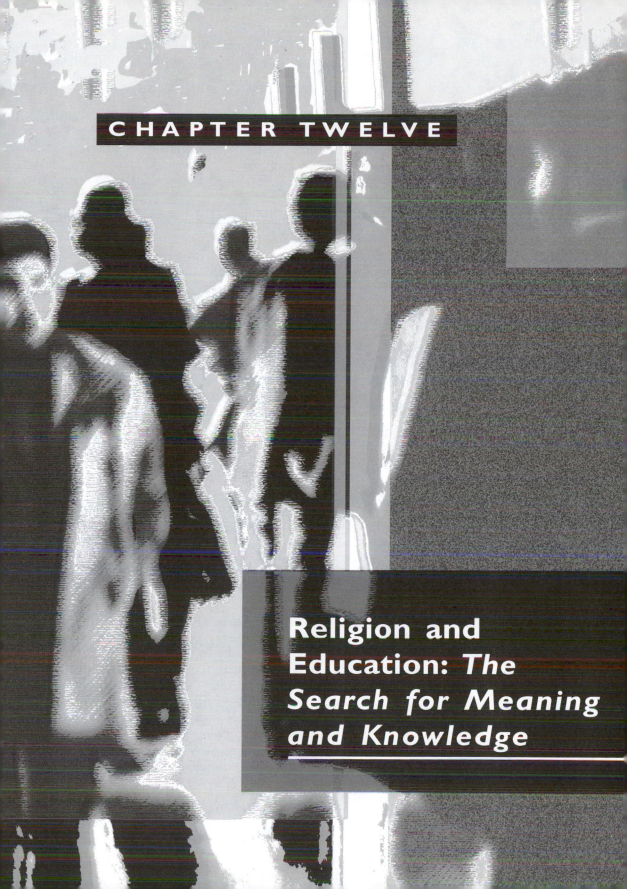

CHAPTER TWELVE

Religion and Education: *The Search for Meaning and Knowledge*

For what or whom would you be willing to die? People willingly give up their lives for a host of reasons. They die to protect important things such as family or country. At times they even give up their lives for something that others would consider trivial. A November 1996 Associated Press release told of a 25-year-old tailor in India who committed suicide to protest the Miss World beauty pageant being held in his city.

Would you kill yourself to protest a beauty pageant? Probably not. Would you die to protect your family? Your country? Perhaps. What about religion? If you are religious, would you die rather than renounce your religion? A great many people of all religions have died because of their faith. Some, like members of Jonestown and Heaven's Gate, died because their leaders declared it was time. Others died because they refused to renounce their faith or insisted on a particular version of their faith. Servetus, a religious man of the sixteenth century who differed from the orthodox Christians of his day about the nature of God, died at the stake rather than accept the beliefs of the Christians who condemned him. His story has parallels in the other religions of the world.

What about education? Would you die for your school? Would you die in defense of knowledge or in defense of someone's right to know? Certainly, history is replete with examples of people who have risked their personal well-being in the pursuit of educational causes. For example, those who broke the law and secretly educated slaves in the United States during nineteenth-century America and those who risked social scorn, physical violence, and imprisonment because they insisted on equal educational rights for women and minorities illustrate the passion that can be aroused by education.

Religion also provokes similar passions. Why? Why would someone die for a religious belief? Why is religion—like education—so important to some people? Are religion and education that fundamental to the quality of life? We will examine these two institutions in the light of such questions.

What Is Religion?

Before reading on, write down your definition of religion. Is God a part of your definition? Worship? Beliefs? Morality? People even use "religion" to refer to the major commitment of an individual as in "her work is her religion" or "he makes a religion out of television sports." In sociological terms, **religion** is the institution which provides meaning through a set of beliefs and practices that are defined as sacred.

Note that the definition does not include God. For instance, Buddhism, one of the major religions of the world that we shall briefly describe below, has no conception of God. The point is, some religions are primarily systems which are called "sacred" because they are said to be superior to and different from the "profane" or "worldly" way of most people. Of course, most religions are **theistic**, centering on God or gods.

Figure 12.1 shows the relative size of the major world religions. Christians constitute the largest group, and Roman Catholics account for more than half of all Christians. Christianity grew out of Judaism. Christians believe in Jesus Christ as the Messiah (Savior) for whom the Jews waited. Christians use the Bible for formulating beliefs and practices. Roman Catholics are Christians under the authority of the Pope. The Popes, according to Catholic doctrine, have ruled over the church since the time, and in accord with the command, of Christ.

Figure 12.1   **Religious Population of the World**

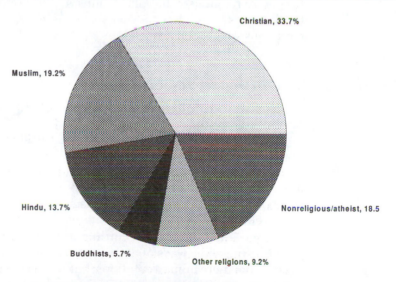

Christian, 33.7%

Muslim, 19.2%

Hindu, 13.7%

Buddhists, 5.7%

Other religions, 9.2%

Nonreligious/atheist, 18.5

Source: U.S. Bureau of the Census 1996d:826.

Islam, the second largest religion, was founded by the prophet Muhammad in about 610 A.D. "Islam" is the Arabic word for "submission to God." Muslims believe that Allah (God) gave the sacred scriptures (the Koran) directly to the prophet and that Muhammad is the last in a series of prophets which include Adam, Abraham, Moses, and Jesus.

Hinduism, the third largest of the world's religions, arose in India more than a thousand years before the birth of Christ. It affirms many gods. Hindus seek release from repeated reincarnation (the belief in a series of rebirths into the world), because life in this world involves suffering. Hindus believe they shall be released through such things as the practice of yoga, obedience to the scriptures (the Veda and Upanishads), and devotion to a personal spiritual adviser.

Buddhism is an offshoot of Hinduism and the two religions share many doctrines, such as reincarnation. Siddhartha Gautama, the Buddha (Enlightened One), founded Buddhism in Nepal in the sixth century B.C. Buddhists focus on achieving enlightenment through meditation and good works.

Obviously, the religions of the world exhibit great diversity in their beliefs and practices. At the same time, all religions, whatever their beliefs and practices, fulfill certain functions for people. Let's consider various ideas about the nature of these functions.

The Functions of Religion

If you are religious, what does your religion do for you? What do you think it does for society? Social scientists have come up with very different answers to those questions.

Religion as the Worship of Society

From a *structural-functionalist* point of view, religion plays an important role in the integration of society, that is, in holding a society together through shared values. Emile Durkheim (1965; orig. 1915) noted that because every known society has some kind of religion, religion must be significant. He concluded that the ultimate object of religion was society itself. Thus, what people call God or the gods is really their own society. Religion is the disguised worship of society and, as such, religion integrates and maintains a society.

To put it another way, according to Durkheim the function of religion is to make the ways of any society sacred. Social norms and values become not mere human creations, but sacred phenomena that demand commitment from the individual. In sum, religion becomes the most extreme form of ethnocentrism, for it puts a divine stamp of approval upon the ways of the society. We shall illustrate the utility of these ideas when we discuss civil religion in the United States later in this chapter.

Religion as an Opiate

Conflict theorists have a different view of religion. Like Durkheim, they often see religion as the reflection of social factors rather than of some supernatural reality. As Engels (1939; orig. 1894) put it: "All religion, however, is nothing but the phantastic reflection in men's minds of those external forces which control their daily life." Engels' mentor, Karl Marx, argued that religion embodies the interests of the ruling class. Religion, he insisted, both expresses people's misery and perpetuates that misery by acting as an opiate that keeps people satisfied by dulling their pain. In other words, religion is a drug that leads the masses to passively accept their exploited and deprived situation.

As an opiate, religion maintains the status quo, which means that religion justifies and supports social inequality. Certainly, there are examples of this function. We noted one in Chapter Ten when we pointed out that women have tended to have subservient roles in religious organizations. In medieval Europe, the estate system was said to be in accord with the will of God. Today, some conservative groups (both Christian and others) still insist on the subordination of women to men and console the poor with the promise of a rich afterlife.

Religion as a Force for Change

Contrary to the Marxist position, religion does not always act as a deterrent to change. In fact, as Weber (1958; orig. 1904–05) showed, religion can be a force for change. Weber analyzed the role of Protestantism in the rise of capitalism. In particular, he examined the role of Calvinism and "Protestant asceticism," which he called the "Protestant ethic." Calvinism refers to the ideas of the sixteenth-century reformer, John Calvin, who put great emphasis on the sovereignty of God and the use of human reason in serving God. Asceticism is the practice of self-denial of goods and pleasures.

Weber defined the "spirit" of capitalism as "that attitude which seeks profit rationally and systematically" (Weber 1958, p. 64) and showed how Protestant teachings facilitated the development of this attitude. Among other things, Calvinism helped create the spirit of capitalism by its stress on the rational ordering of moral life. Protestant asceticism contributed a number of important ideas: wasting time is sinful; it is wrong to engage in the spontaneous enjoyment of life; attaining wealth is a sign of God's blessing; and industry and frugality are marks of the Christian faith. These beliefs and practices lead people to engage in hard work, be productive, and to save (reinvest) their money rather than spend it for personal pleasures—all of which are essential for a capitalist society to develop and grow.

Christianity has been an impetus for change in other ways. The clergy and churches were leaders in the Civil Rights movement that began in the 1950s. In Latin America, liberation theology arose in the Catholic church in the 1960s and justified opposition to oppressive governments and social inequality.

Other religions have also been an impetus to change (Lauer 1991). Japanese religion prior to the nation's modernization contained many of the same elements as the Protestant ethic, including admonitions to work hard, to avoid wasting time, and to be thrifty and honest. Buddhism lent a religious justification to many of the peasant revolts in Chinese history. And Islamic teachings have been called on to legitimate the modernization of Muslim nations. Clearly, religion can be a force for change as well as for maintaining the status quo.

Religion as Transcendent Meaning

Durkheim recognized that religion has important functions for individuals as well as for society. Namely, religion furnishes support and strength as people strive to cope with the exigencies of life. In *symbolic interactionist* terms, religion offers a specific kind of meaning to life—a transcendent meaning—and gives believers a perspective through which they can interpret events. In other words, religion assures people that they are involved in something that goes beyond personal pleasures and pains and that has eternal significance (Berger 1967).

Having transcendent meaning in life appeals to most people. Understandably, then, a good many Americans define themselves as religious. Overall, according to Gallup polls, 58 percent of Americans say that religion is "very important" in their lives (Golay and Rollyson 1996, p. 190). Women (65 percent) are more likely than men (50 percent), African Americans (82 percent) more likely than whites (55 percent), and Protestants (65 percent) more likely than Roman Catholics (51 percent) to agree that religion is very important.

Because transcendent meaning is a source of hope, support, and strength, religious people should fare well in terms of such things as life satisfaction and health. Research supports this hypothesis. Religious people tend to have better mental and physical health (Idler and Kasl 1992; Ventis 1995). They have the resources to deal more effectively with the challenges of aging (Johnson 1995). And as research using a national sample showed, they tend to have a somewhat higher level of life satisfaction (Ellison, Gay, and Glass 1989).

Religion in the United States

Compared to a number of other Western nations, the United States is a very religious nation. Look, for example, at the responses from Gallup polls shown in table 12.1. Let's look at the American way of religion more closely.

Table 12.1	**Religious Beliefs in Three Nations**			
		Percent who agree		
		U.S.	United Kingdom	W. Germany
	No doubts about God's existence	63	24	27
	Believe in God and always have	89	61	58
	Pray at least daily	42	18	21
	Believe in heaven	86	54	43
	Believe in the Devil	65	28	25

Adapted from data in *The American Enterprise* November/December 1992

The Diversity of American Religion

In the early 1990s, there were 257,648 religious congregations in the United States, 47.6 percent of which had fewer than 200 members (U.S. Bureau of the Census 1996, p. 68). In addition to worship, a substantial proportion of the congregations offered people such services as recreation, counseling, meal services, crisis support, and alcohol/drug programs.

The religious identification of Americans has been stable in recent decades (Golay and Rollyson 1996). Virtually every religion in the world has at least some adherents in the United States. About 60 percent of Americans call themselves Protestant and 25 percent identify themselves as Roman Catholic. Protestants, incidentally, are divided among approximately 280 different denominations, with Baptists and Methodists claiming the largest number of members. The Orthodox Church, Mormons, Jews, Muslims, and "other" religions are each claimed by 1 to 2 percent of the population; eight percent of the population does not identify with any religion.

In addition, there are a number of religious orientations that cut across denominations or that are not associated with particular churches. For instance, Pentecostalism is a Christian perspective that stresses such things as being "born again," receiving the baptism of the Holy Spirit, speaking in tongues, uttering prophecies, and faith healing. Pentecostals are found in most Christian denominations, including Roman Catholics.

A completely different orientation is found in the New Age movement—a blend of Eastern, Christian, and other religious ideas. Only a small number of Americans specifically identify themselves as New

Agers (Goldman 1991). But the beliefs attract the more affluent Americans. Bookstores have sections for New Age books, and New Age thinking—or aspects of it—has influenced at least some members in the various denominations.

What, exactly, is New Age religion? It is difficult to say. There are no sacred scriptures and no organization that defines and oversees beliefs. Two beliefs which seem to be widespread among New Agers are reincarnation and channeling. As one New Age advocate put it to us with regard to reincarnation: "We step onto the spiral of life, and spend some lifetimes in various bodies." The goal, presumably, is the same as for Eastern religions—ultimate release from the cycle of rebirths.

The practice of channeling received a good deal of attention when a movie star, Shirley MacLaine, claimed to practice it. In channeling, a dead person—sometimes from the distant past—uses a living person's body and voice to impart needed wisdom.

Miscellaneous other beliefs are common among New Agers, and you can get a sense of these by browsing the New Age section of a bookstore or by surfing the Internet. When we did the latter, in a few minutes we came up with the following assertions:

- Everything that is, whether physical or spiritual, is God.

- You create your own reality.

- The gem, red garnet, should be worn if you feel physically weak because it activates personal power.

- The gem, yellow beryl, should be worn if you're having financial problems; yellow counteracts the effects of the planet Jupiter, and Jupiter affects finances.

- Religion divides, but spirituality unites.

Obviously, New Age religion includes a potpourri of ideas from many sources. Perhaps the bottom line is a belief in a fundamentally spiritual universe and the capacity of every individual to align with spirituality in order to maximize his or her potential.

Religious Membership vs. Participation

Did you notice that while only 8 percent of Americans claim no religious affiliation, a much higher percentage has some doubts about God's existence, does not pray daily, and does not believe in heaven or the Devil (Table 12.1)? When you ask how religious Americans are, then, you need to look at more than religious identification or membership.

One way to determine religiosity is to ask how often people attend a religious service. As we shall note below, about a fifth of Americans attend religious services in any given week. Of course, this means that tens of millions of Americans do participate in about 300 or more different religious groups each week. Why so many different groups? Without going into the history of denominationalism, we can say that the groups cater to differing preferences in worship style, in programs and services, and in the extent to which the theology and views on social issues are liberal or conservative. In recent decades, the more liberal churches have declined, while the more conservative churches (which demand, and receive, more time and money from their members) have grown (Iannaccone, Olson, and Stark 1995).

Thinking Critically

Both popular and scholarly works put weekly attendance at religious services at about 40 percent of Americans. This figure is based on surveys that ask people about their attendance. Three researchers wondered about the validity of the figure and used a combination of *existing data* and *survey research* to get a more accurate count than that provided by people's recollections (Hadaway, Marler, and Chaves 1993).

Their research was motivated by the fact that most major denominations report declines; if attendance was staying at 40 percent, the growing population should result in growth rather than decline. They selected a county in Ohio, surveyed a random sample of people about attendance at religious services and then secured average attendance counts from all Protestant churches in the county. The result was that although 35.8 percent of Protestants claimed to have attended church the preceding week, attendance records showed that only 19.6 percent attended during an average week.

Data from Catholic dioceses around the nation also showed a lower average attendance than that based on people's reports. The researchers concluded that actual attendance is about half that reported in the polls. The discrepancy may be due to a combination of sampling problems, forgetfulness, and the tendency for people to answer polls in a socially desirable way. At any rate, perhaps only a fifth of the population attends religious services in any given week.

Religious Liberals and Conservatives

There is no consensus on precisely what it means to be a religious liberal or conservative. In general, the more conservative an individual, the more likely he or she is to accept the scriptures as literally true and infallible and the doctrines of the group as the only truth. He or she is also more likely to view conservative politics as God's preferred way.

National surveys of Christians from 1984 to 1992 show that between 20 and 25 percent of Americans define themselves as conservative and the same percentage call themselves liberal, while 40 to 45 percent define themselves as moderates (Wuthnow 1996). Compared to conservatives, those defining themselves as liberals were more likely to be younger, have more education, pursue professional careers, and be Democrats rather than Republicans. Compared to liberals, those defining themselves as conservatives were more likely to accept the Bible as literally true and without any error, oppose abortion, and homosexual teachers in public schools, favor voluntary school prayer, oppose more government spending on social programs, and favor the death penalty.

Explorations

A New Experience of Religion

Have each group member identify a religious group with which he or she is unfamiliar or least familiar. Such groups may be located on campus or in the community. Find out the time when the group holds services, and attend one or more of the services as a *participant observer*. Make notes about the service, and, if possible, talk to some of the members about the meaning the religion has for them.

Record your observations and analysis as follows:

Describe the service, including any interaction among the people before and after the service.

What functions did the service appear to hold for the people?

In what ways do the group and their practices differ from the religion with which you are most familiar?

Where would you place the group on the liberal/conservative continuum? Why?

If the entire nation practiced the religion of the group, how, if at all, would this affect the American institutions of government, marriage, family, education, and the economy?

Discuss your findings with each other, then present your conclusions to the class. If you do this as an individual project, select one group and write out your answers to the above questions.

Churches, Sects, and Cults

Another way to view religious diversity in the United States is to look at the distinction between churches, sects, and cults. The distinction between a church and a sect was detailed by Ernst Troeltsch (1931), a student of Max Weber. A **church** is an established religious organization that is an integral part of the larger society (we now call that a denomination). A **sect**, in contrast, is a religious organization that stands apart from the larger society and the Church. Troeltsch and others compared the two on a number of dimensions:

- the Church gains members by birth, the sect by conversion.

- Church members become leaders by formal training, sect members by their **charisma** (extraordinary personal qualities that attract devoted followers).

- the organization and worship of the Church is more formal than that of the sect.

- the Church is more liberal in its doctrines than is the sect.

- the Church compromises with and accepts, while the sect opposes and to some extent rejects, the values of the larger society.

In essence, a sect is like a protest group, while a church is an integral part of the society. Over time, a sect may grow more conservative, and eventually become a Church. The first Methodists were a sect, but the group eventually became a Church. Not all sects evolve into churches, however. The Amish who maintain their separate communities and distinctive lifestyles (e.g., a ban on such modern technologies as electricity and the automobile), and the Jehovah's Witnesses who maintain their distinctive beliefs (e.g., refusing to pledge allegiance to the flag or to receive blood transfusions) are examples of sects that have not become churches.

In contrast to the church and sect, a **cult** is a religious group that repudiates the values of the larger society, opposes all other religions, and demands total commitment from its members. The cult, in other words, maintains an extreme ingroup/outgroup stance. Sects usually arise out of existing religious organizations. Cults usually arise when a charismatic leader offers a substantially new vision of reality. The Jim Jones and Heaven's Gate cults (Chapter One) illustrate the extent to which a cult can command total commitment from its members (although few cults have as devastating consequences for their members).

Cult membership involves radical changes in the lives of those who become members, sometimes including a personality change (Conway and Siegelman 1979). For example, the International Society for Krishna Consciousness (Hare Krishna) is a variation of Hinduism that began in the United States in 1965. The saffron-colored robes and shaved heads of members symbolize the radical change in their lives. All members are expected to be vegetarians, to refrain from drugs (including alcohol) and sex outside of marriage, and to remove themselves as much as possible from such things as science, education, materialism, and even family. Women are subservient to men in the group. In a real sense, the members become different people.

The new vision of reality and radical changes in the lives of members is also illustrated by what is perhaps the best-known of the cults, the Unification Church (Moonies). The Moonies are followers of the Reverend Sun Myung Moon, who started his movement in Korea in 1954. The movement came to the United States five years later and has grown rapidly.

The Reverend Moon's vision of reality is that we are living in the "last days," that God will soon establish His kingdom on earth, and that the task of believers is to prepare the earth for the Messiah's return (Bromley and Shupe 1981). Members are taught to suppress their sexuality. They can only marry if permitted by cult leaders. They also repudiate their families, work up to eighteen hours a day soliciting funds, and give nearly all they make to the Church. The Reverend Moon lives in luxury, but most of his followers deprive themselves of all but the bare essentials in order to support the cause.

Why do people accede to such demands? We believe that people have a fundamental need for transcendent meaning in their lives and that, for whatever reasons, they have not found this meaning anywhere else. They may have an experience with a cult that they believe connects them for the first time with the divine. A young Hare Krishna convert told about her participation in a service of dancing and singing: I was "trying to get that bliss and make it come; and it did . . . I felt like I saw a white light. I felt like I was going to explode" (Conway and Siegelman 1979, p. 138).

A Note on Distinctions

The distinctions we have made so far in this chapter are not always easily applied to religious groups. Baptists are more conservative as a group than are Episcopalians. But liberals, moderates, and conservatives are found in all major groups, so that the more accurate statement is that a larger proportion of Baptists than of Episcopalians are conservative in their beliefs (Wuthnow 1996).

Even the distinction between Church, sect, and cult is not hard and fast. For example, Presbyterians form a Church, but there are Presbyterian members and churches who resemble a sect in that they hold to very conservative beliefs and take stands in opposition to a number of the values of the larger society (such as legalized abortion and homosexual rights). Moreover, some groups are in the process of moving from one type to another. Many scholars believe that Mormons, whose beliefs are based on The Book of Mormon as well as the Bible, comprise a sect that is becoming a Church (denomination). The distinctions are useful tools for understanding religious phenomena, then, but they should not be used in a way that obscures the complexity and dynamic nature of religious groups.

Social Stratification and Religion

Like so many other things, religious participation and beliefs vary by socioeconomic status (Gallup 1990). Measuring socioeconomic status by education and income, Jews have higher status than do Christians. Among Christian groups, the Episcopalians are highest in status, followed by Presbyterians, Lutherans, Methodists, Roman Catholics, and Baptists.

These denominational differences reflect, in part, the liberal/conservative distinction. That is, many people with higher levels of education and income prefer a more liberal religious faith. The differences also partly reflect a preference for a "this-worldly" or "other-worldly" faith. The churches with a larger proportion of people in the lower strata are more likely to have an other-worldly message—a message that stresses the glory of the afterlife.

An other-worldly message would be of obvious comfort to those who are getting less in this world. This may be the reason that a larger proportion of those in the lowest income levels (66 percent) than in the highest levels (48 percent) say that religion is "very important" in their lives (Golay and Rollyson 1996, p. 190). The well-to-do, in contrast, may prefer a this-worldly faith that approves their lifestyle and gives them guidance on living appropriately in this world in the context of their faith.

Civil Religion

Civil religion is a set of beliefs that makes the dominant values of the nation sacred (Bellah and Hammond 1980). In other words, civil religion is not associated with a particular group nor is it confined to one nation. Civil religion is found throughout the world wherever people and their leaders define their national values and institutions as a reflection of God's command or God's preference. To the extent that people practice civil religion, they lend support to Durkheim's argument that religion is fundamentally a worship of society itself.

In the United States, civil religion includes the notion that Americans are the chosen people of God, chosen to implement a way of life that is consistent with God's will for people (Bellah 1992). This notion helped justify such practices as the oppression of Indians and the enslavement of Africans.

Like any religion, civil religion includes a set of beliefs, symbols, sacred writings, rituals, and saints. Consistent with the belief that Americans are a chosen people, the American system of government and the economy are viewed as God's approved ways. To be patriotic is to be godly. To practice free enterprise is to affirm the economic system that God has ordained in the Bible. The American flag, the Declaration of Independence, and the Constitution are sacred and revered like the Bible. The pledge of allegiance and the observance of national holidays like Memorial Day, the Fourth of July, and Veterans' Day are affirmations of faith. George Washington, Thomas Jefferson, and Abraham Lincoln are among the saints.

The practice of civil religion is exemplified by the Christian Coalition, a 1.5 million-member organization of conservative Christians (Frame 1996). The Coalition equates conservative Christian interests

with national interests, and seeks through lobbying, campaign dona-
tions, and voting to influence the political process. Coalition leaders
claim that they are doing nothing more than trying to bring the nation
into line with its traditional values of freedom and individualism (as, of
course, those values are interpreted by Coalition members). Among
other things, the Coalition presses for the abolition of abortion rights,
a Constitutional amendment to permit prayers in public schools, reduc-
tions in spending on social programs, and a balanced federal budget.

Religious Fundamentalism

Fundamentalism is an effort to practice a pure religion based on
a literal interpretation of the sacred scriptures. In recent years, there
has been a resurgence of fundamentalism in religions throughout the
world. For instance, fundamentalist Muslims have taken up arms in a
number of countries in an attempt to establish Islamic societies that
conform to their own understanding of what such societies should be
like.

Among other things, fundamentalists are likely to place women in
a subservient role. In Iran, where Muslims successfully took control of
the government, women are not permitted to appear in public unless
they are veiled. A debate broke out in 1996 about whether Iranian
women should be allowed to ride bicycles (MacFarquhar 1996). The
debate resulted in some new restrictions. Women could still ride their
bicycles in a Tehran park, but only on one five-mile trail which was
secluded behind a fence and watched by the police.

Similarly, when Islamic fundamentalists gained control of most of
Afghanistan, newspapers reported that women were banned from the
work force and schools for girls were closed. In Kabul, soldiers told
members of an international Red Cross relief agency that if any Afghan
women were found working there, both the women and the Red Cross
officials would be hanged.

In the United States, the fastest growing religious groups are those
with the largest proportion of fundamentalists—Southern Baptists, As-
semblies of God, Seventh-Day Adventists, Mormons, and Jehovah's Witnesses. As may be evident from this list, all fundamentalists are not alike.
One group's literal understanding of the Bible is another group's heresy.
Yet all share the passion to be true to the literal meaning of the scriptures
and to practice a pure religion based on that meaning.

Pentecostalism is a type of fundamentalism. Pentecostals have
grown dramatically throughout this century and throughout the world.
Cox (1995) estimates that there are now 400 million Pentecostals in the
world and that they are growing by 20 million a year! At that rate, Pentecostals will outnumber Roman Catholics early in the twenty-first cen-

tury (although these are overlapping categories, because there are Pentecostal Catholics).

Why has fundamentalism grown so much? What is its appeal? Take the United States as an example. Undoubtedly, a number of factors have contributed to the growth of fundamentalism in this country. For one thing, as witnessed by political trends, America has become more conservative generally over the past two decades. A second factor is the rapid pace of change. In the last chapter, we noted the changes occurring in intimate relationships. Rapid and dramatic changes are occurring in other areas as well—from technology to norms to the diversity of the population. When people perceive change to be rapid, they are likely to find it stressful (Lauer 1991). One way to deal with the stress is to find something that is stable and dependable. Fundamentalist groups offer a stable, unambiguous interpretation of ultimate reality to those who are struggling with the instability and ambiguity of a changing society.

A third factor in the growth of fundamentalism is the social ills with which Americans grapple. The seemingly simpler world of the 1950s—the world of the "Leave It To Beaver" television series—came apart in the 1960s. Such things as the strife of the Civil Rights and Women's movements, the mass protests against the Vietnam War, the legalization of abortion, surging divorce rates, political turmoil and scandals (some, such as the resignation of President Nixon, were unparalleled in the nation's history), and increasing violence in the society have left many Americans with a sense of living in a society that is ripping apart at the seams because of moral collapse. Moral issues, of course, are very complex. Yet in fundamentalism, moral issues are straightforward and unambiguous and so is the way to bring morality back to the nation. To those pained by the moral state of the nation, then, fundamentalism offers a solution.

Finally, fundamentalism's growth has been helped by the so-called "electronic church," the preachers and church services that appear on radio and television (Johnstone 1992). The majority of those who pursue such a ministry are fundamentalists. More than 1,000 radio stations and about 60 television stations are owned by religious groups. Hundreds of ministers and thousands of hours of religious programs occur throughout the nation each week. Some of the ministers—Jerry Falwell, Jimmy Swaggart, and Pat Robertson—are among the most recognized names in the nation. Fundamentalism has been marketed extremely well. We do not know how many people have been converted to fundamentalism by the electronic church, nor how many have been brought into Church membership, but one indication of the effectiveness of the ministry is the half-billion dollars that are given to its support each year (Johnstone 1992).

The Functions of Education

Early in American history, religion and education were closely tied together. Education was thought to be essential to religious well-being because it enabled people to read the Bible. A 1648 Puritan law in Massachusetts required heads of families to "catechize their children and servants in the grounds and principles of Religion" (Morgan 1966, p. 88). It also imposed a fine on those who failed in this duty. Religious groups founded many of the nation's colleges and universities, including Harvard.

Gradually, education became separate from family and religion (although religious schools still exist at all levels of education). Education no longer has a primarily religious function. What, then, are its functions? What do you expect out of education? What functions does it serve for you personally? What are its functions for people generally? The chances are you gave one or more of the following as an answer: to create a more effective citizenry; to prepare for upward mobility; and to facilitate personal development.

Socializing Citizens

The Northwest Ordinance of 1787 included a provision that encouraged education because it is "necessary to good government and the happiness of mankind" (Parker 1975, p. 29). Thomas Jefferson added his voice to those who linked education with good citizenry, pointing out that only an educated person can discern the good politician from the demagogue.

From the beginning of the nation, then, people have perceived education to be a crucial factor in the socialization of citizens. Of course, there is no consensus on what, precisely, it means to be a "good" citizen. Is the good citizen one who has learned to know and protect traditional values and ways? Or is the good citizen one who has learned to discern flaws and to press for changes? To put it more concretely, were the young men in the Vietnam era who answered the government's call to go to war the good citizens, or were those who burned their draft cards and marched in protest the good citizens? Or were they all good citizens?

As with most matters, the issues are complex. However, on at least one point, there is some consensus: to be a good citizen is to participate in the political process through informed voting. Education prepares people to be informed voters. Moreover, there is a strong relationship between years of education and the likelihood of voting. In the 1994 congressional elections, for example, the proportion of people who said they voted was 23.2 percent for those with eight years or less education, 40.5 percent for those with a high school education, and 63.1 percent for those with a college degree (U.S. Bureau of the Census 1996, p. 286).

Such figures do not tell you whether the voting was "informed," but they underscore the point that education makes people far more likely to participate in the political process.

Preparing for Upward Mobility

When asking students about their aspirations, we have yet to hear one respond: "I would like to achieve less than my parents have." Americans value upward mobility. Perhaps this is why Americans are such great consumers of books that tell how to become a success. Success usually means, or at least involves, income. A long-standing belief in the United States is that education is necessary in order to maximize the opportunities for financial success. One of the more common reasons we hear from college students for earning a degree is the belief that it will enable them to get a better job. Is this belief correct?

Three things need to be said. First, it is true that even with advanced degrees some people are not upwardly mobile, nor can they secure a job commensurate with their educational qualifications. However, they are only a small minority. Second, as noted in Chapter Eight, among those who are mobile, the amount of mobility is typically small. This reflects the fact that those who attain the highest levels of education tend to come from well-educated families. In other words, they are starting out in a relatively high socioeconomic position. Third, in support of the importance of education, a strong relationship exists between educational level and median income. As shown in Table 12.2, the median income of those at the lowest educational level is only 18.3 percent of those at the highest level.

Table 12.2	**Median Household Income, by Education of Householder**	
	Years of school completed	Median income
	Less than 9th grade	$14,275
	9th to 12th grade (no diploma)	17,543
	High school graduate	30,071
	Some college, no degree	35,879
	Bachelor's degree	52,370
	Master's degree	61,045
	Doctorate degree	78,157

Source: U.S. Bureau of the Census 1996d, p. 462

The point is that, while there are exceptions, your chances of getting into the higher income brackets increase with each additional step you take on the educational ladder. Many of the higher-paying jobs require the specialized knowledge and skills that are provided by education. And many employers require an employee to have a college degree even for positions that could be ably filled by people without a degree.

Facilitating Personal Development

Educators stress the role of education in personal development. That is, education frees you from the constraints of ignorance so that you may maximize your physical, emotional, and intellectual well-being. Education is not merely a way to enhance your income but also a way to enhance the quality of your life in general.

There does seem to be a relationship between educational level and well-being. Education can provide the tools for the "mastery of life" (Winter, Stewart, and McClelland 1978). Three Harvard researchers set out to test the extent to which a liberal arts education facilitates such mastery of life. They concluded that students with a liberal arts education "are better able to formulate valid concepts, analyze arguments, define themselves, and orient themselves maturely to their world" (Winter, Stewart, and McClelland 1978, p. 69).

More recently, using *survey research* to get data from national samples, Ross and Wu (1995) investigated the relationship between education and a number of indicators of well-being. They found that, compared to the poorly educated, the better educated respondents were more likely to have fulfilling jobs, have a greater sense of control over their lives, engage in good health practices, and enjoy better health.

Education, of course, will not *guarantee* your personal development, any more than the lack of education will inevitably frustrate it. However, you do increase your chances of personal development as you increase your educational level.

An Educational Profile of the United States

You were probably aware of one or more of the functions of education discussed above. Your awareness may have been a factor in the value you place on education. How typical are your views? How many Americans share your educational aspirations? How many will attain the years of schooling that you will? Let's look at the state of education in the United States today.

Educational Aspirations

Unless you had no choice in the matter, the fact that you are in college indicates a high level of educational aspiration on your part. Interestingly, the educational aspirations of Americans have increased considerably over the past few decades. A comparison of national surveys of high school seniors in 1972 and 1992 show dramatic changes (National Center for Educational Statistics 1996). In 1972, 34 percent of seniors planned to go to a four-year college and 11 percent planned to attend a two-year college. By 1992, the figures were 54 and 13 percent. In other words, the proportion of seniors planning on additional education rose from 45 to 67 percent.

The increase in educational aspirations occurred for all racial/ethnic groups. The percentage of those planning on attending a four-year college increased: from 35 to 55 percent among whites; from 32 to 52 percent among African Americans; from 11 to 20 percent among Hispanics; and from 47 to 65 percent among Asian Americans. In addition, a third of the seniors, ranging from 32 percent of whites to 43 percent of Asian Americans, planned to pursue their education into graduate school (National Center for Educational Statistics 1996).

Educational Attainment

Aspirations may or may not translate into attainment. Some students who want to obtain a college education will have to drop out because of finances or a family crisis. Or they may discover that they are not suited to higher education. Still, attainment has risen along with aspirations. Higher aspirations are found among adults as well as high school seniors. Many adults have returned to college in recent decades. In particular, increasing numbers of women have enrolled in college after marriage and motherhood (Bradburn, Moen, and Dempster-McClain 1995). Women most likely to enroll are those with some prior college credits, nontraditional gender-role orientations, and such life experiences as part-time work or divorce.

Among all races, then, the proportion of those completing high school rose from 51.9 percent of men and 52.8 percent of women in 1970 to 81.7 percent of men and 81.6 percent of women in 1995; the proportion of those completing four or more years of college rose from 13.5 percent of men and 8.1 percent of women in 1970 to 26.0 percent of men and 20.2 percent of women in 1995 (U.S. Bureau of the Census 1996d, p. 159).

Attainment has risen among all groups. From 1970 to 1995, the proportions of those completing four or more years of college rose from 11.3 to 24.0 percent for whites, 4.4 to 13.2 percent for African Americans, and 4.5 to 9.3 percent for Hispanics (U.S. Bureau of the Census 1996, p. 159). Asian Americans have the highest rates of any group—38.2 percent have completed four or more years of college (U.S. Bureau of the Census 1996d, p. 49).

Academic Achievement

Higher aspirations have meant higher levels of attainment. But what about the quality of the education? What are American students achieving academically? During the 1980s and 1990s, a series of studies and reports criticized the American educational system as plagued by mediocrity (Lauer 1997). One of these reports lamented the fact that too many college graduates are unable to perform simple reading, writing, and mathematical tasks. Another criticized the total number of hours elementary and high school students spend in school (which is less than in many other nations). Additional reports expressed concern over the fact that, on various tests of knowledge, American students did not score as well as their counterparts in other nations.

With regard to global comparisons, U.S. high school students score poorly. In a comparison of U.S. scores with those in 13 other countries, the Americans ranked last in biology and algebra, eleventh in chemistry, twelfth in geometry and calculus, and ninth in physics (U.S. Department of Education 1993). A study of science and math achievement by students in 41 countries found that U.S. students ranked slightly below average in math and slightly above average in science (Applebome 1996). Average math scores ranged from 354 (South Africa) to 643 (Singapore), with the American average at 500. Average science scores ranged from 326 (South Africa) to 607 (Singapore), with the American average at 534.

Similarly, there are disturbing results when examining reading ability. Tests show that only 7 percent of high school seniors are able to read at an advanced level (U.S. Department of Education 1993).

Racial/ethnic variations exist in the academic achievement of high school seniors (National Center for Education Statistics 1996). Whites rank highest in reading proficiency, while Asian Americans rank highest in math and science proficiency. African Americans rank lowest in all three categories.

Two additional facts should be kept in mind as you ponder the above. First, American education is more open than is that of many other nations. If other nations had as high a proportion of young people in school as does the United States (rather than the best of students), their average scores might be lower. Second, while the racial/ethnic differences in academic achievement are still large, the gap between whites and others has been diminishing in recent decades. And if you take into account such things as socioeconomic status differences and quality of schools, students from the various racial/ethnic groups are nearly equal in achievement (Lauer 1997).

EXTENSIONS

Educational Struggles in Egypt

In the United States, education is important for those who wish to maximize their chances for good jobs, high incomes, and personal development. In developing nations, such as Egypt, education is vital to economic advancement (Lauer 1991). Unfortunately, setting up an effective educational system is not a simple matter, as Egypt well illustrates.

In 1994, the president of Egypt, Hosni Mubarak, acknowledged that the nation was very poor, and asserted that the educational system was a "problem of national security." By that, he meant that it was imperative for Egyptians to decrease the amount of illiteracy and to increase the number of employable skills in the population in order to move out of poverty.

Egypt faces an enormous task. An estimated 52 percent of all Egyptians, and 70 percent of Egyptian women, are illiterate. About a fourth of all students drop out of school. Even so, the schools are overcrowded, in poor physical condition, and often lack such basic amenities as libraries, books, desks, and playgrounds. In the early 1990s, the schools were so overcrowded that most had four shifts a day, with each group of children receiving only 1.5 hours of instruction a day.

The fact that Islamic fundamentalists gained control of many schools and are more concerned with religious indoctrination than with a curriculum that will bring about national economic growth exacerbates the problems. The costs of education further compound the problems. In the early 1990s, government spending on education increased considerably. About 5,500 new schools were built. However, the spending per capita was about $25 a year. This is low even for developing nations and is less than 3 percent of the $939 per capita spent on public elementary and secondary education in the United States in 1992 (U.S. Bureau of the Census 1996d, p. 170).

Thus, in Egypt and other developing nations, education poses a dilemma: The needed economic growth will not occur without a better educated populace, but the needed educational system costs more than the economy can bear.

Source: *Africa Research Bulletin*, June 1996.

Education and Social Stratification

We have already shown one way in which education and the social stratification system intersect, namely, the strong relationship between education and income level. The relationship is a reciprocal one. Thus, the higher your educational level is, the higher your income is likely to be. Also, the higher your income the more likely your children are to obtain a high education and income. Poor children may face the same dilemma as a developing nation (see Extensions, this chapter), in the sense that they need an education to be upwardly mobile but lack the resources to obtain that education. Literally millions of families in the nation earn less annually than the cost of room, board, and tuition at an average private university (Lauer 1997). Student loans and scholarships can help, but these resources are becoming less readily available.

Unfortunately, money is not the only handicap to those in the lower strata. Because lower-strata parents are likely to have lower levels of education, they are also less able to provide the kind of family environment that nurtures and encourages cognitive development. Their children, thus, may be at an intellectual disadvantage from the time they enter school. A Carnegie Foundation report asserted that many children begin school with a background of poor health care, parents who are minimally involved with them, few if any preschool opportunities, unsafe neighborhoods, and varying amounts of malnourishment (Chira 1991). As a result, perhaps a third or more of those who come to kindergarten are not prepared to learn even at that level.

Children's social class background continues to affect their school experience beyond the first years. Those from the lower strata are less likely than others to graduate from high school or to go to college if they do graduate from high school. They are also less likely to go to a prestigious school whatever their ability or aspirations (Mortenson 1991; Hearn 1991).

One of the reasons that children from the lower strata do not attain higher levels of education is that their school experiences are less likely to reward and encourage them. Their peers and even their own families may not value education highly. They may need more attention and more support from teachers than other students, but are less likely to receive it than are middle-class children (Lauer 1997).

Teachers' expectations, incidentally, are crucial to children's intellectual growth. In a classic *experiment* in a California elementary school, Rosenthal and Jacobson (1968) assigned arbitrary achievement scores to children just before they were promoted into a new class. The new teachers, thus, had a set of fake achievement scores for each child, and those scores created expectations in the teachers about what the children would do in their class. At the end of the year, students whom the teachers expected to do poorly tended to get lower scores, and those whom they expected to do well tended to get higher scores (even on objective tests, not just according to the subjective evaluation of the teachers). Subsequent research shows that this phenomenon of teacher expectations affects adults as well as children.

The point is that teachers may expect more out of their middle- and upper-class students than those from the lower and working classes. And those expectations, independently of the actual abilities of the children, can affect performance.

Problems in Education

You may think of education as a solution, particularly if you think of it in terms of the functions we discussed earlier. However, education is also a problem, and in this section we will examine a number of the problems in American education today.

Experiences

'She Can't Help It'

People judge one another from their own perspective. A middle-class teacher, therefore, may not deal well with a lower-class pupil because the teacher expects the pupil to act in accord with middle-class values and ways. Unfortunately, even though the teacher is not deliberately insensitive or malicious, the results can be devastating for the educational well-being of the pupil. Phyllis, who is now a teacher herself, recalls an incident from her childhood that sensitized her to the problem of dealing with someone from another social class:

I was in first grade at the time. During recess, our class was playing on the monkey bars. One of the girls came from a very poor family. She usually looked ill-kept. On that particular day, she was playing next to me. As we were turning around on the bars, the other children began to make fun of her and laugh about her dirty underwear.

I don't know why I did it, because I didn't know the girl that well. But the way the others were teasing her made me mad, and I hollered at a group of them: "She can't help it." Well, the words were barely out of my mouth before we all heard the voice of our teacher booming across the school yard: "Yes, she can."

I don't even remember that girl's name. But I do remember the look on her face. She was mortified. She began to cry. And there was nothing more that I could do, because even the teacher showed contempt for her.

Before the end of the year, I guess the girl's family had moved, because she stopped coming to school. I don't know what happened to her, but I recall that she never did seem to try after that playground incident. She never tried to make any friends, and she never got any notice or compliments from the teacher like most of the rest of us.

I've always wished I could have done something more to help her. In a way I am, I suppose, for I am making every effort to treat all my students equally. I am determined that no child in my class will ever be humiliated like she was. I want my children to love education and to go as far as their abilities will allow them.

Academic Quality

We pointed out earlier that a number of studies and reports have questioned the quality of American education, in part, because of the relatively poor scores that American students receive on standardized tests. Concern has also been expressed over the decline in college entrance examination scores (SAT). The scores have fluctuated, but the general trend from the 1950s to the early 1990s has been downward with a slight upward trend since that time. Average verbal scores were 476 in 1952, 422 in 1991, and 428 in 1995, while average math scores were 494 in 1952, 474 in 1991, and 482 in 1995 (U.S. Department of Education 1992, p. 54; U.S. Bureau of the Census 1996d, p. 177).

In response to concerns about the quality of education, a 1989 educational summit established eight national goals which were to be met by the year 2000 (Reichmann 1996):

- All children will be ready to learn when starting school.

- All adults will be literate, able to read and write.

- 90 percent or more will graduate from high school.

- Students will have demonstrated competence in challenging subject matter after leaving grades 4, 8, and 12.

- American students will rank first in the world in math and science.

- Schools will be free of drugs, guns, and violence.

- Schools will be partners in education with parents.

- Teachers will be able to engage in professional development programs.

While some progress has been made (math scores of fourth and eighth graders are up, violence is down, and family reading is more common), there is no progress or even a worsening in a number of the areas. Reading scores at grade 12 have declined, as has teachers' participation in professional development. Drug activity and disruption in classrooms is on the rise. The panel monitoring the nation's progress declared that the goals will probably not be reached by 2000 (Reichmann 1996). It is likely, therefore, that questions will continue to be raised about the quality of American education.

Feminist theorists raise another important issue: the quality of education cannot be measured merely by average scores on standardized tests but by whether students learn materials that intersect with their lives and their identity. Any curriculum that ignores how gender pervades social life and how gender roles are fashioned by social factors is incomplete. Self knowledge is a crucial component of a quality education. And, as we showed in Chapter Ten, little in women's socialization, including education, offers them the kind of insights that feminists advocate.

The Learning Environment

What kind of environment helps you to learn? Perhaps you like music in the background. Or silence and no distractions. Perhaps you prefer a classroom where there is a good deal of discussion, or one in which there is just lecture.

But consider this. How well would you learn if you sat in a dingy, noisy, dilapidated classroom? How well would you learn if you feared for your safety? How well could you concentrate if you knew that your fellow students would despise you if you did well, or if you heard that a number of students intended to beat you up after school?

All of these conditions confront far too many students every day in the United States. For example, a survey of schools in New York City reported that one of every five are so run down that they are a hazard to both students and teachers (Sullivan 1996). The hazards include falling bricks and pieces of concrete from weakening walls and falling windows from rotting moldings. As much as $500 million is needed to repair hundreds of buildings.

Drugs and weapons also combine to create an atmosphere of fear in many schools. Surveys of high school students indicate that 3 percent of whites, 7.1 percent of African Americans, and 10.1 percent of Hispanics do not want to go to school because they fear for their safety (National Center for Educational Statistics 1996, p. 139). The surveys report that about one of every eight students carries a weapon to school, one of 12 has been threatened or injured at school by a weapon, and one of three has had property stolen or deliberately damaged at school. Finally, 24.1 percent of whites, 17.5 percent of African Americans, and 34.1 percent of Hispanics admit that they have been offered, sold, or given an illegal drug while at school.

These figures translate into millions of American students who have experienced fear, violence, theft, or drug dealing at school. Moreover, for some students, the experience is a daily one. The fear, incidentally, is not just of violence, but of derision from one's fellow students. In some lower-class areas, students who want to perform well are hampered by the pressure, threats, and harassment from those in the culture of gangs, drugs, and violence who disparage and even attempt to thwart academic achievement (Shanker 1994).

Inequality in Education

In previous chapters, we noted a number of educational inequalities. Educational attainment varies by social class, racial/ethnic group, and gender. Here we will look briefly at another inequality that affects students: unequal educational resources which result from unequal funding.

Funding of schools is unequal among the states and also among the school districts within each state. Schools in poor areas have a lower tax base from which to draw and are likely, therefore, to have fewer resources to offer students. In 1995, for example, the average expenditure per pupil (based on average daily attendance) ranged from highs of $9,934 in Alaska and $9,860 in New Jersey to lows of $4,123 in Mississippi and $3,668 in Utah (U.S. Bureau of the Census 1996d, p. 170).

These differences in funding mean that an affluent school district may have two to four times as much to spend on each pupil as a poor district. In essence, many children are penalized in terms of the quality of education available to them because of the neighborhood in which they happen to live.

Moreover, funding differences tend to penalize racial minorities and benefit whites. To address this issue, the courts mandated the busing of school children as a way to break down segregation and equalize educational opportunities. Some children from poor neighborhoods would be bused to more affluent schools, and some from well-to-do neighborhoods would be bused to poorer schools. Busing affects only a small proportion of all students, but many parents vigorously oppose it. Although evidence exists that attending desegregated schools enhances the educational quality of poor African Americans, the pressure to bus students eased in recent years (Lauer 1997).

Alternatives to Public Education

Many parents have reacted to the problems of the public schools by searching for alternatives. Two available alternatives are private schools and home schooling.

Private Schools

The use of school vouchers is one of the hot political issues of the day. Rather than forcing people to send their children to public schools or pay extra for private schools while still paying taxes to fund public education, the advocates of vouchers urge the government to use tax money collected for education to allow parents to choose the school they want for their children. Vouchers would be issued to those who opt for a private school.

Private schools are of two types. One type is secular and is either a high-quality school that is restricted to a select set of students or a school employing a particular educational philosophy (such as the Montessori schools). The other type is religious (the parochial school). Parochial school systems have been maintained by Roman Catholics and Lutherans for most of U.S. history. In the last couple of decades, however, a large number of fundamentalist Christian schools have also emerged. The Christian schools are a response to charges that public schools have failed by abandoning values, banning prayer, and teaching evolution. They address these charges by teaching their students to think and behave in ways consistent with their fundamentalist doctrines (Wagner 1990).

Home Schooling

Increasing numbers of parents choose to teach their children at home rather than send them to school. The Department of Education estimates that more than a half-million children are now home schooled; advocates put the figure at 1.2 million (Hawkins 1996). The home schooling movement was given impetus by conservative Christians who believed that their children were not getting moral guidance in the schools. Gradually, home schoolers came to include parents who either were dissatisfied with the quality of education or worried about emotional and physical threats to their children in the schools.

How well are children taught at home? There is no systematic evidence. However, one study of those who were educated in part or in whole at home concluded that they were as successful as those in school in terms of pursuing a higher education and getting good jobs (Webb 1989). And a sample of students schooled at home scored better on a reading test than 79 percent of students in school (Hawkins 1996). Perhaps the greatest challenge to home schooling is not in the ability of parents to educate well but in the extra demands it imposes on their lives.

Critical Thinking Exercise

A popular magazine article offered a number of ways to improve education in the United States (Melcher 1996). These included: federal standards, giving schools and school districts flexibility in the methods used to attain the standards, expanding teacher training, and securing more parental involvement in education. As a social scientist, what comments would you make and what questions would you raise? Could you identify some potentially negative effects of the author's suggested methods of improvement? What information in this chapter bears on the author's suggestions? What kind of research would you want before agreeing with the author's suggestions?

Summary

Religion is the social institution that provides people with meaning through a set of beliefs and practices defined as sacred. Worldwide, Christianity has the most adherents, followed by Islam and Hinduism. More than half of all Christians are Roman Catholics.

Religion has a number of functions. Durkheim identified a social function of religion—it makes the ways of a society sacred. Marxists see religion as an opiate that leads the deprived to accept their lot because they will be rewarded in heaven. In his analysis of the Protestant ethic and the growth of capitalism, Weber showed how religion can be a force for change. In addition, as Durkheim noted, religion provides people with transcendent meaning in their lives.

Religion in the United States is diverse. The majority of people identify themselves as Protestants. But virtually all religions are found to some extent. Moreover, some religious orientations, such as Pentecostalism and New Age, cut across the various denominations. In terms of participation, about a fifth of the population attends religious services each week. American religion is also diverse in terms of the liberal/conservative dimension. About 40 to 45 percent of Americans identify themselves as moderates, with liberals and conservatives splitting the rest.

Another way to look at diversity is the distinction between churches, sects, and cults. Churches are groups that are well integrated in the society. Sects oppose some of the values of the society, and cults make a radical break with the society. Cults demand total commitment from their members.

Religious participation and beliefs vary by socioeconomic status. Denominations can be ranked according to the average socioeconomic status of their members. This relationship reflects varying preferences for liberal or conservative and other-worldly or this-worldly religion.

Civil religion is a set of beliefs that makes the dominant values of a society sacred. In the United States, civil religion is reflected in the belief that Americans are a chosen people of God, chosen to implement a way of life that God wills for all people. American civil religion includes beliefs (e.g., free enterprise is biblical economics), symbols (e.g., the flag), sacred writings (e.g., the Constitution), rituals (e.g., the Fourth of July), and saints (e.g., George Washington).

Fundamentalism is an effort to practice a pure religion based on a literal interpretation of the sacred writings. Generally, fundamentalists put women into a subservient role. Fundamentalism has grown considerably, helped by such things as a general conservative trend, rapid social change, pervasive social ills, and the electronic church.

One of the functions of education is to create a more effective citizenry. Thus, education makes people more likely to vote. A second function is to prepare for upward mobility. There is a strong relationship between education and income level. A third function is to facilitate personal development. Education is related in various ways to people's well-being.

Both the educational aspirations and the educational attainment of Americans have increased among all racial/ethnic groups in recent decades. Concerns have been raised about academic quality, however, fueled by such things as the relatively mediocre showing of American students on various tests of knowledge.

Education intersects with the social stratification system in a number of ways. There is a strong, reciprocal relationship between education and income. And social class background affects a child's chances throughout his or her years in school. Both family environment and teachers' expectations and manner of relating are more likely to be impediments for those in the lower than those in the upper strata.

Education is a problem as well as a solution. Concern over academic quality led to the establishment of national goals to be achieved by the year 2000. Deteriorating physical facilities, violence, drugs, and gang activity make many schools poor learning environments. Inequality in funding means that students in poorer districts have far fewer educational resources than those in more affluent districts.

In reaction to the problems of education, some Americans have sought alternatives to public schools. Private schools, either secular or religious, and home schooling have increased considerably in recent years.

Glossary

Calvinism the system of Christian beliefs deriving from the work of the Protestant reformer, John Calvin (1509–64)

charisma extraordinary personal qualities that attract devoted followers

church an established religious organization that is an integral part of the larger society

civil religion a set of beliefs that makes the dominant values of the nation sacred

cult a religious group that repudiates the values of the larger society, opposes all other religions, and demands total commitment from its members

fundamentalism the effort to practice a pure religion based on a literal interpretation of the sacred texts

religion the institution that provides meaning through a set of beliefs and practices that are defined as sacred

sect a religious organization that stands apart from the larger society and the Church

theism a religion that is centered on God or gods

CHAPTER THIRTEEN

Government and the Economy: *The Search for Order and Sustenance*

We once had a student who called himself a "rational anarchist." In essence, he believed that government is a necessary evil. Government, he maintained, is necessary to protect the citizenry from foreign threats but is an evil when it intrudes into other aspects of life. In particular, he objected strenuously to government interference with the economy and spoke with fervor about the benefits of "pure capitalism."

He also made an interesting statement about how much better off the nation was in the past when the government *did* let the economy run on its own. In this he was mistaken. Governments and economies are, and always have been, tied together. For example, much of European exploration and colonization of North America resulted from direct or indirect government financing. And quickly, government policy permitted the seizure of more and more land from the Indians and employed the military to "protect" the western-bound pioneers.

Government action increasingly affected the economy in the nineteenth century. The Homestead Act of 1862 gave farmers large tracts of land. Business was stimulated by the building of canals and subsidies to railroads. Early governmental aid to science and technology can be seen in such things as the Lewis and Clark expedition and the federal grant to Samuel Morse for building a telegraph line between Baltimore and Washington, D.C. We could go on at length about the many ways in which the government has affected the economy. Variations on the story have been repeated in other nations. For instance, government was at the heart of modernization in Japan (Lauer 1991). In more recent times, government action has been essential in helping developing nations obtain a share of business in the computer industry (Evans 1995).

Governments and economies are interdependent throughout the world. And people's experiences with them are both gratifying and vexing. People will die for a government, and they will die to overthrow a government. They praise the economy when they are well off and curse it when they are hurting financially. Let's try to make sense out of these two institutions which can have such contrary effects on your life.

Government and Social Order

What comes to mind when you hear the word "government"? Does it generate good or bad feelings in you? Most Americans have some ambivalence about government. In a national poll that asked how much of the time the respondents believed they could trust the federal government to do what is right, only 4 percent said always (Golay and Rollyson 1996, p. 36). Fourteen percent said most of the time, 73 percent said only sometimes, and 9 percent said never. Poll results vary from year to year as government scandals, failures, or successes dominate the news. However, public confidence in the government has tended to decline for the last few decades (table 13.1). Do such polls matter? Does it make any difference whether people trust the government? It does, because it affects a central aspect of government: power and authority.

Power and Authority

In one of Aesop's fables, the animals have a public meeting. A rabbit addresses the assemblage and argues for fair shares for each animal. The lions admit that the speech was a good one. But, they note, the speech did not have claws and teeth as the lions did. The fable makes the point that the bottom line in social life is who has the power to coerce. Is this true? Is the image of powerful lions dominating the relatively helpless lesser animals an acceptable image of governing?

Power

Sociologists define **power** as control over the behavior of others—with or without their consent—to attain specific goals. Note that power may be exercised *with or without* consent. Or, to put it another way, power may be either legitimate or illegitimate.

As we shall discuss below, there are governments that are essentially like powerful lions ruling over a relatively helpless citizenry. Even in the United States where government exists at the consent of the governed, there are individuals who view the government as illegitimately and arbitrarily exercising power. Indeed, the various para-military groups that currently operate in the United States exemplify this attitude. Moreover, the very existence of opposing political ideas means that, for every government action, a segment of the population will experience the action as one they oppose. At times this opposition has become sufficiently disgruntled to accuse the government of exercising illegitimate power. Thus, on the one hand, some Americans strongly approved of the civil rights' legislation of recent decades, while others argued that the legislation was a gross misuse of governmental power. Similarly, there are always some Americans who view participation in war or the levying of taxes as a violation of government's legitimate power, while others support the government's actions even if they prefer a different course of action.

The point is, every government policy or action will be opposed by a part of the citizenry. On a particular issue, some citizens will believe that the government exercises its power illegitimately. This does not mean that this segment of the population denies the government's right in general to exercise control. Rather, they feel that government is involved in a specific action that is beyond its realm of authority.

In some cases, however, power is exercised over people who do not accept the right of the rulers to govern at all. In those cases, the rulers must govern by force. This is, as Weber (1947) put it, rule by coercion. Not only is this illegitimate power, it is also neither efficient nor effective because it requires constant vigilance on the part of the rulers. When the vigilance or the resources to control the population weaken, the government is likely to be overthrown by a coup or armed rebellion.

In sum, power is necessarily exercised by governments. But even if they oppose particular actions, most people in the United States as well as other democratic countries will not define the government as illegitimate. Why not? To understand this, we turn to the topic of authority.

Authority

In contrast to coercion, which is an illegitimate exercise of power, Weber (1947) defined **authority** as legitimate power. The question is, on what basis would people define power as legitimate? Why, even though they oppose certain actions of government, would they still agree to its legitimacy?

Weber identified three types of authority. Legal authority has a rational base, a belief in the legality of social norms and the right of those who govern to issue commands within the scope of those norms. Traditional authority rests upon the sanctity of societal traditions and the right of those in high positions to govern in accord with the traditions. Charismatic authority is based upon the right of an individual to govern as a result of his or her extraordinary qualities and personal magnetism.

Although the three types of authority are very different, you can see all three at work in most societies. For example, legal authority is vested in American office holders through the Constitution and laws. A few Americans, such as those who have formed anti-government militias in various states (Smolowe 1995), deny the legitimacy of government, particularly the federal government, and are prepared to take up arms to defend themselves against what they define as government oppression. Yet most Americans are not willing to overthrow the government or even to engage in civil disobedience. This is true even though only a minority, as table 13.1 shows, express a great deal of confidence in national leaders. The figures in the table suggest that Americans believe in the legitimacy of their system and are willing to live with leaders in whom they have less than complete confidence until they can vote to "throw the rascals out."

Table 13.1	**Percent Who Have a Great Deal of Confidence in Government Leaders**

Year	Executive	Congressional
1973	29	24
1975	13	13
1977	28	19
1980	12	9
1983	13	10
1987	19	16
1990	23	15
1993	12	7

Source: Adapted from data in *The American Enterprise*, November/December, 1993, p. 94.

Charismatic authority combines with legal authority when particular leaders seem charismatic to the people. Of course, no one is considered charismatic by everyone. President John F. Kennedy was a charismatic man who commanded the devotion of millions of followers. A colleague told us that for years after Kennedy's assassination, when he asked students (without talking about any individuals beforehand) to identify their heroes, Kennedy was one of the most commonly named. Still, the feelings of many Americans toward Kennedy were quite the opposite, ranging from indifference to contempt and even hatred.

Charismatic individuals can exercise even more power than they could just by virtue of holding office (and thereby possessing legal authority). Or to put it another way, popular leaders may be more influential than those who possess only the power of the office they hold.

In some nations, a charismatic leader has managed to get almost complete control. Fidel Castro in Cuba, the Ayatollah Khomeini in Iran, and Mao Zedong in China are among those whose charismatic authority shaped an entire nation.

Traditional authority is disappearing as a basis for governing. In the past, kings and tribal leaders ruled by traditional authority. The traditions by which they ruled were long-standing and, for the most part, accepted uncritically by the people they ruled. Traditional authority still exists in some areas of social life, however, particularly in religious groups. The Pope has traditional authority among Roman Catholics. But even the Pope's authority varies among Catholics depending upon the extent to which a particular Pope is charismatic and the extent to which papal directives conflict with changing cultural norms.

Experiences

'I'd Give My Life for Him'

Each of the three types of legitimate authority—legal, charismatic, and traditional—enables leaders to exercise power over others. When a leader has more than one type, his or her power is enhanced. One of the authors (Robert) interviewed a Marine who ascribed all three types to his commanding officer. As a result, the Marine greatly respected and was extremely devoted to this officer. Following is a part of the interview between Robert (R) and the Marine (M), along with our notations about the way the enlisted man expressed the different kinds of authority:

R: Unlike what I have heard from a number of other enlisted men, you have great respect for your commanding officer.

M: Oh much more than respect. He's my hero [charismatic authority]. He was wounded in Viet Nam while trying to save some of his men. He'd give his life for us. And I'd give my life for him. If he came to me tomorrow and said we were going on a mission that would mean certain death, I'd be at his side in a minute.

R: You said he was in Viet Nam. Do you recall the My Lai incident where some American soldiers went into a suspected enemy area and killed hundreds of Vietnamese civilians, including women and children?

M: Yes.

R: Many people wondered how American soldiers could do such a thing. Why didn't they question the orders to shoot all those people? What do you think you would have done?

M: If I had been there, and my CO had told me to fire on those people, I would have done it without question. If I had any questions, they would have been raised later.

R: That doesn't pose any ethical problems for you?

M: Not at all. In the Corps, you pride yourself on being able to follow orders [traditional authority]. Where would we be today if every Marine had raised questions about firing on the enemy?

R: I see your point, but it makes me uneasy about how to deal with situations like My Lai.

M: You don't have to deal with it. Those kinds of things happen in war. We were there because our government told us we had to be there [legal authority]. And you don't go and fight a war by checking out everyone before you shoot 'em.

Types of Governments

Governments differ according to the kind of power they exercise. The simplest way to classify them is to distinguish between those that exercise illegitimate power, or coercion, and those that exercise legitimate power, or authority. We call the former authoritarian, and the latter participatory, governments.

Authoritarian Governments

An **authoritarian government** rules by coercion. That is, the people have, legally, little or nothing to say about who governs them and how they are governed. There are, however, varying degrees of authoritarianism in governments.

Some authoritarian governments, like those in Saudi Arabia, Libya, and Cuba, are ruled by a single individual who has either inherited the position (the King of Saudi Arabia) or has gained it by revolution (Qaddafi in Libya and Castro in Cuba). Some are ruled by a group, such as the military juntas that seized power and control such nations as Ethiopia and Chile.

The various authoritarian governments differ in the extent to which they attempt to control the lives of people. Some regimes are content to simply retain their own power and privileges and do not interfere in unrelated matters. Other regimes are **totalitarian governments**; they strive to control the totality of people's lives.

Totalitarian governments may be guided by a utopian vision. In China, Mao Zedong's vision of a Communist nation was a guide for actively shaping all of life (Schurmann and Schell 1967; Robinson 1970). Government policies regulated everything from the economy to education to people's work life and the number of children couples could have. Those who resisted the policies were subject to sanctions, ranging from peer pressure to beatings, imprisonment, and even death.

Participatory Governments

A **participatory government** is one in which people have a voice in who rules them and in how they are ruled. Power ultimately resides with the people; and they can invest it in one or more of the three kinds of authority—legal, traditional, or charismatic. As we illustrated earlier, this does not mean that the people are never coerced or that they agree with all the actions of the government. But at least they can legally bring about changes in leadership and in government policies.

Participatory governments also differ in terms of the structure of leadership and the extent to which people have a voice. Among participatory governments are the constitutional monarchies such as those in Great Britain, Spain, and Norway. At one time, each of these nations had an authoritarian government in the form of a hereditary monarchy. Today, however, the monarchs (kings or queens) are symbolic heads of state while the actual governing is done by political leaders elected by the people and guided by precepts, laws, and/or constitutions.

A **democracy** is government by the people as a whole. Direct democracy exists where the entire citizenry participates directly in running civic affairs. In contrast, a representative democracy is one in which the citizenry elects representatives to govern on their behalf.

The word democracy comes from the ancient Greeks who first practiced democracy in their city states. The Greeks exercised a form of direct democracy in which all citizens regularly assembled and voted on all issues. However, it should be noted that only adult males who owned property were citizens.

Although a direct democracy might be technologically possible today (with citizens voting on issues via the Internet, perhaps), most people would probably prefer the representative type of democracy. Direct democracy is still found at the local level in some New England towns where the Town Hall is the means of making governmental decisions. Otherwise, at every level from the local to the national, the United States government functions as a representative rather than a direct democracy.

You can easily understand the benefits of a representative democracy over a direct democracy by thinking about the time and energy it would require if you were expected to vote on every issue that came before the national, state, and local governments. The sheer volume and complexity of issues would make this an impossible undertaking.

To be sure, voting for your representative rather than voting directly means that political decisions will not always reflect your will or your preference. However, this would also happen in a direct democracy in which the majority rules.

Thinking Critically

In a lengthy letter to a newspaper, a writer complained that the United States is no longer a representative government (*The San Diego Union-Tribune*, January 18, 1997). He pointed out that although people vote, the Electoral College casts the decision; that the courts declare propositions approved by the people unconstitutional; that criminals break the law and then get off on technicalities; and that elected officials are hamstrung by the piles of laws passed by their predecessors. In short, the writer argued, the nation is becoming socialistic and people are losing their freedoms.

We have heard similar arguments from others, but we think that the writer goes too far in his allegations. First, the Electoral College was established by the Constitution—the same document that the writer claimed is being violated. Second, the Constitution created a system of checks and balances. And within the context of that system, the courts established the concept of judicial review which gave them the power to declare propositions and laws unconstitutional. But what proportion of propositions approved by the people are ever declared unconstitutional? The writer gives the impression that this happens routinely.

Third, it is true that some criminals get off on technicalities. But what proportion? As we pointed out in Chapter Seven, the United States has a higher proportion of its population in jails and prisons than any other nation. Fourth, exactly how are elected officials hamstrung by existing laws? True, there are an incredible number of laws, but the writer needs to provide concrete examples of how the number of laws impedes the work of officials and threatens representative government.

Finally, in what sense is the writer correct when he argues that Americans are losing their freedom and their representative government? Does freedom mean that the particular proposition you support must be put into effect regardless of its constitutionality? To what extent is your freedom being curbed if a few criminals get off on technicalities? Indeed, the Constitution protects the rights of the accused so that the rights of the innocent will also be safeguarded. And in what way is representative government being destroyed when officials' hands are tied, if they are, by a mountain of laws passed by duly elected representatives?

The American System of Government

In theory, the people possess the ultimate power in a representative democracy. Yet who really rules in the United States? Every citizen can participate in the political process. But who actually does? We'll look for answers to these questions as we examine the American system of government in greater detail. First, we will consider the way in which the government has grown over time.

The Growth of Government

Do you believe that the government has become too large and powerful in the United States? Do you think that its size and power are a threat to your rights and freedoms as a citizen? A Gallup poll asked these same questions and found that 38 percent answered yes, the federal government has become so huge and powerful that it threatens the rights and freedoms of the citizenry (Golay and Rollyson 1996, p. 37).

Just how large is the government? Just how threatened are you? Three decades ago, Peter Drucker (1968, p.172, 212) addressed both issues: "There is no country in the world today where the entire government establishment of 1910 could not comfortably be housed in the smallest of the new government buildings now going up, with room to spare for a grand-opera house and a skating rink" and " the most despotic government of 1900 would not have dared probe into the private affairs of its citizens as income-tax collectors now do routinely in the freest society." Drucker also asserted that every governmental agency in the nation—local, state, and federal—in the time of Theodore Roosevelt could easily be put into the regional federal building in Denver.

The issues of how much power the government exercises and the extent to which your freedoms are threatened are not easily answered (see Thinking Critically, this chapter). However, the question of the size of the government can be answered from *existing data* provided by the Census Bureau (U.S. Bureau of the Census 1975 and 1996d). In 1816, the earliest date for which data are available, the federal government had 4,837 employees. The number increased to 157,442 in 1891, to 1.042 million in 1940, and to 3.128 million in 1990. Then, as a result of pressure from citizens and some politicians to reduce the scope of government, the number of employees declined to 2.919 million in 1995.

Of course, the population grew through all those years and the role of the federal government expanded. So look at the figures in terms of the number of federal employees per population unit. The figures show that there was a federal employee for every 1790 citizens in 1816, for every 409 citizens in 1891, for every 127 citizens in 1940, and for every 80 citizens in 1990. By 1995, the figure was one federal employee for every 90 citizens.

Keep in mind that the figures are only for federal employees. The number of state and local employees is available only back to 1929. Adding those numbers to the federal figures means that there was a government employee for every 39 citizens in 1929, for every 31 citizens in 1940, and for every 29 citizens in 1990 (the numbers of state and local employees for 1995 were not available as of this writing).

Clearly, government employment has grown much more rapidly than the population. But has that growth entailed the acquisition of excessive power? Consider the question of who rules in America.

Who Rules?

To raise the question of who rules is to ask how power is actually distributed. The question can't be answered merely by referring to the kind of governmental system. Even if the people have the ultimate power in a representative democracy, they may or may not choose to participate in the political process. Who, then, actually exercises power in the United States? The answers to this question vary.

The Pluralist Model

Structural functionalists (and most political scientists) advocate a **pluralist model** in which power is distributed more or less equally among various **interest groups**. Interest groups attempt to influence public opinion and political decisions in accord with their members' particular concerns. The National Rifle Association (NRA), the National Organization for Women (NOW), the National Association for the Advancement of Colored People (NAACP), and the American Association of Retired Persons (AARP) are examples of interest groups.

According to structural functionalists, each interest group has a certain amount of power, and this is necessary if the society is to be an integrated whole rather than a conglomeration of warring groups. Thus, each interest group, either on its own or by a coalition with other groups, is able to sway public opinion and bring about political action that furthers the group's interest. For example, between 1870 and 1930 a number of women's groups were able to get legislation passed that protected women in the workplace with such measures as minimum wage laws (McCammon 1995). Working together and forming coalitions with powerful politicians, the interest groups secured passage of the laws in the face of strong opposition from employers.

If the pluralist view is correct, of course, each interest group will experience defeats as well as victories. For there are likely to be opposing interest groups on every issue. Thus, the NAACP won many legal victories for African Americans and other minorities but was unable to secure its position on a number of presidential political appointees. NOW has influenced a good deal of legislation that helps women but failed to secure passage of the Equal Rights Amendment to the Constitution. The NRA has successfully blocked legislation on gun control at all levels of government but was unable to block passage of a federal law restricting automatic and semiautomatic weapons.

Given the fact that interest groups can exert power in accord with the pluralist model, what about the individual? How much power do you have? To put it bluntly, you have very little apart from your participation in an interest group. You have the power of your vote. You have the power to express your views to office holders. But a letter signed by you will have little impact compared to one that comes from an organization. One of our students wrote a strong letter to her Senator expressing opposition to the Senator's vote on a specific issue. In response, she received a form letter from the Senator's office thanking her for her interest and support.

The Power-Elite Model

Conflict theorists dispute the pluralist model. In the **power-elite model**, as set forth by C. Wright Mills (1956), power is concentrated in a relatively small number of political, economic, and military leaders. In the United States, interest groups wield a middle level of power, mostly through lobbying efforts in Congress. At the bottom of the power pyramid is the bulk of citizens, who Mills characterized as a powerless mass of unorganized people controlled by the power elite.

Among other things, Mills pointed out that the very composition of the government underscores its control by elite members of the society because the majority of American politicians come from the higher socioeconomic strata. How can they truly represent the needs of all Americans? Moreover, those who are leaders in government interact with military and business leaders on a regular basis, and jointly they decide on policies that the nation should pursue.

While not agreeing in all details with Mills, a number of researchers accept the power-elite rather than the pluralist model. Dye (1990) asserted that some 7,000 Americans monopolize political power. These 7,000 are leaders in government (including the military), corporations, and public interest organizations such as the mass media, education, and foundations. Domhoff (1990) has made numerous analyses of decision making in the United States and concludes that the upper class generally rules the nation. The upper class, he contends, uses its resources and influence to directly affect political decision-makers or to indirectly affect them through such things as the mass media, think tanks, and foundations.

The power-elite model is supported by the concentration of wealth in the United States. While the richest Americans receive a smaller proportion of income than they did before World War II (Lauer 1997), income is only one part of wealth. Consider the following facts, reported in *The New York Times*(April 17, 1995):

- The richest 1 percent of American households own nearly 40 percent of the nation's wealth;

- The richest 20 percent of Americans own more than 80 percent of the nation's wealth;

- The poorest 20 percent of Americans receive 5.7 percent, and the richest 20 percent receive 55 percent, of all after-tax income, which is the greatest inequality in any industrial nation.

Such facts support the idea that an elite group of Americans holds a disproportionate amount of power and uses that power to further its own interests.

How, then, do conflict theorists explain welfare programs like Head Start that address the educational disadvantages of the poor, or the Medicare and Medicaid programs that were once vigorously opposed by the American Medical Association? These programs are in the interests of the poor and increase the tax burden of the wealthy elite. A die-hard conflict theorist might say that such programs are a sop thrown to non-elites to maintain the illusion that they have some power. Others would argue that they are evidence that the power-elite model does not fully explain the American political process.

A variation of the power elite model is proposed by *feminist theorists* who argue that the government represents not merely class interests but patriarchal class interests (Eisenstein 1992). In this model, the elite are not merely members of the upper strata, but in particular male members of the upper strata. And, indeed, if you look at names of leaders who hold a monopoly of power, you will find them overwhelmingly to be men.

Our position is that both the pluralist and power elite models have some validity. The pluralist model fails to take into account the extent of concentration of wealth and power in the hands of a relatively few Americans. The power-elite model fails to take into account the extent to which interest groups can affect political decisions and the extent to which some powerful individuals—for whatever reasons—become champions of people who are disadvantaged and relatively powerless. The feminist version gives no weight to the small but increasing number of women in powerful positions or to the fact that wives share some of the power and wealth of their elitist husbands.

If the pluralist model were completely accurate, there would be less inequality in the nation than now exists. If the power-elite model were completely accurate, there would be little point to any kind of political participation by the masses of people. But we believe that there is a point in being politically involved, so let's examine the patterns of participation.

Political Participation

People participate in the political process in a number of ways. They become informed by the mass media. They vote. They join and support political parties and interest groups.

Political parties in the United States date back to the early years of the nation. The current party system, composed of the Democratic and Republican parties, developed in the years immediately preceding the Civil War. For the past 60 years or more the presidential candidates from those parties have received 85 or more percent of the votes cast (U.S. Bureau of the Census 1996d, p. 269). A number of other parties have emerged at various times (including the Union, Socialist, Progressive, States' Rights, Libertarian, Independent, and Reform parties), but few of their candidates have won office at any level of government.

As noted in Chapter Eight, the two major parties are divided to some extent along socioeconomic lines. Thus, the Democratic party has a higher proportion of participants from the lower strata, and the Republican party has a higher proportion of upper-strata supporters. Social class background continues to be an important factor in party identification, but some shifts have occurred in recent years (Hout, Brooks, and Manza 1995). Nonmanagerial white-collar workers and professionals have become more (though not predominantly) Democratic while Re-

Figure 13.1   Presidential Voting Patterns, 1996

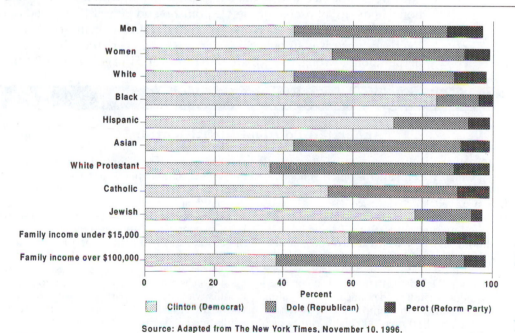

Source: Adapted from The New York Times, November 10, 1996.

publicans have gained support among managers and the self-employed. And skilled blue-collar workers, once strongly Democratic, have become more independent of party identification. The 1996 voting patterns for a number of groups is shown in figure 13.1.

Of course, even those who identify with a particular party do not necessarily vote. Since 1980, less than half of the registered voters say they voted in Congressional election years, and between 57 and 61 percent say they voted in Presidential election years (U.S. Bureau of the Census 1996d, p. 286).

What determines whether someone will participate in the political process? Three factors are related to participation: resources such as time and money, an interest in politics, and being accessible to recruitment efforts (Verba, Schlozman, and Brady 1995).

The mass media can help generate interest and serve as a recruitment mechanism. From a *symbolic interactionist* perspective, political understanding is not based simply on objective data but is socially constructed. And the media are of prime importance in constructing such understanding. For example, the 1991 Congressional hearings on Supreme Court nominee Clarence Thomas turned into a media event when a law professor, Anita Hill, claimed that Thomas had sexually harassed her when she worked for him.

An analysis of the hearings concluded that Thomas and Hill "became unwilling participants in a bizarre, Kafkaesque psychodrama in which both were subjected to a simulated trial-by-media, with a voyeuristic national audience of pseudo-jurors" (Robinson and Powell 1996). Each side worked hard to construct a particular image of the two central characters. Each side portrayed its own character as a victim and the other as a base perpetrator of wrong. It was a war of symbols and images, and the Thomas

Explorations

Inherited Political Identification

Figure 13.1 shows a number of dimensions along which voting patterns differ: gender, racial/ethnic background, religion, and income. Data are available on a variety of other factors, such as age, party identification, region, education, and marital status. But what about family tradition? That is, to what extent do people identify themselves with, and vote for, a particular party because their parents also identified with that party? We believe that there is a considerable amount of inherited political identification.

Have each group member survey 20 adults, 10 women and 10 men. Ask them with which

political party they identify (or if they define themselves an independent). Then ask them with which political party their parents identify or identified.

Let one group member tabulate the results. What proportion of the respondents have the same political identification as their parents? Did the men in the sample differ from the women? How? If the sample is representative of the nation as a whole, to what extent do people identify with the same party as their parents? If you do this as an individual project, interview 20 adults and answer the same questions.

camp eventually won out (in the sense that Thomas was confirmed). The Thomas-Hill conflict may be a prototype of an increasing amount of dramaturgical politics. The bottom line of dramaturgical politics is not who is right but rather who can best convince the populace of his or her rightness.

Threats to Order: Protest, Violence, and War

A primary function of government is to preserve the social order, but in every society there are dissatisfied people who seek through protest or violence to change the system. They pose internal threats to the existing order. There are also external threats from other nations that can lead to war.

Protest and Violence

Do you believe you have the right to protest government policies and practices? Virtually all of our students answer this question in the affirmative. Do you believe you have the right to engage in violent protest if necessary? Most of our students have some difficulty answering this question. They are very aware that often what starts out to be a peaceful protest becomes a violent confrontation. They have seen protests against war, against discrimination, and against brutal treatment by the police turn violent as protesters confronted those who disagreed with them. And the violence concerns them.

However, there are also those who believe that *only* violent protest will be effective. For them, petitions, marches, and picketing are useless in the face of governmental power. William Gamson (1990) studied 53 protest groups that existed in the United States between 1800 and 1945 and whose goals ranged from minor reform to wholesale revolution. He concluded that those groups which resorted to aggressive tactics such as violence, boycotts, and strikes were somewhat more successful than other groups.

The bottom line is that violent protest works to some extent. Yet this is not to say that nonviolent methods would not have worked. Moreover, violence can also be counterproductive (Lauer 1991). For example, support for anti-abortion groups declined in the early 1990s after a number of violent episodes, including shootings and killings, at abortion clinics.

War

Does a government have the right to commit people to war in defense of the nation? Most people agree that it does. Differences occur, however, as to whether a particular war is necessary to defend the nation. The great bulk of Americans supported participation in World War

II. The majority of Americans supported the war in Viet Nam when it first began, but gradually turned against it. They questioned whether the war was really necessary. Was the United States really threatened by the North Vietnamese? Similarly, many Americans questioned whether the interests of the United States were really jeopardized when Iraq invaded Kuwait in 1990. We raise these questions to underscore the complexity of the issue and to illustrate why there has always been a segment of the population that have opposed each war.

War is one of the most destructive of all human experiences, and it has become increasingly destructive for civilians. In the early part of the century, about nine times as many soldiers as civilians died in war; in recent wars, about nine times as many civilians as soldiers have died (Mollica et al. 1994). And children are increasingly the victims (Crossette 1995). From the mid-1980s to the mid-1990s, two million children were killed in wars, another four to five million were disabled, and 12 million were made homeless.

Social scientists have identified a number of reasons why nations go to war (Lauer 1997). One is economic. For example, severe economic problems after World War I were a factor in Germany's aggressive policy which eventually led to World War II. War can also be very profitable for those engaged in the production of military supplies, resulting in support for the war by business leaders.

Political factors are a second reason. A leader in political jeopardy can unite a nation and solidify his or her power by convincing the people of the need for war against an external enemy. Some analysts believe that such a need for solidifying power was a part of Saddam Hussein's willingness to engage in war with the United States in 1990.

Political and economic factors come together in a third reason: leaders may perceive a war as necessary in order to defend "national interest." Thus, political leaders maintained that it was in the interest of the United States to wage a war in Viet Nam because of the Communist threat—a threat which could lead to takeovers in other Southeast Asian countries and have severe economic consequences as well. Similarly, some argued that it was in the nation's interest to wage war against Iraq because of the threat to oil supplies and the threat to the nation's political allies in the Middle East.

Finally, a fourth factor in war is the desire of people everywhere to govern themselves. Wars between African tribes joined in a single nation (e.g., Nigeria, Zaire, and Rwanda), between Serbs, Croats, and Muslims in the former Yugoslavia, and between Russia and some of the provinces in the former U.S.S.R. all reflect a determination of people to be autonomous. People want social order. However, they want an order that they choose and not one that is imposed upon them.

Types of Economies

People not only desire social order but also need sustenance. The economy is the institution that involves the production and distribution of goods and services, some of which are necessary for the maintenance of life and some of which are believed to enhance the quality of life. The two basic forms of economy today are capitalism and socialism. There are also some economies that combine the two.

Capitalism

Capitalism is an economic system with private ownership of the means of production and competitive, for-profit distribution of goods and services. Adam Smith (1965; orig. 1776) wrote the classic treatise on capitalism. He maintained that capitalism is based on selfishness but has a beneficial outcome: individuals' pursuit of their selfish ends promote the public good and the well-being of all. Competition among individuals pursuing profit results in the public being offered goods and services they need and want at prices they can afford to pay. Only those who provide the best goods and services at reasonable prices will survive and profit from the market. Capitalists, then, benefit by efficiently meeting public demand, while the public benefits by having quality goods and services available and affordable. Moreover, according to pure capitalists, any interference by the government in this process only causes havoc.

Do people act on the basis of self-interest? And does this lead to the public good? Deutsch and Krauss (1962) set up an *experiment* in which two people each guided a truck in an electronic game to a particular destination. The players were rewarded for completing the trip, and the reward was greatest for minimizing the time taken. Two routes were available. If the players chose the short route (which would take the least time), they would encounter each other on a one-lane road.

Acting on self-interest, the players chose the short route. When they came to the one-lane road, they had to bargain, each trying to get the other to back up and free up the road. In most cases, neither player was willing to yield because each wanted the maximum reward. The outcome was that both players lost, because both stubbornly refused to allow the other to pass the one-lane road. Neither player collected a reward.

The experiment illustrates the fact that when people behave selfishly for profit, they may act in ways that are counter-productive to their own interests and to the interests of others. Couldn't the same principle hold true for a society? That is, is it possible that a mass of people acting purely in each of their self-interests might generate detriment rather than good to themselves and others?

On the other hand, what if a third party enters in to minimize det-rimental outcomes? What if, for example, the researchers in the experi-ment had intervened, changed the rules, and required the participants to yield to each other on an alternating schedule? They might not have liked the arrangement, but they would both have benefited from the new rules. Similarly, you could argue that pure capitalism, without any gov-ernment intervention in the economy, would not bring about the results envisioned by Adam Smith. To be sure, some people would benefit, but to maximize the benefits for the most people the government would have to take action and create rules. Such a conclusion would be sup-ported by the fact that economic inequality in the United States was greater in the nineteenth century when the government intervened less, than in the twentieth century when government programs and policies aimed at a more equitable distribution of wealth.

Most nations in the world today have a type of capitalist economy, but no nation has a pure capitalist economy. Rather, these economies are more or less controlled by various government practices and policies.

Socialism

Socialism is an economic system with state ownership of the means of production and cooperative distribution of goods and services. So-cialist ideas go back to the ancient Greek myth of the "Golden Age," a time when there was no private property and people lived in peace and harmony (Boas 1948). As a political movement, socialism gained mo-mentum in the nineteenth century, particularly through the work of Karl Marx.

In a pure socialist economy, the state owns all the means of produc-tion and the government regulates all aspects of the economy in the pursuit of collective goals. Advocates of socialism posit a number of advantages over capitalism. Two of the more important are the elimina-tion of the inequalities that mark capitalist economies and avoidance of the economic swings of capitalism—recessions, depressions, and infla-tion.

No nation practices pure socialism, and the number of nations at-tempting to forge any kind of socialist economy is declining. The breakup of the Soviet Union in 1992 ended one of the important at-tempts at socialism. The People's Republic of China is one of the few nations in the world that still practices socialism, and even that nation shows some signs of shifting toward capitalist practices (Nee 1991).

Mixed Economies

A **mixed economy** is an economic system that combines elements of capitalism and socialism. In particular, mixed economies have both private and state-owned enterprises, at least some of which may compete with each other.

The democratic socialism of Sweden is an example of a mixed economy. The government owns and distributes goods and services such as education, health care, and public transportation. However, many kinds of goods and services entail private ownership and competitive, for-profit distribution. There is less inequality in Sweden than in the United States, and the nation provides its citizens with what may be the most comprehensive social services in the world. Sweden has one of the lowest infant mortality rates (U.S. Bureau of the Census 1996d, pp. 835–36). It has also avoided some of the severe economic swings experienced by other nations.

Many other nations have a mix of private and public ownership of various goods and services. Most of the economies of Western Europe are mixed. In fact, virtually all nations have some elements of both public and private ownership. Public ownership is minimal in the United States, for example, but the government does own and operate such things as the postal service and national parks. The point is not that the American economy is mixed but that no economy is completely free of either public or private ownership.

The Changing American Economy

The United States has always had a predominately capitalist economy—moving from agrarian capitalism to industrial capitalism and, finally, to post-industrial capitalism. Before the nation industrialized, agriculture was the dominant form of work with humans and animals providing the primary sources of energy. Early in the nineteenth century, more than eight out of 10 workers were in agriculture. As late as 1850, 65 percent of the energy used in work was supplied by humans and animals (Lenski 1966). However, industrialization developed rapidly after 1850. You will recall that an industrial society is one with new sources of energy (coal, petroleum, etc.) and with industry rather than agriculture as the primary source of wealth.

The changing nature of the economy is seen in the declining proportion of workers in agriculture. From more than 80 percent in 1800, the proportion of workers in farming jobs declined to 19.9 percent in 1900, 7.4 percent in 1950, and 2.8 percent in 1995 (U.S. Bureau of the Census 1975, p. 141 and 1996d, p. 410).

After the middle of the twentieth century, industrial as well as agricultural jobs declined to a point that the United States now has a postindustrial or service economy. In the postindustrial economy, the majority of jobs is in services (trade, transportation, health, recreation, government, etc.) rather than in agriculture or manufacturing. In 1900, 36.0

percent of nonagricultural workers were involved in manufacturing jobs; the proportion dropped to 27.4 percent in 1970 and 16.4 percent in 1995 (U.S. Bureau of the Census 1975, p. 137 and 1996d, p. 410). From the mid-1990s to 2005, the Census Bureau projects that the fastest growing jobs will be in the service area (such as home health aides, occupational and physical therapists, and special education teachers) and in information technology (such as systems analysts and computer engineers) (U.S. Bureau of the Census 1996d, p. 409).

In the last two decades, changes have occurred in the economy that maximize corporate profits but affect many people adversely (Caskey 1994; Harrison 1994). Numerous businesses and corporations have "downsized," that is, reduced the size of their work force, in order to cut operating costs. That such workers were not simply expendable "fat" is indicated by a consequent change: the downsized companies frequently hire contract workers—part-time or temporary workers—to replace the full-time workers they laid off. The company thus saves money because it does not provide contract workers with fringe benefits or health insurance. Ironically, many of those hired as contract workers are former full-time employees of the firms. A Labor Department survey of a national sample of such workers found that 17 percent said they had a "previous different relationship" with the companies they now work for, and a California temporary-help agency reported that 80 percent of the temporary help it sends to Pacific Bell are former employees of the company (Uchitelle 1996).

The net effect of the changing economy is that many American families are worse off in the 1990s than they were in earlier years. Correcting for inflation, the median income of families from 1992 through 1994 was lower than the median from 1986 through 1991 (U.S. Bureau of the Census 1996d, p. 469). As a result, the rate of home ownership among young couples (those with spouses under 35 years of age) has declined and Americans are borrowing more and paying higher rates of interest through the use of credit cards (Ritzer 1995). We do not know if this deterioration of the standard of living is short-term or long-term; future changes in the economy could lead to improvement again, but they could also lead to further decline.

Work in the United States

What do you want to do in terms of work or career? Perhaps you have a dream you are pursuing. Whether that dream can be fulfilled depends on more than your desires and efforts. It also depends on the economy. Think of it this way. If, in a given year, there are 15,000 graduates with degrees in veterinary medicine, but the economy can only absorb an additional 10,000 veterinarians, a third of the graduates will have to find different employment.

A friend of ours dreamed of becoming an aeronautical engineer. He went to a good university and graduated with honors. However, at the time he graduated there were no jobs available in the field. He settled for a sales job in computers. By the time aeronautical engineering jobs were available again, he had invested too much of himself in sales and felt too far removed from engineering to go back to his original dream.

In other words, the kind of work or career you pursue, the wages or salary you will receive, and the likelihood of your remaining steadily employed are all dependent on more than your personal desires and drive. But your work is an essential element in your well-being. As Freud pointed out, love and meaningful work are the two pillars of mental health. So what can you expect from the world of work in the United States, how is it changing, and what problems can you anticipate?

The Labor Force

The **labor force** consists of all civilians who are employed and those who are unemployed but are able and want to work. In other words, the size of the labor force doesn't just tell you how many people are working, but also how many people are either working or looking for work. The American labor force has increased enormously over time. It nearly tripled in the three decades from 1820 to 1850 (from 2.88 to 7.7 million), then nearly quadrupled from 1850 to 1900 (from 7.7 to 29.07 million) (U.S. Bureau of the Census 1975, p. 134). It was this rapid growth of the labor force that made the swift industrialization of the nation possible. By 1996, the labor force was more than 134.1 million (Bureau of Labor Statistics 1996d).

The labor force has grown in diversity as well as in size. Women comprise an increasing proportion of the labor force. In 1900, only 18.1 percent of the labor force was female (U.S. Bureau of the Census 1975, p. 132). The proportion increased to 28.8 percent in 1950 and to 46.1 percent in 1995 (U.S. Bureau of the Census 1996d, p. 396).

As the economy has changed, the kinds of jobs available have also changed. There has been a general upgrading of the occupational structure. The proportion of jobs requiring minimal skills has decreased, and the proportion of those requiring specialized training and skills of various kinds has increased. As the nation moved from an agricultural to an industrial society, the demand for farm workers decreased and the demand for workers in factories and offices increased. When Americans entered a postindustrial era, an expanding range of specialized skills was needed. There are now more than

30,000 different occupations. Some of the fastest growing occupations, such as systems analyst, did not even exist a half century ago. And some of the most rapidly declining occupations, such as letter press and central office operator, reflect the needs of an industrial rather than a postindustrial economy.

The Changing Meaning of Work

What do you expect your work to do for you? No doubt you expect it to provide you with sufficient income to live well. At one time, this was the major consideration for most American workers. Now, however, people want more from their work than an ample income. A national poll reported that only 8 percent of the respondents said they would be willing to keep a job they hated even if it was guaranteed to make them rich (Lauer 1997).

What, then, do people want out of work in addition to a secure income? For one thing, they want work that is meaningful to them. As a secretary told us, "I don't want a job that just consumes my time and gives me a check. I want to feel that I am contributing something to this world."

People also want stimulating work. The labor force has become increasingly educated. Educated workers find that jobs involving repetitive, routine tasks are boring and disheartening. Educated workers today want to be challenged by their work, and this means tasks that require more than routine efforts (Weiss 1990). Barbara Garson (1975) described the ways such jobs create stress and the ways people try to cope with them through mental games. An example of a routine job is provided by a woman who worked in a ping-pong factory:

> My job was stacking the ping-pong paddles into piles of 50. Actually, I didn't have to count all the way up to 50. To make it a little easier they told me to stack them in circles of four with the first handle facing me. When there got to be thirteen handles on the second one from the front, then I'd know I had 50 . . . . As soon as I'd stack 'em, they'd unstack 'em. Maybe it wouldn't have been so bad if I could have seen all the piles I stacked at the end of the day. But they were taking them down as fast as I was piling them up. That was the worst part of the job. (Garson 1975, pp. 1–2)

Americans are less and less willing to hold such jobs (fortunately, routine jobs are declining). They want a sense of accomplishment from their work. As a study of engineers found, the best predictors of job satisfaction were the challenges posed by the work and intrinsic interest in the work (Watson and Meiksins 1991).

Employment in industry refers to manufacturing jobs. "Services" includes public utilities, wholesale and retail trade, transportation and

Comparative Employment Data

As noted in the text, the proportion of U.S. workers in agriculture declined rapidly as the nation industrialized; the proportion in industry declined as the nation moved into a postindustrial era. Is this trend true for other nations with capitalist and mixed economies?

We also noted that the proportion of the labor force that is female increased considerably over time in the United States. How does this compare with other capitalist nations, including those with mixed economies?

Table 13.2 provides data to answer these questions.

Table 13.2   **Civilian Employment**

Percent of the Labor Force

	Agriculture, forestry, fishing	Industry	Services	Female
United States	2	23	74	46
Australia	5	22	72	43
Canada	4	2	75	45
France	5	27	68	44
Germany	3	36	61	43
Italy	8	33	59	35
Japan	6	34	60	40
Sweden	4	25	72	48
United Kingdom	2	26	72	45

Source: U.S. Bureau of the Census 1996d, pp. 841-42.

communication, finance, insurance, real estate, and social services. In all the nations, regardless of the type of economy, employment in the services is far greater than that in industry or agriculture. Not only the United States, but also most Western nations and Japan have moved into a postindustrial era.

The figures on the proportion of the work force that is female in the nations are also remarkably alike. Although it is not shown in the table, the female proportion has increased in each of the nations over the past decades. In sum, in terms of the kinds of work available and the likelihood of women being in the labor force, the developed nations of the world are quite similar to each other.

Problems of Work

Think again about what people want from work. They want a secure and ample income but are prevented from having this by unemployment or underemployment. They want meaningful and stimulating work but are stymied by underemployment and job dissatisfaction. And although most people do not think of work in terms of being a threat to their health, they expect the workplace to be safe. Work hazards pose a threat to safety. It's important to understand how these problems affect workers.

Unemployment and Underemployment

The **unemployment rate** is based on the number of workers who are out of jobs and looking for employment. Thus, the rate does not include those able-bodied adults who, for whatever reasons, are not actively seeking employment. The unemployment rate varies over time and between different groups of workers. As we noted in previous chapters, black and Hispanic unemployment rates tend to be 1.5 to two times as high as those for whites, and women's rates were higher than men's until 1990. The highest unemployment rates occurred during the Great Depression of the 1930s, when rates varied from 14.3 to 24.9 percent (U.S. Bureau of the Census 1975, p. 135). In late 1996, the rate was 5.2 percent. It was slightly higher for adult women (4.7) than for adult men (4.3), and higher for African Americans (10.8) than for Hispanics (8.0) or whites (4.4) (Bureau of Labor Statistics 1996).

Unemployment rates also vary by occupational category and reflect the changing nature of the economy. Higher than average rates are found among those seeking employment in lower status jobs (such as operators and laborers), while lower than average rates are found among those seeking employment in higher status jobs (those in managerial and professional specialties have half or less the rate of unemployment as the national average)(U.S. Bureau of the Census 1996d, p. 414).

Unemployment is traumatic for people, and more individuals are affected by it each year than are victimized by crime (Lauer 1997). If you lose your job—even if you know it is the result of downsizing and has nothing to do with your competence—you may fall victim to a variety of physical and emotional ills. These adverse consequences of unemployment occur in other nations as well as in the United States. Three researchers examined Canadian data and found that the unemployed had higher rates of illness, mortality, and suicide (Jin, Shah, and Svoboda 1995). Data from Sweden also showed that unemployed youth had higher rates of drug use, crime, and morality (especially by suicide and accidents)(Hammarstrom 1994).

Underemployment is also traumatic. **Underemployment** includes full-time work for inadequate wages, work that is below the worker's skill level, or part-time or temporary work for those who desire full-time jobs. Downsizing has increased the amount of underemployment. Since 1982, temporary employment has grown three times faster than the rate of overall employment (Rogers 1995). The underemployed are likely to be dissatisfied with their jobs and find the work not meaningful or stimulating. They are also likely to have various health problems, ranging from back pain to alcohol abuse (Duerksen 1996).

The health problems of underemployment are understandable. Think about work that is completely routine. Can you imagine, for instance, what it would be like to spend eight hours a day, 40 hours a week, stacking ping-pong paddles? Such a job could literally make you sick. Incidentally, the detrimental effects on health and well-being generally from routine, monotonous work have been found in other nations, such as Sweden, as well as in the United States (Waluyo, Ekberg, and Eklund 1996).

Job Dissatisfaction

Job dissatisfaction can stem from underemployment, but it can also result from a variety of other factors. For one thing, your boss may prove to be a difficult person. This problem is sufficiently widespread that numerous books are available on how to deal with problem bosses (e.g., Grothe and Wylie 1987). Problem bosses can be found everywhere, and they can turn an otherwise desirable job into a distasteful one. A friend of ours, a professor at a midwestern university who worked under a tyrannical departmental chairman, told us that she loved teaching, and enjoyed research, but she hated her job because "the chairman is everywhere, making caustic remarks and impossible demands and creating an atmosphere in which no one trusts anyone anymore."

Job dissatisfaction may be rooted in thwarted expectations for advancement. A study of a professional services firm found that those in lower positions were less satisfied than those in higher positions in the organization (Burke 1996a). Similarly, research at a university concluded that, among faculty, those at the lower ranks experienced more stress and reported more job dissatisfaction than those in higher ranks (Abouserie 1996). Even if workers receive promotions, they may be dissatisfied if they have not advanced as rapidly or to as high a position as they believe they should (McElroy, Morrow, and Mullen 1996).

Job dissatisfaction can even be related to such things as the size of the organizational unit in which you work. A study of a firm with 22 units and 1,608 employees reported that those in the larger units had less satisfaction than those in the smaller units (Burke 1996b). These results may reflect the fact that larger units tend to be more impersonal.

How much job dissatisfaction is there? More than eight of 10 Americans say they are either very or moderately satisfied with their jobs, a proportion that has remained fairly constant for at least two decades (Lauer 1997). Still, if nearly 20 percent of the work force has some degree of dissatisfaction, the problem involves more than 20 million people. And the number may be rising. Increasing numbers say they prefer their off-hours to those on the job, and slightly over half of workers say they would choose a different kind of work if they were just beginning (Lauer 1997).

Work Hazards

Perhaps the last thing you expect is for your work or your workplace to pose a threat to your physical well-being. But in 1994, 6,558 American workers were killed on the job, and 3.5 million experienced some kind of disabling injury (U.S. Bureau of the Census 1996, pp. 433–34). The riskiest workplaces, of course, are in industries where people work with and around machinery, such as in meat packing plants, auto plants, and foundries.

As a response to hazards in the workplace, the federal government created the Occupational Safety and Health Administration (OSHA) in 1970. OSHA has about 2,100 inspectors who work with other professionals to create and enforce safety standards in the workplace. As a result, the number of annual workplace deaths has decreased steadily from the 13,800 who died in 1970 (U.S. Bureau of the Census 1996, p. 433).

Office buildings also contain hazards. For example, indoor air pollution frequently occurs in office buildings. Poor ventilation and toxic vapors from such things as copy-machine liquids, paint, rugs, wall paneling, and cleaning solvents can lead to various physical and mood disorders. The Environmental Protection Agency has pointed out that the air in some office buildings is 100 times as polluted as the air outside, creating a "sick building" that causes such things as mucous membrane irritation, eye irritation, headaches, feelings of lethargy, and the inability to concentrate (Soine 1995).

Minimizing Work Problems

We noted that satisfaction with your work is an important factor in your personal well-being. In fact, data from more than a thousand workers nationwide show that job satisfaction has greater impact on people's life satisfaction than does life satisfaction have on job satisfaction (Chacko 1983). It is important, therefore, to avoid or minimize the problems we have discussed in order for work to be meaningful and fulfilling.

This brings us back to government. Various governmental actions affect the unemployment rate in the United States. For example, steps taken by the government to control inflation frequently increase unemployment. You could argue that if the government is going to intervene in the economy to moderate inflation and recession, then the government should take steps to moderate the impact on workers. This is what happens in Japan and Sweden. These nations have more benefits available to the unemployed, and this lessens to some extent the financial and emotional impact on workers. Corporations and businesses can also assume some responsibility for the well-being of workers. For instance, if downsizing is necessary, sufficient advance notice lessens the trauma for workers. Indeed, Nord and Ting (1991) found that a minimum of two months notice will minimize the losses and difficulties of workers.

The point here is not to offer a set of solutions to work problems, but rather to underscore once again the intertwining of government and economy. Leaders in the two institutions need to take cooperative action if the detrimental effects of work problems are to be minimized.

Critical Thinking Exercise

Studies consistently find that unemployment is associated with stress and health problems. But an economist looked at state-level data and concluded that unemployment may lead to lower overall mortality and to lower mortality from several major causes of death, including accidents (Kelley 1997). However, he did find an increase in suicide rates when unemployment rates climbed. The newspaper report of the research said that the finding suggests that *employment* adversely affects people's health, particularly job-related stress and work hazards.

What questions would you raise about this research and the newspaper's interpretation? What are some possible reasons that this research seems to contradict in many respects all other research on the issue (keep in mind such things as the possibility of changes in the relationship between unemployment and stress, variations in that relationship over time and circumstances, or the way the economist may have grouped his data)?

Summary

Government and economy are interrelated institutions. Government actions affect the economy, and they do so throughout the world. Both institutions can vex as well as gratify people.

Power and authority are central aspects of government. Government can exercise different kinds of power. When a government rules by coercion, without the consent of the people, this is the illegitimate use of power. Authority, rule with the consent of the people, is legitimate power. Weber identified three types of authority: legal, charismatic, and traditional. All three may be found in the world today, although traditional authority is becoming less common. Power increases when a leader is able to exercise more than one kind of authority.

Differing types of authority are expressed in various kinds of governments. The simplest way to classify governments is authoritarian (rule by coercion) and participatory (rule by authority). Authoritarian governments may be ruled by individuals or by small groups such as military juntas. Totalitarian regimes represent extreme authoritarianism; they try to control the totality of people's lives.

In participatory governments, people are also coerced on some points. However, they grant legitimacy to the government and are able to change leaders and programs and policies through legal processes. Participatory governments range from constitutional monarchies to representative democracies.

The U.S. government has grown enormously over the course of its history. Both the absolute number of governmental employees and the number per population unit have increased. The question of who really rules the nation in the context of massive government is answered differently by those who maintain the pluralist versus those who support the power-elite models. The pluralist model portrays power as distributed among competing interest groups. The power-elite model portrays power as monopolized by a relatively small number of people, particularly those who are leaders in government, the military, and the corporate world. Neither model fully explains all the facts.

People participate in the political process in a number of ways, including voting, obtaining information from the mass media, and joining political parties and interest groups. Resources, interests, and accessibility to recruitment efforts help determine who will participate.

Protest, violence, and war threaten the social order and must be addressed by government. Violent protest can work, but can also be counterproductive. Wars have various causes—economic, political, and the universal desire for autonomy.

People need sustenance as well as order. They get sustenance from the economy. Capitalism and socialism are the most common economies today. Capitalism involves private ownership of the means of production and competitive, for-profit distribution of goods and services. Most nations are capitalist, but no nation allows the economy to be entirely free of government intervention. Socialism involves state ownership of the means of production and cooperative distribution of goods and services. The number of nations trying to sustain socialism is declining. Many economies are mixed, with elements of both capitalism and socialism.

The American economy has moved from an agricultural to an industrial to a postindustrial economy. Jobs in agriculture and industry have continued to decline, while those in the service and information areas have continued to increase.

A changing economy means a changing world of work. In the United States, the labor force has increased greatly over time. Workers have more education. And the work force has become more diverse with women, including mothers with children, becoming an increasing proportion of the labor force.

The meaning of work for Americans has also changed. In addition to a stable income, Americans want work that is stimulating and meaningful. There are a number of work problems that threaten what people want from work, including unemployment and underemployment, job dissatisfaction, and work hazards.

Unemployment and underemployment vary by social group and by occupational category. Both, however, can cause physical and emotional problems. Job dissatisfaction can stem from underemployment but can also be a result of such things as a difficult boss and thwarted expectations of advancement. As many as a fifth of all workers may suffer from job dissatisfaction. Work hazards are most likely to afflict industrial workers, but office workers also face hazards from indoor pollution. Minimizing work problems will require the cooperative efforts of business and governmental leaders.

Glossary

authoritarian government a government that uses coercion to govern

authority the legitimate exercise of power on the basis of law, tradition, or charismatic leadership

capitalism an economic system with private ownership of the means of production and competitive, for-profit distribution of goods and services

democracy government by the people

interest group a group that tries to influence public opinion and political decisions in accord with the particular interests of the group's members

labor force all civilians who are employed and those who are unemployed but able and wanting to work

mixed economy an economic system that combines elements of capitalismand socialism

participatory government a government that uses authority to govern

pluralist model a model of politics in which power is distributed more or less equally among various interest groups

power-elite model a model of politics in which power is concentrated in political, economic, and military leaders

socialism an economic system with state ownership of the means of production and cooperative distribution of goods and services

totalitarian government a government that is authoritarian and that attempts to control the totality of people's lives

underemployment full-time work for inadequate wages, work that is below the worker's skill level, or part-time or temporary work for those who desire full-time jobs

unemployment rate the proportion of workers who are out of jobs and looking for employment

CHAPTER FOURTEEN

Science, Technology, and Health: *The Search for Personal and Environmental Well-Being*

Today we have the technology to keep people alive even when their physical condition and quality of life makes them long for death. Do you favor or oppose the use of technology in this way? We also have the technology to kill millions of people in less than a day. Would you favor or oppose a ban on this kind of technology? In the future, we may have the technology to allow parents to determine the sex, eye color, hair color, body size, and ultimate height of their children. Would you favor or oppose the use of such technology?

Clearly, technology can be used in ways that generate controversy. Samuel Butler (1968; orig. 1872) raised questions about the diverse uses to which technology can be put in his satirical novel, *Erewhon*. The fictional colony of Erewhon is inhabited by people who have developed a unique society. Among other things, illness, ugliness, and bad luck are punishable crimes, and tedious people are sent to the Hospital for Incurable Bores. The story is told by a sheep farmer who accidentally discovers the isolated colony. Early on, he discovers a room full of old machinery and also realizes that a magistrate is displeased that he had found it. He observes that Erewhonians are about as advanced as Europeans of the twelfth or thirteenth century, yet the machinery in the room is clearly more sophisticated.

Eventually, the farmer determines that the Erewhonians had become alarmed by the detrimental potential of new technologies. After much debate, they agreed to discard all technology that had been discovered over the preceding 271 years and to forbid the development of any new technology. For about 600 years, then, they had lived without any new technology. The Erewhonian solution to the problem of the detrimental use of technology is extreme. But the story illustrates the fact that technology and **science**, the knowledge gained by systematic, rational observation, may be used to exploit and oppress as well as to enhance well-being. As the questions that open this chapter illustrate, science and technology raise ethical considerations for many people. But they are also integral to our standard of living and way of life, including our health. In this chapter we will examine the ways in which science, technology, and health intersect with each other and affect people's lives.

Science as a Human Construction

We defined science as knowledge gained through systematic, rational observation. Does that mean that science is free of all subjective influences, including the human foibles that characterize other social pursuits? Not at all. *Symbolic interactionists* view all human activity, including science, as socially constructed. That is, science is not just knowledge that is "out there" waiting to be discovered. Rather, science is knowledge that results from human action and interaction. And scientists are people who create their systems of knowledge in the context of particular cultures and social structures, and who possess the kinds of biases and personal ambitions that characterize those in other pursuits.

Feminist theorists agree with symbolic interactionists that science is a social process. Arguing that, in particular, it is a male-biased and male-dominated pursuit (Keller 1992). Feminists maintain that science is a male-biased enterprise for at least two reasons. First, the focus has been on domination and use of nature rather than on achieving harmony with nature. Second, the scientific method stresses an intense objectivity that ignores the emotions and perspectives of the scientist and the way in which these influence the research process.

Also, men dominate science. The proportion of doctorates in scientific fields granted to women has increased enormously since 1970, and in some fields—sociology, psychology, and the health sciences—women earn more than half the doctorates. But by 1993 women still only earned 39.9 percent of the doctorates in the biological sciences, 21.9 percent of the doctorates in the physical sciences, and 14.4 percent of the doctorates in the computer sciences (U.S. Bureau of the Census 1996d, p. 193). In addition, a 1996 report pointed out that fewer than one-third of the nation's top jobs in the field of high technology are held by women (Bennett 1996).

The point is, science is not what some of its more enthusiastic advocates have claimed—an infallible guide to utopian living. At the same time, science has thrust humankind into a new dimension of life. What, exactly, is this phenomenon we call science?

The Nature of Science

The attempt to gain knowledge is ancient. Yet throughout human history, people have used diverse methods to gain knowledge. One method is reliance on the supernatural. Many contemporary Christian fundamentalists use this method to insist that the world was created by God a little over 6,000 years ago (a number that comes from a literal interpretation of a number of passages in the Bible). Those who consult astrologers to discover their futures use this method as well. A second method is reliance on authority. In the Middle Ages, all science in Western society had to conform to the teachings of Aristotle, who was held to be an infallible authority.

Intuition provides a third method—believing something is true because you have a "gut feeling" about it or you have had a flash of insight. Reason, and particularly logic, offers a fourth method. Knowledge is that which is reasonable or logical. Of course, one person's intuition or logic is another person's nonsense. Still, some important insights have come through people's intuition and use of reason.

Finally, science is a relatively recent way of gaining knowledge. Science gains knowledge by observation (gathering data, as opposed to armchair speculation or abstract reasoning) and by inferences made from that observation. This method of gaining knowledge did not develop and spread until the seventeenth century (Butterfield 1957).

We can illustrate the difference between science and the other methods by the following. What causes alcoholism? The answer to the question is a piece of knowledge that could help Americans deal with the nation's most serious drug problem. Consider the possibilities. Because most religions condemn excessive drinking, reliance on the supernatural could lead you to conclude that alcoholism is simply a sin.

Reliance on authority might lead you to believe that alcoholism is a disease because you read a book by an expert who medicalizes alcoholism. Other experts disagree with that characterization, but you accept the authority of the expert whose book you read.

Your intuition might lead you to regard alcoholism as a character flaw. Perhaps you have known alcoholics, and your gut feeling about them was that they all lacked self-control. Or your reasoning might lead you to conclude that alcoholism is a response to frustration. A disproportionate number of alcoholics are white, urban males from higher socioeconomic backgrounds (Lauer 1997). It is reasonable to conclude that the frustrations such men encounter as they seek to realize their career and relational aspirations cause them to seek solace in drink.

Obviously, the answers of sin, disease, character flaw, and frustration lead to very different ways to deal with the problem. So knowledge is important if people are to deal constructively with the problems they face. How does science attempt to answer the question of what causes alcoholism? By observation and inference. Researchers pose various questions to guide their observations. How do the work and family experiences of alcoholics differ from those of others? At what age does problem drinking begin, and how do alcohol abusers differ from their nonabusing peers? What is happening in societies when the rate of alcoholism is high? Guided by such questions, researchers gather data. Interpreting those data, they conclude that a variety of factors are related to alcoholism, including peer pressure, role problems, adverse family experiences, and feelings of powerlessness (Lauer 1997).

Note an important fact about the above example: knowledge gained by science tends to be more complex than that yielded by other methods. The reasoning of Aristotle led him to conclude that fire, air, earth, and water were the basic elements of the universe. The science of chemists and physicists has resulted in a far more intricate understanding. Whether the issue is the causes of alcoholism or the nature of matter, the knowledge gained by science is more complex than that gained by other methods.

Thinking Critically

Although many people think of science as gaining certain and valid knowledge, scientific studies may contradict each other. Consider, for instance, the question of whether coffee is detrimental to your health. An article in a popular publication noted a number of scientific studies on the effects of caffeine that yielded contradictory results (Stephens 1990). Among the findings of various studies are: there is a relationship between amount of coffee consumed and cholesterol levels; drinking three cups a day doubles the risk of heart attacks; how the coffee is brewed makes a difference—filtered coffee does not increase cholesterol; caffeine has no effect on blood pressure, heart rate, and cholesterol level; and five or more cups of coffee a day reduces the risk of colon cancer by 40 percent. Finally, a Harvard professor looked at all the research over a ten-year period and

concluded that there is no evidence that normal caffeine consumption is detrimental to health.

You have probably seen similar contradictions about other foods. How do you sort them out? If you're really concerned about, let's say, caffeine, go to a library that has medical journals. Track down the references mentioned in the popular article as well as all others on the topic. Check carefully the samples used. Note the size of the differences; if, for instance, 35.1 percent of noncoffee drinkers and 40.2 percent of coffee drinkers had high cholesterol levels, is that worth worrying about? What other factors could account for the differences? For example, are heavy coffee drinkers also more likely to smoke and to eat unhealthy foods? Were those possibilities taken into account in the research? Are other interpretations of the data possible?

The Development of Science

Although individuals such as Aristotle and Leonardo da Vinci engaged in scientific efforts, science as a method involving observation and inference emerged in the seventeenth century. The *experiment* is a central part of science, of course, and one of the most famous experiments in history took place when Galileo (or perhaps someone else, according to historians) dropped two objects of different weights from the top of the leaning tower of Pisa to test Aristotle's thesis that objects fall at a rate that is proportional to their weights (Butterfield 1957).

The experiment was like an announcement that henceforth a new way of gaining knowledge would be employed. Aristotle's authority would no longer be accepted without question. And Aristotle's method, primarily using pure reason, would no longer be sufficient. The age of science had begun.

The development of science was greatly stimulated by the founding of the Royal Society in London in 1662. Through the Royal Society, the English government gave financial support to scientific work. Robert Merton (1957) studied the scientists who were members of the Royal Society and found that Puritans were disproportionately represented. In a study analogous to Max Weber's analysis of the growth of capitalism and Protestantism, Merton found that a number of Puritan ideas facilitated scientific pursuits. For example, Puritans believed that all should be done for the glory of God, and Puritan scientists believed that their work was a way of glorifying God. The Puritans also affirmed social well-being as a goal of Christians, and Puritan scientists believed their knowledge could enhance that well-being.

A third Puritan idea was the value of diligent work, and science requires such diligence. Fourth, the Puritans emphasized the importance of reason in curbing passions and evaluating the individual's spiritual status. To evaluate one's spiritual status required observation—keeping data—and making appropriate inferences from those data. And that, of course, is science.

However, the growth of science was slow until the middle of the nineteenth century. In fact, until the 1850s, "science was more a gentlemanly than a professional pursuit" (Brown, R. 1993, p. 161). Science was an avocation for most scientists because there were few opportunities to make a living at it. From the 1850s on, however, science became institutionalized in Western society through three processes (Brown 1993). First, scientists in the various disciplines developed standardized methods, procedures, and language. They created a body of knowledge unique to each of their disciplines. Second, research universities emerged, providing resources for full-time and adequately supported scientific work. And third, specialized organizations such as laboratories, institutes, and think tanks developed, offering additional opportunities for scientific work.

The growth of science in the United States means increasing opportunities for work in scientific fields. In 1900, far less than 1 percent of workers were classified as scientists or engineers (U.S. Bureau of the Census 1975, p. 140–41). By 1950, the figure had risen to about 1 percent, and by 1995 it was more than 4 percent (U.S. Bureau of the Census 1996d, p. 405–406).

The growth of science also means increased funds devoted to research and development. The funds come from government, industry, universities and colleges, and other nonprofit organizations. The funds grew from $13.5 billion in 1960 to $171 billion in 1995 (U.S. Bureau of the Census 1996d, p. 601). Even adjusting for inflation, that represents a 154 percent increase. The nation's investment in science has paid off in, among other things, Nobel Prizes in chemistry, physics, and physiology/medicine. As Table 14.1 shows, U.S. scientists have received 40.9 percent of all the prizes awarded in those three sciences from 1901 to 1994 (although we should note that the United Kingdom and Germany both did better if we consider the number of prizes in relationship to population).

Social Factors in Scientific Progress

The figures in Table 14.1 suggest a question: why does scientific work flourish more in certain societies than in others? How can we explain the dominance of a few nations in the kind of basic research that is rewarded a Nobel Prize? Why do some third-world nations have almost no scientific work in progress? Let's consider a number of social factors involved in the progress of science.

Table 14.1 **Nobel Prize Laureates in Chemistry, Physics, and Physiology/Medicine: 1901 to 1994**

	Total	Physics	Chemistry	Physiology/Medicine
Total	425	146	120	159
United States	174	60	39	75
United Kingdom	69	21	24	24
Germany	59	17	28	14
France	24	10	7	7
Soviet Union	10	7	1	2
Japan	4	3	1	0
Other countries	85	28	20	37

Source: U.S. Bureau of the Census 1996d, p. 612

Beliefs and Values

One factor in scientific progress is the number of scientists in a society. And, as Hardy (1974) discovered in his study of the social origins of American scientists, cultural values are related to the number of people who opt for scientific careers. Hardy gathered data on the number of doctorates in science earned in the United States from 1920 to 1961. He found regional differences. Students earning a bachelor's degree in New England were more likely to go on for a doctorate than those in other regions, and those getting a degree in the South were least likely to continue to the doctorate. He also found differences among schools. In the first half of the time period, a disproportionate number of those earning doctorates came from small, liberal arts colleges of Protestant affiliation or origin. A number of women's colleges, including Bryn

Mawr, Mount Holyoke, Radcliffe, and Vassar, also produced a large number of scientists. Finally, religious groups differed in the number of scientists they produced, with liberal Protestants and Jews being highly productive and fundamentalist Protestants and Roman Catholics being least productive.

Hardy accounted for these differences by identifying seven cultural beliefs and values that are associated with producing greater numbers of scientists. The first is naturalism, the belief in an orderly, lawful world (as opposed to viewing the world as capricious or mysterious). The second is a value on learning and knowledge. The third is a belief in human dignity (as opposed to viewing people as powerless or evil). The fourth is a value on dedication to purposeful work (as opposed to an "eat, drink, and be merry" philosophy of life).

The fifth is the value of egalitarianism, viewing all people as having equal rights and all groups as having equal potential. The sixth is an antitraditional value, a dissatisfaction with existing ways, and a questioning, searching mind. And finally, there is a value on this world and the foreseeable future (as opposed to a focus on the afterlife).

Any group or society possessing these seven beliefs and values will be more productive of scientists and scientific work. Liberal Protestants and Jews are more likely to hold to these beliefs and values than are those in other religious groups and, therefore, produce more scientists. Incidentally, in her analysis of American scientists who won Nobel Prizes between 1901 and 1972, Zuckerman (1977) also found religious differences. Seventy-two percent of the laureates were raised Protestant, mostly mainstream rather than fundamentalist, and 27 percent were raised Jewish.

Government and Economy

As indicated by the funding figures quoted earlier, sustaining a strong and productive scientific community is a costly enterprise. Both the government's commitment to science and the economy's health impact a society's ability to pursue scientific work.

For example, the Japanese government proposed an 8 percent increase in basic science programs in 1997 and plans to invest $155 billion in science and technology between 1997 and 2001 (Normile 1997). The $155 billion figure over five years is an average of $31 billion a year— more than the total annual gross national product of many developing nations!

The point is, many governments lack the resources to pour into scientific work. Most research and development in such nations must be funded by nongovernmental sources.

Given adequate resources, the government still must be committed to science. This commitment will vary over time, depending upon the political situation. The United States poured enormous funds into research and development for the space program after the Soviet Union launched the first satellite into space in 1957. The increased governmental support for scientific research in Japan in the late 1990s resulted from an awareness that the nation was falling behind in basic discoveries in science and in technological developments, a situation that threatened continuing economic growth (Imura 1996).

War, and the threat of war, can also stimulate a government to support scientific research. The science of mechanics, with its emphasis on the motion of spherical projectiles, developed during the Renaissance—the age of the cannon. About 10 percent of the research done by the members of the Royal Society in its early years related directly or indirectly to military technology (Ziman 1976, p. 303). The military's need to calculate ballistic tables in World War II led to the funded research that produced the digital computer. Roughly half of all federal research and development funds between 1975 and 1995 were allocated to the Department of Defense (U.S. Bureau of the Census 1996d, p. 603).

Competition

Competition seems to foster scientific and technological progress. The competition may be, as suggested above, between nations. Or it may be between organizations such as universities. For example, Joseph Ben-David (1970) examined differences in scientific productivity in medicine in the United States, England, France, and Germany during the nineteenth century. Using existing data, he created measures of productivity by using the number of scientific discoveries and the number of scientists making the discoveries.

Ben-David found that the greatest progress in medical science in the early part of the century was made in France and England, while more advances were made in Germany and the United States in the second half of the century. What had happened?

Ben-David found the answer in the organization of science in the four nations. France and England maintained centralized university systems, while the U.S. and German systems were decentralized. In other words, rather than one or two major universities monopolizing higher education, the U.S. and German systems involved numerous universities competing with each other for students and status. In order to attract the best professors and the best students, the U.S. and German universities had to expand their facilities, provide the best possible research environments, and encourage cutting-edge work in the rapidly changing field of medicine.

The competition for prestige and money has continued to be at the center of scientific and technological advances. Nations, universities, industrial organizations, and individuals all compete with each other to gain the rewards that come from scientific and technological advances.

For example, the 1977 Nobel Prize in Physiology or Medicine was awarded to three researchers, two of whom were bitter enemies (Wade 1982). The two were originally colleagues, but they separated and formed two different research teams. Each was determined to be the first to identify and characterize hormones used by the brain to control such bodily functions as temperature, reproduction, and growth. In their competition for the prize, the researchers violated many of the norms that are supposed to govern scientific work. For instance, credit is usually given to other scientists working in the same area, but each avoided as much as possible acknowledging the work of the other. Each also refused to share information with the other, working in secret rather than cooperatively. In the end, both achieved the coveted prize, though both lost the effort to win a victory over the other. The competition between the scientists did little for their relationship with each other, but it did spur their efforts and facilitate their scientific triumph.

Whatever effect it may have on interpersonal relationships, competition is a stimulus to scientific progress. Science is more likely to be advanced, therefore, where competition is a part of the culture or built into the social structure.

Explorations

Technology: Savior or Demon?

We began this chapter with some questions about technology and its impact on people. Divide the class into groups of about five people. Let half of the groups take the "pro" side and half the "against" side on the following proposition: Technological developments have reached the point where they create more problems than they solve.

Groups may use library resources, interviews, personal experiences, or other resources to develop their position. Keep in mind that the problems may be purely technical or may be related to health, interpersonal relationships, the functioning of social institutions, ethical issues, and so forth. Let a representative of each group then present its position in a class debate. Be sure to set some ground rules for how the debate will be conducted, and choose a moderator to enforce these rules. Allow time at the end of the debate for class members to discuss whether or not the research and debate changed their perspectives and, if so, in what way.

If you do this as an individual project, search recent popular and professional literature to find examples, and make up a list of the kinds of problems solved and the kinds created by technological developments. What conclusions would you draw about the role of technology in society today?

Technology and Human Progress

If the United States became a modern Erewhon, and a decision were made to eliminate all technology created after a particular date, how would it affect your life? Dramatically, to say the least. If the Erewhonian number of 271 years were selected as the cut-off date, the nation would revert back to the technology available in colonial days. If 1900 were selected, you probably wouldn't have electricity in your home or drive your own car. If 1940 were selected, many aspects of everyday life—from penicillin to microwaveable food to the personal computer—would be unavailable.

These illustrations point out both how recent many of the technologies that you now take for granted are and the way in which technology relates to your lifestyle. Technology has not fulfilled the vision of those nineteenth century writers who argued that it would create a virtual utopia. Yet it has enabled many people to live longer and healthier and at a higher standard than would have been possible in the past.

Prepotent Technologies

Recall that technology is the organization of knowledge for practical purposes. Thus, technology includes everything from the latest innovation for your personal computer to the techniques employed by therapists with their clients. Today, however, there are three types of technology that are particularly powerful and influential in terms of their effects and potential effects on human life: information technology, social engineering, and biological engineering (Lauer 1991).

The impact of information technology can be seen in such things as the use of computers for medical diagnoses, chemical analyses, and the solving of business problems. A computer chip monitors and alerts you to problems in the various systems of your automobile. Sensors developed for the space program can be used to make a thermograph of your house and spot heat loss in places with inadequate insulation. The Internet makes available to you a wealth of information from every conceivable kind of organization and group throughout the world. A magnetized strip on the back of your bank card enables you to withdraw money from banks all over the world (assuming you have money to withdraw).

These are only a few illustrations of a type of technology that continually intersects with your life in one way or another. But each type raises, as well as resolves, problems. Among other things, information technology now involves extremely complex programs, and that complexity can create problems. In 1993, for instance, Britain's nuclear regulatory agency reported safety concerns about a new nuclear power plant (Schwartz 1996). The safety concerns were not about such things as nuclear waste or leakage. Rather, the software created to monitor the plant's operation and shut it down should problems arise had been put through a series of tests and had failed nearly half of them!

Some computer programs are too complex even to test. Those that are tested, like the one at the nuclear power plant, may exhibit a certain number of failures. Unfortunately, no one knows how likely a failure is or when it might occur. If the complex program is integral to the safety of a nuclear power plant, the technology poses some risk to human health and life.

The second type of prepotent technology is **social engineering**, the use of knowledge to control human behavior and organizational processes. Various kinds of therapy have been developed to help people deal with emotional and interpersonal problems. Knowledge about organizational processes has been used by managers and consultants to enhance the effectiveness and efficiency of organizations. Social engineering, then, may intersect with your life if you need help with a problem, if you want to stop smoking, or if you go to work in an organization.

Educational and religious organizations are also affected by social engineering. Policies, programs, and sanctions are designed to control your behavior in one way or another—whether they are the grades you receive in classes or your church's requirement that you have premarital counseling before your wedding can take place.

Like information technology, social engineering creates problems. Brainwashing is a form of social engineering that was used successfully by the Communist Chinese on American prisoners of war in Korea and is used successfully by some cults when they recruit new members. Brainwashing involves physical isolation from a person's usual social network, physical deprivation in the form of minimal food and maximum activity, and continual bombardment with an ideology by friendly, concerned people.

And what do you think of motivational research? How do you feel about social scientists teaching business people ways to sell their products or market their services in the face of apathy or resistance? Advocates of neuro-linguistic programming claim that they can teach lawyers how to sway juries and business people how to sell just about anything to anyone (Conway and Siegelman 1983). In essence, neuro-linguistic programming uses the same principles as those employed in clinical hypnosis. You "get in sync" with other people and thereby influence them. This influence, incidentally, is unrecognized by the other people. Assuming such techniques work, do you believe that it is ethical to use them to sway juries, sell products, or enhance an individual's power in an organization?

The third type of prepotent technology is biological engineering. Biological engineering includes everything from organ transplants in humans to the genetic engineering of plants to make them more disease- and drought-resistant. The possibilities for enhancing the quality of human life are enormous. Among other things, gene manipulation techniques can be used to add vitamins and proteins, and to reduce fatty acids, in the foods people eat (Knauf and Facciotti 1995). Researchers also expect the time to come when gene transplantation in humans will cure various chronic diseases and genetically based disabilities such as cystic fibrosis.

Biological engineering, in other words, may be a crucial factor in your health and longevity. It may also be a factor in your life satisfaction, for advances in biological engineering have enabled many couples to bear children who would have formerly remained childless.

Yet, like information technology and social engineering, biological engineering creates problems. Blank (1988) has argued that, because of the new technologies, Americans must either confront health care policies or face a major crisis. Techniques such as organ transplants, the treatment of disabled infants, and reproductive procedures all pose dilemmas between individual and social rights. For instance, surgeons can transplant a heart into an adult and give that person additional years of life. However, the cost of the transplant is enormous. Should the money go for the care of the individual or should it be used to provide prenatal care for large numbers of poor, pregnant women who would then give birth to healthier babies?

Vexing ethical and legal issues also arise out of biological engineering. In 1985, a young woman accepted $10,000 plus medical expenses to be artificially inseminated and bear a child for an infertile couple. After giving birth to "Baby M," however, the woman said she had made a terrible mistake and that she wanted to keep the child which she now regarded as her own. At the time, there weren't any legal or ethical precedents to help the courts make a decision in the case. This is only one of a series of disputes over the past two decades arising out of the use of reproductive technologies.

Perhaps one of the most controversial challenges in biological engineering began in 1997 when a team of British scientists cloned a sheep (Kolata 1997). A **clone** is an exact biological copy that is produced asexually. The incident raised the possibility of "carbon copies" of humans (produced without sexual relations). Some people immediately called for a ban on efforts to clone humans. Others decried any effort to impede scientific progress. The issue is likely to generate considerable debate for some years to come.

How Technology Changes Society

Technology brings about social change in a number of ways (Lauer 1991). First, technology increases alternatives. People who at one time could not have children may now be able. People who at one time would have died from some disease may now have a cure available. People who at one time were limited in the kind of work they could do or the area in which they could live may now have numerous options. Or think of recreation. How many options were open to your colonial forebears?

How many different ways of engaging in recreation can you think of, and how many of those are the result of technological developments of some kind?

Second, technology changes interaction patterns. The changes may be voluntary because new alternatives are available. For instance, the automobile greatly enlarged the range of possibilities for spending leisure time; people were no longer confined to a particular location or to family and neighbors.

The changes may also be inevitable. Introducing automation in automobile plants affected the frequency and kind of interaction workers have on the job. A researcher who studied a machine plant before and after the installation of a robot found that the new technology was a mixed blessing to those workers whose jobs changed from handling metal to handling the robot control panel (Goleman 1983). All the workers praised the robot for eliminating the fatigue and physical strain from their work. Yet new sources of stress appeared. Before the robot, the worker could joke, sing, or daydream while loading the machine; the robot panel, however, required full attention. As one worker noted, he no longer had time to talk with anyone because it broke his concentration.

Third, technology creates social problems and results in additional change to deal with those problems. For example, you may have heard complaints (or made them yourself) about government regulations. For business people, these regulations are extensive and often nettlesome. How did they come about? The Constitution makes no provision for regulatory agencies. Rather, as Burke (1966) has shown, regulatory powers developed in the nineteenth century and reflected changed attitudes about the government's role in protecting people's well-being. The changed attitudes were encouraged by the use of the steam engine in river traffic. In particular, after a series of explosions of high-pressure engines in which many people were injured or killed, Congress began to consider legislation to prohibit the use of the high-pressure engines. In 1852, Congress passed a bill that set maximum allowable pressures and also established agencies to take action against those who broke the regulations.

Finally, technology brings about change through the domino effect, the tendency for any new technology to stimulate additional technological developments. A new technology may have a number of different applications; e.g., materials developed for the space program have been used for such things as protective padding in professional football helmets and non-stick cookware. The domino effect also occurs in research: scientists discover something accidentally while looking for something else. "Post-it" notes, easily stuck to and easily removed from a sheet of paper, resulted from an effort to find a super-strong glue.

As illustrated by Ruth Cowan (1976), any particular instance of technological development may include more than one or all of the above four processes. Cowan studied the "industrial revolution" in the home in the early twentieth century. She looked particularly at what happened to the middle-class housewife in the 1920s as new devices for doing housework were developed. During the 1920s, electricity replaced gaslamps in a majority of homes, and various electric appliances, from irons to washing machines, soon appeared on the market.

How did these appliances affect the average housewife? Although they are often called "labor-saving devices," they actually increased the number of household tasks. For along with the appliances came new standards for household care. Advertisers warned of the "household germ" and many women developed something close to a fetish about cleanliness, engaging in more intensive and more frequent cleaning and laundering.

As technology altered the role of the housewife, the ideology about this role also changed. Before World War I, housework was generally regarded as drudgery that, if possible, was done by servants. In the 1920s, advertisers both played on women's guilt (don't be one of those mothers whose children get ill because all the germs behind the sink have not been eliminated), and defined housework in terms of glorious mission (laundering is not a chore, but an expression of love).

In sum, the role of the middle-class housewife changed dramatically. Unlike previous generations, she no longer had paid servants in the home to do the housework. She had new appliances but they only meant higher standards to meet. In meeting those standards, she fulfilled a high calling. Thus, she had new alternatives (she could still opt to ignore the new standards) and new patterns of interaction in the home. And she was caught up in what would increasingly become a problem—the subjugation of women to housework.

The Nature and Sources of Health

Survey research that asks Americans about the important factors in their life satisfaction consistently shows that good health is at, or near, the top of the list (Watts 1981). The more health problems you experience, the more likely you are to agree with that assessment. So how satisfied are you with the health care system? Do you believe that Americans receive better health care than anyone else in the world? In terms of perceptions, Americans report less satisfaction with their health care system and more difficulties in paying for care and obtaining needed services, than do Canadians and Germans (Blendon et al. 1995). In terms of objective measures of health (**life expectancy**, infant mortality rates, days of disability due to illness, etc.), Americans tend to rank above most nations but below a few (see Table 14.1). Let's explore these issues of health that are so important to your satisfaction with life.

What Is Health?

The answer to the question may seem obvious to you. But we raise the question to stress the point that health includes both your physical and emotional well-being. You would not be considered healthy if you were severely anxious even if a physical checkup revealed no problems. And you would not be considered healthy if you had chronic arthritis even if you usually felt content and happy.

Indeed, it is unlikely that you would be physically well and emotionally unwell or vice versa. For physical illness sometimes results in emotional problems, and emotional problems can create physical symptoms or illness. For example, people who suffer a heart attack might struggle with depression afterwards as they try to come to terms with their vulnerability and mortality. But depression, it turns out, may also be a harbinger as well as a result of a heart attack. A study of 1,551 people in Baltimore identified 444 as depressed (Kolata 1996). A follow-up survey 13 years later found that those 444 were four times as likely to have suffered a heart attack as were the nondepressed.

Finally, we want to stress that health and illness are social phenomena. *Structural functionalists* make the point by viewing medicine as the social system's mechanism for maintaining health. Illness is a form of dysfunction in the system because it disrupts role functioning. Parsons (1975) pointed out that the **sick role**, the behaviors expected of those who are ill, is a socially approved way of removing people from active involvement in other roles. The sick role also includes the expectations that people will not be blamed for their illness, and that they will define it as undesirable and seek proper medical help.

Experiences

'I Have Been Robbed of a Life I Can Call My Own'

As noted in the text, some people are able to function effectively in spite of serious illness. That doesn't mean, however, that they have no struggle or regrets. Lucille just earned her doctorate and is beginning her practice as a therapist. She is also a wife and a mother. And she has lupus, a chronic inflammatory disease in which the body's immune system attacks healthy tissues and organs. In severe cases, lupus is life-threatening. Even in mild cases, it is debilitating. Lucille tells about her struggles:

> Lupus is a bizarre, cruel disease. It can destroy your will to live and your ability to cope.
>
> When I first became ill, no one seemed to understand what I was going through. At times, I still feel like I have been robbed of a life I can call my own. ☞

☞ I had the disease for five years before I finally found a doctor who diagnosed it. People thought I was a hypochondriac. Friends and family saw me looking well one moment and distressed the next. My family went from annoyance to anger to distress. My former doctor sent me to a psychiatrist because he said nothing was physically wrong with me.

When the disease was finally diagnosed, I felt relief that it had a name and that I wasn't crazy. But I felt distress because this illness would alter all of my plans and dreams. I asked the doctor if I was going to die soon. She couldn't answer the question with any certainty. In the days following, I experienced intense fear and anxiety. I had frightening nightmares. I felt fatigued, helpless, and fearful of becoming dependent on others.

At times, I have been so exhausted I could barely lift my arm to attend to my personal needs. But my husband has stood by me and remained optimistic and encouraging. Eventually, I began to focus on living moment by moment and hour by hour. I came to accept the disease, and the fact that this was my life and I had to live it.

Right now, the disease is in remission. My doctor asked me what kept me going when I had active lupus. I told her I had a mother with an iron will—perhaps I learned from her. My will, of course, can't make the disease disappear. It may become active again. But, with the help of God and my family, I won't let it destroy my spirit.

Social Factors in Health and Illness

What keeps you healthy? What makes you sick? Genes, stress, bacteria, and viruses are all part of the technical answer to the questions. But equally important are the social factors in health and illness.

One important social factor is social class. Conflict theorists point out that social inequality includes differential access to medical care. Medicine, like everything else in a capitalist society, is driven by profit, and it is more profitable to focus on the needs of the well-to-do who are able to afford the best in medical care. Those in the lower classes, therefore, receive less adequate care than those in the upper classes (Feinstein 1993).

Ironically, those in the lower classes also suffer more illnesses. Compared to people in the middle- and upper-strata, those in the lower class have more physical and emotional health problems, more days of restricted activity due to illness, less knowledge about health care services, fewer good health practices such as not smoking and a proper diet, less likelihood of obtaining basic preventive health measures like vaccinations, and less likelihood of carrying health insurance (Feinstein 1993; National Center for Health Statistics 1995; Sundquist 1995).

Social roles are a second factor in health and illness. Many physical and emotional disorders are related to stress, and some roles are inherently more stressful than others. In particular, a number of occupational roles and the traditional female role are related to higher rates of illness. Occupational roles may create high levels of stress because of the work environment (e.g., working with hazardous materials), the nature of the job (such as routine, repetitive work), or the nature of a particular workplace (e.g., a tyrannical boss).

With regard to the female role, although women live longer than men, they have higher rates of illness and make greater use of health care services than do men (Kessler et al. 1994). The higher rates of female illness are probably related to certain characteristics of the traditional female role (Lauer 1997). Traditionally, women are more emotionally involved than are men in the lives of family and friends. Such involvement carries with it the likelihood of greater stress when there are problems in the lives of family members and friends.

The traditional role of the married woman—the role of staying home and taking care of the house and children—is also stressful. Indeed, married mothers who work outside the home are healthier than those who do not. Of course, some women prefer the traditional role and find satisfaction in it. The important thing is to be able to choose. The more satisfied an individual is with his or her roles, the better health that person is likely to have (Wickrama et al. 1995).

The economy is a third factor in health and illness. The transition to industrial economies and to a world economy is related to health and illness in a number of ways. A major source of viral diseases is the movement of people, plants, animals, and products around the world, carrying microbes that are new to particular places or particular populations (Henig 1993). An infectious virus can literally travel around the world in a matter of hours, infecting people who have no prior exposure and no immunity.

Agricultural and industrial workers in modern economies are exposed to carcinogenic materials. As we shall discuss in the next chapter, modern economies also mean that people generally are exposed to a wide variety of pollutants. In Poland, for example, heavily industrialized areas adversely affect people's health (Indulski and Rolecki 1995). Among other things, in comparison to other European countries the Poles have experienced a shortening of their life expectancy (the average number of years people can expect to live), higher rates of cancer and cardiovascular disease, and a higher infant death rate.

Finally, fluctuations in the economy affect health and illness. As noted in the last chapter, both underemployment and unemployment adversely affect both physical and emotional health.

The government is a fourth factor in health and illness. Government funding and policies are important factors in such things as access to medical care. Without Medicaid and Medicare, for example, many, if not most, poor and elderly people would have even less adequate medical care than they have now.

However, the government enters the picture in another way. Consider this: what do you think is the major factor in improved health over the past two centuries? The answer is not improved medical technology and care. Medicine's contribution has increased considerably in the twentieth century. It has been estimated that three of the seven years' increase in life expectancy since 1950 can be attributed to medical care (Bunker 1995). But rates of many infectious diseases that killed people in the past, such as tuberculosis, declined dramatically before physicians knew their cause or had the drugs to treat them.

Rather than medicine, improved nutrition and public health measures (such as sanitation and clean water) have been largely responsible for the decline of infectious diseases and increased life expectancy. Public health measures are the government's responsibility. Public health agencies today also contribute to health through such things as education about good health behavior and diseases, and through the indentification of health hazards in communities (Kisely and Jones 1995).

Extent and Consequences of Health Problems

The chances are high that you or someone in your immediate family has already had to deal with a serious health problem. Americans and those in other developed nations are generally healthier than people in third-world countries. But health problems touch every life at some time or another.

Extent of Physical and Mental Illness

Advances in health in the United States are reflected in the statistics on life expectancy. In 1900, life expectancy was 46.3 years for males and 48.3 years for females; in 1994 the figures were 72.3 years for males and 79.0 years for females (U.S. Bureau of the Census 1975:55 and 1996d:88). A substantial part of the increased longevity is due to lower rates of infant mortality and lower rates of death from infectious diseases.

What are the diseases most likely to cause death? Table 14.2 shows major causes of death today. Except for 1918, when an influenza epidemic was the major cause of death, diseases of the heart have been at the top of the list since 1900 (U.S. Bureau of the Census 1975: 58). However, death rates from heart disease have tended to decline since 1979, and if the trend continues, cancer may replace heart disease as the leading cause of death by the year 2000 (Nelson 1992).

Table 14.2	Major Causes of Death in the U.S.	
	Cause	**Rate per 100,000**
	Diseases of the heart	281.2
	Malignant neoplasms (cancer)	204.7
	Cerebrovascular diseases	60.2
	Chronic pulmonary diseases	39.9
	Accidents (including motor vehicle)	34.1
	Pneumonia and influenza	31.8

**Table 14.2
(Continued)**   **Major Causes of Death in the U.S**

Diabetes mellitus	22.5
AIDS	16.2
Suicide	11.8
Chronic liver disease and cirrhosis	9.5
All other causes	168.2

Source: Rosenberg et al. 1996

The major cause of death varies by age (Rosenberg et al. 1996). From birth through the age of 24, accidents are the leading cause of death. In 1995, **AIDS** (acquired immune deficiency syndrome) was the leading cause of death among those aged 15–24. And cancer was the leading cause for those between 45 and 64 years.

The leading causes of death are similar for those of different races, except that African Americans are seven times more likely than whites to be murdered (U.S. Bureau of the Census 1996d, p. 97). Moreover, while

EXTENSIONS

Some Global Health Comparisons

Table 14.2 shows that the leading causes of death in the United States are chronic diseases. As noted in the text, heart disease has been the most common cause of death since at least 1900. But cancer, the second leading cause of death, caused fewer deaths than infectious diseases like tuberculosis until the early 1920s and fewer than influenza until the late 1930s.

Generally, in the developed nations today, chronic diseases are the major causes of death. But the rates differ enormously between nations, as figure 14.1 shows for heart disease. The variations shown in the figure reflect, among other things, diverse lifestyles (including eating patterns, smoking rates, and stress).

In contrast to the developed nations, infectious diseases are the major cause of death in third-world nations. And the infectious diseases, including some of those against which progress had been made, are on the rise. The World Health Organization declared a global tuberculosis emergency in 1993. Tuberculosis is the greatest killer of adults in the world.

It is estimated that 10.4 million people in East Asia and 13.4 million in Africa will die in the 1990s from tuberculosis (compared to 120,000 in North America). And the problem is compounded by the fact that new strains of tuberculosis have emerged that are resistant to the drugs now used to treat it.

Malaria is another deadly infectious disease on the rise. Between one and three million people died of malaria in 1996. Malaria has killed 10 times as many children as war since the mid-1980s. Unfortunately, this disease is also becoming resistant to the medications that have been used to treat it.

The challenge of infectious diseases, then, is twofold. On the one hand, public **health** measures are needed to curb the spread. On the other hand, medical **science** must find new ways (including new drugs) to cope with the diseases because existing treatments are no longer effective.

Sources: Africa Research Bulletin, March 1996; Kristof 1997; U.S. Bureau of the Census 1996d.

Figure 14.1   **Death Rates from Heart Disease**

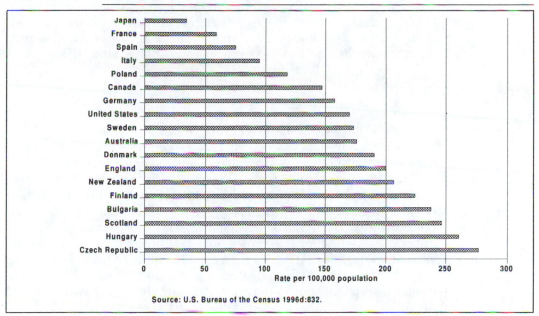

Source: U.S. Bureau of the Census 1996d:832.

the leading causes of death are similar for men and women, there are differences in health problems (Verbrugge 1985). Compared to men, women tend to have higher rates of acute (short-term) diseases, short-term disabilities, and nonfatal chronic diseases. Men tend to have more injuries, more visual and hearing problems, and higher rates of the fatal chronic diseases such as diseases of the heart.

Mental illness includes a wide variety of disorders (American Psychiatric Association 1987). Among the more common are substance use disorders (such as drug abuse), anxiety disorders (including phobias and obsessive-compulsive behavior), affective disorders (such as manic-depressive reaction, a problem of extreme fluctuations in emotions), schizophrenic disorders (those that involve such thinking disorders as hallucinations and fantasies), and personality disorders (such as narcissism, an obsession with personal needs, desires, and image).

How common are such problems? One of the most comprehensive studies involved a national probability sample of 8,098 Americans aged 15 to 54 (Kessler et al. 1994). The researchers found that nearly half of the respondents reported at least one lifetime disorder and nearly 30 percent reported a disorder in the preceding twelve months. The most common disorders reported were depression, alcohol dependence, and phobias of various kinds.

The researchers also found some sex differences. Women have more affective and anxiety disorders, while men have more problems with substance abuse and higher rates of antisocial personality disorder. Finally, rates varied by age and social class, with higher rates of most disorders reported in the younger age groups and the lower socioeconomic strata. Other research confirms the higher rate of depression among women— about double that among men; and the highest rate is found among black women in the 35 to 44 year age group (Blazer et al. 1994).

AIDS

What disease do you most fear? When we asked the question, a number of students said "AIDS." It is a fearsome disease, for there is no cure and the infected individual can develop rare cancers or suffer serious brain damage as the immune system collapses and the individual slowly dies.

HIV, the virus that causes AIDS, spreads through blood or semen. Some people have been infected by blood transfusions given before blood was tested for the virus. The major ways that people are infected, however, are through sex or sharing drug needles and syringes with an infected person. Pregnant women who are infected can also pass the virus on to the fetus. AIDS has been called a "global epidemic" because of the large number of people infected with HIV (Purvis 1997). Keep in mind, however, that not all those infected with the virus have developed AIDS. And at this point, it is not known if all those who test HIV positive inevitably will develop AIDS.

Over 60 percent of those infected with the virus are in sub-Saharan Africa—some 14 million people. Another 5.2 million in South and Southeast Asia are infected. About 750,000 North Americans have the virus.

In the United States, the AIDS virus spreads mainly through male homosexual activity and intravenous drug use. Of all AIDS cases reported through 1995, 85.6 percent were male and 45.3 percent were between 30 and 39 years of age (U.S. Bureau of the Census 1996d, p. 142). A disproportionate number of the cases were African Americans— 35.1 percent; 48.9 percent were white and 14.8 percent were Hispanic.

In other areas of the world, the AIDS virus spreads primarily through heterosexual activity, particularly through the use of prostitutes. About half of the prostitutes in Bombay, India, for example, are infected. In most areas of the world, about 20 percent of the victims are female. In sub-Saharan Africa however, over half are female. Is AIDS truly an epidemic? In terms of the number of people who die from it each year, it certainly ranks far below other infectious diseases (see Extensions, this chapter). And deaths from AIDS may be declining. Nevertheless, it has generated enormous concern, considerable funding for research, and a reputation as one of the more dreaded scourges of the modern world.

Consequences of Health Problems

Think about a time when you, or someone close to you, was seriously ill. What are the three most negative things you recall about the experience? As you recall them, you will relive to some extent the personal and interpersonal consequences of health problems.

One obvious consequence is suffering. The suffering includes both physical and emotional pain. In fact, as noted earlier, any physical problem will likely bring with it some emotional upset, and any emotional problem will likely result in some physical symptoms.

Illness, secondly, has consequences for interpersonal relationships. An illness can put new demands on a spouse or family member. It can alter relationships with friends. Karp (1994) interviewed 35 people who had been treated for depression and found that they longed to be connected to others but were incapable of relating intimately. Those who are depressed also believe that nondepressed people cannot understand them and that openly admitting the problem is stigmatizing.

Third, illness affects your role functioning. Recall that the sick role releases you from responsibilities of other roles. However, when a role involves obligations to others, such as spouse, parent, or employee, you may feel constrained to continue to fulfill at least some of the obligations. You may do so, however, in a way that is not fully satisfactory either to yourself or to the others.

Finally, illness may raise a number of personal issues. Illness disrupts your life. You can't do things you normally do. You may be anxious about the costs of treating your illness, or about the implications the illness has for your long-term health. If the illness is a chronic one, you will probably have to deal with a sense of loss, adjustments to a different lifestyle, and questions about the kind of person you are (Charmaz 1995). And the first time you experience a very serious illness, you may find yourself confronting your own vulnerability and mortality for the first time in your life.

Social Issues in Health and Illness

How good is the health care available to you? What will it be like in the future? Are there ways in which you can get involved in enhancing your own health? Do you believe that you have the right, if you have a terminal disease, to receive help in bringing about your own death? These are some of the social issues surrounding health and illness today.

The Quality of Health Care

At the beginning of the chapter, we noted that Americans are less satisfied with their health care than are people in a number of other nations. This doesn't mean that the American health care system is inferior to those of other nations. Here, then, we will not try to evaluate the various systems, but simply explore why Americans express dissatisfaction. We suggest that the dissatisfaction stems from three factors in the system:

One factor is the cost of health care. Especially for those without health insurance, the cost of care is so high that many Americans have called for government action to implement a national health plan. President Clinton promised such a plan when he took office in 1993. As of this writing, it has not materialized.

A second factor is those patients who suffer as a result of treatment. **Iatrogenic** problems, those caused by physicians in the course of their treatment, are not as common as they were in the past. But they still occur. The problem may be one of putting a patient through the trauma of unnecessary surgery. Barron (1989) estimated that about 20 percent of pacemaker operations are unnecessary. Or the problem may be human error or incompetence. A study of 12 hospitals concluded that a fourth of patient deaths were due to medical errors, ranging from prescribing the wrong drugs to misdiagnosis (Scott 1988). And 53 family physicians who were interviewed in depth described their most serious errors; out of 53 cases reported, 25 resulted in the patient's death (Ely et al. 1995). The physicians attributed the errors to such factors as hurry, distraction, lack of knowledge, and premature diagnosis.

A portion of iatrogenic problems lie in the fact that medicine is an inexact science. A diagnosis may be a judgment call rather than a correct reading of precise data. And the diagnosis and treatment of mental illness are even more inexact than those of physical illness. Therapists are influenced by such things as the sex, race, and social class of a patient (Dixon, Gordon, and Khomusi 1995). In an experiment, researchers gave 209 psychiatrists two case studies to evaluate (Loring and Powell 1988). Both patients had a schizophrenic disorder, but the psychiatrists were only given information about symptoms and, in some cases, the sex and race of the patients. Interestingly, most of the psychiatrists correctly diagnosed the problem when no information on sex or race was given. But when information on sex and race was included, less than a majority made a correct diagnosis and only 21 percent made the correct diagnosis when the patients were said to be white females.

A third factor of importance is the organization of medical care. Increasingly, health care occurs in the context of "managed care," which means that your physician or therapist works for an organization that controls not only the cost but also decisions about treatment (Leyerle 1994). Thus, your doctor may believe that you need a certain test, but the test may be disallowed by staffers at the health care organization. A physician friend told us of an instance when a test he ordered was refused. He angrily called the official who had denied the test and told him that this decision might result in the patient's death. After some angry exchanges, the official finally allowed the test.

Managed care means that health care is driven by the profit motive. Throughout the nation, not-for-profit hospitals are being sold to profit-making enterprises (Miller 1997). What will happen to such things as emergency rooms, charity cases, and typically unprofitable units such as burn centers and facilities for AIDS patients? At this point, no one knows. There is already some evidence, however, that certain groups will not fare well under managed care. In particular, a study of 2,235 patients in Boston, Chicago, and Los Angeles found that the elderly and the poor did not do as well, in terms of an improved health status, under managed care as they did under fee-for-service plans (the use of conventional insurance to pay doctors for each service performed) (Ware et al. 1996).

In sum, medical science continues to make breakthroughs and to develop ever-more sophisticated technology. Yet the present trend in medical care suggests that the quality of your health care will decline rather than improve in the near future.

Promoting Health: Preventive Measures

Fortunately, your health depends upon your choices as well as upon the health care system. You can do a number of things to enhance your health status and to minimize problems of illness. You probably already know that regular exercise, a balanced and low-fat diet, and avoidance of drug abuse (including alcohol and tobacco) help maximize your health status.

Unfortunately, many Americans do not take these preventive measures. As many as 250,000 Americans die each year because they do not exercise regularly (U.S. Department of Health and Human Services 1995). More than 60 percent of adults do not exercise regularly, and a fourth never exercise. Even among those aged 12 to 21 years, just under half exercise regularly, and 14 percent report no recent physical activity (U.S. Department of Health and Human Services 1996). Among young people, inactivity is more common among females than males, and among black females than white females. Among adults, inactivity is more prevalent among females than males, among African Americans and Hispanics than whites, and among those in the lower strata than those in the higher strata.

A balanced diet is important so that your body receives all the nutrients it needs, and a low-fat diet is important to maintain a healthy weight and ward off certain illnesses. But the per capital consumption of fat increased from 52.6 pounds in 1970 to 66.9 pounds in 1994 (U.S. Bureau of the Census 1996d, p. 147). At least a third of adults and a fifth of adolescents in the United States are overweight, and overweight appears to be increasing rather than decreasing (U.S. Department of Health and Human Services 1995). Overweight is more prevalent among some racial and ethnic groups than it is among whites; nearly half of black and Mexican American women are overweight.

Finally, drug use and abuse continues to take its toll, as noted in Chapter Seven. The most dramatic progress occurred in the decline in smoking, the result of intensive government and medical efforts to educate the public on its hazards. Among adult males, the proportion of smokers declined from 51.9 percent in 1965 to 25.0 percent in 1993; among adult females, the decline was from 33.9 percent in 1965 to 22.5 percent in 1993 (U.S. Bureau of the Census 1996d, p. 145). Still, drug abuse is the main preventable cause of illness and premature death in the United States. Each year about 400,000 deaths result from cigarette smoking, l00,000 from alcohol abuse, and 20,00 from the use of illegal drugs (Centers for Disease Control 1995).

The Right to Die

The right to die became a national issue during the 1990s after a Michigan doctor helped a number of people with terminal diseases commit suicide. The issue is complex. Think of it in terms of your responses to the following. Should physicians use all available means to keep people alive? If your answer is no, then should people have the right to refuse life-sustaining treatment such as a heart-lung machine? If your answer is yes, should they have that right even if there is some question about whether their illness is terminal? Finally, should people have the right to physician-assisted suicide?

As may be obvious from the questions, the issue is one of values and beliefs. On the one hand are those who argue that life is sacred and that those who want to end their own life are "playing God" (Paris and Poorman 1995). Many who hold this belief are willing to concede an individual's right to refuse life-sustaining treatment, but not the right to assisted suicide. They also point out that some people express the wish to die and then later change their minds. A study of 200 terminally ill patients reported that 44.5 percent said they *occasionally* wished that death would come soon; only 8.5 percent indicated a serious and continuing desire to die (Chochinov et al. 1995). If physician-assisted suicide were readily available, some might opt for it who would have later changed their minds.

On the other hand, there are those who argue that, while life is indeed sacred, there is no moral duty to preserve it under all circumstances (Paris and Poorman 1995). A few legal decisions support this position. For example, a 1996 court decision ruled that New York State was discriminatory in allowing patients to refuse life-sustaining treatment and not allowing them to end their lives with physician-prescribed drugs (Hermann 1996). And in 1994, Oregon became the first state to allow physician-assisted suicide under specified circumstances (Mullens 1995). As of this writing Oregon is considering the repeal of this law, and the issue of the right to die is under review by the Supreme Court.

Apart from the moral and legal battles, there is the actual practice of assisting death. A national survey of physicians reported that in 39 percent of 2257 cases of death, the physician decided to withdraw or withhold treatment in order to hasten death (Pijnenborg et al. 1995). In over half of the cases, the physician made the decision without any involvement on the part of the patient. And many physicians take the next step, and help terminally ill patients commit suicide by prescribing fatal doses of pain-killing narcotics (Borg 1996). Critical-care nurses sometimes do the same (Asch 1996).

Whatever the courts ultimately decide, then, some of those who work most closely with terminally ill patients accept the right to die. The issue is one thing in the abstract. It is another when you are attending to someone in extreme pain who is going to die in a short time whatever you do.

Critical Thinking Exercise

A number of lawsuits have been brought against manufacturers of silicone breast implants on the grounds that the implants result in serious health problems. As reported in a popular magazine, some medical and legal experts believe that the supposed detrimental effects of the implants are questionable conclusions based on "junk science" (Nash 1996). An Oregon judge agreed and said that the evidence lacked scientific credibility. A law professor cautioned against too hasty a conclusion, noting that plaintiffs were finally proven right about the adverse effects of asbestos and the Dalkon Shield (a contraceptive device). But the writer of the article praised the Oregon judge for trying to "apply rational standards" to a difficult case.

What kinds of questions would you raise about the popular article? What kinds of questions would you pose to the judge? How would you go about trying to determine for yourself whether the implants pose a health hazard?

Summary

Technology and science (the knowledge gained by systematic, rational observation) may be used to exploit and oppress as well as to enhance well-being. Science is socially constructed knowledge. As a way to gain knowledge and solve human problems, science can be contrasted with reliance on the supernatural, reliance on authority, intuition, and abstract reasoning.

Science as a method involving observation and inference emerged in the seventeenth century. Its development was stimulated by the founding of the Royal Society in London in 1662. A disproportionate number of the members were Puritans, and a number of Puritan ideas facilitated scientific work. Science grew slowly until about 1850, when it was institutionalized in Western society through the development of standardized knowledge and procedures, research universities, and specialized scientific organizations.

A number of social factors are involved in the progress of science. Groups that hold to certain values and beliefs—naturalism, learning and knowledge, human dignity, dedication to purposeful work, egalitarianism, antitradition, and a focus on this world—are more productive of scientists and scientific work. The government's commitment to science and the economy's health are important factors in a society's ability to pursue scientific work. Competition of some sort seems to foster scientific and technological progress. The competition may be between nations, organizations, or individuals.

There are three types of technology that are particularly powerful and influential in terms of their effects, and potential effects, on human life: information technology, social engineering, and biological engineering. Each type creates as well as solves problems. Technology changes society by increasing alternatives, changing interaction patterns, creating social problems, and the domino effect.

Health is central to life satisfaction. Health includes both physical and emotional well-being. There are a number of social factors that affect health and illness, including social class, social roles, the economy, and the government.

As indicated by increasing life expectancy, progress has been made in health. The chronic diseases are most likely to result in death in the developed nations, while infectious diseases kill more people in the third world. Diseases of the heart have been the number one cause of death in the U.S. since at least 1900. The most common mental disorders are depression, alcohol dependence, and phobias. There are some differences in both physical and mental illness patterns among men and women.

AIDS has been called a global epidemic. It does not kill as many people as other infectious diseases or the chronic diseases, but tens of millions of people worldwide carry the virus. In the United States the virus is transmitted mainly through homosexual and intravenous drug activity. Heterosexual contact is primarily responsible for its spread in other parts of the world. Among the consequences of health problems are suffering, altered interpersonal relationships, changed role functioning, and a number of personal issues. Social issues surrounding health and illness that confront the nation today are the quality of health care, preventive health measures, and the right to die.

Glossary

AIDS acquired immune deficiency syndrome, a disease that causes the immune system to stop functioning and leads to death

clone an exact biological copy that is produced asexually

health a state of physical and emotional well-being

iatrogenic caused by the physician in the course of treating a patient

life expectancy the average number of years people can expect to live

science the knowledge gained by systematic, rational observation

sick role the behavioral expectations for those who are ill

social engineering the use of knowledge to control human behavior and organizational processes

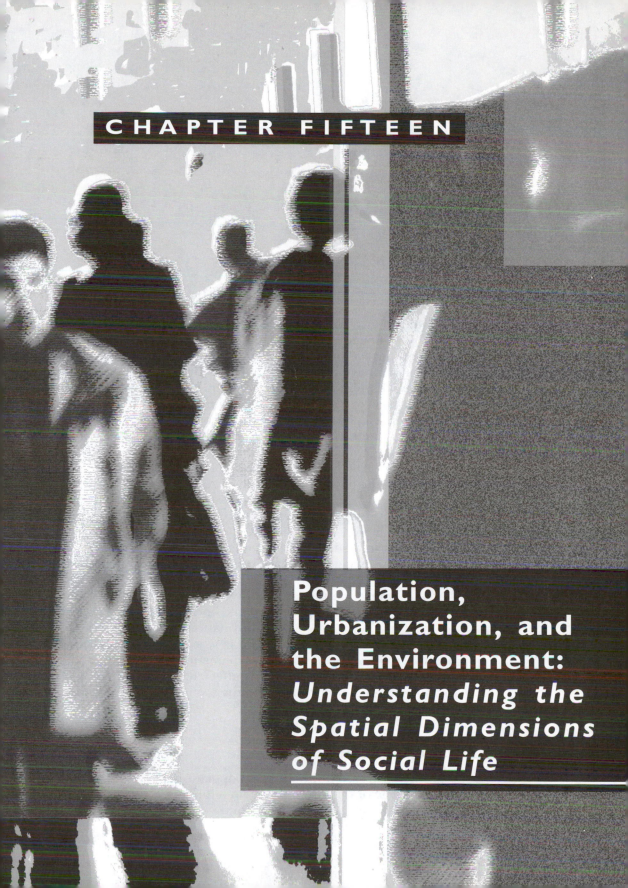

Population, Urbanization, and the Environment: *Understanding the Spatial Dimensions of Social Life*

How many, if any, children do you plan to have? How would you feel if the government placed a one-child limit on all couples and imposed penalties on those who exceeded the limit? How would you react if the government ordered you to live and work in a rural rather than urban area? These questions may sound absurd to you, but they reflect actual policies and practices in China where the government has tried to control population growth and bolster the economy.

The Chinese methods may be unacceptable to you (as they are to many Chinese), but they illustrate the intensity of the government's concern over the growth and distribution of population. In part, this concern reflects the desire for a healthy, growing economy. In part, the concern stems from the menacing environmental impact of a growing and increasingly urban population.

Population, urbanization, and the environment are interrelated issues. And they are issues for all nations. You might not think of the United States as having a population problem, but consider this: a child born in the United States will, during its lifetime, have a 35 times greater impact on the environment than a child in India and more than 250 times the impact of a child born in one of the sub-Saharan African nations (Population Information Network 1996).

It's not surprising, then, that there is worldwide concern about population, urbanization, and the environment. How can you understand that concern? How is human life affected by such things as the size and distribution of population? How are population, urbanization, and the environment interrelated?

Population and Population Trends

Demography is the scientific study of population. In this section, we will look at a few of the topics that demographers study—including the manner in which population size and composition affect everything from crime rates (the greater the proportion of young males in the population, the higher the crime rates) to job opportunities to your chances of marriage. These are topics that are important for social as well as your individual well-being.

Components of Population

One important component of population is *size*. As of 1996, the world's population stood at 5.77 billion and the U.S. population was 265.2 million (Population Reference Bureau 1996). China is the most populous nation of the world, with 1.22 billion people. In other words, more than one of every five people in the world is Chinese!

The *age and sex composition* of the population is a second component. In the United States, females comprise 51.2 percent of the population, and the median age of the population is 34.3 years (U.S. Bureau of the Census 1996d, p. 15). Both sex and age composition shift over time, however. For most of nation's history, males have outnumbered females. The number of females exceeded the number of males for the first time in 1940, and women have remained a majority since 1946 (U.S. Bureau of the Census 1975, p. 9).

The population of the United States has also grown older (however, the population of Japan and most affluent European nations is older). In 1800, the median age of the population was 16.0 years (U.S. Bureau of the Census 1975, p. 19). By 1900, it was 22.9 years, and it reached 30.0 years in 1980 (U.S. Bureau of the Census 1996d, p. 5). The U.S. population is now older than that of many nations. In 1996, 7.3 percent of Americans were under the age of five, compared to 10.7 percent of the world as a whole, and 12.8 percent were 65 or older, compared to 6.5 percent of the world as a whole (U.S. Bureau of the Census 1996d, p. 830).

A third important component of population is the growth rate. A benchmark used by demographers is the amount of time it takes for a population to double in size. That time has shrunk dramatically through the ages (Cohen 1996). At the time of Christ, the world had about 250 million people. It required 1,650 years for the population to double to 500 million, but less than 200 years (to 1830) for it to double again. The population doubled again in 100 years and once more in the next 45 years. Such facts give demographers and others cause for alarm.

How fast is the world's population growing now? A sustained 2 percent growth rate means a doubling of the population in 35 years. You can see present trends in table 15.1.

Table 15.1	**Population Growth Rates in Selected Nations**

Nation	Annual Growth Rate, 1990-2000
World	1.4
Afghanistan	5.9
Australia	1.1
Brazil	1.2
France	0.4
Germany	0.8
Iran	3.7
Kenya	2.4
Mexico	1.9
Nigeria	3.0
Spain	0.2
United Kingdom	0.3
United States	1.0

Source: U.S. Bureau of the Census 1996d, pp. 827-29

The rates vary considerably. Keep in mind that the rates must be sustained for this doubling to occur. If the above rates are sustained, the world population will double in 50 years. Iran's population will double in 19 years, the United States' in 70 years, and Spain's in 330 years.

As the table suggests, the highest rates of growth are in the developing nations. Growth rates in the developing nations are, on the average, 19 times higher than those in the developed nations (Population Reference Bureau 1996).

Thinking Critically

In 1798, minister and economist Thomas Malthus published a dire warning about population growth, claiming that populations tend to grow faster than the food supply. In 1968, a modern Malthusian, biologist Paul Ehrlich (1968), warned that the human race was on a suicidal course because of rampant population growth. A few years later, he wrote: "Man is not only running out of food, he is also destroying the life support systems of the Spaceship Earth" (Ehrlich 1971, p. 364). But the appalling consequences Ehrlich predicted did not happen. Among other things, the rate of population growth has slowed and technological breakthroughs have increased food production. Nevertheless, he and his wife repeated the warning in 1990 (Ehrlich and Ehrlich 1990), noting that at least 200 million people, most of them children, had died of hunger and related diseases since the 1968 book appeared. They also noted that the earth has far less topsoil and groundwater for growing crops than it had in 1968.

Without minimizing the importance of the issues raised, we would point out that the dire warnings of catastrophe predicted by Malthus and the Ehrlichs have not come to pass. Are their conclusions reasonable? Yes. However, they are not the only conclusions that can be drawn from existing knowledge. It is reasonable to argue that there are limits to the size of the population that can be sustained by the earth. But no one really knows what those limits are, and the limits can be expanded somewhat by technological advances. We take Malthus and the Ehrlichs seriously; we do not take them as an infallible guide.

Components of Population Growth

What accounts for growth rates such as those shown in table 15.1? One obvious factor is birth rates. The **crude birth rate** is the number of births in one year per 1,000 persons. As you would expect, the crude birth rate varies considerably among nations. Afghanistan's rate of 43.0 is nearly three times as high as the United States' rate of 14.8, which is 1.5 times as high as Italy's rate of 9.9 (U.S. Bureau of the Census 1996d, p. 831).

A number of factors explain the differing birth rates. For example, cultural values, including religious beliefs, may lead people to believe that they should have or need to have numerous children. *Feminist theorists* view such values and beliefs as an expression of male domination because multiple pregnancies serve both to emphasize women's mothering and homemaker roles and (in some societies) to demonstrate men's manliness. Furthermore, if women are continually involved in child-bearing and child-rearing, they will remain dependent upon their husbands for their sustenance.

In his analysis of *existing data* from three censuses, Heim (1996) showed the impact of culture. He compared the birth rates between immigrant and native-born women in California from 1970 to 1990. She found that the immigrant birth rates were higher than those of the native-born women and that the higher birth rates reflected the countries from which the women had come. As the women, or more particularly their children, become assimilated into American culture, their birth rates will probably drop.

Education also influences birth rates. Historically, birth rates fall as women gain education and move into the labor force (Lauer 1997). Education and job opportunities give women new perspectives and open up new possibilities that cannot be pursued if women are consumed in child-bearing and child-rearing. Moreover, education usually provides women with greater knowledge about their sexuality. What would you think of a situation in which a fifteen-year-old girl about to give birth to her first child comes to a physician, not knowing that she is pregnant and with no idea that sexual intercourse led to her pregnancy? Impossible, you think? It happens to girls such as Somalia Maria, who lives in Brazil, who is illiterate, and who never had anyone tell her the "facts of life" (Goering and Luft 1996).

Government action impacts birth rates too. Certainly, it is important for government to support the formal education of women (in many developing nations women are less likely than men to get an education). In addition, family planning programs are effective. That is, providing women with information and with contraceptives has lowered birth rates in a number of nations (Crossette 1996).

Death rates are the second component of population growth. The **crude death rate** is the number of deaths in one year per 1,000 persons.

Like birth rates, death rates vary considerably between nations. Afghanistan's rate of 18.2 is slightly more than double the United States' rate of 8.8, which is nearly double Mexico's rate of 4.6 (U.S. Bureau of the Census 1996d, p. 831).

Various factors are responsible for the differing death rates. One is the age composition of a nation. Nations with a larger proportion of older people are likely to have higher death rates. A second factor is the health care system of the nation. Modern and generally accessible health care systems contribute to lower death rates. Third, other factors—diet, lifestyles, and economic status—also affect mortality rates.

These factors account for different mortality rates among groups within a nation as well. For example, an analysis of mortality rates in the United States concluded that Asian American rates, which are lower than those of other races, reflect a combination of healthy lifestyles and socioeconomic advantages (Rogers, Hummer, Nam, and Peters 1996). White rates are somewhat higher, primarily because of cigarette smoking. And Mexican American, American Indian, and African American rates are still higher, mainly because of socioeconomic disadvantages.

Migration, the movement of people from one area to another, is the third component of population growth. Migration may be involuntary (e.g., people displaced by war) or it may be voluntary (e.g., people who seek better opportunities). Migration occurs both within and between nations. Not all movement within a nation is viewed as migration. Demographers do not consider a change of residence within a city or a county as migration, only that which crosses county lines. That is, if you move from one county to another within the same state, or from one state to another, you are officially a migrant and you have added to the population growth of the area to which you move.

The migration that is a component of a nation's population growth, of course, is that which involves people coming from other nations. The **immigration rate** is the number of people who have come into the country in one year per 1,000 population. In the United States, that rate has varied from an average of 10.4 in the first decade of the twentieth century to 0.4 during the 1930s (U.S. Bureau of the Census 1996, p. 10).

Figure 15.1 shows how the three components—birth rates, death rates, and immigration rates—have varied in the United States since 1970. Note that birth and death rates have both fluctuated, but the rates in the 1990s were lower than those in 1970. Immigration rates have gone up. The large increase in immigration rates after 1989, incidentally, reflects the granting of permanent residence under an amnesty program to people who had entered the country illegally.

The population growth of any year can be computed by subtracting the death rate from the birth rate and adding the net immigration rate. "Net" immigration rate refers to the fact that migration may flow out of, as well as into, a country. Migration out of the United States is quite small.

Figure 15.1 **Components of Population Growth in the U.S.**

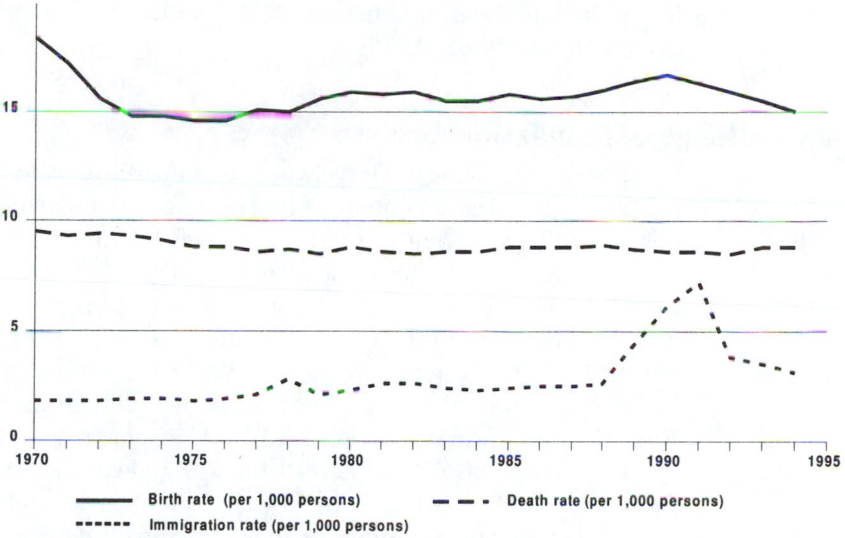

Sources: U.S. Bureau of the Census 1990:9, 62, and 1996d:10, 74.

Thus, in 1994, the birth rate was 15.0, the death rate was 8.8, and the immigration rate was 3.1. The population gain, then, was 15.0 - 8.8 + 3.1, or 9.3 per 1,000 population.

Obviously, the larger the gap between the birth and death rates, the greater the population growth. In fact, it was precisely a widening of the gap after 1750 that resulted in the second doubling of the world population we noted earlier. The widened gap is a part of what demographers call the **demographic transition**, the change from high birth and death rates to low birth and death rates. The demographic transition tends to accompany economic development.

In Europe, the transition accompanied industrialization (Wrigley 1974). Around the middle of the eighteenth century, birth and death rates were both high, with a resulting modest population increase. But as industrialization expanded and health conditions improved, death rates fell dramatically. The population increased rapidly because birth rates remained high. Eventually, by about 1880, birth rates began to decline also, but the death rates were still falling so the population continued to grow rapidly. Finally, birth and death rates both reached relatively low levels, a process not completed until the 1930s. Since then, European population has grown very slowly.

The same process occurred in the United States. In colonial days and the early years of the nation, birth and death rates were both high. In 1800, the birth rate was 55.0, nearly four times the 1994 rate (U.S. Bureau of the Census 1975, p. 49)! Unfortunately, death rates are only available for the entire nation back to 1900. In that year, however, the death rate was 17.2 and the birth rate was 32.3. That's a gap of 15.1, compared to the gap of 8.2 in the late 1930s and 6.2 for 1994. The United States had completed the transition by the 1930s.

The Challenge of Population Growth

The population is too large when resources are inadequate to support people at their desired quality of life, or when the environmental damage has reached a level that jeopardizes people's health and well-being. As we pointed out earlier, technological developments can raise the limit to new levels. At the present level of technology, it has been estimated that the world already has three times the population it could sustain at the standard of living of Western Europe (Van 1996). Or, put somewhat differently, for everyone now living to have a standard as high as that of Western Europe, the natural resources of two additional earths would be needed.

Whether technological developments can ever raise the standards of the entire earth's population to those of the West is debatable. Yet it is clear that if the developing nations are to achieve any kind of economic growth at all, they must go through the demographic transition (Schmid 1995). High rates of population growth more than consume any benefits of economic growth. For example, because of improved agricultural methods there were large gains in grain production in Rwanda between 1950 and 1994 (Brown 1995). But because Rwanda has a very high birth rate, by 1994 the grain output per capita had declined by nearly half in spite of the gains in the overall amount!

In the developed nations, the demographic transition took between one and two hundred years. However, the process must occur more quickly in the developing nations because of pressing needs for food and other resources.

Population growth, as we pointed out earlier, is not merely a problem of the developing nations. Americans consume a disproportionate share of the world's resources and contribute a disproportionate amount to the world's environmental damage. With less than 5 percent of the world's population, Americans use a fourth of all the energy consumed in the world and pour 22 percent of all carbon dioxide into the atmosphere (Elmer-Dewitt 1992). Any growth in the United States' population, therefore, exacerbates the problems of the world.

Nations employ diverse methods in attempts at population control. We pointed out that China has used a one-child policy. The program began in 1979, using the slogan, "one is best, at most two, never a third" (Jacobson 1989). Prior to 1979, the emphasis of the Chinese communist government had been on having no more than two children. The Chinese leadership concluded, however, that even two children per family was detrimental to the nation's well-being. If China was to develop rapidly and minimize the strain on its natural resources, population growth had to be minimized.

The government tried to make the new policy acceptable by providing incentives to those who agreed to limit their families to one child. In urban areas, couples received monthly cash payments for fourteen years and got preferred treatment in housing and jobs. Only children would get special privileges, such as priority medical care and preferred schooling and jobs after graduation. In addition, rural couples were promised extra shares of their commune's income for fourteen years, more private land, and larger grain rations.

By the mid-1980s, the government estimated that 78 percent of urban, though only 31 percent of rural, couples had signed an agreement to limit their families to one child. Rural resistance was rooted in a number of factors. For one thing, Chinese culture has traditionally valued large families and numerous sons. Second, rural reluctance reflected the belief that more children meant more workers in the fields. Finally, sons were seen as a kind of social security, for sons were responsible for taking care of their aging parents. Those in rural areas whose first child was a girl were particularly likely to want a second child, and officials often yielded to their wishes and granted permission (Li 1995).

The overall success of the Chinese effort may be seen in the fact that the most recent growth rate stands at 1.1 percent, which is considerably lower than the 1.9 percent rate of the rest of Asia (Population Reference Bureau 1996). Other nations have pursued various efforts, ranging from family-planning clinics to unofficial incentives that exploit people's ignorance. An example of the latter occurs in the interior regions of Brazil, where politicians offer women free sterilization in exchange for votes (Goering and Luft 1996). The women, ignorant of any alternatives and of the fact that the procedure cannot be reversed, take advantage of the offer in order to avoid the onus of continuous childbearing. In some regions,

Explorations

Control or Exploitation?

Most social scientists view population control as imperative for the well-being of the earth's population. Yet some people see population control as unnecessary or even as a form of exploitation. We had a Nigerian student, for instance, who argued that neither he nor anyone he knew accepted the fact that population control is necessary for people's well-being. "The problem," he insisted, "is how to develop the nation and distribute the benefits equitably." And an African American student argued that population control in the United States is simply another form of racism, a way to continue to exploit the minorities who have high birth rates and who threaten, by their increasing numbers, the white domination of the society. We have had other students, such as Mormons and some Roman Catholics, who have argued against population control on religious grounds.

☞ Your assignment is to explore the population-control attitudes of people from diverse racial and ethnic backgrounds. Divide the class into groups of at least five students and have each student interview four or five people from one of the following categories: international students; African Americans; Hispanics; Asian Americans; American Indians; white Americans.

Ask each person: Do you believe that population control is necessary today? For all nations, or only some of them? Why is it necessary (or not)? For those who believe it is necessary,

ask: How should it be controlled? Whose responsibility is it? And what methods are acceptable?

Summarize the group's findings. How do the people from the various groups compare in terms of their support for population control? What are the reasons given for support or rejection of the need for population control? And how do the respondents feel it should be controlled?

If you do this project alone, select two of the groups, interview five people from each, and compare them along the lines indicated above.

---

more than 40 percent of women have been sterilized, and the birth rate has fallen dramatically over the past two decades.

Urbanization and Urbanism

Population growth is typically accompanied by **urbanization**, the increasing concentration of people living in cities. It is more likely than not that you grew up in a city because a majority of Americans live in cities. It is also more likely than not that your great-grandparents grew up in a rural area, for a majority of Americans did not live in cities until about 1920.

Throughout the world, less than half of people live in urban areas. As we shall discuss below, however, this could change in the near future. Incidentally, different nations have somewhat differing definitions of an urban area. In some Scandinavian nations, 200 or more inhabitants qualify a place as a city, while in Japan a minimum of 30,000 is necessary. In the United States, a city consists of 2,500 or more people.

The Development of Cities

Can you imagine human life without cities? Actually, cities are a relatively recent development in human history. The first cities emerged between 5000 B.C. and 3500 B.C. (Martindale 1962). Prior to cities, people lived in small groups and, eventually, in villages. In peasant villages, the major institution was the family. In the first cities, the central institution was either religion or a simple form of urban government.

Cities brought new roles into prominence. In peasant villages, people essentially were farmers although they also participated in the village council, carried out religious obligations, and shared in the defense of the village against enemies. In the cities, a number of formal nonagricultural roles—"soldiers, bureaucrats, officials, and priests" (Martindale 1962, p. 63)—emerged as central to urban life.

Cities require an agricultural base, of course, so the first cities arose near rivers such as the Euphrates and Tigris in the Middle East, the Nile in Egypt, and the Yellow River in China. Farmers in those areas were able to produce enough surplus to support the people who lived and worked in the cities.

What would an early city have looked like to a visitor? Historians offer the following guided tour of Ur, one of about a dozen cities in Sumer between 3500 and 2800 B.C. (Wallbank et al. 1987)

> As you approach the city, you see farmers at work, their plows pulled by oxen. Ur is on the Euphrates River, where you notice boats carrying farm products into the city. The countryside is flat, and you easily see a platform upon which there is a sanctuary where the local god is worshipped. Once in the city, you would see a great many specialists pursuing their appointed tasks as agents of the community—some craftsmen casting bronze tools and weapons, others fashioning their wares on the potter's wheel, and still others, merchants, arranging to trade grain and manufactures for the metals, stone, lumber, and other essentials not available in Sumer. Scribes would be at work incising tablets of clay . . . memoranda used in administering the temple, which was also a warehouse and workshop. Some of the scribes might be making an inventory of the goats and sheep received that day for sacrificial use; others might be drawing up wage lists. (Wallbank et al. 1987, p. 10-11)

Cities like Ur greatly stimulated the development of the culture and economy. Those developments, in turn, fostered the growth of more cities. For their first few thousand years, the world's cities were small by modern standards. Even at its peak, the ancient city-state of Athens had only between 130,000 and 150,000 free men and 100,000 slaves (Heer 1962).

The Industrial Revolution, however, brought about a surge of growth both in the number and size of cities. Cities were sites of factories and businesses and, thus, were of prime importance in economic development. As people recognized that economic opportunities increasingly resided in the cities, they left rural areas in great numbers to pursue their fortunes.

Urbanization as a Global Process

All nations are striving for economic development. And economic development is associated with cities and with the concentration of resources found in cities. During the twentieth century, therefore, rapid urbanization has marked most nations.

Is Urbanization Necessary?

Why is economic development tied to the growth of cities? Actually, there is a good deal of controversy over the answer to this question (Bradshaw 1987). Some social scientists argue that urban expansion is an inherent part of the transition from a traditional, agricultural society to a modern, industrial society. They point out that rural people come to the cities to take advantage of economic opportunities, and, furthermore, that city life helps to develop the modern ideas and skills necessary for an industrial society.

Other social scientists argue for an urban bias—the notion that government policies which favor urban areas is the real reason for the growth of cities. They point out that urban groups have political power. These groups use their power to influence government to pass such things as investment and tax legislation which favors the location of industrial enterprises in urban areas.

According to world systems theory (which we discussed in Chapter Eight), no inherent relationship exists between economic development and urbanization. If urbanization occurs in the developing nations, they argue, it is because it serves the purposes of the core nations, providing some specialized function in the world economy such as a financial market.

Examining data from 61 developing nations, Bradshaw (1987) concluded that all three theories have some validity. Urbanization is occurring, and government policies favor urban areas. Yet the rapid rate of urbanization causes some problems in the developing nations. Rather than facilitating economic development, it is often a drain on the economy as more people cluster in the cities than can be employed.

The negative consequences of too rapid urbanization are pointed out in a United Nations report which states that as many as 900 million city dwellers reside in substandard housing, 400 million lack adequate sanitation, and 250 million do not have safe drinking water (McMahon 1996). At the same time, according to the report, the urban poor are three to 10 times better off economically than are the rural poor. It is understandable, then, that people continue to crowd into the cities even though they may not be able to find work there.

The Urbanizing World

Just how rapid has urbanization been? From 1750 to 1960 the population of the world increased by about 312 percent, from 728 million to almost three billion (Lauer 1991, p. 357). At the same time, the number of people living in cities of 5,000 or more increased about 3,990 percent, from 22 million to over 900 million! In 1800, London was the only city with a population in excess of one million people. More than a hundred cities now have this many residents.

United Nations figures show that 44.8 percent of the world's population lived in urban areas in 1994. The figure varied from 74.7 percent of those in the developed nations to 37.0 percent in the developing nations. In the poorest countries, less than a fifth of people are urban dwellers. By the year 2025, however, about 61.1 percent of the world's population may reside in cities, including 84.0 percent of those in the developed nations and 57.0 percent of those in the developing nations.

In the United States, only about 5 percent of the population lived in urban areas in 1790, and no city had a population as large as 50,000 (U.S. Bureau of the Census 1975, p. 12). The proportion of those in urban areas increased to 15.3 percent in 1850 (just before rapid industrialization began), to 39.7 percent in 1900, and to a slight majority—51.2 percent—in the 1920 census. Today, more than three-fourths of the U.S. population live in urban areas (U.S. Bureau of the Census 1996d, p. 43).

Suburbs, Megalopolises, and Urban Sprawl

As urban areas continue to grow in size, new aspects emerge. One is the division of the urban area into the central city and **suburbs**. A suburb is an urban area adjacent to a city but outside the jurisdiction of the city's government. People move to suburbs as the central city declines. They seek newer and larger homes, better living conditions (e.g., less **pollution**—harmful alterations to air, land, or water—and less crime), and better governmental services (including schools). Many whites moved to escape the increasing numbers of minorities in the central cities. Businesses moved to be nearer the more affluent customers and to escape high taxes in the city.

Some observers dispute these reasons as the best explanation for urban change. In the *conflict theory* of Gottdiener (1994), the deconcentration away from the central city is tied up with the changing global, capitalist economy. The way in which land is settled reflects the activities of "self-interested profit takers" (Gottdiener 1994, p. 268). It is in their interests to move out of the central cities, obtain cheaper land, use foreign labor, and so on—practices which government policies and actions facilitate rather than discourage. Deconcentration results in the creation and persistence of poverty in the central cities even while it facilitates a growing capitalist economy. Thus, suburbanization raises questions of social justice.

Suburbanization began slowly in the first decades of the twentieth century, then picked up rapidly after 1950. In the 1970s and 1980s, increasing numbers of minorities moved into suburban areas. Two researchers studied 1,773 American suburbs in which more than 15 but less than 50 percent of the residents are racial and ethnic minorities (Phelan and Schneider 1996). They found that African Americans are less likely than other racial/ethnic groups to live in suburban areas. In addition, those suburbs with a significant proportion of African Americans are likely to be poor, have lower home values, higher taxes, and a greater need for governmental services. In contrast, suburbs with large proportions of Asian Americans are likely to be wealthier and have lower taxes. Those with large Hispanic populations fall in between the other two types.

Because suburban areas have their own governments, the tax base of cities is significantly eroded when the more affluent people, businesses, and industries move to the suburbs. The cities are left with a greater proportion of people who need services and with fewer economic resources to meet those needs.

Various efforts at urban renewal attempt to counter the decline of central cities. Many of the approximately 1.3 million public housing units in the United States are being torn down and replaced with more attractive and appealing apartment complexes (Adler and Malone 1996). These efforts are a recognition that central cities and suburbs are interdependent (Downs 1996). The perception of the central city is important if a business wants to operate throughout a metropolitan area. Suburban businesses that employ low-wage workers may have to recruit them from the central city—the only place such workers can afford to live. And many of the cultural opportunities, such as museums, zoos, and symphonies, are likely to be located in the central city but used extensively by suburbanites.

Nevertheless, financial constraints still are a major factor affecting the quality of life in many large cities. Unfortunately, the financial picture isn't very promising. Most of the new housing and commercial construction scheduled for the coming decade will take place in suburban areas. Also about three-fourths of offices are now located in suburbs (Richard 1996). This situation is unlikely to change in the near future because it is usually cheaper to carry on business in the suburbs where they have lower taxes and free parking.

Although there are significant differences between a city and its suburbs, together they form a metropolis. And when growth continues, and suburban areas from one metropolitan area reach those of another, the entire area is called a **megalopolis**. In a megalopolis, such as that between Boston and Washington, D.C., you travel for hundreds of miles passing through one urban area after another.

Thus, the United States, along with some other nations, has reached the point of urban sprawl, the spread of urban areas over great stretches of land. Urban sprawl, which is possible because of the automobile, is an inefficient use of land and resources. For instance, in most European cities there are more people and jobs per unit of land and more walking, bicycling, and use of public transportation.

Urban sprawl has created a number of problems in the United States (Roseland 1996). Compared to the more efficient European cities,

American cities use more energy per person. Urban sprawl has also consumed farmlands, eroded the tax base of central cities, and damaged the environment. We will discuss the latter point in the last section of this chapter.

Urbanism: Life in the City

Think for a moment about life in the city. What words come to your mind when you reflect on city living? Sophistication? Culture? Traffic? Noise? Excitement? Loneliness? Crime? Pollution? Depending on your experience, any or all of these words might apply to city living.

The City as Symbol

As *symbolic interactionists* point out, whether you live in the city or a rural area, you live in a symbolic environment. That is, you construct the meaning of your environment by defining it in particular ways. A city is complex. How do you define an entire city? In the words of Wohl and Strauss (1958, p. 529): ". . . complexity forces us to analogize . . . . The city may be termed or compared with a factory, a madhouse, a frontier, a woman." By thus symbolizing the city, you shape your own response to it.

For instance, John Steinbeck wrote about the way in which New York City changed from something monstrous the first time he visited it, to a "Temptation" on his second visit, to his "village" when he returned to live there. Strauss (1968, p. 5) commented on Steinbeck's experience:

> Each Steinbeck who came to the city was, in some sense, a different man; and each time he perceived, and therefore used, the city quite differently . . . The urban milieu . . . is responded to not merely as physical terrain, a bit of geography, but as symbolic space filled with meaning and peopled with significant persons, artifacts, and institutions.

Similarly, Zukin (1995) has analyzed the modern city in terms of its "symbolic economy." Increasingly, she asserted, urban growth entrepreneurs construct images of their cities to achieve a number of ends. For one thing, they attempt to present a particular city as a world-class area worthy of people's visit and investment. They also try to get residents to define various parts of the city, including recreational and cultural facilities, in terms that will attract them to those places (and, hopefully, exclude others such as the homeless).

In sum, urban entrepreneurs are responding to the ongoing fiscal crises of cities by manipulating symbols in a way that will attract new people and new investments. And a good part of the effort focuses on the cultural resources in the city. Those resources enhance the city's appeal. Cities without many cultural resources may try to increase them.

Thus, a city in Massachusetts with a declining economy attempted to construct a cutting-edge art museum as a way to reverse the trend.

The City as Gesellschaft

Have you ever felt lonely while surrounded by a lot of people? Such an experience is possible, and, in fact, has been experienced by people in large cities throughout the world (Rao 1996). As you may know from experience, you can be in the midst of a large number of people and still feel that you are not an integral part of any of their lives. You can feel this way even though you have daily transactions with many of them. In other words, you can be in a situation where the bulk of your interaction comes from secondary rather than primary relationships.

Dealing with people on a more or less impersonal basis, in secondary relationships, is part of what Tönnies (1957; orig. 1887) called **Gesellschaft** (the German word for society). Modern, industrial society, in his analysis, is characterized by weak family ties, fewer personal and more impersonal relationships, and competition between people. For some observers, the city epitomizes *Gesellschaft*.

Tönnies contrasted *Gesellschaft* with **Gemeinschaft** (the German word for community), a group with a strong sense of community, bound together by tradition, kinship, and personal relationships. In his view, ,*Gemeinschaft* is found in rural communities.

It is debatable whether urban areas are always *Gesellschaft* and rural communities are always *Gemeinschaft*, but it is true that many people have experienced the city as *Gesellschaft*. A prime example are the homeless. Using *participant observation*, Snow and Anderson (1993) lived among and studied homeless people, experiencing as well as hearing about their alienation. One of the factors mentioned by some of the homeless to explain their plight was lack of family support—a characteristic of *Gesellschaft*. In addition, disabilities, minimal skills, and bureaucratic obstacles (also characteristic of *Gesellschaft*) combined to keep them homeless.

We would expect that most people who move to a city experience some degree of loneliness and isolation at first. For the majority, the city eventually becomes something of a *Gemeinschaft* as they are integrated into various groups. For at least some of them, however, the city remains a *Gesellschaft*.

The City as Freedom

In contrast to the relatively bleak portrait of city life implied by *Gesellschaft*, Robert Park (1952) celebrated the city as the locus of human freedom:

> In the freedom of the city every individual, no matter how eccentric, finds somewhere an environment in which he can expand and bring what is peculiar in his nature to some sort of expression. A smaller

community sometimes tolerates eccentricity, but the city often rewards it. (Park 1952, p. 86)

In other words, if you are the kind of person who likes to do your own thing, and if your own thing differs from the conventional behavior of others, you are likely to find the city more accepting than a small town. This is true because, as Park pointed out, the city is a "mosaic" of small and diverse kinds of communities. As we suggested above, then, the city as a whole may be a *Gesellschaft*, but it contains numerous *Gemeinschafts* within it.

Claude Fischer (1984) made a similar point in his subcultural theory of the city, a theory that subcultures of like-minded people emerge in the city and enrich participants' lives. Fischer recognized that a subculture tends to become an ingroup, defining other subcultures as well as the larger society as threatening and/or offensive. Thus, if you are homosexual, you might find yourself stigmatized in a small town, but you can find a community of homosexuals in the city. The subculture supports and enriches members even though others in the city are hostile. If you are an Orthodox Jew, you might feel alienated from the larger society, but you can find cities with communities of Orthodox Jews that support and enrich you. And so on.

There is, then, less pressure to conform to one way of life in the city, because, unlike small towns, the city contains a mix of diverse ways of life. It also offers a broader range of activities, relationships, and life styles.

The City as a Way of Life

Perhaps all of the above can be summed up by saying that the city is a distinctive way of life, distinctive, that is, from life in rural areas, villages, and small towns. In a classic paper on the city as a way of life, Wirth (1938) combined some of the ideas we have explored above. On the one hand, he agreed that there is more freedom and tolerance in cities than in rural areas or small towns. City residents are exposed to a greater range of lifestyles and, thus, are more accepting of diversity. On the other hand, Wirth agreed with Tönnies that the size and diversity of cities create *Gesellschaft*, and that the impersonal nature of city life creates alienation and various kinds of emotional problems.

In essence, then, life in the city is a trade-off. On the one hand, you have more freedom to pursue your own uniqueness and more opportunities for diverse experiences in the city than in small towns and rural areas. On the other hand, the city poses a variety of hazards to your emotional well-being. On balance, it is clear that the bulk of people are willing to risk the hazards in order to take advantage of the city as a way of life.

Experiences

'This City Isn't Fit for Human Habitation'

The contrasting experiences of George, a middle-aged teacher, and Terri, a young businesswoman, illustrate the way in which a city can mean different things to different people. George lived for three decades in a large, Eastern city before moving to the Midwest. Terri has lived in the same Eastern city for a little over ten years, after moving there from the Midwest.

George's experiences in the city impelled him to leave it:

I was mugged twice, once in the morning only a block from the school. I got to the point where I preferred to stay at home at night rather than risk going out and being mugged or attacked. The last straw for me was the day my wife and I were in a taxi in heavy traffic. A man on a bicycle, a messenger, got into some kind of argument with the taxi driver. We tried to ignore it. When the taxi came to a halt at a red light, the man on the bicycle rode up, hopped off his bike, and smashed in the front window of the cab with a hammer. Glass flew all over my wife and me. The guy then just rode off while we sat there stunned.

At that point, I said to my wife that this city isn't fit for human habitation. Fortunately, she felt the same way and within three months we moved. I finally feel comfortable going out at night. I wouldn't move back there for any money in the world.

Terri, in contrast, retains her initial sense of exhilaration over life in that city:

I came from a small town in the Midwest, and all my friends thought I was crazy to move here. But I loved it from the moment I arrived. I find it stimulating and exciting and challenging. It's impossible to be bored in this city. My only fear is that I won't live long enough to take advantage of all the things there are to do.

I'm proud of my Midwestern roots, and I think it was a great place to grow up. But I have no desire to move back there. At least not to the small town where I grew up. I think I would die of boredom if I had to move back there permanently.

The Challenge of the Environment

For more than sixty years, the Gallup poll has asked Americans what they regard as the nation's most serious problems. How would you respond to the question? A colleague, who once wrote a book on social problems, told us that of all the problems she investigated the one that caused her the most dismay was the problem of environmental damage. "It seems," she said, "not only that there is too little concern about the environment, but also that every time we take steps to resolve a particular problem, we create one or more new problems."

Environmental problems are serious. They are made even more serious by the rapidly increasing population of the world and the concentration of an ever-larger proportion of people in cities.

The Earth as an Ecosystem

In your opinion, what is an appropriate attitude for people to have toward the earth? Should people view the earth as a resource to exploit freely for human needs? Or should they view the earth as a partner in sustaining life, a partner that must be guarded and nurtured as well as used for human needs? The majority of people in the developed nations have viewed the earth in the former way—as a resource to exploit freely.

Some people, such as American Indians, view the earth more as a partner in life, a partner to respect and protect as well as use for the fulfillment of human needs. They emphasize the need to live in harmony with nature. For example, the Coeur d'Alene Indians of Idaho regard rivers, ponds, streams, and lakes as sacred (Haynes 1996). The waters are not only the source of food but also are used for a daily spiritual ritual, the "sweat bath." In 1996, the tribe sued mining companies for pouring millions of tons of toxic wastes into the rivers, thereby altering the ecosystem and destroying worship sites.

Increasing numbers of people throughout the world are becoming aware of the fact that the earth is not a limitless resource that can be exploited indefinitely. More and more, people realize that the entire earth is an **ecosystem**, a set of living things and their environment that are interdependent. In other words, humans, animals, vegetation, the land, the atmosphere, and the oceans are all dependent upon one another for their well-being. If something happens to one element in an ecosystem, the effects are felt by the other elements.

Consider the following as a few examples both of the interdependence of all things in the ecosystem and of the way in which human activity can have adverse effects on the ecosystem:

- Photosynthesis is the process in which plants produce oxygen and organic materials that are essential to all animal life; photosynthesis is adversely affected by air pollution, by **pesticides** (chemicals used to kill insects defined as pests) and **herbicides** (chemicals used to kill plant life, particularly weeds), and by the spread of human population into forested areas.

- Biological processes in the soil not only produce coal and oil but also enable farmers to grow food; contamination of the soil by overuse of chemical fertilizers and by various kinds of pollution reduce its effectiveness in growing food.

- The earth is an ecosystem and also a complex of smaller ecosystems in which there is a natural balance; human intervention can alter the balance. Thus, a National Park Service policy allowed the elk in Yellowstone National Park to overpopulate, resulting in deterioration of vegetation, stream banks, and the small animal population (Budiansky 1996).

We will give one more example of the way in which human activity affects ecosystems. Large ships are equipped with ballast tanks to give them stability as they traverse large bodies of water. The current practice is for ballast tanks to be filled with water at the port where cargo is loaded and then dumped out at the destination port. What this means, in effect, is that a ship becomes "a colossal, sloshing, floating aquarium," transporting a huge amount of plant and animal life from one ecosystem to another (Kendall 1996). One estimate is that 3,000 species of plants and animals are taken into ballast tanks and carried around the world every day.

The significance of this movement of plant and animal life to a new location is found in the meaning of an ecosystem, which is, by definition, a balanced system of interdependent relationships. Thus, the invasion of a new form of life will change the balance and can even destroy a part of the ecosystem. For instance, a jellyfish unwittingly imported into the Black Sea has nearly destroyed the anchovy population (Kendall 1996).

We are not saying that all human activity harms ecosystems. Rather, we are saying that great care is necessary and ongoing research is imperative in order for humans to learn how to live in harmony with nature. The notion that humans have the task of conquering nature has resulted in massive problems, as we will outline below. Paul Ehrlich (1971, p. 364) put it this way: "Man, always a threat at the plate, has been hitting Nature hard. It is important to remember, however, that NATURE BATS LAST."

Humans in the Environment

We have already illustrated the impact that human life can have on the environment. Here we will examine more closely this impact as well as the effects the environment has on humans. Remember, in an ecosystem every element affects every other element in some way.

Environmental Impact of Human Activity

Have you ever purchased a new automobile? If so, did it occur to you that you made a contribution to the world's environmental problems? Probably not. Yet the automobile illustrates the two ways in which human activity adversely affects the environment: its use adds to the total amount of pollution and its construction depletes more of the earth's natural resources.

The example of the automobile, incidentally, underscores the dilemmas involved. For we are not suggesting an Erewhonian return to an earlier and simpler life. We are simply pointing out that human activity inevitably has consequences for the environment, and many of those consequences are troublesome. Pollution is one kind of adverse consequence. Some kinds of air pollution are visible, such as the infamous Los Angeles smog. However, a good deal of air pollution is invisible because it is composed of tiny particulate matter and gases, such as carbon monoxide, nitrogen oxides, and sulfur dioxide.

Industrial processes produce a substantial amount of air pollution. About 96.1 percent of the sulfur dioxide and 51.3 percent of nitrogen oxides in the air come from the burning of fossil fuels and other industrial processes (U.S. Bureau of the Census 1996d, p. 234). Automobiles and trucks are another major source of pollution, contributing 28.3 percent of the lead, 62.3 percent of the carbon monoxide, and 31.9 percent of the nitrogen oxides in the air (U.S. Bureau of the Census 1996d, p. 234).

As Table 15.2 shows, progress has been made in the control of air pollution. Nearly all pollutants are lower, either in total amount or a per capita amount, than they were in 1940. Nitrogen dioxides are an exception; ironically, their increase reflects, among other things, changes in gasoline and automobile emission systems.

Table 15.2	**Air Pollutant Emissions (in thousands of tons)**				
	Small Particulates	Sulfur dioxide	Nitrogen dioxides	Carbon monoxide	Lead
1940	15,956	19,953	7,374	93,615	NA
1960	15,558	22,227	14,140	109,745	NA
1980	7,050	25,905	23,281	115,625	.075
1994	3,705	21,118	23,615	98,017	.005
	NA = not available				

Source: U.S. Bureau of the Census 1996d, p. 234

Incidentally, you may think of air pollution as something that you mainly encounter out-of-doors. But indoor air pollution is also serious. A substantial number of buildings in the United States are "sick." They contain areas in which a fifth or more of the employees who work in them experience physical or emotional problems that are eased when they leave the building. Indoor pollution can result from poor ventilation and from toxic vapors from equipment, paint, rugs, and cleaning fluids. Problems associated with the "sick building syndrome" include mucous membrane irritation, eye irritation, headaches, feelings of lethargy, and an inability to concentrate (Soine 1995).

Pollution of water, like that of air, comes from various sources and is of various kinds. Sewage removes oxygen and contaminates the water. Organic chemicals—including insecticides, pesticides, and detergents, and waste heat from power plants and industry discharging hot water— also pollute water. Major sources of pollution in the oceans are waste materials dumped there by nearby urban areas and oil spills. All of these pollutants, including waste heat, can kill fish and other aquatic life.

Some progress has been made in water pollution control. Throughout the nation, rivers, streams, and lakes have been restored and made safe for swimming and fishing. Oil spills have been reduced dramatically, and other kinds of pollutants are declining in many coastal sites (Broad 1997). Yet large amounts of waste are still dumped into the ocean and more than 1.5 million gallons of oil a year still spill in and around U.S. waters (U.S. Bureau of the Census 1996d, p. 233).

Finally, land pollution occurs from chemical wastes, trash and garbage, acid rain, and the use of pesticides and herbicides. Sulfur dioxide and nitrogen oxide emissions cause acid rain. The gasses mix with water vapor and form acids that fall back as rain or snow. Acid rain pollutes both water and land. It kills fish, reduces crop yields, damages forests, and causes deterioration of buildings and monuments. Some scientists warn that acid rain threatens the existence of sugar maple trees in the eastern part of the United States and Canada.

Researchers who examined data collected on a New England forest over more than 30 years concluded that acid rain had altered the soil chemistry and stopped all growth for at least 10 years (Stevens 1996). The forest will take an indeterminate number of years to recover and will only do so if the amount of acid rain can be reduced significantly.

Human activity also causes **environmental depletion**, the increasing scarcity of natural resources. No nation in the world is now self-sufficient in terms of natural resources. The United States has a wealth of resources, but in 1994 the nation imported half or more of 17 minerals and metals—including all of the manganese and mica, 84 percent of the tin, and three-fourths of the chromium (U.S. Bureau of the Census 1996d, p. 701). The problem of natural resources will only become more severe, for Americans are consuming a larger proportion of them *per capita*. Young and Sachs (1995, p. 80) estimate that the consumption of raw materials such as minerals and lumber was 14 times greater in the early 1990s than it was in 1900, while the population was only three times larger.

Depletion, like pollution, is a global problem. Depletion includes the loss of animal and plant species that are important to the stability of the ecosystems of which they are a part (Lockwood and Pimm 1994). Depletion is also seen in the alarming decline in the world's fish population as a result of overfishing to supply food for the growing population (Camhi 1996).

In addition, depletion includes the rapid deforestation occurring in tropical forests. Those forests contain an enormous number of species of animals and plants, including some plants that are used for medicine. The forests also are important in blocking the buildup of carbon dioxide, a major factor in global warming. Whether the earth's temperature really is warming remains a matter of some controversy, but there is considerable evidence that it is. This evidence includes more than two decades of steadily rising average global temperatures and extreme fluctuations in weather conditions (Brown 1995). If global warming is occurring, the polar ice caps could start melting, adding water to the oceans and flooding coastal plains including many large metropolitan areas.

EXTENSIONS

Environmental Disaster in Ethiopia

You may have seen some of the horrifying pictures of starving African children that appear periodically in the news media. How can this kind of thing happen? Actually, such problems typically stem from a combination of natural and human processes, underscoring the point that humans and their environment are interdependent parts of an ecosystem. Ethiopia illustrates the point well; it has been particularly hard hit by problems of drought and famine since the early 1970s.

Ethiopia has two diverse regions, a mountainous plateau—the Highlands—and a number of surrounding lowlands. Most of the people live in the Highlands. After World War II, the government embarked on a program of economic development. Ethiopia was still a feudal system at the time. Economic and political power concentrated in the Southern Highlands, where the capital was located. Government policies allowed aristocrats to be the landlords of large tracts in the north. Increasing numbers of peasants migrated south to find work; those who remained in the north worked hard for absentee landlords and had little left over for themselves.

Government policy also led to the cutting down of forests without replacing the trees. Without the forests, the steep land lost top soil and agricultural production declined rapidly. The first drought occurred in 1973.

Because the people in the north were already living meagerly, and the productivity of the land had declined precipitously, the drought meant disaster for the ecosystem. Famine followed swiftly. And initially the government would not allow international relief agencies into the country because it did not want to acknowledge the problems.

In 1974, a military coup ousted the emperor and set the nation on a socialist course. The new government, however, only intensified the problems. All land was nationalized, deforestation escalated, and soil erosion increased. An even worse drought hit the nation in 1984 and 1985. Millions of Ethiopians, mostly in the north, starved to death. Because the northerners were less supportive of the government, the military leaders did little to help them. Rather, they used the famine to consolidate their power, and let international relief agencies deal with the massive starvation.

In sum, a combination of governmental actions and natural processes led to famine and millions of deaths in Ethiopia. Even without the droughts, government policies would have created serious problems. With the droughts, those policies created a disaster.

Source: Lanz 1996

The Human Impact of Environmental Damage

When pollution and depletion damage the environment, people suffer. We noted one example of this in the "sick building syndrome." Some of the more serious problems that have a known or suspected relationship to the environment are "cancer, reproductive disorders such as infertility and low birth weight, neurological and immune system impairments, and respiratory conditions such as asthma" (U.S. Department of Health and Human Services 1995). One study estimated that annually more than 5,000 deaths in Los Angeles and more than 4,000 in New York are due to particulates that pollute the air in those cities (Hilts 1996). In addition, people suffer emotionally as well as physically. Working with hazardous materials, for example, can lead to increased anxiety and depression (Roberts 1993).

There is also an economic cost to environmental damage. In fact, it is virtually impossible to calculate the total cost when you consider that it includes such things as: damage and death to wildlife, livestock, trees, and crops; pollution-control efforts; increasing expense of procuring ever-scarcer resources; medical care for those whose health is affected; lost productivity because of sickness stemming from exposure to environmental hazards; restoration of ecosystems; and renovation of structures damaged by air pollution and acid rain.

Estimates are available for at least some of the above costs, however. For instance, Brown, R. (1993) estimated that air pollution reduces crops by 5 to 10 percent in the United States. This amounts to an annual loss of $3.5 to $7.0 billion. And expenditures for pollution abatement and control in the nation are more than $109 billion a year (U.S. Bureau of the Census 1996, p. 239).

Population, Urbanization, and Environment: Inseparable Trio

By now it is clear that population, urbanization, and environment are inextricably tied together. In accord with *structural functionalism*, an ecosystem is a complex system of interrelated parts. The system includes not just humans and their social structures and processes, but the natural environment and the spatial distribution of people. In order for the system to survive, all parts must work together. To damage one of the parts is to jeopardize the entire system.

Consider, for example, the environmental impact of cities. Does it make any difference whether 250 million people are dispersed evenly over a nation or concentrated in cities? That is, is the crucial factor the sheer number of people or is the way they are arranged spatially also important?

Clearly, air pollution is worse in cities than in rural areas. There are now 24 cities in the world that have, or will have, a population of 10 million or more by the year 2000. Air pollution information is available on 20 of them. This information reveals that the quality of air in most of them is poor and getting worse because of growing population, traffic, and energy use (Mage et al. 1996). The seven most polluted cities are Mexico City, Beijing, Cairo, Jakarta, Los Angeles, Sao Paulo, and Moscow.

But what would happen if the people in those cities were dispersed? Wouldn't they still do the same amount of environmental damage? Probably not. For one thing, urbanization is necessary for industrial processes, and the industrialized nations generate three-fourths of the world's pollutants and wastes (Population Information Network 1996). Without industrial processes, in other words, environmental damage would be far less. However, even apart from those processes, cities affect the environment in a number of ways:

- Urban buildings and processes make city temperatures warmer than those of surrounding rural areas; a large city can become a heat island, affecting regional climate.

- Urban processes generally result in more clouds and more precipitation than occur in rural areas.

- Urbanization changes the landscape in an area, increasing the amount of runoff water from precipitation and the potential for flooding.

- Urban dwellers use more water per capita than do rural dwellers.

- The concentration of population makes sewage disposal problematic; in some areas of the developing world, 90 percent of sewage is discharged into waters without being treated first.

- Urbanization deprives plants and animals of their natural habitat, endangering the survival of some of them.

Of course, there are environmental advantages as well as disadvantages to urbanization. If urbanization involves apartment buildings, less land is required per person for a dwelling. Apartment living also consumes less energy per capita, because apartment units can be heated and kept cool more efficiently than single housing units.

Critical Thinking Exercise

Many people are trying to come up with ways to revitalize cities that face declining revenues and increasing problems. One author has suggested that Atlantic City provides an example of how to do it (Gilliam-Mosee 1996). Gambling, the author pointed out, has renewed the city. The casino hotels are becoming an integral part of the city's culture and contribute substantially to redevelopment funds. The city's inhabitants have benefited from the stimulation of the local economy and the additional jobs provided by the casinos.

Without making any moral judgements about the desirability of gambling as a source of revenue, how would you respond to the author's suggestion that, on the basis of the Atlantic City experience, gambling can be used to revitalize a city? What kinds of questions would you ask about the author, the data, and the interpretation of the data? What additional information would you like to have? What kind of research would you recommend to test the author's suggestion?

The point is, the very nature of the city—concentrated people in a particular kind of environment—has an impact on the environment. Thus, for technical as well as political and social reasons, the urban areas of the world are a major factor in environmental damage. As the population continues to grow, and increasing numbers of people cluster into cities, the world faces the enormous challenge of learning how to live in harmony with an environment that ultimately bats last.

Summary

Demography is the scientific study of population. Some of the important components of population include size, age and sex composition, and growth rate. Growth rates vary greatly in the world. A sustained growth rate of 2 percent results in a doubling of the population in 35 years.

A number of factors are involved in the growth rate of a population. One is the birth rate. Cultural values, educational levels, and government action all affect birth rates. A second factor is the death rate. Death rates differ among the nations because of such things as the age composition of the population, the health care system, diet, lifestyle, and economic status. Migration is the third factor in population growth. The population growth for any year is the birth rate minus the death rate plus the net immigration rate.

The greater the gap between birth and death rates, the larger the population growth. The demographic transition is a process of moving from high birth and death rates to relatively low rates. Typically, death rates fall before birth rates, widening the gap between the two and resulting in rapid population growth. The developed nations all experienced the demographic transition during industrialization.

Population growth presents a challenge. Rapid growth can impede economic development. When the population is too large, people may not have the resources available to live at their desired quality of life and may be damaging the environment in a way that is hazardous to their well-being. Recognizing these facts, many governments are trying to control the growth of their populations.

Urbanization typically accompanies population growth. Cities first appeared between 5000 and 3500 B.C. Cities required new roles and stimulated the culture and economy. Cities grew rapidly in size and number during the Industrial Revolution.

Urbanization is necessary for economic development and modernization. Although less than half the world's population lives in cities, it is estimated that more than 61 percent will live there by the year 2025. As urban growth continues, suburbs spring up, leading to a number of problems in the central cities. Continuing growth leads eventually to urban sprawl.

Life in the city can be conceptualized in various ways. The city may be seen as a symbol, as *Gesellschaft* (Tönnies), as freedom (Park), or as a way of life that is distinctive from life in rural areas and small towns (Wirth).

Population growth and urbanization create environmental problems. The earth is an ecosystem and contains a multitude of smaller ecosystems. In an ecosystem, all elements depend upon each other for their well-being.

Human activity has an inevitable impact upon the environment. It can bring about harmful changes (pollution) in the air, the water, and the land. Some progress has been made in pollution control, but the problem remains serious. Human activity also depletes the earth's resources. No nation in the world is self-sufficient in terms of natural resources.

Environmental damage has an adverse effect upon humans. Environmental factors bring about a variety of physical and emotional illnesses. The economic costs of the damage are massive.

Population, urbanization, and the environment are inextricably tied together. Each affects the other, as illustrated by the fact that urban areas have an impact on the environment that reflects the concentration of population as well as the size of the population. The challenge is to learn to live in harmony with the environment.

Glossary

crude birth rate   the number of births in one year per 1,000 persons

crude death rate   the number of deaths in one year per 1,000 persons

demographic transition   the change from high birth and death rates to low birth and death rates

demography   the scientific study of population

ecosystem   a set of living things and their environment that are interdependent

environmental depletion   the increasing scarcity of natural resources

Gemeinschaft a group with a strong sense of community, bound together by tradition, kinship, and personal relationships

Gesellschaft a group characterized by weak family ties, individualism, competition, and more impersonal than personal relationships

herbicide a chemical used to kill plant life, particularly weeds

immigration rate the number of people who have come into the country in one year per 1,000 population

megalopolis an urban area formed by the merging of two or more metropolitan areas

migration the movement of people from one area to another

pesticide a chemical used to kill insects defined as pests

pollution harmful alterations to air, land, or water

subcultural theory Fischer's theory that subcultures of like-minded people emerge in the city and enrich participant's lives

suburb an urban area adjacent to a city but outside of the city's government

urbanization the increasing population of people living in cities

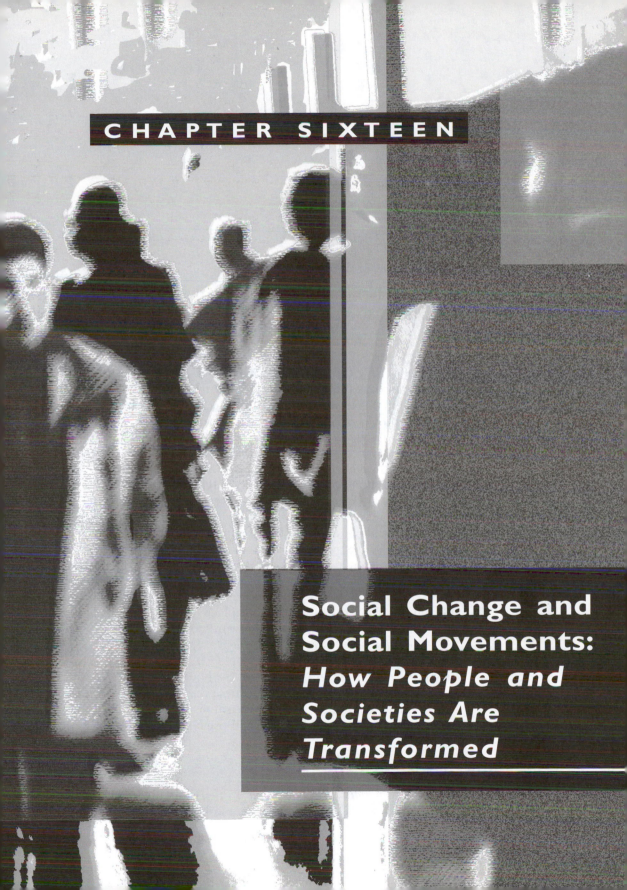

CHAPTER SIXTEEN

Social Change and
Social Movements:
*How People and
Societies Are
Transformed*

Have you heard of the following sayings?

- The more things change, the more they stay the same.
- People always resist change.
- You can't teach an old dog new tricks.

These sayings reflect the conventional wisdom that people don't like change, that they drag their feet when faced with change, and that many things about humans never change. But think about yourself and your own life. Are you exactly the kind of person you were five or 10 years ago? What about your future? Would you prefer to have life be like a videotape where you could press a "pause" button and put everything on hold indefinitely? Or are you anticipating certain changes in your life circumstances that you expect to be gratifying? And what about the country? Are you perfectly content with everything happening in the nation? Try this exercise: in two minutes, how many things can you name that you would like to see changed in the United States?

We raise such questions to underscore our disagreement with all three of the above sayings. Your own experience and reflections no doubt tell you that you don't always resist change—sometimes you actively work to bring it about. Your own reflections and understanding also tell you that the world is a different place now than it was five or 10 years ago. And hopefully you have even known older people who learned some impressive new tricks.

Still, it is true that you often find people who resist change or who are unable to learn or accept new ways. So how can you understand why people sometimes resist and sometimes press for change? If it isn't true that human life remains basically the same, what kinds of changes have occurred in societies? What causes those changes?

The Meaning of Social Change

In her novel, *The Tenant of Wildfell Hall*, Anne Brontë had the narrator say that his father considered "change but another word for destruction"

(Brontë 1994, p. 3; orig. 1848). This negative view of change, which the sayings at the beginning of this chapter also reflect, has been widespread. Let's try to get a more realistic view of change.

Change Is Normal and Pervasive

We will define **social change** as "alterations in social phenomena at various levels of human life from the individual to the global" (Lauer 1991, p. 4). As such, change is normal and pervasive. You can easily identify changes that occur at various levels of society: the nation (e.g., crime rates, migration patterns); the culture (e.g., technological developments, values); institutions (e.g., divorce rates, business cycles); organizations (e.g., productivity, sex composition of the workers); interaction patterns (e.g., racial segregation, male/female interaction in the workplace); and individuals (e.g., attitudes about the environment and the government).

The argument that social change is normal and pervasive accords with *conflict theory* but not with *structural functionalism*, which stresses equilibrium and persistence of such things as values in social systems. Structural functionalists do not deny change, however. Neil Smelser (1959) analyzed the Industrial Revolution from a structural-functionalist perspective. He pointed out that the Industrial Revolution involved both short-term adjustments and long-term structural changes. "Dissatisfaction" with the existing situation and an awareness of what could be achieved for individuals and societies spurred the revolution. Values including personal responsibility, discipline, and a sense of calling, in turn, legitimated the dissatisfaction (recall that Max Weber identified such values as a factor in the rise of capitalism).

However, even values change over time. In the 1980s, Americans appeared to be self-focused, valuing greatly their personal growth and personal well-being. By the mid-1990s, however, Americans placed a greater value on family, on having leisure time, and on making some contribution to society (Judy 1996). And *survey research* on college students in China reported that the students were moving away from some long-standing Chinese values, such as personal sacrifice for the social good and self-discipline (Chunhou 1996).

This is not to deny stability or continuity, but to affirm that change is normal and pervasive. We agree with the philosopher, Alfred North Whitehead (1933, p. 273), who asserted that the only choice for humans is to grow or decay, because "the pure conservative is fighting against the essence of the universe."

Change Is Not Inherently Traumatic

In addition to structural functionalists, other social scientists have contributed to the negative image of change, calling it such things as an "ordeal," a "crisis," and a "foreign and unwanted agent" (Lauer 1991, p. 15). But is change inherently traumatic for people?

Clearly, change is often painful. The West rejoiced when the Communist world began collapsing in 1989. When even Russia ceased to be run by the Community Party, Westerners believed that the Russian people would also rejoice and thrive in their new freedom. Yet by 1996, Russians exhibited ambivalent feelings (Newman 1996). They appreciated some of their new freedoms, but they found themselves in greater poverty and many of them wondered if the old way of central authority and state subsidies was not really better for them.

In addition to such evidence, you could argue that people frequently resist change because it is inherently painful. People may resist even when, at least to an outsider, it appears that the change would benefit them. Thus, a government attempt to introduce new fertilizer to Nigerian peasants failed in spite of the fact that the innovation would have greatly increased productivity. The peasants reacted this way because of past negative experiences with government officials and a lack of understanding about the new fertilizer (Lauer 1991).

Why is there so much resistance to change? After sifting through hundreds of studies on the issue, we have concluded that, if you look at the situation from the point of view of those resisting, there are generally reasonable bases for the resistance. In particular, people resist change when they perceive the change to be:

- *an economic threat or liability*. The American Medical Association vigorously opposed Medicare when it was first proposed because of the assumed economic threat it posed for doctors' incomes.

- *ambiguous or obscure in its consequences*. The Nigerian peasants did not understand the benefits of the new fertilizer; they simply saw it as another directive from a government they mistrusted.

- *imposed on them*. In a classic experiment, Kurt Lewin (1958) and his associates explored ways to get Americans to change their eating habits during World War II when food was rationed. The government wanted women to use meat such as beef hearts, sweetbreads, and kidneys. One approach the researchers tried was to lecture groups of women on the importance of making the change. Another approach was to give some information, then have a group discussion and a group decision. A follow-up showed that only 3 percent of women in the lecture groups served one of the meats, but about a third of those in the group-decision settings served one. In the lecture situation, the change is viewed as imposed. People are far more likely to accept and support change when they participate in the decision-making process.

- *too risky or too costly*. Recall our discussion in the last chapter about the Chinese effort at population control. From the government's point of view, a cost/benefit analysis made the effort eminently worthwhile; from the individual family's point of view, a cost/benefit analysis suggested that the family would suffer more than it would gain.

- *a threat to interpersonal relationships*. Technological innovations in the workplace may be perceived not only as a threat to workers' jobs but also to their work relationships. As noted in Chapter Fourteen, automation can mean changes in the amount and kind of interaction workers have on the job. Such changes are likely to be stressful.

- *inconsistent with their values*. Pro-life people continue to fight against legalized abortion, and pro-choice people continue to resist changes in the legal status of abortion.

- *a threat to their self-esteem*. How would you feel if you were told that your job would be taken over by a robot? People who are displaced or who lose their jobs because of economic or technological change face a struggle with their sense of self-worth.

- *a threat to their status and power*. Graduate sociology students in a small university reacted strongly when the faculty considered abolishing the poorly attended and ineffective graduate student organization. Even though few were interested in participating, they viewed the change as a threat to their status and power.

Even though there is always resistance to change, then, that resistance is usually reasonable when viewed from the perspective of the resistors. Moreover, any change that is resisted is also advocated by someone. Change is not inherently traumatic. However, the *rate* of change is related to trauma. People are likely to be stressed when the change is too rapid; but they are also stressed by too little change (Lauer 1991).

Thinking Critically

For a thousand years, the Chinese bound the feet of women. Around the age of six to eight, the four smaller toes were bent under the foot and the whole foot was kept tightly wrapped. This was an extremely painful procedure and led to a number of physical ills and even death (Mackie 1996). The eventual outcome was a woman with roughly four-inch feet who was crippled and largely housebound for life.

After a thousand years of the practice, it was largely eradicated during the first decade of the twentieth century. This rapid and dramatic change was achieved by a combination of education and natural-foot societies—parent organizations that pledged neither to bind their daughters' feet nor to allow their sons to marry women whose feet had been bound.

Mackie (1996) argues that a similar campaign could end infibulation—female genital mutilation—which is most common among some Islamic peoples in Africa. It involves the removal of the clitoris and part of the labia. The vulva is then sewn together, and a small piece of wood inserted into the vagina to keep the labia from completely growing together and to allow a passage for urine and menstrual flow.

Could educational efforts and parent organizations end the practice of infibulation in a decade? We would hope so, but are skeptical. We do not believe that Mackie's conclusions are wholly reasonable. For over a century, traditional culture in China had been challenged by Western businessmen, missionaries, and educators as well as by internal decay. By the end of the nineteenth century, the old order had eroded and China was susceptible to dramatic change. Educational efforts and parent organizations flourished in this tumultuous atmosphere and they succeeded in ending footbinding.

It is likely that similar social circumstances are needed to bring about an end to infibulation. And perhaps they are needed even more because both religious values and cultural traditions support infibulation. Some African Muslims who have emigrated to the United States have taken their daughters out of the country in order to have the rite performed (Dugger 1996). As one man said, "If I don't do it, I will have failed my children."

Sources of Change

Given that change is normal and pervasive, what causes it? One source of change is social movements, which we will discuss in the last section of this chapter. Here, we will explore five other sources: technology, ideology, competition and conflict, the government and economy, and population.

Technology

In Chapter Fourteen, we noted that technology brings about change by increasing alternatives, changing interaction patterns, creating social problems, and setting into motion a domino effect. Let's look at a few specific changes that result from two technological innovations that consume an increasing part of American's lives: television and personal computers. Both innovations are relatively recent. In 1946, only 8,000 households had television sets (U.S. Bureau of the Census 1975, p. 796). By 1970, 59.6 million households—97.1 percent of the total—had television sets. Today, at least 98 percent of American households have television sets.

Table 16.1	Personal Computers in Use in Homes	
	Year	**Number (millions)**
	1981	.75
	1983	7.64
	1985	14.86
	1988	22.38

Source: U.S. Bureau of the Census 1990, p. 759

Approximately 91 percent of the adult population watches television, a figure which varies little by sex and race/ethnicity (U.S. Bureau of the Census 1996, p. 561). On the average, people watch more than 3,400 hours of television a year.

The impact of all this television viewing is significant. For example:

- Television helps mold the attitudes of children about sex, and may promote promiscuous behavior (American Academy of Pediatrics 1990).

- Television provides relaxation and escape and encourages families to spend time together. But long periods of watching may leave people in worse moods than they were before they began to watch (Roark 1990).

- Television portrays substantial use of alcoholic beverages without any negative consequences; this can be misleading to the young (Lauer 1997).

- An enormous amount of violence appears on television. An analysis of 2,500 hours reported violence in 57 percent of the programs (Farhi 1996). Moreover, perpetrators of violent acts went unpunished 73 percent of the time, and 47 percent of the violent incidents portrayed no harm to the victims. Television violence increases the amount of hostility and aggressive behavior in children and adults (Lauer 1997).

With regard to personal computers, table 16.1 shows that their use grew rapidly after 1981. More than one fourth of American homes now have computers. Like television, they also profoundly affects people's lives. For example:

- Computers facilitate learning and develop new skills in children (Levin 1985).

- Some people become obsessed with the computer, leading to marital and family conflict (*Time*, October 15, 1984, p. 109).

- E-mail can contribute to a sense of overload and time pressure (Heller 1991).

- A study of 220 computer-using fathers found that the more time a father spent on the computer, the less time he gave to household work, recreational activities such as sports, and interacting with his wife, and the more likely he was to report conflict with his wife (Bird, Goss, and Bird 1990).

- Computers are used to commit crime of all kinds, and the problem is so widespread that a number of cities have set up special units to deal with it (Conly and McEwen 1990).

Note that these two technologies are typical of technological innovations generally in the sense that they have both positive and negative consequences. If we have listed more negative consequences, it is because researchers tend to focus on those more than on the positive possibilities. In any case, technology clearly affects human life in many and important ways.

Explorations

Technology and Change

One way to identify the role of technology in social change is to choose a particular development and trace out its consequences. Decide in your group which technological innovation you would like to pursue (an encyclopedia or history of technology can help you identify the date of the innovation), then search the popular and professional literature for consequences. Assign each group member a specific year or period of years to search. Use your library's computerized search program or other sources such as the *Readers' Guide to Periodical Literature*, the *New York Times Index*, *Sociological Abstracts*, *Business Index*, and *Psychological Abstracts*.

Watch for anticipated consequences (speculation about the use and effects of the technology) as well as observed consequences.

The technology may be of any sort, including such things as the bicycle, electricity, the automobile, penicillin, television, behavior modification, in vitro fertilization, personal computers, primal scream therapy, and fax machines. Write up a report assessing the impact of the technology as well as comparing expected consequences with actual consequences.

If you do this project as an individual, pursue the consequences in either the popular or the professional literature rather than both.

Ideology

What do you think of when you hear the word "ideology"? Unfortunately, the word has negative connotations for some people. To social scientists, an **ideology** is a set of interrelated beliefs that explain reality and give directives for action. All groups, whether political, religious, or scientific, have ideologies, for ideologies are a way to make sense out of the world and to guide the behavior of individuals. Ideologies are also an important factor in change and in resistance to change. We will look first at the way in which they can be a barrier or impediment to change and then at ways in which ideologies promote change.

Ideologies as Barriers or Impediments

Religious ideologies have often acted as a barrier or impediment to change. Actually, the same ideology can foster some changes and resist others. Also, diverse ideologies within the same religious tradition can contradict each other. Some Christians oppose the teaching of evolution as contrary to their faith, while others argue that evolution is perfectly consistent with theirs.

It is often debatable whether religious ideologies actually dictate particular actions or are interpreted this way by people pursuing self-interest. For instance, we noted in Chapter Twelve that women in a number of Islamic nations are subservient and in a few situations are forbidden to work outside the home. Yet it can be argued that "Islam itself does not impose any particular restrictions on the labor force activities by women (the prophet Mohammed's wife was a successful trader)" (Weeks 1988, p. 224). In cases of disagreement, those in more powerful positions are able to enforce their version of the faith.

Ideologies are used, then, to require people to think and act in particular ways. And this often means to prevent innovation and change. Christianity has been marked by a history of conflict with science, ranging from the trial of Galileo (condemned by the Catholic church in 1633 for denying that the earth is the center of the universe) to the trial of Scopes in Tennessee (convicted in 1925 for teaching Darwinian evolution in a public school) to the current effort by fundamentalists to outlaw abortion and suppress the rights of homosexuals.

However, other kinds of ideologies also inhibit change. In the U.S.S.R., developments in biology lagged behind the those in the rest of the world because Soviet biology was dominated by Lysenko from the 1940s to the early 1960s. Lysenko convinced the government that Lamarckian rather than Mendelian genetics were consistent with Marx's thought. Lamarck taught that animals can acquire characteristics through living habits (e.g., moles lost their sight after living underground for many generations). Mendel argued that characteristics are inherited from parents. Lamarck's work, then, suggested that successive generations of Russians could be socialized to eventually produce ideal communists. Mendelian genetics, which virtually all biologists accept, were labeled a capitalistic myth. At least one of Russia's world-renowned biologists was banished to Siberia for disagreeing. This impeded biological progress in the U.S.S.R. for decades.

Ideologies as Facilitators of Change

Ideologies can also facilitate change. Recall Weber's work on the Protestant ethic and the development of capitalism. The Protestant ideology motivated people to behave in particular ways, and those ways happened to be what was needed for the growth of a capitalist economy.

Interestingly, elements of the Protestant ethic have been noted in other religions and have produced similar results. Robert Bellah (1957) showed that the religion of the Tokugawa era in Japan (1603–1867) was a crucial factor in the **modernization** of that nation (modernization is the economic, social, and cultural change occurring in the transition from an agrarian to an industrial society). Tokugawa religion included such things as the admonition to work hard, to avoid wasting time, and to be thrifty and honest. The Tokugawa era was followed by rapid modernization in the Meiji era (1867-1912). Bellah argued that Tokugawa religion was an important factor in Japanese modernization because it led to rational economic behavior of the kind conducive to the growth of capitalism.

Even Buddhism, with its strong emphasis on detachment from material concerns, has facilitated economic development in three ways (Von der Mehden 1986). First, the demand to meet religious obligations can encourage an entrepreneurial spirit among people. Second, Buddhist leaders have not confined their activities to purely spiritual purposes but have also become involved in community development projects. And third, Buddhist religious symbols can be powerful tools for mobilizing people: when economic development is sanctified by, or even expected by, transcendent values, devout people will rally to the cause.

Economic and political ideologies also facilitate change. In particular, the ideology of **nationalism** holds central importance in the world today. Nationalism stresses the importance of the nation's interests over those of all outsiders. Nationalism can lead people to revolt against foreign control, to reject foreign ideas, and to restrict foreign immigration and activity within the nation.

Nationalism has been important in all industrializing nations. One of the first great issues in Meiji Japan was that of national unification. The Japanese heeded the call to revere the Emperor and oust the "barbarian" (Lauer 1991, p. 221). As in this case, nationalistic ideologies create solidarity among the people and support for the government.

If you probe a little further and ask exactly how ideologies facilitate change, you will find at least four ways (Lauer 1991). First, an ideology can make a change legitimate. In the United States, the robber barons of the nineteenth century legitimated their ruthless practices through the ideology of Social Darwinism—the idea that business, like nature, is a struggle for existence and results in the survival of the fittest.

Second, an ideology functions to support leaders who implement the change. Religious doctrines justify the changes that have occurred in some Islamic nations, including new, subservient roles for women and new legal procedures. The same doctrines lead to support for the government and its efforts to maintain the new ways.

Third, an ideology motivates individuals. Feminist ideology has motivated women throughout the world to strive for equality between the sexes. Religious ideology motivates some Americans to try to repeal laws legalizing abortion. Political ideology motivates some Americans to try to abolish welfare.

Fourth, an ideology can confront people with a contradiction. Most Americans adhere to a political ideology that includes a value on equality of opportunity. Women and those from racial and ethnic minorities have confronted the rest of the nation with the contradictions between ideology and reality. Of course, the contradictions do not sway everyone, but at least some people will be persuaded to lend support to those who are on the short end of opportunities.

Competition and Conflict

Do you enjoy competing with people? Or would you prefer less competition in such places as school and work? Competition is not strong in all societies, but in the United States it is an integral part of everything from sports to education to the workplace. Some observers believe that this competition is largely negative in its consequences, resulting in higher stress levels, reduced personal trust, and less emotional security (Elleson 1983). Whatever the validity of these arguments, competition is a major factor in change. As we showed in Chapter Fourteen, because of competition medical science progressed much more in the United States and Germany in the nineteenth century than it did in France and England.

Some kind of competition characterizes most organizational life. Universities compete for students, research funds, faculty, and prestige. Hospitals compete for patients, research funds, and the most advanced technology. Businesses compete for customers. Churches compete for members. In a pioneer study of complex organizations, Hage and Aiken (1970) found that the higher the level of competition, the higher the rate of program change in the organizations. Competition creates a dynamic environment, forcing organizations to make changes in their structure and processes in order to remain competitive.

Competition is also a factor in creativity and innovation. As noted in Chapter Fourteen, intense competition for the Nobel Prize has played a role in many scientific breakthroughs. Economic competition between nations facilitates the funding and, thereby, the rapid development of new technology in such fields as electronics and information. Business competition within a nation leads to breakthroughs as corporations sponsor research and development. Competition for church members has led some groups to break away from denominational labels and create the so-called "megachurches" that are found throughout the United States. A megachurch is a religious innovation, a church with a huge membership (sometimes in the tens of thousands), a large physical plant, and no ties to any particular denomination.

As a final example, competition for water and the control of water in arid areas of the American West led to a stratification system of considerable inequality (Arnold 1996). Those who gained control of water were able to amass a disproportionate amount of wealth and power.

Competition, then, is an ongoing source of change. You might consider some of the changes desirable and some not. Certainly, those who lost out in the competition for control of water in the American West would have defined the resulting social system as undesirable. Yet the winners probably praised the society that enabled them to flourish.

Conflict is also an important source of change. As *conflict theorist* Dahrendorf (1959, p. 208) notes: "all that is creativity, innovation, and development . . . is due, to no small extent, to the operation of conflicts between group and group, individual and individual, emotion and emotion within one individual." As we discussed in Chapter One, Dahrendorf argued that pervasive social change characterizes every society, and that every society has pervasive conflict that leads to the change.

An example of conflict between groups leading to major change is Lachmann's (1989) study of state formation in sixteenth and seventeenth century England and France. Lachmann identified conflict between three groups—the clergy, the monarchs, and their officials, and lay landlords—as the "critical dynamic" that explains the way in which the two nations developed. The outcome of the conflict was the establishment of absolutist monarchies. Prior to this time, the people were ruled by various aristocrats, clerics, and others with hereditary rights. Thus, conflict among the three groups exercising power over the peasants was resolved by one of the groups—the monarchs—winning out and gaining total control.

A good deal of research identifies conflict as a force for creative change. Conflict characterized various creative periods of history, including the axial period (900 to 200 B.C.) and the Renaissance (fourteen to sixteen centuries) (Lauer 1991). Conflict, in the form of disputes about such things as procedures and policies, is associated with effective organizations (Lawrence and Lorsch 1967; Van de Vliert 1985).

Of course, conflict can also be destructive. Internal conflict has rendered more than one organization ineffective. Yet if the conflict is managed properly and if it involves contrary ideas rather than personalities, it can be an important stimulus to change.

The relationship between conflict and change tends to be self-sustaining. Conflict can lead to change, which generates more conflict, which leads to further change. Consider the green revolution in Asia (Schneider 1981). The green revolution refers to improved agricultural technology, including new varieties of grains, better methods of irrigation, and the use of fertilizer and pesticides. As a result of the green revolution, India more than tripled its wheat harvest between 1965 and 1980.

In this case, a new technology led to important economic change. However, even though India was able to export grains, millions of its citizens continued to face hunger and even starvation (Barnett 1989). The new technology allowed the large farmers, with their greater access to land, capital, and credit, to profit from the green revolution. Small farmers could not make the necessary investment (as much as ten times the cost of traditional farming methods) in the new techniques. In addition, because the green revolution made land more valuable, rents went up on small farms. At the same time, with the greater yield of grain, prices tended to fall. Thus, the small farmer not only did not benefit, but actually suffered because of the change.

The outcome was conflict between small and large farmers. Landlords evicted some small farmers. Or if they were not evicted, the farmers faced smaller profits (because of lower prices) and increased deprivation. As the conflict intensified, violent confrontations occurred between landlords, displaced farmers, and a number of "land grab" movements. Pressure mounted for land reform programs. Thus, the change led to conflict, which created pressure for additional kinds of change.

The Government and Economy

In Chapter Thirteen we noted a number of ways in which the U.S. government has been involved in changes within the American economy. In nations throughout the world, governments have been of central importance in economic development. In Japan, the government was an integral part of the modernization that began in 1868 and led to Japan becoming a world power (Reischauer 1964). The Meiji government borrowed various tools of modernization from the West, including the Western calendar, methods of administration, the civil service, a national banking system, a modernized currency, and a modern political system that included a cabinet and constitution. Within a few years, the government aimed at universal education in the nation, and Japan became the first Asian nation to have a literate population. Finally, the government stimulated the industrialization of the nation by creating and controlling such crucial areas as the railways, the telegraph, and public utilities, and by stimulating business ventures through government loans and support.

The Japanese government also recognized the importance of science and technology and expended huge sums of money to import foreign technology, teachers, and specialists as well as to send students to study abroad (Lockheimer 1969). As quickly as possible, Japanese scholars and technicians were trained to take over the planning and operation of industrial enterprises.

More recently, the South Korean government illustrated how government can foster economic growth (Alam 1989). What has been called a "miracle" of economic development began in South Korea during the 1960s. For the next decade, the nation experienced an incredible annual growth rate of 9.5 percent in gross domestic products, a significant increase in exports, and a fivefold increase in domestic savings.

Although a number of factors were involved in South Korea's economic development, the government's role was central. By intervening in the economy in such ways as liberalizing trade policies, establishing export goals, providing incentives to increase exports, and regulating closely the national financial system, the government guided the nation into a new era.

Governments are active in other areas, of course. The United States government has funded science and technology. It has been a central factor in the growth of education. Indeed, from its inception the government designated large tracts of public land for educational use, and this policy was continued. For instance, the Morrill Act of 1862 gave public lands to the states, stipulating that money received from the sale of those lands could be used for such practical education programs as agriculture and engineering.

The U.S. government has also implemented numerous social measures. Governmental action is responsible for such things as social security, welfare programs, civil rights' legislation, various efforts to guarantee equal opportunities to women and racial/ethnic minorities, and the regulation of facilities for senior citizens. Had the nation been a pure democracy, with every citizen voting on every issue, it is probable that a number of these actions would not have been taken.

Government-driven changes in the economy, incidentally, illustrate the fact that the domino effect exists in more than the realm of technology. Because all elements of a social system affect other elements, any change in one is likely to reverberate in a sequence of additional changes. Thus, data from eight western European nations and the United States show that increasing prosperity from the 1970s to the early 1990s was associated with a shift in values related to national goals (as opposed to those related to personal goals) (Abramson and Inglehart 1995). In particular, people became somewhat less concerned with materialistic goals such as order and inflation, and more concerned with equality and human rights.

Population

The father of sociology, Auguste Comte (1858), noted that population trends affect social change. Comte argued that both population size and density affect the rate of social change. A higher concentration of people in a specific area creates new desires and new problems. People make changes to accommodate these desires and resolve these problems. If the population growth is too slow, he warned, it will impede progress (see Extensions, this chapter). If it is too high, it will also impede progress because the problems become too demanding and social stability becomes too tenuous.

We noted the validity of Comte's insight in the last chapter when we pointed out that rapid population growth can preclude economic progress. The age, sex, and racial/ethnic composition of a population can also affect change. For example, the age composition has a bearing on crime rates. Young males commit a disproportionate amount of crime. Close to a third of those arrested for serious crimes are under 18 years of age, and more than three-fourths are males (U.S. Bureau of the Census 1996, p. 209). As the age composition of the society shifts, crime rates shift as well: lower proportions of youth usually result in lower crime rates and vice versa (Steffesmeier and Harer 1991).

Age composition also affects a society's capacity to care for people. You would probably agree that the increasing life expectancy of Americans is a change which should be applauded. However, programs like Social Security are already in trouble because of the increasing number of people over 65, and the problem will worsen after 2010 when the baby boomers start swelling the ranks of senior citizens. Moreover, it is still uncertain whether the increased life span will be marked by reasonably good health or will simply mean a greater number of years of disability and decline (Roush 1996). If the latter is the case, providing services to the growing group of senior citizens will severely strain society.

The stresses of an aging population are already being felt in Japan (Oshima 1996). Japan has had well-developed pension and health care systems as well as a strong cultural tradition of children caring for their aging parents. However, the cultural tradition is breaking down as more women work outside the home and more children move away from their home areas to pursue careers. And the existing social services are already incapable of responding to the demands for assistance.

Finally, migration patterns have a bearing on change. As pointed out in the last chapter, the migration of the well-to-do out of central cities has

EXTENSIONS

Dilemmas of Population Growth: Australia

Comte pointed out that a too small rate of population increase impedes economic progress. Although small population size and growth are not a serious problem for any nation today, various nations have needed a larger population at specific points in their history. For example, after the Second World War, the Australian government concluded that the nation needed more people in order to bring about economic growth. There were simply not enough skilled workers in the existing population to fill available positions.

In 1947, therefore, the government instituted an immigration program to increase its pool of skilled workers rapidly. If potential immigrants who applied for the program were accepted, they were given free transportation to Australia. In return, they had to sign an agreement to remain there for a minimum of two years in a job and at a place designated by the government.

Most of the initial immigrants were from central Europe. In time, they also came from southern Europe, the Middle East, Latin America, and Southeast Asia. In the half century since the program was initiated, the population has doubled. And Australia has changed from a mostly rural society with a monolithic culture to a primarily urban and multicultural society.

Some serious problems have accompanied the changed nature of Australian society. A major problem involves the stratification system. Immigrants have generally wound up in the lower levels of the system. Although they came to fill skilled positions, many of them found themselves in jobs that native Australians preferred not to do. Moreover, the immigrants have not been assimilated into the higher levels of institutions such as the government and education. Nor have elements of the diverse immigrant cultures found their way into the mass media and the culture of native Australians.

In essence, then, Australia is a segregated nation. The immigrants moved into run-down, cheap-rent areas of the central cities where they eventually located stores and ethnic restaurants. By turning slum areas into ethnic enclaves, the immigrants have economically enriched the nation. But they remain largely outsiders, and their exclusion from much of mainstream Australian life presents a potential for serious conflict in the nation.

Source: Jamrozik, Boland, and Urquhart 1995.

changed many urban areas from prospering cities to financially strapped and problem-filled communities. In addition, immigration has frequently increased intergroup conflict, particularly when newcomers are seen as economic competitors.

Patterns of Change

Look at figure 16.1. It shows a number of possible patterns of change. Many kinds of change can be conceptualized in terms of such patterns. Actually, few changes in social life are as simple as the linear growth and linear decline patterns. A change may occur this evenly and smoothly over a short period of time but not over the long run.

Cyclic change without any trend is also unlikely over the long run, although the pattern does apply to some phenomena for periods of time.

Figure 16.1   Patterns of Change

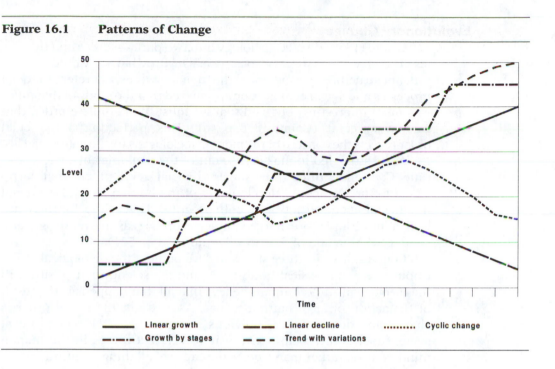

Look back, for example, at figure 15.1. The death rate has followed a cyclic pattern for at least two decades. If the figure were extended to prior decades, you would see a long-term decline. It is even possible, however, that a point of stability has been reached and that there will only be cyclic variations with no further decline in those rates.

Some crime rates are also cyclic. The murder rate was 9.0 in 1994. It was 4.6 in 1910. But in the intervening years it varied from a low of 4.5 in 1955, 1957, and 1958 to a high of 9.7 in 1933. While the rates were lower in the first years of the century, then, they have varied cyclically without any long-term trend since 1910.

Most changes will fit the patterns of growth by stages or a trend with variations. These graphic patterns, of course, are only the bare bones of understanding a particular change. You need to know the substance as well. However, the pattern does give you an important handle on what is happening.

Developmental Change

Developmental change can be conceived as a pattern of growth by stages. In turn, two important variations of developmental change are evolutionary and dialectical change.

Evolutionary Change

Comte (1858) divided sociology into two parts—statics and dynamics. The "statical" aspect of society deals with what we would call the order or structure of society, and the "dynamical" aspect refers to social processes and social change. Comte believed that the study of dynamics was more interesting, but said that we must "contemplate order, that we may perfect it" (Comte 1858, p. 461). This "perfecting" of the social order reflects the concern of the pioneer sociologists to alleviate social ills.

As he struggled to make sense out of the dynamics of society over time, Comte identified three stages of social development that correspond to three stages of development of the human mind. He argued that the mind and society have both progressed over time, for there has been a "more and more marked influence of the reason over the general conduct of Man and of Society" (Comte 1858, p. 521).

Comte called the three stages of development the theological or fictitious; the metaphysical or abstract; and the scientific or positive. In the theological stage, humans believe that all that happens is the result of the action of supernatural beings. As a result, the social order is shaped and dominated by religious authorities. In the metaphysical stage, supernatural beings give way to abstract forces in the human mind. Nature, rather than God, is the cause of all things. Natural rather than divine laws explain human life. In the positive stage, reasoning and observation are the tools of the intellect. And the social order that results from this kind of thinking will maximize the well-being of humankind.

Earlier, we pointed out other views of change as evolutionary: Durkheim's analysis of the movement from mechanical to organic solidarity (Chapter One) and Lenski's analysis of how technological innovations lead to new types of social orders (Chapter Three). More recent analysts also find evolutionary development useful in understanding the changes in societies. For instance, Sanderson (1995) went back to the most primitive societies and raised the question of what caused the transition from hunting and gathering to agrarian societies. He concluded that population pressures led to this development and that the ability to produce a surplus was the key to the direction of the subsequent evolution of societies.

The existence of a surplus allowed the evolution of society into the agrarian age and the further evolution into the feudal and industrial ages. Other factors have also been at work in this evolution, of course, including population changes, technological developments, and urbanization.

In evaluating the evolution of human society, Sanderson came to an interesting conclusion about whether or not it represents progress. Most sociologists, from Comte on, believed that social evolution represented progress even though they have not agreed on the course of, or reasons for, that evolution. Sanderson, however, defined progress in terms of four things: material well-being, work and the workload, extent of equality in a society, and extent to which there is democracy and individual freedom. In terms of those four criteria, he argued, most change has been regressive rather than progressive. The little progress that has occurred has been in the most developed nations of the world.

In sum, there are various kinds of evolutionary analyses of human society, but they all affirm an increasingly complex social structure. Most identify technology as a central impetus of the evolutionary process. Further, most see this evolution in terms of progress toward a more meaningful and fulfilling life for humans.

Dialectical Change

In Chapter One, we briefly discussed the dialectical theory of Marx and Engels. Dialectical theory sets forth contradiction as the essence of all of things and the prime mover of change. Using dialectical theory, Marx and Engels interpreted human history according to the following outline (see Engels 1939; Marx and Engels 1947; Marx 1920):

1. Human relationships are independent of people's will. That is, people relate to each other on the basis of the economic structure of their society rather than on the basis of their ideas or values.

2. Every society has an infrastructure—the economic structure—and a superstructure that includes ideologies, law, government, family, and religion. The infrastructure is the basis upon which the superstructure develops. If the infrastructure changes, it will cause changes in the elements of the superstructure as well.

3. The contradiction between the forces and relations of production drives change. Capitalism produces more than people can absorb because the bulk of profits go to the capitalists and the workers cannot afford all the goods they are producing.

4. The contradiction between the forces and relations of production manifests itself in class conflict. The increasingly prosperous capitalists and the increasingly impoverished workers polarize into two hostile groups.

5. Ultimately, revolution resolves the contradiction. The communist revolution does away with classes and, ultimately, with the state itself (which supported the capitalists).

6. In the resulting classless society, life will be characterized by the principle of from each according to ability and to each according to needs.

History has not been kind to the analysis of Marx and Engels. Where communist revolutions occurred, they did so in agrarian or less industrialized societies rather than in fully developed capitalistic nations. And in many nations where communist governments formerly held power, efforts are now being made to develop capitalistic economies. Still, Marxism has been attractive to people throughout the developing world because of its humane vision of the future and its emphasis on human action in bringing that vision to reality.

Cyclic Change

Where is the human race heading? You probably would answer that it's going somewhere even if you can't say for sure whether its headed in a direction that can be called progress. But what about the idea that humans are going nowhere? That history, like recent death and murder rates, is simply an endless series of cycles? In the ancient world, the Greeks, Romans, and Chinese all thought of human life in terms of historical cycles in which there is no qualitative difference between the past and present.

This notion is foreign to the modern Western mind. Some kinds of change are cyclic, but most social scientists do not see the whole of human history in terms of cyclic change. An exception was Pitirim Sorokin, who analyzed change in Western civilization from 600 B.C. to about 1935 A.D. (Sorokin 1937–41). Sorokin concluded that history is a cyclic variation between three "supersystems" that represent fairly homogeneous cultures. One system is the *ideational*, with its central principle of God as the true reality and value. The second system is the *sensate*, which affirms the sensory world as the true reality and value as its central principle. And the third system is the *idealistic*, which is a combination of the other two—that is, reality and values are partly sensory and partly transcendent. Christian medieval Europe was an ideational culture. The Renaissance was idealistic. And the world at the time of Christ and the twentieth century exemplify sensate cultures.

There are important distinctions between a sensate (or ideational or idealistic) society at different points in history. But Sorokin believed that the fundamental culture is more important than anything else. If a society's emphasis is on spiritual needs and God's truth, this factor is more important than the society's economic system or state of technological development. This is because the ideational culture will structure the way that people behave in the economic system and the way they use technology.

The present sensate age, Sorokin believed, must eventually come to an end and give way to a new ideational or idealistic era. Sorokin expected that change to occur in the near future, for he called our sensate culture, with its heavy emphasis on materialism, "overripe." He used an immense amount of existing data to buttress his arguments. While we do not accept his cyclic view of history, he made important contributions to an understanding of change by stressing the normality and pervasiveness of change, and by showing how even well-integrated cultural systems slowly change, driven by their own internal dynamics to develop eventually into a different system.

Diffusion and Adoption of Innovations

A bra that makes a woman look bustier. An exercise machine designed to give a man a great looking abdomen. A device that can require people to punch in a code number before their call can be completed to your telephone. A device that will take pictures from your camcorder, a videotape, or a photo, and put them into your personal computer. A camera that allows you to view the picture you took instantly, put it on your television screen, or print it out on your computer's color printer. A home-study course that will teach you how to read a book and assimilate its contents in an hour or two.

These are just a few of the recent innovations that continually flood the market. Have you purchased any of them? If something new appears that is related to a major interest of yours, how quickly do you try to obtain it? Questions like these relate to the adoption and diffusion of innovations, a major area in the study of change. Innovations, incidentally, may be inventions—something new in the world—but they also include those things which are new to a particular population.

On the basis of a vast number of studies of many kinds of innovations in diverse settings, it is clear that innovations diffuse through a population in a pattern that is similar to the trend with variations line in figure 16.1. The pattern is actually a logistic curve (s-shaped). At first, the innovation is adopted by a few people, then it diffuses rapidly through the population, and eventually levels off at some point short of the total population. The period of rapid diffusion is not merely the result of marketing; rather, it is a combination of marketing and word-of-mouth influence, of becoming aware of an innovation, and of interacting with people who have adopted it.

For example, the birth rate in Costa Rica declined rapidly between 1960 and 1988 (Rosero-Bixby and Casterline 1994). The decline occurred in all the socioeconomic strata, but there is no evidence that people's preferred family size changed. What caused that decline? In essence, the researchers found a pattern of diffusion of birth control. Once birth-control measures were adopted by a segment of the population, they diffused rapidly to other segments through a kind of social contagion.

Diffusion occurs between as well as within societies. In fact, diffusion is so common in the world that anthropologists claim that as much as 90 percent of any culture is the result of diffusion from other cultures (Lauer 1991).

When the innovation comes from another culture, people may modify it in some way to adapt it to their own culture. Thus, when the Japanese embarked on the modernization of their nation, three of the many things they borrowed from the West were the police, the postal service, and newspapers (Westney 1987). They modified each in accord with their own needs.

They borrowed the police system from the French because the French system was highly centralized and was used for political surveillance and control. They went beyond the French model, however, creating, among other things, the world's first police academy in 1885. They borrowed the postal system from England, but did not use all aspects of that system. And they got the idea for newspapers from Western nations, but were innovative in their use of newspapers. Japanese newsmen used creative formats and advertising that increased circulation rapidly.

Modernization

Modernization fits the pattern of growth by stages shown in figure 16.1. In fact, a number of analysts have specified the stages of modernization (Lauer 1991). Rather than looking at specific stages, however, we will briefly outline the conditions necessary for modernization and some of the social changes that characterize the process.

With regard to conditions, the developing nations today face a number of dilemmas (Dube 1988). One is the dilemma of self-reliance versus interdependence. Nations like China and India have tried to forge a course of development based on self-reliance. Such a course avoids indebtedness to foreign nations and exploitation by foreign nations. Exploitation, as world systems theorists point out, means that the developed nations benefit far more from efforts at modernization than the developing nations themselves. Although a number of studies have supported that conclusion, two researchers who used a different method of analysis examined data on 62 developing nations over two decades and found great benefits of economic growth to the developing nations (Firebaugh and Beck 1994). Still, the governments of developing countries are wary of becoming overly dependent on the developed nations.

Another dilemma is the tension between economic growth and equitable distribution. Can the developing nations avoid the gross inequalities that characterized the West in the early days of capitalism? A third dilemma is whether to try centralized planning or allow the free market to guide the development. Finally, there is the dilemma of the impact of industrialization on the environment. Can the earth sustain an industrial world?

The situation of the developing nations is compounded by the fact that they face a far different international environment than did the developed nations when they began to modernize. The developing nations are not able to engage in large territorial expansion. They are at a severe technological disadvantage. And they have a high rate of population growth that tends to offset any economic growth.

For all of the above reasons, it is difficult to identify precisely the conditions necessary for modernization. But the following are some minimal conditions:

- Social structural conditions include a strong, efficient agricultural sector, popular participation in political life, an open stratification system, a communication system in the form of the mass media, and an educational system that strives toward universal literacy.

- Social psychological conditions include trust in the government, commitment to the goal of modernization, and values and attitudes consistent with a rational economy.

Once the modernization process has begun, there is likely to be pervasive change throughout the society. The population grows and shifts from rural to urban areas. Increasing numbers of specialists and numerous new roles characterize the occupational structure. Status is based increasingly on achievement rather than on ascription. Inequalities in income and power diminish somewhat as increasing numbers of people move into the middle class. The status of women and children tends to rise. National interests begin to take priority over local interests. The political process tends to be democratized but, at least in the developing nations today, political conflict tends to increase (Moaddel 1994). The functions of the government expand enormously. Education becomes increasingly important and an increasing proportion of the population is educated. And the family tends to lose some of its functions to other institutions.

Not all of these changes occur in every case of modernization, but they are typical of what happened in the developed nations and of what is happening in the developing nations. As Sanderson (1995) noted, biological evolution tends toward divergence, but social evolution tends toward convergence—toward societies becoming increasingly alike in important ways.

Social Movements

"What can you do if you want to change something about your society?" we frequently ask students. Invariably, someone says "vote" or "write a letter to your Congressperson." Usually someone also comes up with what we believe is a better answer: "organize people who agree with you or join an existing organization of likeminded people." When you answer in these terms, you are thinking about *social movements*—organized efforts to promote or resist some kind of change.

There are many different kinds of movements, and there may be a large number of organizations within a movement. For instance, prominent social movements in the United States include the labor, women's, civil rights, charismatic, and pro-life movements. Each of these involve a number of different organizations (some of which are hostile to each other). For instance, the civil rights movement has included the National Association for the Advancement of Colored People, the Congress on Racial Equality, the Black Panthers, and other diverse groups.

Social movements often generate countermovements—organized efforts to oppose the aims of the movement. White Citizens' Councils and various white supremacist groups arose to resist the changes sought by civil rights organizations. Pro-choice organizations oppose the changes pursued by pro-life groups.

Why do people join a social movement organization? You may think the answer is obvious—to bring about some change. But let's rephrase the question: why do people who favor the aims of a movement *not* join one of its organizations? More people favor the aims of a movement than join its organization. Do you, for example, favor the aims of the women's movement? The civil rights movement? The pro-life or pro-choice movement? Are you a member of organizations in any of these movements? Why or why not?

The issue of why people do or do not join is critical for leaders as they strive to mobilize as many people to their cause as possible. In fact, leaders face an additional task—not only to get people to join but to get them to participate in the movement (through financial support and volunteer work). We will look first at the explanations for why and how people are brought to participate in a social movement, and then discuss the way in which movements affect social change.

Why People Participate

A number of theories attempt to explain why people participate (Marx and McAdam 1994). **Strain theory** asserts that a social movement is a reaction of people stressed by some kind of serious disruption in the social order. For example, rapid changes in the South between 1920 and 1960, including the collapse of the cotton economy and the migration of large numbers of African Americans to cities, broke down the old social order. The civil rights movement grew out of the stresses of the resulting social disorder.

Resource mobilization theory holds that a social movement depends upon the ability to mobilize crucial resources in the face of opposition. The theory assumes rationality in human action: potential members weigh the costs and benefits of participating. One task of leaders is to convince people that the benefits outweigh the costs. The theorists argue that it is not stress that explains the rise of a movement because there are always stressed people. Rather, the rise of a movement depends on the availability of crucial resources such as leaders, funds, access to mass media, and organizational skills.

Thus, enormous stress has always characterized the lives of African Americans. Only when the necessary resources (leaders, government support, financial support from white liberals, etc.) became available did the civil rights movement emerge.

Political process theory is a variation of resource mobilization, emphasizing the availability of political opportunities as an explanation for the rise of a movement. People who are stressed by their situation form a movement when the opportunity for exerting political power is finally available to them. That opportunity may arise from such things as weakness in the government, increased tolerance in the society, and a commitment to legal equality for all groups. Thus, the civil rights movement flourished in the wake of court decisions and legislation that made segregation and discriminatory treatment illegal. Civil rights activists now had the power to secure the protection of law enforcement officials and to challenge unfair practices in the courts.

Finally, some theorists see the rise of movements in the experience of **relative deprivation**, which is perceived deprivation based on a subjectively defined standard of comparison. In other words, as emphasized by symbolic interactionists, to understand whether someone or some group feels deprived, you have to know with what or with whom the comparison is being made. Or, put another way, you have to understand the size of the gap between what people expect and what they get. When people define that gap as intolerable, they are likely to form a movement to bring about change.

For example, from a feminist point of view, all women are deprived in one way or another (as we discussed at length in Chapter Ten). But not all women, it appears, feel that they are deprived. This is illustrated by a recent national poll which asked a sample of Americans this question: "In general, do you think we need to increase, keep the same, or decrease affirmative-action programs in this country?" Thirty-five percent of the women polled urged an increase, 28 percent said programs should remain the same, and 30 percent said that affirmative action programs should be decreased (Golay and Rollyson 1996, p. 50).

Relative deprivation, then, means that people can feel—or not feel—deprived regardless of how their status might be evaluated by an outsider. Deprivation, like stress, is usually part of the lives of social movement participants. The deprivation is relative, however, in the sense that participants are rarely among the most deprived segments of the population. Rather, there is a gap between what they expect and what they actually receive. The women who belong to NOW and other

Experiences

'I Became a Feminist'

Maggie was a college student in the late 1960s. Her journey from being a questioning and idealistic freshman to a radical student to a feminist occurred within a few years. Now a social worker, and still actively involved in the women's movement, she tells about the experiences that led her to become a feminist:

> When I first started college, I had visions of making the world a better place. I wasn't sure just how I would do it, but I started attending some meetings of a civil rights group on campus. Then I met this guy in one of my classes and he took me to an S.D.S. meeting—that's Students for a Democratic Society. By this time, the war in Vietnam was starting to tear the nation apart. I was appalled by what I heard about our involvement there. I became very antiwar. And soon I became a radical student. I was determined to make the world a better place.
>
> I wasn't into the woman thing yet. Not even by the time I graduated. I was accepted to graduate school at a large mid-western university. Talk about culture shock! There I was, a socialist and anti-war activist, in a bastion of male-dominated conservatism. I can't tell you how isolated I felt. But I didn't feel any hostility. And I didn't feel oppressed. Just lonely and unique.

> I started reading about the women's movement. I started making some female friends. I came across a number of women who were very smart, but who hadn't been able to get into law school or other professional programs. They cared little about my socialism, but they talk enthusiastically about ways to open up opportunities for women. I was on my way to becoming a feminist. As it turned out, it was a group of men who were responsible for my taking the final step. I attended a mass meeting protesting the war in Vietnam. I was welcomed and given the opportunity to make an announcement about a women's meeting which I had organized. I hoped the meeting would attract some like-minded women who were interested in addressing women's issues.
>
> I was astonished at the hateful reaction from the men in charge of the meeting. Those radical, supposedly egalitarian, men treated me with complete contempt. They weren't interested in equality for women, only in protesting the war. I overheard one of them say to another, "Why don't you take her out and bang her? That's all she needs." At that moment, I became a feminist. I was convinced, and still am, that women will never be free and equal unless we demand and fight for our own rights.

women's organizations are largely middle-class rather than poor women. They *are* deprived, but they are not among the *most* deprived.

Similarly, a study of the protest movement in South Korea that led to the fall of the government of Syngman Rhee found that economic deprivation was the most important factor in explaining participation in the protests (Kim 1996). But, again, those who participated were not among the most deprived.

Social Movements and Social Change

Do movements make any difference? They do. The American women's movement, for example, over the last 170 years has achieved such things as the legal right to property, the right to pursue a higher education, the right to vote, and the right to enter any occupation or profession.

Movements can bring about change at multiple levels of social life. Whatever else they do, social movements effect some changes in their members by socializing them into the movement's ideology. Maggie, who shared with us her journey to feminism (see Experiences, this chapter), told us that only after she joined a feminist organization did she fully realize the extent of women's oppression and the way in which sexism pervades the whole of American society.

Movements also help bring about role change. The Communist movement in China greatly altered the role of women in that nation. Women were declared equal to men. Although the reality falls short of the ideology, Chinese women have far more freedom to participate in political life and the work force than they had before the revolution. Similarly, the American women's movement helped bring about role change. Women are no longer expected to be satisfied solely with the homemaker role.

Institutional changes are another outgrowth of social movements. We noted earlier some institutional changes with regard to women. The civil rights movement has effected institutional changes for racial minorities, including the rights to equal access to public accommodations, to integrated housing and education, and to equal economic opportunities.

Finally, social movements tend to generate countermovements—a tendency which alters the political process. People in social movements seldom confront a single opponent (such as the anti-war movement confronting the government). Instead, they confront countermovements as well as the government. Thus the pro-life movement not only has to deal with the government that made abortion legal, but with the pro-choice movement that works to keep it legal. This situation is typical. As Meyer and Staggenborg (1996, p. 1654) put it: "Movement-countermovement interplay has become a veritable fixture . . . in contemporary politics." Movement and countermovement members alike strive to sway political leaders, mold public opinion, and mobilize increasing resources to their cause. Those who can mobilize the most resources and/or most effectively create and use a sense of deprivation of some kind will ultimately prevail.

Given that social movements *can* bring about change, what factors determine whether they will in fact succeed in their aims? We noted Gamson's (1990) study in Chapter Thirteen in which he showed that aggressive tactics are more likely to result in success. Gamson identified four additional factors that relate to the success of a movement: organization, reasonable goals, the support of other organizations and groups, and timing. Organization means some kind of central organization that directs activities and coordinates efforts. Reasonable goals are those that aim at reforms (new policies or laws) rather than revolts (overthrow the government). Such goals are reasonable from the point of view of the larger society.

Having reasonable goals makes a movement more likely to gain support from other organizations and groups. The support may be financial or political or public relational (look at all the others who support our efforts). Finally, timing refers to the fact that success is more likely during times of political crisis or instability. While these are not the only times in which a movement can succeed, the point is that the same efforts can be sympathetically considered or vigorously resisted depending on what else is happening in the society at the time.

The five factors do not guarantee success. But movement participants cannot afford to ignore them if they want to achieve their aims.

Critical Thinking Exercise

Change is pervasive, but some kinds of change are difficult to measure. We were surfing stations on our car radio when we caught a commentator complaining about the liberal bias of the newspapers. He went on to claim that prior to President Franklin Roosevelt, the newspapers reported the news fairly and objectively. Since that time, he argued, they have been slanted to a liberal view.

How would you respond? What kinds of questions would you raise about the statement? What kinds of questions would you put to the commentator? What kind of evidence would you need to accept his statement? What is your own position on the issue he raised, and how would you go about defending it?

Summary

Social change is both normal and pervasive. Change is not inherently traumatic. People find change painful, and resist it, when they perceive it to be an economic threat or liability; ambiguous or obscure in its consequences; imposed on them; too risky or too costly; a threat to interpersonal relationships; inconsistent with their values; a threat to their self-esteem; and a threat to their status and power.

Among the sources of change are social movements, technology, ideology, competition and conflict, the government and economy, and population shifts. Television and personal computers illustrate the broad-ranging impact of technology on change, each having both positive and negative consequences.

All groups have ideologies that enable members to make sense of the world. Ideologies can be a barrier or impediment to change. Ideologies also facilitate change in four ways: they can legitimate the change, they function as a support for the leaders who implement the change, they motivate individuals, and they confront people with a contradiction that needs to be resolved.

Competition and conflict increase the amount of creativity and innovation, although they can also have destructive effects. The relationship between conflict and change tends to be self-sustaining. The government and economy are important factors in change. In most modernizing nations, the government plays a central role in directing and supporting the change. Population growth, migration, and changes in the age and sex composition of the population all foster various kinds of social change.

Change is patterned. Developmental change is growth by stages. Two important kinds of developmental change are evolutionary (illustrated by Comte's analysis) and dialectical (illustrated by Marx's analysis) change. Cyclic change, exemplified by Sorokin's analysis, is ongoing fluctuations without any trend. The diffusion and adoption of innovations follow a logistic curve. Modernization is a form of growth by stages. Modernization brings pervasive change at all levels of social life.

Social movements are organized efforts to promote or resist some kind of change. The explanations of why people participate in social movements are strain theory, resource mobilization, political process theory, and relative deprivation. According to strain theory, people stressed by social disruption form movements. Resource mobilization views people as rational, and potential movement members as deciding whether to participate on the basis of a cost/benefit analysis. Political participation theory emphasizes the availability of political opportunities to people who are stressed. Relative deprivation points to the gap between what people expect and what they get.

Social movements bring about change at a number of levels. They change their members by socializing them into the movement's ideology. They may also effect role change and changes in institutions. They tend to generate countermovements, and the change that occurs in society comes out of the matrix of movement/countermovement struggle. Factors associated with movement success in bringing about change include the use of aggressive tactics, organization, reasonable goals, the support of other organizations and groups in the society, and timing.

Glossary

dialectical theory the theory that contradiction is the essence of all of things and the prime mover of change

ideology a set of interrelated beliefs that explain reality and give directives for action

modernization the economic, social, and cultural change occurring in the transition from an agrarian to an industrial society

nationalism an ideology that stresses the importance of the nation's interests over those of all outsiders

political process theory the theory that a social movement depends upon the availability of political opportunities

relative deprivation the perception of deprivation on the basis of a subjectively defined standard of comparison

resource mobilization theory the theory that a social movement depends upon the ability to mobilize crucial resources in the face of opposition

social change alterations in social phenomena at various levels of human life from the individual to the global

social movements organized efforts to promote or resist some kind of change

strain theory the theory that a social movement is a reaction of people stressed by some kind of serious disruption in the social order

GLOSSARY

abortion expulsion of a fetus from the uterus

achieved status a position one has by virtue of one's efforts

agrarian society a society in which people survive by using animal-drawn plows for cultivating the land

AIDS acquired immune deficiency syndrome, a viral infection that causes the immune system to stop functioning and leads to death

anomie a condition in which norms are weak, inconsistent, or lacking

anorexia nervosa an emotional disorder involving self-starvation

anticipatory socialization the adoption of values, attitudes, and behaviors that an individual perceives to be associated with a role that he or she will, or would like to, assume

anti-Semitism prejudice against Jewish people

ascribed status a position one has by virtue of the circumstances of one's birth

assimilation a process in which a racial/ethnic group adopts the culture of the dominant group, thereby blending into the larger society and losing its distinctive identity

authoritarian government a government that uses coercion to govern

authority the legitimate exercise of power on the basis of law, tradition, or charismatic leadership

beliefs propositions which are unverified or unverifiable

blended family a remarriage in which one or both spouses bring in children from a previous marriage

bulimia an emotional disorder involving repeated binge eating followed by "purging" through forced vomiting or laxatives

bureaucracy a form of organization characterized by specific domains of authority and responsibility, a hierarchy of authority, management based on written documents, expertise of officials and workers, management on the basis of rules, and full-time workers

Calvinism the system of Christian beliefs deriving from the work of the Protestant reformer, John Calvin (1509–64)

capitalism an economic system with private ownership of the means of production and competitive, for-profit distribution of goods and services

caste system a closed form of stratification, based on ascription

charisma extraordinary personal qualities that attract devoted followers

church an established religious organization that is an integral part of the larger society

civil religion a set of beliefs that makes the dominant values of the nation sacred

class system an open form of stratification, based on achievement

clone an exact biological copy that is produced asexually

cohabitation living with someone in an intimate, sexual relationship without being married

comparable worth the principle that equal pay should be given to work that is judged to be of comparable worth

conflict theory a theory that focuses on contradictory interests, inequalities, and the resulting conflict and change

content analysis he determination of the relative frequency of particular ideas or words in the content of some communication or printed materials

contraception the use of devices or techniques to prevent fertilization

control group an experimental group in which there is no manipulation of the independent variable and only the dependent variable is measured

correlation the extent to which two phenomena vary the same way, from 0 to 100 percent

crimes of negligence crimes in which there is an unintended victim or potential victim

crude birth rate the number of births in one year per 1,000 persons

crude death rate the number of deaths in one year per 1,000 persons

cult a religious group that repudiates the values of the larger society, opposes all other religions, and demands total commitment from its members

cultural integration the process whereby various portions of the culture fit together into a more or less coherent whole

cultural relativism the idea that each culture must be evaluated in its own terms rather than in terms of the standards of others

cultural transmission the process by which culture is learned by each succeeding generation

culture everything created by people, including their technology, knowledge and beliefs, art, morals, law, customs, and all other products of their thought and action

definition of the situation when we define a situation as real, it is real in its consequences

democracy government by the people as a whole

demographic transition the change from high birth and death rates to low birth and death rates

demography the scientific study of population

dependent variable the variable in an experiment that is affected in some way by the independent variable

deviance behavior that violates social norms

dialectical materialism the theory that history is a process driven by material forces (rather than ideas) that exist together but that are in contradiction with each other

dialectical theory the theory that contradiction is the essence of all things and the prime mover of change

differential association the theory that illegal behavior results from exposure to more favorable than unfavorable definitions of that behavior

diffusion the spread of culture from one society to another or from one portion of a society to another

discrimination arbitrary, unfavorable treatment of the people in another racial/ethnic group

dramaturgy a method of analyzing human behavior that uses the imagery of the theater

dyad a group of two people

ecosystem a set of living things and their environment that are interdependent

ego the part of the personality that enables the individual to interact with the world in a realistic and effective way

environmental depletion the increasing scarcity of natural resources

estate system a closed form of stratification, based on law as well as birth

ethnic group people with a shared cultural background that leads them to identify with each other

ethnocentrism the belief that one's own culture is the right and best way of life and the tendency to evaluate other cultures in terms of one's own cultural ways

exchange a form of interaction in which people give and receive some kind of valued goods, services, or possessions

experiment the manipulation of some variables, while controlling others, in order to measure the outcome on still other variables

family a group of two or more persons related by birth, marriage, or adoption and residing together in a household

feminism the belief that all gender inequalities should be eliminated

feminist theory a theory that focuses on explaining women's disadvantaged position in society

folkways norms that are defined as not essential to social well-being, thereby incurring only mild sanctions when broken

formal organization a secondary group set up to achieve specific goals

fundamentalism the effort to practice a pure religion based on a literal interpretation of the sacred scriptures

gemeinschaft a group with a strong sense of community, bound together by tradition, kinship, and personal relationships

gender man or woman (social male or female), as distinguished from the biological male or female

gender role the behavior associated with being either a man or a woman

generalizability the extent to which the results of a study apply to other subjects, groups, or conditions

gesellschaft a group characterized by weak family ties, individualism, competition, and more impersonal than personal relationships

ghetto an urban area inhabited predominantly by one minority group

group two or more interacting people who pursue some common goal or interest

health a state of physical and emotional well-being

herbicide a chemical used to kill plant life, particularly weeds

homophobia the irrational fear of homosexuality

horticultural society a society in which the people survive by growing plants in gardens

hunting and gathering society a society in which the people survive by hunting animals and gathering plants

hypothesis a tentative statement about the relationship between phenomena

"I" the unpredictable, the novel, the impulsive part of the self

iatrogenic caused by the physician in the course of treating a patient

Id the seat of the instincts, the source of all psychic energy

ideology a set of interrelated beliefs that explain reality and give directives for action

illegal services crime in which unlawful services such as drugs or prostitution are rendered to a customer

immigration rate the number of people who have come into the country in one year per 1,000 population

impression management an individual's effort to manage the impressions others receive so as to control the way the others define the individual and the situation

independent variable the variable in an experiment that is manipulated in order to see how it affects the dependent variable

industrial society a society with new sources of energy (coal, petroleum, natural gas, etc.) and industry rather than agriculture as its primary source of wealth

informal organization the unofficial, unplanned, but patterned relationships in an organization

ingroup a group to which an individual feels he or she belongs to which he or she is loyal

innovation a discovery or invention that adds something new to a culture

institution a collective solution to a problem of social life

institutional discrimination the maintenance of discriminatory behavior through the policies and practices of institutions

interest group a group that tries to influence public opinion and political decisions in accord with the particular interests of the group's members

intragenerational mobility movement in social class position of an individual or group

intergenerational mobility change in social class position from one generation to the next

knowledge propositions for which there is empirical evidence

labeling theory the theory that people become deviant as they are defined and treated as deviants

labor force all civilians who are employed and those who are unemployed but able and wanting to work

latent functions unintended and unrecognized consequences of social action

laws formalized norms enforced by the state

life expectancy the average number of years people can expect to live

linguistic relativity the thesis that language systems shape our experience of the world and direct our interpretations

macro level large-scale social processes

manifest functions intended and recognized consequences of social action

material culture those objects and artifacts which are made and used by people

"me" the socialized part of the self

mean the average, or all of the scores divided by the number of cases

mechanical solidarity a type of social solidarity in which there are shared ideas and tendencies, the dominance of the group over the individual, and strong sanctions against anyone who deviates from group norms

median the number below which are half of all the scores and above which are the other half

megalopolis an urban area formed by the merging of two or more metropolitan areas

micro level small-scale social processes

migration the movement of people from one area to another

minority a disadvantaged racial or ethnic group

mixed economy an economic system that combines elements of capitalism and socialism

modernization the economic, social, and cultural changes occurring in the transition from an agrarian to an industrial society

monogamy partnered with one person at a time

mores norms considered essential to the well-being of the group, thereby incurring severe sanctions when broken

nationalism an ideology that stresses the importance of the nation's interests over those of all outsiders

nonmaterial culture the beliefs, attitudes, values, and norms that are shared by people

non sequitur a conclusion that does not follow logically from what precedes it

nuclear family a family composed of husband, wife, and children

norm a shared expectation for behavior

objective social class class position as measured by education, income, occupation, or some combination of the three

organic solidarity a type of social solidarity based on people's need of other in a society with a complex division of labor

outgroup a group to which an individual feels he or she does not belong and towards which he or she feels some hostility, dislike, and/or competition

Parkinson's Law the bureaucracy will continue to expand independently of the amount of work to be done

participant observation the study of a social situation in which the researcher also takes part

participatory government a government in which the people have a voice in who rules them and how they are ruled

patriarchy a social system in which men dominate women

performance all the activity of an individual that influences others with whom the individual is interacting

pesticide a chemical used to kill insects defined as pests

Peter Principle individuals in an organization will be promoted to their level of incompetence

pluralism the maintenance of racial/ethnic identities along with equal rights and power

pluralist model a model of politics in which power is distributed more or less equally among various interest groups

political process theory the theory that a social movement depends upon the availability of political opportunities

pollution harmful alterations to air, land, or water

polygyny marriage of one husband with two or more wives

post-industrial society a society in which agricultural and industrial jobs are a minority of all jobs

power control over the behavior of others—with or without their consent—to attain specific goals

power-elite model a model of politics in which power is concentrated in political, economic, and military leaders

power structure the way in which power is distributed among the various units and members of the organization

predatory crime crime involving loss of property or some kind of physical harm

prejudice a negative attitude toward people in another racial/ethnic group that justifies discriminatory behavior

primary deviance deviant acts or behavior by an individual who still defines himself or herself as conforming rather than deviant

primary groups groups that involve face-to-face, personal, intimate interaction

public disorder crimes crimes such as disorderly conduct and public drunkenness that are offensive to an audience

race a group of people with distinguishing biological characteristics that affect their interaction with other groups *racism* the belief that some racial groups are inherently inferior to others

reference group a real or imaginary group that is the audience that approves of an individual's behavior

relative deprivation the perception of deprivation on the basis of a subjectively defined standard of comparison

religion the institution that provides meaning through a set of beliefs and practices that are defined as sacred

representative sample a sample that typifies the population from which it is drawn

resocialization socialization into a role that radically alters an individual's behavior

resource mobilization theory the theory that a social movement depends upon the ability to mobilize crucial resources in the face of opposition

rites of passage ceremonies that mark the transition to a new status in a society

role the social expectations for behavior associated with a particular status

role conflict contrary expectations attached to the same role or incompatible expectations between two or more roles

role distance the gap between social expectations and actual performance

role-making acting in a way to modify a role

role set the set of role relationships involved in occupying a particular social status

role strain difficulty in fulfilling role obligations

role-taking constructing the attitudes of another person in order to anticipate the behavior of that person

sample a small number of people selected by various methods from a larger population

sanctions rewards and punishments used to regulate behavior according to social norms

science the knowledge gained by systematic, rational observation

secondary deviance deviant acts or behavior by an individual who defines himself or herself as a deviant

secondary groups groups based on impersonal relationships and have a specific task

sect a religious organization that stands apart from the larger society and the church

segregation the physical and social separation of racial/ethnic groups of people from each other

self the capacity to observe, respond to, and direct one's own behavior

self concept the set of beliefs and attitudes an individual holds toward him- or herself

self control the internalization of norms that results in self-regulation of behavior *sex* biological male or female

sexism prejudice or discrimination against someone based on that person's sex

sexual harassment unwanted sexual advances by someone in a position of superior power

sick role the behavioral expectations for those who are ill

small group a group in which face-to-face interaction is possible for all of the members

social change alterations in social phenomena at various levels of human life from the individual to the global

social classes groups that are unequal with regard to things valued in a society, whose members share similar values and lifestyles

social control a system of mechanisms for regulating behavior in socially approved ways

social engineering the use of knowledge to control human behavior and organizational processes

socialism an economic system with state ownership of the means of production and cooperative distribution of goods and services

socialization the social process by which an individual develops and learns to function effectively in a group

social mobility movement of individuals and groups within or between social classes

social movements organized efforts to promote or resist some kind of change

social network the totality of an individual's complex system of relationships

social stratification the organization of any society into groups that are unequal with regard to things valued

social structure regularities and patterns in social interaction

society people who share a particular territory and culture

sociological imagination a way of thinking that enables people to understand the impact of culture, society, and group memberships on their behavior

sociology the scientific study of social life

status an evaluated social position

sterilization a surgical procedure that eliminates fertility

strain theory the theory that a social movement is a reaction of people stressed by some kind of serious disruption in the social order

structural-functionalism a theory that focuses on social systems and how their interdependent parts maintain order

subcultural theory Fischer's theory that subcultures of like-minded people emerge in the city and enrich participant's lives

subculture a group within a society that shares much of the culture of the larger society while maintaining certain distinctive cultural patterns of its own

subjective social class the ranking that people give to themselves in the class system

suburb an urban area adjacent to a city but outside the jurisdiction of the city's government

superego the part of the personality that distinguishes right from wrong and urges the individual to perfection

survey research the use of interviews and/or questionnaires to gather data

symbolic interactionism a theory that focuses on the interaction between individuals and the resulting construction of social life

symbols arbitrary signs with shared meaning

technology the organization of knowledge for practical purposes

test of significance a technical way of determining the probability that the findings occurred by chance

theism a religion that is centered on God or gods

theory a set of logically related propositions that explain relationships of social phenomena to each other

totalitarian government a government that is authoritarian and that attempts to control the totality of people's lives

underemployment full-time work for inadequate wages, work that is below the worker's skill level, or part-time or temporary work for those who desire full-time jobs

unemployment rate the proportion of workers who are out of jobs and who are looking for employment

urbanization the increasing concentration of people living in cities

values shared conceptions of what is desirable or undesirable, right or wrong

variable any trait or characteristic or social factor that has multiple values to which numbers can be assigned

voluntary association an organization that people voluntarily join to pursue a particular interest or to support particular ideals.

white-collar crimes crimes committed by respectable people in the course of their work

world system theory analysis of the world as an economic system with a division of labor along national lines

REFERENCES

Abouserie, Reda. 1996. "Stress, coping strategies and job satisfaction in university academic staff." *Educational Psychology* 16: 49-56.

Abramson, Paul R., and Ronald Inglehart. 1995. *Value Change in Global Perspective*. Ann Arbor: University of Michigan Press.

Adams, Susan, Janet Kuebli, Patricia A. Boyle, and Robyn Fivush. 1995. "Gender differences in parent-child conversations about past emotions: A longitudinal investigation." *Sex-Roles* 33: 309-23.

Adelman, Clifford. 1991. *Women at Thirtysomething: Paradoxes of Attainment*. Washington, D.C.: U.S. Department of Education.

Adler, Jerry, and Maggie Malone. 1996. "Keeping track: An inventory of rail service." *Newsweek*, November 4.

Adler, Stephen J. and Wade Lambert. 1993. "Common criminals: Just about everyone violates some laws, even model citizens." *Wall Street Journal*, March 12.

Ager, Susan. 1996. "New girdles hold women in, and back." *The San Diego Union-Tribune* October 25.

Alam, M. Shahid. 1989. "The South Korean 'miracle': Examining the mix of government and markets." *The Journal of Developing Areas* 23: 233-58.

Aloise-Young, Patricia A. 1993. "The development of self-presentation: Self-promotion in 6- to 10-year-old children." *Social Cognition* 11:201-22.

Amato, Paul R. l987. "Family Processes in One-Parent, Stepparent, and Intact Families: The Child's Point of View." *Journal of Marriage and the Family* 49:327-37.

_____. l99l. "Parental Absence During Childhood and Depression in Later Life." *The Sociological Quarterly* 32:543-56.

American Academy of Pediatrics. 1990. "Children, Adolescents, and Television." *Pediatrics* 85: 1119.

American Psychiatric Association. 1987. *Diagnostic and Statistical Manual of Mental Disorders*, 3d ed., rev. Washington, D.C.: American Psychiatric Association.

Andreski, Stanislav, ed. l969. *Herbert Spencer: Principles of Sociology*. London: Macmillan.

Applebome, Peter. 1996. "Americans straddle 'average' mark in math, science." *New York Times*, November 21.

Arendell, Terry. 1986. *Mothers and Divorce: Legal, Economic, and Social Dilemmas*. Berkeley: University of California Press.

_____. 1995. *Fathers and Divorce*. Thousand Oaks, CA.: Sage Press.

Arnold, Thomas Clay. 1996. "Theory, history, and the Western waterscape: The market culture thesis." *Journal of the Southwest* 38: 215.

Asch, David. 1996. "The role of critical care nurses in euthanasia and assisted suicide." *New England Journal of Medicine* 334 (May 23):1374-79.

Asch, S.E. 1958. "Effects of group pressure upon the modification and distortion of judgments." In E.E. Maccoby, T.M. Newcomb, and E.L. Hartley, eds., *Readings in Social Psychology*. New York: Holt, Rinehart and Winston.

Association of American Colleges. 1982. *The Classroom Climate: A Chilly One for Women?* Washington, D.C.: Association of American Colleges.

Aune, R. Kelly. 1994. "The influence of culture, gender, and relational status on appearance management." *Journal of Cross-Cultural Psychology* 25:258-72.

Bahr, Kathleen S. 1994. "The Strengths of Apache Grandmothers: Observations on Commitment, Culture and Caretaking." *Journal of Comparative Family Studies* 25:233-48.

Bandura, A., D. Ross, and S.A. Ross. 1963. "Imitation of film-mediated aggressive models." *Journal of Abnormal and Social Psychology* 66:3-11.

Banerjee, Ruben. 1992. "Where beggars are choosers." *India Today*. February 22, 1992.

Barnett, Tony. 1989. *Social and Economic Development*. New York: Guilford Press.

Barrett, Richard E., and Martin King Whyte. 1982. "Dependency theory and Taiwan: Analysis of a deviant case." *American Journal of Sociology* 87:1064-89.

Barringer, Felicity. 1992. "As American as apple pie, dim sum, or burritos." *New York Times*, December 30.

Barron, James. 1989. "Unnecessary surgery." *The New York Times Magazine*, April 16.

Bastian, Lisa. 1995. "Criminal victimization 1993." *Bureau of Justice Statistics Bulletin* May 1995.

Baumeister, Roy F., Laura Smart, and Joseph M. Boden. 1996. "Relation of threatened egotism to violence and aggression: The dark side of high self-esteem." *Psychological Review* 103:5-33.

Baydo, Gerald R. 1974. *A Topical History of the United States*. Arlington Heights, Il.: The Forum Press.

Beals, Alan R. 1967. *Culture In Process*. New York: Holt, Rinehart and Winston.

Becker, Howard, and Harry Elmer Barnes. 1961. *Social Thought from Lore to Science*, vol. 2, 3rd ed. New York: Dover.

Beggan, James K., David M. Messick, and Scott T. Allison. 1988. "Social values and egocentric bias: Two tests of the might over morality hypothesis." *Journal of Personality and Social Psychology* 55:606-11.

Bellah, Robert N. 1957. *Tokugawa Religion*. New York: The Free Press.

_____. 1992. *The Broken Covenant: American Civil Religion in Time of Trial*. 2nd ed. Chicago: University of Chicago Press.

Bellah, Robert N, and Phillip E. Hammond. 1980. *Varieties of Civil Religion*. New York: Harper and Row.

Ben-David, Joseph. 1970. "Scientific productivity and academic organization in nineteenth-century medicine." In *Comparative Perspectives on Female Organization*, ed. Henry A. Landsberger. Boston: Little-Brown.

Benin, Mary Holland and Barbara Cable Nienstedt. 1985. "Happiness in Single- and Dual-Earner Families: The Effects of Marital Happiness, Job Satisfaction, and Life Cycle." *Journal of Marriage and the Family* 47:975-84.

Bennett, Claudette E. 1993. "The Asian and Pacific Islander population." In the U.S. Bureau of the Census, *Population Profile of the United States: 1993*. Washington D.C.: Government Printing Office.

Bennett, Julie. 1996. "Gender gap: Few women in hi-tech jobs, despite many opportunities." *Chicago Tribune*, December 29.

Berger, Peter. 1967. *The Sacred Canopy: Elements of a Sociological Theory of Religion*. Garden City, N.Y.: Anchor Books.

Berkin, Carol Ruth, and Mary Beth Norton. 1979. *Women of America: A History*. Boston: Houghton Mifflin Company.

Bernard, Jessie. 1972. *The Future of Marriage*. New York: World.

Beutel, Ann M. and Margaret Mooney Marini. 1995. "Gender and values." *American Sociological Review* 60: 436-48.

Binder, Frederick M. and David M. Reimers, eds. 1988. *The Way We Lived, Vol. I: 1607-1877*. Lexington, MA.: D.C. Heath and Company.

Bird, Gerald A., Rosemary C. Goss, and Gloria W. Bird. 1990. "Effects of home computer use on fathers' lives." *Family Relations* 39: 438-42.

Blair, Sampson Lee. l993. "Employment, Family, and Perceptions of Marital Quality Among Husbands and Wives." *Journal of Family Issues* 14:189-2l2.

Blair, Sampson Lee, and Daniel T. Lichter. 1991. "Measuring the division of household labor." *Journal of Family Issues* 12: 91-113.

Blank, Robert H. 1988. *Rationing Medicine*. New York: Columbia University.

Blankenhorn, David, Steven Bayme, and Jean Bethke Elshtain. 1990. *Rebuilding the Nest: A New Commitment to the American Family*. Milwaukee: Family Service America.

Blau, Peter M. and Otis Dudley Duncan. 1967. *The American Occupational Structure*. New York: Wiley.

Blazer, D.G., Ronald C. Kessler, Katherine A. McGonagle, and Marvin S. Swartz. l994. "The prevalence and distribution of major depression in a national community sample." *American Journal of Psychiatry* 151:979-86.

Blendon, R.J. et al. 1995. "Who has the best health care system? A second look." *Health* 14: 220-30.

Blum, Debra E. 1994. "Slow progress on equity." *The Chronicle of Higher Education* October 26.

Blum, Jerome, Rondo Cameron, and Thomas G. Barnes. 1966. *A History of the European World*. Boston: Little, Brown, & Company.

Boas, G. 1948. *Essays on Primitivism and Related Ideas in Antiquity*. Baltimore: Penguin.

Bobo, Lawrence and Camille L. Zubrinsky. 1996. "Attitudes on residential integration: perceived status differences, mere in-group preference, or racial prejudice." *Social Forces* 74: 883-909.

Boffey, Philip M. 1987. "U.S. study finds fraud in top researcher's work on mentally retarded." *The New York Times*, May 24.

Bohanon, Cecil. 1991. "The economic correlates of homelessness in sixty cities." *Social Science Quarterly* 72:817-25.

Borg, Gary. 1996. "Doctors assisting in AIDS suicides." *Chicago Tribune*, July 11.

Borland, Delores. l982. "A Cohort Analysis Approach to the Empty-Nest Syndrome Among Three Ethnic Groups of Women: A Theoretical Position." *Journal of Marriage and the Family* 44:117-29.

Bornschier, Volker, Christopher Chase-Dunn, and Richard Rubinson. 1978. "Cross-national evidence of the effects of foreign investment and aid on economic growth and inequality." *American Journal of Sociology* 84:670-82.

Bradburn, Ellen M., Phyllis Moen, and Donna Dempster-McClain. 1995. "Women's return to school following the transition to motherhood." *Social Forces* 73: 1517-1551.

Bradshaw, York W. 1987. "Urbanization and development: A global study of modernization, urban bias, and economic dependency." *American Sociological Review* 52: 224-39.

_____. 1988. "Reassessing economic dependency and uneven development: The Kenyan experience." *American Sociological Review* 53:693-708.

Brett, P.J., K. Graham, and C. Smythe. 1995. "An analysis of specialty journals on alcohol, drugs and addictive behaviors for sex bias in research methods and reporting." *Journal of Studies on Alcohol* 56:24-34.

Broad, William J. 1997. "Survey of 100 U.S. coastal sites shows pollution declining." *The New York Times*, January 21.

Broman, Clifford L. 1988b. "Satisfaction Among Blacks: The Significance of Marriage and Parenthood." *Journal of Marriage and the Family* 50:45-51.

Bromley, David G., and Anson Shupe, Jr. 1981. *Strange Gods: The Great American Cult Scare*. Boston: Deacon Press.

Bronstein, Phyllis. 1994. "Patterns of parent-child interaction in Mexican families: A cross-cultural perspective." *International Journal of Behavioral Development* 17:423-46.

Bronte, Anne. 1994. *The Tenant of Wildfell Hall*. Hertfordshire: Wordsworth Classics.

Brown, Lester R. 1993. "A new era unfolds." In *State of the World* 1993, Lester R. Brown, et al., eds., pp. 3 21. New York: W. W. Norton.

_____. 1995 "Nature's Limits." In *State of the World 1995*, Lester R. Brown, et al., eds., pp. 3-20. New York: W.W. Norton.

Brown, P. 1995. "Race, class, and environmental health: A review and systematization of the literature." *Environmental Research* 69: 15-30.

Brown, Richard Harvey. 1993. "Modern science: Institutionalization of knowledge and rationalization of power." *The Sociological Quarterly* 34: 153-68.

Browne, Irene. 1995. "The baby boom and trends in poverty, 1967-1987." *Social Forces* 73: 1071-1095.

Budiansky, Stephen. 1996. "Yellowstone's unraveling: The ecosystem is in grave peril and the most damage is caused by elk." *U.S. News & World Report*, September 16.

Bunker, J.P. 1995. "Medicine matters after all." *Journal of the Royal College of Physicians* 29: 105-12.

Bureau of Indian Affairs. 1992. "Indian Lands 1992." *U.S. Department of the Interior*. Washington D.C.: U.S. Government Printing Office.

Bureau of Labor Statistics. 1996. "Employment situation summary, October 1996." Bureau of Labor Statistics Website, November 1.

Burke, John G. 1966. "Bursting boilers and the federal power." *Technology and Culture* 7: 1-23.

Burke, Ronald J. 1996a. "Sources of job satisfaction among employees of a professional services firm." *Psychological Reports* 78: 1231-1234.

_____. 1996b. "Unit size, work experiences and satisfactions: An exploratory study." *Psychological Reports* 78: 763-67.

Burns, Alisa, and Catherine Scott. 1994. *Mother-headed Families and Why They Have Increased*. Hillsdale, N.J., Lawrence Erlbaum.

Butler, Samuel. 1968. *Erewhon*. New York: Lancer Books.

Butterfield, Herbert. 1957. *The Origins of Modern Science*. New York: The Free Press.

Camhi, Merry. 1996. "Overfishing threatens sea's bounty." *Forum for Applied Research and Public Policy* 11: 5.

Canada, Katherine, and Richard Pringle. 1995. "The role of gender in college classroom interactions: A social context approach." *Sociology of Education* 68:161-86.

Cancio, A. Silvia, T. David Evans, and David J. Maume, Jr. 1996. "Reconsidering the declining significance of race." *American Sociological Review* 61: 541-56.

Caskey, John P. l994. *Fringe Banking: Check-Cashing Outlets, Pawnshops, and the Poor*. New York: Sage.

Cavalli-Sforza, Luca, Paolo Menozzi, and Alberto Piazza. 1994. *The History and Geography of Human Genes*. Princeton, N.J.: Princeton University Press.

Cebula, Richard J. and Willie J. Belton. 1994. "Voting with one's feet: An empirical analysis of public welfare and migration of the American Indian." *American Journal of Economics and Sociology* 53: 273-80.

Centers for Disease Control. l994. "Physical violence during the l2 months preceding childbirth." *Journal of the American Medical Association* 271:1152-54.

_____. l995. "Symptoms of substance dependence associated with use of cigarettes, alcohol, and illicit drugs—United States, l992-l994." *Morbidity and Mortality Weekly Report*, 44 (November l0).

Cerulo, Karen A. 1992. "Technological ties that bind: Media-generated primary groups." *Communication Research* 19:109-29.

Chacko, Thomas I. 1983. "Job and life satisfaction: A causal analysis of their relationships." *Academy of Management Journal* 26: 163-69.

Chafetz, Janet Saltzman. 1988. *Feminist Sociology: An Overview of Contemporary Theories*. Itasca, IL.: F.E. Peacock Publishers.

Chagnon, Napoleon. 1992. Yanomamo: *The Fierce People*. 4th ed. New York: Holt, Rinehart, & Winston.

Chakraborty, Jyotimoy. 1994. "Marriage Customs of the Siddis." *Journal of the Anthropological Survey of India* 43:17–23.

Champion, Dean J. 1975. *The Sociology of Organizations*. New York: McGraw-Hill.

Chan, Steve. 1989. "Income inequality among LDCs: A comparative analysis of alternative perspectives." *International Studies Quarterly* 33:45-65.

Chang, Edward C. 1996. "Cultural differences in optimism, pessimism, and coping: Predictors of subsequent adjustment in Asian American and Caucasian American college students." *Journal of Counseling Psychology* 43: 113-23.

Chao, Ruth K. 1996. "Chinese and European American mothers' beliefs about the role of parenting in children's school success." *Journal of Cross-Cultural Psychology* 27:403-23.

Charmaz, Kathy. 1995. "The body, identity, and self: Adapting to impairment." *The Sociological Quarterly* 36: 657-80.

Chassler, Sey. 1997. "What teenage girls say about pregnancy." *Parade Magazine*, February 2.

Chavez, Leo R. 1994. "The power of the imagined community: The settlement of undocumented Mexicans and Central Americans in the United States." *American Anthropologist* 96:52-73.

Chen, C. and H.W. Stevenson. 1995. "Motivation and mathematics achievement: A comparative study of Asian-American, Caucasian-American, and east Asian high school students." *Child Development* 66: 1214-1234.

Cheng, Sheung-Tak. 1996. "A critical review of Chinese koro." *Culture, Medicine and Psychiatry* 20:67-82.

Chia, R. C. et al. l994. "A comparison of family values among Chinese, Mexican, and American college students." *Journal of Social Behavior and Personality* 9:249-58.

Chira, Susan. 1991. "Report says too many aren't ready for school." *New York Times*, December 8.

Chochinov, H.M. et al. 1995. "Desire for death in the terminally ill." *American Journal of Psychiatry* 152: 1185-1191.

Chriswick, Barry R. 1993. "The skills and economic status of American Jewry: Trends over the last half-century." *Journal of Labor Economics* 11: 229-42.

Chunhou, Zhang. 1996. "Student responses to economic reform in China." *Adolescence* 31: 663-76.

Church, George J. 1996. "Ripping up welfare." *Time* August 12, 1996.

Cimons, Marlene. 1990. "U.S. smoking toll put at $52 billion." *Los Angeles Times*, February 21.

Clark, David L. and Sue McKibbin. 1982. "From orthodoxy to pluralism: New views of school administration." *Phi Delta Kappan* 63:669-72.

Clark, Jennifer, and Bonnie L. Barber. 1994. "Adolescents in postdivorce and always-married families: Self-esteem and perceptions of fathers' interest." *Journal of Marriage and the Family* 56:608-14.

Clark-Nicolas, Patricia, and Bernadette Gray-Little. 1991. "Effect of economic resources on marital quality in black married couples." *Journal of Marriage and the Family* 53:645-55.

Coats, Erik J. 1995. "The role of television in the socialization of nonverbal behavioral skills." *Basic & Applied Social Psychology* 17:327-41.

Cohen, Bernard P. and Xueguang Zhou. 1991. "Status processes in enduring work groups." *American Sociological Review* 56:179-88.

Cohen, Joel E. 1996 "Ten myths of population." *Discover*, April.

Cohen, Michael D., James C. March, and Johan P. Olsen. 1972. "A garbage can model of organizational choice." *Administrative Science Quarterly* 17:1-25.

Cohn, Samuel, and Mark Fossett. l995. "Why racial employment in-quality is greater in Northern labor markets: Regional differences in White-Black employment differentials." *Social Forces* 74:511-42.

Coleman, Diane H. and Murray A. Straus. l986. "Marital Power, Conflict, and Violence in a Nationally Representative Sample of American Couples." *Violence and Victims* 1:141-57.

Collins, Sharon M. 1989. "The marginalization of Black executives." *Social Problems* 36: 317-31.

Colombotos, John. 1969. "Physicians and Medicare: A before-after study of the effects of legislation on attitudes." *American Sociological Review* 34:3l8-34.

Combahee River Collective. 1992. "A black feminist statement." In Maggie Humm, ed., *Modern Feminisms.* New York: Columbia University Press.

Comte, Auguste. l858. *The Positive Philosophy*, trans. Harriet Martineau. New York: Calvin Blanchard.

Condon, Richard G., and Pamela R. Stern. 1993. "Gender-role preference, gender identity, and gender socialization among contemporary Inuit youth." *Ethos* 21: 384-416.

Conlin, Joseph. 1984. *The American Past*. New York: Harcourt Brace Jovanovich.

Conly, Catherine H., and J. Thomas McEwen. 1990. "Computer Crime." *NIJ Reports*, January/February, pp. 2 7.

Conway, Flo and Jim Siegelman. 1978. *Snapping: America's Epidemic of Sudden Personality Change*. New York: Dell Publishing Company.

_____. 1983. "The awesome power of the mind-probers." *Science Digest*, September.

Cooley, Charles Horton. 1902. *Human Nature and the Social Order*. New York: Scribner.

Coon, Carleton, S., Stanley M. Garn, and Joseph B. Birdsell. 1950. *Races*. Springfield, IL: Charles C. Thomas.

Cooney, Teresa M. l994. "Young Adults' Relations With Parents: The Influence of Recent Parental Divorce." *Journal of Marriage and the Family* 56:45-56.

Corson, Richard. 1965. *Fashions In Hair*. New York: Hastings House.

Cose, Ellis. 1993. *The Rage of the Privileged Class*. New York: HarperCollins.

Costin, F. and C. Kaptanoglu. 1993. "Beliefs about rape and women's social roles: A Turkish replication." *European Journal of Social Psychology* 23:327-30.

Cowan, Ruth Schwartz. 1976. "The 'Industrial Revolution' in the home: Household technology and social change in the twentieth century." *Technology and Culture* 17: 1-23.

Cox, Harvey. 1995. *Fire from Heaven*. Reading, MA.: Addison-Wesley Publishing Company.

Crabb, Peter B., and Dawn Bielawski. 1994. "The social representation of material culture and gender in children's books." *Sex Roles* 30:69-79.

Croft, William C. l994. "High price for white-collar crime." *Chicago Tribune*, September 7.

Crossette, Barbara. l995. "Children called big losers in small wars." *The San Diego Union-Tribune*, December ll.

_____. 1996. "U.N. survey shows population growth slowing." *The New York Times*, November 17.

Cunningham, Michael. 1996. "Nice guys finish first in mating game: Study debunks theory about women, money." *Chicago Tribune*, August 12.

Curry, Timothy Jon. 1993. "A little pain never hurt anyone: Athletic career socialization and the normalization of sports injury." *Symbolic Interaction* 16:273-90.

Curtis, James E., Edward G. Grabb, and Douglas E. Baer. 1992. "Voluntary association membership in fifteen countries." *American Sociological Review* 57:139-52.

Dahrendorf, Ralf. 1959. *Class and Class Conflict in Industrial Society*. Stanford: Stanford University Press.

D'Amico, Ronald and Nan L. Maxwell. 1995. "The continuing significance of race in minority male joblessness." *Social Forces* 73: 969-91.

Darley, J.M., and B. Latané. 1968. "Bystander intervention in emergencies: Diffusion of responsibility." *Journal of Personality and Social Psychology* 8:377-83.

Davis, Kingsley and Wilbert E. Moore. 1945. "Some principles of stratification." *American Sociological Review* 10:242-49.

Dawson, John M. and Patrick A. Langan. 1994. "Murder In Families." *Bureau of Justice Statistics: Special Report*, July.

Dehyle, Donna. 1995. "Navajo youth and Anglo racism: Cultural integrity and resistance." *Harvard Educational Review* 65: 403-44.

Delaney, Cassandra Halleh. 1995. "Rites of passage in adolescence." *Adolescence* 30:891-97.

del Castillo, Richard G. 1984. *La Familia: Chicano Families in the Urban Southwest, 1848 to the Present*. Notre Dame, IN: University of Notre Dame Press.

DeMaris, Alfred, and K. Vaninadha Rao. 1992. "Premarital Cohabitation and Subsequent Marital Stability in the United States: A Reassessment." *Journal of Marriage and the Family* 54:178-90.

Derne, Steve. 1995. *Culture in Action: Family Life, Emotion and Male Dominance in Banaras, India*. Albany: State University of New York Press.

Deutsch, Morton, and R.M. Krauss. 1962. "Studies of interpersonal bargaining." *Journal of Conflict Resolution* 6: 52-76.

Devine, Joel A., and James D. Wright. 1993. *The Greatest of Evils: Urban Poverty and the American Underclass*. New York: Aldine de Gruyter.

Diamond, Jared. 1991. "Speaking with a single tongue." *Discover*, February, pp. 78-85.

Diener, Ed., Marissa Diener, and Carol Diener. 1995. "Factors predicting the well-being of nations." *Journal of Personality and Social Psychology* 69::851-64.

Dixon, Jo, Cynthia Gordon, and Tasnim Khomusi. 1995. "Sexual symmetry in psychiatric diagnosis." *Social Problems* 42: 429-49.

Dobkin, Patricia L. 1995. "Individual and peer characteristics in predicting boys' early onset of substance abuse." *Child Development* 66:1198-1214.

Domhoff, G. William. 1990. *The Power Elite and the State: How Policy Is Made in America*. New York: Aldine de Gruyter.

Dornbusch, Sanford et al. 1982. "Sexual development, age, and dating: A comparison of biological and social influences upon one set of behaviors." *Child Development* 52:620-30.

Downs, Anthony. 1996. "Are suburbs really independent from central cities?" *National Real Estate Investor* 38: 28.

Drucker, Peter F. 1968. *The Age of Discontinuity*. New York: Harper & Row.

Dube, S.C. 1988. *Modernization and Development: The Search for Alternative Paradigms*. Tokyo: The United Nations University.

Duerksen, Susan. 1996. "Health, work stresses linked." *The San Diego Tribune*, September 2.

Dugger, Celia W. 1996. "Tug of taboos: African genital rite vs. American law." *The New York Times*, December 28.

Duncan, Terry E., Elizabeth Tildesley, Susan C. Duncan, and Hyman Hops. 1995. "The consistency of family and peer influences on the development of substance use in adolescence." *Addiction* 90:1647-60.

Dunn, Ashley. 1994. "Asian-American study reveals hidden poverty." *New York Times*, May 19.

Durant, Robert H., Robert Pendergast, and Carolyn Seymore. l990. "Sexual Behavior Among Hispanic Female Adolescents in the United S States." *Pediatrics* 85:1051-58.

Durkheim, Emile. l933. *The Division of Labor in Society*, trans. George Simpson. New York: Free Press.

_____. 1938. *The Rules of Sociological Method*. 8th ed., trans. S. A. Soloway and J.H. Mueller. Glencoe, IL.: Free Press.

_____. 1951. *Suicide*, trans. John A. Spaulding and George Simpson, ed. George Simpson. New York: Free Press.

_____. 1965. *The Elementary Forms of Religious Life*. New York: The Free Press.

Durkin, Keith F. 1995. " 'Log onto sex': Some notes on the carnal computer and erotic cyberspace as an emerging research frontier." *Deviant Behavior* 16:179-200.

Dvir, T., D. Eden, and M.L. Banjo. 1995. "Self-fulfilling prophecy and gender: Can women be Pygmalion and Galatea?" *Journal of Applied Psychology* 80:253-70.

Dwyer, Kathleen M. l990. "Characteristics of Eighth-Grade Students Who Initiate Self-Care in Elementary and Junior High School." *Pediatrics* 86:448-54.

Dye, Thomas R. 1990. *Who's Running America: The Bush Era*. 5th ed. Englewood Cliffs, NJ.: Prentice-Hall.

East, Patricia L., Marianne E. Felice and Maria C. Morgan. l993. "Sisters' and Girlfriends' Sexual and Childbearing Behavior: Effects on Early Adolescent Girls' Sexual Outcomes." *Journal of Marriage and the Family* 55:953-63.

Easteal, Patricia Weiser. 1994. "Survivors of sexual assault: An Australian survey." *International Journal of the Sociology of Law* 22:329-54.

Eder, Donna, Catherine Colleen Evans, and Stephen Parker. 1995. *School Talk: Gender and Adolescent Culture*. New Brunswick, N.J.: Rutgers University Press.

Edin, Kathryn J. 1995. "The myths of dependence and self-sufficiency: Women, welfare, and low-wage work." *Focus* 17:1-9.

Ehrlich, Paul R. 1968. *The Population Bomb*. New York: Ballantine Books.

_____. 1971. ""Eco-catastrophe!'" In *The Survival Equation: Man, Resources, and His Environment*, R. Revelle, A. Khosla, and M. Vinovskis, eds. Boston: Houghton Mifflin.

Ehrlich, Paul R. and Anne H. Ehrlich. 1990. *The Population Explosion*. New York: Simon & Schuster.

Eisenstein, Zillah. 1992. "The sexual politics of the new right." In Maggie Humm, ed., *Modern Feminisms*. New York: Columbia University Press.

Eitzen, D. Stanley and H. George Sage. 1993. *Sociology of North American Sport*. 5th ed. Dubuque, Iowa: Wm. C. Brown.

Ekman, P. 1973. "Cross-cultural studies of facial expression." In P. Edman, ed., *Darwin and Facial Expression*. New York: Academic Press.

Elleson, Vera J. 1983. "Competition: A cultural imperative?" *Personnel and Guidance Journal* 62: 195-98.

Elliott, Marta. 1996. "Impact of work, family, and welfare receipt on women's self-esteem in young adulthood." *Social Psychology Quarterly* 59:80-95.

Ellison, Christopher G., David A. Gay, and Thomas A. Glass. 1989. "Does religious commitment contribute to individual life satisfaction?" *Social Forces* 68: 100-23.

Ellison, Katherine. 1996. "Suicides are tragic protest symbol among Brazilian Indians." *The San Diego Union-Tribune*, March 23.

Elliston, Deborah A. 1995. "Erotic anthropology: 'Ritualized homosexuality' in Melanesia and beyond." *American Ethnologist* 22:848-67.

Elmer-Dewitt, Philip. 1992. "Rich vs. poor." *Time* June 18.

Ely, J.W., W. Levinson, N.C. Elder, A.G. Mainous, III, and D.C. Vinson. 1995. "Perceived causes of family physicians' errors." *Journal of Family Practice* 40: 337-44.

England, Paula, Melissa S. Herbert, Barbara Stanek, Lori L. Reid, and Lori McCreary Megdal. 1994. "The gendered valuation of occupations and skills: Earnings in 1980 census occupations." *Social Forces* 73: 65-99.

Engels, Friedrich. 1884. *The Origin of the Family, Private Property, and the State*. New York: International Publishers.

_____. 1939. *Anti-Duhring*. New York: International Publishers.

Englemann, Larry. 1995. "The best quotes of 1995." *San Jose Mercury News*, December 31.

Englis, Basil G. 1995. "To be and not to be: Lifestyle imagery, reference groups, and the clustering of America." *Journal of Advertising* 24:13-28.

Erdmans, Mary Patrice. 1995. "Immigrants and ethnics: Conflict and identity in Chicago Polonia." *The Sociological Quarterly* 36: 175-95.

Erikson, Erik H. 1963. *Childhood and Society*. 2nd ed. New York: W.W. Norton.

Etzioni, Amitai. 1961. *A Comparative Analysis of Complex Organizations*. New York: Free Press.

Evans, Peter. 1995. *Embedded Autonomy: States and Industrial Transformation*. Princeton, NJ.: Princeton University Press.

Fagot, B. L., and R. Hagan. 1991. "Observations of parent reactions to sex-stereotyped behaviors: Age and sex effects." *Child Development* 62: 617-28.

Farhi, Paul. 1996. "Harmful violence found to fill TV." *Washington Post*, February 6.

Fausto-Sterling, Anne. 1985. *Myths of Gender: Biological Theories about Women and Men*. New York: Basic Books.

Feagin, Joe R. and Clairece Booher Feagin. 1994. "Theoretical perspectives in race and ethnic relations." In Fred L. Pincus and Howard J. Ehrlich, eds., *Race and Ethnic Conflict Boulder*: Westview Press.

Feagin, Joe R. and Melvin P. Sikes. 1994. *Living with Racism: The Black Middle-class Experience*. Boston: Beacon.

Featherman, David L. and Robert M. Hauser. 1978. *Opportunity and Change*. New York: Aldine.

Fein, Melvyn L. 1990. *Role Change: A Resocialization Perspective*. New York: Praeger.

Fein, O. 1995. "The influence of social class on health status: American and British research on health inequalities." *Journal of General Internal Medicine* 10: 577-86.

Feinstein, Jonathan S. 1993. "The relationship between socio-economic status and health." *The Milbank Quarterly* 71: 279-313.

Feldman-Savelsberg, Pamela. 1995. "Cooking inside: Kinship and gender in Bangangte idioms of marriage and procreation." *American Ethnologist* 22:483-501.

Felson, Richard B., Allen E. Liska, Scott J. South, and Thomas L. McNulty. 1994. "The subculture of violence and delinquency: Individual vs. school context effects." *Social Forces* 73:155-73.

Ferree, Myra Marx, and Elaine J. Hall. 1996. "Gender, race, and class in mainstream textbooks." *American Sociological Review* 61:929-50.

Firebaugh, Glenn, and Frank D. Beck. 1994. "Does economic growth benefit the masses? Growth, dependence, and welfare in the Third World." *American Sociological Review* 59: 631-53.

Fischer, Claude. 1984. *The Urban Experience*. 2nd ed. San Diego: Harcourt Brace Jovanovich.

Fischer, Klauss. 1995. *Nazi Germany: A New History*. New York: Continuum.

Fischman, Joshua. 1984. "Survey results aren't black and white." *Psychology Today*, October, p. 8.

Flexner, Eleanor. 1972. *Century of Struggle: The Woman's Rights Movement in the United States*. New York: Atheneum.

Foner, Nancy. 1995. "The hidden injuries of Bureaucracy: Work in an American Nursing home." *Human Organization* 54:229-37.

Fong, Eric. 1996. "A comparative perspective on racial residential segregation: American and Canadian experiences." *The Sociological Quarterly* 37: 199-206.

Ford, Clellan S. and Frank A. Beach. 1951. *Patterns of Sexual Behavior*. New York: Harper Torchbook.

Ford, M.R., and C.R. Lowery. 1986. "Gender differences in moral reasoning; A comparison of justice and care orientations." *Journal of Personality and Social Psychology* 50:777-83.

Forrest, Jacqueline Darroch, and Susheela Singh. 1990. "The Sexual and Reproductive Behavior of American Women, 1982-1988." *Family Planning Perspectives* 22:206-14.

Fowers, Blaine J. 1991. "His and Her Marriage: A Multivariate Study of Gender and Marital Satisfaction." *Sex Roles* 24:209-21.

Frame, Randy. 1996. "Conservatives gain GOP's attention." *Christianity Today Website*.

Francis, Leslie J., and Susan H. Jones. 1996. "Social class and self-esteem." *The Journal of Social Psychology* 136:405.

Francis, Linda E. 1994. "Laughter, the best mediation: Humor as emotion management in interaction." *Symbolic Interaction* 17:147-63.

Franklin, Clyde W. 1985. "The black male urban barbershop as a sex-role socialization setting." *Sex Roles* 12:965-79.

Freud, Sigmund. 1961. *Civilization and Its Discontents*. Trans. James Strachey. New York: W.W. Norton & Co.

Frey, William H. and Reynolds Farley. 1996. "Latino, Asian, and Black segregation in U.S. metropolitan areas: Are multiethnic metros different?" *Demography* 33: 35-50.

Friedlander, B.Z. 1993. "Community violence, children's development, and mass media." *Psychiatry* 56:66-81.

Friedman, Howard S. et al. 1995. "Psychosocial and behavioral predictors of longevity." *American Psychologist* 50:69-78.

Frijda, Nico H., and Batja Mesquita. 1994. "The social roles and functions of emotions." In Shinobu Kitayama and Hazel Rose Markus, eds., *Emotion and Culture: Empirical Studies of Mutual Influences*. Washington, D.C.: American Psychological Association.

Froelich, Warren, and Kristine Moe. 1985. "Research fraud said infrequent." *The San Diego Union*, September 15.

Futter, Stacy. 1995. "Rape statistics part of story." *Chicago Tribune*, November 12.

Gabardi, Lisa, and Lee A. Rosen. 1991. "Differences Between College Students from Divorced and Intact Families." *Journal of Divorce and Remarriage* 15:175-91.

Galati, Dario, and Riccardo Sciaky. 1995. "The representation of antecedents of emotions in Northern and Southern Italy." *Journal of Cross Cultural Psychology* 26:123-40.

Gallup, George H., Jr. 1990. *Religion in America 1990*. Princeton, NJ.: Princeton Religion Research Center.

Gallup, George, Jr., and Frank Newport. 1991. "Baby-boomers seek more family time." *Gallup Poll Monthly*, #307: 31-41.

Gamson, William A. 1990. *The Strategy of Social Protest*. 2nd ed. Belmont, CA: Wadsworth.

Gándara, Patricia. 1995. *Over the Ivy Walls: The Educational Mobility of Low-income Chicanos*. Albany: State University of New York Press.

Ganong, Lawrence H. and Marilyn Coleman. 1993. "A Meta-Analytic Comparison of the Self-Esteem and Behavior Problems of Step-children to Children in Other Family Structures." *Journal of Divorce and Remarriage* 19:143-63.

_____. 1994. *Remarried Family Relationships*. Thousand Oaks, CA.: Sage.

Garcia, J.M., and P.A. Montgomery. 1991. "The Hispanic population in the United States: March 1990." *Current Population Reports*, Series P-20, No. 449.

Gardner, William L. 1992. "Lessons in organizational dramaturgy: The art of impression management." *Organizational Dynamics* 21:33-46.

Gargan, Edward A. 1996. "In rich Hong Kong, cages for the poor." *The New York Times* July 14, 1996.

Garrow, David J., ed. 1987. *The Montgomery Bus Boycott and the Women Who Started It: The Memoir of Jo Ann Gibson Robinson*. Knoxville: University of Tennessee Press.

Garson, Barbara. 1975. *All the Livelong Day: The Meaning and Demeaning of Routine Work*. New York: Penguin Books.

Gecas, Viktor. 1981. "Contexts of socialization." In Morris Rosenberg and Ralph H. Turner, eds., *Social Psychology: Sociological Perspectives*. New York: Basic Books.

Gee, Alison Dakota. 1996. "The price of beauty." *Asiaweek*, August 2.

Gelles, Richard J. and Murray A. Straus. 1988. *Intimate Violence*. New York: Simon & Schuster.

George, Kenneth D. and Andrew E. Behrendt. 1987. "Therapy for Male Couples Experiencing Relationship Problems and Sexual Problems." *Journal of Homosexuality* 14:77-88.

Gerth, H.H. and C. Wright Mills. 1946. *From Max Weber: Essays in Sociology*. New York: Oxford University Press.

Gilbert, Dennis A. and Joseph A. Kahl. 1993. *The American Class Structure*. 4th ed. Belmont, CA: Wadsworth.

Gilliam-Mosee, Redenia. 1996. "On the boardwalk: Gaming in America." *Forum for Applied Research and Public Policy* 11: 109.

Gilligan, Carol. 1982. *In A Different Voice*. Cambridge, MA.: Harvard University Press.

Gnanadason, Aruna. 1991. "Violence against women: No longer a secret." *One World*, October.

Goering, Laurie, and Kerry Luft. 1996. "Unplanned parenthood: A mix of fear and ignorance in the slums." *The Chicago Tribune*, December 17.

Goffman, Erving. 1959. *Presentation of Self in Everyday Life*. Garden City, N.Y.: Doubleday.

_____. 1961. *Encounters*. Indianapolis: Bobbs-Merrill.

_____. 1967. "On Face Work," *Interaction Ritual*. Garden City: N.Y.: Doubleday.

Golay, Michael and Carl Rollyson. 1996. *Where America Stands 1996*. New York: John Wiley and Sons.

Goldberg, Wendy A., Ellen Greenberger, Sharon Hamill, and Robin O'Neil. 1992. "Role Demands in the Lives of Employed Single Mothers With Preschoolers." *Journal of Family Issues* 13:312-33.

Goldberger, Arthur S., and Charles Manski. 1995. "Review article: *The Bell Curve* by Herrnstein and Murray." *Journal of Economic Literature* 33:762-76.

Goldman, Ari L. 1991. "Portrait of religion in U.S. holds dozens of surprises." *New York Times*, April 10.

Goldscheider, Calvin, and William D. Mosher. 1991. "Patterns of Contraceptive Use in the United States: The Importance of Religious Factors." *Studies in Family Planning* 22:102-15.

Goldscheider, Frances Kobrin, and Linda J. Waite. 1991. *New Families, No Families? The Transformation of the American Home*. Berkeley: University of California Press.

Goleman, Daniel. 1983. "The electronic Rorschach." *Psychology Today*, February.

_____. 1995. *Emotional Intelligence: Why It Can Matter More Than IQ*. New York: Bantam Books.

Goode, William J. 1960. "A theory of role strain." *American Sociological Review* 25:483-96.

Gordon, Margaret T., and Stephanie Riger. 1989. *The Female Fear*. New York: Free Press.

Gottdiener, Mark. 1994. *The Social Production of Urban Space*. 2nd ed. Austin: University of Texas Press.

Gould, Roger M. 1972. "The phases of adult life: A study in developmental psychology." *American Journal of Psychiatry* 129:521-31.

Gouldner, Alvin. 1960. "The norm of reciprocity: A preliminary statement." *American Sociological Review* 25:169-77.

Graber, J.A., J. Brooks-Gunn, R.L. Paikoff, and M.P. Warren. 1994. "Prediction of eating problems: An 8-year study of adolescent girls." *Developmental Psychology* 30: 823-34.

Graham, Gerald. 1984. "Good old company grapevine frequently bears fruit." *The Kansas City Star*, March 25, 1984.

Greenglass, Esther R. 1985. "A Social-Psychological View of Marriage for Women." *International Journal of Women's Studies* 8:24-31.

Greenlaw, Paul S. 1996. "Effects of race on interview ratings in a situational panel interview." *Journal of Applied Psychology* 81: 178-86.

Greenstein, Theodore N. 1996. "Gender ideology and perceptions of the fairness of the division of household labor: Effects on marital quality." *Social Forces* 74:1029-1042.

_____. 1996. "Husbands' participation in domestic labor: Interactive effects of wives' and husbands' gender ideologies." *Journal of Marriage and the Family* 58: 585-95.

Greif, Geoffrey L. 1985. *Single Fathers*. Lexington, Mass.: Lexington Books.

Gross, Edward and Gregory P. Stone. 1964. "Embarrassment and the analysis of role requirements." *American Journal of Sociology* 70:1-15.

Grothe, Mardy, and Peter Wylie. 1987. *Problem Bosses: Who They Are and How to Deal with Them*. New York: Fawcett Crest.

Hadaway, C. Kirk, Penny Long Marler, and Mark Chaves. 1993. "What the polls don't show: A closer look at U.S. church attendance." *American Sociological Review* 58: 741-52.

Hadden, Kenneth and Bruce London. 1996. "Educating girls in the Third World: The demographic, basic needs, and economic benefits." *International Journal of Comparative Sociology* 37: 31-46.

Hage, Jerald, and Michael Aiken. 1970. *Social Change in Complex Organizations*. New York: Random House.

Hagen, John and Ruth Peterson, eds. 1995. *Crime and Inequality*. Stanford, CA.: Stanford University Press.

Halcon, John J. and Maria de la Luz Reyes. 1991. " 'Trickle-down reform: Hispanics, higher education, and the excellence movement." *Urban Review* 23: 117-35.

Hall, Calvin. 1954. *A Primer of Freudian Psychology*. New York: New American Library.

Hall, Peter M. and Dee Ann Spencer Hall. 1982. "The social conditions of the negotiated order." *Urban Life* 11:328-49.

Hall, Richard H. 1982. *Organizations: Structure and Process*, 3rd ed. Englewood Cliffs: Prentice-Hall.

Hammarstrom, Anne. 1994. "Health consequences of youth unemployment." *Social Science and Medicine* 38 (March):699-709.

Hamptom, Robert L. and Richard J. Gelles. 1994. "Violence Toward Black Women in a Nationally Representative Sample of Black Families." *Journal of Comparative Family Studies* 25:105-19.

Hanson, Sandra L. 1996. "Gender, Family Resources, and Success in Science." *Journal of Family Issues* 17 (January):83-113.

Hardy, Kenneth R. 1974. "Social origins of American Scientists and scholars." *Science* 185: 497-505.

Harris, Marvin. 1974. *Cows, Pigs, Wars and Witches*. New York: Vintage Books.

Harrison, Bennett. 1994. *Lean and Mean: The Changing Landscape of Corporate Power in the Age of Flexibility*. New York: Basic Books.

Hart, Daniel. 1988. "A longitudinal study of adolescents' socialization and identification as predictors of adult moral judgment development." *Merrill Palmer Quarterly* 34:245-60.

Hawkins, Dana. l996. "Homeschool battles." *U.S. News & World Report*, February l2.

Hawkins, John David. 1975. "Utopian Values and Communal Social Life." Unpublished Ph.D. dissertation, Northwestern University.

Haynes, V. Dion. 1996. "Indians sue in bid to save heritage: Report may force mines to clean up Idaho Valley." *The Chicago Tribune*, December 25.

Hearn, James C. 1991. "Academic and nonacademic influences on the college destinations of 1980 high school graduates." *Sociology of Education* 64:158 71.

Heck, Ronald H. 1995. "Organizational and professional socialization: Its impact on the performance of new administrators." *Urban Review* 27:31-49.

Heer, Friedrich. 1962. *The Medieval World: Europe 1100-1350*. New York: Mentor.

Heim, Mary. 1996. "Fertility of immigrant women in California." *Population and Environment: A Journal of Interdisciplinary Studies* 17: 391-407.

Heimer, Karen. 1996. "Gender, interaction, and delinquency: Testing a theory of differential social control." *Social Psychology Quarterly* 59:39-61.

Heimer, Karen, and Ross L. Matsueda. 1994. "Role-taking, role commitment, and delinquency: A theory of differential social control." *American Sociological Review* 59:365-90.

Hein, Jeremy. 1995. *From Vietnam, Laos, and Cambodia: A Refugee Experience in the United States*. New York: Twayne Publishers.

Heller, Celia S. 1969. *Structured Social Inequality: A Reader in Comparative Social Stratification*. New York: Macmillan.

Heller, Scott. 1991. "Psychologist looks at life in these postmodern times." *The Chronicle of Higher Education*, June 5.

Henig, Robin Marantz. 1994. *A Dancing Matrix: How Science Confronts Emerging Viruses*. New York: Vintage Books.

Henton, June, Rodney Cate, James Koval, Sally Lloyd, and Scott Christopher. 1983. "Romance and violence in dating relationships." *Journal of Family Issues* 4:467-82.

Hermann, Donald H. J. 1996. "Death wish: It's time to legitimize physician-assisted suicide." *Chicago Tribune*, May 2.

Hernandez, Donald J. 1993. "When families break up." In the U.S. Bureau of the Census, *Current Population Reports*, series P-20 no. 478. Washington, D.C.: Government Printing Office.

Hernandez, Nelda R., and Arden White. 1989. "Pass it on: Errors in direct quotes in a sample of scholarly journal articles." *Journal of Counseling & Development* 67:509-12.

Herring, Cedric and Karen Rose Wilson-Sadberry. 1993. "Preference or necessity? Changing work roles of black and white women, 1973-1990." *Journal of Marriage and the Family* 55: 314-25.

Herrnstein, Richard J., and Charles Murray. l994. *The Bell Curve: Intelligence and Class Structure in American Life*. New York: Free Press.

Hesse-Bilber, Sharlene. 1996. *Am I Thin Enough Yet? The Cult of Thinness and the Commercialization of Identity*. New York: Oxford University Press.

Hetherington, E. Mavis. 1993. "An overview of the Virginia longitudinal study of divorce and remarriage with a focus on early adolescence." *Journal of Family Psychology* 7:39-56.

Hilts, Philip J. 1996. "Fine particles in air cause many deaths, study suggests." *The New York Times*, May 9.

Hirschi, Travis. 1969. *Causes of Delinquency*. Berkeley, CA.: University of California Press.

Hochschild, Arlie. 1989. *The Second Shift; Working Parents and the Revolution at Home*. New York: Viking.

Hogan, Dennis P., David J. Eggebeen, and Clifford C. Clogg. 1993. "The structure of intergenerational exchanges in American families." *American Journal of Sociology* 98: 1428-58.

Holmes, Steven A. 1994. "Survey finds minorities bear own ill will, biases." *The San Diego Union-Tribune* March 3.

Homans, G.C. 1961. *Social Behavior: Its Elementary Forms*. New York: Harcourt Brace Jovanovich.

Hope, Keith. 1982. "Vertical and nonvertical class mobility in three countries." *American Sociological Review* 47: 99-113.

Horney, Julie, D. Wayne Osgood, and Ineke Haen Marshall. 1995. "Criminal careers in the short term: Intra-individual variability in crime and its relation to local life circumstances." *American Sociological Review* 60:655-73.

Horowitz, Ruth. 1982. "Adult delinquent gangs in a Chicano community." *Urban Life* 11:3-26.

Hout, Michael, Clem Brooks, and Jeff Manza. 1995. "The democratic class struggle in the United States, 1948-1992." *American Sociological Review* 60: 805-28.

Hughes, Kathleen A. 1996. "Inconspicuous consumption name of new game." *San Diego Union-Tribune* October 3, 1996.

Hugick, L., and J. Leonard. 1991. "Sex in America." *The Gallup Poll Monthly* #313, October, p. 69.

Hunt, Morton. 1974. *Sexual Behavior in the 1970s*. Chicago: Playboy Press.

Huntington, Gertrude Enders. 1981. "Children of the Hutterites." *Natural History* 90:34-46.

Hyde, J.S., and E.A. Plant. 1995. "Magnitude of psychological gender differences." *American Psychologist* 50:159-61.

Iannaccone, Laurence R., Daniel V.A. Olson, and Rodney Stark. 1995. "Religious resources and church growth." *Social Forces* 74: 705-31.

Idle, Tracey, Ellen Wood, and Serge Desmarais. 1993. "Gender role socialization in toy play situations." *Sex Roles* 28: 679-91.

Isler, Ellen L., and Stanislav V. Kasl. 1992. "Religion, disability, depression, and the timing of death." *American Journal of Sociology* 97: 1052-79.

Imahori, T. Todd and William R. Cupach. 1994. "A cross-cultural comparison of the interpretation and management of face: U.S. American and Japanese responses to embarrassing predicaments." *International Journal of Intercultural Relations* 18:193-2.

Imura, Hiroo. 1996. "Science education in Japan." *Science* 274: 15.

Indulski, J.A. and R. Rolecki. 1995. "Industrialization and environmental health in Poland." *Central European Journal of Public Health* 3: 3-12.

Ishida, Hiroshi, Walter Müller, and John M. Ridge. 1995. "Class origin, class destination, and education: A cross-national study of ten industrial nations." *American Journal of Sociology* 101: 145-93.

Jackall, Robert. 1988. *Moral Mazes: The World of Corporate Managers*. New York: Oxford University Press.

Jackson, Linda A. 1995. "Physical attractiveness and intellectual competence: A meta-analytic review." *Social Psychology Quarterly* 58:108-22.

Jackson, Linda A., John E. Hunter, and Carole N. Hodge, 1995. "Physical attractiveness and intellectual competence," *Social Psychology Quarterly* 58: 108–122.

Jackson, Maggie. 1996. "Women's climb to corporate top is slow progress, survey reports." *The San Diego Union-Tribune*, October 18.

Jacobson, Jodi L. 1989. "Baby budget." *World-Watch*, September/October.

James, William. 1950. *The Principles of Psychology*. New York: Dover.

Jamrozik, Adam, Cathy Boland, and Robert Urquhart. 1995. *Social Change and Cultural Transformation in Australia*. New York: Cambridge University Press.

Jang, Kerry L., W. John Livesley and Philip A. Vernon. 1996. "Heritability of the big five personality dimensions and their facets: A twin study." *Journal of Personality* 64:577-91.

Jin, R. L., C.P. Shah, and T.J. Svoboda. 1995. "The impact of unemployment on health." *Canadian Medical Association Journal* 153 (September 1):529-40.

Johnson, Bette Magyar, Shmuel Shulman, and W. Andrew Collins. 1991. "Systemic patterns of parenting as reported by adolescents." *Journal of Adolescent Research* 6:235-52.

Johnson, Timothy R. 1995. "The significance of religion for aging well." *American Behavioral Scientist* 39: 186-208.

Johnstone, Ronald L. 1992. *Religion in Society*. 4th ed. Englewood Cliffs, NJ.: Prentice-Hall.

Jones, E.F. 1964. *Ingratiation*. New York: Appleton-Century-Crofts.

Jordan, Winthrop D. 1970. "Modern tensions and the origins of American slavery." *In Slavery and Its Aftermath*, P.I. Rose, ed. Chicago: Aldine-Atherton.

Josephson, Wendy L. 1987. "Television violence and children's aggression." *Journal of Personality and Social Psychology* 53:882-90.

Judy, Peter E. 1996. "Emerging trends to have huge impact on marketing." *Marketing News* 30: 6.

Kahn, Arnold. 1984. *Social Psychology*. Dubuque, Ia.: Wm.C. Brown.

Kalick, S. Michael. 1988. "Physical attractiveness as a status cue." *Journal of Experimental Social Psychology* 24: 469-89.

Kanter, Rosabeth Moss. 1977. *Men and Women of the Corporation*. New York: Basic Books.

Karp, David A. 1994. "The dialectics of depression." Symbolic Interaction 17: 341-66.

Keller, Evelyn Fox. 1992. "Feminism and Science." In Maggie Humm, ed., *Modern Feminisms*. New York: Columbia University Press.

Kelley, H.H., and J.W. Thibaut. 1978. *Interpersonal Relations: A Theory of Interdependence*. New York: Wiley.

Kelley, Joanne. 1997. "Study links job loss, longer life." *The San Diego Union Tribune*, January 27.

Kelley, Jonathan and M.D.R. Evans. 1995. "Class and Conflict in Six Western Nations." *American Sociological Review* 60: 157-78.

Kendall, Peter. 1996. "Cargo ships reshape harbors' ecosystems: Invaders thrive after hitching rides in ballasts." *The Chicago Tribune*, October 13.

Kephart, William M. 1991. *Extraordinary Groups*. 4th ed. New York: St. Martin's Press.

Kessler, Ronald C., and William J. Magee. 1993. "Childhood Adversities and Adult Depression: Basic Patterns of Association in a US National Survey." *Psychological Medicine* 23:679-90.

Kessler, Ronald C. et al. 1994. "Lifetime and 12-month prevalence of DSM-III-R psychiatric disorders in the United States." *Archives of General Psychiatry* 51:8-19.

Kilborn, Peter T. 1992. "Sad distinction for the Sioux: Homeland is no. 1 in poverty." *New York Times*, September 20.

Kim, Quee-Young. 1996. "From protest to change of regime: The 4-19 revolt and the fall of the Rhee regime in South Korea." *Social Forces* 74: 1179-1209.

Kimball, E.H., H.I. Goldberg, and M.W. Oberle. 1996. "The prevalence of selected risk factors for chronic disease among American Indians in Washington State." *Public Health Report* 111: 264-71.

Kisely, S., and J. Jones. 1995. "A hive of activity: The future of public health." *Public Health* 109: 227-33.

Kitayama, Shinobu, and Hazel Rose Markus, eds. 1994. *Emotion and Culture: Empirical Studies of Mutual Influences*. Washington, D.C.: American Psychological Association.

Klein, Malcolm W. 1995. *The American Street Gang: Its Nature, Prevalence, and Control*. New York: Oxford University Press.

Kluckhohn, Clyde. 1960. *Mirror For Man*. Greenwich, Conn.: Fawcett.

Knauf, V.C., and D. Facciotti. 1995. "Genetic engineering of foods to reduce the risk of health disease and cancer." *Advances in Experimental Medical Biology* 369: 221-28.

Kohlberg, Lawrence. 1969. *Stages in the Development of Moral Thought and Action*. New York: Holt, Rinehart & Winston.

Kohn, Melvin L. 1971. "Bureaucratic man: A portrait and an interpretation." *American Sociological Review* 36:461-74.

_____. 1977. *Class and Conformity*. 2nd ed. Chicago: University of Chicago Press.

Kolata, Gina. 1983. "Man's world, woman's world? Brain studies point to differences." *New York Times*, February 28.

_____. 1996. "Chance of heart attack increases for those who suffer depression." *New York Times*, December 17.

_____. 1997. "Cloning triumph poses major issues." *The San Diego Union-Tribune*, February 24.

Konar, Ellen et al. 1982. "Status demarcation in the office." *Environment and Behavior* 14:561-80.

Kposowa, Augustine J., K.D. Breault, and Gopal K. Singh. 1995. "White male suicide in the United States: A multivariate individual-level analysis." *Social Forces* 74:315-23.

Kristof, Nicholas D. 1997. "Malaria makes a comeback, deadlier than ever." *New York Times*, January 8.

Kroeber, A. L. 1948. *Anthropology*. New York: Harcourt, Brace & Co.

Kroeber, A. L. 1948. *Anthropology*. New York: Harcourt, Brace.

Kroeger, Otto, and Janet M. Thuesen. 1988. *Type Talk*. New York: Dell Publishing.

Kruttschnitt, Candace, Jane D. McLeod, and Maude Dornfeld. 1994. "The economic environment of child abuse." *Social Problems* 41 (May):299-315.

Kuhse, Helga. 1995. "Clinical ethics and nursing." *Bioethics* 9: 207-19.

Kurdek, Lawrence A., and J. Patrick Schmitt. 1986. "Perceived Emotional Support from Family and Friends in Members of Homosexual, Married, and Heterosexual Cohabiting Couples." *Journal of Homosexuality* 14:57-68.

Lachmann, Richard. 1989. "Elite conflict and state formation in 16- and 17-century England and France." *American Sociological Review* 54: 141-62.

Ladd, Everett Carll. 1986. "Generation Myths." *Public Opinion* November/December.

Lambert, William W., and Wallace E. Lambert. 1973. *Social Psychology*. 2nd ed. Englewood Cliffs, N.J.: Prentice-Hall.

Landry, Bart. 1988. *The New Black Middle Class*. Berkeley: University of California Press.

Lane, Harlan. 1976. *The Wild Boy of Aveyron*. Cambridge: Harvard University Press.

Laner, Mary Riege, and Jeanine Thompson. 1982. "Abuse and aggression in courting couples." *Deviant Behavior* 3:229-44.

Langer, Gary. 1989. "Polling on prejudice: Questionable questions." *Public Opinion*, May/June, pp. 18-19.

Lang-Takac, Esther, and Zahava Osterweil. 1992. "Separateness and connectedness: Differences between the genders." *Sex Roles* 27: 277-89.

Lanz, Tobias J. 1996. "Environmental degradation and social conflict in the northern highlands of Ethiopia: The case of Tigray and Wollo Provinces." *Africa Today* 43: 157-82.

LaPiere, Richard. l934. "Attitudes vs. actions." *Social Forces* 13:230-37.

Lauer, Jeanette C. and Robert H. Lauer. 1981. *Fashion Power: The Meaning of Fashion in American Society*. Englewood Cliffs, N.J.: Prentice-Hall.

_____. 1986. *'Til Death Do Us Part': How Couples Stay Together*. New York: The Haworth Press.

Lauer, Robert H. 1981. *Temporal Man: The Meaning and Uses of Social Time*. New York: Praeger.

_____. 1991. *Perspectives on Social Change*. 4th ed. Boston: Allyn and Bacon.

_____. 1997. *Social Problems and the Quality of Life*, 7th ed. Dubuque, IA: Brown and Benchmark.

Lauer, Robert H., and Warren H. Handel. 1983. *Social Psychology: The Theory and Application of Symbolic Interactionism*. 2nd ed. Englewood Cliffs, NJ: Prentice-Hall.

Lauer, Robert H., and Jeanette C. Lauer. 1988. *Watersheds: Mastering the Unpredictable Crises of Life*. New York: Little, Brown.

_____. 1997. *Marriage and Family: The Quest For Intimacy*, 3rd ed. Dubuque, IA: Brown and Benchmark.

Laumann, Edward O., Robert T. Michael, John H. Gagnon, and Stuart Michaels. 1994. *The Social Organization of Sexuality*. Chicago: University of Chicago Press.

Laursen, Brett. 1995. "Conflict and social interaction in adolescent relationships." *Journal of Research on Adolescence* 5:55-70.

Lawrence, Paul R., and Jay W. Lorsch. 1967. *Organization and Environment*. Boston: Harvard University Press.

Leary, Mark R. 1994. "Self-presentation can be hazardous to your health: Impression management and health risk." *Health Psychology* 13:461-70.

_____. 1993. "The social psychology of tanning and sunscreen use: Self-presentational motives as a predictor of health risk." *Journal of Applied Social Psychology* 23:1390-1406.

Leary, Mark et al. 1994. "Self-presentation in everyday interactions: Effects of target familiarity and gender composition." *Journal of Personality and Social Psychology* 67: 664–673.

Lehman, Anthony F., and David S. Cordray. 1993. "Prevalence of alcohol, drug, and mental disorders among the homeless." *Contemporary Drug Problems* 20:355-84.

Lehman, Wayne E.K., David J. Farabee, Melvin L. Holcom, and D. Dwayne Simpson. 1995. "Prediction of substance use in the workplace." *Journal of Drug Issues* 25:253-74.

Lemert, Edwin M. 1951. *Social Pathology*. New York: McGraw-Hill.

Lempert, Richard, and Karl Monsma. 1994. "Cultural differences and discrimination: Samoans before a public housing eviction board." *American Sociological Review* 59:890-910.

Lenski, Gerhard E. l966. *Power and Privilege*. New York: McGraw-Hill.

Lenski, Gerhard, Jean Lenski, and Patrick Nolan. 1994. *Human Societies: An Introduction to Macrosociology*, 7th ed. New York: McGraw-Hill.

Levin, Gilbert. 1985. "Computers and kids: The good news." *Psychology Today*, August.

Levinson, Daniel J. 1978. *The Seasons of a Man's Life*. New York: Alfred A. Knopf.

Lewin, Kurt. 1958. "Group decision and social change." In *Readings in Social Psychology*, Maccoby, Eleanor E., Theodore M. Newcomb, and Eugene L. Hartley, eds., pp. 197-211. New York: Holt, Rinehart, and Winston.

Leyerle, Betty. l994. *The Private Regulation of American Health Care*. Armonk, N.Y.: M.E. Sharpe.

Li, Jiali. 1995. "China's one-child policy: How and how well has it worked? A case study of Hebei Province, 1979-88." *Population and Development Review* 21: 563-85.

Lieberman, Leonard and Fatimah Linda C. Jackson. 1995. "Race and three models of human origin." *American Anthropologist* 97: 231-41.

Liedtke, Klaus. 1978. "Coca-Cola uber alles." *Atlas World Press Review*, October, pp. 37-38.

Lillard, Lee A., and Linda J. Waite. 1995. " 'Til death do us part': Marital disruption and mortality." *American Journal of Sociology* 100: 1131-56.

Lin, Chien and William T. Liu. 1993. "Intergenerational relationships among Chinese immigrant families from Taiwan." In H. P. McAdoo, ed., *Family Ethnicity: Strength in Diversity*. Newbury Park, CA.: Sage.

Link, Bruce G., Mary Clare Lennon, and Bruce P. Dohrenwend. 1993. "Socioeconomic status and depression: The role of occupations involving direction, control, and planning." *American Journal of Sociology* 98:1351-87.

Linton, Ralph. 1949. "The natural history of the family." In *The Family*, ed. R.N. Anshen. New York: Harper & Brothers.

Lipset, Seymour Martin, and Earl Raab. 1995. *Jews and the New American Scene*. Cambridge, MA.: Harvard University Press.

Liska, Allen E. and Paul E. Bellair. 1995. "Violent crime rates and racial composition: Convergence over time." *American Journal of Sociology* 101:578-610.

Littlepage, G.E. 1991. "Effects of group size and task characteristics on group performance." *Personality and Social Psychology Bulletin*. 17:449-56.

Lloyd, P.C. 1969. *Africa in Social Change*. Baltimore: Penguin.

Locke, Steven, and Douglas Colligan. 1986. *The Healer Within: The New Medicine of Mind and Body*. New York: New American Library.

Lockheimer, F. Roy. 1969. "Prerequisites, receptivity, and change: Government and the development of science in Japan." In *The Social Reality of Scientific Myth: Science and Social Change*, Kalman H. Silvert, ed. New York: American Universities Field Staff.

Lockwood, J.L., and S.L. Pimm. "Biological diversity. Species: Would any of them be missed?" *Current Biology* 4: 455-57.

Lorenzo, May Kwan, Bilge Pakiz, Helen Z. Reinherz, and Abbie Frost. 1995. "Emotional and behavioral problems of Asian American adolescents." *Child and Adolescent Social Work Journal* 12: 197-212.

Loring, Marti, and Brian Powell. 1988. "Gender, race, and DSM-III: A study of the objectivity of psychiatric diagnostic behavior." *Journal of Health and Social Behavior* 29:1 22.

Luster, Tom, and Harriette McAdoo. 1996. "Family and child influences on educational attainment: A secondary analysis of the High/Scope Perry preschool data." *Developmental Psychology* 32:26-39.

MacDonald, William L., and Alfred DeMaris. 1996. "Parenting stepchildren and biological children: The effects of stepparent's gender and new biological children." *Journal of Family Issues* 17: 5-25.

MacFarquhar, Neil. 1996. "Iran's intolerance turns vehement." *The San Diego Tribune*, October 5.

Mackey, Richard A., and Bernard A. O'Brien. 1995. *Lasting Marriages: Men and Women Growing Together*. Westport, Ct., Praeger.

Mackie, Gerry. 1996. "Ending footbinding and infibulation: A convention account." *American Sociological Review* 61: 999-1017.

Maclachlan, James. 1979. "What people really think of fast talkers." *Psychology Today*, November, 113-16.

Mage, D. et al. 1996. "Urban air pollution in megacities of the world." *Atmospheric Environment* 30: 681-86.

Mahon, Noreen E., Adela Yarcheski, and Thomas J. Yarcheski. 1993. "Health Consequences of Loneliness in Adolescents." *Research in Nursing and Health*. 16:23-31.

Marger, Martin N. 1994. *Race and Ethnic Relations: American and Global Perspectives*, 3rd ed. Belmont, CA.: Wadsworth.

Markides, Kyriakos S. and Sue Keir Hoppe. l985. "Marital Satisfaction in Three Generations of Mexican Americans." *Social Science Quarterly* 66:l47-54.

Markman, Howard, Scott Stanley, and Susan L.Blumberg. 1994. *Fighting for Your Marriage: Positive Steps for Preventing Divorce and Preserving Lasting Love*. San Francisco: Jossey-Bass.

Marks, Nadine F. 1995. "Midlife marital status differences in social support relationships with adult children and psychological well-being." *Journal of Family Issues* 16:5-28.

Marshall, Linda L., and Patricia Rose. 1990. "Premarital violence: The impact of family of origin violence, stress, and reciprocity." *Violence and Victims* 6:51-64.

Martindale, Don. 1962. *Social Life and Cultural Change*. Princeton, N.J.: D. Van Nostrand Company, Inc.

Martinez, Estella A. l993. "Parenting Young Children in Mexican American/Chicago Families." In H.P. McAdoo, ed., *Family Ethnicity: Strength in Diversity*. Newbury Park, Cal.: Sage.

Marty, Martin E. 1984. *Pilgrims in Their Own Land*. Boston: Little, Brown.

Marx, Gary T., and Douglas McAdam. 1994. *Collective Behavior and Social Movements: Process and Structure*. Englewood Cliffs, N.J.: Prentice-Hall.

Marx, Karl. 1920. *The Poverty of Philosophy*, trans. H. Quelch. Chicago: Charles K. Kerr.

_____. 1959. *Basic Writings on Politics and Philosophy*. Lewis S. Feuer, ed. New York: Doubleday.

_____. 1964. *Selected Writings in Sociology and Social Philosophy*. Tom Bottomore and Maximilian Rubel, eds. Baltimore: Penguin.

Marx, Karl, and Friedrich Engels. 1947. *The German Ideology*, ed. R. Pascal. New York: International Publishers.

Mason, J.O. l993. "Violence, alcohol and other drugs." *Public Health Reports*, January/February, pp. l-3.

Mastekaasa, Arne. l994. "Marital Status, Distress, and Well-Being: An International Comparison." *Journal of Comparative Family Studies* 25:l83-205.

Matlock, T., J.R. Slate, and D.A. Saarnio. 1995. "Family variables and domestic violence." *Journal of the Arkansas Medical Society* 92: 222-24.

Matthews, Lisa S., Rand D. Conger, and K.A.S. Wickrama. 1996. "Work-family conflict and marital quality: Mediating processes." *Social Psychology Quarterly* 59: 62-79.

McAdoo, John Lewis. l993. "Decision Making and Marital Satisfaction in African American Families." In H.P. McAdoo, ed., *Family Ethnicity: Strength in Diversity*. Newbury Park, Cal.: Sage.

McAneny, Leslie. 1992. "Number of drinkers on the rise again." *Gallop Poll Monthly* #317, pp. 43 47.

McCaghy, Charles H., and Timothy A. Capron. 1994. *Deviant Behavior*. 3rd ed. New York: Macmillan.

McCammom, Holly J. 1995. "The politics of protection: State minimum wage and maximum hours laws for women in the United States, 1870-1930." *The Sociological Quarterly* 36: 217-49.

McClelland, David C., and David A. Pilon. 1983. "Sources of adult motives in patterns of parent behavior in early childhood." *Journal of Personality and Social Psychology* 44:564-74.

McCracken, David. 1993. "Kids of lesbians are well-adjusted: Study." *The Chicago Tribune*, January 17.

McElroy, James C., Paula C. Morrow, and Ellen J. Mullen. 1996. "Intraorganizational mobility and work related attitudes." *Journal of Organizational Behavior* 17: 363-74.

McKenry, Patrick C., and Mark A. Fine. l993. "Parenting Following Divorce: A Comparison of Black and White Single Mothers." *Journal of Comparative Family Studies* 24:99-111.

McLeod, Jane D., and Kevan Edwards. 1995. "Contextual determinants of children's responses to poverty." *Social Forces* 73: 1487-1516.

McLeod, Jane D., and Michael J. Shanahan. 1993. "Poverty, parenting, and children's mental health." *American Sociological Review* 58: 351-66.

McMahon, Colin. 1996. "Hope and poverty gravitate to cities for world's poor." *The Chicago Tribune*, June 2, 1996.

McNamara, Robert P. 1995. *The Times Square Hustler: Male Prostitution in New York City*. Westport, Ct.: Praeger.

Mead, George Herbert. 1934. *Mind, Self and Society*. Charles Morris, ed. Chicago: University of Chicago Press.

Mead, Margaret. 1969. *Sex and Temperament in Three Primitive Societies*. New York: Dell.

Mednick, Martha T. l987. "Single Mothers: A Review and Critique of Current Research." Pp. 184-201 in S. Oskamp, ed. *Family Processes and Problems: Social Psychological Aspects*. Beverly Hills, Ca.: Sage.

Meier, August, Elliott Rudwick, and Francis E. Broderick, eds. 1971. *Black Protest Thought in the Twentieth Century*, 2nd ed. Indianapolis: Bobs-Merrill.

Melcher, Richard A. 1996. "Education: more reform, please." *Business Week*, December 9.

Mellinger, Wayne Martin. 1994. "Negotiated orders: The negotiation of directives in paramedic-nurse interaction." *Symbolic Interaction* 17:165-85.

Melson, Gail F. and Alan Fogel. 1988. "Learning to care." *Psychology Today*, January.

Melville, Herman. 1966. *Moby Dick*. New York: Harper and Row.

Merton, Robert K. 1939. "Social structure and anomie." *American Sociological Review* 3:672-82.

_____. 1957. *Social Theory and Social Structure*. Glencoe, IL.: Free Press.

Metz, Michael E., B.R. Simon Rosser, and Nancy Strapko. 1994. "Differences in conflict-resolution styles of heterosexual, gay, and lesbian couples." *Journal of Sex Research* 31:293-308.

Meyer, David S., and Suzanne Staggenborg. 1996. "Movements, countermovements, and the structure of political opportunity." *American Journal of Sociology* 101: 1628-60.

Milgram, Stanley. l974. *Obedience To Authority*. New York: Harper & Row.

Miller, Jon, and Sanford Labovitz. 1973. "Individual reactions to organizational conflict and change." *The Sociological Quarterly* 14:556-75.

Miller, Linda. 1997. "Sale after sale means medical care as we know it is vanishing rapidly." *The San Diego Union-Tribune*, January 12.

Mills, C. Wright. 1956. *The Power Elite*. New York: Oxford University Press.

_____. l959. *The Sociological Imagination*. New York: Oxford University Press.

Mills, Jeannie. l982. "Jonestown Masada." In Ken Levi, ed., *Violence and Religious Commitment*. University Park, PA.: The Pennsylvania State University Press.

Minick, Ptlene, and Sarah Hall Gueldner. 1995. "Patterns of conflict and anger in women sixty years old or older: An interpretive study." *Journal of Women and Aging* 7:71-84.

Mirowsky, John, and Catherine E. Ross. 1995. "Sex differences in distress: Real or artifact?" *American Sociological Review* 60: 449-68.

Moaddel, Mansoor. 1994. "Political conflict in the world economy: A cross-national analysis of modernization and world-system theories." *American Sociological Review* 59: 276-303.

Mohr, John, and Paul DiMaggio. 1995. "The intergenerational transmission of cultural capital." *Research in Social Stratification and Mobility* 14:167-199.

Mollica, R.F. et al. l994. "The effect of trauma and confinement on functional health and mental health status of Cambodians living in Thailand-Cambodia border camps." *Journal of the American Medical Association* 270 (August 4):58l-86.

Morgan, Edmund S. 1966. *The Puritan Family*. New York: Harper and Row.

Morier, Dean. 1994. "The effect of interpersonal expectancies on men's self-presentation of gender role attitudes to women." *Sex Roles* 31:493-504.

Mortenson, Thomas G. 1991. *Equity of Higher Educational Opportunities for Women, Black, Hispanic, and Low Income Students*. Iowa City, Iowa: ACT.

Mosher, William D., and James W. McNally. l99l. "Contraceptive Use at First Premarital Intercourse: United States, l965-l988." *Family Planning Perspectives* 23:l08-l6.

Mueller, Charles W., Sarosh Kuruvilla, and Roderick D. Iverson. 1994. "Swedish professionals and gender inequalities." *Social Forces* 73: 555-73.

Mullens, A. 1995. "Oregon vote may mark watershed for right-to-die debate in Canada and the U.S." *Canadian Medical Association Journal* 152: 91-2.

Musick, Judith S. 1993. *Young, Poor, and Pregnant: The Psychology of Teenage Motherhood*. New Haven, CT.: Yale University Press.

Mydans, Seth. 1996. "Long-necked women are a tourist attraction." *The New York Times*, October 21.

Myers, D.G. and E. Diener. 1995. "Who is happy?" *Psychological Science* 6:10-19.

Nagel, Joanne. 1995. "Politics and the resurgence of American Indian ethnic identity." *American Sociological Review* 60: 947-65.

Nash, J. Madeleine. 1996. "Ruling out 'junk science.' " *Time*, December 30.

National Center for Educational Statistics. 1990. *1989 Education Indicators*. Washington, D.C.: Government Printing Office.

_____.1996. *The Condition of Education 1996*. National Center for Educational Statistics Website.

National Center for Health Statistics. 1995. "Annual report on nation's health shows continued disparities." Press release, June 22.

_____. l995. *Digest of Education Statistics*. Washington, D.C.: U.S. Department of Education.

_____. 1996. "The condition of education 1996." *National Center for Educational Statistics Website*.

National Clearinghouse for Alcohol and Drug Information. 1995a. "1995 National Household Survey on Drug Abuse." NCADI Website.

_____. 1995b. "Teen drug use rises for fourth straight year." NCADI Website.

National Institute of Mental Health. 1982. *Television and Behavior*. Washington, D.C.: Government Printing Office.

National Institute on Alcohol Abuse and Alcoholism. 1989. "Alcohol and trauma." *Alcohol Alert* January: 1-4.

National Opinion Research Center. 1993. *General Social Surveys, 1972-1992*: Cumulative Codebook. Chicago: National Opinion Research Center.

Nee, Victor. 1991. "Social inequalities in reforming state socialism: Between redistribution and markets in China." *American Sociological Review* 56: 267-82.

Nelson, Harry. 1992. "Cancer may pass heart disease as no. 1 killer." *Los Angeles Times*, February 18.

Newman, Barry. 1996. "Pining for order: Russians are of two minds about new freedoms and the new poverty." *The New York Times*, May 31.

Newport, Frank. 1995. "Americans Think Many Institutions Are Too Powerful." *The Gallup Poll Monthly*. October, 1995 (Number 361).

Nickens, H.W. 1995. "The role of race/ethnicity and social class in minority health status." *Health Service Research* 30: 151-62.

Nord, Stephen, and Yaun Ting. 1991. "The impact of advance notice of plant closings on earnings and the probability of unemployment." *Industrial and Labor Relations Review* 44:681 91.

Normile, Dennis. 1997. "Japanese budget: Basic science spending to jump in 1997." *Science* 275: 21.

Oggins, Jean, Joseph Veroff, and Douglas Leber. l993. "Perceptions of Marital Interaction Among Black and White Newlyweds." *Journal of Personality and Social Psychology* 65:494-511.

O'Keefe, Nona K., Karen Brockopp, and Esther Chew. 1986. "Teen dating violence." *Social Work* 31:465-68.

Oliver, J.M. 1995. "Self-esteem and self-efficacy: Perceived parenting and family climate and depression in university students." *Journal of Clinical Psychology* 51:467-81.

Oliver, Melvin L., and Thomas M. Shapiro. 1995. *Black wealth/White wealth: New perspectives on racial inequality.* New York: Routledge.

O'Neill, Barry. 1994. "The history of a hoax." *The New York Times Magazine*, March 6.

Orcutt, James D., and J. Blake Turner. 1993. "Shocking numbers and graphic accounts: Quantified images of drug problems in the print media." *Social Problems* 40:190-206.

Osgood, D. Wayne, Janet K. Wilson, Patrick N. O'Malley, Jerald G. Bachman, and Lloyd D. Johnston. 1996. "Routine activities and individual deviant behavior." *American Sociological Review* 61: 635-55.

Oshima, Sumiko. 1996. "Japan: Feeling the strains of an aging population." *Science Magazine* 273: 44.

Ostling, Richard N. 1992. "The second reformation." *Time*, November 23.

Ouchi, William G. 1981. *Theory Z: How American Business Can Meet the Japanese Challenge.* Reading, Ma.: Addison-Wesley.

Pandey, Janak. 1986. "Sociocultural perspectives on ingratiation." *Progress in Experimental Research* 14: 205-29.

Park, Robert E. 1952. Human Communities. Glencoe, IL.: The Free Press.

Parker, Franklin. 1975. "What's right with American education." In G. Smith and C.R. Parker, eds., *Myth and Reality*, 2nd ed. Boston: Allyn and Bacon.

Parkinson, C. Northcote. 1970. *The Law of Delay.* London: John Murray.

Paris, J.J., and M. Poorman. 1995. " 'Playing God' and the removal of life-prolonging therapy." *Journal of Medical Philosophy* 20: 403-18.

Parsons, Talcott. 1955. "Family structure and the socialization of the child." In T. Parsons and R.F. Bales, eds., *Family, Socialization and Interaction Process.* Glencoe, IL.: The Free Press.

_____. 1967. *Sociological Theory and Modern Society.* New York: Free Press.

_____. 1975. "The sick role and the role of the physician reconsidered." *Milbank Medical Fund Quarterly, Health and Society* 53: 257-78.

_____, and Robert F. Bales. 1953. *Family Socialization and Interaction.* Glencoe, Ill.: Free Press.

Patterson, James, and Peter Kim. 1991. *The Day America Told the Truth: What People Really Believe About Everything that Really Matters.* New York: Prentice Hall.

Pedersen, Nancy L., Robert Plomin and G.E. McClearn. 1994. "Is there G beyond g?" *Intelligence* 18:133-43.

Peretti, Peter O., and Anthony di Vitorrio. 1993. "Effect of loss of father through divorce on personality of the preschool child." *Social Behavior and Personality* 21:33-38.

Perrow, Charles. 1972. *Complex Organizations: A Critical Essay.* Glenview, Ill.: Scott, Foresman.

_____. 1982. "Disintegrating social sciences." *Phi Delta Kappan* 63:684-88.

Peter, Laurence J., and Raymond Hull. 1969. *The Peter Principle: Why Things Always Go Wrong*. New York: William Morrow.

Peterson, Richard R. 1996. "A re-evaluation of the economic consequences of divorce." *American Sociological Review* 61:528-36.

Petronio, Sandra, and Thomas Endres. l985/86. "Dating and the Single Parent: Communication in the Social Network." *Journal of Divorce* 9:83-l05.

Pettigrew, Thomas F. 1994. "New patterns of prejudice: The different worlds of 1984 and 1964." In Fred L.Pincus and Howard J. Ehrlich, eds., *Race and Ethnic Conflict*. Boulder: Westview Press.

Pfeffer, Jeffrey, and Jerry Ross. 1990. "Gender-based wage differences." *Work and Occupations* 17: 55-78.

Phelan, Jo, Bruce G. Link, Ann Stueve, and Robert E. Moore. 1995. "Education, social liberalism, and economic conservatism: Attitudes toward homeless people." *American Sociological Review* 60:126-40.

Phelan, Thomas J., and Mark Schneider. 1996. "Race, ethnicity, and class in American suburbs." *Urban Affairs Review* 31: 659-80.

Piaget, Jean, and Barbel Inhelder. 1969. *The Psychology of the Child*. New York: Basic Books.

Pietromonaco, Paula R., Jean Manis, and Hazel Markus. l987. "The Relationship of Employment to Self-Perception and Well-Being in Women: A Cognitive Analysis." *Sex Roles* l7:467-77.

Pijnenborg, L. et al. 1995. "Withdrawal or withholding of treatment at the end of life: Results of a nationwide study." *Archives of Internal Medicine* 155: 286-92.

Pincus, Fred L. 1994. "From individual to structural discrimination." In Fred L. Pincus and Howard J. Ehrlich, eds., *Race and Ethnic Conflict*. Boulder: Westview Press.

Pizer, Stuart A., and Jeffrey R. Travers. 1975. *Psychology and Social Change*. New York: McGraw-Hill.

Pollock, Griselda. 1992. "Feminism and Modernism." In Maggie Humm, ed. *Modern Feminisms*. New York: Columbia University Press.

Population Information Network. 1996. "Earth Day feature: Consumption and the Earth's future." *Population Today* 24: 5-8.

Population Reference Bureau. 1996. *World Population Data Sheet*. Washington, D.C.: Population Reference Bureau.

Powers, Daniel A., and Christopher G. Ellison. 1995. "Interracial conflict and Black racial attitudes: The contact hypothesis and selectivity bias." *Social Forces* 74: 205-26.

Purvis, Andrew. 1996. "The global epidemic." *Time*, December 30.

Queen, Stuart A., Robert W. Habenstein, and Jill Sobel Quadagno. l985. *The Family In Various Cultures*. 5th ed. New York: Harper & Row.

Quillian, Lincoln. 1995. "Population, perceived threat, and prejudice in Europe." *American Sociological Review* 60: 586-611.

Rand, Erica. 1995. *Barbie's Queer Accessories*. Durham, NC: Duke University Press.

Rao, R. Raj. 1996. "The poetry of Bombay City." *The Journal of Commonwealth Literature* 31: 63.

Redelmeier, Donald A. and Robert J. Tibshirani. 1997. "Association between cellular-telephone calls and motor vehicle collisions." *New England Journal of Medicine* 336;453-58.

Redlinger, Lawrence J., and Philip K. Armour. 1982. "Changing worlds: Observations of the processes of resocialization and transformations of subjective social reality." In Ken Levi, ed., *Violence and Religious Commitment*. University Park: The Pennsylvania State University Press.

Reich, Jerome R. 1994. *Colonial America*. 3rd. ed. Englewood Cliffs, NJ: Prentice Hall.

Reichmann, Deb. 1996. "Little progress toward meeting education 2000 goals." *The Chicago Tribune.*

Reischauer, Edwin O. 1964. *Japan: Past and Present.* Tokyo: Charles E. Tuttle.

Reiss, Ira L., and Gary R. Lee. 1988. *Family Systems in America*, 4th ed. New York: Holt, Rinehart, and Winston.

Remland, M.S., T.S. Jones, and H. Brinkman. 1995. "Interpersonal distance, body orientation, and touch: Effects of culture, gender, and age." *Journal of Social Psychology* 135:281-97.

Rich, Adrienne. 1992. "Of woman born: Motherhood as experience and institution." In Maggie Humm, ed., *Modern Feminisms.* New York: Columbia University Press.

Richard, Geoffrey. 1996. "Office market finds short cut to recovery—through the suburbs." *National Real Estate Investor* 38: 92.

Richards, Leslie N. and Cynthia J. Schmiege. 1993. "Problems and Strengths of Single-Parent Families: Implications for Practice and Policy." *Family Relations* 42:277-85.

Ritzer, George. 1995. *Expressing America: A Critique of the Global Credit Card Society.* Thousand Oaks, CA.: Pine Forge Press.

Roark, Anne C. 1990. "TV: It can leave you tense and passive, studies find." *Los Angeles Times*, April 29.

Roberts, J. Timmons. 1993. "Psychosocial effects of workplace hazardous exposures: Theoretical synthesis and preliminary findings." *Social Problems* 40:74 89.

Roberts, Robert E.L. and Vern L. Bengtson. 1996. "Affective ties to parents in early adulthood and self-esteem across 20 years." *Social Psychology Quarterly* 59:96-106.

Robins, Lee N., and Dariel A. Regier. 1991. *Psychiatric Disorders in America.* New York: Free Press.

Robinson, Cherylon and Lawrence Alfred Powell. 1996. "The postmodern politics of context definition: Competing reality frames in the Hill-Thomas spectacle." *The Sociological Quarterly* 37: 279-305.

Robinson, Dawn T. and Lynn Smith-Lovin. 1992. "Selective interaction as a strategy for identity maintenance: An affect control model." *Social Psychology Quarterly* 55:12-28.

Robinson, Joan. 1970. *The Cultural Revolution in China.* London: Penguin Books.

Robinson, Nancy S. 1995. "Evaluating the nature of perceived support and its relation to perceived self-worth in adolescents." *Journal of Research on Adolescence.* 5:253-80.

Roethlisberger, F.J. and W.J. Dickson. 1939. *Management and the Worker.* Cambridge: Harvard University Press.

Rogers, Jackie Krasas. 1995. "Just a temp: Experience and structure of alienation in temporary clerical employment." *Work and Occupations* 22 (May):137-66.

Rogers, Richard G., Robert A. Hummer, Charles B. Nam, and Kimberley Peters. 1996. "Demographic, socioeconomic, and behavioral factors affecting ethnic morality by cause." *Social Forces* 74: 1419-1438.

Rollins, Judy. 1986. "Single Men and Women: Differences and Similarities." *Family Perspective* 20:117-25.

Romer, D. 1994. "Using mass media to reduce adolescent involvement in drug trafficking." *Pediatrics* 93:1073-77.

Roper, Burns W., and Edward B. Keller. 1988. "Thoughts of Youth." *Public Opinion*, March/April, pp. 16-17, 58-59.

Roper Center. 1996. "Race in the United States: It's not a matter of black and white." *The Public Perspective* February/March.

Roseland, Mark. 1996. "Taming urban sprawl: Healthy cities and towns." *Northwest Report*, #19: 1-6.

Rosenbaum, Jill. 1987. "Social control, gender, and delinquency: An analysis of drug, property, and violent offenders." *Justice Quarterly* 4: 117-32.

Rosenberg, H. M. et al. 1995. "Births and deaths: United States, 1995." *Monthly Vital Statistics Report*: 45: 31.

Rosenfeld, Anne, and Elizabeth Stark. 1987. "The prime of our lives." *Psychology Today*, May, pp. 62-72.

Rosenthal, Robert, and Lenore Jacobson. 1968. "Self-fulfilling prophecies in the class-room: Teachers' expectations as unintended determinants of pupils' intellectual competence." In M. Deutsch, I. Katz, and A. R. Jensen, eds., *Social Class, Race, and Psychological Development*. New York: Holt, Rinehart and Winston.

Rosero-Bixby, Luis, and John B. Casterline. 1994. "Interaction diffusion and fertility transition in Costa Rica." *Social Forces* 73: 435-62.

Ross, Catherine E., and Chia-Ling Wu. 1995. "The links between education and health." *American Sociological Review* 60:719-45.

Ross, Catherine E., and John Mirowsky. 1992. "Households, employment, and the sense of control." *Social Psychology Quarterly* 55: 217-35.

Ross, Catherine E., and Marieke Van Willigen. 1996. "Gender, parenthood, and anger." *Journal of Marriage and the Family* 58: 572-84.

Rossides, Daniel W. 1990. *Social Stratification*. Englewood Cliffs, N.J.: Prentice-Hall.

Roush, Wade. 1996. "Demography: Live long and prosper." *Science Magazine* 273: 42.

Rubenstein, Carin and Phillip Shaver. 1982. *In Search of Intimacy*. New York: Delacorte Press.

Rudofsky, Bernard. 1971. "The Fashionable Body." *Horizon* 13: 56-65.

Ruggles, Steven. 1994. "The origins of African-American family structure." *American Sociological Review* 59: 136-51.

Rushton, J. Philippe. 1994. "The equalitarian dogma revisited." *Intelligence* 19:263-80.

Saad, Lydia. 1995. "A special report: Immigrants see U.S. as land of opportunity." *The Gallup Poll Monthly*, July.

Sack, William H., Morton Beiser, Gloria Baker-Brown, and Roy Redshirt. 1994. "Depressive and Suicidal Symptoms in Indian School Children: Findings From the Flower of Two Soils." *American Indian and Alaska Native Mental Health Research* 4:81-96.

Sadker, Myra, and David Sadker. 1994. *Failing at Fairness: How America's Schools Cheat Girls*. New York: Charles Scribner's Sons.

Saluter, Arlene. 1996. "Age at first marriage at record high, Census Bureau reports." *United States Department of Commerce News*. Washington D.C.: U.S. Census Bureau.

Sammons, Mary Beth. 1997. "May I polish that apple for you?" *The Chicago Tribune*, January 26.

Sampson, Robert J., and John H. Lamb. 1990. "Crime and deviance over the life course: The salience of adult social bonds." *American Sociological Review* 55:609-27.

Sanderson, Stephen K. 1994. *Social Transformation: A General Theory of Historical Development*. Oxford: Blackwell.

Scanzoni, John. 1972. *Sexual Bargaining*. Englewood Cliffs, N. J.: Prentice-Hall.

Schaefer, Richard T. 1993. *Racial and Ethnic Groups*. 5th ed. New York: HarperCollins.

Schaie, K. W. 1994. "The course of adult intellectual development." *American Psychologist* 49: 304-13.

Scheff, Thomas. 1966. *Being Mentally Ill*. Chicago: Aldine.

Schlenker, Barry R. 1994. "The impact of self-presentations on self-appraisals and behavior: The power of public commitment." *Personality and Social Psychology Bulletin* 20:20-33.

Schmid, Josef. 1995. "Development under population pressure and shortage of resources: An alternative path to demographic transition." *Journal of Sociology and Social Policy* 15: 8-10, 95-118.

Schneider, Keith. 1981. "The Green Revolution: How much further can it go?" *The New York Times*, August 21.

Schulenburg, Joy. 1985. *Gay Parenting*. New York: Anchor Press.

Schurmann, Franz, and Orville Schell, eds. 1967. *Communist China*. New York: Vintage Books.

Schwartz, Evan I. 1996. "Trust me, I'm your software." *Discover*, May.

Scott, Donald M., and Bernard Wishy, eds. 1982. *American Families: A Documentary History*. New York: Harper & Row.

Scott, Janny. 1988. "Study links nine common medical errors to deaths." *Los Angeles Times*, October 1.

Segura, Denise A. 1991. "Ambivalence or continuity? Motherhood and employment among Chicanas and Mexican immigrant women workers." *Aztlan* 20:119-50.

Seidman, Stuart N., and Ronald O. Rieder. 1994. "A Review of Sexual Behavior in the United States." *American Journal of Psychiatry* 151:330-41.

Seifert, Kelvin L., Robert J. Hoffnung, and Michele Hoffnung. 1997. *Lifespan Development*. Boston: Houghton Mifflin.

Seligman, Martin E.P. 1990. *Learned Optimism: How to Change Your Mind and Your Life*. New York: Simon & Schuster.

Senge, Peter. 1990. *The Fifth Discipline: the Art and Practice of the Learning Organization*. New York: Doubleday.

Shankar, Arti. 1994. "Organizational context and ingratiatory behavior in organizations." *Journal of Social Psychology* 134:641-47.

Shanker, Albert. 1994. "The crab bucket syndrome." *The New York Times*, June 19.

Shepelak, Norma J., Anita Curry-Jackson, and Vernon L. Moore. 1992. "Critical thinking in introductory sociology classes: A program of implementation and evaluation." *Teaching Sociology* 20:18-27.

Sherman, Lawrence W., Patrick R. Gartin, and Michael E. Buerger. 1989. "Hot spots of predatory crime: Routine activities and the criminology of place." *Criminology* 27: 27-55.

Sigelman, Lee. 1995. "Blacks, Whites, and anti-Semitism." *Sociological Quarterly* 36: 649-56.

Sigelman, Lee, Timothy Bledsoe, Susan Welch, and Michael W. Combs. 1996. "Making contact? Black-White social interaction in an urban setting." *American Journal of Sociology* 101: 1306-32.

Simenauer, Jacqueline, and David Carroll. 1982. Singles: *The New Americans*. New York: Simon and Schuster.

Singer, Jerome L., Dorothy G. Singer, and Wanda S. Rapaczynski. 1984. "Family patterns and television viewing as predictors of children's beliefs and aggression." *Journal of Communication* 34:73-89.

Smelser, Neil J. 1959. *Social Change in the Industrial Revolution*. Chicago: University of Chicago Press.

Smircich, Linda. 1983. "Concepts of cultural and organizational analysis." *Administrative Science Quarterly* 28: 339-58.

Smith, Adam. 1965. *An Inquiry into the Nature and Causes of the Wealth of Nations*. Edwin Cannan, ed. New York: Modern Library.

Smith, Drake S. 1985. "Wife Employment and Marital Adjustment: A Cumulation of Results." *Family Relations* 34:483-90.

Smock, Pamela J. 1994. "Gender and short-run economic consequences of marital disruption." *Social Forces* 73: 243-62.

Smolowe, Jill. 1995. "Enemies of the state." *Time*, May 8, pp. 58-69.

Snow, David A., and Leon Anderson. 1993. *Down on Their Luck: A Study of Homeless Street People*. Berkeley: University of California Press.

Soine, L. 1995. "Sick building syndrome and gender bias." *Social Work and Health Care* 20 (no. 3):51-65.

Solano, Cecilia H., and Mina Dunnam. 1985. "Two's company: Self-disclosure and reciprocity in triads versus dyads." *Social Psychology Quarterly*. 48:183-87.

Solorzano, Daniel G. 1991. "Mobility aspirations among racial minorities, controlling for SES." *Sociology and Social Research* 75: 182-88.

Sommers-Flanagan, Rita, John Sommers-Flanagan, and Britta Davis. 1993. "What's happening on music television? A gender role content analysis." *Sex Roles* 28: 745-53.

Sonenstein, Freya L., Joseph H. Pleck, and Leighton C. Ku. 1991. "Levels of Sexual Activity Among Adolescent Males in the United States." *Family Planning Perspectives* 22: 162-67.

Sorensen, Annemette and Heike Trappe. 1995. "The persistence of gender inequality in earnings in the German Democratic Republic." *American Sociological Review* 60: 398-406.

Sorokin, Pitirim. 1937-41. *Social and Cultural Dynamics*, 4 vols. New York: American Book Company.

South, Scott J. 1993. "Racial and ethnic differences in the desire to marry." *Journal of Marriage and the Family* 55:357-70.

South, Scott J., and Kim M. Lloyd. 1995. "Spouse alternatives and marital dissolution." *American Sociological Review* 60:21-35.

Southworth, Suzanne and J. Conrad Schwarz. 1987. "Post-Divorce Contact, Relationship with Father, and Heterosexual Trust in Female College Students." *American Journal of Orthopsychiatry* 57:371-82.

Stake, Jayne E. 1992. "Gender differences and similarities in self-concept within every-day life contexts." *Psychology of Women Quarterly* 16: 349-63.

Stammer, Larry B. 1990. "Rain forests disappearing 50% quicker than feared." *Los Angeles Times*, June 8.

Stander, Valerie, and Larry Jensen. 1993. "The relationship of value orientation to moral cognition: Gender and cultural differences in the United States and China Explored." *Journal of Cross-Cultural Psychology* 24:42-52.

Stares, Paul B. 1996. *Global Habit: The Drug Problem in a Borderless World*. Washington, D.C.: Brookings Institution.

Steffesmeier, Darrell, and Miles D. Harer. 1991. "Did crime rise or fall during the Reagan presidency? The effects of an 'aging' U.S. population on the nation's crime rate." *Journal of Research in Crime and Delinquency* 28:330 59.

Steinberg, Laurence, Nina S. Mounts, Susie D. Lamborn, and Sanford M. Dornbusch. 1991. "Authoritative parenting and adolescent adjustment across varied ecological niches." *Journal of Research on Adolescence* 1:19-36.

Stephens, Ray. 1990. "New coffee research brews quandary." *AARP Bulletin*, January.

Stets, Jan E. 1993. "The Link Between Past and Present Intimate Relationships." *Journal of Family Issues* 14:236-60.

Stevens, William K. 1996. "Study reveals impact of acid rain." *The New York Times*, April 16.

Stevenson, William B. 1986. "Change in the structure of bureaucracy: A longitudinal analysis." *Sociological Perspectives* 29: 307-36.

Stoller, Eleanor Palo. 1996. "Sauna, Sisu and Sibelius: Ethnic identity among Finnish Americans." *The Sociological Quarterly* 37: 145-75.

Stoner, Carroll and Jo Anne Parke. 1977. *All Gods Children*. New York: Penguin Books.

Strauss, Anselm L. 1968. *The American City: A Sourcebook of Urban Imagery*. Chicago: Aldine Press.

_____. 1978. *Negotiations: Varieties, Context, Processes, and Social Order*. San Francisco; Jossey-Bass.

Strauss, Anselm L., et. al. 1963. "The hospital and its negotiated order." In E. Friedson, ed., *The Hospital in Modern Society*. New York: Free Press.

Strutton, David. 1995. "Sex differences in ingratiatory behavior: An investigation of influence tactics in the salesperson-customer dyad." *Journal of Business Research* 34:35-45.

Stryker, S., and R. Serpe. 1982. "Towards a theory of family influence in the socialization of children." In A. Kerckhoff, ed., *Research in Sociology of Education and Socialization*. Vol. 4. Greenwich, CT: JAI Press.

Suitor, J. Jill. 1991. "Marital quality and satisfaction with the division of household labor across the family life cycle." *Journal of Marriage and the Family* 53: 221-30.

Sullerot, Evelyne. 1974. *Woman, Society, and Change*. New York: McGraw-Hill.

Sullivan, John. 1996. "Hazards seen at one-fifth of New York City schools." *The New York Times*, November 19.

Sumner, W.G. 1906. *Folkways*. New York and Boston: Ginn.

Sundquist, J. 1995. "Ethnicity, social class and health: A population-based study on self-reported illness in 223 Latin American refugees, 333 Finnish and 126 south European labour migrants and 841 Swedish controls." *Social Science and Medicine* 40: 777-87.

Sutherland, Edwin H. 1939. *Principles of Criminology*. Philadelphia: J.B. Lippincott.

Sutherland, Edwin H., and Donald R. Cressey. 1955. *Principles of Criminology*. 5th ed. Philadelphia: J. B. Lippincott.

Swartz, Marc J. and David K. Jordan. 1976. *Anthropology: Perspective on Humanity*. New York: John Wiley & Sons.

Swim, Janet K. 1995. "Sexism and racism: Old-fashioned and modern prejudices." *Journal of Personality and Social Psychology* 68 (February):199-214.

Tackett, Michael. 1996. " 'My opponent is a drunken, syphilitic swindler.' " *The Chicago Tribune*, July 21.

Takaki, Ronald. 1989. *Stranger from a Different Shore: A History of Asian-Americans*. Boston: Little, Brown.

Tallis, R.C. 1996. "Burying Freud." *The Lancet* 347: 669.

Tang, Joyce. 1993. "The career attainment of Caucasian and Asian engineers." *The Sociological Quarterly* 34: 467-96.

Tannahill, Reay. 1980. *Sex In History*. New York: Stein and Day.

Tannen, Deborah. 1990. *You Just Don't Understand: Women and Men in Conversation*. New York: William Morrow and Company.

Tarrow, Sidney. 1997. "Cycles of collective action: Between moments of madness and the repertoire of contention." In D. McAdam and D.A. Snow, eds. *Social Movements*. Los Angeles: Roxbury Publishing Company.

Tasker, F., and S. Golombok. 1995. "Adults raised as children in lesbian families." *American Journal of Orthopsychiatry* 65: 203-15.

Telles, Edward E. 1992. "Residential segregation by skin color in Brazil." *American Sociological Review* 57: 186-97.

Testa, Maria. 1995. "Social influences on drinking during pregnancy." *Psychology of Addictive Behaviors* 9:258-68.

Thomas, William I. 1937. *The Unadjusted Girl*. Boston: Little, Brown.

Thomson, Elizabeth, Thomas L. Hanson, and Sara S. McLanahan. 1994. "Family Structure and Child Well-Being: Economic Resources vs. Parental Behaviors." *Social Forces* 73:221-42.

Thorne, Barrie. 1993. *Gender Play: Girls and Boys in School*. New Brunswick, N.J.: Rutgers University Press.

Tice, Dianne M. 1995. "When modesty prevails: Differential favorability of self-presentation to friends and strangers." *Journal of Personality and Social Psychology* 69:1120-38.

Tiefer, Leonore. 1978. "The Kiss." *Human Nature* l (July):28-45.

Tönnies, Ferdinand. 1957. *Community and Society*. Translated and edited by Charles P. Loomis. East Lansing: Michigan State University Press.

Tonry, Michael H. 1995. *Malign Neglect: Race, Crime and Punishment in America*. New York: Oxford University Press.

Torassa, Ulysses. 1996. "Violence is darker side of self-esteem." *The San Diego Union-Tribune*, February 16.

Toth, Jennifer. 1991. "Number of children living on America's streets swells." *The Los Angeles Times*, October 31.

Traeen, Bente. 1996. "Sexual socialization and motives for intercourse among Norwegian adolescents." *Archives of Sexual Behavior* 25: 289-302.

Troeltsch, Ernst. 1931. *The Social Teachings of the Christian Churches*. New York: Macmillan.

Tumin, Melvin M. 1985. *Social Stratification: The Forms and Functions of Inequality*. 2nd ed. Englewood Cliffs, N.J.: Prentice-Hall.

Turner, Ralph H. 1962. "Role-taking: Process versus conformity." In A. Rose, ed., *Human Behavior and Social Processes*. Boston: Houghton Mifflin.

Uchitelle, Louis. 1996. "More downsized workers are returning as rentals." *The New York Times*, December 8.

Udry, J. Richard. l995. "Sociology and biology: What biology do sociologists need to know?" *Social Forces* 73:l267-78.

Ulmer, Jeffery T. 1994. "Revisiting Stebbins: Labeling and commitment to deviance." *The Sociological Quarterly* 35:135-57.

U.S. Bureau of the Census. 1975. *Historical Statistics of the United States, Colonial Times to 1970, Bicentennial Edition*. Washington, D.C.: Government Printing Office.

_____. 1990 *Statistical Abstract of the United States*. Washington, D.C.: Government Printing Office.

_____. 1995. *Statistical Abstract of the United States*. Washington, D.C.: Government Printing Office.

_____. 1996a. *Current Population Survey: March 1996*. Census Bureau Website.

_____. 1996b. *Facts from the Census Bureau for Black History Month*. Census Bureau Website.

_____. 1996c. *Income and Poverty*. Washington, D.C.: Government Printing Office.

_____. 1996d *Statistical Abstract of the United States*. Washington, D.C.: Government printing office.

_____. 1996e. *Poverty 1995*. Census Bureau Website.

_____. 1996f. *United States Population Estimates, by Age, Sex, Race, and Hispanic Origin, 1990 to 1995*. Census Bureau Website.

U.S. Department of Education. 1992. *The Condition of Education, 1992*. Washington, D.C.: Government Printing Office.

U.S. Department of Education. l993. *National Excellence: A Case for Developing America's Talent*. Washington, D.C.: Government Printing Office.

U.S. Department of Health and Human Services. 1995. *Healthy People, 2000*. Washington, D.C.: Public Health Service.

_____. 1996. *Physical Activity and Health: A Report of the Surgeon General*. Washington, D.C.: The President's Council on Physical Fitness and Sports.

U.S. Department of Justice. 1983. *The Prosecution of Felony Arrests, 1979*. Washington, D.C.: Government Printing Office.

_____. 1988. *Report to the Nation on Crime and Justice*. 2nd ed. Washington, D.C.: Government Printing Office.

U.S. Federal Bureau of Investigation. 1995. *Crime in the United States, 1994 Uniform Crime Reports*. Washington, D.C.: Government Printing Office.

University of Michigan News and Information Services. 1995. "Drug use rises again in 1995 among American teens." Press release, December 11.

Useem, Michael and Jerome Karabel. 1986. "Pathways to corporate management." *American Sociological Review* 51: 184-200.

Van, Jon. 1996. "Population boom slowing: Even so, earth is overburdened, experts say." *The Chicago Tribune*, February 11.

Van Ausdale, Debra, and Joe R. Feagin. 1996. "The use of racial and ethnic concepts by very young children." *American Sociological Review* 61: 779-93.

Van de Vliert, Evert. 1985. "Escalative intervention in small-group conflicts." *Journal of Applied Behavioral Science* 21: 19-36.

Veblen, Thorstein. 1953. *The Theory of the Leisure Class*. New York: Mentor Books.

Ventis, W. Larry. 1995. "The relationships between religion and mental health." *Journal of Social Issues* 51: 33-48.

Ventura, Michael. 1995. "Are we living in a fatherless world?" *The Austin Chronicle*, June 9.

Verba, Sidney, Kay Lehman Scholzman, and Henry E. Brady. 1995. *Voice and Equality: Civic Volunteerism in American Politics*. Cambridge, MA.: Harvard University Press.

Verbrugge, Lois M. 1985. "Gender and health; an update on hypotheses and evidence." *Journal of Health and Social Behavior* 26:156 82.

Vigil, James Diego. 1996. "Street baptism: Chicano gang initiation." *Human Organization* 55:149-58.

Von der Mehden, Fred R. 1986. *Religion and Modernization in Southeast Asia*. Syracuse, N.Y.: Syracuse University Press.

Wade, Nicholas. 1981. *The Nobel Duel: Two Scientists' 21-year Race to Win the World's Most Coveted Research Prize*. New York: Anchor Press.

Wagner, Melinda Bollar. 1990. *God's Schools: Choice and Compromise in American Society*. New Brunswick, N.J.: Rutgers University Press.

Walker, Lawrence J. 1991. "Verbal interactions within the family context." *Canadian Journal of Behavioural Science* 23:441-54.

Wallbank T. Walter et al. 1987. *Civilization: Past and Present*. Glenview, Ill.: Scott, Foresman and Company.

Wallerstein, Immanuel. 1979. *The Capitalist World-Economy*. New York: Cambridge University Press.

Wallerstein, Judith S. 1986. "Women after divorce: Preliminary report from a ten-year follow-up." *American Journal of Orthopsychiatry* 56:65 77.

Wallerstein, Judith S. and Sandra Blakeslee. 1989. *Second Chances: Men, Women and Children a Decade After Divorce*. New York: Ticknor & Fields.

Walsh, Anthony, and Robert A. Gordon. 1995. *Biosociology: An Emerging Paradigm*. Westport, CT: Praeger.

Waluyo, Lieke, Kerstin Ekberg, and Jorgen Eklund. 1996. "Assembly work in Indonesia and in Sweden: Ergonomics, health, and satisfaction." *Ergonomics* 39: 199-212.

Wann, Daniel L., and Michael A. Hamlet. 1996. "Being a 'joiner' and psychological well-being." *Psychological Reports* 79: 1186.

Ward, Russell A. 1981. "The Never-Married in Later Life." Pp. 342-56 in P. J. Stein, ed., *Single Life: Unmarried Adults in Social Context*. New York: St. Martin's.

Ware, J. E. Jr., M. S. Bayliss, W. H. Rogers, M. Kosinski, and A. R. Tarlov. 1996. "Differences in four-year health outcomes for elderly and poor, chronically ill patients treated in HMO and fee-for-service systems." *Journal of the American Medical Association* 276: 1039-47.

Watson, James M., and Peter F. Meiksins. 1991. "What do engineers want? Work values, job rewards, and job satisfaction." *Science, Technology, and Human Values* 16:140 72.

Watts, William. 1981. "Americans' hopes and fears: The future can fend for itself." *Psychology Today*, September.

Webb, Julie. 1989. "The outcomes of home-based education: Employment and other issues." *Educational Review* 41: 121 33.

Weber, Max. 1947. *The Theory of Social and Economic Organization*. Trans. A. M. Henderson and Talcott Parsons. New York: The Free Press.

_____. 1958. *The Protestant Ethic and the Spirit of Capitalism*. Trans. T. Parsons. New York: Charles Scribner's Sons.

Weber, Michael P. 1975. "Social mobility in 19th-century America: Myth or Reality?" *The Forum Series* St. Charles, MO: The Forum Press.

Weeks, John R. 1988. "The demography of Islamic nations." *Population Bulletin* 43: 26.

Weiss, Robert S. 1990. *Staying the Course: The Emotional and Social Lives of Men who Do Well at Work*. New York: The Free Press.

Weitzman, Lenore J. 1985. *The Divorce Revolution: The Unexpected Social and Economic Consequences for Women and Children in America*. New York: Free Press.

_____. 1996. "The economic consequences of divorce are still unequal: Comment on Peterson." *American Sociological Review* 61:537-38.

Weitzman, Lenore J., D. Eifler, E. Hokada, and C. Ross. 1972. "Sex-role socialization in picture books for preschool children." *American Journal of Sociology* 77:1125-50.

Wellington, Alison J. 1994. "Accounting for the male/female wage gap among whites: 1976-1985." *American Sociological Review* 59: 839-48.

Westney, D. Eleanor. 1987. *Imitation and Innovation: The Transfer of Western Organizational Patterns to Meiji Japan*. Cambridge: Harvard University Press.

Wharton, Edith. 1989. *The Custom of the Country*. New York: Signet.

White, James M. 1989. "Reply to Comment By Trussell and Rao: A Reanalysis of the Data." *Journal of Marriage and the Family* 51:540-44.

White, Lynn K. and Alan Booth. 1985. "Stepchildren in Remarriages." *American Sociological Review* 50:689-98.

Whitehead, Alfred North. 1933. *Adventures of Ideas*. New York: Mentor Books.

Whitman, David. 1996. "A bad case of the blues." *U.S. News and World Report*, March 4.

Whorf, Benjamin Lee. 1940. "Science and linguistics." *Technology Review* 42:229-231.

Whyte, Martin King. 1990. *Dating, Mating, and Marriage*. New York: Aldine de Gruyt.

Wickrama, K.A.S., Rand D. Conger, Fredrick O. Lorenz, and Lisa Matthews. 1995. "Role identity, role satisfaction, and perceived physical health." *Social Psychology Quarterly* 58: 270-83.

Wilkie, Dana. 1997. "Welfare recipients get little relief in state plan." *The San Diego Union-Tribune*, January 10.

Williams Christine L. 1995. *Still a Man's World: Men Who Do "Women's Work"*. Berkeley and Los Angeles: University of California Press.

Williams, J. Allen, JoEtta A. Vernon, Martha C. Williams, and Karen Malecha. 1987. "Sex-role socialization in picture books: An update." *Social Science Quarterly* 68:148-56.

Williams, Louis. 1993. "Dennis': The relationship between a black barbershop and the community that supports it." *Human Mosaic* 27:29-33.

Williams, Robin M., Jr. 1970. *American Society*, 3rd ed. New York: Alfred A. Knopf.

Wilson, George. 1996. "Toward a revised framework for examining beliefs about the causes of poverty." *The Sociological Quarterly* 37: 413-28.

Wilson, William Julius. 1987. *The Truly Disadvantaged*. Chicago: University of Chicago Press.

Wilson-Moore, Margot. 1996. "Servants and daughters: Out of wedlock pregnancy and abandonment of women in Bangladesh." *Human Organization* 55:170-77.

Winfree, L. Thomas, Jr., Lawrence Kielich, and Robert E. Clark. 1984. "On becoming a prosecutor: Observations on the organizational socialization of law interns." *Work and Occupations* 11:207-26.

Winkler, Karen J. 1985. "Estrogen's link to heart disease unclear." *The Chronicle of Higher Education*, November 6.

Winter, David G., Abigail J. Stewart, and David C. McClelland. 1978. "Benefits of a liberal arts education." *Psychology Today*, September.

Wirth, Louis. 1938. "Urbanism as a way of life." *American Journal of Sociology* 44: 1-24.

Wohl, R. Richard, and Anselm Strauss. 1958. "Symbolic representation and the urban milieu." *American Journal of Sociology* 63: 523-32.

Wolff, Kurt. 1950. *The Sociology of George Simmel*. New York: Free Press.

Wolfinger, Nick, Jerome Rabow, and Michael D. Newcomb. 1993. "The different voices of helping: Gender and drunk driving interventions." Paper presented at the American Sociological Association annual meeting.

Wolin, Steven J. and Sybil Wolin. 1993. *The Resilient Self: How Survivors of Troubled Families Rise above Adversity*. New York: Villard Books.

Wong, Sin-Kwok. 1990. "Understanding cross-national variation in occupational mobility." *American Sociological Review* 55: 560-73.

Wood, Katherine C. 1996. "African Americans' and European Americans' mutual attributions: Adjective generation technique (AGT) stereotyping." *Journal of Applied Psychology* 26:884-912.

Wood, Katherine C., and Bem P. Allen. 1996. "African Americans' and European Americans' mutual attributions." *Journal of Applied Social Psychology* 26: 884–912.

Wright, James D. and Sonia R. Wright. 1976. "Social class and parental values for children: A partial replication and extension of the Kohn thesis." *American Sociological Review* 4:527-37.

Wrigley, E.A. 1974. *Population and History*. New York: McGraw-Hill.

Wuthnow, Robert. 1996. "Restructuring of American religion: Further evidence." *Sociological Inquiry* 66: 303-29.

Yankelovich, Daniel. 1981. "New rules In American Life: Searching for Self-Fulfillment in a World Turned Upside Down." *Psychology Today*, April.

Young, John E., and Aaron Sachs. 1995. "Creating a sustainable materials economy." In Lester R. Brown, et al. eds., *State of the World 1995*. New York: W.W. Norton.

Zabarenko, Deborah. 1996. "Study gives women top scores in management." *The San Diego Union-Tribune*, September 19.

Zajonc, Robert. 1967. "Social facilitation." In E.P. Hollander and R.J. Hunt, eds., *Current Perspectives in Social Psychology*. 2nd ed. New York: Oxford University Press.

Zawitz, Marianne. 1994. "Violence between intimates." *Bureau of Justice Statistics: Selected Findings* (Washington, D.C.: U.S. Department of Justice).

Zhou, Min and Yoshinori Kamo. 1994. "An analysis of earnings patterns for Chinese, Japanese, and non-Hispanic white males in the United States." *The Sociological Quarterly* 35: 581-602.

Zhou, Xueguang, Nancy Brandon Tuma, and Phyllis Moen. 1996. "Stratification dynamics under state socialism: The case of urban China, 1949-93." *Social Forces* 74:759-96.

Zill, Nicholas, and Charlotte A. Schoenborn. 1990. "Developmental Learning and Emotional Problems: Health of Our Nation's Children, United States, 1988." Advance Data, No. 190, *Vital and Health Statistics of the National Center for Health Statistics*.

Ziman, John. 1976. *The Force of Knowledge: The Scientific Dimensions of Society*. London: Cambridge University Press.

Zuckerman, Harriet. 1977. *Scientific Elite: Nobel Laureates in the United States*. New York: The Free Press.

Zukin, Sharon. 1995. *The Cultures of Cities*. Cambridge, MA.: Blackwell Publishers.

AUTHOR INDEX

SUBJECT INDEX